WITHDRAWN

ARGUMENTATION AND DEBATE:

A Classified Bibliography

Second edition

by
Arthur N. Kruger

The Scarecrow Press, Inc.
Metuchen, N.J.   1975

Library of Congress Cataloging in Publication Data

Kruger, Arthur N
    Argumentation and debate.

    First ed. published in 1964 under title: A classi-
fied bibliography of argumentation and debate.
    1.   Debates and debating--Bibliography.   I.   Title.
Z7161.5.K75 1974   016.80853   74-17198
ISBN 0-8108-0749-1

To Eleanor, Bob, and Mary

TABLE OF CONTENTS

PREFACE TO THE SECOND EDITION

This revised edition attempts to bring up to date the original work which was published some ten years ago. As a result, approximately two thousand entries have been added to the original work, bringing the total to about six thousand. Of these, approximately 650 are doctoral dissertations and masters' theses.

One of the most notable additions to this new work is a detailed subject index, which should be of considerable value to both students and scholars. Several minor changes have also been made. The category of Persuasion and Rhetorical Theory, for example, has been divided into two sub-categories, one dealing with classical and historical perspectives, the other with modern treatments. Some new categories have been added, such as Decision-Making and Beliefs and Values (see Section XXI), and some attempt was made to fill in the lacunae alluded to in the Preface to the first edition. I am aware, of course, that there will always be unintentional oversights, but, hopefully, these have been kept to a minimum.

In speaking of the value of a bibliography of this type, I can do no better than reiterate the sentiments so well expressed by two other compilers of a bibliography, namely: "A potential researcher, not quite settled on his subject, has at hand in this general bibliography an instrument enabling him better to cope with the recent explosion in publication, providing him in one sitting with information with which to make preliminary judgments on what has and what has not been done on his theme, and even suggesting to him endless musings on research ideas that could easily fill his lifetime. "*

In concluding, I would like to express my appreciation for

the enthusiastic response which the first edition seems to have received. Encouraged by this response, I have tried in this revised edition to develop an even more comprehensive tool for research by not only classifying but also indexing all entries. As a result of the new index and new entries, the book has grown considerably in size. I think--at least I hope--that the reader will find a proportionately even greater increase in value.

Acknowledgments

I would like to thank my graduate students Jacqueline Schillig, Carolyn Annucci, Charles Tichy, and Ted Gluckman, and my daughter Mary for helping me prepare various parts of the manuscript, and the Research Committee of C.W. Post College for paying some of the expenses incurred in this preparation.

Arthur N. Kruger

---

*James W. Cleary and Frederick W. Haberman, Rhetoric and Public Address: A Bibliography, 1947-1961 (Madison: University of Wisconsin Press, 1964), v.

PREFACE TO THE FIRST EDITION

This book represents the first comprehensive bibliography of argumentation and debate and as such is designed to provide a convenient reference for teachers, student debaters, graduate students specializing in debate, and debate coaches and professors interested in writing articles or doing research in the field of debate. The sections containing entries of masters' theses and doctoral dissertations should prove helpful and suggestive to graduate students in debate. To the best of my knowledge, this material is relatively complete and up to date.

In general, the emphasis is on works published in the United States during the twentieth century. Foreign entries and those published before the twentieth century were included only when the data were readily accessible. Preference throughout was given to those writers who worked or who are now working directly in the field of argumentation and debate. This accounts for the extensive listing of articles which have appeared in journals devoted primarily to debate (the Gavel of Delta Sigma Rho, the Forensic of Pi Kappa Delta, the Speaker of Tau Kappa Alpha, the Bulletin of the Debating Association of Pennsylvania Colleges, the Debaters Magazine, the Rostrum, the Platform News, and the Register of the American Forensic Association) as well as in those speech journals which frequently contain articles on debate (the Quarterly Journal of Speech, Speech Monographs, Speech Teacher, Western Speech, Southern Speech Journal, Central States Speech Journal, and Today's Speech.) Unfortunately, several of the former journals are now defunct and hence often difficult to locate.

Since argumentation and debate spills over into many other disciplines, a major problem in compiling a work of this nature was determining where to draw the line, particularly with regard to works in the field of public address. The yardstick for including such works was whether or not they were directed primarily to debaters. Thus, only selected articles on such topics as delivery and audience adaptation were included. Similarly with works in the field of logic and scientific method. For the most part, the entries here were confined to articles applying directly to debate and to certain basic works such as textbooks.

The reader may note that occasionally the major divisions of this work overlap. This was unavoidable. To borrow a favorite debate expression, the divisions are intended primarily to meet practical needs. Similarly, it may be seen that certain entries might easily have fit into several different categories. In such cases the entry was put into the category which seemed to correspond with the particular emphasis of the entry. An entry like Bruno Jacobs' "Why NFL Will Retain Cross-Examination Style," for example, might appropriately have been placed into four different categories: "High School Debating," "Leagues," "Cross-Examination," "Debate Tournament." It was ultimately placed into "Cross-Examination" because the emphasis of the article seemed to be here. However, for purposes of cross-reference the number of the entry was cited at the end of the other three sections. This same practice was followed with other over-lapping entries. Where the title of a work does not indicate the nature of the subject, a brief comment is appended.

Although I have tried to make this bibliography as complete as possible, undoubtedly certain items were overlooked. Such lacunae of course were unintentional and will, I trust, be regarded indulgently. Perhaps a future edition will make the necessary amends. Finally, it is my hope that this book will not only provide a guide to systematic study but also motivate future contributors to the literature of argumentation and debate.

LIST OF ABBREVIATIONS

This list does not include all of the journals or publishers cited in the Bibliography, but only those most frequently cited; others are spelled out in full where cited.

PERIODICALS

Am	America
An	Analysis
Ar	Arena
AA	American Anthropologist
AAA	Annals of the American Academy of Political and Social Science
AAUPB	American Association of University Professors' Bulletin
ABAJ	American Bar Association Journal
ABS	American Behavioral Scientist
AC	American City
AEB	Adult Education Bulletin
AEM	Agricultural Education Magazine
AFAR	American Forensic Association Register [superseded by Journal of the American Forensic Association]
AHR	American Historical Review
AJE	American Journal of Education
AJLH	American Journal of Legal History
AuJP	Australasian Journal of Philosophy
AJPh	American Journal of Philology
AJPsy	American Journal of Psychology
AJS	American Journal of Sociology
AL	Adult Leadership
AbLR	Alabama Law Review
AlLR	Albany Law Review
ArLR	Arkansas Law Review
APsy	American Psychology
APQ	American Philosophical Quarterly
APSR	American Political Science Review
ASQ	Administrative Science Quarterly
ASR	American Sociological Review
B	Bookman
BA	Bachelor of Arts
BBE	Baltimore Bulletin of Education
BCLR	University of British Columbia Law Review

BDAPC	Bulletin of the Debating Association of Pennsylvania Colleges
BJP	British Journal of Psychology
BJPS	British Journal for the Philosophy of Science
BLR	Buffalo Law Review
BNAP	Bulletin of the National Association of Secondary School Principals
BaS	Balance Sheet
BeS	Behavioral Science
Ce	Century
Ch	Chautauquan
Chr	Christendom
Com	Commonweal
Con	Contemporary
CBJ	Canadian Bar Journal
CC	Christian Century
CD	Congressional Digest
ChD	Child Development
CE	Contemporary Education
CEJ	Chambers' Edinburgh Journal
CER	Catholic Educational Review
CF	Canadian Forum
CH	Clearing House
CHSQ	California Historical Society Quarterly
CJ	Classical Journal
CJER	California Journal of Educational Research
CJSE	California Journal of Secondary Education
CLQ	Cornell Law Quarterly
CrLQ	Criminal Law Quarterly
CLR	Columbia Law Review
CiLR	Cincinnati Law Review
CO	Current Opinion
CP	Classical Philology
CPP	College of the Pacific Publication
CQ	Classical Quarterly
CR	Classical Review
CaSJ	Catholic School Journal
CoSJ	Colorado School Journal
CSMM	Christian Science Monitor Magazine
CSSJ	Central States Speech Journal
CULR	Catholic University Law Review
CUQ	Columbia University Quarterly
CW	Classical Weekly
CWRLR	Case Western Reserve Law Review
D	Dial
Di	Dialogue
DCBJ	District of Columbia Bar Journal
DCPR	Dialogue: Canadian Philosophical Review
DLJ	Duke Law Journal
DLR	Drake Law Review
DM	Debaters' Magazine

Ed	Education
Etc	Etcetera
Eth	Ethics
EJ	English Journal
EM	Educational Method
EO	Educational Outlook
EQ	Emerson Quarterly
ER	Educational Review
EcR	Eclectic Review
ERF	Educational Research Forum
ES	Educational Screen
ET	Educational Theory
EV	Education for Victory
F	Forensic of Pi Kappa Delta
Fo	Forum
FA	Foreign Affairs
FR	Fortnightly Review
G	Gavel of Delta Sigma Rho [superseded by Speaker and Gavel]
GLR	Georgetown Law Review
GaLR	Georgia Law Review
GO	Government and Opposition
GPO	Government Printing Office
H	Hobbies
HER	Hawaii Educational Review
HGM	Harvard Graduates' Magazine
HLJ	Hastings Law Journal
HLR	Harvard Law Review
HM	Harpers Magazine
HP	High Points
HR	Human Relations
HSCP	Harvard Studies in Classical Philology
HSJ	High School Journal
HST	High School Teacher
I	Independent
In	Inquiry
IAVE	Industrial Arts and Vocational Education
IATEB	Illinois Association of Teachers of English Bulletin
IC	International Conciliation
IE	Illinois Education
IIENB	Institute International Education News Bulletin
IdJE	Idaho Journal of Education
InJe	International Journal of Ethics
IJOAR	International Journal of Opinion and Attitude Research
IJRE	International Journal of Religious Education
ILJ	Insurance Law Journal
ILR	Iowa Law Review

J	Judicature
JABS	Journal of Applied Behavioral Science
JAD	Journal of Adult Education
JAFA	Journal of the American Forensic Association
JAP	Journal of Applied Psychology
JAbP	Journal of Abnormal Psychology
JASP	Journal of Abnormal and Social Psychology
JBE	Journal of Business Education
JC	Journal of Communication
JCJ	Junior College Journal
JCR	Journal of Conflict Resolution
JEd	Journal of Education
JEx	Journal of Expression
JEE	Journal of Experimental Education
JExP	Journal of Experimental Psychology
JER	Journal of Educational Research
JES	Journal of Educational Sociology
JGE	Journal of General Education
JGP	Journal of General Psychology
JHE	Journal of Higher Education
JHI	Journal of the History of Ideas
JHP	Journal of the History of Philosophy
JHR	Journal of Human Relations
JIAP	Journal of the Indian Academy of Philosophy
JJ	Jurimetrics Journal
JLE	Journal of Legal Education
JLR	Journal of Legal Reasoning
JNE	Journal of Negro Education
JPer	Journal of Personality
JPhil	Journal of Philosophy
JPol	Journal of Politics
JPsy	Journal of Psychology
JPL	Journal of Public Law
JPR	Journal of Peace Research
JPS	Journal of Public Speaking
JPSP	Journal of Personality and Social Psychology
JQ	Journalism Quarterly
JR	Juridical Review
JSE	Journal of Secondary Education
JSHD	Journal of Speech and Hearing Disorders
JSP	Journal of Social Psychology
JUL	Journal of Urban Law
JVI	Journal of Value Inquiry
JVLB	Journal of Verbal Learning and Verbal Behavior
KLJ	Kentucky Law Journal
KLR	Kansas Law Review
KSBJ	Kentucky State Bar Journal
KSJ	Kentucky School Journal
KSSJ	Kansas State Speech Journal
KT	Kansas Teacher

LA	Living Age
LoA	Logique et Analyse
LASJ	Los Angeles School Journal
LD	Literary Digest
LISA	Long Island Speech Association Express
LJ	Library Journal
LLR	Louisiana Law Review
LS	Language and Speech
LSR	Law and Society Review
Ma	Mademoiselle
Mi	Mind
Mo	Monist
MASAL	Michigan Academy of Science, Arts, and Letters
MJE	Minnesota Journal of Education
MJPS	Midwestern Journal of Political Science
MLJ	Manitoba Law Journal
MnLR	Maine Law Review
MoLR	Modern Law Review
MqLR	Marquette Law Review
MP	Modern Philology
MeS	Medieval Studies
MoS	Modern Schoolman
Na	Nation
Ne	Newsweek
No	Nous
NAR	North American Review
NCA	Nineteenth Century and After
NCEAB	National Catholic Education Association Bulletin
NDJFL	Notre Dame Journal of Formal Logic
NDUQJ	North Dakota University Quarterly Journal
NE	New Era
NEAJ	National Education Association Journal
NEJ	Nebraska Educational Journal
NFLB	National Forensic League Bulletin [superseded by Rostrum]
NL	New Leader
NLR	Nebraska Law Review
NPT	National Parents Teachers
NR	New Republic
NSch	Nation's Schools
NSchol	New Scholaticism
NSta	New Statesman
NStu	New Student
NYLF	New York Law Forum
NYSBJ	New York State Bar Journal
NYSEF	New York State Education Journal
NYTM	New York Times Magazine
Ou	Outlook
Overl	Overland

Overs   Overseas
OC   Open Court
OS   Ohio Schools
OSJ   Ohio Speech Journal

Pe   The Personalist
Ph   The Phoenix (Toronto)
Phil   Philosophy
Pu   Public
PAM   Pan American Monthly
PAPA   Proceedings of the American Philosophical Asso-
             ciation
PAS   Proceedings of the Aristotelian Society
PB   Psychological Bulletin
PE   Popular Education
PG   Popular Government
PJ   Personnel Journal
PaJ   Parliamentary Journal
PLR   University of Pennsylvania Law Review
PoLR   Portia Law Review
PaM   Parent's Magazine
PsM   Psychological Monographs
PMLA   Publications of the Modern Language Association
PN   Platform News
POQ   Public Opinion Quarterly
PPR   Philosophy and Phenomenological Research
PQ   Philological Quarterly
PhQ   Philosophical Quarterly
PR   Philosophical Review
PhR   Philosophy and Rhetoric
PsyR   Psychological Review
PsyRd   Psychological Record
PsyRt   Psychological Reports
PS   Philosophy of Science
PaS   Pacific Speech
PhS   Philosophical Studies
PsyS   Psychonomic Science
PSA   Pennsylvania Speech Annual
PSJ   Pennsylvania Speech Journal
PSM   Popular Science Monthly
PSQ   Political Science Quarterly
PSR   Public Speaking Review
PhT   Philosophy Today

QJS   Quarterly

R   Rostrum
Ra   Ratio
Re   Recreation
Rep   Reporter
Ro   Rotarian
RD   Reader's Digest

RLR	Rutgers Law Review
RM	Review of Metaphysics
RP	Review of Politics
RQ	Restoration Quarterly
RR	Review of Reviews
S	Speaker of Tau Kappa Alpha [superseded by Speaker and Gavel]
Sch	School
Schol	Scholastic
So	Sociometry
Sp	Spectator
Spec	Speculum
Sun	Sunset
Sur	Survey
Sy	Synthese
SA	Speech Activities
SchA	School Activities
SAQ	South Atlantic Quarterly
SC	School and Community
SD	Scholastic Daily
SE	Safety Education
SoE	Social Education
SEN	Sierra Educational News
SER	School of Education Record
StG	State Government
SuG	Survey Graphic
SJP	Southern Journal of Philosophy
S(L)	Speech (London)
SL	School Life
SLJ	Southwestern Law Journal
SM	Speech Monographs
ScM	Scribner's Magazine
SN	Speech News (of the Illinois Speech Association)
SP	Studies in Philology
SPG	Speaker and Gavel
SQ	Sociological Quarterly
SaR	Saturday Review
SchR	School Review
SchS	School and Society
SoS	Social Studies
SrS	Senior Scholastic
SSCJ	Southern Speech Communication Journal
SSJ	Southern Speech Journal
SSR	Sociology and Social Research
ST	Speech Teacher
STLJ	South Texas Law Journal
T	Time
Tr	Trial
TCJ	Teachers College Journal
TES	Times Education Supplement

TH	Today's Health
TLQ	Trial Lawyer's Quarterly
TnLR	Tennessee Law Review
TxLR	Texas Law Review
TO	Texas Outlook
TQ	Television Quarterly
TS	Today's Speech

UCLA	UCLA Law Review
UDA	University Debater's Annual
USOEB	United States Office of Education Bulletin

VLR	Vanderbilt Law Review
VS	Vital Speeches

WB	Wilson Bulletin
WEJ	Washington Educational Journal
WJE	Wisconsin Journal of Education
WLB	Wilson Library Bulletin
WmLJ	Willamette Law Journal
WLLR	Washington and Lee Law Review
WaLR	Washburn Law Review
WiLR	Wisconsin Law Review
WsLR	Washington Law Review
WPQ	Western Political Quarterly
WS	Western Speech
WUSLL	Washington University Studies in Language and Literature
WVLR	West Virginia Law Review

YLJ	Yale Law Journal
YLR	Yale Law Review

PUBLISHERS

Academic	Academic Press
Allen	G. Allen and Unwin, Ltd.
Allyn	Allyn and Bacon, Inc.
American	American Book Company
Antioch	The Antioch Press
Appleton	Appleton-Century-Crofts, Inc.
Atheneum	Atheneum Publishers

Badger	Richard G. Badger
Banks	Banks Law Publishing Company
Banta	George Banta Publishing Company
Barnes	Barnes and Noble, Inc.
Bell	George Bell and Son
Black	Adam and Charles Black
Bobbs	Bobbs Merrill Company

Boni	Boni and Liveright
Brown U.	Brown University Press
Brown	William C. Brown Company
Burgess	Burgess Publishing Company
Butterworth	Butterworth and Company
California	University of California Press
Cambridge	Cambridge University Press
Capitol	Capitol Publishing Company
Carswell	Carswell Company
Catholic	Catholic University of America Press
Century	The Century Company
Chapman	Chapman and Grimes
Chicago	University of Chicago Press
Clarendon	Clarendon Press
Columbia	Columbia University Press
Cordon	The Cordon Company
Cornell	Cornell University Press
Coward	Coward-McCann Geoghagan, Inc.
Crofts	F. S. Crofts and Company
Cromarty	Cromarty Law Book Company
Crowell	Thomas Y. Crowell Company
Crown	Crown Publishers
Current	Current Literature Publishers Company
D. Appleton	D. Appleton-Century
Dennison	T. S. Dennison and Company
Dial	Dial Press
Dodd	Dodd, Mead, and Company
Doubleday	Doubleday, Doran, and Company
Dover	Dover Publications, Inc.
Drake	F. J. Drake Company
Dryden	Dryden Press
Duke	Duke University Press
Dutton	E. P. Dutton and Company
Educator	Educator Supply Company
Excelsior	Excelsior Publishing House
Expression	Expression Company
Farrar	Farrar and Rinehart, Inc.
Follett	Follett Publishing Company
Foundation	The Foundation Press
Fraude	Henry Fraude
Free	The Free Press of Glencoe
Funk	Funk and Wagnalls
Garcia	R. P. Garcia Publishing Company
Ginn	Ginn and Company
Handy	Handy Book Corporation
Harcourt	Harcourt, Brace, and Company

Harper	Harper and Brothers
Harrap	George A. Harrap and Company
Harvard	Harvard University Press
Heath	D. C. Heath and Company
Hedrick	H. L. Hedrick
Heffer	W. Heffer and Sons
Heinemann	William Heinemann
H. Holt	Henry Holt and Company
Hinds	Hinds and Noble
H. Liveright	Horace Liveright
Hodder	Hodder and Stoughton
Holt	Holt, Rinehart and Winston
Houghton	Houghton Mifflin Company
Humanities	Humanities Press
Illinois	University of Illinois Press
Imperial	Imperial Press
Indiana	University of Indiana Press
Ivers	M. J. Ivers and Company
Ives	Ives Washburn
Kaiser	F. P. Kaiser
Kerr	C. H. Kerr and Company
King's	King's Crown Press
Knopf	Alfred A. Knopf, Inc.
Library	The New American Library
Lippincott	J. B. Lippincott Company
Little	Little, Brown, and Company
Liveright	Liveright Publishing Corporation
Longmans	Longmans, Green, and Company
LSU	Louisiana State University Press
Macmillan	The Macmillan Company
McGraw	McGraw-Hill Book Company, Inc.
McKay	David McKay Company, Inc.
McKnight	McKnight and McKnight
Meridian	Meridian World Publishing Co., Inc.
Merrill	Press of Merrill and Webber Company
Methuen	Methuen and Company
Michigan	University of Michigan Press
Minnesota	University of Minnesota Press
Missouri	University of Missouri Press
MIT	Massachusetts Institute of Technology Press
Mosher	Thomas Bird Mosher
National	National Textbook Company
Naylor	The Naylor Company
N. Carolina	University of North Carolina Press
Neale	Neale Publishing Company
Nebraska	University of Nebraska Press
Nelson	Thomas Nelson and Sons

New	New Century Press
Noble	Noble and Noble
Northwestern	Northwestern University Press
Norton	W. W. Norton and Company
Nostrand	D. Van Nostrand Company, Inc.
Ohio State	Ohio State University Press
Olgilvie	J. S. Olgilvie Publishing Company
Oliver	Oliver and Boyd
Orange	Orange Chronicle Company Printers
Oxford	Oxford University Press
Paul	K. Paul, Trench, Trubner, and Company
Penguin	Penguin Books, Ltd.
Penn	The Penn Publishing Company
Penn State	Pennsylvania State University Press
Pergamon	Pergamon Press, Inc.
Philosophical	Philosophical Library
Pitman	Sir Isaac Pitman and Sons
Pittsburgh	University of Pittsburgh Press
Platform	Platform News Publishing Company
Prentice	Prentice-Hall, Inc.
Princeton	Princeton University Press
Public	Public Affairs Press
Putnam's	G. P. Putnam's and Sons
Random	Random House
Rinehart	Rinehart and Company, Inc.
Robertson	Robertson and Mullens
Ronald	The Ronald Press Company
Routledge	George Routledge and Sons
Rutgers	Rutgers University Press
Scarecrow	Scarecrow Press
Scott	Scott, Foresman, and Company
Scribner's	Charles Scribner's Sons
Simon	Simon and Schuster
SMU	Southern Methodist University Press
Spartan	Spartan Books, Inc.
Springer	Springer Publishing Company
Stanford	Stanford University Press
Stevens	Stevens and Sons
Stockwell	A. H. Stockwell
Stokes	F. A. Stokes Company
Sweet	Sweet and Maxwell
Thomas	Charles Thomas & Son
Van Nostrand	Van Nostrand Reinhold
Viking	Viking Press
Wadsworth	Wadsworth Publishing Company

Wahr	George Wahr
Walch	J. Weston Walch, Publisher
Wiley	John Wiley and Sons Inc.
Williams	L. Williams
Wilson	H. W. Wilson Company
Winston	The John C. Winston Company
Wisconsin	University of Wisconsin Press
Wolfe	L. R. Wolfe
Yale	Yale University Press

UNPUBLISHED THESES AND DISSERTATIONS

M. A.	Master of Arts
M. S.	Master of Science
Ph. M.	Master of Philosophy
Ph. D.	Doctor of Philosophy

COLLEGES AND UNIVERSITIES

Akron	University of Akron
Alabama	University of Alabama
Arkansas	University of Arkansas
Baylor	Baylor University
Bowling Green	Bowling Green State University
Brigham Young	Brigham Young University
Brooklyn	Brooklyn College of the City University of New York
California, L. B.	California State College at Long Beach
C. Missouri	Central Missouri State College
Chicago	University of Chicago
Cincinnati	University of Cincinnati
Colorado	University of Colorado
Colorado State	Colorado State University
Columbia	Columbia University
Cornell	Cornell University
C. W. Post	C. W. Post College of Long Island University
Denver	University of Denver
Florida	University of Florida
Florida State	Florida State University
Fresno	Fresno State College
Harvard	Harvard University

Hawaii	University of Hawaii
Illinois	University of Illinois
Illinois State	Illinois State University, Normal
Indiana	University of Indiana
Iowa	University of Iowa
Johns Hopkins	Johns Hopkins University
Kansas	University of Kansas
Kansas State	Kansas State Teachers College at Emporia
Kent State	Kent State University
LSU	Louisiana State University
Mankato	Mankato State Teachers College
Marquette	Marquette University
Michigan State	Michigan State University
Minnesota	University of Minnesota
Missouri	University of Missouri
Missouri, K. C.	University of Missouri at Kansas City
Montana	University of Montana
Montana State	Montana State University
Nebraska	University of Nebraska
New Mexico	University of New Mexico
N. Dakota	North Dakota State University
N. Illinois	Northern Illinois State University
Northwestern	Northwestern University
Ohio	University of Ohio
Ohio State	Ohio State University
Oklahoma	University of Oklahoma
Oregon	University of Oregon
Oregon State	Oregon State University
O. Wesleyan	Ohio Wesleyan University
Penn State	Pennsylvania State University
Pittsburgh	University of Pittsburgh
Purdue	Purdue University
Sacramento	Sacramento State College
San Jose	San Jose State College
St. Cloud	St. Cloud College of Minnesota
S. California	University of Southern California
S. Dakota	University of South Dakota
S. Illinois	Southern Illinois University
S. Mississippi	University of South Mississippi
Stanford	Stanford University
SUNY	State University of New York
Syracuse	Syracuse University

Temple	Temple University
Texas	University of Texas
UCLA	University of California at Los Angeles
Washington	University of Washington
Wash. State	Washington State University
Wayne State	Wayne State University
W. Kentucky	Western Kentucky University
Wisconsin	University of Wisconsin
Wyoming	University of Wyoming

I. GENERAL PRINCIPLES

1. Textbooks and Manuals

Adler, Mortimer. Dialectic. New York, Harcourt, 1927.   1

Africa, Francisco M. The Art of Argumentation and Debate.
Manila, Garcia, 1952.   2

Alden, Raymond M. Art of Debate. New York, H. Holt, 1900.   3

American Institute of Banking. Debate Handbook. New York,
1947.   4

Anderson, Jerry M., and Dovre, Paul J., eds. Readings in
Argumentation. Boston, Allyn, 1968.   5

Arnold, John H. The Debater's Guide. Harrisburg, Pa., Handy,
rev. and enl., 1923.   6

Babcock, Robert W., and Powell, John H., Jr. How to Debate.
Philadelphia, Lippincott, 1923.   7

Baggaridge, James B., and Masel, Philip. The Art of Debating.
Melbourne, Australia, Robertson, 3d ed., 1939.   8

Baird, A. Craig. Argumentation, Discussion, and Debate. New
York, McGraw, 1950.   9

_____. Outline of Argumentation and Debate, Prepared for Stu-
dents in Bates College. Auburn, Me., Merrill, 1922.   10

_____. Public Discussion and Debate. New York, Ginn, 1937. 11

Baker, George P., and Huntington, Henry B. The Principles of
Argumentation. New York, Ginn, new ed., 1925.   12

Barksdale, Ethelbert C. The Art and Science of Speech: A Textbook for Student and Coach. San Antonio, Texas, Naylor,
1937.   13

Barron, H.M. How to Argue. London, Williams, 1932.   14

_____. How to Debate and the Science of Argument. London,
Stockwell, 1933.   15

Bauer, Otto F.   Fundamentals of Debate: Theory and Practice.
    Chicago, Scott, 1966.   16

Baylor University.   Suggestions on Debating.   Waco, Texas, De-
    bater's Research, 1926.   17

Behl, William A.   Discussion and Debate; An Introduction to
    Argument.   New York, Ronald, 1953.   18

Bell, Edwin.   The Principles of Argument.   Toronto, Canada Law
    Book Co., Ltd., 1910.   Philadelphia, Cromarty Law Book
    Co., 1910.   19

Bennett, William.   Pragmatic Debate.   Evanston, Ill., Champion-
    ship, 1971.   20

Bogoslavski, Boris.   The Technique of Controversy.   New York,
    Harcourt, 1928.   21

Borden, Richard C., and Busse, Alvin C.   How to Win an Argu-
    ment.   New York, Harper, 1926.   22

Bosmajian, Haig A.   Dissent: Symbolic Behavior and Rhetorical
    Strategies.   Boston, Allyn, 1972.   23

Braden, Waldo W., and Brandenburg, Ernest.   Oral Decision-
    Making; Principles of Discussion and Debate.   New York,
    Harper, 1955.   24

Bradley, Mark E., and Daniel, David W.   Better Speaking; A
    Textbook of Public Speaking, Discussion, and Debating.   New
    York, Nostrand, 1941.   25

Brandt, William J.   The Rhetoric of Argumentation.   Indianapolis,
    Bobbs, 1970.   26

Brown, C. W.   Complete Debater's Manual.   Chicago, Drake,
    1902.   27

Brumbaugh, Jesse F.   Legal and Public Speaking.   Indianapolis,
    Indiana, Bobbs, 1932.   28

Buck, Gertrude, and Mann, Kristine.   A Handbook of Argumenta-
    tion and Debating.   Orange, New Jersey, Orange, 1906.   29

Bump, Malcolm A.   The Debate Case: Modern Competitive De-
    bate.   New York, Debaters "600" Club, 1967.   30

Buys, W. E., and others.   Discussion and Debate.   Chicago,
    National Debate Research Company, Box 1161, 1957.   31

Capp, Glenn R.   Manual of Debate Principles Applied to Federal

Aid to Education. Waco, Texas, Debaters Research Bureau, Baylor University, 1941. 32

_____, and Capp, Thelma R. Principles of Argumentation and Debate. Englewood Cliffs, New Jersey, Prentice, 1965. 33

_____ and _____. Workbook in Principles of Argumentation and Debate. Waco, Texas, Baylor Book Store, Baylor, 1965. 34

Carr, Clarence F., and Stevens, Frederick E. How to Speak in Public. London, Pitman, 2nd ed., 1929. (A "ready guide to fluency in debate.") 35

Case, Keith. Basic Debate. Minneapolis, Minnesota, Northwestern, 1936. 36

Chenoweth, Eugene C. Debate and Discussion; Manual and Workbook on the Debate Proposition and Discussion Questions. Bloomington, Indiana, The Author, 1948. 37

_____. Discussion and Debate. Dubuque, Iowa, Brown, 1951. 38

Colbourn, Frank E. The Art of Debate. Lecture (1969) recorded by Listening Library, Inc., 1 Park Ave, Old Greenwich, Conn. (Printed copies of text available.) 38a

Colburn, C. William. Strategies for Educational Debate. Boston, Holbrook Press, 1972. 39

Collins, George R., and Morris, John S. Persuasion and Debate. New York and London, Harper, 1927. 40

Cosper, Russell. Teaching Debate in Secondary Schools. Ann Arbor, Michigan, Wahr, 1940. 41

Courtney, Luther W., and Capp, Glenn R. Practical Debating. New York, Lippincott, 1949. 42

Covington, Harry F. The Fundamentals of Debate. New York, Scribner's, 1918. 43

_____. A Pamphlet on Debating and Brief-Drawing. Princeton, New Jersey, The Author, 1903. 44

_____. Suggestions for Debaters. Princeton, New Jersey, Cliosophic Society, 1903. 45

Crocker, Lionel. Argumentation and Debate. New York, American, 1944. 46

_____. Argumentation and Debate. New York, American Institute of Banking, 1962. 47

Davis, Henry C., and Smith, Reed.   Debating for High Schools.
Columbia, South Carolina, The University, 1920.   (Bulletin of
the University of South Carolina, No. 83, February, 1920.)   48

Davis, William H.   Training for Debate.   Lawrence, Kansas:
The University, 1910.   49

Debating and Debating Societies.   University of California Bulletin.
Berkeley, California, California, 1914.   50

Debating and Public Discussion.   Extension Division Bulletin, 11,
No. 6.   Bloomington, Indiana, Indiana, 1913.   51

Deering, Ivah E.   Let's Try Thinking.   Yellow Spring, Ohio,
Antioch, 1942.   52

Denney, Joseph V., Duncan, Carson S., and McKinney, Frank C.
Argumentation and Debate.   New York and Cincinnati, American,
1910.   53

Dick, Robert C.   Argumentation and Rational Debating.   Dubuque,
Iowa, Brown, 1972.   54

The Dime Debater and Chairman's Guide.   New York, Ivers, 1900.
                                                                        55
Ehninger, Douglas, and Brockriede, Wayne.   Decision by Debate.
New York, Dodd, 1963.   56

Eisenberg, Abne M., and Ilardo, Joseph A.   Argument: An Alternative to Violence.   Englewood Cliffs, New Jersey, Prentice,
1972.   57

Everett, G.A., and Phipps, G.R.   Principles of Debate.   Ithaca,
New York, Cornell Country Life, Ser. No. 149, 1919.   58

Ewbank, Henry L., and Auer, J. Jeffrey.   Discussion and Debate;
Tools of a Democracy.   New York, Appleton, 2nd ed., 1951. 59

Fort, Lyman M.   Argumentation and Debate.   Mitchell, South Dakota, Educator Supply Co., 1925.   60

_____.   Oral English and Debate.   New York, H. Holt, 1929.   61

Foster, William Horton.   Debating for Boys.   New York, Sturgis
and Walton Co., 1915.   Also, New York, Macmillan, 1922.   62

Foster, William T.   Argumentation and Debating.   Boston, Houghton,
2nd ed. rev., 1969.   63

_____.   Essentials of Exposition and Argument.   Boston and New
York, Houghton, 1911.   (A manual for high schools, academies,
and debating clubs.)   64

Fox, Andrew N.   Modern Debating.   Chicago, Follett, 1932.   65

Freeley, Austin J.   Argumentation and Debate.   Belmont, California, Wadsworth, 3rd ed. , 1969.   66

Fritz, Charles A.   The Method of Argument.   New York, Prentice,
1931.   67

_____.   The Principles of Argument.   New York, N. Y. U. Book-
store, 1941.   68

Gardiner, John H.   The Making of Arguments.   Boston, Ginn,
1912.   69

Gibson, Laurence M.   Handbook for Literary and Debating Societies.
London, Hodder, 5th ed. , 1907.   70

Gislason, Haldor B.   Effective Debating.   University of Minnesota
Bulletin, General Series No. 14.   Minneapolis, Minnesota,
Minnesota, 1919.   71

Gordon, Albert I.   Debate Manual.   New York, Young People's
League of the United Synagogues of America, 1927.   72

Graves, Harold F.   Argument.   New York, Cordon, 1938.   73

_____ and Oldsey, Bernard S.   From Fact to Judgment.   New
York, Macmillan, 2nd ed. , 1963.   74

_____ and Spotts, Carle B.   The Art of Argument.   New York,
Prentice, 1927.   75

Gulley, Halbert E.   Essentials of Discussion and Debate.   New
York, Holt, 1955.   76

Haney, Thomas K.   An Introduction to Debate.   Boston, Ginn, 1965.
                                                                77
Harlan, Roy E.   Strategic Debating.   Boston, Chapman, 1940.   78

Hayworth, Donald, and Capel, R. B.   Oral Argument.   New York,
Harper, 1934.   79

Holm, James N.   How to Debate Successfully, with all Illustrations
from the Topic of the Welfare State.   Portland, Maine, Walch,
1950.   80

_____.   Successful Discussion and Debate; Illustrated by the Farm
Policy Topic.   Portland, Maine, Walch, 1956.   81

_____.   Ibid. ; Illustrated by the Increasing Educational Opportuni-
ties Topic.   Portland, Maine, Walch, 1955.   82

_____.   Ibid. ; Illustrated by the Selection of Presidents Topic.

Portland, Maine, Walch, 1953.   83

_____ and Kent, Robert.   How to debate successfully; Illustrated
by the Federal World Government Topic.   Portland, Maine,
Walch, 1947.   84

_____ and _____.   Ibid.; Illustrated by the Nationalization of Basic
Industries Topic.   Portland, Maine, Walch, 1949.   85

Howes, Raymond F., comp. and ed.   Debating.   Boston and New
York, Heath, 1931.   86

Huber, Robert B.   Influencing through Argument.   New York, Mc-
Kay, 1963.   87

Hungerford, Herbert.   The Success Club Debater.   New York, The
Success Company, 1901.   88

Jones, Leo.   A Manual for Debaters.   Bulletin of the University of
Washington, Exten. Ser. No. 8, Gen. Ser. No. 75.   Seattle,
Washington, The University, 1913.   89

Kahn, Theresa G., and Murphy, Richard.   A Series of Six Radio
Talks on Debating.   (Broadcast from the University of Pittsburgh
Studio of KDKA; Radio Publication No. 55.)   Pittsburgh, Pennsyl-
vania, University of Pittsburgh, 1929.   90

Ketcham, Victor A.   Argumentation and Debate.   New York, Macmillan, 1928.   91

_____.   The Theory and Practice of Argumentation and Debate.
New York, Macmillan, 1914.   92

Key, Percy C.   Theory and Practice of Argument.   Ann Arbor,
Michigan, Edwards Brothers, Inc., 1933.   93

Kleiser, Grenville.   How to Argue and Win.   New York and London,
Funk, 1910.   94

_____, comp. and ed.   Kleiser's Complete Guide to Public Speaking,
Comprising Extracts from the World's Great Authorities upon Pub-
lic Speaking, Oratory, Preaching, Platform and Pulpit Delivery,
Voice Building and Management, Argumentation, Debate, Reading,
Rhetoric, Expression, Gesture, Comport, etc.   New York and
London, Funk, 1915.   95

Kline, R. E. Pattison.   Argumentation and Debate.   Chicago, La
Salle Extension Institute, 1910.   96

Klopf, Donald W., and McCroskey, James C.   The Elements of Debate.   New York, Arco Publishing Co., 1969.   97

Kolb, J. H., and Wileden, A. F.   Why Not Have a Debate?   Madison,

Wisconsin, University of Wisconsin Agricultural Extension Service, 1927.   98

Kruger, Arthur N.   Counterpoint: Debates About Debate.   Metuchen,
New Jersey, Scarecrow, 1968.   99

_____. Effective Speaking: A Complete Course.   New York, Van
Nostrand, 1970.   100

_____. Modern Debate: Its Logic and Strategy.   New York, Mc-
Graw, 1960.   101

Laycock, Craven, and Scales, Robert L.   Argumentation and Debate.
New York, Macmillan, 1907.   102

Lockridge, Ross F.   Debating and Public Discussion; Manual for
Civic Discussion Clubs.   Indiana University Bulletin 11, No. 6.
Indianapolis, Indiana, The University, 1913.   103

Lyman, Rollo La Verne.   The Principles of Effective Debating.
Madison, Wisconsin, University Extension, rev. ed., 1908.   104

_____. Public Discussion and Debate.   Norman, Oklahoma, Uni-
versity Extension, 1913.   105

MacPherson, William.   How to Argue Successfully.   New York,
Dutton, 1914.   106

Marriott, James W.   Q. E. D.; Some Hints on Arguing.   London,
Harrap, 1944.   107

McBath, James H., ed.   Argumentation and Debate.   New York,
Holt, 1963.   (Revised edition of book formerly edited by David
Potter, infra.)   108

_____, ed.   Essays in Forensics.   Hannibal, Missouri, American
Forensic Association, 1970.   (Twenty essays from The AFA
Register.)   109

McBurney, James H., and Mills, Glen E.   Argumentation and Debate.   New York, Macmillan, 2nd ed., 1964.   110

_____, O'Neill, James M., and Mills, Glen.   Argumentation and
Debate.   New York, Macmillan, 1951.   111

McDonald, Daniel.   The Language of Argument.   Scranton, Chandler
Press, 1971.   112

Miller, Arthur B., and Fausti, Remo P.   Elements of Deliberative
Debating.   Belmont, California, Wadsworth, 1969.   113

Miller, Carl G.   Argumentation and Debate.   New York and Chicago,
Scribner's, 1930.   114

Miller, Gerald R., and Nilsen, Thomas R.   Perspectives on Argumentation.   Chicago, Scott, 1966.   115

Mills, Glen E.   Reason in Controversy.   Boston, Allyn, 2nd ed.,
1968.   116

Mitchell, H. B., and Marshall, K. D., eds.   A Handbook for Debaters.   Seminole, Oklahoma, N. P., 1946.   117

Moulton, Eugene R.   The Dynamics of Debate.   New York, Harcourt, 1966.   118

Murphy, James J., and Ericson, Jon M.   The Debater's Guide.
New York, Bobbs, 1961.   119

Musgrave, George McCoy.   Competitive Debate; Rules and Techniques.   New York, Wilson, 3rd ed., 1957.   120

Natanson, Maurice, and Johnstone, Henry W., Jr., eds.   Philosophy, Rhetoric, and Argumentation.   University Park, Pa., Penn
State, 1965.   121

Naylor, G. K., and Naylor, T. E.   Rules and Conduct of Debate.
London, (N. P.), 1905.   122

Newman, Robert P.   The Pittsburgh Code of Academic Debate.
Pittsburgh, Pennsylvania, Pittsburgh, 1963.   123

Nichols, Alan.   Discussion and Debate.   New York, Harcourt,
1941.   124

Nichols, Egbert R., and Baccus, Joseph H.   Modern Debating.
New York, Norton, 1936.   125

Olgilvie, John S.   How to Talk and Debate.   New York, Olgilvie,
1902.   126

O'Neill, James M.   A Manual of Debate and Oral Discussion for
Schools, Societies, and Clubs.   New York, Century, 1920.   127

_____.   Principles of Effective Debating and How to Judge a Debate.
Bulletin of the University of Wisconsin.   Madison, Wisconsin,
The University, 1925.   128

_____ and Cortright, Ruport L.   Debate and Oral Discussion.
New York, Century, 1931.   129

_____, Laycock, Craven, and Scales, Robert L.   Argumentation
and Debate.   New York, Macmillan, 1917.   130

_____ and McBurney, J. H.   The Working Principles of Argument.
New York, Macmillan, 1932.   131

Osborne, Margherita O.   Debating.   Philadelphia, Penn, 1934. 132

Pacilio, John, Jr., and Stites, William H.   Introduction to Debate:
A Programed Handbook.   Boulder, Colorado, Pruett Press,
1967.   133

Pattee, George K.   Practical Argumentation.   New York, Century,
rev., 1915.   134

Pellegrini, Angelo M., and Stirling, Brents.   Argumentation and
Public Discussion.   Boston and New York, Heath, 1936.   135

Pelsma, John R.   Essentials of Debate.   New York, Crowell, 1937.
                                                                             136
Perelman, Chaim.   The Idea of Justice and the Problem of Argument.   New York, Free, 1963.   137

_____.   An Historical Introduction to Philosophical Thinking (trans-
lated by Kenneth A. Brown).   New York, Free, 1965.   138

_____, and Olbrechts-Tyteca, L.   The New Rhetoric: A Treatise on
Argument (translated by John Wilkinson and Purcell Weaver).
Notre Dame, Indiana, and London, Univ. of Notre Dame Press,
1969.   139

Perry, France M.   An Introductory Course in Argumentation.   New
York, American, 1906.   140

Potter, David, ed.   Argumentation and Debate.   New York, Dryden,
1954.   (Rev. Ed. edited by J. McBath, supra.)   141

Public Discussion and Debate.   University of North Carolina Record
No. 115, Extension Series No. 6.   Chapel Hill, North Carolina,
University of North Carolina Extension Service, 1914.   142

Quimby, Brooks.   So You Want to Debate.   Portland, Maine, Walch,
1948.   143

_____.   Ibid., as Illustrated by the International Organization
Topic.   Portland, Maine, Walch, 1952.   144

_____.   So You Want to Discuss and Debate.   Portland, Maine,
Walch, 2nd ed., 1954.   145

Reeves, J. Walter.   The Fundamentals of Argumentation and Debate.
Boston and New York, Heath, 1928.   146

_____ and Hudson, Hoyt H.   Principles of Argument and Debate.
Boston, Heath, 1941.   147

Riddell, George A. R.   Some Things That Matter.   London, Hodder,
1922.   148

Rigg, John. Platform Oratory and Debate for Schools and Colleges.
New York, Stokes, 1929. London, Allen, 1929.   149

Sandford, William P., and Yeager, Willard H. Problems for Debate Practice. New York, Nelson, 1933.   150

Schopenhauer, Arthur. The Art of Controversy (Selected and translated by T. Bailey Saunders). London, Allen, 1921.   151

Shaw, Warren C. The Art of Debate. New York, Allyn, 1922. 152

_____ and Weaver, Andrew T. Information for Debates; a Pamphlet
for Use in English IX and English X at Dartmouth College.
Hanover, New Hampshire, The Dartmouth Press, 1913.   153

Shepard, David W., and Cashman, P. H. A Handbook for Beginning
Debaters. Minneapolis, Minnesota, Burgess, 2nd ed., 1961. 154

Sherman, Douglas R. A Manual for Beginning Debating. Detroit,
Wayne State University Press, 1956.   155

Shurter, Edwin D. How to Debate. New York and London, Harper,
1917.   156

_____. Science and Art of Debate. New York, Neale, 1908. 157

_____. The Science and Art of Effective Debating. New York,
Noble, 1925.   158

Shurter, Robert L., and Helm, George M. Argument. New York,
Rinehart, 1939.   159

_____ and Pierce, John R. Critical Thinking: Its Expression in
Argument. New York, McGraw, 1966.   160

Sims, John G., Jr. Elements of Debating. Nashville, Tennessee;
and Dallas, Texas, Publishinghouse of M. E. Church, 1905. 161

Sloan, J. R., Jr. Successful Debater; Arranged for the Use of Debate Coaches and Public Speaking Teachers. Jermyn, Texas,
National Debaters' Bureau, 1933.   162

Smith, Craig R., and Hunsaker, David M. The Bases of Argument:
Ideas in Conflict. Indianapolis, Bobbs, 1972.   163

Smith, Elmer W. Handbook of Debate. Hamilton, New York, New
Century Press, 1912.   164

Smith, Reed. Effective Debating. Columbia, South Carolina, University of South Carolina, 1917.   165

Smith, Roy M. Public Speaking and Debate. Canton, Missouri,
Culver-Stockton College, 1930.   166

Speaker and Debater; a complete book of self-instruction in speaking
and debating, based on Gibson's Handbook for Literary and Debating Societies. Rev. with additional material by Rodney Bennett.
London, English Universities Press, 1938.   167

Spotts, Carle B.   Debate and Discussion; a Syllabus and Workbook.
Boston, Expression, 1941.   168

Stone, Arthur P., and Garrison, Stewart L.   Essentials of Argument.   New York, H. Holt, 1916.   169

Summers, Harrison B., Whan, Forest L., and Rousse, Thomas A.
How to Debate, a Textbook for Beginners.   New York, Wilson,
1950.   170

Taylor, Vernon L.   The Art of Argument.   Metuchen, New Jersey,
Scarecrow, 1971.   171

Terry, Donald R., ed.   Modern Debate Case Techniques.   Skokie,
Ill., National, 1970.   172

Thayer, Albert R.   Twenty Cases for Informal Debate.   Portland,
Maine, Walch, 1966.   173

Thomas, Ralph W.   A Manual of Debate.   New York and Cincinnati,
American, 1910.   174

Thompson, Wayne N.   Modern Argumentation and Debate: Principles and Practices.   New York, Harper, 1971.   175

Toulmin, Stephen E.   The Uses of Argument.   New York, Cambridge, 1958.   176

Wagner, Russell H.   Handbook of Argumentation.   New York, Nelson, 1936.   (Emphasis on cross-examination.)   177

Welday, John O.   Debaters' Manual.   Girard, Kansas, Appeal to
Reason, 1916.   178

Willhoft, Waldo O.   Modern Debate Practice.   New York, Prentice,
1929.   179

Wilson, Louis R.   Public Discussion and Debate.   North Carolina
University Extension Series.   Chapel Hill, North Carolina: The
University, 1914.   Raleigh, North Carolina, Edwards and
Broughton Printing Co., 1917.   180

Winans, James A., and Hudson, Hoyt H.   A First Course in Public
Speaking, with Debating and Oral Reading.   New York and London, Century, 1931.   181

_____ and Utterback, William E.   Argumentation.   New York,
Century, 1930.   182

Windes, Russell R., and Hastings, Arthur.   Argumentation and
   Advocacy.   New York, Random, 1965.   183

_____ and O'Neill, Robert N.   A Guide to Debate.   Portland,
   Maine, Walch, 1964.   184

Wood, Roy V.   Strategic Debate.   Skokie, Ill., National, 1968. 185

2.   Theses and Dissertations

Bevilacqua, Vincent M.   A Comparative Analysis of Richard Whately's Elements of Rhetoric and Contemporary Argumentation Texts.
   M. A. Emerson College.   1958.   186

De Boer, Holle G.   A Workbook in Elementary Debate.   M. A.
   Colorado State Teachers College.   1935.   187

Earney, Michael D.   The Place of the Non-Logical Proofs in Contemporary American Debate Textbooks.   M. A. Michigan State.
   1953.   188

Ecroyd, Donald H.   An Analysis of the Theory of Persuasion in Selected American Works on Argumentative Speaking.   M. A. Iowa.
   1945.   189

Higgins, Albert J., Jr.   An Analysis of Personality Differences Between Debaters and Non-Debaters.   M. S. Kansas State.   1964.
                                                                    190
Lahman, Carroll P.   A Handbook of Debate.   M. A. Wisconsin.
   1929.   191

Link, Alma T.   Critical Analysis of Nine College Debate Texts.
   M. A. Iowa.   1928.   192

Maddox, Thomas K.   The Treatment of Logic in Textbooks on Argumentation and Debate.   M. A. L. S. U.   1942.   193

Miller, E. W.   The College Debate; Principles of Proof and Evidence.
   M. A. Ohio Wesleyan University.   1922.   194

Nilsen, Thomas R.   A Survey of the Concept and Function of Logic
   and the Works of Selected American Writers in the Fields of
   Argumentation and Discussion.   M. A. University of Washington.
   1948.   195

Patrick, Charlotte W.   The Argumentation Theory of George Pierce
   Baker.   M. A. Wyoming.   1969.   196

Phelps, Emma S.   The Place of Deductive Logic in Representative
   Works on Argumentation, Debate, and Discussion.   M. A. Iowa.
   1946.   197

Rexroad, Chloe E.   The Importance of Dialectic in Argumentation.
    M. A.   Kansas State.   1969.   198

Spicher, Lynn.   Debate: A Handbook for Beginners.   M. A.   Brad-
    ley University.   1966.   199

II. WRITINGS BEFORE 1900

A. DEBATE

1. Books

Baker, George P. The Principles of Argumentation. Boston and London, Ginn, 1896.   200

_____, comp. Specimen Briefs Drawn by Students of Harvard College. Cambridge, Mass., The University, circa 1892.   201

_____, comp. Specimens of Argumentation. New York, H. Holt, 1893.   202

Barrows, L. D. Rudiments of Public Speaking and Debate. New York, Methodist Book Concern, 1861.   203

Buck, Gertrude. A Course in Argumentative Writing. New York, H. Holt, 1899.   204

Carey, Thomas J. The Complete Debater. New York, Excelsior, 1884.   205

Colston, John R. Reports of Forensic Meetings. Swansea, England, Ivey and Pearse; London; Simpkin, Marshall, and Co., 1849. 206

Cooke, Peter J. Forensic Eloquence; Or, The Eloquence of the Bar: A Practical Handbook for Barristers and Solicitors. London, G. Barker, 1897.   207

Craig, Asa H. Pros and Cons, Complete Debates. New York, Hinds, 1897.   208

Dwight, Theodore, Jr., ed. President Dwight's Decisions of Questions Discussed by the Senior Class in Yale College, in 1813 and 1814. New York, Jonathan Leavitt, 1833. (Forty-one disputes on questions like "Should Capital Punishment be Inflicted?") 209

Gibbons, Frederick Brian de Malbisse. On Debating Societies: Their Use and Value, Political and Educational. London, Temple Publishing Co., 1890. (16pps.)   210

Gore, James H. Congressional Manual of Parliamentary Practice, Deduced from the Rules and Rulings of the Congress of the United

States.   Syracuse, N.Y., C.W. Bardeen, 1893.   211

Hall, Charles C.   The Value of the Debating Society (An Address to
  Young Men).   Brooklyn, N.Y., The Author, 1890.   (19pps.) 212

Hart, Albert B., and Baker, George P.   Harvard Debating; Subjects
  and Suggestions for Courses in Oral Discussion.   Cambridge,
  Mass., The University, 1896.   213

Henry, William H.F.   The Practical Debater, An Outline of Instruction in the Law and Practice of Parliamentary Assemblies.   Indianapolis, Indiana, J.E. Sherrill, 1884.   214

Holyoake, George J.   Public Speaking and Debate; A Manual for
  Advocates and Agitators.   London, T.F. Unwin, 1895.   (First
  published in outline form under the title Rudiments of Public
  Speaking and Debate.)   215

_____.   Rudiments of Public Speaking and Debate; Or, Hints on the
  Application of Logic.   (With an essay on sacred eloquence by
  Henry Rogers.)   New York, Carlton and Porter, 1861.   216

How to Debate.   Glasgow, n.p., 1883.   (35pps.)   217

Jones, John G.   An Address Delivered, on Thursday, April 3d,
  1806...on the Opening of the British Forum.   A Society for Rational and Temperate Discussion...Including the Rules and Regulations of the Institution.   London, The Author, 1806.   (13pps.)
                                                          218
Kinnamon, A.J.   Debater's Handbook.   Chicago, Dennison, 1887.
  (On parliamentary law and debating.)   219

Kinsey, O.P.   The Normal Debater.   Cincinnati, Ohio, G.E. Stevens
  and Co., 1874.   220

Knowles, James S.   The Debater's Handbook.   Boston, Lee and
  Shepard, 1887.   221

Lee, Albert S.   Literary Manual: A Convenient Handbook for the
  Use of Colleges, Schools, and Debating Societies.   Cincinnati,
  Ohio, The Author, 1880.   222

Lewis, George C.   An Essay on the Influence of Authority in Matters of Opinion.   London, Longmans, 1875.   (Discusses the criteria of reliable authority.)   223

MacEwan, Elias J.   The Essentials of Argumentation.   Boston,
  Heath, 1898.   224

McElligott, James N.   The American Debater.   New York, Ivison,
  Blakeman, Taylor and Co., rev. ed., 1882.   225

Neely, Thomas B.   The Church Lyceum; Its Organization and Man-

agement. Introduction by Bishop Henry W. Warren. New York:
Phillips and Hunt, 1882.   226

Palgrave, Reginald F. D. The Chairman's Handbook; Suggestions
and Rules for the Conduct of Chairmen of... Rules... Drawn from
the Practice of Parliament. London, Sampson Low and Co.,
1895.   227

Robinson, William. Forensic Oratory; A Manual for Advocates.
Boston, Little, 1893. (Principles and types of oratory; sections
on cross-examination.)   228

Rowton, Frederick. The Debater: A New Theory of the Art of
Speaking. London, Longman, Brown, Green, and Longmans, 2d
ed., 1850.   229

_____. How to Conduct a Debate. New York, Dick and Fitzgerald,
circa 1847.   230

_____ and Payne, F. M. Nine Complete Debates... Especially
Adapted to Literary and Debating Societies. New York, Excelsior, 1893.   231

Sidgwick, Alfred. The Process of Argument; A Contribution to
Logic. London, Black, 1893.   232

Society for Political Education. Question for Debate in Politics and
Economics. New York, The Society for Political Education,
1889.   233

Thayer, James B. Preliminary Treatise on Evidence at the Common Law. Boston, Little, 1898.   234

Warford, Aaron A. How to Debate. New York, F. Tousey, 1884.
                                                                       235
Whately, Richard. Elements of Rhetoric: Comprising an Analysis
of the Laws of Moral Evidence and of Persuasion, with Rules for
Argumentative Composition and Elocution. Boston and Cambridge,
James Munroe and Co., rev. ed., 1861.   236

Yale University Brothers in Unity. Subjects for Debate. New
Haven, Conn., The University, 1847.   237

2. Articles

Bacon, Cecil F. Intercollegiate Debating. Fo, 26 (October, 1898),
222-28.   238

Bagehot, Walter. On the Emotion of Conviction. In The Works of
Walter Bagehot ed. by Forrest Morgan. Hartford, Conn.,
Travelers Insurance Co., 1891. Vol. II, pp. 326-38.   239

Baker, George P. Debating at Harvard. HGM, 7 (March, 1899),
363-72.   240

Brodt, Philip E. Debating Societies at Columbia. Columbia University Quarterly, 1 (December, 1898), 47-52. (Historical notes
and statement on the functions of debating societies.)   241

Buckham, John W. The Ethics of Expression. Ed, 17 (February,
1897), 326-31.   242

Buckley, James M. Debate and Composition: Their Relation to
Symmetrical Culture. Ch, 13 (1889), 18.   243

_____. Preparation and Action in Debate. Ch, 18 (1894), 659-64.
                                                                244
_____. Principles and Practice of Debate. Ch, 18 (1894), 402-
407.   245
_____. Public Oral Debate. Ch, 18 (1894), 532-36.   246

Dangers of Debating. Bentley's Miscellany, 19 (1891), 615.   247

Dickens, Charles. Our Debating Society. All the Year Round, 43
(July 12, 1879), 85-89.   248

Discussion Classes (Editorial). CEJ, 9 (February 12, 1848), 107-
109. (On debating clubs.)   249

Emery, V.J. On the Definition of Some Rhetorical Terms. AJPh,
18, 70 (1897), 206-13.   250

English, C.D. Inefficiency of Argument. Overl, 17 (1891), 59.
                                                                251
Gordy, J.P. The Test of Belief. PR, 3 (May, 1894), 257-77. 252

McElligott, James N. Debating as a Means of Educational Discipline. AJE, 1 (March, 1856), 237-56; (May, 1856), 495-502.253

Miller, Marion M. Debating in American Colleges. BA, 2 (January, 1896), 208-15.   254

Pierce, Charles S. The Critic of Arguments. OC, 6 (1892), 3391-
94; 3415-18.   255

Ringwalt, Ralph C. Intercollegiate Debating. Fo, 22 (January,
1897), 633-40.   256

Ritchie, David G. The Relation of Logic to Psychology. PR, 7
(January, 1897), 1-17.   257

Smith, G.J. On Teaching Argumentation. ER, 14 (October, 1897),
285-91.   258

Stevenson, Robert Louis. Debating Societies. In Letters and Miscellanies of Robert Louis Stevenson. New York, Scribner's, 1900. Vol. XXII, pp. 42-3.   259

Village Debating Societies. Knickerbocker's, 45 (1855), 156-66. 260

Vrooman, Carl. College Debating. Ar, 10 (October, 1894), 677-83.   261

Williams, A. M. The Scottish School of Rhetoric. Ed, 13 (November, 1892), 142-50; (December, 1892), 220-27; (January, 1893), 281-90; (February, 1893), 344-54; (March, 1893), 427-34; (April, 1893), 488-96.   262

B. RELATED FIELDS: LOGIC

Books

Abbott, Austin. A Brief on the Modes of Proving the Facts Most Frequently in Issue or Collaterally in Questions on the Trial of Civil or Criminal Cases. New York, Diossy Law Book Co., 1891.   263

Arnauld, A. The Port Royal Logic. Edinburgh, Sutherland and Knox, 1851.   264

Bacon, Francis. Novum Organum. Oxford, Clarendon, 1889. 265

Bain, A. Logic, Deductive and Inductive. New York, Appleton, 1887.   266

Boole, George. An Investigation of the Laws of Thought. London, Walton and Materly, 1854.   267

Bosanquet, Bernard. Logic, or the Morphology of Knowledge. Oxford, Clarendon, 1888.   268

Gilbart, James W. Logic for the Million. London, Bell and Daldy, 1865.   269

Hamilton, William. Lectures on Logic. Edinburgh, W. Blackwood and Sons, 1859-1860.   270

Hegel, F. W. Wissenschaftder Logik. Nuremburg, Schrag, 1812-1816.   271

Hyslop, James H. The Elements of Logic, Theoretical and Practical. New York, Scribner's, 3d ed., 1894.   272

_____. Logic and Argument. New York, Scribner's, 1899. 273

Mill, John Stuart. A System of Logic. London, Harper, 1887. 274

Überweg, F.   A System of Logic (translated by T. M. Lindsay).
      London, Longmans, 1871.   275

Wallace, William.   The Logic of Hegel.   Oxford, Oxford, 1873. 276

Whately, Richard.   Elements of Logic.   London, J. W. Parker and
      Son, 9th ed., 1859.   277

B.   RELATED FIELDS: PERSUASION AND RHETORIC

Books

Adams, John Quincy.   Lectures on Rhetoric and Oratory.   Cam-
      bridge, Mass., Hilliard and Metcalf, 1810.   278

Aristotle.   Aristotle's Treatise on Rhetoric.   Analysis by Thomas
      Hobbes.   Analytical Questions on the Rhetoric.   Oxford, D. A.
      Talboys, 2d ed., 1833.   279

Bain, Alexander.   The Senses and the Intellect.   London, Longman,
      Green, Longman, Roberts and Green, 1864.   280

Blair, Hugh.   Lectures on Rhetoric and Belles Lettres.   1783 (Many
      editions).   281

Campbell, George.   The Philosophy of Rhetoric.   New York, Harper,
      new ed., 1851.   282

Cicero, M. T.   De Oratore (translated by F. B. Calvert).   Edinburgh,
      Edmonston, 1870.   283

_____.   De Oratore (translated with introduction and notes by
      Augustus S. Wilkins).   Oxford, Clarendon, 1890-1893.   3 Vols.
                                                                 284
_____.   The Three Dialogues on the Orator.   Ed. by William
      Guthrie.   New York, Harper, 2d American ed., 1860.   285

Cope, E. M.   An Introduction to Aristotle's Rhetoric.   London and
      Cambridge, Macmillan, 1867.   (An excellent commentary and
      analysis.)   286

Frieze, Henry S.   The Tenth and Twelfth Books of the Institutions
      of Quintilian, with Explanatory Notes.   New York, American, new
      rev. ed., 1888.   287

Genung, John F.   Handbook of Rhetorical Analysis.   Boston, Ginn,
      1895.   288

_____.   Outlines of Rhetoric.   Boston, Ginn, 1896.   289

_____.   The Practical Elements of Rhetoric.   Boston and New

York, Ginn, 1899.   290

Grant, Alexander.   Aristotle.   Philadelphia, Lippincott, 1877.   291

Hill, Adam S.   The Foundations of Rhetoric.   New York, Harper,
    1897.   292

_____.   The Principles of Rhetoric.   New York, Harper, rev. ed.
    enl., 1895.   293

Miller, D. F.   Rhetoric as an Art of Persuasion; From the Stand-
    point of a Lawyer.   Des Moines, Iowa, Mills and Co., 1880. 294

Moir, George, and Spalding, William.   Poetry, Modern Romance,
    and Rhetoric.   Edinburgh, Black, 1851.   (Section on rhetoric by
    Spalding, based on the work of Aristotle, Campbell, and Whately.)
                                                                        295
Waldstein, Charles.   The Balance of Emotion and Intellect.   London,
    Osgood, McIlvaine and Co., 1896.   296

Walker, John.   The Academic Speaker, Or, A Selection of Parlia-
    mentary Debates..., and Speeches from the Best Writers.   Lon-
    don, Cadell and Davies, 1817.   297

III. HISTORY

1. Books

Beam, Jacob N. The American Whig Society of Princeton University. Princeton, N. J., The Society, 1933. (A history of the Whig Literary Society, including an account of the speaking and debating practices of the 19th century.) 298

Bonner, S. F. Roman Declamation in the Late Republic and Early Empire. Berkeley, California, California, 1949. 299

Coulter, E. Merton. College Life in the Old South. New York, Macmillan, 1928. 300

Dagget, Naphtali. Argumenta Recita in Aula Yalensi, 1947. Mss. in Yale University Library. 301

Demosthenes Demobilized: A Record of Cambridge Union Society Debates, February, 1919-June, 1920, by the Four Presidents. With a preface by Austen Chamberlain and an introduction by J. R. Tanner. Cambridge, W. Heffer and Sons, 1920. (101pps.) 302

Fairley, John A. The Pantheon: An Old Edinburgh Debating Society. Edinburgh, Scotland, The Edinburgh Club, 1909. (Extracted from the first volume of The Book of the Old Edinburgh Club, March, 1909.) 303

Ferguson, C. L. History of the Magpie and Stump Debating Society, 1866-1926. Cambridge, Mass., 1931. 304

Green, E. W. Fifty Years of the St. Albans Debating Society, 1888-1933. St. Albans, 1933. 305

Hay, Denys, ed. The Renaissance Debate. New York, Holt, 1965. 306

John of Salisbury. Metalogicon (translated by Daniel D. McGarry). Berkeley, California, California, 1955. (Discusses Aristotle's contribution to the art of disputation.) 307

Little, A. G., and Pelster, F. Oxford Theology and Theologians, A. D. 1282-1302. Oxford, Oxford Historical Society, 1934. (Contains a summary of the typical disputation process.) 308

Meriwether, Colyer. Our Colonial Curriculum, 1607-1776. Washington, D. C. , Capitol, 1907.   309

Milne-Rae, Lettice, ed.   Ladies in Debate: Being a History of the
Ladies' Edinburgh Debating Society, 1865-1935.   Edinburgh,
Oliver and Boyd, 1936.   (Chapter VII contains a record of debate
subjects used from 1867-1935.)   310

Morrah, Herbert A.   The Oxford Union, 1823-1923.   London, Cas-
sell and Co. , 1923.   311

O'Connor, Lillian.   Pioneer Women Orators.   New York, Columbia,
1954.   312

Oliver, Robert T.   A History of Public Speaking in America.   Boston, Allyn, 1965.   313

Potter, David.   Debating in the Colonial Chartered Colleges.   New
York, Columbia, 1944.   314

Roach, Helen P.   History of Speech Education at Columbia, 1754-
1950.   New York, Columbia, 1950.   315

Stephens, Frank F.   A History of the University of Missouri.   Columbia, Missouri, Missouri, 1962.   316

Wallace, Karl R. , ed.   History of Speech Education in America.
New York, Appleton, 1954.   317

Waterman, Thomas H.   Cornell University: A History.   New York,
Cornell, 1905.   318

2.   Theses and Dissertations

Bauer, Otto F.   A Century of Debating at Northwestern University,
1855-1955.   M. A.   Northwestern.   1955.   319

Caldwell, Evelyn.   The History and Tendencies of the American
Lyceum.   M. A.   S. California.   1927.   320

Callison, Norman.   A History of the Department of Speech and Dra-
matics at Southwestern College in Winfield, Kansas.   M. S.
Kansas State.   1967.   321

Capp, Glenn R. , Jr.   History and Analysis of Intercollegiate Debating in America.   M. A.   Baylor.   1967.   322

Cowperthwaite, Lowery L.   A History of Intercollegiate Forensics
at the State University of Iowa, 1874-1946.   M. A.   Iowa.   1946.
                                                                         323
Gillis, Herbert R.   History, Theory, and Practice of Speech Education at Georgetown, 1789 to 1900.   Ph. D.   Western Reserve.
1958.   324

Graham, Mary W. The Lyceum in Ohio from 1840 to 1860. Ph. D. Ohio State. 1950. 325

Harrison, Carolyn P. American Intercollegiate Debate: A General Survey with Emphasis on Past and Present Controversies, 1892-1968. M. A. W. Kentucky. 1968. 326

Hicks, Wreatha. The First Seventy-Five Years of Forensic Activities of the University of Kansas (1867-1942). M. A. Kansas. 1962. 327

Hughes, Thomas. A Study of the Forensic Activities at Michigan State College from 1857-1937. M. A. Michigan State. 1952. 328

Irwin, James R. Student Public Address Activities at Wayne University, 1918-1956. M. A. Wayne State. 1967. 329

Kyle, Judy M. A History of the Ohio State University Department of Speech. M. A. Ohio State. 1964. 330

Marderosian, Haig Der. A Partial History of Debate at Emerson College. M. S. Emerson. 1957. 331

Martin, Boyd N. The History of Men's Debating at Muskingum College. Michigan. 1952. 332

McBride, Sara A. Forensic Activities at the University of Florida, 1905-1932: With Special Attention to Literary Societies. M. A. Florida. 1949. 333

Miller, Enid. Development of Intercollegiate Debating in the United States, Including a Specific Study of Northwestern and Chicago Universities. M. A. Northwestern. 1926. 334

Mowder, Barbara J. The History of Forensic Activity at Illinois State Normal University. M. A. Illinois State Normal. 1960. 335

Nabors, D. J. The Historical Development of Intercollegiate Forensic Activities, 1915-1956. Ph. D. Oklahoma. 1957. 336

Olson, Donald O. Debating at the University of Nebraska. M. S. Wisconsin. 1947. 337

Price, Paula. History of Debate at F. S. U. M. A. Florida State. 1967. 338

Quimby, Frank B. A Decade of International Debating. M. A. Harvard. 1931. 339

Rice, P. Jeannine. The Development of an Active Speech Program at Miami University, 1900-1940. M. A. Miami University, Ohio. 1967. 340

Rohrer, Daniel. Young Ladies' Literary Society of Oberlin College
1835-1860. M. S. Wisconsin. 1969.   341

Ross, Raymond S. Preliminary Research Toward a History of Intercollegiate Debating at Marquette University. M. A. Marquette.
1951.   342

Shelby, Annette N. The Development of the Theory of Argumentation
and Debate, 1895-1970. Ph. D. L. S. U. 1973   342a

Sillars, Malcolm S. A History of Intercollegiate Debate at the University of Redlands. M. A. Redlands. 1949.   343

Tewell, Fred. A History of Intercollegiate Debating in the State
Collegiate Institutions of Louisiana. M. A. L. S. U. 1949. 344

Thomas, Ota. The Theory and Practice of Disputation at Yale,
Harvard, and Dartmouth from 1700 to 1800. Ph. D. Iowa. 1941.
                                                              345
Waller, Charlie F. A History of Debate at Stephen F. Austin State
College. M. A. Stephen F. Austin State College. 1952.   346

Weaver, Richard L. Forum for Ideas: The Lyceum Movement in
Michigan 1818-1860. Ph. D. Indiana. 1969.   347

White, Jacqueline A. An Historical Study of the Forensic Program
at Ohio University from 1812 to 1860. M. A. Ohio. 1969. 348

3. Articles

Bauer, Otto F. The Harvard-Yale Myth. AFAR, 11 (Winter, 1963),
20-23. (Contends that the first American intercollegiate debate
was not between Harvard and Yale.)   349

Boase, Paul H. Interdenominational Forensics on the Ohio Frontier.
G, 35 (March, 1953), 55-57.   350

Bohman, George V. A Study in Pre-Revolutionary American Political Oratory, 1761-1776. M. A. Wisconsin. 1934.   351

Braden, Waldo W. The Beginnings of the Lyceum, 1826-1840. SSJ,
20 (Winter, 1954), 125-35.   352

Carmack, Paul A. Controversial Speaking Campaigns in American
History. G, 44 (January, 1962), 20-24.   353

Clark, Donald L. An Extension of Bromley Smith's Article. QJS,
35 (February, 1949), 82-83. (Article referred to is "Extracurricular Disputations: 1400-1650, " infra.)   354

_____. Some Values of Roman Declamatio. QJS, 35 (October,
1949), 280-83.   355

Clarke, M. L.   The Thesis in the Roman Rhetorical Schools of the
Republic.   CQ, new series 1 (1951), 159-66.   (Contends that controversia did not develop from thesis in Roman rhetorical teaching but that controversia was an established method of education
from the earliest days of Roman rhetoric.)   356

Davis, Frank B.   Debating in the Literary Societies of Selected
Southern Universities.   SSJ, 15 (December, 1949), 91-99.   357

Diem, W. Roy.   History of Intercollegiate Debating in Ohio.   CSSJ,
1 (November, 1949), 43-53.   358

_____.   Ohio Wesleyan Debate History.   G, 43, (May, 1961), 64-66.
359

Dovre, Paul J.   Historical-Critical Research in Debate.   JAFA, 2
(May, 1965), 72-79.   360

Dutton, Joseph.   Debating of Yesteryear.   G, 27 (May, 1945), 55.
Also in DM, 1 (July-September, 1945), 96-97.   361

Emerson, J. Gordon.   A Half-Century of the Carnot-Joffre.   G, 27
(March, 1945), 35-42.   (On the annual debate between Stanford
and the University of California.)   362

_____.   The Old Debating Society.   QJS, 17 (July, 1931), 362-75.
363

Ewbank, Henry L.   Debating in the "Good Old Days."   G, 34 (November, 1951), 3-4.   364

Giles, Leona H.   Debate History of Oklahoma.   Scholastic Debater,
1 (January, 1945), 7.   365

Gunderson, Robert G.   Early Coeds Win the Right to Speak.   G,
32 (January, 1950), 29-30.   366

Kennedy, George.   Speech Education in Greece.   WS, 31 (Winter,
1967), 2-8.   367

Kuebler, Roy R.   Debating at Dickinson College: Historical Note.
BDAPC, 13 (March 1, 1947), 19-24.   368

Lillich, Richard B.   The First Ladies Literary Society.   G, 39
(November, 1956), 5-7.   369

MacKendrick, Paul.   The Classical Origins of Debate.   CSSJ, 12
(Autumn, 1960), 16-20.   370

McNally, James R.   Dux Illa Directrixque Artrium: Rudolph
Agricola's Dialectical System.   QJS, 52 (December, 1966), 337-
347.   371

Meador, Prentice A., Jr.   Speech Education at Rome.   WS, 31
(Winter, 1967), 9-15.   372

Morrison, Robert.   History of Debate in American Colleges--North
    Carolina University.   DM, 3 (Autumn, 1948), 150-52.   373

Mundt, Karl E.   Free Speech Two Thousand Years Ago.   R, 16
    (November, 1941), 2.   374

Murphy, James J.   Two Medieval Textbooks in Debate.   JAFA, 1
    (January, 1964), 1-6.   375

Nadeau, Ray.   Hermogenes on "Stock Issues" in Deliverative Speak-
    ing.   SM, 25 (March, 1958), 59-66.   376

Nichols, Egbert R.   A Historical Sketch of Intercollegiate Debating.
    QJS, 22 (April, 1936), 213-20; 22 (December, 1936), 591-602;
    23 (April, 1937), 259-78.   377

Patterson, Walter G.   Debate Club, 1846 Style.   SchA, 18 (March,
    1947), 207-209.   378

Pellegrini, Angelo M.   Renaissance and Medieval Antecedents of
    Debate.   QJS, 28 (February, 1942), 14-19.   379

Pence, James W., Jr.   The Decline of the Literary and Debating
    Societies at the University of Virginia.   SSJ, 26 (Spring, 1961),
    214-23.   380

Perril, H. Bruce.   Development of Debating as Revealed in Early
    References.   G, 17 (May, 1935), 57-58.   (Contains a good de-
    scriptive bibliography of many articles listed in Section 2.) 381

Polk, Lee R.   Historical Research in Forensics: Its Status and
    Guidelines for the Future.   JAFA, 7 (Winter, 1970), 36-41. 382

Post, Robert M.   Forensic Activities at Trinity College, Dublin, in
    the Eighteenth Century.   CSSJ, 19 (Spring, 1968), 19-25.   383

Potter, David.   Footnotes for a History of Debating.   S, 29 (Janu-
    ary, 1947), 45.   384

_____.   Glimpses of Extra-Curricular Debating 1722-1783.   DM,
    3 (March, 1947), 32-33, 63.   385

_____.   The Literary Society.   In History of Speech Education in
    America.   Ed. by Karl R. Wallace.   New York, Appleton, 1954.
                                                                  386
_____.   More Footnotes for a History of Debating.   F, 32 (May,
    1947), 94-96.   387

_____.   Our Debate Tradition.   In Argumentation and Debate.   Ed.
    by David Potter.   New York, Dryden, 1954.   pp. 3-22.   388

_____.   The Old Princeton Debating Societies.   DM, 3 (December,
    1947), 208-10.   389

_____. A Postscript to the History of Debating in the American Colleges. G, 43 (May, 1961), 57-59.   390

_____. Significant Changes in Collegiate Debating, 1748-1948. G, 30 (May, 1948), 73-74.   391

_____. Some Aspects of Speaking in Town Meetings of Colonial New England. SSJ, 22 (Spring, 1957), 157-63.   392

Rayment, Charles S. Three Notes on Roman Declamation. Classical Weekly, 45 (1952), 225-28.   393

Roach, H. P. Early Speaking Societies at Columbia College. AAUPB, 41 (December, 1955), 639-44.   394

Seifrit, William C. Literary Societies at West Virginia Wesleyan. West Virginia History, 23 (1961), 42-49.   395

Smith, Bromley. Extra-Curricular Disputations; 1400-1560. QJS, 34 (December, 1948), 473-76.   396

_____. Father of Debate: Protagoras of Abdera. QJS, 4 (March, 1918), 196-215.   397

_____. Queen Elizabeth at the Cambridge Disputations. QJS, 15 (November, 1929), 495-502.   398

_____, and Ehninger, Douglas. The Terra Filial Disputations at Oxford. QJS, 36 (April, 1940), 333-39.   399

Smith, Donald K. Origin and Development of Departments of Speech. In History of Speech Education of America, ed. by Karl R. Wallace. New York, Appleton, 1954.   400

Snyder, Henry N. The College Literary Society. Sewanee Review, 12 (1904), 91ff.   401

Stites, Ruth E. Eighty Years of Forensics at Rockford. G, 16 (January, 1934), 26-27.   402

Taylor, John A. The Evolution of College Debating. PSR, 2 (December, 1912), 97-105. (A review of intercollegiate debating twenty years after its beginning; discusses selection of teams, judging, ethics.)   403

Tewell, Fred, and Braden, Waldo W. Brief History of Debating in Louisiana. SSJ, 18 (May, 1953), 226-32.   404

Tozier, R. B. A Short Life History of the Chautauqua. American Journal of Sociology, 40 (July, 1934), 69-73.   405

Trueblood, Thomas C. A Chapter on the Organization of College Courses in Public Speaking. QJSE, 12 (1926), 6ff.   406

Williams, Donald E.   College Literary Societies and the Founding
   of Departments of Speech.   JAFA, 3 (January, 1966), 29-33. 407

Yoakam, Doris G.   The First Female Fumer.   G, 17 (January,
   1935), 20-22.   (On the career of Frances Wright.)   408

Yoder, Jess.   The Frankenthal Debates: An Example of Sixteenth
   Century Religious Disputation.   QJS, 53 (October, 1967), 264-
   271.   409

Zacharias, Donald W. , and Johannesen, Richard L.   McElligott's
   American Debater: Argumentation in a Debating Society Context.
   JAFA, 4 (Fall, 1967), 83-86.   410

IV. NATURE, AIMS, VALUES, AND CRITICISMS

1. Books

Biddle, W. W. Propaganda and Education. Teachers College Contributions to Education, No. 52. New York, Columbia, 1932.
411

Hook, Sidney. Education for the Modern Man. New York, Dial, 1946.
412

Mill, John Stuart. Utilitarianism, Liberty, and Representative Government. London, Dent, 1910. (Contains the well-known chapter on freedom of thought, discussion, and debate, pp. 78-113.)
413

Rapoport, Anatol. Fights, Games, and Debates. Ann Arbor, Mich., Michigan, 1960.
414

Schreiber, Julius, ed. It Pays to Talk It Over. Washington, D. C. , National Institution of Social Relations, 1947.
415

Sims, John G. , Jr. Debating as an Educator. Fort Worth, Texas, The Author, 1926.
416

Vaihinger, Hans. The Philosophy of "As If. " New York, Harcourt, 1925.
417

Van Loon, Hendrik W. Tolerance. New York, Boni, 1925.   418

Walch, J. Weston. Why Debate. Portland, Me. , Platform, 1936.
419

Wiese, M. J. Let's Talk It Over. Chicago, Ill. , Chicago, 1936.
420

2. Theses and Dissertations

Allen, Ronald R. The Effects of Interpersonal and Concept Compatibility on the Encoding Behavior and Achievement of Debate Dyads. Ph. D. Wisconsin. 1960.
421

Beckman, Vernon E. An Investigation and Analysis of the Contributions to Critical Thinking Made by Courses in Argumentation and Discussion in Selected Colleges. Ph. D. Minnesota. 1956. 422

Brembeck, Winston L. The Effects of a Course in Argumentation on Critical Thinking Ability. Ph. D. Wisconsin. 1947.   423

Carmack, William R. , Jr.   An Experiment Comparing Discussion
With Debate as Methods for Imparting Factual Information to an
Audience.   M. A.   Florida State.   1953.   424

Cleary, James W.   A Justification of Debate Within and Without the
Curriculum of a Contemporary American Jesuit University by
Reason of Early Jesuit Educational Practice.   M. A.   Marquette.
1951.   425

Courter, Gene W.   Relationships Between Claimed Benefits of De-
bating and Estimates of Personal Skills and Attitudes Reported by
Former Varsity Debaters from Central Michigan College.   M. A.
Michigan.   1956.   426

Fields, Marsha.   An Investigation of the Attitudes of Former Louisiana State University Debaters.   M. A.   L. S. U.   1962.   427

Jackson, Teddy R.   The Effects of Intercollegiate Debating on Critical Thinking Ability.   Ph. D.   Wisconsin.   1961.   428

Jensen, Leonard.   Analysis of the Speech Needs and Abilities of
College Freshmen with Previous Training in Debate.   M. A.
Iowa.   1935.   429

Jones, Alfred K.   Speech Objectives and the Discussion Element in
Debating.   M. A.   Michigan.   1942.   430

Keele, Reba L.   A Study to Determine the Ability of Debaters to
Identify the Elements of Argument.   M. A.   Brigham Young.
1966.   431

Level, Dale A.   Objectives and Effects of Debate as Reported by
Sponsors of Pi Kappa Delta.   M. A.   Purdue.   1956.   432

Lunde, Ralph.   A Study of the Values of Debate as Seen by Former
Minnesota High School Debaters.   M. A.   Mankato.   1967.   433

Monson, Allwin D.   A Comparison of Debate and Discussion for Developing Skills in Social Integration.   M. A.   Denver.   1942. 434

Mulvaney, Annette.   An Investigation of the Problem-Solving Ability
of Debaters and Non-Debaters at the National Pi Kappa Delta
Convention.   M. A.   S. Illinois.   1964.   435

Murphy, John W.   A Follow-up Study of Former Intercollegiate Debaters.   Ph. D.   Wisconsin.   1953.   436

Phelps, Waldo.   A Comparison of Debate with Discussion for Allness
Behavior.   M. A.   Denver.   1941.   437

Ray, William T. D.   Personality Differences Between Debaters and

Non-debaters.   M. A.   Alabama.   1939.   438

Robinson, Rex E.   Study of the Relationship Between Intercollegiate
    Debating at the State University of Iowa and Vocational Success.
    M. A.   Iowa.   1933.   439

Sloan, Thomas O.   Academic Adjustment of College Forensic Stu-
    dents.   M. A.   Southern Illinois.   1952.   440

Tame, Ellwood R.   An Analytic Study of the Relationship Between
    Ability in Critical Thinking and Ability in Contest Debate and
    Discussion.   Ph. D.   Denver.   1958.   441

Thompson, Morris L.   A Behavioral Theory of the Function of Argu-
    mentation in the Political System.   M. S.   Kansas State.   1970.
                                                                       442
Trew, Marsha Ann.   An Exploratory Study of the Effects of Train-
    ing in Argumentation on Student Opinion Change.   Ph. D.   Michi-
    gan State.   1969.   443

Wall, K. Wayne.   The Open and Closed Minds of College Debaters.
    Ph. D.   Ohio.   1970.   (Concludes that debaters are more open-
    minded than non-debaters.)   444

Williams, Donald E.   The Effects of Training in College Debating
    on Critical Thinking Ability.   M. S.   Purdue.   1951.   445

Williams, Terry W.   Analysis of Correlation and Variance of Rat-
    ings of Debate Values.   M. S.   Kansas State.   1964.   446

Workun, Arthur E.   Forensic Success and Freshman Entrance Ex-
    aminations.   M. S.   Illinois Normal.   1955.   447

Zimmerman, Leland L.   A Personality Study of Debaters and Drama
    Students at the High School and College Levels.   M. S.   Wisconsin.
    1950.   448

3.   Articles

Aarnes, Hale.   Debating From Aristotle to Atoms.   DM, 2 (Decem-
    ber, 1946), 215-18.   449

Abernathy, Elton.   Things I Dislike in Debate.   SSJ, 15 (March,
    1950), 216-18.   450

Allen, Edna, and Capp, Glenn E.   As the Debaters See It.   SA, 6
    (Winter, 1950), 151-53, 172.   451

Allen, Leroy.   Why Not Debate in College?   DM, 1 (July-September,
    1945), 103.   452

Allen, R. R.   The Effects of Interpersonal and Concept Compatibility

of the Encoding Behavior and Achievement of Debate Teams.
CSSJ, 14 (February, 1963), 23-26.   453

Allyn, S. C. Speech and Leadership in Business. QJS, 34 (Febru-
ary, 1948), 36-39.   454

Aly, Bower. How Not to Debate. ScA, 7 (September, 1935), 22-
23.   455

Anderson, Hurst A. A University President Speaks on Speech. G,
36 (May, 1954), 88.   456

Anderson, Paul R. Another College President Speaks on Speech.
G, 37 (November, 1954), 18.   457

Anderson, Ray L. Argumentation and Rhetoric. SPG, 4 (January,
1967), 36-41.   458

Arnold, William E. Debate and the Lawyer. JAFA, 3 (January,
1966), 26-28.   459

Auer, J. Jeffrey. Discussion and Debate. G, 21 (January, 1939),
48-49.   460

_____. Tools of Social Inquiry: Argumentation, Discussion and
Debate. QJS, 25 (December, 1949), 533-39.   461

Baird, A. Craig. Aims and Objectives in Argumentation and Debate.
Speech Bulletin. Supplement QJS, 2 (December, 1930), 2-3. 462

_____. Argumentation as a Humanistic Subject. QJS, 10 (June,
1924), 258-64.   463

_____. Debate and Discussion in Post-War Service to Democracy.
G, 27 (January, 1945), 20-21, 32. Also in DM, 1 (July-August-
September, 1945), 1-5.   464

_____. Discussion and Debate in the Space Age. CSSJ, 10 (Spring,
1959), 48-52.   465

_____. General Education and the Course in Argumentation. G,
38 (March, 1956), 58-59, 86.   466

Baird, John E. Confucius Say: Debate is Great. JAFA, 8
(Winter, 1972), 139-140.   467

Baker, J. Thompson. The Future of Debate. PN, 6 (March-April,
1940), 2-3.   468

Balfour, Arthur J. Public Speaking. In A. J. Balfour as Philosopher and Thinker. Sel. and arr. by Wilfrid M. Short. London,
Longmans, 1912. (On the importance of skill in debating.) 469

Ballantine, Arthur A. vs Miller, Clyde R.   Are We Really? G, 13
    (November, 1930), 17-18.   (Excerpts from articles expressing
    conflicting views on the value of debating.)   470

Barker, Burt B.   As a Lawyer Finds It.   G, 14 (January, 1932),
    7-8.   Also in G, 38 (March, 1956), 60, 78.   (Former Vice-
    President of the University of Oregon.)   471

Barnard, R. H.   Debate and Discussion, a Good Team.   S&S, 47
    (March 5, 1938), 311-13.   472

Barra, E. R.   Ancient Art of Debate.   NYSE, 42 (December, 1954),
    197.   473

Bastian, Dwight.   What Johnny Does Know.   F, 47 (October, 1962),
    10.   (On freedom of speech as related to debate.)   474

Beckman, Vernon E.   Let Debate Go On.   DM, 3 (December, 1947),
    195-96.   (Reply to W. F. Dunbar's article, infra.)   475

Belloc, Hillaire.   An Essay on Controversy.   LA, 304 (May 13,
    1920), 667-70.   476

_____.   On Controversy.   NS, 14 (February 7, 1920), 523-24. 477

_____.   On Convincing People.   NS, 15 (April 17, 1920), 42-43.
                                                                       478
_____.   The Technique of Controversy.   LA, 274 (September 14,
    1912), 676-83.   479

Biddick, William.   Forensic Training as an Aid to Student Leader-
    ship.   F, 26 (January, 1941), 42-43.   480

Biddle, Phillips R.   The Space Between.   F, 45 (January, 1960),
    9.   481

Blackwell, Barbara.   Speech in Public Health.   G, 39 (November,
    1956), 16, 23.   482

Bluhm, Jeanette.   Women Lawyers on Wall Street.   F, 30 (May,
    1945), 82-85.   483

Blyton, Gifford.   Debate for Democracy.   KSJ, 30 (October, 1951),
    34-36.   484

Bowman, Georgia.   College Forensics Helps Women to Enter Radio.
    F, 28 (May, 1943), 115-16.   485

Bowser, Hallowell.   The Revived Art of Debating.   SR, 45 (May 12,
    1962), 78ff.   486

Brack, Harold A.   The Center Pole.   DM, 3 (September, 1947),
    165-166.   487

_____. Why Pre-Ministerial Students Need Forensic Training. G,
39 (January, 1957), 41-2, 52.   488

Braden, Waldo E., ed. A Symposium: What Is the Place of De-
bating in a Democratic Society? S, 36 (January, 1953), 13-17.
(Contributors include Paul D. Brandes, Annabel D. Hagood,
Gregg Phifer, William S. Smith, Douglas Ehninger, and Henry
Y. Warnock.)   489

_____. What Happens to Debaters and Why. F, 44 (May, 1959),
107.   490

Brann, Vincent C., ed. Briefly Speaking; A Symposium: What Is
the Single Most Important Contribution Which Intercollegiate Debate Offers to the Debater? BDAPC, 19 (December, 1953), 21-
25. (Contributors include Henry J. Abraham, Parke G. Burgess,
David Carson, Robert E. Connelly, Robert P. Newman, Joseph
H. Riggs, and Clayton H. Schug.)   491

Brembeck, Winston L. The Effects of a Course in Argumentation
on Critical Thinking Ability. SM, 16 (September, 1949), 177-
89.   492

Bridgman, Donald S. Success in College and Business. PJ, 9
(June, 1930), 1-19.   493

Brigance, W. Norwood. The Contribution of Speech to National Defense. G, 25 (November, 1942), 9-10.   494

_____. The Debate as Training for Citizenship; Reply to A. Com-
stock. ER, 72 (November, 1926), 222-25. (See Comstock's
Article, infra.)   495

_____. Public Address. DM, 2 (March, 1946), 9-11. Reprinted
from CE (October, 1945).   496

Brown, Charles T. An Experimental Diagnosis of Thinking on Controversial Issues. SM, 17 (November, 1950), 370-77.   497

_____. Debate and Personality. S, 39 (March, 1957), 10-11. 498

Buehler, E. C. The Basic Philosophy. G, 32 (January, 1950), 27,
34, 35.   499

_____. Debate and Parliamentary Practice Contribute to Demo-
cratic Processes. BNAP, 38 (January, 1954), 86-90.   500

_____. A Definition of Good Debating. G, 24 (May, 1942), 68-69,
83.   501

_____. A Word for the Cause. G, 31 (January, 1949), 23, 30.
                                                                                  502

Burns, Janette M. Debate and the Teacher in Training. BDAPC,

15 (December 10, 1948), 18-21.   503

Burrowes, Hillier M.   Debaters in Uniform.   BDAPC, 15 (December 10, 1948), 5-8.   504

_____.   Training for Democracy.   F, 27 (January, 1942), 41-43.
                                                           505
Burrows, Albert H.   Forensics and Scholarship.   F, 25 (January,
1940), 33-37.   506

Bursch, James F.   Is a Substitute for Debate Needed to Provide
Training in Scientific Group Thinking?   CJSE, 6 (April, 1931),
254-56.   507

Byers, Burton H.   Debate as a Social Methodology.   SSJ, 18 (May,
1953), 233-56.   508

Callender, W. P. , Jr.   Thoughts with Expression: the Values of
Debate in Schools.   E, 78 (October, 1957), 117-20.   509

Capp, Glenn R.   Discussion and Debate in Life Activities.   BNAP,
38 (January, 1954), 67-70.   510

Carleton, William G.   Effective Speech in a Democracy.   SSJ, 17
(September, 1951), 2-13.   511

_____.   Let Us Keep Debating in Our Schools.   VS, 15 (September
1, 1949), 703.   512

_____.   What Debating Has Meant to Me.   S, 31 (November, 1948),
3.   513

Carmen, M. J.   Basic Tools of Democratic Communication.   CJSE,
26 (March, 1951), 160-62.   514

Carrell, Martha.   Argumentation, Debate, Public Speaking, and the
Legal Profession.   PaS, 1 (October, 1966), 9-14.   515

Caswell, George.   From Forensics to Artillery.   F, 27 (January,
1942), 45.   516

Cessna, R. W.   "Ladies and Gentlemen..."   CSMM, (January 30,
1943), 4.   517

Chafee, Zechariah, Jr.   Free Speech in America.   SR, 24 (August
9, 1941), 3-4.   518

Champions Become College Presidents.   F, 33 (January, 1948), 23.
                                                          519
Chesterton, Cecil.   The Technique of Controversy.   LA, 274 (September 14, 1912), 676-83.   520

Chief Faults of Debaters.   F, 33 (March, 1948), 47-48, 54.   (Short

lists of faults by E. R. Nichols, Martin Holcomb, E. O. Wood
and Glenn Capp.)   521

Christophersen, Merrill G.   A More Rational Philosophy of College
Debate.   AFAR, 8 (Spring, 1960), 17-20.   522

Church, Carrie E.   The Value of Debate in Attaining Social and
Political Leadership.   In Reevaluation of the Place of Speech in
the Educational Process.   Comp. and ed. by Egbert R. Nichols.
Redlands, Cal., Univ. of Redlands Debate Bur., 1935.   pp. 58-
63.   523

Clark, Robert D.   Discussion-Debate: Dichotomy or Continuum?
DM, 2 (December, 1946), 213-15, 241.   524

_____.   These Truths We Hold Self-Evident.   QJS, 34 (December,
1948), 445-50.   (On the social values of rhetorical skills.)   525

Clevenger, Theodore, Jr.   Speaker and Society: The Role of Freedom of Speech in a Democratic Society.   SSJ, 26 (Winter, 1960),
93-99.   526

Coffee, Thomas G.   Where Training in Debate and Public Speaking
Will Pay Big Dividends.   G, 14 (January, 1932), 12-13.   527

Cole, Nancy.   Trials and Tribulations of a Woman Debater.   G, 39
(March, 1957), 69-70.   528

College Debating and Writing.   Na, 90 (May 5, 1910), 452-53.   (Opposed to technical subjects and complicated briefs; advocates
training in speech as well as in thought.   Answered by C. Green,
infra.)   529

Collegiate Debating.   NR, 79 (July 11, 1934), 221.   ("If debating is
worthwhile, it is as training in conversion of opinion, not as an
exhibition of 'public speaking,' or forensic quackery." See rejoinder by R. H. Wagner, NR, 80 (October 24, 1934), 313.) 530

Comstock, Aizada.   Cost of Debating.   ER, 70 (June, 1925), 24-25.
(On the dangers growing out of certain debate practices.   Answered by W. N. Brigance, supra.)   531

Conant, James B.   Free Inquiry or Dogma?   AM, 155 (April, 1935),
436-42.   532

Coors, D. Stanley.   I Learned Six Important Things.   G, 18 (March,
1936), 39-40.   Also in R, 10 (April, 1936), 4-5.   533

Cordell, Christobel M.   A Thought for Debaters.   PN, 3 (November, 1936), 3.   (On the freedom of American students to debate.)
534
Cortright, Rupert L.   Forensic Values for the College.   G, 16
(November, 1933), 8.   535

Cousins, R. B.   Athletics and Forensics; Their Type, Scope, Purpose, Value, and Administration in 1929.   NEA Proceedings
(1929), 887-92.   536

Crane, Wilder W. , Jr.   The Function of Debate.   CSSJ, 5 (Fall,
1953), 16-17.   537

Crocker, Lionel.   Democracy Thrives on Debate.   G, 27 (May,
1945), 54, 58.   Also in DM, 2 (June, 1946), 83-84, 110.   538

———.   Does Debating Do Preachers More Harm Than Good?   G,
24 (January, 1942), 28-30.   539

———.   Extracurricular Perceptions; Value of Public Speaking and
Debate.   VS, 14 (May 1, 1948), 447-48.   540

———.   Important Phases of Public Speaking Interestingly Phrased.
S, 27 (November, 1942), 5-6.   541

———.   Leadership and the Spoken Word.   DM, 1 (July-September,
1945), 13-15.   Rep. from R, 19 (November, 1942).   542

———.   Public Speaking and Current Affairs.   DM, 3 (September,
1947), 162.   543

———.   Training to Exercise Freedom of Speech.   G, 32 (March,
1950), 56, 65.   544

———.   The Value of Debating.   R, 25 (November, 1950), 8, 11.
                                                                        545
———.   Debate and General Education.   S, 40 (March, 1958), 23-
24.   546

———.   Preparing for Leadership.   SPG, 5 (March, 1968), 87-89.
                                                                        547
Cromwell, Harvey.   Effective Speaking; Address, November 18,
1960.   VS, 27 (January 15, 1961), 217-18.   548

———.   What's Wrong with Debate?   SSJ, 18 (March, 1953), 176-
79.   549

———.   Your Speech Is Important to All of Us.   F, 46 (March,
1961), 3-5.   550

———.   Speech and the Honors Program.   F, 50 (October, 1964),
19-21.   551

Cronen, Vernon E.   Forensics and Behavioral Science: A Response
to Walwik and McGlone.   JAFA, 7 (Spring, 1970), 92-96.   552

———.   The Functions of the Debater: Orator, Critic, Pedagogue.
CSSJ, 20 (Winter, 1969), 261-268.   ("Defines the role of the debater in terms of oratorical, critical, and pedagogical functions.

This delineation of functions is based on a new means of distinguishing among the terms of rhetoric, argumentation, and debate. ")   553

Culp, Ormond S.   Speech Training for the Physician.   G, 37 (November, 1954), 18.   554

Culp, Richard.   Friends of Debate.   G, 44 (March, 1962), 33-35.
                                                                         555
Curry, Herbert L.   Debate and Law Courts.   G, 12 (January, 1930), 17-19.   556

Dahlberg, W. A.   The Harvard Committee Approves.   G, 31 (January, 1949), 31-32.   557

Davis, B.   Adapting Forensics to Social Living.   TO, 20 (July, 1936), 35.   558

Davis, William H.   Debating as Related to Non-Academic Life.
QJS, 1 (July, 1915), 105-13.   559

_____.   Is Debating Primarily a Game?   QJS, 2 (April, 1916), 171-79.   560

_____.   What Is Debating For?   QJS, 9   (April, 1923), 194.   561

Debaters and Orators.   Ou, 121 (April 9, 1919), 622-23.   562

Debaters Go 'Round and 'Round.   HENB, 27 (November, 1951), 22-23.   563

Delta Sigma Rho Members Honored by Rotary.   G, 40 (November, 1957), 7-8.   564

De Voros, Evelyn K.   The Purpose of College Debate.   Ws, 18 (May, 1954), 191-94.   565

Dickey, Dallas C.   Debate Training and Citizenship.   SSJ, 8 (January, 1943), 77-79.   566

Dike, Clarence S.   Academic Debate, Its Aims and Methods.   Ed, 42 (February, 1922), 339-42.   (Reply to article with same title by William A. Wetzel, infra.)   567

A Disconcerted Editor and Others.   QJS, 1 (April, 1915), 79-84.
(On the value, philosophy, and ethics of academic debate.)   568

Drushal, J. Garber, Ralph, David C., Schug, Clayton S., and Miller, N. Edd.   Report of the Special Committee on Standards and Objectives.   G, 37 (May, 1955), 73-80.   (Committee of Delta Sigma Rho.)   569

Dunbar, Willis F.   Let's Not Debate; Pupils Should Learn the Tech-

niques of Settlement, Not Argument in Our Schools.   CH, 21
(October, 1946), 67-71.   Also in DM, 3 (December, 1947), 193-
95.   570

Dunn, James A.   Shall Windy Words Have No End?   JEd, 124 (October, 1941), 225-26.   571

Durkee, J. Stanley.   How My Debate Training Helps Me in My Life
Work.   G, 18 (March, 1936), 46-47.   572

Ehninger, Douglas.   Debating as Critical Deliberation.   SSJ, 24
(Fall, 1958), 22-30.   573

_____.   Decision by Debate: a Re-Examination.   QJS, 45 (October,
1959), 282-87.   574

_____.   Discussion and Debate: Another Analysis.   G, 21 (May,
1939), 62-63.   (Answer to J.J. Auer's article, G, 21 (January,
1939), 48-49.)   575

_____.   Debate as Method: Limitations.   ST, 15 (September,
1966), 180-185.   576

Ehrlich, Larry G.   Philosophic Risk in the Forensic Art.   JAFA,
9 (Summer, 1972), 266-273.   577

Ehrsam, Theodore G.   Debating and Truth, BDAPC, 7 (May 30,
1936), 2.   578

Eighty-Four Delta Sigma Rho Alumni Listed as "Leaders in Education."   G, 16 (March, 1934), 36-38.   579

Eisenstadt, Arthur.   Debate, Discussion and Decision-Making.   VS,
27 (November 1, 1958), 62-63.   580

_____.   Education and Debate.   R, 25 (March, 1951), 8-9.   581

Emperor, John B.   Two Paradoxes of Debating and a Doubtful Solution.   SSJ, 3 (November, 1937), 9-11.   582

Endsley, Lorraine.   Speech Work Has Thirty-Seven-Year History.
F, 49 (March, 1964), 1-2.   (In praise of debate coach.)   583

England, Frank.   The Latest Edition of the 3M Bookshelf Games.
SPG, 9 (March, 1972), 72.   (In response to the question: does
debate meet its avowed objectives?)   584

Evans, Charles F. , Jr.   Forensics Is. . . .   SPG, 9 (January, 1972),
43-44.   (Comment on promoting forensics.)   585

Ewbank, Henry L.   Four Hundred Sixty-One Delta Sigma Rho Alumni
in Who's Who in America.   G, 21 (January, 1939), 35-47.   586

_____ . Sixty-Four More Delta Sigma Rho Alumni in "Leaders in
Education. " G, 16 (May, 1934), 62-63.   587

_____ . Teaching Speech for Human Relations. ST, 1 (January,
1952), 9-13. Also in G, 34 (March, 1952), 6-9.   588

_____ . Three Hundred and Eight Delta Sigma Rho Alumni in Who's
Who in America. G, 16 (May, 1934), 52-59.   589

_____ . What Becomes of Our College Orators? G, 7 (June, 1924),
17-18.   590

_____ . What Happens to College Debaters? G, 31 (March, 1949),
44.   591

_____ . What's Right with Debate. QJS, 37 (April, 1951), 197-
202.   592

_____ and Auer, J. Jeffrey. Decision Making; Discussion and
Debate. BNAP, 32 (January, 1948), 34-49.   593

Fausti, Remo P. Debate and Discussion--A Holisitic Approach.
G, 43 (March, 1961), 49-50.   594

Faxon, Glen S. Forensics in Public Administration. G, 38 (November, 1955), 6, 26.   595

Fenner, Frances. The Value of Forensic Training in Domestic
Life. G, 37 (March, 1955), 50, 67.   596

Feris, F. F. It's Not Debatable. DM, 4 (Summer, 1948), 71-73.
                                                                    597
Fest, Thorrel B. For Effective Speech in a Free Society. Delta
Sigma Rho Golden Anniversary Issue. National Office of Delta
Sigma Rho, 1956.   598

_____ . Forensic Programs and Dynamic Democracy. G, 31 (January, 1949), 32-34.   599

_____ . Society and Speech in the Future. G, 39 (March, 1957),
59, 78.   600

_____ . Who Must Speak for Forensics. G, 40 (May, 1958), 59-
60, 74.   601

_____ and Schindler, Barbara. Can Forensics Survive the Educational Revolution? G, 39 (January, 1957), 27-30, 55.   602

Fink, Cornelius W. The Function of Debate in Adult and Adolescent
Education. BDAPC, 13 (March 1, 1947), 2-7.   603

Forensics in Education. QJS, 38 (April, 1952), 209.   604

Foulkes, William R.   The Four Fundamentals of Debate.   Schol,
   13 (January 5, 1929), 6-7.   14 (February 16, 1929), 8.   605

Fox, Wayne O.   The Value and Application of Speech Training to
   My Profession.   G 36 (May, 1954), 97.   606

Frank, Glenn.   Parliament of the People.   Ce, 98 (1919), 401-16.
                                                                 607
Franklin, Benjamin.   The Cash Value of Speaking Ability.   F, 28
   (March, 1943), 90-93.   608

Freeley, Austin J.   An Anthology of Commentary on Debate.   G,
   41 (March, 1959), 43-45.   Also in AFAR, 7 (Winter, 1959), 23-
   27, and ST, 9 (March, 1960), 121-26.   609

_____. Social Rehabilitation Through Debate.   G, 28 (January,
   1946), 26.   Also in DM, 2 (March, 1946), 60.   (On the Norfolk
   Prison debaters.)   610

Fretwell, E. K.   Debating.   Twenty-fifth Yearbook of the National
   Society for the Study of Education.   Bloomington, Ill., Public
   School Publishing Co., 1926.   Part II, pp. 173-175.   611

Furtado, Manuel.   Debater Enters Politics.   F, 32 (October, 1946),
   8-10.   612

Garland, J. V.   What Debaters Learn.   G, 22 (January, 1940), 30-
   33.   613

Gates, Thomas S.   Debating in a University.   G, 14 (January,
   1932), 5-6.   (Former president of the University of Pennsylvania.)   614

Gibson, George M.   How to Conduct a Controversy.   Chr, 9, 3
   (1944), 302-16.   615

Gibson, James W.   Research Report #50: Some Characteristics of
   the College Debater.   CSSJ, 15 (November, 1964), 293-295. 616

Giffin, Kim.   Non-Academic and Academic Debate Through the Eyes
   of a Student of Public Address.   AFAR, 5 (Spring, 1957), 4-9.
                                                                 617
_____ and Linkugel, Will.   The Place of Debate in Modern Education.   BNAP, 42 (November, 1959), 180-85.   618

Gislason, Haldor B.   Debating as Preparation for Life.   PSR, 2
   (October, 1912), 40-42.   (Teaches the student to know and express truth.)   619

Goldberg, Murray A.   Developing Democratic Responsibility Through
   Discussions of Controversial Issues.   EJ, 34 (February, 1945)
   66-71.   620

Graham, Gladys M.   Speech in the Service of Deliberation.   In A
   Program of Speech Education in a Democracy.   Ed. by W. A.
   Cable.   Boston, Expression, 1932.   pp. 242-256.   621

Graham, John.   Dangers in Debate.   JAFA, 2 (September, 1965),
   94-103.   622

_____.   Usefulness of Debate in a Public Speaking Course.   ST,
   15 (March, 1966), 136-139.   623

Granell, Lee E.   What the Students Say About Forensics.   G, 40
   (March, 1958), 45-46, 56.   624

Gray, Clifton D.   Debating--Cui Bono?   G, 14 (January, 1932), 5.
   (Former president of Bates College.)   625

Green, Clarence.   Debating at School.   Na, 90 (June 23 1910), 627.
   (Answer to "College Debating and Writing," supra.)   626

Grether, E. T.   Debating Coach Sums Up Main Speakers' Ideals.
   G, 12 (January, 1930), 23.   (Excerpts from a newspaper article
   on the ideals of debate which appeared in the Daily Californian,
   Univ. of California.)   627

Griffin, Whitmore.   Debates Have Real Value.   Sch (Elem. ed.),
   32 (October, 1943), 150-51.   628

Gruner, Charles R., Huseman, Richard C., and Luck, James L.
   Debating Ability, Critical Thinking Ability, and Authoritarianism.
   SPG, 8 (March, 1971), 63-65.   629

Gulley, Halbert.   Debate versus Discussion.   QJS, 28 (October,
   1942), 305-307.   630

Haakenson, Robert, ed.   Briefly Speaking; A Symposium: Can College Debating Be of Special Service to the Nation in the Present
   Crisis?   BDAPC, 17 (December 15, 1951), 32-34.   (Statements
   by Karl E. Mundt, Arthur N. Kruger, and Barrett Davis.)   631

Haiman, Franklyn S.   A Critical View of the Game of Forensics.
   JAFA, 1 (May, 1964), 62-66.   632

Hale, Robert.   Evils of Themes and Debates.   JEd, 83 (March 23,
   1916), 319-20.   633

Halladay, John.   Nixon, Kennedy, Fifty-Five Statesmen Advise Student Debaters.   Freedom and Union Magazine (October, 1960),
   4.   634

Hance, Kenneth G.   Discussion, Public Speaking, and Debating.
   BNAP, 29 (November, 1945), 66-78.   Also in DM, 2 (September,
   1946), 139-44, 207.   635

_____. Rhetorical Education and Liberal Education. G, 45 (May, 1963), 73-74.   636

_____. Some Values of a Study of Rhetoric and Public Address in a Liberal or General Education. SSJ, 23 (Summer, 1958), 179-88.   637

Hancher, Virgil M. The Debater's Preparation--His Information and Thought. F, 34 (October, 1948), 4-6. (Address delivered at the Iowa High School Forensic League by the President of the State University of Iowa.)   638

Hanks, L. D. Comparison, Philosophy, or Situation. DM, 1 (July-September, 1945), 106-108.   639

Harding, Harold F. The College Student as a Critic. G, 35 (November, 1952), 11-14.   640

Harding, James F., Jr. College Debating as Preparation for Advocacy. F, 43 (October, 1957), 3-4.   641

Harrington, Elbert W. Debater Balance. G, 16 (January, 1934), 29-30. (Criticism of egotistical types.)   642

Harris, Thomas E., and Smith, Robert M. A Systems Analysis of the Current Debate Controversy. JAFA, 9 (Winter, 1973), 355-360.   643

Harshbarger, H. C. Debate Purposes. QJS, 17 (February, 1931), 95-99.   644

Hayhurst, J. S. Critical Materials. DM, 3 (September, 1947), 151-53.   645

Hellerich, Mahlon H. A Survey of Relationship Between Debating and Social Science Instruction in Pennsylvania Colleges and Universities. BDAPC, 18 (December, 1952), 20-30.   646

Hellman, Hugo E. Debating is Debating--and Should Be. QJS, 31 (October, 1945), 295-300. Also in DM, 1 (October-December, 1945), 14-19. (Rejoinder to W. N. Thompson's Discussion and Debate: A Re-Examination, QJS, 30 (October, 1944), 293-99.)
                                                                647
_____. Why Debating? NEAJ, 36 (March, 1947), 188-89.   648

Henderson, Richard D. Debate: Vital in the Educational Program. G, 44 (November, 1961), 9-10.   649

Hetlinger, Duane F., and Hildreth, Richard A. Personality Characteristics of Debaters. QJS, 47 (December, 1961), 398-401.
                                                                650
He Who Affirms Has Proved: Testimony Department. DM, 1 (January-February, 1945), 9-10. (Letters on the value of debate.)
                                                                651

Hicks, Philip M. The New Spirit in Debating. In A Course of Study in Speech Training and Public Speaking for Secondary Schools. Comp. and ed. by A. M. Drummond. New York, Century, 1925. pp. 174-80.   652

Hinds, George L. Forensics in Banking. G, 38 (November, 1955), 7-8.   653

Hogstrom, Harold R. The Wind of Controversy. TS, 5 (November, 1957), 21-27. (Amusing dialogue on the values and ethics of rhetoric and persuasion.)   654

Holladay, Howard. Paid Haters of Debate. F, 43 (March, 1958), 67-68. (Comments on the criticism evoked by the national collegiate debate topic on compulsory unionism.)   655

Hollander, Katharine R. On the Art of Being Articulate. G, 21 (May, 1939), 68-70. (Contends that debaters should speak for a humane social order.)   656

Holm, James N. The Educational Purpose of Debate. PN, 8 (October, 1941), 14-16.   657

_____. Listening in at the Cleveland Convention. PN, 5 (January-February, 1939), 3-5. (Comments on the advantages and disadvantages of debate.)   658

Holt, H. Q. Arguing Differences in Open Debate. PE, 40 (1925), 449.   659

Hoogestraat, Wayne E. Three Things That Debate Is Not. F, 47 (Marcy, 1962), 5-6.   660

Hoover, Kenneth H. Using Controversial Issues to Develop Democratic Values Among Secondary Social Studies Students. JEE, 36 (Winter, 1967), 64-69.   661

_____. Debate: Valid Teaching Method? CH, 40 (December, 1965), 232-235.   662

Hope, Walter E. Debate Dividends. G, 18 (May, 1936), 60.   663

Horrocks, John E. Democracy Demands Debate. SoS, 34 (December, 1943), 350-52.   664

Howe, Jack H. The Changing Face of Forensics. SPG, 8 (November, 1970), 3-7.   665

Howell, William S. Debate and Critical Thinking. R, 16 (February, 1942), 4-5.   666

_____. Is Forensic Experience Valuable After College? G, 35 (May, 1953), 85-86.   667

_____. Persuasive Utility of the Treason Charge. G, 32 (May, 1950), 76-77, 86. (On the relationship between free speech and debate.)   668

Huebner, Lee W. The Debater, the Public Persuasion. JAFA, 7 (Winter, 1970), 1-12. (Text of speech delivered at the 20th Anniversary luncheon of the AFA on the advantages of debate training.)   669

Hughes, Paul. Debate Training Helped Paul Hughes Become War's Outstanding Historical Novelist. F, 31 (March, 1946), 69-71.
                                                        670
Humphrey, Hubert H. The Real Voice of America. G, 39 (November, 1956), 13-14, 24. (Remarks at the Delta Sigma Rho Jubilee Banquet.)   671

Huseman, Richard C. , Ware, Glen, and Gruner, Charles R. Critical Thinking, Reflective Thinking, and the Ability to Organize Ideas: A Multi-Variate. JAFA, 9 (Summer, 1972), 261-265.
                                                        672
Hutton, Ralph. Some Immediate Returns to the Debater. DM, 3 (September, 1947), 160-61.   673

Ihde, Ira C. Must Debating "Pay Out?" PN, 5 (November, 1938), 3-4.   674

Innes, James. The Function of Discussion and Debate. DM, 1 (July-September, 1945), 60.   675

Interest in Debate in High School and Success in College. G, 21 (January, 1939), 53. (Statistical evidence of the correlation between debate training and academic success.)   676

Jacobson, Clarence. Objectives of Debate Training. R, 12 (October, 1937), 9-10. Also in PN, 4 (October, 1937), 5-6.   677

Jay, J. A. Debate and Character Development. HST, 6 (September, 1930), 292.   678

Jennes, Larry. A Debate Philosophy to Grow With. F, 35 (October, 1949), 8-9.   679

Johnson, George E. Debating and the Lawyer. G, 14 (January, 1932), 6-7.   680

Johnston, M. M. Junior Forensic League; Speech Improvement for Grades. Catholic School Journal, 68 (November, 1968), 30-31.
                                                        681
Jones, Cecil H. Speech Training Helps Preaching. G, 37 (November, 1954), 17.   682

Jones, Robert W. The Profession of Journalism Views Debating. G, 14 (January, 1932), 9.   683

Judson, Lyman S.   Talent and Tithe.   G, 20 (May, 1938), 51.   684

Juleus, Nels.   John Stuart Mill and the "Utility" of Debate.   G, 40
(March, 1958), 43-44, 54.   685

Kaltenborn, H. V.   Value of Debate Training.   R, 11 (January,
1936), 8.   Also in G, 18 (May, 1936), 59.   686

Kehm, Harold D.   Speech and the Professional Soldier.   G, 21
(January, 1939), 50-52.   687

Kelley, Hubert.   Democracy Goes to School.   AMag, 119 (1935),
27.   688

Kellog, L. L.   Reality of Debating.   Ou, 132 (November 1, 1922),
354.   689

Kelso, Robert W.   How My Debate Training Helps Me in My Life
Work.   G, 19 (March, 1937), 42-44.   690

King, Thomas R., and Phifer, Gregg.   The College Debater as
Seen by Himself and by His Peers.   JAFA, 5 (Spring, 1968), 48-
52.   691

Kinney, Richard.   Debate and the Adversary System.   G, 20 (January, 1938), 26-27.   (On the value of debate to lawyers.)   692

Klingbeil, Henry C.   Debate or Politics?   QJS, 14 (April, 1928),
218-23.   693

Klopf, Donald W.   Practical Experience in Human Relations for Debaters.   G, 43 (May, 1961), 55-56, 65.   694

Knee, Robert C. (Mrs.).   What Happens to a Woman Debater?   S,
23 (March, 1939), 4.   695

Knoll, Paul X.   A Restatement of the Purpose of Debate Training.
G, 13 (January, 1931), 9-14.   Also in Program of Speech Education in a Democracy, op. cit., 217-26.)   696

Kully, Robert D.   Forensics and the Speech Communication Discipline.   JAFA, 8 (Spring, 1972), 192-199.   697

Lahman, Carroll P.   Debate and Discussion--Rivals or Allies?
DM, 3 (May, 1947), 3-5, 27.   (Comments on W. Thompson's
article, infra.)   698

_____.   Should a High School Debater Continue to Debate in Col-
lege?   DM, 1 (April-June, 1945), 76-77.   699

Lamers, William M., and Dewey, Kenneth A.   A Suggested Norm
in College Debating.   QJS, 19 (February, 1933), 82-84.   700

Larmon, Sigurd S. A Hall of Fame for Debaters. VS, 24 (September 15, 1958), 728. (Remarks delivered at the West Point National Debating Tournament.) 701

Larson, Carl E. The Chronic Refuter. G, 45 (January, 1963), 31-33. (On the over-zealous debater who refutes "at every opportunity." Believes that there is too much emphasis in debate training on denial.) 702

Larson, P. Merville. Objective of Junior College Debating. JCJ, 3 (1932). 703

_____. A Total Pattern for a Democratic Way of Life. DM, 1 (October-December, 1945), 19-22. 704

Lawton, J. H. Choice Between Discussion and Debate? CER, 61 (December, 1963), 577-587. 705

Lee, Irving J. Freedom from Speech. SSJ, 14 (September, 1948), 27-32. (On the need for viability in debating social problems.) 706

Lee, Josh. The Importance of Training in Public Speaking. S, 24 (November, 1939), 3-4. 707

Level, Dale, Jr. Objectives and Effects of Debate. F, 42 (January, 1957), 42-44. 708

Levine, I. N. Activity for Citizenship Training. HP, 37 (June, 1955), 70-74. 709

Lilienthal, N. Case for Debate. SchA, 33 (April, 1962), 241-42. 710

Lippmann, Walter. The Indispensable Opposition. AtM, 164 (August, 1939), 186-90. 711

_____. Our Need for a Public Philosophy. AtM, 195 (April, 1955), 43-49. 712

Lomas, Charles W. Controversy in Wartime. BDAPC, 12 (January 1, 1943), 3-6. 713

_____. Is Free Speech Worth Having? BDAPC, 13* (December 15, 1939), 3-6. 714

_____. Persuasion or Discussion? BDAPC, 11* (December 12, 1941), 6-8. 715

*Prior to the December 19, 1940 issue of the BDAPC, there were no volume numbers listed. This issue was identified as Volume X, No. 14. Consequently, all references to earlier issues of this journal are to the number of total issues which had appeared. This (cont. on p. 72)

Long, Raswell C.   Permanent Values in Debate Training.   G, 19
(January, 1937), 31-32.   716

Longo, E. M.   Debate, An Essential in Economics.   BaS, 45 (February, 1964), 254-255.   717

A Look at Our Members' Achievements.   G, 36 (May, 1954), 101-
105.   (Post-debate achievements of former Delta Sigma Rho members.)   718

Lull, P. E.   Enemies of Academic Debating.   DM, 3 (Autumn, 1948),
109-10.   719

MacInnis, M.   Encourage Your Child to Debate.   NPT, 53 (February, 1959), 30-32.   720

Magee, Lawrence T.   Why Debate?   ArT, 24 (September, 1936),
10-11.   721

Maguire, R.   What Is the Next Curriculum Breakthrough?   JSE, 38
(November, 1963), 81-83.   722

Mahon, George H.   Congressman Values Speech Training.   F, 46
(March, 1961), 9.   Rep. from March, 1937 issue.   723

Manning, Robert N.   A Liberal View of Contemporary Debate.   SPG,
5 (May, 1968), 162-164.   724

Markgraf, Bruce.   An Examination of the Humanistic Side of Debate.
ST, 14 (September, 1965), 240-241.   725

Marts, Arnaud C.   A College President Looks at Debate.   BDAPC,
10 (December 19, 1940), second page cover.   (Former president
of Bucknell University.)   726

Maurer, Irving.   Benefits.   G, 19 (January, 1937), 24.   (Former
president of Beloit.)   727

Maxwell, Pearl.   Informal Debating.   HP, 18 (May, 1936), 41-42.
                                                                              728
Mayer, J. Edmund.   Personality Development Through Debating.
QJS, 22 (December, 1936), 607-11.   Condensed version in DM,
3 (Spring, 1948), 3-4.   729

_____ et al.   Character Education Through Debating.   KT, 35
(May, 1932), 17-19.   730

---

accounts for the apparent discrepancy between the higher number preceding the date of the 1939 issue and that preceding the date of the
1941 issue.   The number 11 which precedes the date of the latter issue is a reference to the volume, or number of years published,
whereas the number which precedes the date of the 1939 issue is a
reference to the total number of issues published to that date.

McAdoo on Debating. G, 16 (March, 1934), 45. (Secretary of the
    Treasury under Woodrow Wilson.)   731

McBath, James H. Beyond the Seventies. JAFA, 8 (Spring, 1972),
    175-177.   732

McBurney, James H. The Role of Discussion and Debate. G, 30
    May, 1948), 64-66.   733

McClaugherty, John. Are Debaters Disagreeable? G, 34 (January,
    1952), 28.   734

McClelland, Samuel D. Function of Debating. EJ, 36 (February,
    1947), 91-93.   735

McCroskey, James C. The Effect of College Speech Training on
    Academic Marks. AFAR, 10 (Winter, 1962), 6-11.   736

McCulloch, Catharine W. Advice from an Experienced Auditor. G,
    17 (March, 1935), 37-39.   737

McGuckin, Henry E. Forensics in the Liberal Education. WS, 34
    (Spring, 1970), 133-138.   738

———. Better Forensics: An Impossible Dream. JAFA, 8 (Spring,
    1972), 182-185.   739

McKay, Frederick B. High School and College Debating: Shall We
    Have More of It? ASch, 18 (March, 1925), 124-30.   740

McKean, Dayton D. Debate or Conference? QJS, 20 (April, 1934),
    223-36.   741

———. The Educational Value of Debate. CoSJ, 44 (February,
    1929), 5-7.   742

Merritt, Frank W. How Can We Improve the Educational Value of
    Intercollegiate Debating? BDAPC, 17 (December 15, 1951), 9-
    12.   743

Meyer, Samuel L. Speech in the Training of a Scientist. F, 45
    (October, 1959), 5-6.   744

Michaelis, Clayton. Life Insurance Selling and Forensics. G, 36
    (March, 1954), 58.   745

Miller, Emerson W. Skill in Debate. QJS, 11 (April, 1925), 150-
    57.   746

Miller, Justin. Oral Argument. G, 28 (March, 1946), 42-43.
    (Former Congressman.)   747

Mills, Glen E. Argumentation in General Education. SSJ, 26 (Summer, 1961), 313-17.   748

Mills, William B.   Demosthenes and Blackstone.   PN, 6 (December, 1939), 11, 13-14.   (On the relationship between law and debating.)   749

Mizer, Jean E.   Are Debate and Declamation Worth Their Salt? IdJE, 26 (December, 1944), 105.   750

Moore, W. M.   What Are the Values in Debate?   HST, 9 (June, 1933), 236.   751

Morgan, Geoffrey F.   Why All This Debating?   S, 25 (January, 1941), 9.   752

Moses, Elbert R. , Jr.   Debate--A Tool of Practical Educators. SSJ, 6 (November, 1940), 23-25.   753

_____.   Debate Vs. Discussion; Reply to F. B. Riggs.   SchS, 64 (August 3, 1946), 84-85.   (See Riggs' article, infra.)   754

Mosher, Joseph A.   Debate and the World We Live In.   QJS, 10 (November, 1924), 332-39.   755

Mundt, Karl E.   Debating as a Molder of Public Opinion.   NFL, 8 (November, 1933), 2.   756

_____.   Debating Is Not Dull.   R, 16 (February, 1942), 2.   757

_____.   Free Speech Protects Human Rights.   R, 21 (April, 1947), 6.   758

_____.   Speech Education and Public Service.   BNAP, 38 (January, 1954), 5-7.   759

_____.   Speech in Our Modern World.   F, 31 (January, 1946), 33-36.   Also in DM, 2 (June, 1946), 77-78, 102.   760

_____.   Speech Is a Weapon for Freedom.   R, 25 (November, 1950), 9-10.   761

_____.   Why Speech Education in Schools?   R, 27 (December, 1952), 9-10.   762

Munro, Harry C.   Differences Between Argument and Discussion. IJRE, 18 (November, 1941), 12-13.   763

Murphy, Jack.   Mr. Average Debater.   SA, 9 (Spring, 1953), 3, 24.   764

Murphy, Richard.   The Forensic Mind.   In Studies in Speech and Drama in Honor of Alexander M. Drummond.   Ed. by Herbert A. Wichelns and others.   Ithaca, N. Y. , Cornell, 1944.   pp. 451-

72.   765

Murphy, Roy D.   Do You Want to be President?   F, 31 (May,
    1946), 93-94, 100.   766

Murray, Jerry B. , Shaugnessy, Daniel E. , and Vince, Thomas L.
    Debate and the Challenge of Business.   G, 45 (March, 1963),
    44-45.   767

Musgrave, George M.   A Challenging Point of View.   DM, 1 (Octo-
    ber-December, 1945), 22-23.   (Reply to W. N. Thompson's Dis-
    cussion and Debate: A Re-examination, infra.)   768

Muskie, Edmund S.   Debating as an influence in the Career of a
    Public Servant.   VS, 24 (October 15, 1957), 30-31.   Also in TS,
    6 (January, 1958), 3-4.   (Former Governor of Maine, now U. S.
    Senator; debated at Bates College as an undergraduate.)   769

Musser, William M. , Jr.   Debate.   Pennsylvania Bar Association
    Quarterly, 30 (1959), 364-70.   (Contends that the practice of law
    suffers because debate is not sufficiently respected.)   770

Nabors, D. J.   First Province Produced Leaders.   F, 58 (January,
    1973), 15.   771

Newman, Robert P.   Be a Philosopher.   PSA, 17 (September, 1960),
    26-34.   (Be philosophical about debate; drawn from the theories
    of Hume.)   772

Nichols, Alan.   The Discussion-Debate Duality.   SSJ, 7 (March,
    1942), 100-102.   773

Nichols, Egbert R.   Editorially Speaking.   DM, 1 (October-Decem-
    ber, 1945), 104-106.   (Debate versus discussion.)   774

_____.   Speech in the West, 1949:   The Influences in Forensics.
    WS, 13 (January, 1949), 12-14.   775

Nichols, Egbert R. , Jr.   Value of Forensic Training.   DM, 1
    (April-June, 1945), 86-87.   (Author was an Army Lieutenant at
    the time.)   776

Nichols, Henry W.   The After-College Values of Forensics.   G, 34
    (January, 1952), 24-25.   777

Nilsen, Thomas R.   Free Speech, Persuasion, and the Democratic
    Process.   QJS, 44 (October, 1958), 235-43.   778

_____.   Persuasion and Human Rights.   WS, 24 (Autumn, 1960),
    201-204.   779

Nobles, W. Scott, and Cohen, Herman.   The Disjunctive Premise
    about Forensics.   ST, 8 (November, 1959), 316-20.   780

Norman, Nelson F. Speaking to the Soviet Public. G, 42 (Novem-
ber, 1959), 13-14.   781

Oliver, Robert T. A National Speech Program for the War.
BDAPC, 12 (January 1, 1943), 1-3.   782

Olson, Donald O. An Evaluation of Debate. G, 30 (January, 1948),
31-34. Also in DM, 4 (Summer, 1948), 64-68.   783

O'Meara, Julia A. The Art of Debate. NYSEJ, 14 (January, 1927),
298-99.   784

O'Neill, James M. Game or Counterfeit Presentment. QJS, 2
(April, 1916), 193-97.   785

Ostergren, Carl F. Public Speaking in Business. G, 14 (January,
1932), 13-14.   786

Ostlund, Leonard A. Case Discussion Learning in Human Relations.
JHR, 16 (1968), 212-219. (Recommends activities, including debating, as useful procedures for classroom instruction in human
relations.)   787

Outcomes of School Debating. NEAJ, 21 (January, 1932), 4. (Twen-
ty-seven objectives of debate as developed at a sectional meeting
of the Illinois Association of Teachers of Speech.)   788

Overstreet, Harry A. When Words Go Forth to Battle. JAD, 10
(January, 1938), 5-11.   789

Owens, Chester D. Demosthenes in Prison. S, 23 (May, 1939),
4-5. (On how prison inmates benefit from debate.)   790

Paget, Edwin H. Debate Questionnaire; An Analysis of Debating.
G, 14 (March, 1932), 20-22. (An interesting questionnaire on
many aspects of academic debate.)   791

Palmieri, Ron. A Foundation of Competition. SPG, 9 (March,
1972), 73. (In response to the question: does debate meet its
avowed objectives?)   792

Palzer, Edward. Are Debaters "Propaganda-Proof?" PN, 7 (Octo-
ber, 1940), 24-25.   793

Pelham, Howard. The Justification for Debate Must Be Expanded.
SPG, 9 (January, 1972), 45-47. (A comment on promoting
forensics.)   794

Pellegrini, Angelo M. Argumentation and Personal Success. QJS,
29 (February, 1943), 22-32.   795

Perkins, Joseph. Excellence in What? SPG, 9 (March, 1972), 74.
(In response to the question: does debate meet its avowed ob-

jectives?) 796

Perry, I. D. Debating. LASJ, 10 (April 25, 1927), 28-29. 797

Phifer, Gregg. Let's Debate. AdT, 5 (August, 1952), 9-11. 798

Phillips, Gerald M. Effects of Debate on the Student. AFAR, 10 (Spring, 1962), 15-19. 799

Pitchell, Robert J. Speechmaking and the Politician. JAFA, 2 (May, 1965), 47-52. 800

Pitkanen, Allan M. Appraisal of Debate. SchA, 13 (March, 1942), 259-60. 801

Pitt, Carl A. Debating Improves Social Adjustment. DM, 3 (Autumn, 1947), 143-46. 802

_____. Speech Training as Preparation for the U. S. Senate. SPG, 5 (March, 1968), 91-93. 803

Plummer, Robert N. The Place of Debate in War Time. DM, 1 (April-June, 1945), 87. 804

Pollock, Art. The Relationship of a Background in Scholastic Forensics to Effective Communication. SPG, 10 (November, 1972), 16-17. 805

Prentiss, Henrietta, and Parks, Sara R. New Ideals in Debating. NYSEJ, 12 (May, 1925), 610-13. 806

Quimby, Brooks. Debate Goes Educational. PN, 5 (September, 1938), 24-25, 30. 807

_____. It's Not the Championships. G, 34 (March, 1952), 2-4. 808

_____. Maine, Muskie, and Delta Sigma Rho. G, 37 (November, 1954), 16. (Senator Muskie, formerly Governor of Maine, was a member of the Bates College debate team, coached by author, when he was an undergraduate. See Muskie article supra.) 809

_____. "Sure, I Remember Him." R, 13 (October, 1938), 4-5, 13. (Achievements of former debaters at Bates College.) 810

Quiz, Quintus (pseud. for Shillito, Edward). Why Are Public Debates Futile? CC, 59 (July 8, 1942), 856. 811

Rafferty, Ruth S. The Durable Value of Debate. G, 2 (November, 1919), 8-9. 812

Ray, William T. D. Democracy in Debating. S, 25 (November, 1940), 10-11. 813

Reed, Marshall R.   How My College Forensic Activities Helped My Career.   G, 38 (January, 1956), 52.   (Value of debate as training for the clergy.)   814

Reeves, J. Walter.   Debate and the Public Interest.   G, 14 (January, 1932), 15.   815

Report of the PSA [Pennsylvania Speech Association] Forensics Section on Debate Evaluation.   BDAPC, 17 (December 15, 1951), 21-24.   (The committee consisted of Howard H. Martin, chairman; Jean Isherwood, Melvin Moorhouse, and Mildred A. Ditty.)
                                                                                816
Rice, George P., Jr.   Student Attitudes Toward Free Speech and Assembly.   ST, 8 (January, 1959), 53-57.   817

_____.   What Do Students Care About Freedom of Speech?   TS, 3 (November, 1955), 19-21.   818

Richards, Darrel S.   Debate Days.   Kiwanis Krier, 44 (November 13, 1962), 2.   819

Richmond, W. H. L.   Young America; Results of International Student Debates.   Sp, 178 (May 16, 1947), 551.   820

Rickey, John T.   Persistent Criticisms of Debate.   G, 38 (January, 1956), 37-41.   821

Riggs, Francis B.   School Debates.   SchS, 63 (March 2, 1946), 155. (See rejoinder by E. R. Moses supra.)   822

Ringwalt, Ralph C.   Intercollegiate Debating.   Na, 71 (December 20, 1900), 489.   823

Robbins, E. Clyde.   College Debating.   Na, 90 (June 2, 1910), 556.
                                                                                824
Robertson, Roger.   Debate's Excuse.   SPG, 7 (January, 1970), 64.
                                                                                825
Robinson, James A.   A Recent Graduate Examines His Forensic Experience.   G, 3 (March, 1956), 62, 88.   (Believes that the annual research done by a conscientious college debater is equivalent to the work done for a master's thesis.)   826

Roegiers, Charles, and Tubbs, Stewart.   Intercollegiate Debate: Its Practical Values.   F, 53 (May, 1968), 25-27.   827

Rosenbaum, Milton E.   The Effect of Verbalization of Correct Responses by Performers and Observers on Retention.   ChD, 38 (September, 1967), 615-622.   (On the value of debaters observing other debaters.)   828

Ross, Herold T.   Widening Horizons.   G, 42 (March, 1961), 37. ("No activity on the college campus can better equip college graduates for their responsibilities than debating.")   829

Rotary International Honors Six Delta Sigma Rho Members. G, 41
(May, 1959), 59-60.   830

Salsbury, Martha. Can We Compete to Cooperate? F, 47 (October,
1961), 3-4.   831

Schick, Guy A. The Dismal Science, Etcetera, and Debate. SPG,
2 (May, 1965), 143-144.   832

Schilling, Elsa A. Why the Debate Student Should be Able to Recognize Propaganda. SSJ, 7 (September, 1941), 15-17.   833

Schmidt, Doris. Psychiatric Nursing and Debate Training. G, 40
(March, 1958), 47-48, 54. (Former debater at Mt. Mercy College, Pittsburgh, Pa.)   834

Schug, Clayton H. "Speak Up for Peace!" BDAPC, 13 (March 1,
1947), 24-25.   835

_____. A Study of Attitude Toward Debate. ST, 1 (November,
1952), 242-52.   836

Schulte, F. B. Training for Articulate Leadership. NCEAB, 58
(August, 1961), 283-86.   837

Scott, Robert L. A Fresh Attitude Toward Rationalism. ST, 17
(March, 1968), 134-139. ("The argument of this paper has...an
aura of absurdity about it, " being an "attempt to build a rational
case against rationalism. ")   838

Secord, A. E. , and Thomas, R. H. Speech in Extra-Curricular Program. DM, 2 (March, 1946), 5-9. (Rep. from BNAP.)   839

Shannon, J. R. Post-College Success of Party Debaters. TCJ, 14
(May, 1943), 108-109.   840

Sharp, Harry, Jr. , and Milliken, Joyce. Reflective-Thinking Ability
and the Product of Problem-Solving Discussion. SM, 31 (June,
1964), 124-127.   841

Shaw, Elton R. The Value of My Training in Debate. G, 14 (January, 1932), 8.   842

Sherbondy, Donald. Speech Training Provides Solid Background for
Industrial Relations. G, 37 (November, 1954), 16.   843

Shiffrin, Steven. Forensics, Dialectic, and Speech Communication.
JAFA, 8 (Spring, 1972), 189-191.   844

Sikkink, Donald E. The Need for Research on the Value of Debate.
AFAR, 8 (Convention Issue, 1960), 12-14.   845

Silverman, Franklin. Forensic Therapy. QJS, 46 (October, 1960),

305-306.   846

Sloan, Thomas O., and Talley, C. Horton. The Academic Adjustment of College Forensic Students. G, 37 (January, 1955), 29-
30.   847

Smith, Carney C. Debating: A Training School for Life. QJS, 23
(October, 1937), 426-31.   848

_____. Speech and Business. G, 39 (January, 1957), 43-44, 50.
                                                                              849
Smith, D. K., and Howell, W. S. Debate: The Fallacy of Inherent
Evil. SchA, 22 (May, 1951), 293-94.   850

Smith, Henry P. The Relationship Between Scores on the Bell Adjustment Inventory and Participation in Extra-Curricular Activities. Journal of Educational Psychology, 38 (1947), 11-16. 851

Smith, Horace G. Debate and the Ministry. G, 14 (January, 1932),
12. Also in G, 38 (March, 1956), 60, 68.   852

Smith, Robert W. The Law in Debate: 1. Freedom of Speech. G,
42 (March, 1960), 43-44, 46. (The first in a series of three
articles on the relationship between legal practice and debate.)
                                                                              853
Statements on the Value of Debate (in answer to a questionnaire by
Austin J. Freeley). F, 44 (March, 1959), 89-90, 92-94. (Short
statements by Erwin D. Canham, George W. Norris, Clarence P.
Quimby, Walter Lippmann, Alexander Meiklejohn, Seymour E.
Harris, David D. Henry, and Hubert H. Humphrey.)   854

Stevens, W. E. Integrity, Integration, and Academic Responsibility.
G, 35 (May, 1953), 83-85.   855

Stewart, Irwin. A University President Views Intercollegiate Debate.
BDAPC, 19 (December, 1953), 12-13. (President of West Vir-
ginia University.)   856

Stewart, John R., and Merchant, Jerrold J. Perceived Differences
between Debaters and Non-Debaters. JAFA, 6 (Spring, 1969),
67-72. (Concludes that debate experience develops identifiable
communication characteristics and that audiences perceive debaters to be better speakers than non-debaters.)   857

Stiles, Karl A. The Scientist and Speech. G, 14 (January, 1932),
11.   858

Streeter, Don. Speech and the Superior Student. ST, 9 (September,
1960), 223-26.   859

Student Forum: Does Debate Meet Its Avowed Objectives? SPG, 9
(March, 1972), 71-74. (Short articles by John Saxon, Frank England, Ron Palmieri, and Joseph Perkins.)   860

Student Forum: Why Debate? SchA, 39 (October, 1967), 2-4.
(Comments by three 1967 graduates of New Trier High School
East, Winnetka, Illinois: J. Garrett, B. Kuenzel, and N. Corn-
blath.)   861

Swallow, Alan, and Stevens, Edwin L. The Value of Debate and
Discussion in Wartime. DM, 1 (July-September, 1945), 65. 862

Swift, Walter B. Mental Attitudes in Debate. JAP, 3 (June, 1919),
156-66. (On the role of the mind and the emotions in debate.)
                                                                  863
Swigert, J. Mack. Can Debating Survive? NStu, 8 (April, 1929),
7-9. (A student evaluates traditional debating and recommends
more entertaining and fairer practices.)   864

Sykes-Marshall, J. G. Debating as an Aid to Character. EO, 12
(1937), 25.   865

A Symposium: Values of Debate. G, 18 (March, 1936), 38-40.
(Contributions include the following: Cross, Ira B. Olden Days
at Wisconsin. p. 38; Clausen, Bernard C. I Have Debated
Several Thousand Times. p. 39; Coors, D. Stanley. I Learned
Six Important Things. pp. 39-40. Supra.; Cross, Edward W.
Finest Achievement. p. 40.)   866

Tallmadge, John A. , ed. An Alumni Forum [on the Value of Debate
Training]. BDAPC, 11 (December 12, 1941), 12-19. (Contribu-
tions include the following: Ditter, Mabel B. "Debate Aids in
the Law. " Pp. 12-13; Burrowes, H. McC. "Cross-Examining an
Alumnus Debater. " Pp. 13-15; Mindlin, Morris. "The Uses of
Speech. " Pp. 15-17; McCole, Mary M. "What Debating Has
Meant to Me. " Pp. 17-19; Pullinger, Anne B. "What Debating
Did for Me. " P. 19.)   867

Tauber, Abraham. New Aims for Debate. QJS, 21 (June, 1935),
389-92. Also in HP, 17 (June, 1935), 29-32.   868

Thompson, Richard N. Character Education Through Debating.
CoSJ, 45 (1930), 45. Also in Montana Education, 6 (January,
1930), 7-8.   869

_____. How Do Debaters Rank in Intelligence? NFL, 3 (January,
1929), 6-7.   870

Thompson, Wayne N. A Broader Philosophy for Debaters. F, 30
(March, 1945), 49-52. Also in G, 27 (May, 1945), 52-53, 57,
and DM, 1 (April-June, 1945), 17-20.   871

_____. Discussion and Debate: A Re-Examination. QJS, 30 (Oc-
tober, 1944), 293-99.   872

Thonssen, Lester. Discussion and Debate. EQ, 19 (December,
1938), 7-8.   873

_____. The Social Values of Discussion and Debate. QJS, 25
(February, 1939), 113-17.   874

Timmons, William M.   Public Address to Provoke Thought.   QJS,
28 (October, 1942), 301-305.   875

Tinkcom, H. M.   Debating for Citizenship.   PSJ, 79 (May, 1931),
602.   876

Tooze, Russell.   Educational Thorn.   SchA, 14 (January, 1943),
173-74.   877

_____. Gavel.   SchA, 15 (March, 1944), 233-34.   878

Townsend, D. E.   Training the Mind Through Debating.   KSJ, 26
(November, 1947), 34.   879

Tucker, Charles O.   Forensics and Behavioral Science Research in
the Law.   JAFA, 2 (May, 1965), 59-65.   880

Tucker, Raymond K. , Kochler, Jerry W. , and MLady, Lynne.
The Image of the College Debater.   JAFA, 4 (Winter, 1967), 1-
9.   881

Tussman, Joseph.   Controversy and Academic Freedom.   WS, 19
(October, 1955), 251-56.   882

Underwood, William A.   A Survey of Lawyers' Training in and Attitudes toward Speech in Illinois.   JAFA, 6 (Spring, 1969), 108-
110.   883

Utterback, William E.   The Influence of Committee Discussion and
Debate on Student Thinking: A Study of the Delta Sigma Rho Congress of 1953.   G, 36 (March, 1954), 66-73.   884

Value of Debate.   Na, 90 (February 17, 1910), 154-155.   885

The Values of Debate.   F, 47 (January, 1962), 19.   886

Van Emden, Bernard.   The Value of Forensic Training for Engi-
neers.   G, 42 (November, 1959), 3-4, 14.   887

Vasilew, Eugene.   A Pilot Study of Debaters' Attitudes Toward Debating.   AFAR, 7 (Spring, 1959), 20-34.   888

Veatch, W. H.   As the Speech Professor Sees It.   G, 14 (January,
1932), 14.   889

Vermes, Hal G.   Let's Have an Argument.   Ro, 55 (December,
1939), 43.   890

Vickrey, James F. , Jr.   The Legislator on Leadership.   SPG, 9
(November, 1971), 8-13.   891

Wagner, Russell H.   Collegiate Debating Today; Reply to Collegiate
Debating.   NR, 80 (October 24, 1934), 313.   (Rejoinder to an
editorial attacking intercollegiate debating, NR, 79 (July 11,
1934), 221.)   892

Walch, J. Weston.   Confidentially.   PN, 3 (January, 1937), 14-15.
(Answer to an attack on debate by H. A. Overstreet, who char-
acterized debaters as "slanters.")   893

Walker, Joseph E., Olsen, William H., and Callahan, Charles W.
Remuneration from Wartime Debating.   SchA, 16 (December,
1944), 128-31.   894

Watts, Lowell.   From Forensics to Radio.   F, 27 (January, 1942),
46.   895

Weaver, A. T.   Some Values in Forensics.   G, 39 (November,
1956), 3-4, 12.   896

Wecter, Dixon.   In Defense of Talk.   SaR, 32 (November 5, 1949),
9-11, 36-38.   897

West, Robert.   The Prospect for Speech Education.   QJS, 30 (April,
1944), 143-46.   898

Westfall, Alfred, ed.   Anthology of Remarks on Value of Debate.
DM, 1 (July-September, 1945), 98-100.   Rep. from F, 30 (May,
1945).   899

_____.   The Mission of the Debater.   F, 8 (January, 1923), 1-2.
                                                                        900
_____.   What Speech Students May Do to Help Win the War.   F,
28 (October, 1942), 8-12.   901

Wetherby, Joseph C.   Academic Status Seekers.   SSJ, 27 (Fall,
1961), 1-6.   902

Wetzel, William A.   The Academic Debate: Its Aim and Method.
Ed. 42 (September, 1921), 39-42.   (Claims that academic debate
provides poor moral training.   See answer by C. S. Dike, supra.)
                                                                        903
White, Trumbull.   Cultivating the Knowledge Crop.   New Outlook,
165 (1935), 25-28.   904

Williams, H. M.   What Should We Do in the Field of Public Address?   DM, 2 (June, 1946), 111, 133.   905

Williams, Donald E.   Group Discussion and Argumentation in Legal
Education.   QJS, 41 (December, 1955), 397-401.   906

Wingate, J. D.   Democratic Living.   Ed, 60 (February, 1940), 328-
30.   907

Wishart, Charles F.   The Enduring Art of Public Speech.   G, 22
    (March, 1940), 49.   (Former president of Wooster.)   908

Withington, Robert.   The Value of Inquiry.   SAQ, 41 (January,
    1942), 45-52.   909

Woolbert, Charles H.   The Debater and His Standing as a Scholar.
    PSR, 2 (May, 1912), 5-7.   (Believes that debate encourages
    original work and the ability to analyze a problem.)   910

Wrage, Ernest J.   E. L. Godkin and The Nation: Critics of Public
    Address.   SSJ, 15 (1949), 100-111.   911

Yeager, W. Hayes, and Utterback, William E., eds.   Communica-
    tion and Social Action.   AAA, 250 (March, 1947), 1-11, 32-40,
    70-75, 113-120.   912

Zelko, Harold P.   Is Debate Training for Life?   BDAPC, 21 (De-
    cember, 1955), 24-29.   913

V. THE DEBATE PROPOSITION

A. SELECTING, PHRASING, AND CHARACTERISTICS

1. Books

Baier, Kurt. The Moral Point of View. New York, Cornell, 1958.
914

Hare, R. M. Freedom and Reason. Oxford, Oxford, 1963. 915

_____. The Language of Morals. Oxford, Clarendon, 1952. 916

Lepley, Ray. Verifiability of Value. New York, Columbia, 1957.
917
_____, ed. The Language of Value. New York, Columbia, 1956.
(Fifteen essays on the nature and status of value.) 918

Stevenson, Charles. Facts and Values: Studies in Ethical Analysis.
New Haven, Yale, 1963. 919

_____. Ethics and Language. New Haven, Yale, 1960. 920

Wellman, Carl. The Language of Ethics. Cambridge, Harvard,
1961. 921

2. Theses and Dissertations

Kourilsky, Marilyn. An Adversary Approach to Propositions of
Policy in Economics. Ph. D. UCLA. 1968. 922

Schunk, John F. Probability and Desirability Determinants of Relationships Among Beliefs in Rhetorical Propositions. Ph. D.
Illinois. 1967. 923

3. Articles

Beck, Clive. Utterances Which Incorporate a Value Statement.
APQ, 4 (October, 1967), 291-299. 924

Belfour, C. S. Selecting a National Debate Question. SchA, 9
(1938), 354-56. 925

Brock, Bernard L. New Criteria for Selecting National Debate

Questions.   JAFA, 5 (Spring, 1968), 43-47.   926

Cordell, Christobel M.   Are Simpler Debate Topics Desirable?
    No! PN, 7 (March-April, 1941), 5-7.   (Opposing viewpoint ex-
    pressed by J. T. Miller, infra.)   927

Crawford, Richard J.   A Proposition Revolt in Intercollegiate De-
    bate.   WS, 35 (Spring, 1971), 116-123.   (Discusses the harmful
    effects of the "single proposition" on debate practice.)   928

Cripe, Nicholas M. , and Walwik, Theodore J.   Selecting the Nation-
    al Proposition: A Proposal.   JAFA, 1 (Winter, 1967), 10-12.
                                                                        929
Cronkhite, Gary.   Propositions of Past and Future Fact and Value:
    A Proposed Classification.   JAFA, 3 (January, 1966), 11-16. 930

Debate Propositions for 1922-1923.   F, 8 (November, 1922), 33-34.
                                                                        931
Debate Questions--Westfall's Report.   F, 7 (May-June-October,
    1921), 19.   932

Diem, Roy W.   Types of Debate Questions.   EQ, 8 (May, 1928),
    15-16.   933

Douds, J. B.   The Selection and Phrasing of Debate Questions.
    BDAPC, 11 (May 25, 1938), 2-4.   934

Ducasse, C. J.   Is a Fact a True Proposition--A Reply.   JPhil, 39
    (February 26, 1942), 132-36.   935

Fest, Thorrel B.   Intercollegiate Debate and Discussion.   QJS, 34
    (December, 1948), 505-6.   (On the selection of national collegiate
    topics.)   936

Finley, G. W.   How Pi Kappa Delta Selects Its Official Debate Ques-
    tion.   G, 14 (November, 1931), 16.   937

_____.   Notes from the Secretary's Office.   F, 18 (May, 1933),
    177.   938

Freeley, Austin J.   The Implications of the Use of a Different
    Proposition.   G, 42 (November, 1959), 15.   939

_____.   The Right Expert--At the Right Time.   QJS, 46 (February,
    1960), 81-82.   (An answer to W. F. Stromer, infra, on selecting
    the national debate topic.)   940

_____.   A Proposal to Improve the Quality of National Debate
    Propositions.   JAFA, 6 (Fall, 1969), 168-172.   Also in F, 55
    (October, 1969), 8-10 and SPG, 7 (November, 1969), 3-7.   941

Graham, Mary W.   Relevancy and Debate Propositions.   QJS, 54
    (April, 1968), 161-163.   942

Gregg, Richard.   The Case for Two Propositions.   G, 41 (November, 1958), 15-16.   943

Hansen, John D.   How About a Fact Proposition for a Change?   F, 34 (May, 1949), 97-99.   944

Hellman, Hugo E.   The New College Debate Question.   G, 26 (November, 1943).   945

How We Get the College Debate Proposition: 1945-1946.   DM, 1 (April-June, 1945), 21-28.   946

Howard, Hal.   The Classification of the Argumentative Proposition. QJS, 50 (February, 1964), 75-76.   (Rejoinder to Terris, infra.)
                                                                        947
Howe, Jack.   Report on Procedures for Selecting the National Debate Proposition.   AFAR, 8 (Convention Issue, 1960), 21-25. (Members serving on the committee, of which Howe was the chairman, were Herbert James, Glen Mills, and Franklin Shirley.)   948

Infante, Dominic A.   Predicting Attitude from Desirability and Likelihood Ratings of Rhetorical Propositions.   SM, 38 (November, 1971), 321-326.   949

Kendall, Richard H., and Fractenberg, David.   Empty Generalities and False Scholarship: The Problems of Debating Foreign Policy Questions.   JAFA, 5 (Winter, 1968), 10-15.   950

Kruger, Arthur N.   The Nature of Controversial Statements.   (Submitted to ST December, 1973.)   951

_____.   Some Characteristics of a Debate Resolution.   BDAPC, 22 (December, 1956), 22-24.   952

MacArthur, J.R.   Will You Be There?   F, 5 (March-April, 1919), 1-2.   (Proposes a common topic for debate for those attending the annual Pi Kappa Delta Convention.)   953

Margolis, J.   Value Judgments and Value Predicates.   JVI (1968), 161-171.   954

Markgraf, Bruce.   The Selection of the National Debate Topic. AFAR, 10 (Winter, 1962), 24-25.   955

Mauser, Anthony.   How Did Kant Define "Analytic"?   An, 28 (June, 1968), 197-199.   956

Mazzola, John P.   The Wording of the Resolution.   BDAPC, 6 (May 29, 1935), 1.   957

McBath, James H., and Aurbach, Joseph.   Origins of the National Debate Resolution.   JAFA, 4 (Fall, 1967), 96-103.   958

Miller, Gerald R. Questions of Fact and Value: Another Look.
   SSJ, 28 (Winter, 1962), 116-22.   959

Miller, John T. Are Simpler Debate Topics Desirable? Yes!
   PN, 7 (March-April, 1941), 4, 6. (See opposing stand by C. M.
   Cordell, supra.)   960

Murphy, Richard. Flexible Debate Topics. QJS, 28 (April, 1942),
   160-64.   961

Murphy, Roy D. Selecting Topics for Debate and Discussion.   F,
   48 (January, 1963), 13-14.   962

National Collegiate Debate and Discussion Propositions.   JAFA, 6
   (Fall, 1969), 167-168.   963

Newman, Robert P. Ours Just to Reason Why. WS, 33 (Winter,
   1969), 2-9. (On the nature of "directional," "positional," and
   "prediction" statements.)   964

Nichols, Egbert R. Requisites of a Good Debate Proposition.   DM,
   1 (January-February, 1945), 48. (Passage from a textbook written jointly with J. H. Baccus.)   965

_____. The Variety of Debate Subjects. QJS, 22 (February, 1936),
   121-22.   966

_____. Third Business Session. F, 19 (May, 1934), 124.   967

Numerous Questions Being Used Widely This Year. S, 13 (November, 1927), 47-49.   968

The Official Question. F, 10 (October, 1924), 20.   969

Oliver, Robert T. What's Wrong with Debate Questions. DM, 2
   (March, 1946), 12-13, 48.   970

Ostergaard, H. The Proposition for Debate. Speech Bull. Supp.
   QJS, 2 (December, 1930), 17-32. (Urges the adoption of propositions that are simple, interesting, and timely.)   971

Phifer, Gregg. On the Subject of Subjects. F, 32 (May, 1947), 93,
   117. Also in DM, 3 (September, 1947), 161-62.   972

The Pi Kappa Delta Debate Question. F, 8 (November, 1922), 16.
                                                                     973
Porter, William C. A Word Concerning Draftsmanship.   BDAPC,
   12 (January 16, 1939), 17-18. (On the phrasing of debating
   propositions.)   974

Rahskopf, Horace G. Questions of Fact Vs. Questions of Policy.
   QJS, 17 (February, 1932), 60-70.   975

Reinhardt, L. R.   Propositions and Speech Acts.   MJPS, 76 (April,
    1967), 166-183.   976

Rose, Forrest H.   Apropos the Annual Debate Question--College.
    DM, 1 (July-September, 1945), 66-67.   977

_____.   Selecting the Debate Question.   DM, 2 (September, 1946),
    151-52.   978

_____.   A Historical Review of Debate Question Selection.   F, 55
    (October, 1969), 3-7, 24.   979

Ross, Raymond S. , and Davis, Margaret.   Choosing Controversial
    Speech Subjects.   ST, 5 (March, 1956), 109-110.   980

_____ and Osborne, Wilbur J.   Controversial Speech Topics: De-
    termination and Use.   CSSJ, 14 (May, 1963), 103-110.   981

Schug, Clayton H.   A Study of Attitude Change Toward Debate Prop-
    ositions Among High School and College Debaters.   ST, 3 (Jan-
    uary, 1954), 15-19.   982

Shepard, David W.   The Ad Interminum.   JAFA, 3 (January, 1966),
    17-21.   (On the meaning of value judgments.)   983

_____.   Logical Propositions and Debate Resolutions.   CSSJ, 11
    (Spring, 1960), 186-90.   984

Stromer, Walter F.   Questions on Questions.   QJS, 45 (October,
    1959), 321-22.   (On selecting the national collegiate debate
    topic.)   985

Taylor, Carl, and Barnard, Raymond H.   Questioning the Debate
    Question; How Should a Debate Proposition be Phrased?   QJS,
    16 (June, 1930), 355-360.   986

Terris, Walter F.   The Classification of the Argumentative Proposi-
    tion.   QJS, 49 (October, 1963), 266-73.   987

_____.   Ibid.   QJS, 50 (February, 1964), 76-77.   (Reply to H.
    Howard, supra.)   988

Thompson, Wayne N.   Criteria for Choosing a National Debate
    Topic.   F, 47 (October, 1962), 14-16.   989

Torrence, Donald L.   Intercollegiate Debate.   QJS, 51 (October,
    1965), 333-334.   990

Walch, J. Weston.   What Becomes of Old Debate Topics?   PN, 5
    (December, 1938), 6-8.   991

Wilson, W. A.   Questions of Degree.   MoLR, 32 (1969), 361.   992

Zelko, Harold P.   Once Again--Our Problem of Questions.
    BDAPC, 12 (January 16, 1939), 19-21.   993

B.   SPECIFIC PROPOSITIONS

1.   Books

Aly, Bower, ed.   Debate Handbook.   Published annually since 1926
    at Columbia, Missouri (Lucas Brothers; Artcraft), by the Com-
    mittee on Debate Materials and Interstate Cooperation of the Na-
    tional University Extension Association (NUEA) and distributed
    through the University of Wisconsin Extension Division, Madison
    5, Wisconsin.   994

Askew, John B.   Pros and Cons: A Newspaper Reader's and De-
    bater's Guide to the Leading Controversies of the Day.   Sixth
    edition revised and rewritten by Hilderic Cousens.   New York,
    Dutton, 1920.   (Superseded by Glover's work, infra.)   995

Bennett, Guy V.   Live Questions for Debate for the Schools of Cali-
    fornia.   Sacramento, Cal. , State Printing Office, 1912.   996

Berkhof, Louis.   Subjects and Outlines.   Grand Rapids, Mich. ,
    Eerdmans-Sevensma Co. , 1918.   997

Both Sides: Briefs for Debate.   New York, The Independent, 1915.
                                                                           998
Brookings, Walter D. , and Ringwalt, Ralph C. , eds.   Briefs for
    Debate on Current Political, Economic, and Social Topics.   New
    York, Longmans, 1911.   (Contains a short statement by Albert
    B. Hart on the "Art of Debate. ")   999

Buehler, Ezra C. , ed.   Debater's Helpbook.   New York, Noble,
    1934-1941.   1000

Carpenter, Oliver C.   Debate Outlines on Public Questions.   New
    York, Mail and Express Co. , 8th rev. ed. , 1947.   1001

Debate; An Impartial Magazine Presenting All Views.   Springfield,
    Mass. , Pro-Con Publishing Co. , Inc. , 1934.   1002

Debate Handbooks.   Normal, Illinois, Midwest Debate Bureau.   (Pub-
    lished annually as an aid to high school and college debaters.)
                                                                          1003
Debate Service, 1922-1923.   Albany, N. Y. , State Library, 1923.
    (List of debate questions on which package libraries containing
    briefs, books, pamphlets, and clippings are furnished.)   1004

Debaters' Handbook Series.   Minneapolis and New York, Wilson,
    1909-1918.   (Arguments pro and con on various topics.)   1005

Glover, Samuel.   Pros and Cons; A Newspaper Reader's and De-
    bater's Guide to the Leading Controversies of the Day.   London,
    Routledge, 13th ed., rev., 1960.   1006

Green, Mark.   Illustrations for Argumentation.   Washington, D. C.,
    The Author, 1937.   (Contains proverbs, maxims, anecdotes,
    analogies, and parables.)   1007

Matson, Henry.   References for Literary Workers, With Introduc-
    tions to Topics and Questions for Debate.   Chicago, A. C. Mc-
    Clurg and Co., 8th ed., 1911.   1008

Pittenger, William.   The Debater's Treasury; Comprising a List of
    Over 200 Questions for Debate, With Arguments Both Affirmative
    and Negative.   Philadelphia, Penn, 1910.   1009

Reference Shelf.   New York, Wilson, 1922-present.   (Selected ma-
    terials on topics of current interest, together with bibliographies
    and suggestions for debate analysis.)   1010

Ringwalt, Ralph C.   Briefs on Public Questions, With Selected Lists
    of References.   New York, Longmans, 1905.   1011

Shurter, Edwin D., and Taylor, Carl C.   Both Sides of 100 Public
    Questions Briefly Debated; with Affirmative and Negative Refer-
    ences.   New York, Hinds, Noble, and Eldredge, 1913.   Revised
    Edition, Noble, 1925.   1012

Walch, J. Weston.   Debate Handbooks.   Portland, Me., Walch.
    (Published annually as an aid to high school and college de-
    baters.)   1013

2.   Articles

Cromwell, Harvey.   Report of the National Questions Committee.
    F, 44 (October, 1958), 19-20; 45 (October, 1959), 7, 23; 46 (Oc-
    tober, 1960), 6-7; 47 (October, 1961), 15, 20.   1014

The Chief Debate Questions for 1932-1933.   G, 15 (November, 1932),
    5-11.   1015

Debate Propositions Chosen.   F, 31 (January, 1957), 3.   1016

Debate Questions for 1928-1929.   G, 11 (November, 1928), 8-10.
                                                                   1017
Debate Questions for 1929-1930.   G, 12 (November, 1929), 7-11.
                                                                   1018
Debate Questions for 1930-1931.   G, 13 (November, 1930), 13-17.
                                                                   1019
Debate Topics for 1933-1934.   G, 16 (November, 1933), 7.   1020

Debaters Review Season's Question.   G, 32 (May, 1950), 80-82.

(Short articles by student debaters: Barbara Lighthall, "It Was a Poor Topic"; Beverly Starika and Court Peterson, "We Liked the Question. ")   1021

Debating Activities, 1926-1927: Subjects of High School Debates; College Questions. WB, 3 (January-March, 1927), 48-49, 65.
                                                                        1022
Debating, 1927-1928. WB, 3 (January, 1928), 159-61.   1023

Drummond, A. M. Subjects of Interest. QJS, 2 (July, 1916), 309-12. (On the Value of the New Republic as a Source of Debatable Subjects; long list cited.)   1024

Fifty Years of Questions. F, 47 (January, 1962), 4-7.   1025

Hatcher, Caro C. A Formulation of the National Debate Question of 1945-1946 for Use in the Discussion Progression Method. DM, 1 (July-September, 1945), 61-62.   1026

Jacob, Bruno E. The 1951 Debate Question. R, 24 (May, 1950), 2.   1027

Keiber, A. E. Quisling Debate Questions. R, 16 (October, 1941), 4-6, 10. Also in PN, 8 (December, 1941), 18-20. (Voices objections to the 1940 and 1941 national high school debate questions; recommends the formation of a committee to work on phrasing the national question.)   1028

List of Questions for Debate. NFLB, 4 (November, 1929), 5. 1029

N. A. T. S. and Debate Fraternities Join in Their 1941-1942 Topic. CD, 20 (November, 1941), 257.   1030

Norton, Larry. Report of the 1957 National Questions Committee. F, 43 (October, 1957), 9-10.   1031

Parrish, W. M. Suggested Debate Proposition. QJS, 11 (November, 1925), 390.   1032

Phifer, Gregg. Our 1950-1951 Debate Resolution. S, 33 (May, 1951), 17-18.   1033

Prominent Debate Questions for 1931-1932. G, 14 (November, 1931), 10-14.   1034

Questions Being Debated in American Colleges and Universities. QJS, 15 (February, 1929), 149-51.   1035

Questions for Debate in 1927-1928; Debate Questions Suggested for 1927-1928; Questions Found Suitable Last Year. G, 10 (November, 1927), 5-7.   1036

Questions Recently Debated. G, 1 (March, 1914), 149.   1037

Rose, Forrest H.   International Debate Subject.   QJS, 31 (October, 1945), 377.   1038

Subjects for Debate.   PSR, 4 (October, 1914), 47-49.   1039

Topics of Current Interest Suitable for Debate.   G, 2 (November, 1919), 11.   1040

Walch, J. Weston.   How This Year's "Complete Handbook" Was Born.   PN, 8 (September, 1941), 6-7.   1041

_____.   National Debate Topics Survive the War.   PN, 8 (January-February, 1942), 3.   1042

VI. THE CASE

A. DEFINITION OF TERMS

1. Book

Robinson, R. Definition. Oxford, Clarendon, 1950.   1043

2. Theses and Dissertations

Benjamin, Robert L. Definition: Its Nature and Function in Argumentative Discourse. Ph. D. Wisconsin. 1951.   1044

Woodward, Michael L. A Comparative Analysis and Evaluation of Definitions of Major Terms as Used in Selected Debate Texts. M. A. Brigham Young. 1970.   1045

3. Articles

Black, Max. The Gap Between "Is" and "Should." PR, 73 (April, 1964), 165-181.   1046

Bond, David J. The Fact Value Myth. SoE, 34 (February, 1970), 186-194. (Believes there is little difference between facts and values.)   1047

Brick, Adolph H. Graphic Interpretation of the Proposition for Debate. QJS, 7 (April, 1921), 149-57.   1048

Butler, J. F. On Definition. Monist, 46 (January, 1936), 1-12.   1049

Corey, Kathy. The Spirit of '72: A Response to David Shepard. JAFA, 9 (Winter, 1973), 364-366. (Defends unusual definitions of key terms in the debate resolution.)   1050

Dahl, Norman O. "Ought" and Blame-worthiness. JPhil, 64 (1967), 418-428.   1051

DeMougeot, William R. Interpersonal Debate: Interpersonal, But Still Unrealistic. ST, 21 (March, 1972), 135-137. (Criticizes illogical definitions of key terms.)   1052

Freshley, Dwight L., ed. Briefly Speaking; A Symposium: What

Does "Should" in a Proposition Mean To You? BDAPC, 18 (December, 1952), 31-33. (Contributors include Wycliffe Griffin, Thomas A. Hopkins, and Alice Healy.) 1053

Glossop, Ronald J. Hume's Rejection of "Ought." JPhil, 64 (1967), 451-453. 1054

Gronbeck, Bruce E. From "Is" to "Ought": Alternative Strategies. CSSJ, 19 (Spring, 1968), 31-39. 1055

Hastings, Arthur. On the Meaning of "Should." SPG, 4 (November, 1966), 8-10. 1056

Hellman, Hugo E. Analyzing the Proposition. DM, 1 (October-December, 1945), 55-66. (On the proposition of Compulsory Military Service for Male Citizens Under Twenty-Four.) 1057

_____. Defining the Proposition. DM, 2 (September, 1946), 165-69, 172. (On the proposition of Complete Medical Care.) 1058

_____. Defining the Proposition and Locating the Issues. DM, 3 (September, 1947), 167-71. 1059

_____. A Definition of Terms. DM, 1 (July-September, 1945), 67-73. (Compulsory military service topic.) 1060

_____. Why Study Definitions? DM, 1 (October-December, 1945), 54-55. 1061

Hollingsworth, H. L. The Meanings of "Ought." In his Psychology and Ethics. New York, Ronald, 1949. 1062

Hubbeling, H. G. The Logic of Criteria in Ethics and Philosophy of Religion. Mi, 79 (1970), 58-66. (On distinguishing between characteristics and norms.) 1063

Humphrey, Chris. The Testability of Value Claims. JVI, 3 (Fall, 1969), 221-227. (Argues that Popper's basic theorems for testing factual claims can be converted to parallel theorems for testing value claims.) 1064

Johnson, Prescott. The Fact-Value Question in Early Modern Value Theory. JVI, 1 (Spring, 1967), 64-71. 1065

Keeton, Morris T. On Defining the Term "Fact." JPhil, 39 (February 26, 1942), 123-32. 1066

Konrad, Richard. There is No Fact-Value Gap for Hume. JVI, 4 (1970), 126-33. 1067

Kruger, Arthur N. Honest Definitions Are the Best Policy. BDAPC, 19 (December, 1953), 4-11. 1068

————. Interpreting the Debate Question. BDAPC, 18 (December, 1952), 13-19.   1069

Lambertson, Floyd W.   The Meaning of the Word "Should" in a
   Question of Policy.   QJS, 28 (December, 1942), 421-24.   1070

Mackenzie, P. T.   Fact and Value.   MJPS, 76 (April, 1967), 228-
   237.   1071

Margolis, Joseph.   One Last Time, Ought Implies Can.   Pe, 48
   (January, 1967), 33-41.   1072

Nelson, Roy C.   And Now to Define the Terms.   G, 31 (March,
   1949), 48-49, 51.   1073

Nichols, Alan.   Debate Propositions and Contexts.   QJS, 21 (June,
   1935), 355-70.   1074

Ritter, John, and Brink, T. L.   Adjuncts: "Extra-Topical" But Ac-
   ceptable.   JAFA, 8 (Spring, 1972), 223-224.   1075

Rives, Stan.   More About Squirrels.   JAFA, 9 (Summer, 1972),
   291.   (Criticizes unrealistic definitions of terms.)   1076

Roma, Emilio III.   "Ought"-"Is" And the Demand for Explanatory
   Completeness.   JVLB, 4 (1970), 302-307.   1077

Schrader, George.   The Status of Value.   JVI, 3 (Fall, 1969), 196-
   204.   (Claims that "value can be regarded as equivalent to meaning"; a world free of values is meaningless.)   1078

Searle, John.   How to Derive "Ought" from "Is."   PR, 73 (January,
   1964), 43-58.   1079

Shepard, David W.   Burden of What?   JAFA, 9 (Winter, 1973), 361-
   363.   (Criticizes illogical definitions and declares that judges
   should not accept them.)   1080

Sloman, Aaron.   "Ought" and "Better."   Mi, 79 (1970), 385-94.
   (Considers the possible uses of "ought" in reasoning.)   1081

Stack, George J.   Value and Facts.   JVI, 3 (Fall, 1969), 205-216.
   (Discusses the interrelationships between "facts" and "values,"
   emphasizing that the distinction between the two is not at all
   clear.)   1082

Winsor, Jerry L.   Toward Honest Definitions and Limitations.   F,
   52 (October, 1966), 21.   1083

(See also works listed in Language Section, 2903-3071.)

B.   ANALYSIS, ORGANIZATION, BRIEFING, DEVELOPMENT, AND STRATEGY

1.   Books

Brock, Bernard, Chesebro, James W., Cragan, John F., and
  Klumpp, James F.   Public Policy Decision-making: Systems
  Analysis in Comparative Advantages Debate.   New York, Random,
  1973.   1084

Cooley, Roger W., ed.   Brief Making and the Use of Law Books.
  St. Paul, Minn., West Book Publishing Co., 4th ed., 1924. 1085

Joiner, Charles W.   The Trial Brief.   In Advocacy and the King's
  English.   Ed. by George Rossman.   New York, Bobbs, 1960.
                                                                         1086
Maxcy, Carroll L.   The Brief: With Selections for Briefing.   Bos-
  ton, Houghton, 1916.   1087

Ringwalt, Ralph C.   Brief Drawing.   New York, Longmans, 1929.
                                                                         1088
Shaw, Warren C.   The Brief-Maker's Notebook for Argumentation
  and Debate.   New York, Ginn, 1916.   1089

Simmons, Henry T.   How Lawyers Should Argue Cases on Appeal.
  In Advocacy and the King's English.   Ed. by George Rossman.
  New York, Bobbs, 1960.   1090

Zarefsky, David, ed.   The Comparative Advantage Case.   Evanston,
  Ill. and Brunswick, Me., Championship, 1970.   1091

2.   Theses and Dissertations

Barber, Sharla J.   The Rhetoric of Confrontation: A Prescriptive
  Analysis for the Beginning Debater.   M. A.   St. Cloud.   1970.
                                                                         1092
Biddle, Phillips.   Presumption and Burden of Proof in Selected
  Twentieth-Century Textbooks on Argumentation.   M. A.   Illinois.
  1963.   1093

Boucher, Daniel K.   An Application of Criteria and Rules to Com-
  parative Analysis in Academic Debate.   M. A.   Akron.   1970.
                                                                         1094
Brittain, Dennis F.   An Examination of the Inherency Issue in
  Legislative and Academic Debate.   M. A.   Wyoming.   1968. 1095

Brundridge, Jerry A.   Argumentative Validity and Advantages of Affirmative Approaches: Assumption and Methods.   M. A.   Southwest Missouri State College.   1969.   1096

Eichmeier, Herman C.   The Critical Analysis of the Comparative
  Advantage Cases as Presented in Modern Textbooks.   M. A.

Cincinnati.   1969.   1097

Farnham, Joseph R.   A Study of Prima Facie in Academic Debating.
M. A.   Colorado.   1969.   1098

Foster, George M.   Development of Rhetorical Stasis for Deliberative Speaking.   Ph. D.   Northwestern.   1970.   1099

Gallagher, F. X.   A Handbook of Strategy for Modern College Debating.   M. A.   Johns Hopkins.   1951.   1100

Grissom, Mary A.   A Survey of Attitudes of Judges and Debaters
toward Comparative Advantage Cases.   M. A.   Baylor.   1969.
                                                                 1101
Gronbeck, Bruce E.   Archbishop Richard Whately's Doctrine of
Presumption and Burden of Proof: A Historical-Critical Analysis.
M. A.   Iowa.   1966.   1102

Henning, J. H.   An Experimental Study of the Role of Presumption
and Burden of Proof in Problem Solving.   Ph. D.   Northwestern.
1946.   1103

Isaacs, Mildred H.   A Study of Arthur N. Kruger's Treatment of
the Concepts of Inherency and Comparative Advantage.   M. A.
C. W. Post.   1972.   1104

Larmer, Larry E.   Production of a Filmed Message Concerning the
Use of the Stock Issues for Analyzing a Debate Resolution.   M. S.
Kansas State.   1964.   1105

Newton, Kenneth.   Placement of Affirmative Plan: Attitude Change
and Informative Gain.   M. A.   Illinois State.   1968.   1106

Parker, M. J.   An Application of Stasis Theory to the Treatment of
Issues in Intercollegiate Debating.   Ph. D.   S. Illinois.   1970.
                                                                 1107
Quist, Allen J.   An Investigation of the Opinions of Debate Coaches
on the Nature and Use of the Comparative Advantage Case.   M. A.
Mankato.   1968.   1107a

Wells, Earl W.   A Study of the Technique of Argumentative Analysis
as Treated by Ancient and Modern Writers.   M. A.   Wisconsin.
1927.   (Summary in QJS, 14 (June, 1928), 470-72.)   1108

3.   Articles

Abernathy, Elton.   The Second Affirmative Speech.   SSJ, 19 (September, 1953), 53-56.   1109

Barber, Sharla J.   In Defense of a Deficiency.   F, 54 (January,
1969), 8-9.   1110

Bean, Charles H.   The Psychology of Adherence to the Old and Ac-
    ceptance of the New.   JSP, 4 (August, 1933), 340-51.   1111

Behl, William A.   A New Look at the Debate Brief.   ST, 10 (Sep-
    tember, 1961), 189-93.   Condensed version in G, 43 (May, 1961),
    60-61.   1112

Brock, Bernard L.   The Comparative Advantages Case.   ST, 16
    (March, 1967), 118-123.   1113

_____.   The "Comparative Advantages" Case: A Disadvantage--A
    Rejoinder.   SPG, 5 (November, 1967), 3-6.   (A rejoinder to
    A. N. Kruger, infra.)   1114

Brooks, George E.   A Revised Method of Case Analysis.   QJS, 27
    (February, 1941), 46-51.   1115

Brown, Charles T.   Beneath the Case.   SSJ, 9 (September, 1943),
    17-18.   1116

Cannon, Martin A.   The 1950 Debate Question and the Burden of
    Proof.   R, 25 (February, 1951), 8, 13.   1117

Chenoweth, Eugene C.   Bearing the Affirmative Burden.   SA, 6
    (Summer, 1950), 51-52, 85.   (On the obligations of an affirma-
    tive team.)   1118

_____.   Steps in the Discussion of a Problem.   DM, 2 (December,
    1946), 248-50.   1119

Chesebro, James W.   Beyond the Orthodox: The Criteria Case.
    JAFA, 7 (Winter, 1971), 208-215.   1120

_____.   The Comparative Advantages Case.   JAFA, 5 (Spring,
    1968), 57-63.   1121

Christie, G. C., and Pye, A. K.   Presumptions and Assumptions in
    the Criminal Law: Another View.   DLJ (1970), 919ff.   1122

Cleary, James W.   Debating Technique.   F, 35 (January, 1950),
    47-49.   (On determining the philosophy underlying policy proposi-
    tions.)   1123

Costigan, J.   Special Debate Techniques.   SchA, 39 (October, 1967),
    16-17.   1124

Cragan, John F., and Shields, Donald C.   The Comparative Advan-
    tage Negative.   JAFA, 7 (Spring, 1970), 85-91.   1125

Craig, A. H., and Edgerton, A. C.   Art of Successful Debating.
    World Review, 7 (1928), 182.   1126

Criminal Presumption and Inference Instructions.   WmLJ, 6 (1970),

497ff.   1127

Cronen, Vernon E.   Comparative Advantage: A Classification.
CSSJ, 19 (Winter, 1968), 243-249.   1128

Cullison, A. D.   Logical Analysis of Legal Doctrine: The Normative
Structure of Positive Law.   ILR, 53 (June, 1968), 1209-1268.
(On the role of Hohfeldian and deontic systems in the analysis of
norms.)   1129

Diem, W. Roy.   "Our Plan. "   G, 18 (January, 1936), 23-24.   1130

Ditty, Mildred A. , ed.   Briefly Speaking; A Symposium: What Does
Defining the Issues of a Debate Mean to You?   BDAPC, 16 (July
10, 1950), 27-30.   (Contributors include C. W. Fink, Mary Hamilton, Melvin P. Moorhouse, and Joseph F. O'Brien.)   1131

_____.   Briefly Speaking; A Symposium: How Specific Should an
Affirmative Proposal Be?   BDAPC, 16 (July 10, 1950), 35-37.
(Contributors include Jon Hopkins, Gordon F. Hostettler, and
Howard H. Martin.)   1132

Dodds, Keith.   "Comparative Advantage":   Negative Options.   R,
40 (March, 1967), 10-11.   1133

Drum, Dale D.   "Crossword Puzzle" Preparation in Debate.   G,
38 (November, 1955), 9-10.   1134

Durkin, Helen E.   Trial and Error, Gradual Analysis, and Sudden
Reorganization; An Experimental Study of Problem Solving.   AP,
210 (May, 1937), 85 pp.   1135

Duties of Affirmative Speakers--A Symposium.   ST, 8 (March,
1959), 139-49.   (Contributors include Glenn R. Capp, Robert
Huber, and Wayne C. Eubank.)   1136

Emerson, James G.   The Case Method in Argumentation.   QJS, 31
(February and October, 1945), 8-15; 282-91; 32 (February, 1946),
1-12.   1137

Ewbank, Henry L.   The Elements of Good Strategy.   Speech Bulletin.   Supplement QJS, 2 (December, 1930), 22-27.   1138

Fadely, L. Dean.   The Validity of the Comparative Advantages Case.
JAFA, 4 (Winter, 1967), 28-35.   1139

Fletcher, G. P.   Presumption of Innocence in the Soviet Union.
UCIA, 15 (June, 1968), 1203-1239.   1140

_____.   Two Kinds of Legal Rules: A Comparative Study of Burden-
of-Persuasion Practices in Criminal Cases.   YLJ, 77 (April, 1968),
880-935.   1141

Freshley, Dwight L., ed. Briefly Speaking; A Symposium: Is Constitutionality an Issue in Debate? BDAPC, 18 (December, 1952), 38-39. (Only contributor: Mildred A. Ditty.)   1142

_____. The Responsibilities of the Affirmative Case. BDAPC, 17 (December 15, 1951), 24-25.   1143

Garn, Harvey A. A Further Look. AFAR, 10 (Winter, 1962), 25-27. (On the "need for change" issue.)   1144

Gibson, Harold E. Planning the Affirmative. SchA, 21 (December, 1949), 120-122, 143.   1145

Giffin, Kim, and Megill, Kenneth. Stock Issues in Tournament Debates. CSSJ, 12 (Autumn, 1960), 27-32.   1146

_____. A Study of Case Construction in Tournament Debates. G, 44 (November, 1961), 11-14.   1147

Gough, Harry B. Formulas for the Special Issues. PSR, 3 (November, 1913), 5-8. ("Formulas" to simplify analysis of policy questions.)   1148

Graham, W. B. Problem Solving. DM, 1 (April-July, 1945), 96-98.   1149

Haakenson, Robert. The Responsibilities of the Negative Case. BDAPC, 17 (December 15, 1951), 25-26.   1150

Harries, O. Six Ways of Confusing Issues. FA, 40 (April, 1962), 443-52.   1151

Hellman, Hugo E. Building Your Constructive Case. DM, 2 (December, 1946), 235-38. (Illustrated by the topic of compulsory health insurance.)   1152

Herzog, E. G. Patterns of Controversy. POQ, 13 (1949), 39-52.   1153

Hester, J. Gordon. Trick Case in Debate. G, 21 (January, 1939), 54. Also in PN, 5 (January-February, 1939), 10.   1154

Hope, B. W. Nothing But Need-Remedy? AFAR, 9 (Convention Issue, 1961), 15-16.   1155

Huber, Robert B. Affirmative--Kiss of Death? S, 40 (January, 1958), 11-14.   1156

Hultzen, L. S. Studies in Deliberative Analysis. In The Rhetorical Idiom, ed. D. C. Bryant. Ithaca, New York, Cornell, 1958, 97-123.   1157

Huntington, Henry B. The Relation of the Brief to the Argument. PSR, 4 (May, 1914), 1-10.   1158

James, Fleming, Jr.   Burdens of Proof.   Virginia Law Review, 47
    (1961), 51-70.   1159

Knoll, P. X.   Presumption in the Introduction to the Argumentative
    Speech.   QJS, 18 (November, 1932), 637-42.   1160

Knower, Franklin H.   A Brief Tragedy of Errors.   G, 17 (Novem-
    ber, 1934), 8-11.   (Affirmative and negative briefs on the ques-
    tion Resolved, That the United States Should Adopt the Essential
    Features of the British Broadcasting System.)   1161

_____. Studies in the Organization of Speech Material.   JER, 39
    (November, 1945), 220-30.   1162

Kolberg, O. W.   Duties of Debate Speakers.   R, 19 (October, 1944),
    6.   Also in DM, 1 (January-February, 1945), 17-18.   1163

Kruger, Arthur N.   Logic and Strategy in Developing the Debate
    Case.   ST, 3 (March, 1954), 89-106.   1164

_____. The Meaning of Inherency.   G, 45 (March, 1963), 46-47,
    54.   1165

_____. The "Comparative Advantage" Case: A Disadvantage.
    JAFA, 3 (September, 1966), 104-111.   1166

_____. The Comparative Advantage Case: A Critique.   (Sub-
    mitted to SSCJ, November, 1973.)   1167

_____. The Inherent Need: Further Clarification.   JAFA, 2 (Sep-
    tember, 1965), 109-119.   1168

_____. The Underlying Assumptions of Policy Questions: I. Pre-
    sumption and Burden of Proof.   SPG, 2 (November, 1964), 2-
    17.   1169

_____. Ibid. : II. Indictment of the Status Quo.   SPG, 2 (January,
    1965), 60-62.   1170

_____. Ibid. : III. Inherent Evil.   SPG, 2 (March, 1965), 79-82.
                                                                       1171
_____. Ibid. : IV. Major Change of the Status Quo.   SPG, 2 (May,
    1965), 134-136.   1172

_____. Ibid. : A Postscript.   SPG, 3 (March, 1966), 71-72. 1173

Lambertson, Floyd W.   Plan and Counter-Plan in a Question of
    Policy.   QJS, 29 (February, 1943), 48-52.   1174

_____. Test in Debate Theory and Practice.   G, 20 (March, 1938),
    3942.   1175

Larson, Robert G.   The Law of Presumption: A Look at Confusion,

Kentucky Style. KLJ, 57 (1968), 7-50. (On presumption and burden of proof in the courtroom.)   1176

Lembke, Russell W. On 3x5s and the Sublime. F, 35 (January, 1950), 31-33, 40. (Advocates that "solution to problem" be uppermost with debaters.)   1177

Levitas, Louise. How to Win an Argument. Catholic Digest (October, 1954), 105-108. Reprinted from This Week, August 1, 1954.   1178

Ling, David A., and Seltzer, Robert V. The Role of Attitudinal Inherency in Contemporary Debate. JAFA, 7 (Spring, 1971), 278-283.   1179

Mader, Thomas F. The Inherent Need to Analyze Stasis. JAFA, 4 (Winter, 1967), 13-20.   1180

Markert, M. G. He Stacked the Cards. PN, 7 (November, 1940), 15, 18-20. (Answer to J. W. Walch article on counterplans, infra.)   1181

Markgraf, Bruce. The Prima Facie Case: A Modest Proposal. S&G, 1 (November, 1963), 27-28. (Proposes the adoption of a courtroom procedure, namely, that a decision be awarded to the negative team if after the second affirmative constructive speech the affirmative has failed to present a prima facie case.)   1182

Marsh, Patrick O. Prima Facie Case: The Perennial Debate Topic. G, 45 (November, 1962), 13-15.   1183

_____. Is Debate Merely a Game for Conservative Players? SPG, 1 (January, 1964), 46-53.   1184

_____. A Model for Arguing Directive Propositions. JAFA, 6 (Winter, 1969), 1-11.   1185

_____. Terminological Tangle: A Reply to Prof. Kruger. SPG, 2 (January, 1965), 54-59.   1186

_____. The Terminal Tangle: A Final Reply to Prof. Kruger. SPG, 2 (May, 1965), 137-139.   1187

Moore, Wilbur E. Assumptions Underlying Analysis in Debate. F, 33 (March, 1948), 45-46, 51.   1188

Musgrave, George M. The Double-Summary Technique in Debate. QJS, 32 (December, 1946), 458-68.   1189

_____. Information Please. DM, 2 (June, 1946), 112-13. (Answers miscellaneous questions about debating, some of them pertaining to analysis and strategy.)   1190

_____. Here Are the Answers. DM, 3 (March, 1947), 44. (Answers various questions about analysis and strategy.)   1191

_____. Basic Case Possibilities in a Question of Policy. DM, 2 (September, 1946), 193-94.   1192

_____. The Conventional Case--The 1945-46 College Topic: Negative Possibilities. DM, 1 (October-December, 1945), 76-81.
1193

_____. How To Improve Your Batting Average. DM, 1 (October-December, 1945), 71-74. (Strategy on the question of compulsory military service.)   1194

_____. Organization of Debate Cases. DM, 1 (July-September, 1945), 9-12. Also F, 34 (October, 1948), 7-9.   1195

_____. Some Unfamiliar Strategy. DM, 2 (March, 1946), 14-16, 48.   1196

_____. Technically Speaking. DM, 2 (September, 1946), 195-96; 2 (December, 1946), 256-57; 3 (March, 1947), 44-45. (Answers various questions about analysis and strategy.)   1197

_____. What is the Easiest Way to Lose Debates? DM, 2 (September, 1946), 192-93.   1198

Myers, Wilfred. What Is My Duty? R, 21 (January, 1947), 6-7. Also in DM, 3 (March, 1947), 45-47.   1199

Nadeau, Ray. Some Aristotelian and Stoic Influences on the Theory of Stases. SM, 26 (November, 1959), 248-254.   1200

Nebergall, Roger E. The Negative Counterplan. ST, 6 (September, 1957), 217-20.   1201

Newman, Robert P. Analysis and Issues: A Study of Doctrine. CSSJ, 13 (1961), 43-54.   1202

_____. The Inherent and Compelling Need. JAFA, 2 (May, 1965), 66-71. (A reply to A. N. Kruger's "The Meaning of Inherency.")
1203

Nichols, Egbert R. Methods in Debating. In Intercollegiate Debates. New York, Noble, 1920. Pp. 9-24.   1204

_____. Treatise on Need Debating. SA, 7 (Summer, 1951), 39-42.   1205

Olson, Donald O. A Survey of Attitudes on the Spread. SPG, 8 (March, 1971), 66-69. (The "spread" refers to the 15 minutes of consecutive speaking time which the negative team has in orthodox intercollegiate debating.)   1206

Patterson, J. W.   Obligations of the Negative in a Policy Debate.
    ST, 11 (September, 1962), 208-13.   1207

Pelsma, John R.   A Difficult Problem for the Debater--The Special
    Issues.   PSR, 3 (November, 1913), 1-4.   (Analysis of a proposi-
    tion--proof possibilities for the two sides.)   1208

Pruett, Robert E.   The Issue of Inherency.   F, 55 (March, 1970),
    9-11.   (Distinguishes between structural and philosophical in-
    herency.)   1209

_____.   The Process of Dialectics: A Starting Point for Argument.
    OSJ, 8 (1970), 42-47.   1210

Robie, Fred S.   Teaching a Definition of Issues.   BDAPC, 16 (July
    10, 1950), 13-17.   1211

Robinson, Frederick B.   A New Briefing Device.   PSR, 4 (Novem-
    ber, 1914), 82-91.   (Suggests a three-column brief: 1. in-
    ferences, 2. facts, 3. sources.)   1212

Rowell, Edward Z.   Argumentative Analysis.   In Cultural and Sci-
    entific Speech Education Today, comp. and ed. by W. A. Cable.
    Boston, Expression, 1930. Pp. 88-95.   1213

Schultz, W. A.   Statutory Onus of Proof in Criminal Cases.   CBJ,
    10 (November, 1967), 492-504.   (On burden of proof as it relates
    to statutes.)   1214

Scott, Robert L.   On the Meaning of the Term Prima Facie in Argu-
    mentation.   CSSJ, 12 (Autumn, 1960), 33-37.   1215

Shaw, Warren C.   Systematic Analysis of Debating Problems.   QJS,
    2 (October, 1916), 344-51.   ("Exhaustive lists of hypothetical is-
    sues under every type of proposition.")   1216

_____.   The Use of Strategy in Debate.   QJS, 11 (November,
    1925), 368-72.   1217

Sillars, Malcolm.   Concerning That Negative Burden of Proof.   F,
    36 (October, 1950), 5-6.   1218

Smith, Robert G.   Resolved: That Debaters Should Learn to Listen.
    G, 43 (March, 1961), 35-36, 52.   1219

Smith, Robert W.   The Law in Debate.   II. Burden of Proof.   G,
    42 (May, 1960), 59-60.   1220

A Symposium: Must the Negative Present a Counterplan? BDAPC,
    15 (December 10, 1948), 49-50.   (Contributors include Gordon F.
    Hostettler, Frank W. Merritt, and Joseph F. O'Brien.)   1221

Thomas, David A.   Response to Cragan and Shields: Alternative

Formats for Negative Approaches to Comparative Advantage Cases.
JAFA, 8 (Spring, 1972), 200-206.   1222

_____ and Anderson, Jerry M.   Negative Approaches to the Comparative Advantages Case.   SPG, 5 (May, 1968), 153-157.   1223

Thomas, Sid B., Jr.   The Status of the Generalization Principle.
APQ, 5 (July, 1968), 174-182.   (Defends the notion that "what is
right [or wrong] for one person in a set of circumstances is right
[or wrong] for any similar person in similar circumstances.")
                                                           1224

Thompson, Ernest.   Does Organization Really Make a Difference?
AFAR, 8 (Spring, 1960), 12-16.   1225

Thompson, Wayne N.   The Effect of a Counterplan upon the Burden
of Proof.   CSSJ, 13 (1962), 247-52.   1226

_____. Plan Meets Need.   F, 49 (October, 1963), 8.   (Satirical
comments.)   1227

Torrence, Donald L.   Need Issue Includes Value Judgment.   SPG,
4 (November, 1966), 6-7.   1228

Walch, J. Weston.   On the Other Hand!   A Defense of the "Negative
Alternative."   PN, 7 (October, 1940), 8-10.   (See rejoinder by
M. G. Markert, supra.)   1229

Ward, Leo R.   Aristotle on Criteria of Moral Good.   JPol, 30 (October, 1968), 476-498.   1230

Wells, Earl W.   A Study of the Technique of Argumentative Analysis
as Treated by Ancient and Modern Writers.   QJS, 4 (June, 1928),
470-72.   (Abstract of a thesis.)   1231

White, H. A.   They Offered No Plan.   G, 17 (May, 1935), 52-53.
                                                           1232
_____. Col. J. B. Ladd's Tactical Commandments.   G, 13 (Novem-
ber, 1930), 7.   (Analogy between combat and debate tactics.)
                                                           1233
Wick, Robert.   Burden of Proof.   S, 34 (March, 1952), 16-17.1234

Wiggam, A. E.   How to Win an Argument.   AMag, 110 (November,
1930), 41.   1235

Yeager, Raymond.   Aristotle's Topics as Sources of Proof.   AFAR,
5 (Convention Reports Issue, 1957), 4-7.   1236

Zarefsky, David.   The "Traditional Case"--"Comparative Advantage
Case" Dichotomy: Another Look.   JAFA, 6 (Winter, 1969), 12-
20.   1237

C. REFUTATION AND REBUTTAL

1. Books

Allen, Frank B. Modern Refutation, Illustrated by the Anglo-American Alliance Topic. Portland, Me., Platform, 1938. 1238

_____. A Practical Guide to Rebuttals, Illustrated by the State Medicine Topic. Portland, Me., Platform, 1935. 1239

_____. Ibid., Illustrated by the Government Ownership of Electric Utilities Topic. Portland, Me., Platform, 1936. 1240

Gibson, Harold E. Your Guide to Effective Rebuttals. Jacksonville, Illinois, Mid-West Debate Bureau, 1938. 1241

2. Theses and Dissertations

Boren, Robert A. An Analysis of Methods of Refutation Used in Championship Debates. M. A. Brigham Young. 1964. 1242

Enholm, Donald K. The Use of Rhetorical Topoi for Attack and Defense of Extrinsic Persuasion. M. S. Kansas State. 1966. 1243

Willett, Thomas H. A Quantitative Analysis of Selected Speech Content Variables in Winning and Losing First Affirmative Rebuttal Speeches. M. A. Nebraska. 1967. 1244

3. Articles

Akers, Charles W. The Second Negative Rebuttal Speech. G, 42 (March, 1960), 41-42, 45. 1245

App, Austin J. The "Retort Courteous" in Debate. BDAPC, 13 (December 15, 1939), 6-8. 1246

Aristotle. On Sophistical Refutations. From the Organon, translated by W. A. Pickard-Cambridge, in The Basic Works of Aristotle. New York, Random, 1941. 1247

Carmack, Paul. Technique of Refutation. DM, 2 (June, 1946), 115-16. 1248

Criminal Trial Process--the Fight for Truth. CWRLR, 19 (April, 1968), 713-747. (On legal refutation.) 1249

Cromwell, Harvey. For Better Refutation. R, 36 (November, 1961), 4-7. 1250

Ditty, Mildred A. Evidence and Refutation. BDAPC, 17 (December 15, 1951), 26-31. 1251

Faules, Don.   Measuring Refutation Skill: An Exploratory Study.
     JAFA, 4 (Spring, 1967), 47-52.   1252

Gibson, Harold E.   Defeating the Affirmative Case.   SchA, 7 (De-
     cember, 1935), 17-19.   1253

_____.   Defeating the Negative Case.   SchA, 7 (January, 1936),
     25-26.   1254

_____.   Negative Rebuttal Ideas.   SchA, 8 (January, 1937), 201-
     203.   1255

_____.   Negative Rebuttal Plans.   SchA, 6 (December, 1934), 11-
     13.   1256

Harkness, P. J.   In Rebuttal.   F, 31 (January, 1946), 40-41.   1257

Irwin, C. E.   An Intelligent Guide to Refutation.   QJS, 25 (April,
     1939), 248-53.   1258

Mader, Thomas F.   The Second Affirmative Rebuttal Speech.   G,
     42 (March, 1960), 40, 42.   1259

Mazza, Joseph M., and Polisky, Jerome B.   A Macroscopic View
     of Rebuttal.   AFAR, 11 (Winter, 1963), 16-19.   1260

Mills, Glen E.   Pure Refutation as a Negative Case.   BDAPC, 20
     (December, 1954), 8.   1261

Olson, Donald O.   The Techniques of Questioning in Conventional
     Debate.   SPG, 3 (January, 1966), 57-59.   1262

Palzer, Edward.   Streamline Your Rebuttals.   PN, 7 (October,
     1940), 20-21.   1263

_____.   Strategy in Refutation.   PN, 7 (January-February, 1941),
     16-17.   1264

Parkhurst, Charles E.   The First Negative Rebuttal Speech.   G,
     42 (November, 1959), 5-6, 14.   1265

Smallwood, Osborne T.   The First Affirmative Rebuttal Speech.   G,
     42 (November, 1959), 7-8, 12.   1266

Thistlethwaite, D. L., and Kamenetzky, J.   Attitude Change Through
     Refutation and Elaboration of Audience Counterarguments.   JASP,
     51 (1955), 3-12.   1267

_____, _____, and Schmidt, Hans.   Refutation and Attitude
     Change.   SM, 23 (March, 1956), 14-25.   1268

Toussaint, Sylvester R.   Refutation in Team Debating.   NFLB, 4
     (January, 1930), 1-7.   Also in F, 17 (October, 1933), 116. 1269

Waltz, Waldo C. Some Problems of Rebuttal: An Appraisal. QJS,
    20 (June, 1934), 378, 83.   1270

Watkins, Lloyd I. Whither Rebuttal? QJS, 44 (October, 1958),
    308-10. (An inquiry into the effectiveness of rebuttal speeches.)
                                                                 1271
Willett, Thomas H., and Gruner, Charles R. A Quantitative Analy-
    sis of First Affirmative Rebuttal Speeches from "Winning" and
    "Losing" Debates. SPG, 6 (November, 1968), 16-20. (Concludes
    that explanation was the technique most favored in first affirma-
    tive rebuttal speeches. Found few quantifiable differences be-
    tween winning and losing rebuttals.)   1272

VII.   RESEARCH AND EVIDENCE

1.   Books

Best, William M.   Principles of the Law of Evidence, with Elementary Rules for Conducting the Examinations and Cross-Examinations of Witnesses.   American edition from the Seventh English Edition by C. F. Chamberlayne, Boston, C. C. Soule, 1883. (Same title, London, Sweet, 1922.)   1273

Boller, Paul F.   Quotesmanship: The Use and Abuse of Quotations for Polemical and Other Purposes.   Dallas, SMU, 1967.   1274

Croxton, F. E., and Cowden, D. J.   Applied General Statistics.   New York, Prentice, 1939.   1375

Fogelin, Robert J.   Evidence and Meaning.   London, Routledge and Kegan Paul, 1967.   1276

Garrett, H. E.   Statistics in Psychology and Education.   New York, Longmans, 3rd edition.   1946.   1277

Gray, C. T., and Votaw, D. F.   Statistics Applied to Education and Psychology.   New York, Ronald, 1939.   1278

Guilford, J. P.   Fundamental Statistics in Psychology and Education. New York, McGraw, 2nd edition.   1950.   1279

_____.   Psychometric Methods.   New York, McGraw, 1936.   1280

Jerome, H.   Statistical Methods.   New York, Harper, 1924.   1281

Johnson, Allen.   The Historian and Historical Evidence.   New York, Scribner's, 1926.   1282

Kelley, Truman L.   Fundamentals of Statistics.   Cambridge, Mass., Harvard, 1947.   1283

Lindquist, E. F.   First Course in Statistics.   New York, Houghton, 2nd edition.   1942.   1284

Maguire, John N.   Evidence, Common Sense and Common Law. Brooklyn, Foundation, 1947.   1285

McCroskey, James C.   Studies of the Effects of Evidence in Per-

suasive Communication. SCRL, 4-67. East Lansing, Michigan,
1967.   1286

Mills, Frederick C. Statistical Methods Applied to Economics and
Business. New York, H. Holt, 2nd edition. 1938.   1287

Morgan, Edmond M., Maguire, John M., and Weinstein, Jack B.
Evidence: Cases and Materials. Brooklyn, Foundation, 1957.
                                                          1288
Newman, Robert P., and Newman, Dale R. Evidence. Boston,
Houghton, 1969.   1289

Paton, George W. A Text-Book of Jurisprudence. New York, Oxford, 1946.   1290

Pearson, Frank A., and Bennett, K.R. Statistical Methods. New
York, Wiley, 1942.   1291

Radin, Max. The Law and You. New York, Library, 1948.   1292

Ross, C. C. Measurement in Today's Schools. New York, Prentice,
1942.   1293

Rubenstein, Ronald. John Citizen and the Law. Middlesex, England, Penguin, 1947.   1294

Rugg, Harold O. Statistical Methods Applied to Education. New
York, Houghton, 1927.   1295

Smith, G. M. A Simplified Guide to Statistics. New York, Farrar,
2nd edition. 1946.   1296

Thurstone, Louis L. The Fundamentals of Statistics. New York,
Macmillan, 1925.   1297

Tracy, John E. Handbook of the Law of Evidence. New York,
Prentice, 1952.   1298

Treloar, A. E. Elements of Statistical Reasoning. New York,
Wiley, 2nd edition. 1939.   1299

Vincent, John M. Aids to Historical Research. New York, Appleton, 1934.   1300

von Mises, R. Probability Statistics and Truth. New York, Macmillan, 1939.   1301

Weaver, Richard M. The Ethics of Rhetoric. Chicago, Regnery,
1953.   1302

Wigmore, John H., comp. A Pocket Code of the Rules of Evidence
in Trials at Law. Boston, Little, 1910.   1303

_____. The Science of Judicial Proof as Given by Logic, Psychology, and General Experience, and Illustrated in Judicial Trials. Boston, Little, 3d edition, 1937.   1304

Winks, Robin W., ed. The Historian as Detective: Essays on Evidence. New York, Harper, 1969.   1305

2. Theses and Dissertations

Benjamin, Robert L. Authority: Its Nature and Influence in Oral Argument. M. S. Wisconsin, 1947.   1306

Benson, James A. The Use of Evidence in Intercollegiate Debate. Ph. D. Purdue. 1969.   1307

Brittin, Marie E. Concepts of Evidence in Rhetoric. Ph. D. Northwestern. 1949.   1308

Gregg, Richard B. A Contemporary Applicability of the Legal Rules of Testimonial Evidence for Argument. Ph. D. Pittsburgh. 1963.   1309

Harte, Thomas B. A Test of Audience Ability to Apply the "Tests of Evidence." M. A. Illinois. 1969.   1310

Kline, John A. Interaction of Evidence and Readers' Intelligence on the Effects of Short Messages. M. A. Iowa. 1968.   1311

Kowitz, Albert C. The Effects of Varying Amounts of Factual Information on the Acceptance of Propositions of Fact and Policy. Ph. D. Indiana. 1969.   1312

McKee, Paul R. An Analysis of the Use of Evidence in Ten Intercollegiate Debates. M. A. Kansas. 1959.   1313

Purnell, Sandra. A Study of Evidence in Intercollegiate Debate. M. A. Wayne State. 1966.   1314

Russell, Jensen E. A Description of the Uses of Evidence in Championship Debate. M. A. Brigham Young. 1970.   1315

Underwood, Willard A. An Analysis and Comparison of Evidence in Law and Debate. M. S. Illinois State. 1967.   1316

3. Articles

Abernathy, Elton. Canned Debate Material. SSJ, 8 (September, 1942), 26-27.   1317

Adams, J. R. Scientific Evidence and the Law. NYLF, 13 (Winter, 1967), 658-671.   1318

Anderson, Betty.   Debate Handbooks for 1971-1972:   A Critical Per-
    spective.   JAFA, 8 (Winter, 1972), 165-167.   1319

Anderson, Loren A.   An Experimental Study of Reluctant and Biased
    Authority-Based Assertions.   JAFA, 7 (Spring, 1970), 79-84.
                                                                    1320
Anonymous.   "Of all the Nerve"... or, Was There Really Rotten-
    ness in Denmark?   G, 15 (March, 1933), 17.   (A criticism of
    bureaus supplying notes and evidence for interscholastic and inter-
    collegiate debaters.)   1321

Arnold, William E. , and McCroskey, James C.   The Credibility of
    Reluctant Testimony.   CSSJ, 18 (May, 1967), 97-103.   1322

Barnard, Raymond H.   The Use of Charts in Debate.   QJS, 13
    (February, 1927), 54-56.   1323

Baxter, P. G.   Use and Abuse of Documents: An Introduction to
    Questioned Document Examination.   Medicine, Science, and the
    Law, 9 (1969), 39ff.   1324

Beaird, T. M.   Report of Committee on Debate Materials and Inter-
    state Cooperation of the N. U. E. A.   [National University Extension
    Association] G, 14 (November, 1931), 17-18.   1325

Benson, James A.   The Use of Evidence in Intercollegiate Debate.
    JAFA, 7 (Spring, 1971), 260-270.   1326

Bishop, Brad.   The Master Index.   SPG, 10 (March, 1973), 77-79.
    (On a method of handling evidence without having to shuffle through
    cards.)   1327

Bitzer, Lloyd F.   A Reevaluation of Campbell's Doctrine of Evi-
    dence.   QJS, 46 (April, 1960), 135-40.   1328

Blackman, Charles B.   The Proposed Federal Rules of Evidence--
    How Will They Affect the Trial of Cases?   WLLR, 27 (1969-70),
    17-43.   1329

Bostrum, Robert N. , and Tucker, Raymond K.   Evidence, Personal-
    ity, and Attitude Change.   SM, 36 (March, 1969), 22-27.   1330

Brandes, Paul D.   Evidence in Aristotle's Rhetoric.   SM, 28
    (March, 1961), 21-28.   1331

Buehler, E. C.   The Role of Opinion as Related to Persuasion and
    Contest Debate.   SSJ, 25 (Fall, 1959), 21-26.   1332

Callaghan, J. Calvin.   Are Public-Opinion Polls Evidence?   BDAPC,
    10 (December 19, 1940), 1-5.   Reprinted in BDAPC, 16 (July 10,
    1950), 18-22.   1333

Campbell, W. A.   The Laws of Evidence.   PSQ, 33 (February,

1967), 31-37.   1334

Cathcart, Robert S.   Four Methods of Presenting Evidence.   SM,
   22 (August, 1955), 227-33.   1335

Colister, E.G., Jr.   Expertise: The Expert and the Learned
   Treatise.   KLR, 17 (November, 1968), 167-179.   (On what constitutes expert witness in courtroom.)   1336

Collier, Christopher.   Who Discovered America?:   A Review of Recent Historiography.   SAQ, 66 (Winter, 1967), 31-41.   (Examines
   the ways in which men are convinced by history.)   1337

Conviction upon Plea of Nolo Contendere Impeaching Evidence.
   ArLR, 21 (Spring, 1967), 124-130.   1338

Critical Appraisal of the Best Evidence Rule.   RLR, 21 (Spring,
   1967), 526-546.   1339

Crocker, Lionel.   The Debater and His Handling of Facts.   AFAR,
   11 (2 Spring, 1963), 18-22.   1340

Dresser, William R.   The Impact of Evidence in Decision Making.
   JAFA, 3 (May, 1966), 43-47.   1341

_____.   Effects of "Satisfactory" and "Unsatisfactory" Evidence in
   a Speech of Advocacy.   SM, 30 (August, 1963), 302-306.   1342

_____.   The Use of Evidence in Ten Championship Debates.   JAFA,
   1 (September, 1964), 101-106.   1343

Evidence.   AlLR, 34 (1970), 481.   1344

Evidence Symposium.   Indiana Legal Forum, 3 (1970), 309.   1345

False Statements as Substantive Evidence.   WmLJ, 5 (1969), 253.
                                                                                1346
Finkelstein, Michael O., and Fairley, William B.   A Bayesian Approach to Identification Evidence.   HLR, 83 (1970), 489ff.   1347

Fotheringham, Wallace C.   The Law of Evidence and the Debater.
   AFAR, 6 (Spring, 1958), 18-36.   1348

_____.   Statistical Proof in Debate.   G, 36 (May, 1954), 91-93.
                                                                                1349
Garland, J.V.   Debate Preparation... Random or Regimented?   G,
   23 (March, 1941), 55-56, 60.   1350

Gartland, Henry J.   Debate Reference--Aid to Democracy.   WLB,
   15 (April, 1941), 658-60.   1351

Giffin, Kim, and McKee, Paul R.   An Analysis of Evidence in Debates.   AFAR, 10 (Winter, 1962), 1-5.   1352

Glenn, Norval D.   Problems of Comparability in Trend Studies with
     Opinion Poll Data.   POQ, 34 (1970), 82-91.   (On problems in-
     volved in using opinion poll data to suggest trends.)   1353

Green, Thomas F., Jr.   Highlights of the Proposed Federal Rules
     of Evidence.   GaLR, 4 (1969), 1-42.   (On admissibility of evi-
     dence in Federal Courts.)   1354

Gregg, Richard B.   The Rhetoric of Evidence.   WS, 31 (Summer,
     1967), 180-188.   (Differentiates between logical and psychological
     effects of evidence and suggests that both are involved in argu-
     mentation.)   1355

Hargis, Donald E.   The Forms of Support.   WS, 14 (March, 1950),
     18-22.   1356

Harris, Albert M.   Does the Distribution of Briefs on Public Ques-
     tions Produce More Good than Harm?   QJS, 1 (June, 1915), 177-
     84.   1357

Hart, Peter.   Codification of the Law of Evidence: The American
     Precedent.   MLJ, 2 (1967), 201-217.   1358

Harte, Thomas B.   Audience Ability to Apply Tests of Evidence.
     JAFA, 8 (Fall, 1971), 109-115.   1359

Hellman, Hugo E.   The Varsity Debate Researchers.   G, 28 (May,
     1946), 52, 54.   Also in DM, 2 (September, 1946), 196-97.   1360

Horn, Gunnar.   Debater's Classroom Library.   SchA, 16 (Novem-
     ber, 1944), 98-99.   1361

Howe, Jack.   Disappearing Research.   F, 45 (March, 1960), 5-6.
                                                                         1362
Huff, Darrell.   How to Lie With Statistics.   HM, (August, 1950),
     97-101.   1363

Hufford, Roger.   The Case of the Missing Evidence.   F, 52 (Octo-
     ber, 1966), 15-17.   1364

_____.   Use of Statistical Evidence in Debating.   F, 50 (January,
     1965), 17-20.   1365

Insalata, S. John.   The Persuasive Use of Evidence in Formal Ar-
     gument.   F, 45 (March, 1960), 9-11.   1366

Johnsen, J., comp.   New Debate Material.   WLB, 6 (February,
     1932), 433-5.   1367

Judicial Use, Misuse, and Abuse of Statistical Evidence.   JUL, 47
     (1969-70), 165ff.   1368

Kadish, Mortimer, R.   A Note on the Grounds of Evidence.   JPhil,

(April, 1914), 229-43.   1369

Kline, John A.   Interaction of Evidence and Readers' Intelligence on
the Effects of Short Messages.   QJS, 55 (December, 1969), 407-
13.   (Concludes that factual evidence enhances the expertness and
trustworthiness of the source.)   1370

_____.   Dogmatism of the Speaker and Selection of Evidence.   SM,
38 (November, 1971), 354-356.   1371

_____.   A Q-Analysis of Encoding Behavior in the Selection of Evi-
dence.   SM, 38 (August, 1971), 190-197.   1372

Kramer, D. N.   Scientific Evidence and the Law.   ABAJ, 53 (February, 1967), 165-166.   (Calls for a realistic perspective of the
tests of evidence.)   1373

Lampel, Anita K., and Anderson, Norman H.   Combining Visual and
Verbal Information in a Impression-Formation Task.   JPSP, 9
(August, 1968), 1-6.   (Suggests that poor visual aids detract seri-
ously from information presented, and that good visual aids en-
hance the presentation.)   1374

Major Changes Under the Proposed Federal Rules of Evidence.
TnLR, 37 (1969-70), 556-80, 759-75.   1375

Makosky, John D.   It Can't Happen Here!   BDAPC, 13 (December
15, 1939), 1-3.   1376

Manning, Peter K.   Problems in Interpreting Interview Data.   SQ,
51 (April, 1967), 302-316.   1377

Martin, R. M.   Facts, What They Are and What They Are Not.
APQ. 4 (October, 1967), 269-280.   1378

Material for Debates.   I, 70 (March 2, 1911), 483.   1379

McCormick, M.   Opinion Evidence in Iowa.   DLR, 19 (1970), 245ff.
                                                                   1380
McCroskey, James C.   A Summary of Experimental Research on
the Effects of Evidence in Persuasive Communication.   QJS, 55
(April, 1969), 169-176.   (Summarizes research findings dealing
with (a) evidence and source credibility, (b) credibility of sources
of evidence, (c) evidence, delivery and media of message presentation, (d) evidence and prior knowledge of audience, (e) effects
of evidence on sustained attitude change.)   1381

_____.   The Effects of Evidence in Persuasive Communication.
WS, 31 (Summer, 1967), 189-198.   1382

_____.   The Effects of Evidence as an Inhibitor of Counter-Persua-
sion.   SM, 37 (August, 1970), 188-194.   1383

_____ and Klopf, Donald W.   Primary Sources as Debate Evidence. SPG, 2 (March, 1964), 78-80.   1384

Miller, H. B.   Beyond the Law of Evidence.   S. California Law Journal, 40 (1967), 1-37.   1385

Montrose, J. L.   Basic Concepts of the Law of Evidence.   Law Quarterly Review, 70 (October, 1954), 527-55.   1386

Moore, J. D.   Facts and Figures.   AuJP, 47 (August, 1969), 145-160.   1387

Morrison, C. A.   Some Features of the Roman and the English Law of Evidence.   Tulane Law Review, 33 (1959), 577-94.   1388

Murray, Frank S.   Judgments of Evidence.   AJPsy, 81 (1968), 319-333.   (College students' confidence in their judgments increased when they were presented "stronger" evidence, but not when they were only presented more evidence.)   1389

Muscio, Bernard.   The Influence of the Form of a Question.   BJP, 8 (September, 1916), 351-89.   (An experiment on evidence involving certain question forms.)   1390

Musgrave, George M.   Library Research by Debaters.   DM, 1 (October-December, 1945), 28-30.   1391

Neurath, Otto.   Visual Aids and Arguing.   NE, 25 (April, 1944), 51-6.   1392

Newman, Robert P. , and Sanders, Keith R.   A Study in the Integrity of Evidence.   JAFA, 2 (January, 1965), 7-13.   (Findings indicate that college debaters sometimes invent evidence.)   1393

Nichols, Egbert R.   The Use of Charts, Graphs, and Visual Aids. DM, 4 (Spring, 1948), 43-4.   1394

Olson, Donald O. , Tompkins, Phillip, and Temple, Gloria.   The Co-Operative Squad File.   G, 40 (November, 1957), 15.   1395

Orvis, M. B.   Wisconsin's Package Libraries.   I, 73 (August 22, 1912), 436-9.   1396

Our Own Words or Others?   Brief selections from: Texas Interscholastic Leaguer, "Knock-Out Debate Material;" and Bulletin, Nebraska High School Debating League, 1931, "Find it Yourself. " G, 14 (November, 1931), 21-22.   1397

Perlman, P.   Demonstrative Evidence.   KSBJ, 33 (1969), 5.   1398

Peterson, Cameron R. , and Beach, Lee Roy.   Man as an Intuitive Statistician.   PB, 68 (July, 1967), 29-46.   1399

Pitt, Carl A.   Upgrading the Debater's Research Methods.   SPG,
    7 (January, 1970), 44-46.   1400

Poffenberger, A. J.   Psychology and the Law.   In his Applied Psy-
    chology, New York and London, Appleton, 1929.   Pp. 473-94.
    (Deals with testimony and the evaluation of evidence.)   1401

Rabbitt, Patrick M.   Learning to Ignore Irrelevant Information.
    AJPsy, 80 (March, 1967), 1-13.   1402

Robinson, Frederick B.   Evidence in Academic Debate.   PSR, 2
    (November, 1912), 68-73.   1403

Robinson, James A.   Why Spend Your Time...   G, 35 (March,
    1953), 58-66.   (A criticism of debate handbooks.)   1404

Reuther, Jean.   The Importance of Primary Research.   F, 52 (Oc-
    tober, 1966), 19-20.   1405

Sanders, J. W.   Anatomy of Proof in Civil Actions.   LLR, 28
    (April, 1968), 297-311.   (On what constitutes sufficient evidence
    in court cases.)   1406

Sanders, Keith R.   Toward a Solution to the Misuse of Evidence.
    JAFA, 3 (January, 1966), 6-10.   1407

Schulman, P. W.   Evidence Challenging Credibility.   MLJ, 2 (1967),
    287-294.   (Suggests ways of testing evidence in courtroom cross-
    examination period.)   1408

Scott, Robert L.   Discourage Handbooks?   AFAR, 9 (Convention
    issue, 1961), 14.   1409

Seiler, William J.   The Effects of Visual Materials on Attitudes,
    Credibility, and Retention.   SM, 38 (November, 1971), 331-334.
                                                                  1410

Smith, Harold E.   The Use of Statistical Data in Debate.   QJS, 26
    (October, 1940), 426-31.   1411

Smith, Robert W.   The Law in Debate: III. Hearsay Evidence.   G,
    43 (January, 1961), 23-24; 31-2.   1412

Soper, Paul.   The Debaters' Handbook Evil.   S, 25 (November,
    1940), 4.   1413

Stern, William.   The Psychology of Testimony.   JASP, 34 (January,
    1939), 3-20.   1414

Tarver, Jerry L.   Reflections on a New Debate Handbook.   JAFA,
    2 (January, 1965), 25-27.   1415

Thurber, E.   Debate Material.   WB, 8 (September, 1933), 54-5.
                                                                  1416

Timmons, William M.   Discussion, Debating and Research.   QJS,
    27 (October, 1941), 415-21.   1417

Trautman, P. A.   Motions Testing the Sufficiency of Evidence.
    WsLR, 42 (April, 1967), 787-816.   1418

Trueblood, Thomas C.   Evidence in Debate.   PSR, 1 (December,
    1911), 116.   1419

Van Voorhis, J.   Expert Opinion Evidence.   NYLF, 13 (Winter,
    1967), 651-658.   (On the definition of legal expert opinion evi-
    dence.)   1420

Walch, J. Weston.   What About Debate Handbooks?   PN, 8 (March-
    April, 1942), 5-7.   (A defense of the use of handbooks by an
    author of many.)   1421

Weinstein, Jack B. , and Berger, Margaret A.   Basic Rules of Rel-
    evancy in the Proposed Federal Rules of Evidence.   GaLR, 4
    (1969), 43-109.   (Relevancy of evidence as a standard for admis-
    sibility.)   1422

Weld, H. P. , and Roff, M.   A Study in the Formation of Opinions
    Based on Legal Evidence.   AJPh, 51 (1938), 609-628.   1423

Whitehead, Jack L. , Jr.   Effects of Authority-Based Assertion on
    Attitude and Credibility.   SM, 38 (November, 1971), 311-315.
                                                                       1424
Wichelns, H. A.   Some Weaknesses of Public Opinion Polls.   In
    Eastern Public Speaking Conference.   New York, Wilson, 1940.
    Chapter 15, pp. 334ff.   1425

VIII.   LOGIC, REASONING, AND ARGUMENT

1.   Books

Adams, E. M.   The Fundamentals of General Logic.   New York, Longmans, 1954.   1426

Aikins, H. A.   The Principles of Logic.   New York, H. Holt, 1902.   1427

Angell, Richard B.   Reasoning and Logic.   New York, Appleton, 1964.   1428

Anton, John P.   Aristotle's Theory of Contrariety.   London, Routledge, 1957.   1429

Aristotle.   Organon (translated by W. D. Ross).   Oxford, Clarendon, 1928.   1430

Avery, A. E.   The Function and Forms of Thought.   New York, H. Holt, 1927.   1431

Ballantine, W. G.   The Basis of Belief; Proof by Inductive Reasoning.   New York, Crowell, 1930.   1432

Barker, Stephen F.   The Elements of Logic.   New York, McGraw, 1965.   1433

Barry, Brian.   Political Argument.   New York, Humanities, 1965.   1434

Beardsley, Monroe C.   Thinking Straight.   Englewood Cliffs, New Jersey, Prentice, 2nd edition, 1956.   1435

Bennett, A. A., and Bayliss, C. A.   Formal Logic.   New York, Prentice, 1939.   1436

Berne, Eric.   The Mind in Action.   New York, Simon, 1947.   1437

Bilsky, Manuel.   Logic and Effective Argument.   New York, H. Holt, 1956.   1438

Black, Max.   Critical Thinking.   New York, Prentice, 1946.   1439

Blandshard, Brand.   The Nature of Thought.   London, Allen, 1939.   1440

120

Blyth, John W.   A Modern Introduction to Logic.   Boston, Houghton, 1957.   1441

Bruner, Jerome S. , Goodnow, Jacqueline J. , and Austin, George A. A Study of Thinking.   New York, Wiley, 1956.   1442

Boas, George.   Our New Ways of Thinking.   New York, Harper, 1930.   1443

Bode, B. H.   An Outline of Logic.   New York, H. Holt, 1910. 1444

Boole, George.   The Mathematical Analysis of Logic.   Oxford, Blackwell, 1948.   1445

Bosanquet, Bernard.   Implication and Linear Reference.   London, Macmillan, 1920.   1446

_____.   Logic.   Oxford, Oxford, rev. ed. , 2 vols. , 1911.   1447

Bradley, F. H.   Principles of Logic.   Oxford, Oxford.   2nd ed. , 2 vols.   1922.   1448

Bridgman, P. W.   The Intelligent Individual and Society.   New York, Macmillan, 1938.   1449

Brown, W. (ed.) Psychology and the Sciences.   London, Black, 1924.   1450

Brumbaugh, Jesse F.   Legal Reasoning and Briefing.   Indianapolis, Bobbs, 1917.   1451

Burtt, E. A.   Right Thinking.   New York, Harper, 1946.   1452

Carlson, H. S.   Information and Certainty in Political Opinions. Iowa City, Iowa, Department of Publication, State University of Iowa, 1931.   1453

Carnap, Rudolf.   Formalization of Logic.   Cambridge, Cambridge, 1944.   1454

Carney, James D. , and Scheer, Richard K.   Fundamentals of Logic. New York, Macmillan, 1964.   1455

Castell, Alburey.   A College Logic.   New York, Macmillan, 1939.
                                                              1456
Chapman, F. M. , and Henle, P.   The Fundamentals of Logic.   New York, Scribner's, 1933.   1457

Chase, Stuart.   Guides to Straight Thinking.   New York, Harper, 1956.   1458

Chisholm, R.   Theory of Knowledge.   Englewood Cliffs, New Jersey, Prentice, 1966.   1459

Clarke, Edwin L.   The Art of Straight Thinking.   New York, Appleton, 1929.   1460

Cohen, Morris R.   A Preface to Logic.   New York, H. Holt, 1944.
                                                                    1461
_____ and Nagel, Ernest.   An Introduction to Logic and Scientific
Method.   New York, Harcourt, 1934.   1462

Columbia Associates in Philosophy.   An Introduction to Reflective
Thinking.   Boston, Houghton, 1923.   1463

Copi, Irving M.   Introduction to Logic.   New York, Macmillan,
1953.   1464

Creighton, J. E.   An Introductory Logic.   New York, Macmillan,
4th edition, 1920.   1465

_____ and Smart, H. R.   An Introductory Logic.   New York, Macmillan, 1933.   1466

Demarest, Theodore.   Hints for Forensic Practice; a Monograph on
Certain Rules Appertaining to the Subject of Judicial Proof.   New
York, Banks, 1905.   1467

De Morgan, A.   Formal Logic.   La Salle, The Open Court Publishing Company, 1926.   1468

Dewey, John.   Essays in Experimental Logic.   Chicago, Chicago,
1918.   1469

_____.   How We Think.   New York, Heath, new ed., 1933.   1470

_____.   Logic.   The Theory of Inquiry.   New York, H. Holt, 1938.
                                                                    1471
_____.   Studies in Logical Theory.   Chicago, Chicago, 1919.   1472

Diesing, Paul.   Reason in Society: Five Types of Decisions and
Their Social Conditions.   Urbana, Illinois, Illinois, 1962.   1473

Dimnet, Ernest.   The Art of Thinking.   New York, Simon, 1932.
                                                                    1474
Dotterer, R. H.   Beginner's Logic.   New York, Macmillan, 1924.
                                                                    1475
Eaton, R. M.   General Logic.   New York, Scribner's, 1931.   1476

Evans, D. L., and Gamertsfelder, W. S.   Logic.   Garden City, New
York, Doubleday, 1937.   1477

Fearnside, W. Ward, and Holther, William B.   Fallacy: The Counterfeit of Argument.   Englewood Cliffs, New Jersey, Prentice,
1959.   1478

Fischer, David H.   Historians' Fallacies.   New York, Harper

Torchbooks, 1970.   1479

Flesch, Rudolph.   The Art of Clear Thinking.   New York, Harper,
    1951.   1480

Frye, A. M. , and Levi, A. W.   Rational Belief.   New York, Har-
    court, 1941.   1481

Hamblin, Charles L.   Fallacies.   London: Methuen, 1970.   (An
    historical account of the treatment of fallacies; contains much
    material of particular interest to students of argumentation and
    debate.)   1482

Hazlitt, Henry.   Thinking as a Science.   New York, Dutton, 1916.
                                                           1483
Hepp, Maylon H.   Thinking Things Through: An Introduction to
    Logic.   New York, Scribner's, 1956.   1484

Hibbon, J. G.   Logic: Deductive and Deductive.   New York, Scrib-
    ner's, 3rd edition, 1923.   1485

Hollingworth, H. L.   The Psychology of Thought.   New York, Apple-
    ton, 1926.   1486

Holmes, Roger W.   The Rhyme of Reason.   New York, Appleton,
    1939.   1487

Jastrow, Joseph.   Effective Thinking.   New York, Simon, 1931.
                                                           1488
_____.   Fact and Fable in Psychology.   New York, Houghton,
    1901.   1489

Jeffrey, Richard.   The Logic of Decision.   New York, McGraw,
    1965.   1490

Jensen, Otto C.   The Nature of Legal Argument.   Oxford, Black-
    well, 1957.   1491

Jepson, R. W.   Clear Thinking.   London, Longmans, 1936.   1492

Jevons, W. S.   Elementary Lessons in Logic.   London, Macmillan,
    1928.   1493

_____.   The Principles of Science.   New York, Macmillan, 1905.
                                                           1494
_____.   Studies in Deductive Logic.   New York, Macmillan, 1908.
                                                           1495
Johnson, W. E.   Logic.   Cambridge, Cambridge, 1931.   3 vols.
                                                           1496
Johnstone, Henry W.   Elementary Deductive Logic.   New York,
    Crowell, 1954.   1497

_____.   Philosophy and Argument.   University Park, Pennsylvania,

Pennsylvania State University Press, 1959.   1498

Jorgenson, J.   Treatise of Formal Logic.   Oxford, Oxford, 1931.
                                                               1499
Joseph, H. W. B.   An Introduction to Logic.   Oxford, Oxford, 2nd
    edition, 1916.   1500

Kahane, Howard.   Logic and Contemporary Rhetoric: The Use of
    Reason in Everyday Life.   Belmont, California, Wadsworth,
    1971.   1501

_____.   Logic and Philosophy.   Belmont, Wadsworth, 1969.   1501a

Kerr, Harry P.   Opinion and Evidence: Cases for Argument and
    Discussion.   New York, Harcourt, 1962.   (A supplementary work
    for argumentation and discussion courses.)   1502

Keynes, John M.   A Treatise on Probability.   New York, Macmil-
    lan, 1921.   1503

Keynes, J. N.   Formal Logic.   London, Macmillan, 1906.   1504

Klubertanz, George P.   St. Thomas Aquinas on Analogy: a Textual
    Analysis and Systematic Synthesis.   Chicago, Loyola University
    Press, 1960.   1505

Kneale, W. C.   Probability and Induction.   Oxford, Clarendon, 1949.
                                                               1506
Kyburg, Henry E., Jr.   Probability and the Logic of Rational Be-
    lief.   Middletown, Connecticut, Wesleyan University Press,
    1961.   1507

_____ and Nagel, Ernest, ed.   Induction: Some Current Issues.
    Middletown, Connecticut, Wesleyan University Press, 1963. 1508

_____ and Smokler, Howard E., eds.   Studies in Subjective Proba-
    bility.   New York, Wiley, 1964.   1509

Langer, Susanne K.   Introduction to Symbolic Logic.   Cambridge,
    Harvard, 1937.   1510

Larrabee, H. A.   Reliable Knowledge.   Boston, Houghton, 1945.
                                                               1511
Levi, Edward.   An Introduction to Legal Reasoning.   Chicago, Chi-
    cago, 1948.   1512

Levy, B. H.   Cardozo and the Frontiers of Legal Thinking.   New
    York, Oxford, 1938.   1513

Lewis, C. I.   Knowledge and Valuation.   New York, Open Court,
    1946.   1514

Mace, Cecil A.   The Principles of Logic.   London, Longmans,

1933.   1515

Mander, A. E.   Logic for the Millions.   New York, Philosophical,
1947.   1516

Manicas, Peter T. , ed.   Logic as Philosophy.   New York, Van
Nostrand, 1971.   1517

_____ and Kruger, Arthur N.   Essentials of Logic.   New York,
American, 1968.   1518

_____ and _____.   Workbook for Essentials of Logic.   New York,
American, 1968.   1519

McKeon, Richard, (ed.)   Introduction to Aristotle.   New York, The
Modern Library, 1947.   1520

Michalos, Alex C.   Improving Your Reasoning.   Englewood Cliffs,
N. J. , Prentice, 1970.   1520a

Morris, C.   How Lawyers Think.   Cambridge, Mass. , Harvard,
1937.   1521

Munsterberg, H.   On the Witness Stand.   New York, The Clark
Boardman Company, 1927.   1522

Murphy, Arthur E.   The Uses of Reason.   New York, Macmillan,
1943.   1523

Northrop, F. S. C.   The Logic of the Sciences and the Humanities.
New York, Macmillan, 1947.   1524

Patterson, Charles H.   Principles of Correct Thinking.   Minneapolis, Minn. , Burgess, 1936; New York, Longmans, 1939.   1525

Patzig, Gunther.   Aristotle's Theory of the Syllogism.   Netherlands,
Reidel, 3rd ed. , 1969.   1526

Peirce, Charles S.   Chance, Love, and Logic.   New York, Harcourt, 1923.   (Edited by Morris R. Cohen with supplementary
essay on the pragmatism of Peirce by John Dewey.)   1527

_____.   Collected Papers.   Vols. II and III.   Cambridge, Harvard,
1931-37.   1528

Pitt, Jack, and Leavenworth, Russell E.   Logic for Argument.
New York, Random, 1966.   1528a

Poincaré, H.   Science and Hypothesis.   New York, Dover Publishing Company, 1952.   1529

Prichard, H. A.   Knowledge and Perception.   London, Clarendon,
1950.   1530

Quine, Willard V. O.   From a Logical Point of View.   Cambridge, Harvard, 1964.   1531

_____ .   Methods of Logic.   New York, Holt, 1959.   1532

Radin, Max.   Law as Logic and Experience.   New Haven, Yale, 1940.   1533

Reiser, Oliver L.   Humanistic Logic for the Mind in Action.   New York, Crowell, 1930.   1534

Rignani, Eugenio.   The Psychology of Reasoning.   (Trans. by Winifred A. Hall).   New York, Harcourt, 1927.   1535

Ritchie, A. D.   Scientific Method.   New York, Harcourt, 1923. 1536

Robinson, Daniel S.   Illustrations of the Methods of Reasoning. New York, D. Appleton, 1927.   1537

_____ .   The Principles of Reasoning.   New York, D. Appleton, 2nd edition.   1930.   1538

Robinson, James H.   The Mind in the Making.   New York, Harper, 1921.   1539

Ruby, Lionel.   The Art of Making Sense.   Philadelphia, Lippincott, 1954.   1540

_____ .   Logic: An Introduction.   Philadelphia, Lippincott, 2nd edition, 1960.   1541

Russell, Bertrand.   An Inquiry into Meaning and Truth.   New York, Norton, 1940.   1542

_____ .   Scientific Method in Philosophy.   Oxford, Clarendon, 1914.   1543

Salmon, Wesley C.   Logic.   Englewood Cliffs, New Jersey, Prentice, 1967.   1544

Schiller, F. C. S.   Formal Logic.   London, Macmillan, 1912.   1545

_____ .   Logic for Use.   New York, Harcourt, 1930.   1546

Searles, Herbert L.   Logic and Scientific Methods.   New York, Ronald, 2nd edition, 1956.   1547

Sellars, R. W.   Essentials of Logic.   Boston, Houghton, 1925. 1548

Shaw, Charles G.   Logic in Theory and Practice.   New York, Prentice, 1935.   1549

Sherwood, John C.   Discourse of Reason: A Brief Handbook of Semantics and Logic.   New York, Harper, 1960.   1550

Sidgwick, Alfred. The Application of Logic. New York, Macmillan, 1910. 1551

_____. The Use of Words in Reasoning. London, Black, 1901. 1552

Smart, H. R. The Logic of Science. New York, Appleton, 1931. 1553

Smith, H. B. How the Mind Falls into Error. New York, Appleton, 1933. 1554

Smith, William R. History as Argument. Hague, Mouton Co., 1966. 1555

Stebbing, L. Susan. A Modern Introduction to Logic. New York, Humsinger Press, 6th edition, 1948. 1556

_____. Thinking to Some Purpose. Middlesex, England, Penguin, 1939. 1557

Stone, Julius. Legal System and Lawyers' Reasonings. Stanford, Cal., Stanford, 1964. 1558

Strawson, P. F. Introduction to Logical Theory. New York, Wiley, 1952. 1559

Sullivan, Daniel J. Fundamentals of Logic. New York, McGraw, 1963. 1560

Symonds, Percival M. Education and the Psychology of Thinking. New York and London, McGraw, 1936. (A supplementary aid in the study of problem solving.) 1561

Tarski, Alfred. Introduction to Logic. Oxford, Oxford, 1941. 1562

Templin, Olin, and McCracken, Anna. A Guide to Thinking. Garden City, New York, Doubleday, 1927. 1563

Thouless, R. H. How to Think Straight. New York, Simon, 1939. 1564

_____. Straight and Crooked Thinking. New York, Simon, 1932. London, Hodder, 1930. 1565

Toulmin, Stephen E. The Place of Reason in Ethics. New York, Cambridge, 1958. 1566

_____. Uses of Argument. Cambridge, Cambridge, 1958. 1567

Veatch, Henry B. Two Logics: The Conflict between Classical and Neo-Analytic Philosophy. Evanston, Ill., Northwestern, 1969. 1568

Venn, J. Principles of Empirical or Inductive Logic. London, Macmillan, 2nd edition, 1907. 1569

Von Wright, George H.   A Treatise on Induction and Probability.
New York, Harcourt, 1952.   1570

Walcott, G. D.   An Introductory Logic.   New York, Harcourt, 1931.
                                                             1571
Wallas, Graham.   The Art of Thought.   New York, Harcourt, 1926.
                                                             1572
Weil, R.   The Art of Practical Thinking.   New York, Simon, 1940.
                                                             1573
Werkmeister, W. H.   Introduction to Critical Thinking.   Lincoln,
Nebraska, Johnsen Publishing Company, 1948.   1574

Wertheimer, Max.   Productive Thinking.   New York, Harper, 1945.
                                                             1575
Whitehead, Alfred North, and Russell, Bertrand.   Principia Mathe-
matica.   Cambridge, Cambridge, 2nd edition, 1950.   1576

Wigmore, J. H.   The Principles of Judicial Proof.   Boston, Little,
1937.   1577

_____.   The Student's Textbook of the Law of Evidence.   New
York, Foundation, 1935.   1578

Wilbur, William A.   Argumentation in English Rhetoric.   Washington, D. C. , George Washington University Press, 1913.   1579

Williams, D. C.   The Ground of Induction.   Cambridge, Harvard,
1947.   1580

Williams, Frederick.   Reasoning with Statistics.   New York, Holt,
1968.   1581

Wilson, J. C.   Statement and Inference.   Oxford, Oxford, 1926.
2 vols.   1582

Wolf, A.   Essentials of Scientific Method.   London, Allen, 1928.
                                                             1583
_____.   Textbook of Logic.   London, Allen, 1936.   1584

2.   Theses and Dissertations

Barwind, Jack.   Status of the Toulmin Model of Logic in Educational Debate.   M. A.   Bowling Green.   1966.   1585

Berman, Sanford I.   A Comparative Treatment of Fact, Inference,
and Causation in the Theory of Argumentation and General Semantics.   Ph. D.   Northwestern.   1958.   1586

Brown, Charles T.   An Experimental Diagnosis of Thinking on Controversial Issues.   Ph. D.   Wisconsin.   1949.   1587

Carter, Elton S.   Doctrines of Cassius J. Keyser in Relation to

Argumentation and Discussion Theories. Ph. D. Northwestern.
1950. 1588

Cockerham, Louis W. John Locke's Theory of Logical Proof.
M. S. Oregon. 1959. 1589

Cole, Terry. A Comparison of Cicero's Theory of Positions with
Modern Argumentation. M. A. Fresno. 1968. 1590

Cronin, Michael W. A Study of Causal Reasoning in Intercollegiate
Debate. M. A. Wayne State. 1967. 1591

Cypher, Patricia M. An Empirical Test of Contemporary Definitions of the Enthymeme: Believe Major Premises and Truncation
of the Enthymeme. M. A. Wayne State. 1967. 1592

Dudley, Lloyd P. The Relation of Formal Logic to Debate Theory
and Practice. M. A. S. California. 1934. 1593

Dunn, Miriam F. The Psychology of Reasoning: An Experimental
Study. Ph. D. Catholic University. 1926. (Reprinted in Studies
in Psychology and Psychiatry, 45 [June, 1926], 141 pp.) 1594

Erickson, Richard O. Brockriede and Ehninger's Interpretation and
Adaptation of Toulmin: A Critique. M. A. Minnesota. 1965.
1595

Foster, Teddy J. An Analysis of Cause and Effect Reasoning in
Selected Modern College Debate Textbooks. M. A. S. Illinois.
1959. 1596

Fried, Esther. Standards of Proof in Contemporary Public Discussion. M. A. Cornell. 1938. 1597

Greg, John B. The Enthymeme in Modern American Argumentation
and Debate Theory. M. A. Wayne State. 1963. 1597a

Hastings, Arthur C. A Reformulation of the Modes of Reasoning in
Argumentation. Ph. D. Northwestern. 1962. 1598

Heidt, Raymond. Toulmin's Argument Model as an Instrument for
the Criticism of Speeches. M. A. San Jose. 1968. 1599

Jones, William M. An Exploratory Study of the Effects of Two
Media of Presentation On Performance in Reasoning. Ph. D.
Washington. 1962. 1600

Keil, Charles R. An Experimental Study of an Application of Game
Theory to the Selection of Arguments by College Debaters. Ph. D.
S. California. 1969. 1601

Martin-Trigona, Helen. Logical Proof and Imaginative Reason in
Selected Speeches of Francis Bacon. Ph. D. Illinois. 1968.
1602

McBurney, James H.   The Place of the Enthymeme in Rhetorical
   Theory.   Ph. D.   Michigan.   1935.   1603

Measell, James S.   Foundations of the Concept of Analogy in Greek
   Mathematics and Rhetoric.   M. A.   Illinois.   1968.   1604

_____.   Development of the Concept of Analogy in Philosophy,
   Logic, and Rhetoric to 1850.   Ph. D.   Illinois.   1970.   1605

Merrill, Beverley J.   A Comparison of the Aristotelian Enthymeme
   as a Syllogistic Deep Structure with the Toulmin Structure.   M. A.
   San Diego State College.   1970.   1606

Nelson, William F.   An Historical Critical and Experimental Study
   of the Function of Topoi in Human Information Retrieval.   Ph. D.
   Penn State.   1969.   1607

O'Connell, Sandra E.   The Development, Use, and Evaluation of
   Classroom Materials Employing Toulmin's Model of Argument.
   M. A.   Michigan.   1964.   1608

Redfern, Donna D.   George Pierce Baker's Theory of Argumentation.
   M. A.   Oregon.   1959.   1609

Rowland, A. Westley.   A Study of the Changes in Methods and Procedures in Argumentation.   M. A.   Michigan.   1942.   1610

Rutherford, Lewis R.   An Interpretation of Aristotle's Theory of
   the Modes and Forms of Proof.   Ph. D.   S. Illinois.   1970. 1611

Shadow, Michael J.   A Comparative Analysis of the Relationship of
   Logos to Oral Communication in Selected Works of Heraclitus
   and Aristotle.   M. A.   California, Long Beach.   1968.   1612

Shields, Donald C.   The Teaching of Logos by Missouri Public High
   School Teachers.   M. A.   Missouri, Kansas City.   1968.   1613

Simonson, Solomon.   A Re-Statement of Fallacies.   Ph. D.   Northwestern.   1943.   1614

Smith, Mary J.   A Study of Argument in Selected Works in Argumentation and Debate.   M. A.   Alabama.   1967.   1615

Spicer, Holt V.   Toulmin's Functional Analysis of Logic and Ethics
   and Its Relation to Rhetoric.   Ph. D.   Oklahoma.   1964.   1616

Trent, Jimmie D.   Stephen E. Toulmin's Argument Model as an Instrument for Criticism of Forensic Speeches.   Ph. D.   Purdue.
   1966.   1617

Tucker, Raymond K. , and Rebstock, Eugene.   Implication and Inference Making.   Unpublished Research Study, Northwestern University.   Evanston, Illinois.   1955.   1618

Vancil, David L.   Induction in Modern American Argumentation and
   Debate Theory.   M. A.   Wayne State.   1965.   1619

Wise, Charles N.   An Investigation of Choice Among Modes of
   Reasoning.   M. A.   Oklahoma.   1966.   1620

3.   Articles

Aldrich, Julian C.   Developing Critical Thinking.   SoE, 12 (1948),
   115-18.   1621

Aly, Bower.   Enthymemes: The Story of a Light-Hearted Search.
   ST, 14 (November, 1965), 265-275.   1622

Anderson, Ray L., and Mortensen, C. David.   Logic and Market-
   place Argumentation.   QJS, 53 (April, 1967), 143-151.   1623

App, Austin J.   The Use of Analogy in Debate.   BDAPC, 12 (January 16, 1939), 8-10.   1624

Armstrong, Robert L.   Reduction and Deduction of Syllogisms.
   NSchol, 44 (1970), 273-277.   (Demonstrates how all valid syllogisms can be derived from Barbara and Celarent.)   1625

Ball, V. C.   The Moment of Truth: Probability Theory and Standards of Proof.   VLR, 14 (1961), 807-830.   1626

Barwind, J. Alan, and Blubaugh, Jon A.   The Status of the Toulmin
   Model of Logic in Educational Debate in Higher Education.   OSJ,
   5 (1967), 51-54.   1627

Berry, George.   Logic with Platonism.   Sy, 19 (December, 1968),
   215-249.   (Examines ontological views of logic.)   1628

Bertolotti, John.   The Role of Formal Logic in Argumentation.
   SPG, 10 (March, 1973), 69-70.   1629

Bettinghaus, Erwin, Miller, Gerald, and Steinfatt, Thomas.   Source
   Evaluation, Syllogistic Content, and Judgments of Logical Validity
   by High and Low Dogmatic Persons.   JPSP, 16 (1970), 238-244.
   (Investigates the factors which affect audience evaluations of the
   formal validity of an argument.)   1630

Bird, Otto.   The Formalizing of the Topics in Medieval Logic.
   NDJFL, 1 (1960), 138-149.   1631

_____.   The Re-Discovery of the Topics: Professor Toulmin's In-
ference-Warrants.   Mi, 70 (October, 1961), 534-539.   1632

_____.   Topic and Consequence in Ockham's Logic.   NDJFL, 2
(1961), 65-78.   1633

_____. The Tradition of the Logical Topics: Aristotle to Ockham. JHI, 23 (1962), 207-223.   1634

Bitzer, Lloyd F. Aristotle's Enthymeme Revisited. QJS, 45 (December, 1959), 399-408.   1635

Bodenheimer, Edgar A. A Neglected Theory of Legal Reasoning. JLR, 21 (1968-1969), 373-402. (Discusses practical use of various modes of argumentation in legal reasoning; discusses importance of probability and plausibility as opposed to certainty.)
                                                                        1636

Bormann, Ernest G. An Empirical Approach to Certain Concepts of Logical Proof. CSSJ, 12 (1961), 85-91.   1637

Broad, C. D. On the Relation Between Induction and Probability (I). Mi, 27 (1918); Ibid., (II). Mi, 29 (1920).   1638

Broadie, Alexander. The Practical Syllogism. An, 29 (October, 1968), 26-28. (Describes the relationship between the premises and conclusion of the Aristotelian "practical syllogism" as the relationship between "form and matter.")   1639

Broadrick, King. The Relationship of Argument to Syllogistic and Experimental Logic. QJS, 36 (December, 1950), 476-82.   1640

Brockriede, Wayne E. A Standard for Judging Applied Logic in Debate. AFAR, 10 (Spring, 1962), 10-14.   1641

_____ and Ehninger, Douglas. Toulmin on Argument: An Interpretation and Application. QJS, 46 (February, 1960), 44-53.   1642

Brown, Robert. The Burden of Proof. APQ, 7 (January, 1970), 74-82. (Analyzes the conditions under which the burden of proof can be appropriately assigned in a philosophical debate.)   1643

Brutian, George. On the Conception of Polylogic. Mi, 77 (July, 1968), 351-359. (Discusses the differences between dialectical logic, traditional formal logic, and mathematical or symbolic logic.)   1644

Buchanan, Paul S. Logic or Bunkum in Persuasion. QJS, 11 (April, 1925), 157-62.   1645

Burke, Richard J. Aristotle on the Limits of Argument. PPR, 27 (March, 1967), 386-400.   1646

Butler, J. D. Preface to a Logic; with Discussion. ET, 14 (October, 1964), 229-260.   1647

Cahalan, John C. On the Proving of Causal Propositions. MoS, 44 (January, 1967), 129-142.   1648

_____. Remarks on Father Owens' "The Causal Proposition Revisited. "   MoS, 44 (January, 1967), 152-160.   1649

Care, N. S.   On Avowing Reasons.   MJPS, 76 (April, 1967), 208-
216.   1650

Casteel, John L.   Debate and Scientific Attitude.   QJS, 19 (April,
1933), 186-92.   1651

Centore, F. F.   The "Sneaky O" Proposition.   NSchol, 44 (1970),
600-02.   (Indicates that the E-form proposition is better interpreted as a conjunction of an I and an O.)   1652

Chattopadhyaya, Debiprasad.   Can Induction Be Justified?   JIAP, 6
(1967), 75-91.   1653

Cheng, Chung-Ying.   A Note on Charles Peirce's Theory of Induction.   JHP, 5 (October, 1957), 361-364.   1654

Childs, Ralph De Someri, and Koch, Gustav A.   Speech and Logic.
JAD, 13 (October, 1941), 414-17.   1655

Church, David A. , and Cathcart, Robert S.   Some Concepts of the
Epicheireme in Greek and Roman Rhetoric.   WS, 29 (Summer,
1965), 140-147.   1656

Churchman, C. West, and Buchanan, Bruce G.   On the Design of
Inductive Systems: Some Philosophical Problems.   BJPS, 20
(1969), 311-323.   (Argues that no inductive system can be rational.)   1657

Cleave, J. P.   The Notion of Validity in Logical Systems with Inexact Predicates.   BJPS, 21 (1970), 269-74.   1658

Coffa, J. Alberto.   Two Remarks on Hemple's Logic of Confirmation.   Mi, 79 (1970), 591-96.   1659

Cook, Walter W.   Legal Logic.   CLR, 31 (January, 1931), 108-15.
1660
_____.   Scientific Method and the Law.   ABAJ, 13 (June, 1927),
303-310.   1661

Cronkhite, Gary L.   The Enthymeme as Deductive Rhetorical Argument.   WS, 30 (Spring, 1966), 129-134.   1662

d'Angelo, Gary.   A Schema for the Utilization of Attitude Theory
within the Toulmin Model of Argument.   CSSJ, 22 (Summer,
1971), 100-109.   1663

Davidson, Donald.   Actions, Reasons, and Causes.   JPhil, 60
(1963), 685-700.   1664

_____ and Vendler, Zeno.   Symposium: Causal Relations.   JHP,
64 (1967), 691-713.   1665

Delia, Jesse G.   The Logic Fallacy, Cognitive Theory, and the
   Enthymeme: A Search for the Foundations of Reasoned Discourse.
   QJS, 56 (April, 1970), 140-148.   (Stresses the psychological pro-
   cess that underlies the enthymeme.)   1666

Dewey, John.   Logical Method in Law.   CLQ, 10 (December, 1924),
   17-27.   1667

————.   Some Stages of Logical Thought.   PR, 9 (September,
   1900), 465-89.   1668

Dick, Robert C.   Topoi: An Approach to Inventing Arguments.   ST,
   13 (November, 1964), 313-319.   1669

Douglass, Rodney B.   On Analysis of Logos: A Methodological Inquiry.   QJS, 56 (February, 1970), 22-32.   1670

Duerlinger, James.   Aristotle's Conception of Syllogism.   Mi, 77
   (July, 1968), 480-499.   1671

Dunlap, Knight.   A Theory of the Syllogism.   In University of California Publications in Philosophy.   I. Berkeley, University of
   California Press, 1904.   pp. 227-35.   1672

Dwight, Charles A. S.   Dwight's Reasoning Test.   Ed, 45 (February,
   1925), 338-44.   (A college test on valid and invalid arguments.)
                                                                  1673
Edney, C. W.   George Campbell's Theory of Logical Truth.   SM,
   15 (1948), 19-32.   1674

Ehninger, Douglas.   Argument as Method: Its Nature, Its Limitations and Its Uses.   SM, 37 (June, 1970), 101-110.   1675

Eisenberg, J. A.   The Logical Form of Counterfactional Conditionals.
   DCPR, 8 (1969), 310-314.   1676

Ellis, B. D.   Explanation and the Logic of Support.   AuJP, 48 (August, 1970), 177-89.   1677

Evolving Methods of Scientific Proof.   NYLF, 13 (Winter, 1967),
   679-774.   1678

Fawcett, Harold P.   The Nature of Proof.   JHR, 17 (1969), 382-
   404.   (On the role of basic assumptions in reasoning.)   1679

Feigel, Jerry D.   The Mystery of the Epicheireme.   WS, 31 (Spring,
   1967), 109-114.   1680

Fisher, Walter R.   Uses of the Enthymeme.   ST, 13 (September,
   1964), 197-203.   1681

Fogelin, Robert J.   Inferential Constructions.   APQ, 4 (January,
   1967), 15-27.   1682

Frase, Lawrence T.   Associative Factors in Syllogistic Reasoning.
  JExP, 76 (March, 1968), 407-415.   (Discusses methods for teaching reasoning.)   1683

Friedman, N.   Rhetoric of Logic.   JGE, 17 (January, 1966), 287-
  294.   1684

Gasink, Warren A.   Your Causal Relationships.   F, 49 (May, 1964),
  8-9.   1685

Giannon, Carlo.   A Defense of Logical Conventionalism.   Ra, 11
  (1969), 89-101.   1686

Gibson, A. Boyce.   Reason in Practice.   AuJP, 45 (May, 1967),
  1-14.   1687

Gibson, H. E.   Fallacies in Debate, How to Meet Them.   SchA, 28
  (December, 1956), 119-20.   1688

Gilman, Wilbur E.   Logic and Public Speaking.   QJS, 26 (December, 1940), 667-72.   1689

Goguen, J. A.   The Logic of Inexact Concepts.   Sy, 19 (April, 1969),
  325-373.   (On a logic for use with vague, ambiguous, or ambiv-
  alent terms.)   1690

Good, I. J.   Human and Machine Logic.   BJPS, 18 (August, 1967),
  144-147.   1691

Goulding, Daniel J.   Aristotle's Concept of the Enthymeme.   JAFA,
  2 (September, 1965), 104-108.   1692

Graham, Gladys M.   Analogy--A Study in Proof and Persuasion
  Values.   QJS, 14 (November, 1928), 534-42.   1693

_____.   Cohen's Law and the Social Order.   QJS, 19 (November,
  1933), 67-68.   1694

_____.   A Laboratory Course in Straight Thinking.   SchS, 24 (No-
  vember 27, 1926), 658-62.   (Based on the analysis of arguments
  from everyday sources.)   1695

_____.   Logic and Argumentation.   QJS, 10 (November, 1924), 350-
  62.   1696

_____.   The Natural Procedure in Argument.   QJS, 11 (November,
  1925), 319-337.   1697

_____.   The Place of Reason in Speech.   QJS, 18 (June, 1932),
  462-63.   1698

Graves, Harold F. , and O'Brien, Joseph F.   Argumentation Without
  Debate.   QJS, 19 (November, 1933), 528-33.   1699

Gregg, Richard B.   Some Psychological Aspects of Argument.   WS,
28 (Fall, 1964), 222-229.   1700

Gruner, Rolf.   Plurality of Causes.   Phil, 42 (October, 1967), 367-
374.   (Rejects the view that "the same effect never arises but
from the same cause"; offers counter-arguments and examples.)
                                                                      1701
_____.   Historical Facts and the Testing of Hypotheses.   APQ, 5
(April, 1968), 124-129.   (Claims that establishing historical fact
differs from inquiry in other disciplines not necessarily requiring
the answering of questions or testing of hypotheses.)   1702

Harris, James F.   Quine on Analyticity and Logical Truth.   SJP, 7
(Fall, 1969), 249-255.   (Argues that the notion of logical truth
requires acceptance of analyticity.)   1703

Hausman, Alan.   Hume's Theory of Relations.   No, 1 (August,
1967), 255-282.   1704

Heidbreder, E. F.   Reasons Used in Solving Problems.   JExP, 19
(October, 1927), 397-414.   1705

Heidelberger, Herbert.   The Indispensability of Truth.   APQ, 5
(July, 1968), 212-217.   (Refutes the "redundancy theory" of
truth.)   1706

_____.   Knowledge, Certainty, and Probability.   In, 6 (1963), 242-
250.   1707

Henle, Mary.   On the Relation between Logic and Thinking.   PsyR,
69 (July, 1962), 366-378.   1708

Hoag, C. G.   The Logic of Argument.   Haverford Essays, Haverford,
Pa., 1909.   1709

Holm, James N.   The Opposition is Essential.   F, 28 (March,
1943), 87-89.   (Rejoinder to Moore's "New Patterns for Debate,"
infra.)   1710

Hook, J. N.   Logic, Grammar, and Rhetoric: A Presumptuous Essay on Their Relationships.   EJ, 55 (April, 1966), 417-424. 1711

Howell, Wilbur S.   The Position of Argument: An Historical Examination.   In Papers in Rhetoric, ed. by D. C. Bryant.   St.
Louis.   The Editor, 1940.   Pp. 8-17.   1712

Howell, William S.   Critical Thinking and Persuasion.   G, 30 (4
May, 1948), 67-72.   1713

Hudson, Roy F.   Sound Thinking; Not Sounding Off.   G, 37 (March,
1955), 47-49.   1714

Hufford, Roger.   The Logician, the Historian, and Rhetorical Criticism. JAFA, 2 (January, 1965), 14-16. 1715

Hunt, Everett L. Dialectic: A Neglected Method of Argument.
QJS, 7 (June, 1921), 211-32. 1716

Infante, Dominic A. The Influence of a Topical System on the Discovery of Arguments. SM 38 (June, 1971), 125-128. 1717

Jager, Ronald. Truth and Assertion. Mi, 79 (1970), 161-69. (On
the relationships between assertions and propositions.) 1718

Janis, Irving L., and Frick, F. The Relationship Between Attitudes
Toward Conclusions and Errors in Judging Logical Validity of
Syllogisms. JExP, 33 (July, 1943), 73-77. 1719

Johnson, Alma. An Experimental Study in the Analysis and Meas-
uerment of Reflective Thinking. SM, 10 (1943), 83-96. 1720

Johnson, Donald M. A Modern Account of Problem-Solving. PB,
41 (April, 1944), 201-29. 1721

Johnson, Oliver A. Begging the Question. Di, 6 (September, 1967),
135-150. 1722

Johnson-Laird, P. N. Reasoning with Ambiguous Sentences. BJP,
60 (1969), 17-23. (Argues that natural language is too ambiguous
a vehicle for logical reasoning.) 1723

Johnstone, Henry W., Jr. A New Theory of Philosophical Argumentation. PPR, 15 (1954), 244-52. (Reply by Chaim Perelman,
Ibid., 16 (1955), 245-247.) 1724

Kaplan, Abbott. The Lost Art of Controversy. AL, 3 (June, 1954),
2-3. 1725

Karns, C. Franklin. Causal Analysis and Rhetoric: A Survey of
the Major Philosophical Conceptions of Cause Prior to John
Stuart Mill. SM, 32 (March, 1965), 36-48. 1726

Kaufmann, Harry, and Goldstein, Stephen. The Effects of Emotional Value of Conclusions upon Distortion in Syllogistic Reasoning.
Psychological Science, 7 (1967), 367-368. (Compares the effective recognition of valid and invalid syllogisms.) 1727

Kennedy, J. E. Valuing Federal Matter in Controversy: An Hol-
fedian Analysis in Symbolic Logic. TnLR, 35 (Spring, 1968),
423-441. (Attempts to relate modern symbolic logic to legal
language.) 1728

Kerr, Harry P. Baker's Principles of Argumentation. ST, 11
(March, 1962), 120-23. 1729

Kirwan, Christopher. Logic and the Good in Aristotle. PhQ, 17

(April, 1967), 97-114.   1730

Klemke, E. D.   The Argument from Design.   Ra, 11 (1969), 102-
    106.   1731

Knapp, H. G.   Some Logical Remarks on a Proof by Leibniz.   Ra,
    12 (1970), 125-137.   1732

Knox, John, Jr.   Can a Valid Argument be Based on Differential
    Certainty?   Mi, 79 (1970), 275-77.   1733

Kosman, L. A.   Aristotle on Inconvertible Modal Propositions.   Mi,
    79 (1970), 254-58.   (Contends that Aristotle is correct in arguing
    that contingent E propositions are not convertible.)   1734

Kozy, John, Jr.   The Argumentative Use of Rhetorical Figures.
    PhR, 3 (Summer, 1970), 141-51.   (Discusses analogical reason-
    ing.)   1735

Kyburg, Henry E. , Jr.   On a Certain Form of Philosophical Argu-
    ment.   APQ, 7 (July, 1970), 229-37.   1736

_____.   The Justification of Induction.   JPhil, 53 (1956), 394-400.
                                                               1737
Lakoff, George.   Linguistics and Natural Logic.   Sy, 22 (December,
    1970), 151-271.   1738

Larson, Robert G.   The Order of Presentation as a Factor in Jury
    Persuasion.   KLJ, 56 (Summer, 1967), 523-555.   (On the order
    of presentation in jury trials.)   1739

Lasswell, Harold D.   Self-Analysis and Judicial Thinking.   InJE,
    40 (April, 1930), 354-62.   ("A need for free-fantasy as well as
    logic in training the mind to cope with problems of reality. ")
                                                               1740
LeBlanc, H.   A Rationale for Analogical Inference.   PhS, 20 (Jan-
    uary-February, 1969), 29-30.   1741

Lefford, A.   Influence of Emotional Subject Matter On Logical Rea-
    soning.   JGP, 34 (April, 1946), 127-151.   1742

Lehrer, Keith.   Induction: A Consistent Gamble.   No, 3 (1969),
    285-298.   1743

_____.   Induction, Reason and Consistency.   BJPS, 21 (1970), 103-
    14.   1744

_____.   Knowledge, Truth and Evidence.   An, 25 (1964-1965), 168-
    175.   1745

Levi, Isaac.   Information and Inference.   Sy, 17 (December, 1967),
    369-391.   1746

Lewis, Albert. Stephen Toulmin: A Reappraisal. CSSJ, 23
   (Spring, 1972), 48-55.   1747

Lewis, J. U. Sir Edward Coke (1552-1633): His Theory of "Artificial Reason" as a Context for Modern Basic Legal Theory.
   Law Quarterly Review, 84 (July, 1968), 330-342. (On legal
   principles of argumentation.)   1748

Loevinger, Lee. Jurimetrics. Modern Uses of Logic in Law. 59
   (September, 1959), 15-16.   1749

Lyon, Ardon. Causality. BJPS, 18 (May, 1967), 1-20.   1750

MacIver, A. M. Knowledge. PAS, supp. vol., 32 (1958), 1-24.
                                                                           1751
Madden, Edward H. A Third View of Causality. RM, 23 (1969),
   67-84. (Suggests an alternative to the Humean and entailment
   theories of causality.)   1752

_____. Aristotle's Treatment of Probability and Signs. PS, 24
   (1957), 167-172.   1753

Magrish, James L. Relating Ethical Arguments. LoA, 10 (June,
   1967), 157-166.   1754

Makinson, David. Remarks on the Concept of Distribution in Traditional Logic. No, 3 (February, 1969), 103-108. (Clarifies the
   meaning of "distributed" and "undistributed" terms.)   1755

Mandell, Geoffrey. Action and Causal Explanation. MJPS, 76
   (January, 1967), 34-48.   1756

Manicas, Peter T. On Toulmin's Contribution to Logic and Argumentation. JAFA, 3 (September, 1966), 83-94. (Highly critical
   of Toulmin's layout of arguments.)   1757

Margolis, Joseph. Reasons and Causes. DCPR, 8 (1969), 68-83.
                                                                           1758
Marino, Herman J. Collegiate Debate: The Confessions of a Frus-
   trated Debater. SPG, 10 (March, 1973), 63-68. (Discussion of
   Toulmin's approach to argument.)   1759

Maxwell, Paul A. Solving Problems of Action: A Proposed Procedure for the Solution of Practical Problems. JEE, 6 (September, 1937), 101-5.   1760

McBurney, James H. The Place of the Enthymeme in Rhetorical
   Theory. SM, 3 (1936), 49-74.   1761

_____. Some Recent Interpretations of the Aristotelian Enthymeme.
   Papers of the Michigan Academy of Science, Arts and Letters,
   21 (1935), 489-500.   1762

McCall, Sorrs. Connexive Implication and the Syllogism. MJPS,
76 (July, 1967), 346-356.   1763

McCoy, Thomas R. Logic vs. Value Judgment in Legal and Ethical
Thought. VLR, 23 (1969-70), 1277-96.   1764

McCroskey, James C. Toulmin and the Basic Course. ST, 14
(March, 1965), 91-100.   1765

_____, and Combs, Walter H. The Effects of the Use of Analogy
on Attitude Change and Source Credibility. JC, 19 (December,
1969), 333ff. ("This study examined the effects of two types of
analogy on attitude change and source credibility. ")   1766

McEdwards, Mary G. The Student and His Logic. ST, 14 (January, 1965), 35-37.   1767

McKeon, Richard. Aristotle's Conception of the Development in the
Nature of Scientific Method. JHI, 8 (1947), 3-44.   1768

Meador, Prentice A., Jr. The Classical Epicheireme: A Re-
Examination. WS, 30 (Summer, 1966), 151-155.   1769

_____. Minucian, On Epicheiremes: An Introduction and a Trans-
lation. SM, 31 (March, 1964), 54-63.   1770

Michalos, Alex C. An Alleged Condition of Evidential Support. Mi,
78 (July, 1969), 440-441.   1771

Miller, Byers. Whither Do We Go? F, 26 (May, 1941), 122-23.
(On emphasizing reasoning in debate.)   1772

Miller, Gerald R. Some Factors Influencing Judgments of the Logical Validity of Arguments: A Research Review. QJS, 55 (October, 1969), 276-286.   1773

Mills, Glen E., and Petrie, Hugh G. The Role of Logic in Rhetoric. QJS, 54 (October, 1968), 260-267.   1774

Minnick, Wayne C. Teaching the Analogy. SSJ, 20 (Fall, 1954),
46-49.   1775

Moore, Omar K., and Anderson, Alan R. The Formal Analysis of
Normative Concepts. ASR, 22 (1957), 9-17.   1776

Moore, Wilbur E. After the War, What? F, 29 (January, 1944),
37-39, 44. (A criticism of Aristotelian logic.)   1777

_____. New Patterns for Debate. F, 28 (January; 1943), 43-47,
61. (A criticism of Aristotelian logic from the standpoint of
Korzybski's General Semantics.)   1778

Morgan, John J. B.   Effect of Non-Rational Factors on Inductive
Reasoning.   JEP, 34 (February, 1944), 159-68.   1779

_____ and Morton, J. T.   The Distortion of Syllogistic Reasoning
Produced by Personal Convictions.   JSP, 20 (1944), 35-59.   1780

Mortensen, C. David, and Anderson, Ray L.   The Limits of Logic.
JAFA, 7 (Spring, 1970), 71-78.   1781

Mudd, Charles S.   The Enthymeme and Logical Validity.   QJS, 45
(December, 1959), 409-414.   1782

Mundt, Karl E.   Loquacity vs. Logic.   R, 10 (February, 1936), 2.
                                                                    1783
Murphy, Jeffrie G.   Kant's Second Analogy as an Answer to Hume.
Ra, 11 (June, 1969), 75-81.   1784

_____.   Law Logic.   Eth, 77 (April, 1967), 193-201.   (Examines
the logic of legal decisions and argues that the connection between "reasons" and "decisions" in the law rests upon certain
conventions.)   1785

Musgrave, George M.   Avoiding the Irrelevant.   DM, 2 (June,
1946), 114, 116.   1786

Musselwhite, D. C.   Medical Causation Testimony in Texas: Possi-
bility vs. Probability.   SLJ, 23 (1969), 622-630.   1787

Nagel, Ernest.   Principles of the Theory of Probability.   International Encyclopedia of Unified Science, 1, No. 6 (1947).   1788

_____.   Probability and Non-Demonstrative Inference.   PPR, 5
(1945).   1789

Nelson, Everett J.   Metaphysical Presuppositions of Induction.
PAPA, 40 (1966-1967), 19-33.   1790

Nelson, William F.   Topoi: Functional in Human Recall.   SM, 37
(June, 1970), 121-126.   1791

Oldenquist, Andrew.   The Good Reasons Paradox.   JVI, 3 (Spring,
1969), 52-54.   (Argues that sound moral judgments rest on "good
reasons. ")   1792

Oliver, J. Willard.   Formal Fallacies and Other Invalid Arguments.
MJPS, 76 (October, 1967), 463-478.   1793

Overstreet, Harry A.   The Basal Principle of Truth-Evaluation.   In
the University of California Publications in Philosophy, 1.   Berkeley University Press, 1904.   Pp. 236-262.   1794

_____.   Reason and the Fight Image.   NR, 33 (December 20,
1922). 94-97.   1795

Owens, Joseph. The Causal Proposition Revisited. MoS, 44 (January, 1967), 143-151.   1796

Page, William T. John Dewey's Theory of Propositions: Some Implications for the Study of Argumentation. M. A. Illinois. 1966.   1797

Paget, Edwin H. Logic and Persuasion. SchS, 28 (October 13, 1928), 438-442.   1798

Palzer, Edward. Argument's Fourth Dimension. SSJ, 7 (November, 1941), 46-49.   1799

_____. Formal Logic Shall Not Die. R, 16 (October, 1941), 8-10.   1800

Patton, T. E. Reasoning in Moral Matters. JPhil, 53 (August, 1956), 523-531.   1801

Peirce, Charles S. The Fixation of Belief. PSM, 1877. (Reprinted in large part as "The Ways of Justifying Belief, " Readings in Philosophy, ed. by Randall, John A. , et al. College Outline Series. New York, Barnes and Noble, 1946.)   1802

Pence, Orville L. Logical Proof in the Rhetoric of Whately. SM, 20 (March, 1953), 23-38.   1803

Perry, Ralph B. The Appeal to Reason. PR, 3 (March, 1921), 131-169.   1804

Perry, Thomas D. Judicial Method and the Concept of Reasoning. Eth, 80 (1969), 1-20.   1805

Petrie, Hugh G. Practical Reasoning: Some Examples. PhR, 4 (Winter, 1971), 29-41.   1806

_____. Does Logic Have any Relevance to Argumentation? JAFA, 6 (Spring, 1969), 55-60. (Argues that objections to modern formal logic as a means of persuasion are based on confusion and misunderstanding.)   1807

Pomeroy, Ralph S. Whately's Historic Doubts: Argument and Origin. QJS, 49 (February, 1963), 62-74.   1808

Popper, Karl R. New Foundations for Logic. Mi, 56 (1947), 133-235. (Rules for deductive inference.)   1809

Prado, C. G. A Note on Analogical Predication. NSchol, 44 (1970), 603-04.   1810

Pratt, Jerie M. The Appropriateness of a Toulmin Analysis of Legal Argumentation. SPG, 7 (May, 1970), 133-137.   1811

Preston, Ivan L.   Logic and Illogic in the Advertising Process.
  JQ, 13 (Summer, 1967), 231-239.   1812

Prior, A. N.   Fact, Propositions and Entailment.   Mi, 57 (1948).
                                                                 1813
Przelecki, Marian, and Wojcicki, Ryszard.   The Problem of Ana-
  lyticity.   Syn, 19 (April, 1969), 374-399.   (On the recent contri-
  butions of Polish logicians to the field of logical methodology.)
                                                                 1814
Ragsdale, J. D.   Invention in English Stylistic Rhetorics: 1600-1800.
  QJS, 51 (April, 1965), 164-167.   1815

Reichenbach, Hans.   The Syllogism Revised.   Philosophy of Science,
  19 (January, 1952), 1-16.   1816

Rhoads, John K.   The Type as a Logical Form.   SQ, 51 (April,
  1967), 347-360.   1817

Richman, Robert J.   Reasons and Causes: Some Puzzles.   AuJP,
  47 (May, 1969), 42-50.   1818

Ringwalt, Ralph C.   More Implication.   QJS, 12 (February, 1926),
  66-68.   (On G. M. Graham's article concerning the persuasive
  value of implied argument, QJS, 11 (November, 1925), 319-37.)
                                                                 1819
Romano, Joseph J.   How Many Logics are There?   NSchol, 44
  (1970), 440-48.   (Argues that traditional [Aristotelian] logic can
  be applied to the humanities but that it is difficult to apply modern symbolic logic to these areas.)   1820

Rooney, M. T.   Law and the New Logic.   Proceedings of the American Catholic Philosophical Association, 1940.   1821

Rowell, Edward Z.   Prolegomena to Argumentation.   QJS, I. 18
  (February, 1932), 1-13; II. 18 (April, 1932), 224-48; III. 18
  (June, 1932), 381-405; IV. 18 (November, 1932), 585-606.   1822

Sacksteder, William.   Presentational Arguments.   Ra, 11 (1969),
  129-136.   1823

Salmon, Wesley C.   Symposium: The Philosophy of Rudolf Carnap--
  Carnap's Inductive Logic.   JPhil, 64 (1967), 725-739.   1824

Schiller, F. C. S.   Logic: A Game or an Agent of Value.   Pe, 19
  (January, 1938), 16-31.   1825

Schoenberg, Judith.   The Respecting of Indeterminacy.   Mi, 79
  (1970), 347-68.   (Shows how in reasoning indeterminacy may be
  taken into account in the premises.)   1826

Shepard, David W.   The Role of Logic.   QJS, 55 (April, 1969), 310-
  312.   (A rejoinder to article by Glen E. Mills and Hugh G. Petrie, "The Role of Logic in Rhetoric, " supra.)   1827

Simmons, James R.   The Nature of Argumentation.   SM, 27 (November, 1960), 348-50.   1828

Simon, Rita J.   "Beyond a Reasonable Doubt"--An Experimental Attempt at Quantification.   JABS, 6 (1970), 203-209.   (Quantitative analysis of a jury's interpretation of the meaning of the "beyond reasonable doubt" standard.)   1829

Simonson, Solomon.   The Inconsistencies of Francis Bacon on Fallacies.   QJS, 30 (October, 1944), 306-8.   1830

Smith, William S.   Formal Logic in Debate.   SSJ, 27 (Summer, 1962), 330-38.   1831

_____.   What are the Principles of Argument?   ST, 2 (March, 1953), 134-38.   1832

Smullyan, A.   The Concept of Empirical Knowledge.   PR, 65 (1956).
                                                                       1833
Solmsen, Friedrich.   Discovery of the Syllogism.   PR, 50 (July, 1941), 410-21.   1834

Starbuck, E. D.   The Human Animal That Thinks It Thinks.   College of the Pacific Publications, 1 (1932).   1835

Stewart, Daniel K.   Communication and Logic: Evidence for the Existence of Validity Patterns.   JGP, 64 (1961), 297-305.   1836

Tallet, Jorge.   On the Symmetry of Many-Valued Logical Systems.   LoA, 51 (1970), 302-22.   1837

Tammelo, I.   Logic as an Instrument of Legal Reasoning.   JJ, 10 (1970), 89ff.   1838

Taylor, Anita.   Is It Persuasion or Argumentation?   G, 44 (November, 1961), 5-6, 10.   (An answer to Wigley, 4105.)   1839

Thistlethwaite, Donald.   Attitude and Structure as Factors in the Distortion of Reasoning.   JASP, 45 (July, 1950), 442-58.   1840

Thompson, Janna L.   Third Possibilities.   Mi, 78 (April, 1969), 229-239.   (Discusses whether the principle of the excluded middle is ontological or not.)   1841

Todd, W.   Probability and the Theorem of Confirmation.   MJPS, 76 (April, 1967), 260-263.   1842

Trent, Jimmie D.   Toulmin Model of an Argument: An Examination and Extension.   QJS, 54 (October, 1968), 252-259.   1843

Utterback, William E.   Logic and Argumentation.   QJS, 11 (April, 1925), 175.   1844

_____ and Harding, Harold F.   Some Factors Conditioning Response to Argument.   SM, 22 (November, 1955), 303-8.   1845

Validity of an Inference on an Inference in Iowa.   DLR, 19 (1970),
    452ff.   1846

Verma, Roop R.   Vagueness and the Principles of the Excluded
    Middle.   Mi, 79 (1970), 67-77.   (Indicates that in one form or
    another the principle of the excluded middle is necessary to all
    logics.)   1847

Wallace, Karl.   On Analogy: Redefinition and Some Implications.
    In Studies in Speech and Drama in Honor of Alexander M. Drum-
    mond, ed. by H. A. Wichelns and others.   Ithaca, N.Y. , Cornell,
    1944.   Pp. 412-26.   1848

Walter, Otis M. , Jr.   Descartes on Reasoning.   SM 18 (March,
    1951), 47-53.   1849

_____ .   Thinking and Speaking About Causes.   TS, 9 (3 September,
    1961), 12-14; 9 (November, 1961), 20-21.   1850

Weber, Earl.   A Critique of a Technique.   TS, 8 (1 February,
    1960), 26-30.   (On Bogoslovsky.)   1851

Wedeking, Gary A.   Are There Command Arguments?   An, 30
    (April, 1970), 161-66.   1852

Wellman, R. R.   Dewey's Theory of Inquiry; the Impossibility of Its
    Statement.   ET, 14 (April, 1964), 103-110.   (See also, Eddy, P.
    Reply with Rejoinder.   ET, 15 (October, 1965), 321-329.)   1853

Wheatley, Jon.   Logical Connection.   APQ, 4 (January, 1967), 65-
    71.   1854

Wichelns, Herbert A.   Analysis and Synthesis in Argumentation.
    QJS, 11 (June, 1925), 266-72.   (Also in Letter to the Editor,
    QJS, 11 (November, 1925), 386-8, in answer to Utterback's arti-
    cle on Aristotle's contribution.)   1855

Wick, Warner A.   The Argument in Philosophy.   JGE, 7 (1953),
    81-8.   (On the importance of being able to follow an argument.)
                                                                                   1856
Wiener, F. B.   On the Improvement of Oral Argument.   NYSBJ, 39
    (June, 1967), 187-193.   1857

Wilcox, W. C.   The Antilogism Extended.   Mi, 78 (April, 1969),
    266-269.   (Establishes rules for using antilogisms as proof of
    the validity of categorical syllogisms.)   1858

Wiley, Earl W.   The Enthymeme: Idiom of Persuasion.   QJS, 42
    (February, 1956), 19-24.   1859

Williamson, Colwyn. Analyzing Counterfactuals. DCPR, 8 (1969), 310-314.   1860

Woolbert, Charles H. The Place of Logic in a System of Persua- sion. QJS, 7 (January, 1918), 19-39.   1861

Yeager, Raymond. Aristotle's Topics as Sources of Proof. F, 45 (March, 1960), 12-14.   1862

Yost, Mary. Argument from the Point of View of Sociology. QJS, 3 (April, 1917), 109-24.   1863

IX. PERSUASION AND RHETORICAL THEORY

A. CLASSICAL AND HISTORICAL PERSPECTIVES

1. Books

Adams, Charles D. Demosthenes and His Influence. New York, Longmans, 1927.   1864

Aristotle. The Rhetoric of Aristotle (translated by Lane Cooper). New York, D. Appleton, 1932. (This edition is especially adapted to the needs of public speaking students.)   1865

_____. The Works of Aristotle (translated by W. D. Ross). Oxford, Clarendon, 1928; New York, Oxford, 1928.   1866

Breitenbach, Harold P. The Decomposition of Dionysius of Halicarnassus Considered with Reference to the Rhetoric of Aristotle. Chicago, Chicago, 1911.   1867

Brown, Hazel L. Extemporary Speech in Antiquity. Menasha, Wisconsin, Banta, 1914. (Greek and Roman oratory.)   1868

Bryant, Donald C., ed. Ancient Greek and Roman Rhetoricians: A Biographical Dictionary. Columbia, Missouri, Art Craft Press, 1968.   1869

Butler, Harold E. The Institutio Oratoria of Quintilian, with an English Translation. London, Heinemann; New York, Putnam's, 1921-22. 4 vols.   1870

Charlton, Kenneth. Education in Renaissance England. Toronto, Univ. of Toronto Press, 1965.   1871

Clark, Donald L. Rhetoric in Greco-Roman Education. New York, Columbia, 1957.   1872

Clarke, Martin L. Rhetoric at Rome. London, Cambridge, 1935.
                                                                                                              1873
Crocker, Lionel. The Rhetorical Theory of Henry Ward Beecher. Chicago, Chicago, 1933.   1874

Daly, Lowrie J. The Medieval University, 1200-1400. New York, Sheed and Ward, 1961.   1875

Davidson, Hugh M.   Audience, Words, and Art: Studies in Seven-
teenth-Century French Rhetoric.   Columbus, Ohio State, 1965.
                                                          1876
Demetrius.   A Medieval Latin Version of Demetrius' De Elocutione.
Edited for the First Time from a Fourteenth-Century Manuscript
at the University of Illinois.   With an Introduction and Critical
Notes by Bernice V. Wall.   Washington, D. C. , Catholic University of America, 1937.   1877

_____.   On Style (translated and edited by T. A. Moxon).   New
York, Dutton, 1934.   1878

_____.   On Style; the Greek Text of Demetrius' De Elocutione.
(Edited after the Paris Manuscript with an Introduction, Facsimi-
lies, etc. , by W. Rhys Roberts.) London, Cambridge, 1902.
                                                          1879
De Quincey, Thomas.   De Quincey's Literary Criticism.   (Edited
with an Introduction by H. Darbishire.) London, Fraude, 1909.
(Sections on Whately and De Quincey's ideas on rhetoric and public speaking.)   1880

Dionysius.   The Three Literary Letters.   (Translated and edited by
W. Rhys Roberts.) London, Cambridge, 1901.   1881

Edwards, William A.   The Suasoriae of Seneca the Elder.   Cambridge, Cambridge, 1927.   1882

Eskridge, James B.   The Influence of Cicero Upon Augustine in the
Development of his Oratorical Theory for the Training of the
Ecclesiastical Orator.   Menasha, Wisconsin, Banta, 1912.   1883

Fiske, George C. , and Grant, Mary A.   Cicero's De Oratore and
Horace's Ars Poetica.   Madison, Wisconsin, 1929.   1884

Golden, James L. , and Corbett, Edward P. J.   The Rhetoric of
Blair, Campbell and Whately.   New York, Holt, 1968.   1885

Gwynn, Aubrey O.   Roman Education from Cicero to Quintilian.
Oxford, Oxford, 1926.   1886

Haarhoff, Theodore.   Schools of Gaul.   Oxford, Clarendon, 1922.
(Discusses the influence of Roman schools throughout the Western
world.)   1887

Holland, L. Virginia.   Counterpoint: Kenneth Burke and Aristotle's
Theories of Rhetoric.   New York, Philosophical, 1959.   1888

Howell, Wilbur S.   Logic and Rhetoric in England, 1500-1700.
Princeton, Princeton, 1956.   1889

_____, ed. and trans.   The Rhetoric of Alcuin and Clarlemagne.
Princeton, Princeton, 1941.   1890

Howes, Raymond F. , ed.   Historical Studies of Rhetoric and
    Rhetoricians.   Ithaca, Cornell, 1961.   1891

Hubbell, Harry M.   The Influence of Isocrates on Cicero, Dionysius,
    and Aristides.   New Haven, Yale, 1914.   1892

_____.   The Rhetoric of Philodemus.   New Haven, Yale, 1920.
                                                                1893
Isacus.   Works (translated by Edward Seymour Forster).   London,
    Heinemann, 1927.   1894

Isocrates.   Works of Isocrates (translated by George Noclin).   Lon-
    don, Heinemann, 1928-29.   3 vols.   1895

James, William.   The Will to Believe and Other Essays in Popular
    Philosophy.   New York, Longmans, 1921.   1896

Kennedy, George.   The Art of Persuasion in Greece.   Princeton,
    New Jersey, Princeton, 1963.   1897

Laughlin, (Sister) Mary F. , ed.   Rhetorica Nova Attributed to Ja-
    cobus Izelgrinus.   Washington, D.C. , Catholic University of
    America Press, 1947.   1898

Lechner, (Sister) Joan Marie.   Renaissance Concepts of the Com-
    monplaces.   New York, Pageant Press, 1962.   1899

Lloyd, G.E.R.   Polarity and Analogy: Two Types of Argumentation
    in Early Greek Thought.   Cambridge, Cambridge, 1966.   1900

Longinus.   On the Sublime.   (Ed. by W. Rhys Roberts.)   London,
    Cambridge, 2nd edition, 1907.   1901

McCall, Marsh H. , Jr.   Ancient Rhetorical Theories of Simile and
    Comparison.   Cambridge, Harvard, 1969.   1902

McCurdy, Frances L.   Stump, Bar, and Pulpit: Speechmaking on
    the Missouri Frontier.   Columbia, Missouri, Missouri, 1969.
                                                                1903
Milne, Marjorie J.   A Study of Alcidamas and his Relation to Con-
    temporary Sophistic.   Bryn Mawr, Pennsylvania, 1924.   1904

Mure, Geoffrey R.   Aristotle.   New York, Oxford, 1932.   1905

Murphy, James J. , ed.   A Synoptic History of Classical Rhetoric.
    New York, Random, 1972.   1906

Parks, Brother Edelbert.   The Roman Rhetorical Schools as a
    Preparation for the Courts under the Early Empire.   The Johns
    Hopkins Univ. Studies in History and Political Science, Series
    58, No. 2.   Baltimore, Johns Hopkins, 1945.   1907

Plato.   Phaedrus, Ion, Gorgias, and Symposium, with Passages

from the Republic and Laws. (Translated with Introduction and
Notes, by Lane Cooper.) London, Oxford, 1938.   1908

Platz, Mabel. The History of Public Speaking. New York, Noble,
1935.   1909

Quintilian. The Institutes of Oratory. London, Loeb Classical Library, 1922.   1910

_____. The Institutio Oratoria of Quintilian (with an English Trans-
lation by H. E. Butler). London, Heinemann; New York, Putnam's, 1921-22.   1911

Rainolde, Richard. The Foundacion of Rhetorike. (Introduction by
Francis R. Johnson.) New York, Scholars' Facsimiles and Re-
prints, 1945.   1912

Rashdall, Hastings. Universities of Europe in the Middle Ages
(new ed. by F. M. Powicke and A. B. Emden). 3 Vols. Oxford,
Oxford, 1936.   1913

Sandford, William P. English Theories of Public Address, 1530-
1828. Columbus, Ohio, Hedrick, 1931.   1914

Schmitz, Robert M. Hugh Blair. New York, King's, 1948. 1915

Seneca, Lucius Annaeus. The Suasoriae of Seneca the Elder. (Introductory Essay, Text, Translation and Explanatory Notes by
William A. Edward.) London, Cambridge, 1928.   1916

Sonnino, Lee A. A Handbook to Sixteenth Century Rhetoric. New
York, Barnes, 1968.   1917

Topliss, Patricia. The Rhetoric of Pascal: A Study of His Art of
Persuasion in the "Provincales" and the "Pensees." New York,
Humanities, 1966.   1918

Wallace, Karl R. Francis Bacon on Communication and Rhetoric;
or, The Art of Applying Reason to Imagination for the Better
Moving of the Will. Chapel Hill, North Carolina, 1943. 1919

Wallach, Luitpold, ed. The Classical Tradition: Literary and Historical Studies in Honor of Harry Caplan. Ithaca, N. Y., Cornell, 1966.   1920

Wilson, Thomas. Arte of Rhetorique. (Ed. by G. H. Mair.) Oxford, Clarendon, 1909.   1921

2. Theses and Dissertations

Adkinson, H. M. The Principles of Arrangement as Developed by
Aristotle, Cicero, Quintilian, and Winans. M. S. S. California.

1931.   1922

Anderson, Dorothy I.   Edward T.   Channing's Philosophy and Teach-
    ing of Rhetoric.   Ph. D.   Iowa.   1944.   1923

Backes, James G.   The Relation of John Stuart Mill's Logical The-
    ories and Rhetorical Practices.   M. A.   S. Illinois.   1962. 1924

Backus, Robert.   An Historical Survey of Selected Classical and
    Modern Concepts of Ethics and Oral Persuasion.   M. A.   Colo-
    rado.   1961.   1925

Benson, Frank T.   A Comparative Analysis of George Campbell's
    Philosophy of Rhetoric.   Ph. D.   Minnesota.   1962.   1926

Bitzer, Lloyd F.   The Lively Idea: a Study of Hume's Influence on
    George Campbell's Philosophy of Rhetoric.   Ph. D.   Iowa.   1962.
                                                                1927
Boast, William M.   The Rhetorical and Pedagogical Concepts of
    Isocrates as a Classical Communication Methodology.   Ph. D.
    Denver.   1960.   1928

Bradley, Bert E. , Jr.   John Ward's Theory of Rhetoric.   Ph. D.
    Florida State.   1955.   1929

Brentlinger, Brock W.   The Aristotelian Conception of Truth in
    Rhetorical Discourse.   Ph. D.   Illinois.   1959.   1930

Brunton, M. E.   Invention, as Developed by Aristotle, Cicero, and
    Quintilian (Confined to Logical Persuasion).   M. A.   S. California.
                                                                1931
Burkowsky, Mitchell R.   René Bary's Rhétorique Françoise.   M. A.
    Wayne State.   1960.   1932

Byker, Donald.   Plato's Philosophy of Natural Law as a Key to His
    View of Persuasion.   Ph. D.   Michigan.   1969.   1933

Carrino, Elnora.   Conceptions of Dispositio in Ancient Rhetoric.
    Ph. D.   Michigan.   1959.   1934

Cerino, Dorothy V.   The Rhetoric and Dialectic of Isidorus of Se-
    ville: Translation and Commentary.   M. A.   Brooklyn College.
    1938.   1935

Christian, William K.   Some Theories of Mass Persuasion Held by
    Ancient and Modern Writers.   M. A.   Cornell.   1938.   1936

Cloer, Roberta K.   Emerson's Philosophy of Rhetoric.   Ph. D.   S.
    California.   1969.   1937

Cockerham, Louis W.   Alexander Bain's Philosophy of Rhetoric.
    Ph. D.   Illinois.   1968.   1938

Cohen, Herman.   The Rhetorical Theory of Hugh Blair.   Ph. D.
     Iowa.   1954.   1939

Crawford, John W.   The Rhetoric of George Campbell.   M. A.
     Northwestern.   1947.   1940

Dieter, Otto A.   The Rhetoric of Notker Labeo.   Ph. D.   Iowa.
     1939.   1941

East, James R.   Book Three of Brunetto Latini's Tresor: An Eng-
     lish Translation and Assessment of Its Contribution to Rhetorical
     Theory.   Ph. D.   Stanford.   1960.   1942

Edney, Clarence W.   George Campbell's Theory of Public Address.
     Ph. D.   Iowa.   1946.   1943

Ehninger, Douglas W.   Selected Theories of Inventio in English
     Rhetoric, 1759-1828.   Ph. D.   Ohio.   1949.   1944

Gietzen, Albin J.   A Study of Massilon's Use of Amplification.
     M. A.   Michigan.   1959.   1945

Glenn, Robert.   Rhetoric and Sympathy from Hume to Whately.
     M. A.   Northwestern.   1968.   1946

Golden, James L.   The Rhetorical Theory and Practice of Hugh
     Blair.   M. A.   Ohio.   1948.   1947

Guthrie, Warren A.   The Development of Rhetorical Theory in
     America, 1635-1850.   Ph. D.   Northwestern.   1940.   1948

Hance, Kenneth G.   The Rhetorical Theory of Phillips Brooks.
     Ph. D.   Michigan.   1937.   1949

Harding, Harold F.   English Rhetorical Theory, 1700-1750.   Ph. D.
     Cornell.   1937.   1950

Hewlett, Marilyn N.   An Analysis of Theories of Speech Arrange-
     ment as Developed by Selected Ancient Rhetoricians.   M. A.
     Iowa.   1947.   1951

Hildreth, Richard A.   Quintilian--The Good Man and Ethical Proof.
     M. A.   Wisconsin.   1949.   1952

Hill, Charles L.   An Exposition and Critical Estimate of the Philos-
     ophy of Philip Melanchton.   Ph. D.   Ohio.   1938.   (Considers his
     theory of rhetoric and dialectic.)   1953

Holland, Laura V.   Aristotelianism in the Rhetorical Theory of Ken-
     neth Burke.   Ph. D.   Illinois.   1954.   1954

Hoshor, John P.   A Study of the Principles of Ethical Proof in the
     Works of Certain Ancient and Modern Rhetoricians.   M. A.   Wash-

ington.   1940.   1955

_____.   The Rhetorical Theory of Chauncey Allen Goodrich.   Ph. D.
Iowa.   1947.   1956

Huber, Paul.   A Study of the Rhetorical Theories of John A.
    Broadus.   Ph. D.   Michigan.   1956.   1957

Huseman, Richard C.   The Concept of Appropriateness as an Ele-
    ment of Style in Classical Rhetoric.   Ph. D.   Illinois.   1965.
                                                                    1958
James, Herbert L.   A Comparative Analysis of the Major Rhetori-
    cal Treatises of Plato, Aristotle, Cicero, and Quintilian, To-
    gether with Tabular Outlines and Diagrams of Their Theories.
    M. A.   Ohio.   1951.   1959

Jones, Elbert W.   A Study of "Interest Factors" and "Motive Ap-
    peals" in Rhetorical Theory with Special Reference to Invention,
    Style, and Arrangement.   Ph. D.   Northwestern.   1950.   1960

Keane, Helen.   Study and Practice in Quintilian's Theory of Oratori-
    cal Training.   M. A.   Cornell.   1925.   1961

Keesey, Ray E.   The Rhetorical Theory of John Lawson.   Ph. D.
    Ohio.   1950.   1962

Klein, Willette C.   A Restatement of Plato's Contribution to the
    Theory of Persuasion.   M. A.   Brooklyn College.   1937.   1963

Laine, Joseph B.   Rhetorical Theory in American Colleges and Uni-
    versities, 1915-1954.   Ph. D.   Northwestern.   1958.   1964

Lamb, John H.   An Analysis of the Aristotelian Concept of Ethical
    Proof in Representative Contemporary Speech Literature.   M. A.
    Iowa.   1949.   1965

Lee, Irving J.   A Study of Emotional Appeal in Rhetorical Theory
    with Special Reference to Invention, Arrangement and Style.
    Ph. D.   Northwestern.   1939.   1966

Loving, Ida H.   The Treatment of Language by the Eighteenth Cen-
    tury Rhetoricians: Hugh Blair, George Campbell, Joseph Priestly,
    Thomas Sheridan, and William Barron.   M. A.   Florida.   1959.
                                                                    1967
McConnell, Harry.   Three Elements in the Philosophy of Alfred
    North Whitehead and Their Implications for Rhetorical Theory.
    M. A.   Pittsburgh.   1962.   1968

McGrew, J. Fred.   A Study of the Treatment of Speech Composition
    by English Writers from Cox to Whately.   M. A.   Wisconsin.
    1926.   1969

McLaughlin, Ted J.   Modern Social Psychology and the Aristotelian

Concept of Ethical Proof.   Ph. D.   Wisconsin.   1952.   1970

McMahon, Fred R. , Jr.   A History of the Concepts of Style in English Public Address: 1600-1700.   Ph. D.   S. California.   1958.
1971
Morago, (Sister) M. Teresa Avila.   A Discussion of De Rhetorica
by Cassiodorus.   M. A.   St. Louis.   1960.   1972

Nadeau, Raymond E.   The Index Rhetoricus of Thomas Farnaby.
Ph. D.   Michigan.   1951.   1973

Neale, John V.   An Essay on the Rhetoric of Aristotle.   M. A.
Cornell. 1939.   1974

O'Neil, Marion R.   The Opinions of Ancient Rhetoricians Concerning
the Audience.   M. A.   Cornell.   1940.   1975

Ostler, Margaret E.   A Translation of the Rhetoric of Julius Victor,
with Introduction and Notes.   M. A.   Northwestern.   1938.   1976

Pence, Orville L.   The Concept and Function of Logical Proof in
the Rhetorical System of Richard Whately.   Ph. D.   Iowa.   1946.
1977
_____.   A Study of the Principles of Pathetic Appeal in the Works
of Certain Classical Rhetoricians.   M. A.   Washington.   1939.
1978
Petelle, John.   A Critical Evaluation of the Contribution of Cicero
to Modern Rhetorical Theory.   M. A.   Nebraska.   1960.   1979

Phillips. Gerald M.   The Theory and Practice of Rhetoric at the
Babylonian Talmudic Academies, from 70 C. E. to 500 C. E. As
Evidenced in the Babylonian Talmud.   Ph. D.   Western Reserve.
1956.   1980

Pollock, Wallace S.   The Rhetorical Theory of William G. T. Shedd.
Ph. D.   Northwestern.   1962.   1981

Ried, Paul E.   The Philosophy of American Rhetoric as it Developed
in the Boylston Chair of Rhetoric and Oratory at Harvard University.   Ph. D.   Ohio.   1959.   1982

Robinson, Kenneth W.   Some Classical Discussions of Style.   M. A.
Cornell.   1931.   1983

Rockey, Edward.   Roman Rhetorical Theory on Modes of Delivery.
M. A.   Brooklyn.   1962.   1984

Ruys, Constance R.   The Chambers of Rhetoric of the Netherlands.
M. S.   UCLA.   1951.   1985

Sattler, William M.   Conceptions of Ethos in Rhetoric.   Ph. D.
Northwestern.   1941.   1986

Shafter, Edward.   A Study of Rhetorical Invention in Selected English Rhetorics, 1550-1600.   Ph. D.   Michigan.   1956.   1987

Shapiro, Leo.   A Dictionary of Some Normative Terms in Aristotle's
 Rhetoric.   Ph. D.   Northwestern.   1947.   1988

Shearer, Ned A.   The Rhetorical Theory of Alexander Bain.   Ph. D.
 Wisconsin.   1967.   1989

Shirley, Raymond A.   The Rhetoric of Alexander Campbell in Theory
 and Practice.   M. A.   Tennessee.   1962.   1990

Snoddy, Rowena.   The Classical Bases of John Quincy Adams' Theory of Rhetorical Arrangement.   M. A.   Oklahoma.   1948.   1991

Spencer, Floyd A.   The Influence of Isocrates in Antiquity.   Ph. D.
 Chicago.   1924.   1992

Stretch, Evelyn A. M.   Whately's Rhetorical Theory, the Relationship of Logic and Rhetoric.   M. A.   Stanford.   1950.   1993

Summers, Dorothy.   The Classical Bases of J. Q. Adams' Theory of
 Rhetorical Invention.   M. A.   Oklahoma.   1942.   1994

Torrence, Donald L.   A Philosophy for Rhetoric Constructed from
 the Writing of Bertrand Russell.   Ph. D.   Illinois.   1957.   1995

Van Arsdale, Beryl.   John Quincy Adams, Professor of Rhetoric
 and Oratory.   M. S.   Northern Illinois State.   1958.   1996

Vardaman, George T.   An Analysis of Some Factors Relating to the
 Dialectic of Plato, Aristotle, and Cicero.   Ph. D.   Northwestern.
 1952.   1997

Wallace, Karl R.   Aristotle's Account of the Logical Means of Securing Belief.   M. A.   Cornell.   1931.   1998

———.   Bacon's Theory of Public Address.   Ph. D.   Cornell.
1933.   1999

Welch, Dale D.   The Rhetorical Theory of Aristotle and the Practice of Demosthenes.   M. A.   Cornell.   1928.   2000

White, Mrs. H. M. S.   The Principles of Ethical and Emotional Persuasion as Developed by Aristotle, Cicero, Quintilian and Campbell.   M. A.   S. California.   1931.   2001

Wittig, John W.   John Diebold's Theory of Persuasion.   M. A.   Florida.   1967.   2002

Witty, Robert G.   Isaac Watts and the Rhetoric of Dissent.   Ph. D.
 Florida.   1959.   2003

3. Articles

Allen, Ronald R.   The Rhetoric of John Franklin Genung.   ST, 12
(September, 1952), 238-41.   2004

Anderson, Dorothy I.   Edward T. Channing's Definition of Rhetoric.
SM, 14 (1947), 81-92.   2005

Anderson, Floyd D.   Aristotle's Doctrine of the Mean and Its Relationship to Rhetoric.   SSJ, 34 (Winter, 1968), 100-107.   2006

_____ and Anderson, Ray L.   Plato's Conception of Dispositio.
SSJ, 36 (Spring, 1971), 195-208.   2007

Anderson, William S.   Juvenal and Quintilian.   Yale Classical Studies, 17 (1961), 3-93.   2008

Auer, J. Jeffrey, and Banninga, Jerald L.   The Genesis of John
Quincy Adams' Lectures on Rhetoric and Oratory.   QJS, 49
(April, 1963), 119-132.   2009

Baca, Albert R.   The Art of Rhetoric of Aeneas Silvius Piccolomini.
WS, 34 (Winter, 1970), 9-15.   2010

Backes, James G.   Aristotle's Theory of Stasis in Forensic and Deliberative Speech in the Rhetoric.   CSSJ, 12 (Autumn, 1960), 6-
8.   2011

Bennett, Charles E.   An Ancient Schoolmaster's Message to Present-
Day Teachers.   CJ, 4 (February, 1909), 149-64.   (On Quintilian's
principles.)   2012

Berman, Eleanor D. , and McClintock, E. C. , Jr.   Thomas Jefferson
and Rhetoric.   QJS, 33 (February, 1947), 1-8.   2013

Berquist, Goodwin.   An Ancient Who is Not Antiquated.   TS, 2
(April, 1954), 11-13.   (On Isocrates' precepts.)   2014

Bevan, Edwyn R.   Rhetoric in the Ancient World.   In Essays in
Honour of Gilbert Murray.   London, Allen, 1936.   Pp. 189-213.
                                                            2015
Bevilacqua, Vincent M.   Philosophical Origins of George Campbell's
Philosophy of Rhetoric.   SM, 32 (March, 1965), 1-12.   2016

_____ .   Philosophical Assumptions Underlying Hugh Blair's Lectures
on Rhetoric and Belles Lettres.   WS, 31 (Summer, 1967), 150-
164.   2017

_____ .   James Beattie's Theory of Rhetoric.   SM, 34 (June, 1967),
109-124.   2018

_____ .   Rhetoric and the Circle of Moral Studies: An Historio-
graphic View.   QJS, 55 (December, 1969), 343-357.   2019

Black, Edwin. Plato's View of Rhetoric. QJS, 44 (December,
1958), 361-74.   2020

Bolton, Janet. The Garnishing of the Manner of Utterance. WS,
28 (Spring, 1964), 83-91.   2021

Bormann, Ernest G. The Rhetorical Theory of William Henry Milburn. SM, 36 (March, 1969), 28-37.   2022

Brake, Robert J. On "Speechifiers Well Snubbed": Some Rhetorical Viewpoints of Montaigne. QJS, 56 (April, 1970), 105-113.
                                                                   2023
_____. Michel Montaigne: A Skeptic's Views on Rhetoric. SSJ,
33 (Fall, 1967), 29-36.   2024

_____. Pedants, Professors, and the Law of the Excluded Middle:
On Sophists and Sophistry. CSSJ, 20 (Summer, 1969), 122-129.
                                                                   2025
Brandes, Paul D. The Composition and Preservation of Aristotle's
Rhetoric. SM, 35 (November, 1968), 482-491.   2026

Brockriede, Wayne E. Bentham's Criticism of Rhetoric and Rhetoricians. QJS, 41 (December, 1955), 377-82.   2027

Brownstein, Oscar L. Plato's Phaedrus: Dialectic as the Genuine
Art of Speaking. QJS, 51 (December, 1965), 392-397.   2028

Bryant, Donald C. Aspects of the Rhetorical Tradition: The Intellectual Foundation. QJS, 36 (April, 1950), 169-76.   2029

_____. Aspects of the Rhetorical Tradition: Emotion, Style, and
Literary Association. QJS, 36 (October, 1950), 326-332.   2030

Burke, Kenneth. Rhetoric--Old and New. JGE, 5 (1951), 202-9.
(Burke writes: "The key term for the old rhetoric was 'persuasion' and its stress was upon deliberate design. The key term
for the 'new' rhetoric would be 'identification,' which can include
a partially 'unconscious' factor in appeal.")   2031

Cohen, Herman. William Leechman's Anticipation of Campbell.
WS, 32 (Spring, 1968), 92-97.   2032

Colum, Padraic. Cicero and the Rhetoricians. D, 86 (January,
1929), 52-8.   2033

Cooper, Lane. The Rhetoric of Aristotle. QJS, 21 (February,
1935), 10-19.   2034

Dieter, Otto A. L., and Kurth, William C. The De Rhetorica of
Aurelius Augustine. SM, 35 (March, 1968), 90-108.   2035

Dolph, Phil. Taste and "The Philosophy of Rhetoric." WS, 32
(Spring, 1968), 104-113. (On Campbell.)   2036

Dreher, John, and Crump, James I., Jr.   Pre-Han Persuasion:
    The Legalist School.   CSSJ, 3 (March, 1952), 10-14.   2037

Durham, Weldon B.   The Elements of Thomas De Quincey's Rhet-
    oric.   SM, 37 (November, 1970), 240-248.   2038

Eakins, Barbara.   The Evolution of Rhetoric: A Cosmic Analogy.
    SSJ, 35 (Spring, 1970), 193-203.   2039

Ehninger, Douglas.   Bernard Lami's L'Art de Parler: A Critical
    Analysis.   QJS, 32 (December, 1946), 429-34.   (An analysis of
    the Port Royal Rhetoric.)   2040

_____.   Campbell, Blair, and Whately: Old Friends in a New
    Light.   WS, 19 (October, 1955), 263-69.   2041

_____.   Campbell, Blair, and Whately Revisited.   SSJ, 28 (Spring,
    1963), 169-82.   2042

_____.   The Classical Doctrine of Invention.   G, 39 (March, 1957),
    59-62, 70.   2043

_____.   Dominant Trends in English Rhetorical Thought, 1750-1800.
    SSJ, 18 (September, 1952), 3-12.   2044

_____.   George Campbell and the Revolution in Inventional Theory.
    SSJ, 15 (May, 1950), 270-76.   2045

_____.   George Campbell and the Rhetorical Tradition: A Reply to
    LaRusso.   WS, 32 (Fall, 1968), 276-279.   2046

Ettlich, Ernest.   Introduction [to a symposium on George Campbell].
    WS, 32 (Spring, 1968), 84.   2047

_____.   John Franklin Genung and the Nineteenth Century Definition
    of Rhetoric.   CSSJ, 17 (November, 1966), 283-288.   2048

Fisher, B. Aubrey.   I. A. Richards' Context of Language: An Over-
    looked Contribution to Rhetorico-Communication Theory.   WS, 35
    (Spring, 1971), 104-111.   2049

Flemming, Edwin G.   A Comparison of Cicero and Aristotle on
    Style.   QJS, 4 (January, 1918), 61-71.   2050

Flynn, Lawrence J., S. J.   Aristotle: Art and Faculty of Rhetoric.
    SSJ, 21 (Summer, 1956), 244-54.   2051

Gerhard, W. A.   Plato's Theory of Dialectic.   NSchol, 21 (April,
    1947), 192-211.   2052

Golden, James L.   The Rhetorical Theory of Adam Smith.   SSJ, 33
    (Spring, 1968), 200-214.   2053

_____. James Boswell on Rhetoric and Belles-Lettres.   QJS, 50
(October, 1964), 266-276.   2054

Goodfellow, Donald M.   First Boylston Professor of Rhetoric and
Oratory.   New England Quarterly, 19 (September, 1946), 372-89.
                                                                      2055
Graves, Wallace.   The Uses of Rhetoric in the Nadir of English
Morals.   WS, 28 (Spring, 1964), 97-105.   2056

Greenwood, James G.   The Legal Setting of Attic Oratory.   CSSJ,
23 (Fall, 1972), 181-187.   2057

Gregg, Richard B.   Implications of Schiller's Logic for Rhetorical
Theory.   PSA, 19 (September, 1962), 29-36.   2058

Gronbeck, Bruce E.   Gorgias on Rhetoric and Poetic: A Rehabilitation.   SSCJ, 38 (Fall, 1972), 27-38.   2059

Guthrie, Warren.   The Development of Rhetorical Theory in America: 1635-1850.   SM, 13 (1946), 14-22; SM, 14 (1947), 38-54;
SM, 15 (1948), 61-71; SM, 16 (1949), 98-114.   2060

Haberman, Frederick.   De Quincey's Theory of Rhetoric.   In Eastern Public Speaking Conference, ed. by Harold F. Harding.   New
York, Wilson, 1940.   Pp. 191-203.   2061

Hack, Roy K.   Quintilian Again.   CJ, 5 (February, 1910), 161-4.
                                                                      2062
Hale, Edward E., Jr.   Ideas on Rhetoric in the 16th Century.
PMLA, 18 (1903), 424-44.   2063

Hance, Kenneth G.   The Elements of the Rhetorical Theory of
Phillips Brooks.   SM, 5 (1938), 16-39.   2064

Harding, Harold F.   Quintilian's Witnesses.   SM, 1 (September,
1934), 1-20.   2065

Heller, John L.   Ancient Rhetoric in the Modern College Course in
Speech.   CW, 29 (December 16, 1935), 57-9.   2066

Herrick, Marvin T.   The Early History of Aristotle's Rhetoric in
English.   PQ, 5 (July, 1926), 242-57.   2067

Hildebrandt, Herbert W.   Sherry: Renaissance Rhetorician.   CSSJ,
11 (Spring, 1960), 204-9.   2068

Hillbruner, Anthony.   Plato and Korzybski: Two Views of Truth in
Rhetorical Theory.   SSJ, 24 (4 Summer, 1959), 185-96.   2069

Hinks, D. A. G.   Tisias and Corax and the Invention of Rhetoric.
CQ, 35 (April, 1940), 59-69.   2070

Howell, Wilbur S.   Aristotle and Horace on Rhetoric and Poetics.

QJS, 54 (December, 1968), 325-349.   2071

_____. Classical and European Traditions of Rhetoric and Speech
Training. SSJ, 23 (Winter, 1957), 73-8.   2072

_____. De Quincey on Science, Rhetoric and Poetry. SM, 13
(November 1, 1946), 1-13.   2073

_____. Nathaniel Carpenter's Place in the Controversy between
Dialectic and Rhetoric. SM, 1 (September, 1934), 20-41.   2074

Huby, Pamela M. The Date of Aristotle's Topics and Its Treatment
of the Theory of Ideas. CQ, 12 (1962), 72-80.   2075

Hudson, Hoytt. Compendium Rhetorices by Erasmus: A Translation. In Studies in Speech and Drama in Honor of Alexander M.
Drummond, ed. by H. A. Wichelns and others. Ithaca, N. Y.,
1944. Pp. 326-40.   2076

_____. De Quincey on Rhetoric and Public Speaking. In Studies
in Rhetoric and Public Speaking in Honor of J. A. Winans. Pp.
119-26.   2077

_____. Jewel's Oration Against Rhetoric. QJS, 14 (June, 1928),
374-92. (Introduction to and translation of John Jewel's oration
against rhetoric.)   2078

Hudson, Roy F. Richard Sibbe's Theory and Practice of Persuasion.
QJS, 44 (April, 1958), 137-48.   2079

Hudson-Williams, H. L. I. Thucydides, Isocrates, and the Rhetorical Method of Composition. CQ, 42 (1948), 76-81.   2080

Hunt, Everett L. An Introduction to Classical Rhetoric. QJS, 12
(June, 1926), 201-4.   2081

_____. Plato on Rhetoric and Rhetoricians. QJS, 6 (June, 1920),
33-53.   2082

_____. Plato and Aristotle on Rhetoric and Rhetoricians. In Stud-
ies in Rhetoric and Public Speaking in Honor of J. A. Winans, by
pupils and colleagues. New York, Century, 1925. Pp. 3-60.
                                                           2083
_____. Classical Rhetoric and Modern Communicology. WS, 34
(Winter, 1970), 2-8.   2084

Huseman, Richard C. Aristotle's Doctrine of the Mean: Implications for Rhetorical Style. WS, 34 (Spring, 1970), 115-121. 2085

_____. Aristotle's System of Topics. SSJ, 30 (Spring, 1965), 243-
252.   2086

_____. Modern Approaches to the Aristotelian Concept of the Special Topic.   CSSJ, 15 (February, 1964), 21-26.   2087

Irvine, James R.   Juan Huarte: A Mentalist Concept of Rhetoric.
    SM, 38 (March, 1971), 49-55.   2088

_____.   The Rhetorica of Philodemus.   WS, 35 (Spring, 1971), 96-
    103.   2089

Jaeger, Werner.   Plato's Phaedrus: Philosophy and Rhetoric; Politi-
    cal Culture and the Panhellenic Ideal.   In Paidera: the Ideals of
    Greek Culture (translated by Gilbert Highet).   New York, Oxford,
    1944.   Pp. 182-96.   2090

_____.   The Rhetoric of Isocrates and its Cultural Ideal.   Ibid.,
    pp. 46-83.   2091

Johnson, Francis R.   Two Renaissance Textbooks of Rhetoric:
    Aphthonius' Progymnasmata and Rainolde's A Booke Called the
    Foundacion of Rhetorike.   Huntington Library Quarterly, 6 (Au-
    gust, 1943).   2092

Kennedy, George A.   The Earliest Rhetorical Handbooks.   AJPh, 80
    (April, 1959), 169-78.   2093

_____.   An Estimate of Quintilian.   AJPh, 83 (April, 1962), 130-
    46.   ("Shallow Scholar.")   2094

_____.   The Ancient Dispute over Rhetoric in Homer.   AJPh, 78
    (1957), 23-35.   2095

LaRusso, Dominic.   Root or Branch?   A Re-Examination of Camp-
    bell's "Rhetoric."   WS, 32 (Spring, 1968), 85-91.   2096

Leathers, Dale G.   Whately's Logically Derived Rhetoric: A
    Stranger in Its Time.   WS, 33 (Winter, 1969), 48-58.   2097

Lockwood, D. P.   Roman Rhetoric as Training for the Bar.   Pro-
    ceedings of the American Philological Association, 57 (1926),
    xxiii.   2098

Loukas, Christ.   The Psychology of Aristotle: a Logical Arrange-
    ment of his De Anima and Allied Treatises.   JGP, 6 (January,
    1932), 157-89.   2099

Macksoud, S. John.   Kenneth Burke on Perspective and Rhetoric.
    WS, 33 (Summer, 1969), 167-174.   2100

Makay, John J.   John Milton's Rhetoric.   CSSJ, 22 (Fall, 1971),
    186-195.   2101

Marsh, Robert.   Aristotle and the Modern Rhapsode.   QJS, 39
    (December, 1953), 491-98.   2102

Marsh, Thomas H.   Aristotle versus Plato on Public Speaking.   SSJ,
     18 (March, 1953), 163-66.   2103

Martin, Howard H.   Puritan Preachers on Preaching: Notes on
     American Colonial Rhetoric.   QJS, 50 (October, 1964), 285-292.
                                                                        2104
McBurney, James H.   Some Contributions of Classical Dialectic and
     Rhetoric to a Philosophy of Discussion.   QJS, 23 (February,
     1937), 1-13.   2105

McCain, John W., Jr.   Oratory, Rhetoric and Logic in the Writings
     of John Heywood.   QJS, 25 (February, 1940), 44-7.   2106

McCord, Clarence W.   On Sophists and Philosophers.   SSJ, 29
     (Winter, 1963), 146-149.   2107

McDermott, Douglas.   George Campbell and the Classical Tradition.
     QJS, 49 (December, 1963), 403-409.   2108

McGuire, William J., and Papageorgis, Demetrios.   Effectiveness
     of Forewarning in Developing Resistance to Persuasion.   POQ,
     26 (1926), 24-34.   2109

McKeon, Richard.   Aristotle's Conception of Language and the Arts
     of Language.   CP, 41 (October, 1946), 193-206; 42 (January,
     1947), 21-50.   2110

_____.   Poetry and Philosophy in the Twelfth Century: The Ren-
     aissance of Rhetoric.   MP, 43 (May, 1946), 217-34.   2111

_____.   Rhetoric in the Middle Ages.   Spec, 17 (January, 1942),
     1-32.   2112

McMahon, Fred R.   Elocutio in Mid-Seventeenth Century England.
     WS, 28 (Spring, 1964), 92-96.   2113

Meador, Prentice A., Jr.   Quintilian's Vir Bonus.   WS, 34 (Sum-
     mer, 1970), 162-169.   2114

_____.   Skeptic Theory of Perception: A Philosophical Antecedent
     of Ciceronian Probability.   QJS, 54 (December, 1968), 340-351.
                                                                        2115
Miller, Gerald R.   Thomas Baker: A Sceptic's Attack on Rhetoric.
     WS, 27 (Spring, 1963), 69-76.   2116

Mills, Glen E.   Daniel Webster's Principles of Rhetoric.   SM, 9
     1942), 124-40.   2117

Mohrmann, G. P.   George Campbell: The Psychological Background.
     WS, 32 (Spring, 1968), 99-103.   2118

Moore, Dwain E.   Morley's Concept of the Nature and Function of
     Rhetoric.   WS, 32 (Fall, 1968), 252-265.   2119

Moore, Wilbur E. Samuel Johnson on Rhetoric. QJS, 30 (April, 1944), 165-8. 2120

Mosier, Kenneth. Quintilian's Implications Concerning Forensics. AFAR, (Spring Issue, 1963), 1-7. 2121

Murphy, James J. John Gower's Confessio Amantis and the First Discussion of Rhetoric in the English Language. PQ, 41 (1962), 401-11. 2122

_____. Saint Augustine and the Christianization of Rhetoric. WS, 22 (Winter, 1958), 24-9. 2123

_____. "Modern" Elements in Medieval Rhetoric. WS, 28 (Fall, 1964), 206-211. 2124

_____. St. Augustine and Rabanus Maurus: The Genesis of Medieval Rhetoric. WS, 31 (Spring, 1967), 88-95. 2125

_____. The Arts of Discourse, 1050-1400. MS, 23 (1961), 194-205. 2126

_____. Aristotle's Rhetoric in the Middle Ages. QJS, 52 (April, 1966), 109-115. 2127

_____. The Earliest Teaching of Rhetoric at Oxford. SM, 27 (1960), 345-347. 2128

Nadeau, Ray. Delivery in Ancient Times: Homer to Quintilian. QJS, 50 (February, 1964), 53-60. 2129

_____. Rhetorica Ad Herennium: Commentary and Translation of Book 1. SM, 16 (August, 1949), 57-69. 2130

Nelson, Norman E. Peter Ramus and the Confusion of Logic, Rhetoric, and Poetry. University of Michigan Contributions to Modern Philology, No. 2. Ann Arbor, Mich., Michigan, 1947. 2131

Nobles, W. Scott. The Paradox of Plato's Attitude Toward Rhetoric. WS, 21 (Fall, 1957), 206-10. 2132

Olian, J. Robert. The Intended Uses of Aristotle's Rhetoric. SM, 35 (June, 1968), 137-148. 2133

Olson, Elder J. Argument of Longinus on the Sublime. MP, 39 (February, 1942), 225-38. 2134

Pack, Roger. Two Sophists and Two Emperors. CP, 42 (1947), 17-20. 2135

Parrish, Wayland M. Whately and His Rhetoric. QJS, 15 (February, 1929), 58-79. 2136

Rahskopf, Horace G.   John Quincy Adams: Speaker and Rhetorician.
    QJS, 32 (December, 1946), 435-41.   2137

Rice, George P., Jr.   Aristotle's Rhetoric and Introductory Public
    Address.   WS, 7 (May, 1943), 2-5.   2138

Ried, Paul E.   The Boylston Chair of Rhetoric and Oratory.   WS,
    24 (Spring, 1960), 83-87.   2139

Riley, Floyd K.   St. Augustine, Public Speaker and Rhetorician.
    QJS, 22 (December, 1936), 572-78.   2140

Roberts, W. Rhys.   Aristotle on Public Speaking.   FR, 122 (Aug-
    ust 1, 1924), 201-210.   2141

_____.   Notes on Aristotle's Rhetoric.   AJPh, 45 No. 180 (1924),
    351-61.   2142

Rousseau, Lousene G.   The Rhetorical Principles of Cicero and
    Adams.   QJS, 2 (October, 1916), 397-409.   2143

Sattler, William M.   Conceptions of Ethos in Ancient Rhetoric.
    SM, 14 (1947), 55-65.   2144

_____.   Some Platonic Influences in the Rhetorical Works of Cicero.
    QJS, 35 (April, 1949), 64-69.   2145

Seiver, George O.   Cicero's De Oratore and Rabelais.   PLMA, 59
    (September, 1944), 655-71.   2146

Sloan, Thomas O.   A Renaissance Controversialist: Thomas
    Wright's Passions of the Minde in Generall.   SM, 36 (March,
    1969), 38-54.   2147

Smith, Bromley.   Corax and Probability.   QJS, 7 (February, 1921),
    13-42.   2148

_____.   Hippias and a Lost Canon of Rhetoric.   QJS, 12 (June,
    1926), 129-45.   2149

_____.   Thrasymachus: a Pioneer Rhetorician.   QJS, 13 (June,
    1927), 278-91.   2150

Sochatoff, A. Fred.   Basic Rhetorical Theories of the Elder Seneca.
    CJ, 34 (March, 1939), 345-54.   2151

Solmsen, Friedrich.   Aristotelian Tradition in Ancient Rhetoric.
    AJPh, 62 (January, 1941), 35-50; 62 (April, 1941), 169-90. 2152

Speer, Diane P.   Milton's Defensio Prima: Ethos and Vituperation
    in a Polemic Engagement.   QJS, 66 (October, 1970), 277-283.
                                                                    2153
Speer, Richard.   John of Salisbury: Rhetoric in the Metalogicon.

CSSJ, 20 (Summer, 1969), 92-96.   2154

Steele, Edward D.   The Role of the Concept of Choice in Aristotle's
Rhetoric.   WS, 27 (Spring, 1963), 77-83.   2155

Stovall, Thera.   Brushing the Cobwebs off Quintilian.   SSJ, 9 (January, 1944), 54-8.   2156

Symposium: The Rhetorical Theory of George Campbell.   WS, 32
(Spring, 1968), 84-113. (Contributions by E. Ettlich, D. La-
Russo, H. Cohen, G. P. Mohrmann, and P. Dolph.)   2157

Symposium: The Rhetoric of the English Renaissance.   WS, 28
(Spring, 1964), 69-105. (Contributions by F. McMahon, K. Wallace, J. Bolton, and W. Graves.)   2158

Talley, Paul M.   DeQuincey on Persuasion, Invention, and Style.
CSSJ, 16 (November, 1965), 243-54.   2159

Thompson, Claud A.   Rhetorical Madness: An Ideal in the Phaedrus.
QJS, 55 (December, 1969), 358-363.   2160

Thompson, Wayne N.   The Symposium: A Neglected Source for
Plato's Ideas on Rhetoric.   SSCJ, 37 (Spring, 1972), 219-232.
                                                             2161
Thonssen, Lester W.   A Functional Interpretation of Aristotle's
Rhetoric.   QJS, 16 (June, 1930), 297-310.   2162

Utterback, William E.   Aristotle's Contribution to the Psychology of
Argument.   QJS, 11 (June, 1925), 218-25.   2163

Van Hook, La Rue.   The Criticism of Photius on the Attic Orators.
Transactions of the American Philological Associations, Haverford, Pa., 38 (1907), 41-47.   2164

Wagner, Russell H.   The Meaning of Dispositio.   In Studies in
Speech and Drama in Honor of A. M. Drummond.   Ithaca, N. Y.,
Cornell, 1944.   Pp. 285-94.   2165

_____.   The Rhetorical Theory of Isocrates.   QJS, 8 (November,
1922), 323-37.   2166

_____.   Thomas Wilson's Arte of Rhetorique.   QJS, 15 (June,
1929), 423-5.   2167

_____.   Thomas Wilson's Contributions to Rhetoric.   In Papers in
Rhetoric, ed. by D. C. Bryant.   St. Louis, The Editor, 1940.
Pp. 1-7.   2168

Wallace, Karl R.   Bacon's Conception of Rhetoric.   SM, 3 (1936),
21-48.   2169

_____.   Bacon's Contribution to the Theory of Rhetoric and Public

Address.   In Humanistic Studies in Honor of John Calvin Metcalf.
University of Virginia Studies 1.   Charlottesville, Va., The University, 1941.   Pp. 282-313.   2170

_____.   Early English Rhetoricians on the Structure of Rhetorical
Prose.   In Papers in Rhetoric, ed. by D. C. Bryant.   St. Louis,
Mo., The Editor, 1940.   Pp. 18-26.   2171

_____.   The English Renaissance Mind.   WS, 28 (Spring, 1964),
70-82.   2172

_____.   Francis Bacon on Understanding, Reason, and Rhetoric.
SM, 38 (June, 1971), 79-91.   2173

Weedon, Jerry L.   Locke on Rhetoric and Rational Man.   QJS, 56
(December, 1970), 378-387.   2174

Wilcox, Stanley.   Corax and the Prolegomena.   AJPh, 64 (January,
1943), 1-23.   2175

_____.   Isocrates' Fellow-Rhetoricians.   AJPh, 66 (April, 1945),
171-86.   2176

_____.   Scope of Early Rhetorical Instruction.   HSCP, 53 (1942),
121-55.   2177

Wilson, Harold S.   Gabriel Harvey's Orations on Rhetoric.   A Journal of English Literary History, 12 (September, 1945), 167-82.
                                                                2178

_____.   George of Trebizond and Early Humanist Rhetoric.   SP,
40 (July, 1943), 367-79.   2179

B.   MODERN TREATMENTS

1.   Books

Abelson, Herbert J.   Persuasion: How Opinions and Attitudes are
Changed.   New York, Springer, 1959.   2180

Abernathy, Elton.   The Advocate: A Manual of Persuasion.   New
York, McKay, 1964.   2181

Anderson, Kenneth E.   Persuasion: Theory and Practice.   Boston,
Allyn, 1971.   2182

Atgeld, John P.   Oratory, Its Requirements and Its Rewards.   Chicago, Kerr, 1901.   2183

Auer, J. Jeffrey, ed.   The Rhetoric of Our Times.   New York,
Appleton, 1969.   2184

Bailey, Dudley, ed. Essays of Rhetoric. New York, Oxford, 1965.
2185

Baird, A. Craig. Rhetoric: A Philosophical Inquiry. New York,
Ronald, 1965.   2186

Benson, Thomas W., and Prosser, Michael H. Readings in Classical Rhetoric. Boston, Allyn, 1969.   2187

Bernays, Edward L. Crystallizing Public Opinion. New York,
Liveright, 1923.   2188

_____. Propaganda. New York, Liveright, 1928.   2189

Bettinghaus, Erwin P. Persuasive Communication. New York,
Bobbs, 1968.   2190

Bosmajian, Haig A., ed. Readings in Speech. New York, Harper,
1965.   2191

Brembeck, Winston L., and Howell, William S. Persuasion, a
Means of Social Control. New York, Prentice, 1952.   2192

Brooks, George E. Dynamic Speaking; a Thesis in the Psychology
of Persuasion. Newport News, Virginia, Franklin Printing Company, 1932.   2193

Brown, J. A. C. Techniques of Persuasion. Baltimore, Penguin,
1963.   2194

Brown, M. Ralph. Legal Psychology: Psychology Applied to the
Trial of Cases, to Crime and its Treatment, and to Mental States
and Processes. Indianapolis, Indiana, Bobbs, 1926.   2195

Bryant, Donald C., ed. Papers in Rhetoric. St. Louis, The Editor, 1940.   2196

_____. The Rhetorical Idiom: Essays in Rhetoric, Oratory, Lan-
guage, and Drama. Ithaca, Cornell, 1958.   2197

Burke, Kenneth. A Grammar of Motives. New York, Prentice,
1952.   2198

Burtt, Harold E. Legal Psychology. New York, Prentice, 1931.
2199

Campbell, Karlyn K. Critiques of Contemporary Rhetoric. Belmont, California, Wadsworth, 1971.   2200

Clark, Fred G. How to be Popular Though Conservative. New
York, Nostrand, 1948.   2201

Clevenger, Theodore, Jr. Audience Analysis. Indianapolis, Bobbs,
1966.   2202

Cohen, Arthur R.   Attitude Change and Social Influence.   New York,
    Basic Books, 1964.   2203

Corbett, Edward P. J.   Classical Rhetoric for the Modern Student.
    New York, Oxford, 1965.   2204

Corder, Jim W.   Uses of Rhetoric.   Philadelphia, Lippincott, 1971.
                                                                    2205
Crocker, Lionel, and Carmack, Paul A., eds.   Readings in Rhet-
    oric.   Springfield, Ill., Thomas, 1964.   2206

Cronkhite, Gary.   Persuasion: Speech and Behavioral Change.   In-
    dianapolis, Bobbs, 1969.   2207

De Armond, Frederick F.   How to Sell and Unsell Ideas.   Chicago,
    Wolfe, 1954.   2208

Doob, Leonard W.   Propaganda.   New York, H. Holt, 1935.   2209

_____.   Public Opinion and Propaganda.   New York, H. Holt,
    1948.   2210

Dowd, Jerome.   Control in Human Societies.   New York, D. Apple-
    ton, 1936.   2211

Ehninger, Douglas, ed.   Contemporary Rhetoric: A Reader's
    Sourcebook.   Glenview, Ill., Scott, 1972.   2212

Eisenson, Jon, Auer, J. Jeffrey, and Irwin, John V.   The Psychol-
    ogy of Communication.   New York, Appleton, 1963.   2213

Faris, Ellsworth.   The Nature of Human Nature.   New York and
    London, McGraw, 1937.   (Cf. "Attitudes and Behavior," pp. 144-
    54; "Concept of Social Attitudes," pp. 132-43; and "Social Atti-
    tudes," pp. 127-31.)   2214

Festinger, Leon.   Conflict, Decision, and Dissonance.   Stanford,
    California, California, 1964.   2215

Fotheringham, Wallace C.   Perspectives on Persuasion.   Boston,
    Allyn, 1966.   2216

Genung, John F.   The Working Principles of Rhetoric.   Boston,
    Ginn, 1900.   2217

Graves, Harold F., and Bowman, John S.   Types of Persuasion.
    New York, Cordon, 1938.   2218

Graves, W. Brooks, ed.   Readings in Public Opinion.   New York,
    D. Appleton, 1928.   2219

Harrington, Elbert W.   Rhetoric and the Scientific Method of Inquiry:
    a Study of Invention.   University of Colorado Studies, Series in

Language and Literature, No. 1. Boulder, Colorado, University
of Colorado Press, 1948.   2220

Harter, D. Lincoln, and Sullivan, John. Propaganda Handbook: a
Guide to Mass Persuasion. Philadelphia, Twentieth Century Publishing Company, 1952.   2221

Harvey, Jan. The Technique of Persuasion. New York, British
Book Center, 1951.   2222

Higgins, Howard H. Influencing Behavior Through Speech. Boston,
Expression, 1930.   2223

Hill, David J. The Science of Rhetoric. New York, American,
1905.   2224

Hoffer, Eric. The True Believer. New York, Harper, 1951. 2225

Hollingworth, H. L. The Psychology of the Audience. New York,
American, 1935. (Cf. "The Psychology of Persuasion." pp. 109-
139.)   2226

Hovland, Carl I. The Order of Presentation in Persuasion. New
Haven, Connecticut, Yale, 1957.   2227

_____ and Janis, Irving. Personality and Persuasibility. New
Haven, Yale, 1959.   2228

_____, _____, and Kelley, Harold H. Communication and Per-
suasion. New Haven, Connecticut, Yale, 1953. (Chapter 1:
"The Order of Presentation in Persuasion." Chapter 7: "Ac-
quiring Conviction Through Active Participation.")   2229

_____, Lumsdaine, Arthur H., and Sheffield, Fred D. Experi-
ments on Mass Communication. Volume 3 of Studies in Social
Psychology in World War II. Princeton, N. J., Princeton,
1949.   2230

Howell, Wilbur S., ed. Problems and Styles of Communication.
New York, Crofts, 1945.   2231

Hummel, Paul, and Huntress, Keith. The Analysis of Propaganda.
New York, Dryden, 1949.   2232

Husband, Richard W. Applied Psychology. New York and London,
Harper, 1934. (Cf. "Appeals in Advertising," pp. 367-409.)
                                                              2233
Jastrow, Joseph. The Betrayal of Intelligence. New York, Green-
berg, 1938.   2234

_____. The Psychology of Conviction; a Study of Beliefs and Atti-
tudes. Boston, Houghton, 1918.   2235

Johannesen, Richard L., ed. Contemporary Theories of Rhetoric:
    Selected Readings. New York, Harper, 1971.   2236

Johnson, Wendell. Your Most Enchanted Listener. New York,
    Harper, 1956.   2237

Jones, Marshall R., ed. Nebraska Symposium on Motivation. Lin-
    coln, Nebraska, Nebraska, 1962.   2238

Karlins, Marvin, and Abelson, Herbert I. How Opinions and Atti-
    tudes Are Changed. New York, Springer, 2nd ed., 1970. 2239

Katz, Daniel, ed., et. al. Public Opinion and Propaganda. New
    York, Dryden, 1954.   2240

Keatinge, Maurice W. Suggestion in Education. London, Black,
    1907.   2241

Kelley, Stanley, Jr. Political Campaigning: Problems in Creating
    an Informed Electorate. Washington, D. C., Brookings Institution,
    1960.   2242

Keynes, John Maynard. Essays in Persuasion. New York, Har-
    court, 1932.   2243

Lasswell, Harold D. Democracy Through Public Opinion. Menasha,
    Wisconsin, Banta, 1941.   2244

_____ and Blumenstock, Dorothy. World Revolutionary Propaganda.
    New York, Knopf, 1939.   2245

Lee, Alfred M., and Lee, Elizabeth B. The Fine Art of Propa-
    ganda. New York, Harcourt, 1939.   2246

Lerbinger, Otto. Design for Persuasive Communication. Engle-
    wood Cliffs, N. J., Prentice, 1972.   2247

Lewin, Kurt. Field Theory in Social Science. New York, Harper,
    1951.   2248

Lippmann, Walter. Public Opinion. New York, Macmillan, 1923.
                                                            2249
_____. The Phantom Public. New York, Harcourt, 1925.   2250

Lowell, Abbott L. Conflicts of Principle. Cambridge, Mass.,
    Harvard, 1932.   2251

_____. Public Opinion and Popular Government. New York, Long-
    mans, New ed., 1914.   2252

_____. Public Opinion in War and Peace. Cambridge, Mass.,
    Harvard, 1923.   2253

Lowenthal, Leo, and Guterman, Norbert.   Prophets of Deceit: a
    Study of the Techniques of the American Agitator.   New York,
    Harper, 1949.   2254

Lumley, Frederick E.   Means of Social Control.   New York, Cen-
    tury, 1925.   2255

_____.   The Propaganda Menace.   New York, D. Appleton, 1933.
                                                                    2256
Lundholm, Helge.   The Psychology of Belief.   Durham, North Caro-
    lina, Duke, 1936.   2257

Mackin, John H.   Classical Rhetoric for Modern Discourse.   New
    York, Free, 1969.   2258

MacPherson, William.   The Psychology of Persuasion.   London,
    Methuen, 1920.   2259

Marsh, Patrick O.   Persuasive Speaking: Theory--Models--Prac-
    tice.   New York, Harper, 1967.   2260

McCarty, Dwight G.   Psychology for the Lawyer.   New York,
    Prentice, 1929.   2261

Menninger, Karl A.   The Human Mind.   New York, Knopf, 1930.
                                                                    2262
Merton, Robert K., and others.   Mass Persuasion.   New York,
    Harper, 1946.   2263

Meyerhoff, Arthur E.   The Strategy of Persuasion.   New York,
    Coward, 1965.   (On the use of advertising skills in fighting the
    cold war.)   2264

Miller, Clyde R.   The Process of Persuasion.   New York, Crown,
    1946.   2265

Minnick, Wayne.   The Art of Persuasion.   New York, Houghton,
    2nd ed., 1968.   2266

Muehl, William.   The Road to Persuasion.   New York, Oxford,
    1956.   2267

Murray, Edward J.   Motivation and Emotion.   Englewood Cliffs,
    N.J., 1964.   2268

Musafer, Sherif.   The Psychology of Social Norms.   New York,
    Harper, 1936.   2269

Nichols, Marie H.   Rhetoric and Criticism.   Baton Rouge, La.,
    LSU, 1963.   2270

Odegard, Peter H.   Pressure Politics.   New York, Columbia, 1928.
                                                                    2271

Oliver, Robert T.   Persuasive Speaking.   New York, Longmans,
    1950.   2272

_____.   The Psychology of Persuasive Speech.   New York, Long-
    mans, 1957.   2273

Overstreet, Harry A.   Influencing Human Behavior.   New York,
    Norton, 1925.   2274

Pear, Thomas H.   The Psychology of Effective Speaking.   London,
    Paul, 1933.   2275

Pigors, Paul.   Leadership or Domination.   Boston, Houghton, 1935.
                                                                 2276
Pillsbury, Walter B. , and Meader, Clarence L.   The Psychology of
    Language.   New York, D. Appleton, 1928.   2277

Prescott, Daniel A. , ed.   Emotion and the Educative Process.   Re-
    port of the Committee on the Relation of Emotion to the Educa-
    tive Process.   Washington, D. C. , American Council of Educa-
    tion, 1938.   2278

Propaganda; How to Recognize it and Deal with it.   New York, In-
    stitute for Propaganda Analysis, 1938.   2279

The Prospect of Rhetoric: Report of the National Development Pro-
    ject.   Englewood Cliffs, N. J. , Prentice, 1971.   2280

Public Opinion in a Democracy.   Proceedings of the Institution of
    Human Relations Held at Williamstown, Mass. , August 1937.
    Special Supplement to January, 1938, Edition of the POQ.   (96
    pps.)   2281

Raines, Lester C.   The Effect of Emotionally-Toned Literature,
    Vocally Expressed, upon an Audience.   Columbus, Ohio, Hedrick,
    1928.   2282

Remmers, H. H.   Further Studies in Attitudes.   Series 2, Bulletin
    of Purdue University, Vol. 37, No. 4.   Studies in Higher Educa-
    tion, 31.   Lafayette, Indiana, Purdue University, 1936.   (298 pp.)
                                                                 2283
Richards, Ivor A.   The Philosophy of Rhetoric.   New York, Oxford,
    1936.   2284

Rivers, William H.   Psychology and Politics; and Other Essays.
    London, Paul, 1923.   2285

Rosenthal, Solomon P.   Change of Socio-Economic Attitudes Under
    Radical Motion Picture Propaganda.   Archives of Psychology, No.
    166.   New York, 1934.   (46 pp.)   2286

Rosnow, Ralph L. , and Robinson, Edward J.   Experiments in Per-
    suasion.   New York, Academic, 1967.   2287

Ross, Edward A. Social Control. New York, Macmillan, 1916.
2288

Rossman, George, ed. Advocacy and the King's English. Indianapolis, Bobbs, 1960. (Sixty-five essays on various aspects of
advocacy.)   2289

Scheidel, Thomas M. Persuasive Speaking. Glenview, Ill., Scott,
1967.   2290

Schramm, Wilbur, ed. The Process and Effects of Mass Communication. Urbana, Illinois, Illinois, 1954.   2291

Schwartz, Joseph, and Rycenza, John A. The Province of Rhetoric.
New York, Ronald, 1965.   2292

Scott, Walter D. Influencing Men in Business. New York, Ronald.
2nd edition, 1919.   2293

_____. The Psychology of Public Speaking. Philadelphia, Pearson
Brothers, 1906.   2294

_____ and Howard D. T. Influencing Men in Business. New York,
Ronald, 1928.   2295

Shaffer, L. F. The Psychology of Human Adjustment. Boston,
Houghton, 1936. (Cf. "Human Conduct and Scientific Method,"
pp. 3-21.)   2296

Sherif, Carolyn W., Sherif, Muzafer, and Nebergall, Roger E. Attitude and Attitude Change. Philadelphia, W. B. Saunders Co.,
1965.   2297

Sidis, Boros. The Psychology of Suggestion. New York, D. Appleton, 1898.   2298

Staley, Delbert M. Psychology of the Spoken Word. Boston,
Badger, 1914.   2299

Stinchfield, Sara M. The Psychology of Speech. Boston, Expression, 1928.   2300

Stryker, Lloyd P. The Art of Advocacy. New York, Simon, 1954.
2301

Swift, Edgar J. How to Influence Men; The Use of Psychology in
Business. New York, Scribner's, 1927.   2302

Thomson, Mehran K. The Springs of Human Action. New York,
D. Appleton, 1927.   2303

Thonssen, Lester. Selected Readings in Rhetoric and Public Speaking. New York, Wilson, 1942.   2304

_____ and Baird, A. Craig. Speech Criticism: the Development

of Standards for Rhetorical Appraisal. New York, Ronald, 1948.
2305

Thorndike, E. L.   The Psychology of Wants, Interests, and Attitudes.
New York, Appleton, 1935.   2306

Thouless, Robert H.   The Control of the Mind; a Handbook of Applied Psychology.   London, Hodder, 1928.   2307

Wait, Wallace T.   The Science of Human Behavior.   New York,
Ronald, 1938.   ("Some of man's ways of behaving as a part of a
social group, " and "what the mainsprings of behavior are, " pp.
112-33, 222-42.)   2308

Wallas, Graham.   Human Nature in Politics.   Boston and New York,
Houghton, 2nd edition.   1919.   2309

White, Wendell.   The Psychology of Dealing with People.   New
York, Macmillan, 1936.   2310

Wiener, Norbert.   The Human Use of Human Beings.   New York,
Doubleday, 1954.   2311

Worsham, James A.   Art of Persuading People.   New York, Harper, 1938.   2312

Wright, Philip Q. , ed.   Public Opinion and World Politics.   Chicago, Chicago, 1933.   2313

Young, Kimball, ed.   Social Attitudes.   New York, H. Holt, 1931.
2314
_____.   Social Psychology.   New York, Crofts, 1945.   2315

_____, ed.   Source Book for Social Psychology.   New York, Knopf,
1927.   (Deals with phases of social behavior.)   2316

Young, Paul.   Motivation of Behavior.   New York, Wiley, 1936.
2317

2.   Theses and Dissertations

Andersen, Kenneth E.   An Experimental Study of the Interaction of
Artistic and Non-Artistic Ethos in Persuasion.   Ph. D.   Wisconsin.   1961.   2318

Anderson, Delmar C.   The Effect of Various Uses of Authoritative
Testimony in Persuasive Speaking.   M. A.   Ohio State.   1958.
2319
Banks, Marion S.   The Treatment of Source Credibility in Selected
College Textbooks on Speech Communication Published since 1960.
M. A.   C. W. Post.   1973.   2319a

Barnett, Suzanne E.   Persuasion and Prejudice: An Experimental
Study of the Effects upon Listener Attitudes of the Addition of Ex-

treme and Moderate Ideas to Persuasive Speeches.   Ph. D.   Indiana.   1962.   2320

Benedict, Ted W.   An Experimental Study of Social Status as a Dimension of Ethos.   Ph. D.   S. California.   1958.   2321

Bettinghaus, Erwin P., Jr.   The Relative Effect of the Use of Testimony in a Persuasive Speech Upon the Attitudes of Listeners.
M. A.   Bradley University.   1953.   2322

Biddle, Phillips R.   An Experimental Study of Ethos and Appeal for Overt Behavior in Persuasion.   Ph. D.   Illinois.   1966.   2323

Blatt, Stephen J.   The Consistency Between Verbal and Behavioral Attitude Response as a Function of High and Low Controversial Social Issues.   Ph. D.   Ohio.   1969.   2324

Bowers, John W.   Language Intensity, Social Introversion, and Attitude Change.   Ph. D.   Iowa.   1962.   2325

Burgess, Parke G.   A Concept of Social Responsibility in Rhetoric.
Ph. D.   Northwestern.   1956.   2326

Burks, Donald M.   Psychological Egoism and Its Refutation in Rhetorical Theory.   Ph. D.   Wisconsin.   1962.   2327

Cathcart, Robert S.   An Experimental Study of the Relative Effectiveness of Selective Means of Handling Evidence in Speeches of Advocacy.   Ph. D.   Northwestern.   1953.   Condensed version in SM, 22 (August, 1955), 227-33.   2328

Chapel, Ralph E.   The Influence of Court Oratory Upon American Oratory in General.   M. A.   Wisconsin.   1926.   2329

Clark, Anthony J.   A Study of Order Effect in Persuasive Communication.   Ph. D.   Denver.   1969.   2330

Costello, Charles S.   A Psychological Approach to Public Speaking.
M. A.   Loyola.   1930.   2331

Costley, Dan L.   An Experimental Study of the Effectiveness of Quantitative Evidence in Speeches of Advocacy.   M. A.   Oklahoma.
1958.   2332

Cryan, Mary E.   A Consideration of Form and Content in Rhetoric and Oratory.   M. A.   Wisconsin.   1927.   2333

Day, Dennis G.   The Treatment of Ethos in Twentieth-Century College Textbooks on Public Speaking.   M. A.   Illinois.   1960. 2334

De Mougeot, William R.   Modern Conceptions of Invention and Disposition.   M. A.   Cornell.   1950.   2335

Dresser, William R.   Studies of the Effects of "Satisfactory" and
    "Unsatisfactory" Evidence in a Speech of Advocacy.   Ph. D.
    Northwestern.   1962.   Condensed version in SM, 30 (August,
    1963), 302-6.   2336

Ehrensberger, Ray.   An Experimental Study of the Relative Effec-
    tiveness of Certain Forms of Emphasis in Public Speaking.
    Ph. D.   Syracuse.   1937.   2337

Ertle, Charles.   A Study of the Effects of Ethos and One-Sided vs.
    Two-Sided Presentation of Arguments in Persuasive Communica-
    tion.   M. A.   Michigan State.   1967.   2338

Gabriel, Charles.   An Experimental Investigation of the Effects of
    Organization on Speaker Ethos.   M. A.   Hawaii, 1967.   2339

Gantt, Vernon W.   Attitude Change as a Function of Source Credi-
    bility and Levels of Involvement.   Ph. D.   Ohio.   1970.   2340

Gibson, James W.   Direct and Indirect Attitude Scale Measurements
    of Positive and Negative Argumentative Communications.   Ph. D.
    Ohio State.   1962.   2341

Goetz, Emily.   Attitude Instability, Persuasibility, and Dogmatism.
    M. A.   Kansas.   1965.   2342

Goss, Blaine.   Source Credibility and Its Effects upon Perceived
    Speech Organization.   M. A.   San Jose.   1968.   2343

Green, Charles P.   Conceptions of Rhetorical Delivery.   Ph. D.
    Northwestern.   1948.   2344

Griffin, Robert S.   A Historical and Psychological Study of the Con-
    viction-Persuasion Concept in Public Speaking.   Ph. D.   S. Cal-
    ifornia.   1942.   2345

Grissinger, James A.   An Analysis and Evaluation of the Use of an
    Electronic "Opinion Meter" in Measuring the Comparative Effect
    upon Audience Opinion of Panel Discussion and Formal Debate.
    M. A.   Ohio State.   1949.   2346

Gulley, Halbert E.   A Study of the Relative Effectiveness of Debate
    and Discussion upon Audience Opinion.   M. A.   Iowa.   1941. 2347

Haiman, Franklyn S.   An Experimental Study of the Effects of Ethos
    in Public Speaking.   M. A.   Northwestern.   1948.   2348

Halley, Richard D.   An Experimental Study of the Effects of Dogma-
    tism and Source Credibility on the Effectiveness of Persuasion
    Communications.   M. A.   Bowling Green.   1965.   2349

Haney, William V.   Measurement of the Ability to Discriminate Be-
    tween Inferential and Descriptive Statements.   Ph. D.   North-

western.   1953.   2350

Hansen, Edna.   An Experimental Study of the Effect of Negative
and Positive Argument on the Attitude of Listeners.   M. A.
Minnesota.   1936.   2351

Hansen, Norman J.   Audience Interest Factors in Debate.   M. A.
Nobraska.   1949.   2352

Hayes, Harold B.   Source Credibility and Documentation as Factors
of Persuasion in International Propaganda.   Ph. D.   Iowa.   1966.
                                                                        2353
Hettinger, E.   A Study of the Treatment of Speech Purposes by
Writers on Rhetoric.   M. A.   Wisconsin.   1927.   2354

Hildreth, Richard.   Experimental Study of Audiences' Ability to Distinguish between Sincere and Insincere Speakers.   Ph. D.   S. California.   1953.   2355

Irwin, Ramon L.   A Survey of Principles of Disposition in Speech
Making.   M. A.   Cornell.   1937.   2356

Jones, Merritt B.   An Experimental Study of the Effects of Speech
Rate on Audience Judgments in Debate Situations.   Ph. D.   S.
California.   1956.   2357

Judd, Larry.   The Relative Effectiveness of Face-to-Face and Recorded Persuasive Speeches in Attitude Change.   M. A.   Oklahoma.   1964.   2358

Kiepe, Paul E.   An Empirical Approach to Persuasion.   M. A.   S.
California.   1933.   2359

Kimball, Emily A.   The Use and Abuse of the Appeal to Human
Drives in Persuasion.   M. A.   Northwestern.   1923.   2360

Kipp, Eugene W.   A Synthesis of Recent Persuasive Theory.   M. A.
Miami Univ. of Ohio.   1969.   2361

Locke, Charlton.   The Psychology of Speaking to an Audience.   M. A.
Ohio Wesleyan.   1920.   2362

Lomas, Charles W.   An Experimental Study of Some of the Effects
of Provocative Language on Audience Reaction to Political
Speeches.   Ph. D.   Northwestern.   1940.   2363

Losee, George D.   A Test of the Law of Primacy in Agree, Neutral,
and Disagree Attitude Conditions.   M. A.   Colorado State.   1970.
                                                                        2364
Ludlum, Thomas S.   A Study of Techniques for Increasing the
Credibility of a Communication.   Ph. D.   Ohio.   1956.   2365

Lull, Paul E.   An Objective Study of the Effectiveness of Humor in

Persuasive Speeches.   Ph. D.   Wisconsin.   1939.   2366

Lundman, Alma T.   Humor as Interpreted by the American Audience.
M. A.   Wisconsin.   1937.   2367

Marsh, Patrick O.   An Empirical Study of the Effects of Two Types
of Conflict-Arousing Arguments upon Retention and Attitude Change.
Ph. D.   Washington.   1961.   2368

McCroskey, James C.   Experimental Studies of the Effect of Ethos
and Evidence in Persuasive Communication.   D. Ed.   Penn State.
1966.   2369

Messner, Carolann G.   Some Aspects of Ethos as Compared with
Other Persuasive Devices.   M. A.   Akron.   1967.   2370

Miller, Fred R.   An Experiment to Determine the Effect Organization Has on the Immediate and Delayed Recall of Information.
M. A.   Miami.   1966.   2371

Nebergall, Roger E.   An Experimental Study of Rhetorical Theory.
Ph. D.   Illinois.   1956.   2372

Norton, Robert W.   A Dissonance Approach to Persuasion.   M. A.
New Mexico.   1969.   2373

Ostermeier, Terry H.   An Experimental Study of the Type and Frequency of Reference as Used by an Unfamiliar Source in a Message and Its Effect Upon Perceived Credibility and Attitude Change.
M. A.   Michigan State.   1966.   2374

Pokorny, Gary F.   An Experimental Study of the Impact of Satiric
Material Included in an Argumentative Speech.   M. A.   Nebraska.
1965.   2375

Pross, Edward L.   A Critical Analysis of Certain Aspects of Ethical Proof.   Ph. D.   Iowa.   1942.   2376

Richardson, Don R.   A Study of the Effectiveness of Various Posi-
tionings of Ethical, Logical, and Emotional Arguments in a Persuasive Speech.   Ph. D.   Ohio.   1964.   2377

Rickard, Paul B.   An Evaluation of Various Types of Oral Presentation in Terms of Audience Comprehension.   M. A.   Wayne State.
1939.   2378

Roerig, Ronnie A.   A Survey of Rhetoric, 1950 to 1970.   M. A.
Colorado State.   1970.   2379

Samples, Eual M.   An Experimental Study of the Effectiveness of
Scripture in Persuasive Speeches Upon Attitudes of the Audience.
M. A.   S. Mississippi.   1956.   2380

Sawyer, Thomas M., Jr. Shift of Attitude Following Persuasion as Related to Estimate of Majority Attitude. Ph.D. Michigan. 1953. 2381

Schrader, Helen W. Approach to the Study of Rhetorical Style. Ph.D. Northwestern. 1949. 2382

Simonson, Solomon. Restatement of Rhetoric: Its Nature, Purpose, and Place in Society. M.A. Brooklyn College. 1939. 2383

Sponberg, Harold E. An Experimental Study of the Relative Effectiveness of Climax and Anti-Climax. M.A. Minnesota. 1942. 2384

Stachowiak, Ray J. The Relationship Between Change in Attitudes and the Ability to Re-evaluate Arguments. Ph.D. Wisc. 1940. 2385

Talley, Charles H. A Study of Motivation, Particularly to the Problem of the Public Speaker. M.A. Northwestern. 1931. 2386

Taylor, Vernon L. The Concept of Illustration in Rhetorical Theory. Ph.D. Northwestern. 1959. 2387

Tiffany, Albert C. Ethos and Argument: Oral Persuasion in Legislative Advocacy. M.A. California, Santa Barbara. 1968. 2388

Tucker, Raymond K. An Experimental Study of the Effects of the Implicative Sequence in Persuasive Speaking. Ph.D. Northwestern. 1956. 2389

Utzinger, V.A. An Experimental Study of the Effects of Verbal Fluency upon the Listener. Ph.D. S. California. 1952. 2390

Wagener, Billy B. An Experimental Examination of Continuance and Context Effect as a Result of the Use of a "Contradictor" in a Persuasive Communication Series. Ph.D. Ohio State. 1968. 2391

Wagner, Gerard A. An Experimental Study of the Relative Effectiveness of Varying Amounts of Evidence in a Persuasive Communication. M.A. S. Mississippi. 1958. 2392

Walter, Otis M., Jr. The Measurement of Ethos. Ph.D. Northwestern. 1948. 2393

Watling, Thomas O. The Effects of Audience Orientation on Concept Meaning and Opinion Change. Ph.D. Denver. 1967. 2394

Welch, Charles E. Subjective Probability and Source Credibility. Ph.D. Denver. 1969. 2395

Welden, Terry A. The Effect on Attitudes and Retention of Message Order in Controversial Material. Ph.D. Michigan State. 1961. 2396

Weston, John R.   Argumentative Message Structure and Prior Familiarity as Predictors of Source Credibility and Attitude Change.
Ph. D.   Michigan State.   1967.   2397

Wills, John W.   An Empirical Study of the Behavioral Characteristics of Sincere and Insincere Speakers.   Ph. D.   S. California.
1960.   (Abstract by Milton Dickens in SM, 28 (June, 1961), 77.)
                                                                 2398

3. Articles

Adams, H. F.   The Effect of Climax and Anticlimax Order.   JAP,
4 (December, 1920), 330-38.   2399

Adams, W. Clifton.   The Interrelationships Among Need for Social
Approval, Persuasibility and Activation.   CSSJ, 23 (Fall, 1972),
188-192.   2400

Albert, Stuart, and Dabbs, James M. , Jr.   Physical Distance and
Persuasion.   JPES, 15 (1970), 265-270.   (Suggests that persuasion is affected by speaker's distance from the audience.)   2401

Allport, Gordon W.   Attitudes.   In Handbook of Social Psychology,
edited by Carl Murchison.   Worcester, Mass. , Clark University
Press, 1935.   Pp. 798-844.   2402

Aly, Bower.   Rhetoric: Its Natural Enemies.   ST, 17 (January,
1969), 1-10.   2403

Anderson, Dwight.   What is Propaganda?   PN, 6 (November, 1939),
18; 22-3.   2404

Anderson, John R.   The Audience as a Concept in the Philosophic
Rhetoric of Perelman, Johnstone, and Natanson.   SSCJ, 38 (Fall,
1972), 39-50.   2405

Anderson, Kenneth, and Clevenger, Theodore, Jr.   A Summary of
Experimental Research in Ethos.   SM, 30 (June, 1963), 59-78.
                                                                 2406
Angell, Ernest.   Some Experiments in Group Persuasion.   JES, 19
(September, 1945), 57-8.   2407

Arnold, Carroll C.   Perelman's New Rhetoric.   QJS, 56 (February,
1970), 87-92.   2408

_____.   Rhetorical and Communication Studies: Two Worlds or
One?   WS, 36 (Spring, 1972), 75-81.   2409

Aronson, Elliot, and Golden, Burton W.   The Effect of Relevant and
Irrelevant Aspects of Communicator Credibility on Opinion Change.
JPer, 30 (1962), 135-46.   2410

Asch, S. E. , Block, Helen, and Hertzman, Max.   Studies in the

Principles of Judgments and Attitudes: 1. Two Basis Principles of Judgment. JPsy, 5 (April, 1938), 251ff.   2411

Baker, Eldon E., and Redding, W. Charles. The Effects of Perceived Tallness in Persuasive Speaking: an Experiment. JC, 12 (1962), 51-3.   2412

Baldwin, Charles S. College Teaching of Rhetoric. ER, 48 (June, 1914), 1-20.   2413

Baskerville, Barnet. In the Regional Journals. QJS, 43 (1957), 179-84. (Critical commentary on articles on rhetoric found in the regional speech journals.)   2414

Bauer, E. Jackson. Opinion Change in a Public Controversy. POQ, 26 (1962), 212-26.   2415

Bauer, Raymond A. The Communicator and the Audience. In People, Society and Mass Communication, ed. Lewis A. Dexter and David M. White. New York, Macmillan, 1964.   2416

_____. The Obstinate Audience. APsy, 19 (1964), 319-328. 2417

Becker, Samuel L. Research on Emotional and Logical Proofs. SSJ, 28 (Spring, 1963), 198-207.   2418

Beighley, Kenneth C. An Experimental Study of the Effect of Four Speech Variables on Listener Comprehension. SM, 19 (November, 1952), 249-58.   2419

_____. An Experimental Study of the Effect of Three Speech Variables on Listener Comprehension. SM, 21 (November, 1954), 248-53.   2420

Bennett, William H. The Role of Debate in Speech Communication. ST, 21 (November, 1972), 281-288.   2421

Berlo, David K., and Gulley, Halbert E. Some Determinants of the Effect of Oral Communication in Producing Attitude Change and Learning. SM, 24 (March, 1957), 10-20.   2422

Bernays, Edward L. The Engineering of Consent. AAA, 250 (1947), 113-21. ("Concept of persuasion in a complex society.")   2423

Bettinghaus, Erwin P. The Operation of Congruity in an Oral Communication Situation. SM, 28 (August, 1961), 131-142.   2424

_____. Cognitive Balance and the Development of Meaning. JC, 13 (June, 1963), 94-105.   2425

Black, John W. A Basis for Speech Study. F, 35 (March, 1950), 55-58, 72. (On the importance of rhetoric in speech education.)   2426

Block, Ralph.   Propaganda and the Free Society.   POQ, 12 (1948-
    49), 677-86.   2427

Bloom, Margaret.   Rhetoric For Anti-Rhetoricians.   SchS, 31 (Jan-
    uary 4, 1930), 18-19.   2428

Bonner, Stanley F.   Rhetorica.   CR, 61 (December, 1947), 84-6.
                                                                     2429
Bostrom, Robert N. , and Tucker, Raymond K.   Evidence, Person-
    ality, and Attitude Change.   SM, 36 (March, 1969), 22-27. 2430

Bowers, John W.   The Congruity Principle of Oral Communication.
    CSSJ, 14 (May, 1963), 88-91.   2431

_____.   Language Intensity, Social Introversion, and Attitude
    Change.   SM, 30 (November, 1963), 345-352.   2432

_____ and Phillips, William A.   A Note on the Generality of Source-
    Credibility Scales.   SM, 34 (June, 1967), 185-186.   2433

Brake, Robert J.   The Substance of Rhetoric: Good Reasons: Aris-
    totle Re-Examined.   QJS, 50 (April, 1964), 184-185.   (Comment
    on Karl R. Wallace, infra.)   2434

Brandenburg, Ernest S.   Factors in Listening to Informative and
    Persuasive Speeches.   CSSJ, 5 (Fall, 1953), 12-15.   2435

Brembeck, W. L.   Content of a College Course in Persuasion.   ST,
    13 (November, 1964), 277-282.   2436

Brigance, William N.   Can We Redefine the James Winans Theory
    of Persuasion?   QJS, 21 (February, 1935), 19-26.   2437

_____.   A Genetic Approach to Persuasion.   QJS, 17 (June, 1931),
    329-39.   2438

Brockriede, Wayne.   Toward a Contemporary Aristotelian Theory of
    Rhetoric.   QJS, 52 (February, 1966), 33-40.   2439

_____.   Dimensions of the Concept of Rhetoric.   QJS, 54 (Febru-
    ary, 1968), 1-12.   2440

Brown, Charles T.   An Experimental Diagnosis of Thinking on Con-
    troversial Issues.   SM, 17 (November, 1950), 370-377.   (Con-
    cludes that men and women do not differ significantly in choosing
    the best reason in support of a conclusion.)   2441

Bryant, Donald C.   Some Problems of Scope and Method in Rhetori-
    cal Scholarship.   QJS, 23 (April, 1937), 182-9.   2442

_____.   Rhetoric: Its Functions and Its Scope.   QJS, 39 (1953),
    401-424.   2443

Burtt, H. E., and Falkenberg, D. B. The Influence of Majority and
Expert Opinion on Religious Attitudes. JSP, 14 (November,
1941), 269-78. 2444

Butler, Jack H. Russian Rhetoric: A Discipline Manipulated by
Communism. QJS, 50 (October, 1964), 229-240. 2445

Callaghan, J. C., ed. A Symposium: Other Available Means of
Persuasion. TS, 3 (November, 1955), 26-34. (The articles include: Angell, Clarence S., "From the Discipline of Philosophy," 26-9; Ness, Ordean G., "From the Discipline of Social
Psychology," 29-32; and Smith, Charles D., "From the Discipline of Literary Criticism," 33-4.) 2446

———. Social Facilitation in Persuasion. QJS, 26 (December,
1940), 643-56. 2447

Campbell, Ernest Q. Scale and Intensity Analysis in the Study of
Attitude Change. POQ, 26 (1962), 227-35. 2448

Carmack, William R., Jr., and Phifer, Gregg. An Experiment
Comparing Discussion with Debate. SSJ, 21 (Spring, 1956), 189-
94. (On the effects of information on an audience.) 2449

Cartier, Francis A. Listenability and "Human Interest." SM, 22
(March, 1955), 53-56. 2450

Cervin, V. B., and Henderson, G. P. Statistical Theory of Persuasion. PsyR, 68 (May, 1961), 157-66. 2451

Chapman, Hugh H., Jr. Persuasion and Sweet Talk. TS, 5 (September, 1957), 5. (On the derivation of the word "persuasion.")
2452

Chen, William K-C. The Influence of Oral Propaganda upon Students' Attitudes. AP, 150 (April, 1933), 5-43. 2453

Clarke, Peter, and James, Jim. The Effects of Situation, Attitude
Intensity and Personality on Information-Seeking. So, 30 (1967),
235-245. (Indicates that persons preparing a discussion or debate tend to seek information which supports attitudes already
held.) 2454

Collie, M. J. Information vs. Persuasion: A Note on Critical
Method. Essays in Criticism (Oxford), 6 (1956), 241-5. 2455

Collins, George R. The Relative Effectiveness of the Condensed
and Extended Motive Appeal. QJS, 10 (June, 1924), 221-30. 2456

Cook, Thomas D. Competence, Counter-arguing, and Attitude
Change. JPer, 37 (1969), 342-358. (Report of two studies
which examine relationships among source credibility, arguments,
and attitude change.) 2457

Covington, Harry F.   On Imaginative Suggestion.   QJS, 2 (April,
    1916), 180-85.   (As related to argument and debate.)   2458

Cowan, Phillip A., Weber, J., Hodinott, B.A., and Klein, J.
    Mean Length of Spoken Response as a Function of Stimulus, Ex-
    perimenter, and Subject.   ChD, 38 (March, 1967), 191-203. 2459

Crane, Edgar.   Immunization: With and Without Use of Counter-
    Arguments.   JQ, 39 (1962), 445-50.   (An experiment to test the
    effect of the first controversial speech on an audience and the ef-
    fect of subsequent arguments.)   2460

Crane, Loren D.   Toward a Theory of Arrangement.   QJS, 1 (1962),
    11-17.   2461

Crocker, Lionel.   Repetition in Public Address.   EJ, 16 (September,
    1927), 510-14.   2462

_____ .   The Rhetorical Theory of Harry Emerson Fosdick.   QJS,
    22 (April, 1936), 207-13.   2463

Cromwell, Harvey.   An Experimental Design for Determining In-
    duced Changes in the Attitudes of Others.   SSJ, 16 (March, 1951),
    198-206.   2464

_____ .   The Persistency of the Effect of Argumentative Speeches.
    QJS, 41 (April, 1955), 154-58.   2465

_____ .   The Persistency of the Effect on Audience Attitude of the
    First Versus the Second Argumentative Speech of a Series.   SM,
    21 (November, 1954), 280-84.   2466

_____ .   The Relative Effect on Audience Attitude of the First
    Versus the Second Argumentative Speech of a Series.   SM, 17
    (June, 1950), 105-22.   2467

Cronkhite, Gary L.   Logic, Emotion, and the Paradigm of Persua-
    sion.   QJS, 50 (February, 1964), 13-18.   2468

_____ .   Toward a Real Test of Dissonance Theory.   QJS, 52
    (April, 1966), 172-178.   2469

Day, Dennis G.   Persuasion and the Concepts of Identification.   QJS,
    46 (October, 1960), 270-73.   2470

Dearin, Ray D.   The Philosophical Basis of Chaim Perelman's The-
    ory of Rhetoric.   QJS, 55 (October, 1969), 213-224.   2471

Demos, Raphael.   Art of Communication or Rhetoric.   JGE, 1 (Jan-
    uary, 1947), 136-42.   2472

Dietrich, John E.   The Relative Effectiveness of Two Modes of Radio
    Delivery in Influencing Attitudes.   SM, 13 (No. 1, 1946), 58-66.
                                                                  2473

Doob, Leonard W.   Some Factors Determining Change in Attitude.
    JASP, 35 (October, 1940), 549-65.   2474

Dresser, William R.   Studies of the Effects of Evidence: Implica-
    tions for Forensics.   AFAR, 10 (Fall, 1962), 14-19.   2475

Duhamel, P. Albert.   The Function of Rhetoric as Effective Expres-
    sion.   JHI, 10 (1949), 344-56.   2476

Edwards, A. L.   Political Frames of Reference as a Factor Influ-
    encing Recognition.   JASP, 30 (January, 1941), 34-50.   2477

Edwards, Allen, and Kilpatrick, F. P.   A Technique for the Con-
    struction of Attitude Scales.   JAP, 32 (October, 1948), 374-84.
                                                                2478

Ehninger, Douglas.   On Rhetoric and Rhetorics.   WS, 31 (Fall,
    1967), 242-249.   2479

_____.   Validity as Moral Obligation.   SSJ, 33 (Spring, 1968),
    215-222.   2480

Ehrensberger, Ray.   An Experimental Study of the Relative Effec-
    tiveness of Certain Forms of Emphasis in Public Speaking.   SM,
    12 (1945), 94-111.   2481

Ernest, Carole H.   Listening Comprehension as a Function of Type
    of Material and Rate of Presentation.   SM, 35 (June, 1968), 154-
    158.   2482

Eubanks, Ralph T. , and Baker, Virgil L.   Toward an Axiology of
    Rhetoric.   QJS, 48 (April, 1962), 157-68.   2483

Ewing, T. N.   A Study of Certain Factors Involved in Changes of
    Opinion.   JSP, 16 (August, 1942), 63-88.   2484

Feather, N. T. , and Armstrong, D. J.   Effects of Variations in
    Source Attitude, Receiver Attitude, and Communication Stand on
    Reactions to Source and Content of Communications.   JPer, 35
    (September, 1967), 435-455.   2485

_____ and Jeffries, D. G.   Balancing and Extremity Effects in Re-
    actions of Receiver to Source and Content of Communications.
    Jper, 35 (June, 1967), 194-213.   2486

Fest, Thorrel B.   The Place of Persuasion.   WS, 22 (Summer,
    1958), 141-48.   2487

Fisher, Walter R.   Advisory Rhetoric: Implications for Forensic
    Debate.   WS, 29 (Spring, 1965), 114-119.   2488

_____.   Rhetoric: A Pedagogic Definition.   WS, 25 (1961), 168-
    70.   2489

Frank, Jerome D. Experimental Studies of Personal Pressure and
Resistance. JGP, 30 (January, 1944), 23-64.   2490

Freedman, Philip I. Race as a Factor in Persuasion. JEE, 35
(Spring, 1967), 48-51.   2491

Fried, Edrita. Techniques of Persuasion. In Propaganda by Short
Wave, ed. by H. L. Childs and John B. Whitton. Princeton,
New Jersey, Princeton, 1942. Pp. 261-302.   2492

Fulton, R. Barry. Motivation: Foundation of Persuasion. QJS,
48 (April, 1962), 295-307.   2493

Furbay, Albert L. The Influence of Scattered versus Compact Seating on Audience Response. SM, 32 (June, 1965), 144-148. 2494

Gard, Willis L. A Preliminary Study of the Psychology of Reasoning. AJPsy, 18 (October, 1907), 490-504.   2495

Giffin, Kim. Sensitivity Training: A Fool's Paradise. JAFA, 1
(January, 1964), 21-22.   2496

_____ and Warner, Donald. A Study of the Influence of an Audience on the Rate of Speech in Tournament Debates. S, 45 (November, 1962), 10-13.   2497

Gilkinson, Howard. The Influence of Party Preference upon the Responses of an Audience to a Political Speech. So, 5 (January,
1942), 72-79.   2498

_____, Paulson, Stanley F., and Sikkink, Donald E. Effects of
Order and Authority in an Argumentative Speech. QJS, 40 (April,
1954), 183-92.   2499

Gislason, Haldor B. An Approach to Persuasion. QJS, 19 (April,
1933), 175-86.   2500

Gonchar, Ruth M. Common Ground: Positive and Negative Identification. SPG, 8 (January, 1971), 45-48.   2501

Gouran, Dennis S. Attitude Change and Listeners' Understanding of
a Persuasive Communication. ST, 15 (November, 1966), 289-
294.   2502

Graham, Gladys M. More Implication. QJS, 12 (April, 1926), 196-
97.   2503

Graves, Harold F. Public Speaking in Propaganda. QJS, 27 (February, 1941), 29-39.   2504

Gray, Giles W. Gestalt Again. QJS, 18 (February, 1929), 85-92.
                                                         2505
_____. Gestalt, Behavior and Speech. QJS, 14 (June, 1928), 334-

59. (Rejoinder to W. M. Parrish's "Implications of Gestalt Psychology," QJS, infra.) 2506

Greenberg, Bradley S., and Miller, Gerald R. The Effects of Low Credible Sources in Message Acceptance. SM, 33 (June, 1966), 127-136. 2507

Greenwald, A. G. Behavior Change Following a Persuasive Communication. JPer, 33 (September, 1965), 370-391. 2508

Gregory, Joshua. The Relation Between the Word and the Unconscious. BJP, 10 (November, 1919), 66-80. 2509

Grissinger, James A. The Comparative Influence on Opinion of Panel Discussion and Formal Debate. SM, 22 (March, 1955), 60-67. 2510

Gruner, Charles R. A Further Experimental Study of Satire as Persuasion. SM, 33 (June, 1966), 184-185. 2511

_____. An Experimental Study of Satire as Persuasion. SM, 32 (June, 1965), 149-153. 2512

_____. Effect of Humor on Speaker Ethos and Audience Information Gain. JC, 17 (September, 1967), 228-233. 2513

Guiliani, Allesandro. The Influence of Rhetoric on the Law of Evidence and Pleading. JR, 7 (1962), 216-51. 2514

Hagan, Michael R. A Missing Chapter in Argumentation Texts. JAFA, 9 (Summer, 1972), 274-278. 2515

Halle, Louis J. Raw Materials of Persuasion. SaR, 33 (March 11, 1950), 9-10; 34-8. 2516

Hammond, Lewis M. Rhetoric and Dialectic. In Eastern Public Speaking Conference, ed. by H. F. Harding. New York, Wilson, 1940. Pp. 173-82. 2517

Harding, Harold F., and Utterback, William E. Factors Conditioning Response to Argument. SM, 22 (November, 1955), 303-308. 2518

Harms, L. S. Listener Judgments of Status Cues In Speech. QJS, 47 (April, 1961), 164-168. 2519

Harrington, Elbert W. The Academic and Rhetorical Modes of Thought. QJS, 42 (February, 1956), 25-30. 2520

_____. A Modern Approach to Invention. QJS, 48 (December, 1962), 373-8. 2521

Hartmann, George W. Immediate and Remote Goals as Political Motives. JASP, 33 (January, 1938), 86-99. 2522

_____. Experiment on Comparative Effectiveness of "Emotional" and "Rational" Political Leaflets. JASP, 21 (1936), 99-114. 2523

Hay, D.   Debate and the Measurement of Attitudes.   QJS, 22 (February, 1936), 62-66.   2524

Heinberg, P.   Relationships of Content and Delivery to General Effectiveness.   SM, 30 (June, 1963), 105-107.   2525

Heisey, D. Ray.   H. J. C. Grierson--Modern Scottish Rhetorician. WS, 30 (Fall, 1966), 248-251.   2526

Higgins, Howard H.   Bases of Influencing Behavior Through Speech: Psychology in the Public Speaking Course.   In A Program of Speech Education in a Democracy, ed. by W. A. Cable.   Boston, Expression, 1932.   Pp. 210-16.   2527

_____. Psychology in Speech-Making.   EQ, 13 (May, 1933), 5-6.
                                                                                                          2528
_____. How Audiences Help to Improve Debating.   G, 12 (January, 1930), 9.   2529

Hochmuth, Marie.   Kenneth Burke and the "New Rhetoric."   QJS, 37 (April, 1952), 133-44.   2530

Holtzman, Paul D.   Confirmation of Ethos as a Confounding Element in Communication Research.   SM, 33 (November, 1966), 464-466.
                                                                                                          2531
Hoshor, John P.   Lectures on Rhetoric and Public Speaking by Chauncey Allen Goodrich.   SM, 14 (1947), 1-37.   2532

Hovland, I., and Mandell, W.   An Experimental Comparison of Conclusion-Drawing by the Communicator and by the Audience. JASP, 47 (July, 1952), 581-88.   2533

_____ and Weiss, W.   The Influence of Source Credibility on Communication Effectiveness.   POQ, 15 (Winter, 1951), 635-50. 2534

How to Detect Propaganda.   PN, 6 (November, 1939), 19-22.   (Reprinted from the Bulletin of the Institute of Propaganda Analysis.)   2535

Howell, Wilbur S.   Role of Persuasion in Debate.   AFAR, 10 (Fall, 1962), 20-23.   2536

Howes, Raymond F.   In Defense of Rhetoric.   QJS, 15 (February, 1929), 80-5.   2537

_____. Rhetoric--the Useful Art of Influencing an Audience.   SC, 22 (May, 1936), 199-200.   2538

Hudson, Hoyt T.   Can We Modernize the Theory of Invention?   QJS, 7 (November, 1921), 324-34.   2539

_____. The Field of Rhetoric. QJS, 9 (April, 1923), 167-80.
                                                                2540

Hunt, Everett L. Rhetoric and General Education. QJS, 35 (October, 1949), 275-79.   2541

Hyman, Herbert H., and Sheatsley, Paul B. Some Reasons Why Information Campaigns Fail. POQ, 11 (Fall, 1947), 412-23.2542

Irwin, Charles E. Effective Teaching is Salesmanship. TS, 4 (January, 1956), 18-19.   2543

Janis, Irving L., and Feshbach, S. Effects of Fear-Arousing Communications. JASP, 48 (January, 1953), 78-92.   2544

_____ and Field, Peter B. A Behavioral Assessment of Persuasibility: Consistency of Individual Differences. So, 19 (1956), 241-59.   2545

_____ and Milholland, H. C., Jr. The Influence of Threat Appeals on Selective Learning of the Content of a Persuasive Communication. JPol, 37 (January, 1954), 75-80.   2546

Jarrett, R. F., and Sheriffs, Alex C. Propaganda, Debate, and Impartial Presentation as Determiners of Attitude Change. JASP, 48 (January, 1953), 33-41.   2547

Jenness, Arthur. Social Influences in the Change of Opinion. JASP, 27 (April-June, 1932), 29-34.   2548

Johannesen, Richard J. Richard Weaver's View of Rhetoric and Criticism. SSJ, 32 (Winter, 1966), 133-145.   2549

Johnson, [Sarett] Alma. Propaganda Analysis and Public Speaking. SSJ, 4 (January, 1939), 12-15.   2550

Johnstone, Henry W., Jr. The Relevance of Rhetoric to Philosophy and of Philosophy to Rhetoric. QJS, 52 (February, 1966), 41-46.   2551

Jones, Ernest. Rationalization in Everyday Life. JASP, 3 (August-September, 1908), 161-69.   2552

Jones, R. A., and Brehm, J. W. Persuasiveness of One- and Two-sided Communications as a Function of Awareness There Are Two Sides. JSP, 6 (1970), 47-56.   2553

Jones, Richard F. Moral Sense of Simplicity; the Anti-Rhetorical Movement. Washington University Studies in Language and Literature, No. 14 (1942), 265-87.   2554

Judson, Lyman S. Stressing the "Exact" Audience Situation. Speech Bulletin. Supp. QJS, 3 (December, 1930), 10-13. (Recommends that debate be adapted to the audience.)   2555

Katz, Daniel. Psychological Barriers to Communication. AAA, 250 (March, 1947), 17-25.   2556

Kay, Lillian. An Experimental Approach to Prestige Suggestion. JPsy, 24 (July, 1947), 71-82.   2557

Kelman, H. C., and Hovland, C. I. "Reinstatement" of the Communicator in Delayed Measurement of Opinion Change. JASP, 48 (July, 1953), 327-35.   2558

Kerr, Harry P. The Rhetoric of Political Protest. QJS, 45 (April, 1959), 146-52.   2559

King, Thomas R. An Experimental Study of the Effect of Ethos upon the Immediate and Delayed Recall of Information. CSSJ, 17 (February, 1966), 22-28.   2560

Kirkendall, Lester. A Study of the Changes, Formation, and Persistence of Attitudes of Pacifism. JES, 2 (December, 1937), 222-8.   2561

Klapper, Joseph T. Mass Media and the Engineering of Consent. AS, 17 (Autumn, 1948), 419-29.   2562

Klapper, Paul, et. al. A Symposium on Rhetoric and General Education. QJS, 35 (December, 1949), 419-26.   2563

Knower, Franklin H. I. A Study of the Effect of Oral Argument on Changes of Attitude. JSP, 6 (August, 1935), 315-47.   2564

_____. II. A Study of the Effect of Printed Argument on Changes in Attitude. JASP, 30 (January-March, 1936), 522-32.   2565

_____. III. Experimental Studies of Changes in Attitude--Some Incidence of Attitude Changes. JAP, 20 (February, 1936), 114-27.   2566

Kretsinger, Elwood A. An Experimental Study of Gross Bodily Movement as an Index to Audience Interest. SM, 19 (November, 1952), 244-48.   2567

Kriesberg, Martin. Opinion Research and Public Policy. IJOAR, 3 (1949), 373-84.   2568

Kruger, Arthur N. Speech Communication and Debate. SSCJ, 39 (Spring, 1974), 233-40. (A rejoinder to William H. Bennett, supra.)   2569

Krugman, Herbert E. The Role of Resistance in Propaganda. IJOAR, 3 (1949), 235-50.   2570

Kulp, D. H. Prestige as Measured by Single-Experience Changes and Their Permanency. JER, 27 (April, 1934), 663-72.   2571

Lambertson, Floyd W.   The Persuasive Value of Humor.   EQ, 16
(November, 1935), 9-10.   2572

_____.   The Psychology of Conciliation.   G, 18 (May, 1936), 53-
55.   2573

La Russo, Dominic A.   Rhetorical Education: Italy, 1300-1450.
WS, 24 (Autumn, 1960), 213-19.   2574

Lawson, Robert G.   The Law of Primacy in the Criminal Courtroom.   JSP, 77 (1969), 121-131.   2575

Lee, Irving J.   Some Conceptions of Emotional Appeal in Rhetorical
Theory.   SM, 6 (1939), 66-86.   2576

Lemmon, Martha L.   A Psychological Consideration of Analogy.
AJPsy, 51 (April, 1938), 304-56.   2577

Leventhal, Howard, and Perloe, Stanley.   Relationship between Self-
Esteem and Persuasibility.   JASP, 64 (1962), 385-388.   2578

Lindsley, Charles F.   A Footnote in the Psychology of Persuasion.
QJS, 7 (June, 1921), 233-57.   2579

Logue, Cal M.   Persuasion as an Aspect of Problem-Solving.   ST,
22 (January, 1973), 81-82.   2580

Long, Chester C.   The Substance of Rhetoric: Good Reasons: Reason vs. Substance.   QJS, 50 (April, 1964), 182-184.   (Comment
on Karl R. Wallace, infra.)   2581

Lorge, Irving.   Prestige, Suggestion, and Attitudes.   JSP, 7 (November, 1936), 386-402.   2582

Luchins, A. S., and Luchins, E. H.   The Effects of Order of Presentation of Information and Explanatory Models.   JSP, 80 (1970),
63-70.   2583

Ludlum, Thomas S.   Effects of Certain Techniques of Credibility
upon Audience Attitude.   SM, 25 (November, 1958), 278-84. 2584

Lull, P. E.   The Effectiveness of Humor in Persuasive Speeches.
SM, 7 (1940), 26-40.   2585

Lumsdaine, Arthur, and Janis, Irving L.   Resistance to "Counter-
propaganda" Produced by One-Sided and Two-Sided "Propaganda"
Presentations.   POQ, 17 (1953), 53-4.   2586

Lund, Frederick H.   The Psychology of Belief.   JASP, 20 (April,
1925), 63-81; 20 (July, 1925), 174-96.   2587

Lundy, Richard M., Simonson, Norman R., and Landers, Audrey
D.   Conformity, Persuasibility, and Irrelevant Fear.   JC, 17

(March, 1967), 39-54.   2588

Lurie, Walter A.   The Measurement of Prestige and Prestige-Sug-
gestibility.   JASP, 9 (May, 1939), 219-25.   2589

Marple, C. H.   The Comparative Susceptibility of Three Age Levels
to the Suggestion of Group Versus Expert Opinion.   JSP, 4 (May,
1933), 176-86.   2590

Maslow, A. H.   A Theory of Human Motivation.   PsyR, 50 (July,
1943), 370-96.   2591

Matthews, Jack.   The Effect of Loaded Language on Audience Comprehension of Speeches.   SM, 14 (1947), 176-86.   2592

Matthews, James B.   Persuasion and Controversy.   Ou, 82 (January 13, 1906), 86-91.   2593

McCroskey, James C.   Scales for the Measurement of Ethos.   SM,
33 (March, 1966), 65-72.   2594

_____ and Dunham, Robert E.   Ethos: A Confounding Element in
Communication Research.   SM, 33 (November, 1966), 456-463.
                                                                 2595
_____ and Mehrley, R. Samuel.   The Effects of Disorganization
and Non-Fluency on Attitude Change and Source Credibility.   SM,
36 (March, 1969), 13-21.   2596

McEwan, W. J., and Greenberg, B. S.   The Effects of Message Intensity on Receiver Evaluations of Source, Message and Topic.
JC, 20 (1970), 340-50.   (More intense messages were judged
clearer and more credible than less intense messages.)   2597

McGuire, William J.   The Effectiveness of Supportive and Refuta-
tional Defenses in Minimizing and Restoring Beliefs Afainst Persuasion.   So, 24 (1961), 184-97.   2598

_____ .   Resistance to Persuasion Conferred by Active and Passive
Prior Refutation of the Same and Alternative Counter-Arguments.
JASP, 63 (1961), 326-32.   2599

McKean, Dayton D.   Public Speaking and Public Opinion.   QJS, 17
(November, 1931), 510-22.   2600

McKeon, Richard.   Discourse, Demonstration, Verification, and
Justification.   LoA, 41-42 (June, 1968), 37-63.   (Argues that the
rhetoric of Aristotle has been broadened to become, "...a new
architectonic art which transforms the methods of inquiry and
discussions in all fields. ")   2601

Mehling, Reuben.   A Study of Non-Logical Factors of Reasoning in
the Communication Process.   JC, 9 (September, 1959), 118-126.
                                                                 2602

Menefee, Selden C.   The Effect of Stereotyped Words on Political
     Judgments.   ASR, 1 (August, 1936), 514-21.   2603

_____.   Scare Words and the Public.   NR, 87 (July 15, 1936),
     291-2.   2604

_____ and Granneberg, Audrey G.   Propaganda and Opinions on
     Foreign Policy.   JSP, 11 (May, 1940), 393-404.   2605

Miller, Gerald R., and Basehart, John.   Source Trustworthiness,
     Opinionated Statements, and Response to Persuasive Communica-
     tion.   SM, 36 (March, 1969), 1-7.   ("Examined the persuasive-
     ness of communications stressing the harmful social consequences
     of failure to conform with message recommendations.")   2606

_____ and Hewgill, Murray A.   The Effect of Variations in Non-
     Fluency on Audience Ratings of Source Credibility.   QJS, 50
     (February, 1964), 36-44.   2607

Millson, William A. D.   Experimental Work in Audience Reaction.
     QJS, 18 (February, 1932), 13-30.   2608

_____.   Problems in Measuring Audience Reactions.   QJS, 18 (No-
     vember, 1932), 621-37.   2609

_____.   Analysis of Audience-Reaction to the Cross-Examination
     Debate.   University Debaters' Annual, 1935-1936.   Ed. by Edith
     M. Phelps.   New York, Wilson, 1936.   Pp. 199-206.   2610

_____.   Analysis of Audience-Reaction to Symposium and Debate.
     University Debaters' Annual, 1933-1934.   Ed. by Edith M. Phelps.
     New York, Wilson, 1934.   Pp. 251-60.   2611

_____.   Audience Reaction to Symposium.   QJS, 21 (February,
     1935), 43-53.   2612

Minnick, Wayne C.   The Philosophy of Persuasion.   ST, 9 (Septem-
     ber, 1960), 211-15.   2613

Montague, C. E.   Three Ways of Saying Things.   Schol, 24 (May 12,
     1934), 7-8.   (Statement, overstatement, and understatement.)
                                                               2614
Moore, Henry T.   The Comparative Influence of Majority and Expert
     Opinion.   AJP, 32 (January, 1921), 16-20.   2615

Moos, Malcolm, and Kostlin, Bertram.   Prestige, Suggestion, and
     Political Leadership.   POQ, 16 (Spring, 1952), 77-93.   2616

Morse, Andrew.   The Effect of Popular Opinion Campaign Slogans--
     An Illustration.   POQ, 13 (1949), 507-10.   2617

Munn, Norman L.   The Effect of Knowledge of the Situation upon
     Judgments of Emotions from Facial Expressions.   JASP, 35

(July, 1940), 324-38.   2618

Murrish, Walter H.   Training the Debater in Persuasion.   JAFA, 1
(January, 1964), 7-12.   2619

Nadeau, Ray.   A Philosophy of Debate for Americans or De Gusti-
bus Non Est Disputandum.   CSSJ, 1 (March, 1950), 40-44.   (On
audience analysis.)   2620

Natanson, Maurice.   The Limits of Rhetoric.   QJS, 41 (April,
1955), 133-39.   2621

_____.   Rhetoric and Philosophical Argumentation.   QJS, 48 (1962),
24-30.   2622

Newman, John D.   Rhetoric and Semantics.   TS, 7 (September,
1959), 28-30.   2623

Nichols, Ralph G.   Factors in Listening Comprehension.   SM, 15
(No. 2, 1948), 154-63.   2624

Nishiyama, Kazuo.   Interpersonal Persuasion in a Vertical Society--
the Case of Japan.   SM, 38 (June, 1971), 148-154.   2625

Ogden, R. M.   Gestalt, Behavior, and Speech.   QJS, 14 (November,
1928), 530-4.   2626

Oliver, Robert T.   The Argumentation--Persuasion Duality in De-
bate.   BDAPC, 17 (December 18, 1951), 2-5.   2627

_____.   Human Motivation: Intellectuality, Emotionality, and Ra-
tionalization.   QJS, 22 (February, 1936), 62; 77.   2628

_____.   A Rhetorician's Criticism of Historiography.   In Eastern
Public Speaking Conference: 1940.   Ed. by H. F. Harding.   New
York, Wilson, 1940.   Pp. 161-72.   2629

Olson, Donald O. , and Petelle, John L.   A New Look at Ethos and
Ethical Proof.   SPG, 1 (March, 1964), 93-97.   2630

Osterhouse, Robert, and Brock, T. C.   Distraction Increases Yield-
ing to Propaganda by Inhibiting Counterarguing.   JPSP, 15 (1970),
344-58.   2631

Ostermeier, Terry H.   Effects of Type and Frequency of Reference
upon Perceived Source Credibility and Attitude Change.   SM, 34
(June, 1967), 137-144.   2632

Paget, Edwin H.   Suggestion.   QJS, 13 (June, 1927), 275-8.   2633

Palzer, Edward.   Speech Audience Affinities.   SchA, 14 (February-
March, 1943), 212-16, 254-58.   2634

Papageorgis, Demetrius. Warning and Persuasion. PB, 70 (October, 1968), 271-282. (On the effects of advance information about topic on audience's opinion.) 2635

_____ and McGuire, William J. The Generality of Immunity to Persuasion Produced by Pre-Exposure to Weakened Counter-Arguments. JASP, 62 (1961), 475-81. 2636

Parker, John P. Some Organizational Variables and Their Effect upon Comprehension. JC, 12 (March, 1962), 27-32. 2637

Parker, W. B. The Psychology of Belief. PSM, 51 (October, 1897), 750. 2638

Parrish, Wayland Maxfield. Implications of Gestalt Psychology. QJS, 14 (February, 1928), 8-29. 2639

Paulson, Stanley F. The Effects of the Prestige of the Speaker and Acknowledgment of Opposing Arguments on Audience Retention and Shift of Opinion. SM, 21 (November, 1954), 267-71. 2640

_____. Social Values and Experimental Research in Speech. WS, 26 (Summer, 1962), 133-139. (On the relative effectiveness of emotional and logical appeals.) 2641

Pear, Tom H. Modern Psychological Problems of Speaking. S(L), 1 (October, 1935), 25-8. 2642

Pekeson, Joseph. The Functioning of Ideas in Social Groups. PsyR, 25 (1918), 214-226. 2643

Pence, Orville L. Emotionally Loaded Argument: Its Effectiveness in Stimulating Recall. QJS, 40 (October, 1954), 272-76. 2644

Perritt, H. Hardy. Cybernetics and Rhetoric. SSJ, 20 (Fall, 1954), 7-15. 2645

Petelle, John. A Schematic Interpretation of Two Levels of Persuasion. SPG, 2 (May, 1965), 140-142. 2646

Phillips, David C. But Do the Dogs Like It? TS, 6 (January, 1958), 5-6. (Complains that intercollegiate debaters are indifferent to their audience.) 2647

Phillips, Robert L. Effects of Emotional Conflict on Learning and Persuasiveness in a Broadcast Discussion. SM, 34 (November, 1967), 448-454. 2648

Poffenberger, A. J. The Condition of Belief in Advertising. JAP, 7 (March, 1923), 1-9. 2649

Postman, Leo. Learned Principles of Organization in Memory. Psychological Monographs: General and Applied, 68, no. 3;

whole no. 374, 1954.   2650

Powell, Frederick. Open-and-Closed-Mindedness and the Ability to
    Differentiate Source and Message. JASP, 65 (1962), 61-64. 2651

Powers, Francis F. The Influence of Intelligence and Personality
    Traits upon False Beliefs. JSP, 2 (November, 1931), 490-3.
                                                                 2652
Probert, Walter. Law and Persuasion: The Language Behavior of
    Judges. PLR, 108 (November, 1959), 35-58.   2653

Rahe, Herbert E. What is Rhetoric? WS, 10 (December, 1946),
    11-13.   2654

Ramsey, Benjamin. In Defense of Satire: A Kind Word for the In-
    strument Which Pinches. SPG, 5 (May, 1968), 158-161. (Points
    out that satire has long been recognized as an effective debating
    device.)   2655

Rank, Vernon. Rationalization as a Factor in Communication. TS,
    4 (April, 1956), 10-21.   2656

Ray, Jack L. The Substance of Rhetoric: Good Reasons; QJS, 50
    (February, 1964), 71-72. (Rejoinder to Karl R. Wallace, infra.)
                                                                 2657
Reader, Mark. The Politics of Avoidance: On the Contours of
    Ambiguity. Eth, 77 (July, 1967), 268-283. (On the role of per-
    suasion as a derivative of the interpretation of ambiguous evi-
    dence.)   2658

Redding, W. Charles. Audience Analysis. WS, 11 (October, 1947),
    19-20.   2659

Reiser, Oliver L. The Structure of Thought. PsyR, 31 (January,
    1924), 51-73.   2660

Rosenthal, Paul I. The Concept of Ethos and the Structure of Per-
    suasion. SM, 33 (June, 1966), 114-126.   2661

───────. Specificity, Verifiability, and Message Credibility. QJS,
    57 (December, 1971), 393-401.   2662

Rosnow, R. L. Whatever Happened to the Law of Primacy? JC,
    16 (March, 1966), 10-31.   2663

Rosnow, Ralph, and Goldstein, J. H. Familiarity, Saliency, and the
    Order Presentation of Communications. JSP, 73 (1967), 97-110.
                                                                 2664
Ross, Herold. Laboratory in Persuasion. G, 43 (November, 1960),
    2. ("The Fall [1960] campaign will once again provide students
    of persuasion with many excellent examples of public speak-
    ing. ")   2665

Rothman, Richard M. The Substance of Rhetoric: Good Reasons: Further Comment. QJS, 50 (February, 1964), 74-75. (Rejoinder to Karl R. Wallace, infra.) 2666

Rowell, Edward Z. The Conviction - Persuasion Duality. QJS, 20 (November, 1934), 469-89. 2667

Ruechelle, Randall C. An Experimental Study of Audience Recognition of Emotional and Intellectual Appeals in Persuasion. SM, 24 (March, 1958), 49-59. 2668

Russell, Bertrand. Psychology and Politics. D, 80 (March, 1926), 179-88. 2669

_____. The Springs of Human Action. AtM, 189 (March, 1952), 27-31. 2670

Saadi, M., and Farnsworth, P. R. The Degrees of Acceptance of Dogmatic Statements and Preferences for Their Supposed Makers. JASP, 29 (1934), 143-50. 2671

Salper, Donald. The Imaginative Component of Rhetoric. QJS, 51 (October, 1965), 307-310. 2672

Sanborn, George A. The Unity of Persuasion. WS, 19 (May, 1955), 175-83. 2673

Sartain, A. Q. Shift in Attitude Toward the Negro after Rational and Emotional Arguments. SSJ, 9 (November, 1943), 34. 2674

Sawyer, Thomas M., Jr. Persuasion and Estimate of Majority Attitude. SM, 22 (March, 1955), 68-78. 2675

Scanlon, Ross. Advertising, Rhetoric, and Public Opinion. TS, 2 (April, 1954), 9-11. 2676

_____. Two Views of "Propaganda." TS, 1 (April, 1953), 13-4. 2677

Schanck, R. L., and Goodman, C. Reactions to Propaganda on Both Sides of a Controversial Issue. POQ, 3 (January, 1939), 107-12. 2678

Scheffler, Israel, and Winslow, C. N. Group Position and Attitudes Toward Authority. JSP, 32 (November, 1950), 177-90. 2679

Scheidel, Thomas M. Sex and Persuasibility. SM, 30 (November, 1963), 353-358. ("Women are significantly more persuasible [than men]... and significantly less retentive.") 2680

Schouls, Peter A. Communication, Argumentation, and Presupposition in Philosophy. PhR, 2 (Fall, 1969), 183-199. 2681

Schrier, William. Debating is Salesmanship. NDUQJ, 20 (March, 1930), 118-25.   2682

Schulman, Gary I., and Norrall, Chrysoula. Salience, Source Credibility and the Sleeper Effect. POQ, 34 (Fall, 1970), 371- 80.   2683

Schunk, John F. Attitudinal Effects of Self-Contradiction in a Per- suasive Communication. CSSJ, 20 (Spring, 1969), 20-29.   2684

Schweickhard, Dean M. Power of Persuasion. IAVE, 31 (March, 1942), 41.   2685

Schweitzer, Don A. The Effect of Presentation on Source Evalua- tion. QJS, 56 (February, 1970), 33-39.   2686

_____. A Note on Whitehead's "Factors of Source Credibility." QJS, 55 (October, 1969), 308-310.   2687

Scott, William A. Attitude Change by Response Reinforcement: Replication and Extension. So, 22 (1959), 328-35. (Involves elimination debate contest.)   2688

_____. Cognitive Consistency, Response, Reinforcement, and Atti- tude Change. So, 22 (1959), 219-29.   2689

Sebald, Hans. Limitations of Communication: Mechanisms of Image Maintenance in Form of Selective Perception, Selective Memory, and Selective Distortion. JC, 12 (September, 1962), 142-149.
                                                                      2690

Sereno, Kenneth K., and Hawkins, Gary J. The Effects of Varia- tions in Speakers' Non-Fluency upon Audience Ratings of Attitude toward the Speech Topic and Speakers' Credibility. SM, 34 (March, 1967), 65-73.   2691

Sharp, Harry, Jr., and McClung, Thomas. Effects of Organization on the Speaker's Ethos. SM, 33 (June, 1966), 182-183.   2692

Shepard, David W. Rhetoric and Formal Argument. WS, 30 (Fall, 1966), 241-247.   2693

Shepard, Walter J. Public Opinion. AJS, 15 (July, 1909), 32-60. (The importance of the public platform as a moulder of public opinion.)   2694

Shields, Ellis G. The Flowers of Rhetoric. Educational Leader, 23 (July, 1959), 7-15. (An apology for the teaching and practice of certain aspects of classical rhetoric.)   2695

Siegel, Elliot R., Miller, Gerald, and Woting, Edward. Source Credibility and Credibility Proneness: A New Relationship. SM, 36 (June, 1969), 118-125.   2696

Sikkink, Donald E.   An Experimental Study of the Effects on the Listener of Anticlimax Order and Authority in an Argumentative Speech.   SSJ, 22 (Winter, 1956), 73-78.   2697

_____.   A Shift of Opinion Study of the Stanford-University of London Debate.   G, 38 (November, 1955), 18-19.   2698

Sillars, Malcolm.   Rhetoric as Act.   QJS, 50 (October, 1964), 277-84.   2699

Silverman, Irwin, and Shulman, Arthur D.   A Conceptual Model of Artifact in Attitude Change Studies.   So, 33 (March, 1970), 97-107.   2700

Simons, Herbert W.   Requirements, Problems, and Strategies: A Theory of Persuasion for Social Movements.   QJS, 56 (February, 1970), 1-11.   2701

Smith, Donald K. , and Scott, Robert L.   Motivation Theory in Teaching Persuasion: Statement and Schema.   QJS, 47 (December, 1961), 378-83.   2702

Smith, Raymond G.   An Experimental Study of the Effects of Speech Organization upon Attitudes of College Students.   SM, 18 (November, 1951), 292-301.   2703

Smith, Robert W.   A Rhetoric of Commitment.   QJS, 49 (April, 1963), 190-193.   2704

Smith, T. V.   Compromise: Its Contest and Limits.   Eth, 53 (October, 1942), 1-13.   2705

Sponberg, Harold.   The Relative Effectiveness of Climax and Anti-Climax Order in an Argumentative Speech.   SM, 13 (No. 1, 1946), 35-44.   2706

Steele, Edward D. , and Redding, W. Charles.   The American Value System: Premises for Persuasion.   WS, 26 (Spring, 1962), 83-91.   2707

Stevens, Wilmer E.   No Reason for Argument?   In Revaluation of the Place of Speech in the Educational Process, ed. by E. R. Nichols.   Redlands, Cal. , University of Redlands Debate Bureau, 1935.   Pp. 52-57.   (Persuasion theory might encourage sophistry.)   2708

Summers, Harrison B.   Debating for the Audience.   G, 10 (November, 1927), 11-13.   2709

Symposium: Value Theory and Rhetoric.   WS, 26 (Spring, 1962), 70-91.   (Contains the following essays: Edward D. Steele, "Social Values, the Enthymeme, and Speech Criticism, " 70-5; Theodore Balgooyen, "A Study of Conflicting Values, " 76-83; Edward

D. Steele, and W. Charles Redding. "The American Value System: Premises for Persuasion," 83-91.)   2710

Taylor, W. S.   Rationalization and its Social Significance.   JASP, 17 (January-March, 1923), 410-18.   2711

Thistlethwaite, Donald L., de Haan, Henry, and Kamenetzky, Joseph. The Effects of "Directive" and "Non-Directive" Communication Procedures on Attitudes.   JASP, 51 (1955), 107-13.   2712

Thomas, Gordon L., and Ralph, David C.   A Study of the Effect of Audience Proximity on Persuasion.   SM, 26 (November, 1959), 300-307.   2713

Thompson, Ernest.   An Experimental Investigation of the Relative Effectiveness of Organizational Structure in Oral Communication. SSJ, 26 (Fall, 1960), 59-69.   2714

_____.   Some Effects of Message Structure on Listener's Comprehension.   SM, 34 (March, 1967), 51-57.   2715

Thompson, Richard N.   Debate Audiences and What They Want.   EJ, 20 (col. ed., September, 1931), 590-92.   2716

Thompson, Wayne N.   A Conservative View of a Progressive Rhetoric.   QJS, 49 (February, 1963), 1-7.   2717

Thonssen, Lester W.   Recent Literature in Rhetoric.   QJS, 39 (December, 1953), 501-4.   2718

Thorndike, Edward L.   The Influence of Primacy.   JExP, 10 (February, 1927), 18-29.   2719

Thorne, E. J.   Teaching Is Not Salesmanship.   TS, 3 (September, 1955), 5-6.   2720

_____.   Teaching 1,2 Salesmanship 1,2.   TS, 4 (November, 1956), 21-4.   2721

Thurston, L. L.   The Measurement of Opinion.   JASP, 22 (January-March, 1928), 415-30.   2722

Tompkins, Philip K.   The McCroskey--Dunham and Holtzman Reports on "Ethos": A Confounding Element in Communication Research.   SM, 34 (June, 1967), 176-179.   2723

_____ and Samovar, Larry A.   An Experimental Study of the Effects of Credibility on the Comprehension of Content.   SM, 31 (June, 1964), 120-123.   2724

Torrence, Donald L.   A Philosophy for Rhetoric from Bertrand Russell.   QJS, 45 (April, 1959), 153-165.   2725

Tressider, Angus.   Psychology and Public Speaking.   SSJ, 3 (November, 1937), 16-19.   2726

Trueblood, C. K.   Beliefs and Personality.   JASP, 34 (April, 1939), 200-24.   2727

Tubbs, Stewart L.   Explicit versus Implicit Conclusions and Audience Commitment.   SM, 35 (March, 1968), 14-19.   2728

Tucker, Raymond K.   General Systems Theory: A Logical and Ethical Model for Persuasion.   JAFA, 8 (Summer, 1971), 29-35.   2729

_____, Koehler, Jerry W., and Mlady, Lynne.   The Image of the College Debater.   JAFA, 4 (Winter, 1967), 1-9.   2730

_____ and Ware, Paul D.   Persuasion Via Mere Exposure.   QJS, 57 (December, 1971), 437-443.   2731

Utterback, William E.   An Appraisal of Psychological Research in Speech.   QJS, 23 (April, 1937), 175-82.   2732

_____.   Opining.   AJPsy, 46 (July, 1934), 503-6.   (Cases on formulation of opinion.)   2733

_____.   A Psychological Approach to the Rhetoric of Speech Composition.   QJS, 10 (February, 1924), 17-23.   2734

_____.   A Psychological View of Argumentation.   In Studies in Rhetoric and Public Speaking in Honor of James Albert Winans. By pupils and colleagues.   New York, Century, 1925.   Pp. 283-99.   (Belief is an aspect of attention.)   2735

_____.   The Influence of Conference on Opinion.   QJS, 36 (October, 1950), 365-70.   2736

_____.   Measuring the Reaction of the Audience to an Argumentative Speech.   QJS, 8 (April, 1922), 181-83.   2737

Wall, Victor D., Jr.   Evidential Attitudes and Attitude Change.   WS, 36 (Spring, 1972), 115-123.   2738

Wallace, Karl R.   The Substance of Rhetoric: Good Reasons.   QJS, 49 (October, 1963), 239-249.   (Answers by Jack L. Ray, Richard M. Rothman, and Chester C. Long, supra.   Rejoinder by Wallace, QJS, 50 (February, 1964), 73-74.)   2739

Walster, Elaine, and Festinger, Leon.   The Effectiveness of "Overheard" Persuasive Communications.   JASP, 65 (1962), 305-402.   2740

Walter, Otis M.   On Views of Rhetoric, whether Conservative or Progressive.   QJS, 49 (December, 1963), 367-382.   2741

_____. Rhetoric as a Liberal Art. SSJ, 20 (Summer, 1955), 309-
15.   2742

_____. Toward an Analysis of Motivation. QJS, 41 (October,
1955), 271-8.   2743

_____. What You Are Speaks So Loud. TS, 3 (April, 1955), 3-6.
                                                              2744
Warren, Irving D. The Effect of Credibility in Sources of Testimony on Audience Attitudes Toward Speaker and Message. SM,
36 (November, 1969), 456-458.   2745

Wasby, Stefn L. Rhetoricians and Political Scientists: Some Lines
of Converging Interest. SSJ, 36 (Spring, 1971), 231-242.   2746

Weinberg, Harry L. A Redefinition of Rhetoric. TS, 6 (4 November, 1958), 9-11.   2747

Weiss, Franklin R. How the Lawyer Uses Rhetoric. TS, 7 (September, 1959), 6-8, 15.   2748

Weiss, R. F. Repetition of Persuasion. PsyRt, 25 (October, 1969),
669-670.   2749

Weiss, Robert O. Tournament Audiences. G, 43 (November,
1960), 7-8.   2750

Weiss, Walter. A "Sleeper" Effect in Opinion Change. JASP, 48
(1953), 173-180.   2751

Wheeler, David, and Jordan, Howard. Change of Individual Opinion
to Accord with Group Opinion. JASP, 24 (July-September, 1929),
203-206.   2752

Wheeless, Lawrence R. The Effects of Comprehension Loss on
Persuasion. SM, 38 (November, 1971), 327-330.   2753

White, H. Adelbert. English Rhetorics. G, 33 (November, 1950),
8-10.   2754

Whitehead, Jack L., Jr. Factors of Source Credibility. QJS, 54
(February, 1968), 59-63.   2755

Whittaker, J. O. Consistency of Individual Differences in Persuasibility. JC, 15 (March, 1965), 28-34.   2756

Whittier, Duane H. Basic Assumption and Argument in Philosophy.
Mo, 48 (October, 1964), 486-500.   2757

Wichelns, Herbert A. Audience Analysis. QJS, 11 (November,
1925), 386-88. (Favors emphasis on subject analysis rather than
on audience analysis.)   2758

Wickert, Frederic. A Test for Personal Goal Values. JSP, 11

(May, 1940), 259-74.   2759

Wilkie, Walter.   An Experimental Comparison of the Speech, the Radio, and the Printed Page as Propaganda Devices.   AP, 169 (June, 1934), 1-32.   2760

Willis, Edgar E.   The Relative Effectiveness of Three Forms of Radio Presentation in Influencing Attitudes.   SM, 7 (1940), 41-47.   2761

Winans, James A.   Persuasion.   PSR, 3 (March, 1914), 196-200.
                                                                2762
Winterowd, W. Ross.   Style: A Matter of Manner.   QJS, 56 (April, 1970), 161-167.   2763

Woodward, Howard S.   Measurement and Analysis of Audience Opinion.   QJS, 14 (February, 1928), 94-111.   2764

Woolbert, Charles H.   The Audience.   PsM, 22 (1916), 37-54. 2765

_____.   A Behavioristic Account of Intellect and Emotions.   PsyR, 31 (July, 1924), 265-72.   2766

_____.   Conviction and Persuasion: Some Considerations of Theory.   QJS, 3 (July, 1917), 249-64.   2767

_____.   Persuasion: Principles and Method.   QJS, 5 (January, March, May, 1919), 12-25; 101-119; 211-238.   2768

_____.   Psychology from the Standpoint of a Speech Teacher.   QJS, 16 (February, 1930), 9-18.   2769

Wright, Warren E.   Judicial Rhetoric: A Field for Research.   SM, 31 (March, 1964), 64-72.   2770

Zelko, Harold P.   Do We Argue, Persuade, or Convince?   QJS, 25 (October, 1939), 385-92.   2771

X. ETHICS

A. GENERAL PRINCIPLES

1. Books

Christopherson, Myrvin F.   Ethics of Speech Communication.
Dubuque, Iowa, Brown, 1967.   2772

Fromm, Erich.   Man for Himself: An Inquiry into the Psychology
of Ethics.   New York, Rinehart, 1947.   2773

Gusdorf, Georges.   Speaking (trans. by Paul T. Brockelman).
Evanston, Ill. , Northwestern, 1965.   2774

Johannesen, Richard L. , ed.   Ethics and Persuasion.   New York,
Random, 1967.   2775

Leys, Wayne A. R.   Ethics for Policy Questions.   Englewood Cliffs,
New Jersey, Prentice, 1952.   2776

Nilsen, Thomas R.   Ethics of Speech Communication.   Indianapolis,
Bobbs, 1966.   2777

Oates, Whitney J.   Aristotle and the Problem of Value.   Princeton,
N. J. , Princeton, 1963.   2778

Parson, Donn W. , and Linkugel, Wil A.   The Ethics of Controversy:
Politics and Protest.   Lawrence, Kansas, Dept. of Speech and
Drama, Kansas, 1968.   Also, The House of Usher, 1968.   (Proceedings of the First Annual Symposium on Issues in Public Communication.)   2779

Perelman, Chaim.   The Idea of Justice and the Problem of Argument.   Translated from the French by John Petrie.   New York,
Humanities, 1963.   2780

2. Theses and Dissertations

Buice, Lee.   The Treatment of Forensic Ethics in Argumentation
and Debate Textbooks.   M. A.   North Texas State.   1966.   2781

Gantt, Vernon.   A Descriptive Study of Unethical Practices in Competitive Debate.   M. A.   Ohio.   1968.   2782

Holton, Robert F.   An Examination of Contemporary Concepts of
Ethics in Persuasion.   M. A.   Southern Illinois.   1960.   2783

Johnson, Robert. The Teaching of Rhetorical Ethics in Beginning
  Speech Courses in the State Colleges and University of California.
  M. A. Sacramento. 1969.   2784

Larson, Carl E. Ethical Considerations in the Attitudes and Practices of College Debaters. M. A. Kansas. 1962.   2785

Moore, Carl. The Treatment of Ethics in College Textbooks of Debate. M. A. Arizona. 1965.   2786

Northwall, John H. A Study of Some Implications of Existentialism
  for Rhetorical Ethics. M. A. Colorado. 1969.   2787

Peterson, Gary L. Ethics in Intercollegiate Debating. M. A. Ohio.
  1961.   2788

Schillig, Jacqueline. Arthur Kruger's Treatment of the Ethics of
  Persuasion and Debate. M. A. C. W. Post. 1974.   2788a

Van Woert, Edwin D. A Suggested Ethic of Rhetoric. M. A.
  Arkansas. 1959.   2789

3. Articles

Barrett, Edward F. The Adversary System and the Ethics of Advocacy. Notre Dame Lawyer, 37 (1962), 479-88.   2790

Betz, Edward S. Is Debating Immoral? NEJ, 15 (September,
  1936), 278-9.   2791

Brandenburg, Ernest. Quintilian and the Good Orator. QJS, 34
  (February, 1948), 23-9.   2792

Burks, Don M. On the Ethics of Speaking. ST, 15 (November,
  1966), 336-339.   2793

Byers, Burton H. Speech Sportsmanship. ST, 3 (March, 1954),
  133-5.   2794

Capel, Robert B. , and Cariker, George. A Debate Code of Ethics.
  F, 47 (October, 1961), 6-7; 30.   2795

Chesebro, James W. A Construct for Assessing Ethics in Communication. CSSJ, 20 (Summer, 1969), 104-114. ("Describes and
  relates contemporary ethical standards and then concentrates upon
  when and how to apply ethical standards to communication behavior. ")   2796

Cohn, G. Bernard. The Ethics of Debate. F, 46 (March, 1961),
  5. (By a student.)   2797

Cordell, Christobel M. How Are Your Ethics? PN, 4 (October,

1937), 3, 30.   2798

Crocker, Lionel. Public Speaking and the Truth; Should the Orator
    Exploit His Audience? VS, 9 (May, 1943), 444-6.   2799

_____. Sinclair Lewis on Public Speaking. QJS, 21 (April, 1935),
    232-37.   2800

_____. Truth Through Personality. QJS, 39 (February, 1953),
    1-5.   2801

Cunningham, J. V. Is Debating Immoral? HP, 16 (October, 1934),
    58-60.   2802

Dahlstrom, Carl. A Proposed Preface to a Text on Public Speaking.
    QJS, 24 (October, 1938), 418-24.   2803

Day, Dennis G. The Ethics of Democratic Debate. CSSJ, 17 (Feb-
    ruary, 1966), 5-14.   2804

Diggs, B. J. Persuasion and Ethics. QJS, 50 (December, 1964),
    359-373.   2805

_____. Ethics and Persuasion: Author's Reply. QJS, 51 (Octo-
    ber, 1965), 331-333. (Rejoinder to Howard H. Martin, infra.)
                                                                                      2806

Ellis, A. Carroll. Good Man Speaking Well. SSJ, 11 (March,
    1946), 85-89.   2807

Ewbank, Henry L., Jr. On the Ethics of Teaching Speech Content.
    CSSJ, 8 (Fall, 1956), 23-25.   2808

Flynn, Lawrence J. The Aristotelian Basis for the Ethics of Speak-
    ing. ST, 6 (September, 1957), 179-87.   2809

Flynt, Wayne. The Ethics of Democratic Persuasion and the
    Birmingham Crisis. SSJ, 35 (Fall, 1969), 40-53.   2810

Funk, Alfred A. Logical and Emotional Proofs: A Counter-View.
    ST, 17 (September, 1968), 210-216. (A rejoinder to Arthur N.
    Kruger, infra.)   2811

Grant, W. Leonard. Cicero on the Moral Character of the Orator.
    CJ, 38 (May, 1943), 472-8.   2812

Grisez, Germain G. The Concept of Appropriateness: Ethical Con-
    siderations in Persuasive Argument. JAFA, 2 (May, 1965), 53-
    58.   2813

Haiman, Franklyn S. Democratic Ethics and the Hidden Persuaders.
    QJS, 44 (December, 1958), 385-92.   2814

_____. A Re-examination of the Ethics of Persuasion. CSSJ, 3

(1952), 4-9.   2815

Haitema, John S. Ethics and Its Applications to Debating, Especially to Contest Debating. JEX, 3 (September, 1929), 169-80. 2816

Hefferline, Ralph F. Communication Theory: II. Extension to Interpersonal Behavior. QJS, 41 (December, 1955), 365-76. 2817

Holtzoff, A. The Ethics of Advocacy. BLR, 16 (Spring, 1967),
583ff.   2818

Hook, Sidney. The Ethics of Controversy. NL, (February 1, 1954),
12-14.   2819

Jacob, Bruno E. Integrity in High School Debating. R, 11 (6 February, 1937), 4-7.   2820

Jensen, J. Vernon. An Analysis of Recent Literature on Teaching
of Ethics in Public Address. ST, 8 (September, 1959), 219-28.
                                                                    2821
Klopf, Donald, and McCroskey, James C. Ethical Practices in Debate. JAFA, 1 (January, 1964), 13-16.   2822

Kruger, Arthur N. The Ethics of Persuasion: A Re-Examination.
ST, 16 (November, 1967), 295-305.   2823

Lillywhite, Herold. Ground Rules for Responsible Communication.
Ed, 77 (1956), 74-9. (A summary of experts' views on the
ethics of persuasion.)   2824

_____. Standards of Ethical Communication in Contemporary So-
ciety. G, 45 (January, 1963), 21-24; 30.   2825

MacKendrick, Paul. Cicero's Ideal Orator--Truth and Propaganda.
CJ, 43 (March, 1948), 339-47.   2826

Martin, Howard H. Ethics and Persuasion: Impertinent Rejoinder.
QJS, 51 (October, 1965), 329-331. (A rejoinder to B. J. Diggs,
supra.)   2827

Michigan High School Forensic Bulletin. Ethics of Speech Contest.
R, 24 (February, 1950), 2.   2828

Mixon, Harold. Ethics and Debate. SchA, 40 (October, 1968), 2-
3.   2829

Murphy, Richard. Preface to an Ethic of Rhetoric. In The Rhetori-
cal Idiom, ed. by D. C. Bryant. Ithaca, N. Y., Cornell, 1958.
                                                                    2830
_____. Speech for the Masses. G, 28 (January, 1946), 20-5.
(Reprinted from the University of Colorado Studies, Series B
(Studies in the Humanities), Vol. 2, No. 4, October, 1945.) 2831

Murray, Elwood.   Pertaining to the Ethics of Rhetoric.   Ed, 51
(October, 1930), 107-12.   2832

Newman, Robert P.   The Ethics of Persuasion.   PSA, 11 and 12
(June, 1955), 3-6.   2833

_____.   Ethical Presuppositions of Argument.   G, 42 (May, 1960),
51-4, 58, 62.   2834

Oliver, Robert T.   Ethics and Efficiency in Persuasion.   SSJ, 26
(Fall, 1960), 10-15.   2835

Pellegrini, Angelo M.   Public Speaking and Social Obligations.   QJS,
20 (June, 1934), 345-51.   2836

Peterson, Gary L.   Whence Cometh Debate Ethics?   S, 44 (May,
1962), 18-20.   2837

Pross, Edward L.   Practical Implications of the Aristotelian Concept of Ethos.   SSJ, 17 (May, 1952), 257-64.   2838

Question of College Morals in Debating.   PSR, 2 (May, 1912), 20-
1.   (Two letters on the problem of college debaters' requests to
"buy, and rent, or borrow" references, speeches, and rebuttals.)
                                                            2839
Rieke, Richard D., and Smith, David H.   The Dilemma of Ethics
and Advocacy in the Use of Evidence.   WS, 32 (Fall, 1968), 223-
233.   2840

Rives, Stanley G.   Ethical Argumentation.   JAFA, 1 (September,
1964), 8-12.   2841

Rogers, A. K.   Prolegomena to a Political Ethics.   In Essays in
Honor of John Dewey.   New York, H. Holt, 1929.   2842

Rogge, Edward.   Evaluating the Ethics of a Speaker in a Democracy.
QJS, 45 (December, 1959), 419-25.   2843

_____.   Rejoinder.   QJS, 46 (April, 1960), 197.   (A rejoinder to
Robert W. Smith, infra.)   2844

Rudin, John J.   "Ethical Proof" in Debate.   F, 30 (March, 1945),
43-48, 61.   2845

Sattler, William M.   Ethical Persuasion in Debating.   S, 26 (November, 1941), 7-8.   (Also in DM, 1 (January-February, 1945),
15-16.)   2846

Schrier, William.   The Ethics of Persuasion.   QJS, 16 (November,
1930), 476-86.   2847

Shawcross, (Sir) Hartley W.   Functions and Responsibilities of an
Advocate.   South Dakota Bar Journal, 27 (January, 1959),

16-32.   2848

Simrell, V. E.   Mere Rhetoric.   QJS, 14 (June, 1928), 359-74.
  (On the nature and ethics of rhetoric.)   2849

Smith, Carney C.   Sportsmanship in Debating.   QJS, 23 (February,
  1937), 83-6.   (Sportsmanship as it relates to debating in high
  schools.)   2850

Smith, Robert W.   Ethics--Relative and Absolute.   QJS, 46 (April,
  1960), 196-197.   (A rejoinder to Edward Rogge, supra.)   2851

Wallace, Karl R.   An Ethical Basis of Communication.   ST, 4 (January, 1955), 1-9.   2852

Watkins, Lloyd I. , ed.   Ethical Problems in Debating--a Symposium.
  ST, 8 (March, 1959), 150-6.   (Opinions by Mrs. Richard D.
  Gillen; Archie M. Thomas; Goodwin F. Berquist, Jr. ; and Claude
  E. Kantner.)   2853

Weinberg, Harry L.   An Ethics for Public Speaking: A Semantic
  Approach.   PSA, 11 and 12 (June, 1955), 7-12.   2854

Wieman, Henry N. , and Walter, Otis M.   Toward an Analysis of
  Ethics for Rhetoric.   QJS, 43 (October, 1957), 266-70.   2855

Zelko, Harold P.   Debate Training and Human Relations: Consistent
  or Incompatible?   BDAPC, 16 (July 10, 1950), 8-12.   2856

B.   DEBATING BOTH SIDES

1.   Theses and Dissertations

Welden, Geraldine S.   Shifts of Opinion of Selected Pennsylvania
  College Debaters on the 1955-56 National Topic as a Function of
  Debating One or Both Sides of the Proposition.   M. A.   Pitts-
  burgh.   1957.   2857

2.   Articles

Baird, A Craig.   The College Debater and the Red China Issue.
  CSSJ, 6 (Spring, 1955), 5-7.   2858

Bassett, T. Robert.   Can We Debate the Labor Question? BDAPC,
  11 (December 12, 1941), 1-4.   (Article followed by a short rejoinder by Howard W. Runkel, "On the Other Hand, " p. 4.) 2859

Bowra, D.   From Sydney, Australia.   ETC, 13 (Winter, 1955-56),
  153.   (Comment on Grant article, infra.)   2860

Burns, James M. Debate Over Collegiate Debate. NYTM (December 5, 1954), 12, 30. (Reply by E. Vasilew, January 2, 1955, p. 4.)   2861

Crampton, Angela C. The Nature of Language: A Question of Ethics in Debating Both Sides. SPG, 4 (May, 1967), 88-92. (Opposes switch-sides debating.)   2862

Cripe, Nicholas. Debating Both Sides in Tournaments Is Ethical. ST, 6 (September, 1957), 209-12.   2863

Debate on Red China. Com, 61 (December 3, 1954), 240.   2864

Deil, George W. In Defense of Debating Both Sides. ST, 7 (January, 1958), 31-34.   2865

Ehninger, Douglas. The Debate About Debating. QJS, 44 (April, 1958), 127-36.   2866

Eisenberg, Meyer. To Debate, or Remain Silent. G, 37 (January, 1955), 38-40. (Concerning the Communist China topic.)   2867

Fest, Thorrel. We Hold These Truths. G, 37 (November, 1954), 2-3, 6. (In defense of debates on the Communist China topic.)
                                                                           2868
Festinger, Leon, and Carlsmith, James M. Cognitive Consequences of Forced Compliance. JASP, 58 (March, 1959), 203-10.   2869

French, Warren G. On Debates and Debating: Reply to Mr. Grant. ETC, 13 (Winter, 1955-56), 148-51.   2870

Gough, Harry B. A Reply to Roosevelt. PSR, 3 (October, 1913), 37-41. (See Roosevelt's views, infra.)   2871

Grant, W. B. Debate on Debates. ETC, 12 (Spring, 1955), 238-39. (Later correspondence in ETC, 13 (Winter, 1955-56), 148-54; 14 (Autumn, 1956), 70-72.)   2872

Greenwald, Anthony G. When Does Role-Playing Produce Attitude Change? JPSP, 16 (1970), 214-19. (Investigates the effects of forcing students to write essays on both sides of controversial topics.)   2873

Howell, Wilbur S. The National Debate Topic: A Defense. QJS, 40 (December, 1954), 434-35. (Communist China topic.)   2874

Huber, Walter G. Should College Students be Allowed to Debate the Question of the Recognition of Red China by the United States? G, 37 (January, 1955), 28, 30.   2875

Janis, Irving L., and King, Bert T. The Influence of Role Playing in Opinion Change. JASP, 49 (April, 1954), 211-18.   2876

_____. Comparison of the Effectiveness of Improvised Versus Non-Improvised Role Playing in Producing Opinion Changes. HR, 9 (1956), 177-86.   2877

Klopf, Donald W., and McCroskey, James C. Debating Both Sides Ethical? Controversy Pau! CSSJ, 15 (February, 1964), 36-39.
2878

Kruger, A. N. Censorship on the Campus. TS, 3 (January, 1955), 5-6. (A criticism of colleges that refused to permit their students to debate the recognition of Communist China topic.) 2879

_____. Is It Educational? Yes. BDAPC, 22 (December, 1956), 4-9. (Contends that switch-sides debating is both ethical and educational. Article followed by short rejoinder by Brooks Quimby, 9-10, and preceded by Quimby's article, infra.) 2880

Lutherans Show Civil Courage; Stand of Augustana Lutheran Colleges on Collegiate Debate. CC, 71 (December 22, 1954), 1540. (On the recognition of Communist China topic.) 2881

McCroskey, James C. Still More Debate Over Debate. F, 47 (October, 1962), 7-9. (An Answer to Professor Thomas, infra.)
2882

Moore, H. A., Jr. Debate on Red China Raises Issue of Intellectual Freedom. NSch, 55 (January, 1955), 48-9. 2883

Mundt, Karl E. Anent Vocal Ambidexterity! R, 9 (June, 1935), 3.
2884

Murphy, Richard. The Ethics of Debating Both Sides. ST, 6 (January, 1957), 1-9. 2885

_____. Rejoinder, Debating Both Sides. ST, 6 (September, 1957), 255-6. 2886

_____. The Ethics of Debating Both Sides, II. ST, 12 (September, 1963), 242-7. 2887

Newman, Robert P., ed. Briefly Speaking; A Symposium: Do You Think the Current National Debate Topic Is a Suitable One for College Students? BDAPC, 22 (December, 1956), 20-22. (Contributors include Robert E. Connelly, Richard Mechling, and Thomas A. Hopkins.) 2888

Olson, Ronald H. The Debate Over Debate. F, 47 (January, 1962), 3, 7. 2889

Quimby, Brooks. But Is It Educational? SA, 9 (Summer, 1953), 30-31. Also in BDAPC, 22 (December, 1956), 2-3. (A criticism of switch-sides debating. See rejoinder by A. N. Kruger, followed by Quimby's rejoinder, in BDAPC.) 2890

Recognition of Red China as Debate Topic. Am, 92 (November 6, 1954), 143. 2891

Red-Hot Issue.   Ne, 44 (November 29, 1954), 72.   (Red China
   topic.)   2892

Roosevelt, Theodore.   Roosevelt on Debate in "Chapters of a Possible Autobiography. "   Ou, 103 (February 22, 1913), 406.   ("Per-
   sonally I have not the slightest sympathy with debating contests
   in which each side is arbitrarily assigned a given proposition and
   told to maintain it without the least reference to whether those
   maintaining it believe in it or not. ")   2893

Rothman, Richard.   Debate Really Can.   F, 49 (October, 1963), 7-
   8.   (Favors switch-sides debating.)   2894

Shepard, David W.   The Debate on Debating: A Rebuttal.   ETC,
   14 (Autumn, 1956), 70-72.   (Rejoinder to Grant, supra.)   2895

Sikkink, Donald.   Evidence on the Both Sides Controversy.   ST, 11
   (January, 1962), 51-54.   2896

Smith, Donald K.   Letter to the Editor: "Debating Both Sides. "
   ST, 6 (November, 1957), 336.   2897

Subject for Debate.   T, 64 (November 29, 1954), 43.   (Red China
   topic.)   2898

Thomas, J. D.   Cor Cordium: More of the Debate Over Debate.
   F, 47 (March, 1962), 3-5.   ("Speakers should talk the way they
   would vote. ")   2899

Williams, Hazel B.   Cooperative Creative Thinking.   ETC, 13
   (Winter, 1955-56), 151-52.   (Rejoinder to Grant, supra.)   2900

Windes, Russel R. , Jr.   Competitive Debating: The Speech Program, the Individual, and Society.   ST, 9 (March, 1960), 99-
   108.   2901

Wits versus Convictions.   Ou, 104 (June 7, 1913), 271-2.   (Indict-
   ments of debating by Theodore Roosevelt and H. V. Kaltenborn.)
                                                                 2902

XI. PRESENTATION

A. LANGUAGE

1. Books

Alexander, Hubert G.   Language and Thinking.   New York, Van
Nostrand, 1967.   2903

Anshen, Ruth Manda, ed.   Language: An Inquiry into Its Meaning
and Function.   New York, Harper, 1957.   2904

Austin, J. L.   How to Do Things with Words.   Cambridge, Mass.,
Harvard, 1962.   2905

Ayer, A. J.   Language, Truth, and Logic.   New York, Dover, 1946.
                                                                   2906

Benjamin, Robert L.   Semantics and Language Analysis.   Indianapolis, Bobbs, 1970.   2907

Black, Max, ed.   The Importance of Language.   Englewood Cliffs,
New Jersey, 1962.   2908

_____.   Models and Metaphors: Studies in Language and Philoso-
phy.   Ithaca, New York, Cornell, 1962.   (Contains much material on logic as well as on language.)   2909

Breal, M. J. A.   Semantics.   New York, Dover, 1964.   2910

Bridgman, P. W.   The Way Things Are.   New York, Viking, 1961.
                                                                   2911

Britton, Karl.   Communication.   New York, Harcourt, 1939.   2912

Brown, Roger.   Words and Things.   New York, Free, 1958.   2913

Carnap, Rudolph.   Introduction to Semantics.   Cambridge, Harvard,
1942.   2914

_____.   The Logical Syntax of Language.   New York, Harcourt,
1937.   2915

Cassirer, Ernst.   The Philosophy of Symbolic Forms, Vol. 1.   New
Haven, Yale, 1953.   2916

Chase, Stuart.   Power of Words.   New York, Harcourt, 1954. 2917

_____. The Tyranny of Words. New York, Harcourt, 1938. 2918

Christensen, N. E. On the Nature of Meanings. Copehagen, Munks-
gaard, 1961.   2919

Condon, John C. Semantics and Communication. New York, Mac-
millan, 1966.   2920

DeVito, Joseph. The Psychology of Speech and Language. New
York, Random, 1970.   2921

Edwards, Paul. The Logic of Moral Discourse. Glencoe, Illinois,
Free, 1954.   2922

Empson, William. Seven Types of Ambiguity. New York, Meridian,
1955.   2923

Flesch, Rudolph. The Art of Plain Talk. New York, Harper,
1946.   2924

Flew, A. G. N. , ed. Logic and Language: First and Second Series.
New York, Doubleday, 1965.   2925

Gellner, Ernest. Words and Things. London, Gollancz, 1959. 2926

Greenough, J. B. , and Kittredge, G. L. Words and Their Ways in
English Speech. New York, Macmillan, 1906.   2927

Harris, Robert T. , and Jarrett, James L. Language and Informal
Logic. New York, Longmans, 1956.   2928

Hayakawa, S. I. Language in Action. New York, Harcourt, 1941.
                                                                                            2929
_____. ed. Language, Meaning, and Maturity. New York, Harper,
1954.   2930

_____. Language in Thought and Action. New York, Harcourt,
1949.   2931

_____, ed. The Use and Misuse of Language. Greenwich, Conn.,
Fawcett Publications, 1962.   2932

Hill, Forbes I. Language and Style. Indianapolis, Bobbs, 1969.
                                                                                            2933
Hospers, John. An Introduction to Philosophical Analysis. Engle-
wood Cliffs, New Jersey, 1953.   2934

_____. Meaning and Truth in the Arts. Chapel Hill, North Caro-
lina, North Carolina, 1946.   2935

Huse, H. R. The Illiteracy of the Literate. New York, D. Apple-
ton, 1933.   2936

Jespersen, Otto. Language. London, Allen, 1922.   2937

Johnson, Alexander B.   A Treatise on Language (ed. by D. Rynin).
    Berkeley, California, California, 1959.   2938

Johnson, Wendell.   People in Quandaries: The Semantics of Per-
    sonal Adjustment.   New York, Harper, 1946.   2939

Kecskemeti, Paul.   Meaning, Communication, and Value.   Chicago,
    Chicago, 1952.   2940

Korzybski, Alfred.   Science and Sanity.   New York, The Internation-
    al Non-Aristotelian Library Publishing Company, 2nd edition,
    1941.   2941

Langer, Susanne K.   Philosophy in a New Key.   New York, NAL,
    1948.   2942

Lee, Irving J.   Customs and Crises in Communications: Cases for
    the Study of Some Barriers and Breakdowns.   New York, Harper,
    1954.   2943

_____.   The Language of Wisdom and Folly.   New York, Harper,
    1949.   2944

_____.   Language Habits in Human Affairs.   New York, Harper,
    1941.   2945

Lewis, H. D., ed.   Clarity Is Not Enough.   New York, Humanities,
    1963.   2946

Linsky, Leonard, ed.   Semantics and the Philosophy of Language.
    Urbana, Ill., Illinois, 1952.   2947

Makaye, J.   The Logic of Language.   Hanover, Dartmouth College
    Publication, 1939.   2948

Martin, R. M.   Truth and Denotation: A Study in Semantical Theory.
    Chicago, Chicago, 1958.   2949

McDonald, Daniel.   The Language of Argument.   Scranton, Pennsyl-
    vania, Chandler Publishing Co., 1971.   2950

Mead, G. H.   Mind, Self, and Society.   Chicago, Chicago, 1934.
                                                            2951
Mellinkoff, David.   The Language of the Law.   Boston, Little,
    1963.   2952

Morris, C. W.   Foundations of the Theory of Signs.   International
    Encyclopedia of Unified Science, Vol. 1, No. 2.   2953

_____.   Signs, Language and Behavior.   New York, Prentice,
    1946.   2954

Nesbit, F. F.   Language, Meaning, and Reality.   New York, Exposition, 1955.   2955

Ogden, C. K. , and Richards, Ivor A.   The Meaning of Meaning.
New York, Harcourt, 1948.   2956

Pap, Arthur.   Elements of Analytic Philosophy.   New York, Macmillan, 1949.   2957

Partridge, Eric, Comp. with an Introduction by.   A Dictionary of
Cliches.   New York, Dutton, 1963.   2958

Patrick, Max, and Evans, Robert O. , eds.   Style, Rhetoric, and
Rhythm: Essays by Morris W. Croll.   Princeton, N. J. , Princeton, 1965.   2959

Philbrick, F. A.   Understanding English: An Introduction to Semantics.   New York, Macmillan, 1947.   2960

_____.   Language and the Law: The Semantics of Forensic English.
New York, Macmillan, 1949.   2961

Quine, Willard V. O.   Word and Object.   Cambridge, MIT, 1964.
                                                                    2962
Rapoport, Anatol.   Operational Philosophy.   New York, Harper,
1953.   2963

Reiss, Samuel.   The Universe of Meaning.   New York, Philosophical, 1953.   2964

Russell, Bertrand.   An Inquiry into Meaning and Truth.   Baltimore,
Maryland, Penguin, 1962.   2965

Salomon, Louis B.   Semantics and Common Sense.   New York,
Holt, 1966.   2966

Schaff, Adam.   Introduction to Semantics.   (Translated by Wojtasiewicz, Olgierd.)   New York, Pergamon Press, 1962.   (Contains
an extensive bibliography on semantics.)   2967

Sidgwick, Alfred.   The Use of Words in Reasoning.   London, Black,
1901.   2968

Sondel, Bess.   The Humanity of Words: A Primer of Semantics.
New York, World Publishing Company, 1958.   2969

Studebaker, John W.   Plain Talk.   Washington, The National Home
Library Foundation, 1936.   2970

Thayer, Lee, ed.   Communication: General Semantics Perspectives.
New York, Spartan, 1970.   2971

Ullman, Stephen.   Semantics: An Introduction to the Science of

Meaning. New York, Barnes, 1962.   2972

_____. Words and Their Use. New York, Philosophical, 1951.
                                                              2973
_____. The Principles of Semantics. New York, Barnes, 1959.
                                                              2974
Urban, W. M. Language and Reality. New York, Macmillan, 1939.
                                                              2975
Walpole, Horace. Semantics. New York, Norton, 1951.   2976

Weekley, E. The Romance of Words. London, J. Murrey Com-
    pany, 4th edition, 1925.   2977

Weinberg, Harry L. Levels of Knowing and Existence. New York,
    Harper, 1960.   2978

Wheelwright, Philip. Metaphor and Reality. Bloomington, Indiana,
    Indiana, 1962.   2979

Whorf, Benjamin L. Language, Thought, and Reality. Cambridge,
    MIT, 1956.   2980

Ziff, Paul. Semantic Analysis. Ithaca, New York, Cornell, 1960.
                                                              2981

2. Theses and Dissertations

Adrian, Paula J. A Study of the Relationship Between Language
    Usage Congruency and Perceived Ethos. M. A. Iowa. 1967.
                                                              2982
Allbritten, Robert. Language Intensity and Affective Response: An
    Exploration of Force Dynamics in Style. Ph. D. Ohio. 1970.
                                                              2983
Borchers, Gladys L. A Study of Oral Style. Ph. D. Wisconsin.
    1928.   2984

Franzwa, Helen H. The Use and Effectiveness of Evaluative-Dy-
    namic Language in Persuasion. Ph. D. Illinois. 1967. 2985

Gordon, Elizabeth M. Principles of Oral Style. M. A. Cornell.
    1940.   2986

Hamilton, Peter K. An Experimental Study of the Persuasibility of
    Debate Speeches Differing in Reading Ease. M. A. Nebraska.
    1967.   2987

McGuckin, Henry L. , Jr. An Experimental Study in the Persuasive
    Force of Similarity in Cognitive Style between Advocate and Audi-
    ence. Ph. D. Stanford. 1966.   2988

Pitkin, William M. A Study of Loaded Words. M. A. Wisconsin.
    1931.   2989

Stewart, John R. Rhetoricians on Language and Meaning: An Ordinary
Language Philosophy Critique. Ph.D. S. California. 1970. 2990

Wegener, Ruth A. Views of Meaning: Locke and Semantics. M.A.
Colorado State. 1967.   2991

3. Articles

Aly, Bower. The Rhetoric of Semantics. QJS, 30 (February,
1944), 23-30.   2992

Auer, J. Jeffery. A Program for Improving Ethical Language Usage
in a Free Society. G, 45 (2 January, 1963), 19-20, 30. (From
a "Symposium on Ethics.")   2993

Babcock, C. Merton. The Importance of Perspective in Communication. CSSJ, 6 (Fall, 1954), 3-6.   2994

Barnard, Raymond H. General Semantics and the Controversial
Phases of Speech. QJS, 26 (December, 1940), 602-6.   2995

Beisecker, Thomas. Verbal Persuasive Strategies in Mixed-Motive
Interactions. QJS, 56 (April, 1970), 149-160.   2996

Benjamin, Robert L. A Case for Semantics. WS, 16 (October,
1952), 255-62.   2997

Beutel, Frederick. Elementary Semantics: Criticism of Radical
and Experimental Jurisprudence. JLE, 13 (1960), 67-75.   2998

Bois, J. Samuel. The Art of Awareness: A Textbook on General
Semantics. Dubuque, Iowa, Brown, 1966.   2999

Bowers, John W. Some Correlates of Language Intensity. QJS, 50
(December, 1964), 415-420.   3000

_____ and Osborn, Michael M. Attitudinal Effects of Selected
Types of Concluding Metaphors in Persuasive Speeches. SM, 33
(June, 1966), 147-155.   3001

Bryngelson, Bryng. A Prelude to General Semantics. SSJ, 9
(March, 1944), 90-4.   3002

Capp, Glenn R. General Semantics for the Debater. SSJ, 19 (May,
1954), 294-303.   3003

Carpenter, Ronald H. The Essential Schemes of Syntax: An Analysis of Rhetorical Theory's Recommendations for Uncommon Word
Orders. QJS, 55 (April, 1969), 161-168.   3004

_____ . Style and Emphasis in Debate. JAFA, 6 (Winter, 1969),
27-31.   3005

Cathcart, Robert.   A Point of Emphasis in Audience Debating.   G,
36 (3 March, 1954), 55-8.   3006

Christopherson, Merrill G.   The Necessity for Style in Argument.
ST, 9 (March, 1960), 116-20.   3007

———.   The Style of the Great Debaters: Eighteenth Century.
AFAR, 19 (Spring, 1962), 1-8.   3008

Coleman, E. B.   Improving Comprehensibility by Shortening Sentences.   JAP, 46 (1962), 131-4.   3009

Darnell, Donald K.   The Relation Between Sentence Order and Comprehension.   SM, 30 (June, 1963), 97-100.   3010

DeVito, Joseph A.   Style and Stylistics: An Attempt at Definition.
QJS, 53 (October, 1967), 248-255.   3011

Dickens, Milton.   A Note on Wendell Johnson's Semantics.   WS, 10
(December, 1946), 8-9.   3012

Diem, W. Roy.   Do We Teach English?   G, 31 (March, 1949), 47,
51.   3013

Douds, J. B.   Propaganda Techniques in Debating.   S, 24 (January,
1940), 3.   3014

Emswiler, Thomas, Jr.   The Importance of Clarity in Debate.   F,
46 (March, 1961), 8-9.   (By a student.)   3015

Finfgeld, Thomas E.   The Ability to Select Words to Convey Intended Meaning.   QJS, 52 (October, 1966), 255-258.   3016

Fisher, Walter R.   The Importance of Style in Systems of Rhetoric.
SSJ, 26 (Spring, 1962), 173-82.   3017

Fowler, Russell.   What are the Characteristics of Unethical Language and What is the Climate Which Nurtures It?   G, 45 (January, 1963), 25-6.   (From a "Symposium on Ethics.")   3018

Franzwa, Helen H.   Psychological Factors Influencing Use of "Eval-
uative-Dynamic" Language.   SM, 36 (June, 1969), 103-109. 3019

Friedman, Robert P.   Resolved: That American Debaters Should
Abandon the Use of Clichés.   SPG, 2 (March, 1965), 86-89. 3020

Gibson, James W.   Research Reports, No. 95.   Oral Vocabulary of
High School Debaters.   Edited by Frank E. X. Dance.   CSSJ, 18
(November, 1967), 310-312.   3021

Gilkinson, Howard, Paulson, Stanley F., and Skkink, Donald E.
Conditions Affecting the Communication of Controversial Statements in Connected Discourse: Forms of Presentation and the

Political Frame of Reference of the Listener. SM, 20 (November, 1953), 253-60.   3022

Gorman, Margaret. A Critique of General Semantics. WS, 31 (Winter, 1967), 44-50.   3023

Grant, C. K. On Using Language. Philosophical Quarterly, 6 (1956), 327-43. (Style analyzed from the standpoint of logic.)   3024

Gregory, Kathleen M. The Application of General Semantics to College Debate. F, 54 (October, 1968), 3-7.   3025

Gruner, Charles R., Kibler, Robert J., and Gibson, James W. A Quantitative Analysis of Selected Characteristics of Oral and Written Vocabularies. JC, 17 (June, 1967), 152-158.   3026

Hallie, P. P. A Criticism of General Semantics. Ce, 14 (1952), 17-23.   3027

Hamburg, John H. How to Double-Cross Your Own Debaters. PN, 8 (September, 1941), 11-12. (Criticizes debaters for excessive reading of quotations; advises paraphrasing.)   3028

Hastings, Arthur. Metaphor in Rhetoric. WS, 34 (Summer, 1970), 181-193.   3029

Hollander, Katherine R. On the Art of Being Articulate. G, 21 (May, 1939), 68-70.   3030

Hoogestraat, Wayne E., and McCleary, William R. Fluency and Stylistic Bloopers. F, 53 (March, 1968), 5-6. (Examples of stylistic inaccuracies in debate speeches.)   3031

Jersild, A. T. Modes of Emphasis in Public Speaking. JAP, 12 (December, 1928), 611-20.   3032

Kanouse, David E., and Abelson, Robert P. Language Variables Affecting the Persuasiveness of Simple Communications. JPSP, 7 (1967), 158-163. (Compares the persuasiveness of "syllogistic" communications on four topics when premises contain a "positive, manifest verb," a "negative, subjective verb," and two evidence conditions, "concrete evidence" and "abstract evidence.")   3033

Kruger, Arthur N. Debate Terminology. PSA, 11 and 12 (June, 1955), 18-25. (Discusses commonly used debate terms.)   3034

Lee, Irving J. General Semantics. QJS, 38 (February, 1952), 1-12.   3035

_____. Why Discussions Go Astray. F, 33 (October, 1947), 1-3. Also in DM, 4 (Spring, 1948), 22-3.   3036

Machotaka, Pavel. Defensive Style and Esthetic Distortion. JPer,

35 (1967), 600-622.   3037

McGuckin, Henry E., Jr.   The Persuasive Force of Similarity in
    Cognitive Style Between Advocate and Audience.   SM, 34 (June,
    1967), 145-151.   3038

Miller, Edd.   Speech Introductions and Conclusions.   QJS, 32
    (April, 1946), 181-3.   3039

Mills, Glen E.   Use of Humor in Speech.   R, 13 (December, 1938),
    7-9.   3040

Musgrave, G. M.   Making it Easier for the Judge and Audience.
    DM, 2 (September, 1946), 194.   (Recommends internal sum-
    maries.)   3041

Nebergall, Roger E.   An Experimental Investigation of Rhetorical
    Clarity.   SM, 25 (November, 1958), 243-54.   3042

Nichols, Egbert R.   Debate Terminology.   DM, 4 (Spring, 1948),
    37.   3043

Oliver, Robert T.   Modern Witch Doctors; the Politician Heads
    Parade of Word-Smiths.   EQ, 20 (April, 1940), 3-4.   3044

Palzer, Edward.   Check Those Transmission Wires.   PN, 7 (No-
    vember, 1940), 22-3.   (Criticizes the colorless speech style of
    much debating.)   3045

_____.   Make Your Statistics Vital!   PN, 5 (January-February,
    1939), 11-12.   3046

_____.   Perspective Through Speech.   SchA, 14 (January, 1943),
    168-70.   3047

_____.   Solecisms of Forensic Speech.   SchA, 13 (November,
    1941), 93-5.   3048

Parrella, Gilda.   Image and Mirror: Empathy in Language Devices.
    WS, 36 (Fall, 1972), 251-260.   3049

Pence, R. W.   "Up With Which We Can No Longer Put!"   QJS, 35
    (April, 1949), 199-201.   (Rhetorical aspects of grammatical er-
    rors.)   3050

Probert, W.   Law Through the Looking Glass of Language and Com-
    municative Behavior.   JLE, 29 (1968), 253-277.   3051

Ramsey, Benjamin.   In Defense of Satire: A Kind Word for the In-
    strument Which Pinches.   SPG, 5 (May, 1968), 158-161.   3052

Reinsch, N. Lamar, Jr.   An Investigation of the Effects of the
    Metaphor and Simile in Persuasive Discourse.   SM, 38 (June,

1971), 142-145.   3053

Robbins, James. Words are Deeds. G, 41 (November, 1958), 11-
12. (On the importance of words in argumentation and persuasion; "words spell action. ")   3054

Roethlisberger, F. J. Barriers to Communication Between Men.
ETC, 9 (Winter, 1952), 89-93.   3055

Rogers, Clement F. The Use of Ridicule in Controversy. Church
Quarterly Review, 141 (January, 1946), 219-27.   3056

Rynin, David. Semantics. WS, 20 (Winter, 1956), 35-44.   3057

Schug, Clayton. What is at Stake? G, 27 (January, 1955), 26-27.
(On the importance of using words correctly.)   3058

Seagle, William. Can Lawyers Talk English? AtM, 181 (March,
1948), 95-7.   3059

Shannon, Mary E. Debating in Oral Language. New Haven Teachers Journal, 21 (April, 1928), 11.   3060

Shepard, David W. "I Have Proved Conclusively... " S, 41 (January, 1959), 13-15.   3061

Sibley, Edward C. An Innocent Abroad. G, 18 (November, 1935),
11. (Urges the use of more humor and the avoidance of "dry
logic" in debate.)   3062

Singer, R. G. Forensic Misconduct by Federal Prosecutors--"And
How It Grew!" AbLR, 20 (Summer, 1968), 227-279. (An analysis of the lawyer's language--inflammatory and prejudicial.) 3063

Skelly, Loretta. The Jargon of Debating. F, 25 (October, 1940),
3-4, 15.   3064

Tiffin, Joseph, and Steer, Max D. An Experimental Analysis of
Emphasis. SM, 4 (1937), 69-74.   3065

Tucker, Raymond K. "You Implied as Much... ???" G, 42 (March,
1960), 47. (On the "method of implication;" contends that it is
more persuasive to present the facts first and draw conclusions
from them, than to state the conclusions first and then the
facts.)   3066

Utterback, W. E. Psychological Approach to the Rhetoric of Speech
Composition. QJS, 10 (February, 1924), 17-22.   3067

Valentine, Milton. Irresponsible Use of Language as a Threat to
Democratic Discussion. G, 42 (2 January, 1963), 27-30. (From
a "Symposium on Ethics. ")   3068

Walch, J. W.   Student Audiences Demand Realism With Humor.   PN,
    4 (April-May, 1938), 15.   3069

Weiler, G.   Degrees of Knowledge.   PhQ, 15 (1965), 317-327. 3070

Zelko, Harold P.   Let's Not Call Names.   BDAPC, 11 (December
    12, 1941), 5-6.   (Urges the use of moderate language in attack
    and defense.)   3071

(For the interested reader, the following periodicals deal wholly or
in part with articles on semantics: Analysis, ETC, Mind, and
Philosophical Review.)

B.   DELIVERY

1.   Books

Allport, G. W.   Pattern and Growth in Personality.   New York,
    Holt, 1961.   3072

_____.   Personality.   New York, H. Holt, 1937.   3073

Eisenson, Jon.   The Psychology of Speech.   New York, Appleton,
    1938.   3074

Mortensen, C. David.   Communication: The Study of Human Inter-
    action.   New York, McGraw, 1972.   3075

Murphy, Gardner.   Personality: A Biosocial Approach to Origins
    and Structure.   New York, Harper, 1947.   3076

Murray, Elwood.   The Speech Personality.   Philadelphia, Lippin-
    cott, rev. edition, 1944.   3077

Pear, T. H.   Voice and Personality.   New York, Wiley, 1932. 3078

Scott, Walter D.   The Psychology of Public Speaking.   New York,
    Noble, 1926.   3079

2.   Theses and Dissertations

Gonzalez, Frank S. H.   The Effect of Delivery in the Transmission
    of Information.   M. A.   Montana State.   1959.   3080

Goodman-Malamuth, Leo.   An Experimental Study of the Effects of
    Speaking Rate Upon Listenability.   Ph. D.   S. California.   1956.
                                                                3081
Jackson, James H.   An Experimental Study of Listeners' Evaluations
    of Speech Content as Compared with Speech Delivery.   Ph. D.
    S. California.   1957.   3082

Lantz, William C.   An Experimental Study of Listeners' Perceptions of Speech Content as Compared with Delivery.   Ph. D.   S. California.   1955.   3083

3. Articles

Addington, David W.   The Effect of Vocal Variations on Ratings of Source Credibility.   SM, 38 (August, 1971), 242-247.   3084

Allport, Gordon W., and Cantril, H.   Judging Personality from Voice.   JSP, 5 (February, 1934), 37-54.   3085

Angell, Clarence S.   Emphasizing Debating Skill without Neglecting Substance: A Marriage of Convenience.   G, 39 (January, 1957), 35-37, 40.   3086

App, Austin J.   A Graphic Style in Debating.   BDAPC, 11 (May 25, 1938), 5-6.   3087

Barnard, Raymond H.   Why Bow to the Fetish of Conversational Delivery.   PN, 5 (September, 1938), 7-8.   3088

Berquist, Goodwin F., Jr.   The Standard the Judge Never Mentions. G, 45 (March, 1963), 48.   3089

Bettinghaus, Erwin.   The Operation of Congruity in an Oral Communication Situation.   SM, 28 (August, 1961), 131-142.   3090

Borchers, Gladys.   An Approach to the Problem of Oral Style. QJS, 22 (February, 1936), 114-17.   3091

Brack, Harold A.   Is Effective Public Speaking "Conversational"? ST, 14 (November, 1965), 276-277.   3092

Brigance, William N.   How Fast Do We Talk?   QJS, 12 (November, 1926), 337-42.   3093

————.   What Is a Successful Speech?   QJS, 11 (November, 1925), 372-7.   3094

Brother Alexander.   Are You Perfectly Satisfied?   R, 21 (December, 1946), 9.   3095

Buehler, E. C.   Delivery in Debate.   G, 34 (January, 1952), 21-23. Also in SA, 8 (Spring, 1952), 12-13.   3096

————.   Voice as a Factor in Forensics.   G, 29 (March, 1947), 36.   3097

Cabat, Richard C.   Belligerent Discussion and Truth Seeking.   InJE, 9 (October, 1898), 29-53.   3098

Clevenger, Theodore, Jr. Toward a Point of View for Contest Debate. CSSJ, 12 (Autumn, 1960), 21-26.   3099

Diehl, Charles F., White, Richard C., and Burk, Kenneth W. Rate and Communication. SM, 26 (August, 1959), 229-32. 3100

_____, _____ and Satz, Paul H. Pitch Change and Comprehension. SM, 27 (March, 1961), 65-68.   3101

Dressel, Harold A. Debating for the Audience. QJS, 16 (April, 1930), 227-31.   3102

English, W. Francis. The Western Lawyer as a Speaker. QJS, 30 (October, 1944), 285-8.   3103

Eppinga, Peter L. An Ancient Force in Action Today--Ethos. F, 47 (March, 1962), 14-16.   3104

Erhart, Joseph F. X., S. J. Logic and Debate. BDAPC, 21 (December, 1955), 21-23.   3105

Eulalia, (Sister) Mary. Debating as an Art. BDAPC, 10 (December 19, 1940), 5-7.   3106

Fairbanks, Grant, and Kodman, Frank, Jr. Word Intelligibility as a Function of Time Comprehension. Jour. of the Accoustical Society of America, 29 (May, 1957), 636-641.   3107

_____, Guttman, Newman, and Miron, Murray S. Auditory Comprehension in Relation to Listening Rate and Selective Verbal Redundancy. JSHD, 22 (March, 1957), 23-32.   3108

_____, _____ and _____. Auditory Comprehension of Repeated High-Speed Messages. JSHD, 22 (March, 1957), 20-22. 3109

_____, _____ and _____. Effects of Time Compression upon the Comprehension of Connected Speech. JSHD, 22 (March, 1957), 10-19.
                                                                                      3110
Faries, Clyde J. The Debater Has No Case. F, 54 (January, 1969), 5-7.   3111

Fay, Paul J., and Middleton, Warren C. The Ability to Judge Sociability from the Voice as Transmitted Over a Public Address System. JSP, 13 (1941), 303-9.   3112

_____. The Ability to Judge Truth-Telling or Lying from the Voice as Transmitted Over a Public Address System. JGP, 24 (1941), 211-15.   3113

_____. Judgment of Spranger Personality Types from the Voice as Transmitted over a Public Address System. Character and Personality, 8 (September 1939-June, 1940), 144-155.   3114

Foulke, E. , and Sticht, T. G.   Review of Research on the Intelligi-
    bility and Comprehension of Accelerated Speech.   PB, 72 (July,
    1969), 50-62.   (Detailed study of the effects of speaking rapidly
    upon intelligibility and comprehension.)   3115

Gilbert, Russell W.   Electrocution in Debate.   S, 2 (January, 1939),
    4-6.   (On adaptation to the audience.)   3116

Glasgow, George M.   A Semantic Index of Vocal Pitch.   SM, 19
    (March, 1952), 64-68.   3117

Gorden, William I.   A Comparison of Two Types of Delivery of a
    Persuasive Speech.   SSJ, 27 (Fall, 1961), 74-9.   3118

Gray, Giles W.   "Quote - Unquote. "   SSJ, 10 (March, 1945), 92-4.
                                                                       3119
Haiman, Franklyn S.   An Experimental Study of the Effects of Ethos
    in Public Speaking.   SM, 16 (1949), 190-202.   3120

Hance, Kenneth G.   The Concept of Ethical Proof in Persuasion and
    Debate.   AFAR, 6 (Spring, 1958), 5-12.   3121

Harding, Harold F.   The Principles of Poor Speaking.   G, 31 (4
    May, 1949), 80-1.   (Reprinted from Scientific Monthly, 66 (Jan-
    uary, 1948).)   3122

Harms, L. S.   Listener Comprehension of Speakers of Three Status
    Groups.   LS, 4 (1961), 109-112.   3123

Harwood, Kenneth A.   Listening Ability and Rate of Presentation.
    SM, 22 (March, 1955), 57-9.   3124

_____ .   Listening Ability and Readability.   SM, 22 (March, 1955),
    49-52.   3125

Hatlen, Theodore.   Give Speech a Chance in Debate.   WS, 4 (May,
    1950), 13-14.   3126

Heinberg, Paul.   Relationship of Content and Delivery to General
    Effectiveness.   SM, 30 (June, 1963), 105-107.   3127

Hildebrandt, Herbert W. , and Stevens, Walter W.   Manuscript and
    Extemporaneous Delivery in Communicating Information.   SM, 30
    (November, 1963), 369-372.   3128

Hostlettler, Gordon A.   The Use and Abuse of Notes.   TS, 3 (Jan-
    uary, 1955), 7-8.   3129

Kanungo, R. N.   Effects of Verbal Repetition on Meaning Intensity
    and Retention of Functions.   PsyRt, 22 (June, 1969), 771-779.
                                                                       3130
Keller, I. C.   Is It Debating?   QJS, 21 (November, 1935), 506-10.
    (Criticizes reading of debate speeches.)   3131

Kline, Donald F.   Effect of Debate Skills on Delivery.   G, 35
(March, 1953), 59–60.   3132

Lambertson, F. W.   Extemporaneous Speaking Versus Oratory.   G,
15 (March, 1933), 9.   3133

Lindsley, Charles F.   Delivery in Debate.   QJS, 4 (January, 1918),
116–18.   3134

Lucas, R. L. , and Jaffee, C. L.   Effects of High–Rate Talkers on
Group Voting Behavior in the Leaderless–Group Problem–Solving
Situation.   PsyRt, 25 (October, 1969), 471–477.   3135

Mays, Morley J.   Courtesy in Debate.   BDAPC, (May 28, 1937),
2.   3136

McBath, James H.   Speech and the Legal Profession.   ST, 10 (Jan-
uary, 1961), 44–47.   3137

_____ and Cripe, Nicholas M.   Delivery: Rhetoric's Rusty Canon.
JAFA, 2 (January, 1965), 1–6.   3138

McKinney, Fred.   Psychological Aspects of Public Speaking.   G,
18 (May, 1936), 61–63.   3139

Michael, William, and Crawford, C. C.   An Experiment in Judging
Intelligence by the Voice.   Journal of Educational Psychology,
18 (1927), 107–114.   3140

Moses, Paul J.   The Study of Personality from Records of the
Voice.   Journal of Consulting Psychology, 4 (1942), 257–61. 3141

Mundt, K. E.   According to Aesop.   R, 11 (February, 1937), 2.
(Calls for vividness in presentation.)   3142

_____ .   One Hundred Sad Debates.   R, 11 (8 April, 1936), 2–3.
(Complains that delivery in tournament debates tends to become
too dehumanized and formal.)   3143

_____ .   "Vocabulation, " the Cardinal Vice.   R, 10 (November,
1935), 2–3.   Also in G, 18 (January, 1936), 26.   (Complains
that school debaters often speak gibly with little knowledge.) 3144

Palzer, Edward.   Let Your Eyes Speak, Too!   PN, 6 (January-
February, 1940), 11–13.   3145

_____ .   Personal Adjustment Under Stress.   R, 18 (December,
1943), 8–9.   3146

_____ .   Position Problem in Platform Speech.   SchA, 12 (March-
April, 1941), 271–3, 307–10.   3147

_____ .   Speech–Making in Miniature.   F, 26 (May, 1941), 120–

121.   3148

_____. This Thing Called Microphone Technique. PN, 6 (March-
April, 1940), 14-15.   3149

_____. A Thought for Debaters. R, 15 (April, 1941), 8.   3150

_____, ed. The Acid Test--A Symposium. PN, 7 (September,
1940), 10-13. (Further discussion of extemporaneous debating
by Karl F. Robinson, Ray Kesslar Immel, and L.R. Breniman.)
                                                           3151
Parrish, W.M. The Concept of Naturalness. QJS, 37 (December,
1951), 448-54.   3152

Paulette, (Sister) Mary. Teach Our Youth to Speak. CaSJ, 54
(March, 1954), 98.   3153

Pelsma, J.R. Flux de Bouche. F, 24 (May, 1939), 107-15. (On
speaking.)   3154

Porter, Ebenezer. The Gesture in Public Speaking. PN, 7 (September, 1940), 28-30.   3155

Ragsdale, J. Donald. Effects of Selected Aspects of Brevity on
Persuasiveness. SM, 35 (March, 1968), 8-13.   3156

_____. Problems of Some Contemporary Notions of Style. SSJ,
35 (Summer, 1970), 332-341.   3157

Rothman, Richard M. Let's Think about the Listener. F, 49
(March, 1964), 4-5.   3158

Sapir, Edward. Speech as a Personality Trait. AJS, 32 (May,
1927), 892-905.   3159

Shearn, Donald, Sprague, Robert, and Rosenzweig, Sandford. A
Method for the Analysis and Control of Speech Rate. Journal of
Experimental Analysis of Behavior, 4 (1961), 197-201.   3160

Swift, W.B. Hygiene of the Voice Before Debates. QJS, 1 (July,
1915), 114-26.   3161

Swinney, James P. The Relative Comprehension of Contemporary
Tournament Debate Speeches. JAFA, 5 (Winter, 1968), 16-20.
                                                           3162
Symposium on Nonverbal Communication. JC, 11 (June, 1961), 51-
99.   3163

Taylor, Harold C. Social Agreement on Personality Traits as
Judged from Speech. JSP, 5 (May, 1934), 244-8.   3164

Thomas, Stafford H. Effects of Monotonous Delivery on Intelligibility. SM, 36 (June, 1969), 110-113.   3165

Turner, Frederick H. , Jr. The Effect of Speech Summaries on Audience Comprehension. CSSJ, 21 (Spring, 1970), 24-29. 3166

Van Buren, Ruth. Get Your Audience--and Hold It. PN, 8 (December, 1941), 14-15. 3167

Vohs, John L. An Empirical Approach to the Concept of Attention. SM, 31 (August, 1964), 355-360. 3168

Voor, John B. , and Miller, Joseph M. The Effect of Practice upon the Comprehension of Time-Compressed Speech. SM, 32 (November, 1965), 452-454. 3169

Walch, J. Weston. Ferdinand, the Debater. PN, 7 (September, 1940), 13-14. (A criticism of memorized debate speeches.) 3170

_____. When the Formula Doesn't Work. PN, 8 (October, 1941), 8-9. (On extemporaneous debating and how to develop it.) 3171

Woolbert, Charles H. Speaking and Writing--A Study of Differences. QJS, 8 (June, 1922), 271-285. 3172

XII.   TEACHING AND COACHING

1.   Books

Lahman, Carroll P.   Debate Coaching, A Handbook for Teachers
and Coaches.   New York, Wilson, 1936.   3173

McKown, Harry C.   Extracurricular Activities.   New York, Macmillan, rev. ed., 1952.   (Includes a section on literary societies,
debating and speaking.)   3174

Walch, J. Weston.   An Outline of Debating and Debate Coaching.
Portland, Me., Platform, 1937.   (A pamphlet.)   3175

Weaver, Andrew T., Borchers, Gladys L., and Smith, Donald K.
The Teaching of Speech.   New York, Prentice, 1952.   3176

2.   Theses and Dissertations

Carter, Jack.   A Survey and Analysis of the Methods and Philosophies of Selected Directors of Intercollegiate Tournament Debating.   M. A.   Alabama.   1953.   3177

Clark, Patricia A.   Some Analytical Skills a Forensic Student May
Gain from the Study of English and Political Science.   M. A.
Pacific Lutheran University.   1970.   3178

Eggeling, Rae.   How to Teach an Effective Course in Debating.
M. A.   Texas.   1948.   3179

Pribil, Rosemarie.   A Survey of the Coaching Philosophies and
Practices of Intercollegiate Debate Coaches in the United States.
M. S.   Wisconsin.   1958.   3180

Stovall, Richard L.   An Investigation to Determine the Criteria
Used in Selecting Argumentation and Debate Textbooks.   M. A.
C. W. Post.   1969.   3181

Thaler, Margaret.   An Introductory Study of Inference Mechanism in
the Teaching of Public Speaking.   M. A.   Denver.   1945.   3182

3. Articles

Anderson, Dorothy I.   Edward T. Channing's Teaching of Rhetoric.
   SM, 16 (1949), 69-81.   3183

Auser, Cortland P., and Bayless, Ovid L.   The Persuasion Course
   at the U.S. Air Force Academy.   ST, 16 (January, 1967), 33-
   37.   3184

Babcock, Maud M.   Courses in Debating.   QJS, 1 (April, 1915),
   91-2.   (Contains list of colleges offering courses in debate.)3185

Bickford, Ethel S.   Speak the Speech Trippingly.   Ed, 57 (December, 1936), 209-13.   (Suggestions based on experiences in organizing a debate course at a small teachers' college.)   3186

Bowman, Georgia.   Memorial Service.   F, 56 (May, 1971), 5-6.
   (On the deaths of three directors of forensics: Forrest Rose,
   Dale Stockton, and Ted Nelson.)   3187

Brandes, Paul.   Aristotle for the Undergraduate.   SSJ, 14 (March,
   1949), 264-69.   3188

Brembeck, Winston L.   The Content of the College Course in Persuasion.   ST, 13 (November, 1964), 277-282.   3189

_____.   Teaching the Course in Persuasion.   ST, 9 (September,
   1960), 216-221.   3190

Brewer, Robert, and Willett, Tom.   Debate Via Telelecture.   F,
   56 (October, 1970), 3-5, 30.   (Recommends the use of the telephone, amplified over loud speakers, as a research tool and as
   a vehicle for practice debates between interested schools.)   3191

Brigance, William N.   "Demagogues, 'Good' People, and Teachers
   of Speech."   ST, 1 (1952), 157-62.   3192

Buehler, E. C.   What Constitutes a Superior Director of Forensics?
   G, 30 (May, 1948), 63.   3193

Cable, W. Arthur.   Vitalizing the Course of Study in Argumentation
   and Debate.   QJS, 12 (June, 1926), 182-95.   3194

Capp, Glenn R.   Training College Debaters.   SSJ, 1 (March, 1936),
   11-15.   3195

Clarke, Presley W.   What's Wrong with Our Debate Training?   G,
   17 (March, 1935), 46-7.   3196

Collins, G. Rowland.   Problems in Teaching Debate.   QJS, 7 (June,
   1921), 261-71.   3197

Courses in Debating.   QJS, 1 (April, 1915), 91-2.   3198

A Debate Course Broadcast Direct from the Classroom. G, 16
(January, 1934), 21. (On the contents of Speech 111, Advanced
Public Discussion and Debate, offered at Iowa by A. Craig
Baird.)   3199

Dickens, Milton C. Turning a Corner in Debate. JE, 4 (June,
1930), 65-70. (Problems confronting debate coaches and suggested solutions.)   3200

Dovre, Paul J. The Basic Course in Argumentation: A Prospectus.
CSSJ, 22 (Winter, 1971), 236-241.   3201

Durkee, Frank M. Simplified Coaching of Debate. SchA, 12 (May,
1941), 335-6.   3202

Geary, (Sister) Theophane. Some Observations of the Training of
Debaters. BDAPC, 15 (December 10, 1947), 9-12.   3203

Graham, John. The Value of Common Materials in the Debate
Course. SSCJ, 37 (Spring, 1972), 290-303.   3204

Grandy, Adah G. Some Work in Debates. EJ, 2 (June, 1913),
389-90.   3205

Gronbeck, Bruce E. Four Approaches to Studying Argument in
Graduate Programs. JAFA, 9 (Fall, 1972), 350-354.   3206

Gunderson, Robert G. Teaching Critical Thinking. ST, 10 (March,
1961), 100-4.   3207

Hance, Kenneth. Adapting "the Teaching Cycle" to Debate. QJS,
30 (December, 1944), 444-50.   3208

Harmon, Carol. Speech Coaches: A Tribute. F, 56 (October,
1970), 7-8. (A tribute to debate coaches.)   3209

Hastings, Arthur. Recent Texts: New Aspects of Argumentation.
JAFA, 1 (January, 1964), 34-36.   3210

Hatch, R. W. Teaching Controversial Issues in the Classroom. Ed,
47 (1936), 140-44.   3211

Heisey, D. Ray. An Honors Course in Argumentation. ST, 17
(September, 1968), 202-204.   3212

Hellerich, Mahlon H. The Social Science Instructor and Intercollegiate Debating. BDAPC, 16 (July 10, 1950), 3-7.   3213

Hess, Maurice A. How Much Should the Coach Do? G, 14 (March,
1932), 10-13.   3214

Hilliard, Otis L. The Art and Practice of Coaching Debate. Cori-
cana, Texas: Debate Coaches Bureau, 1938. 21 pp.   3215

How's Your Speech "I. Q. ?" (Test Your Knowledge of Speech and
Debate Rules.) PN, 4 (February-March, 1938), 7-8.   3216

Hutton, Ralph. Coaching Non-Academic Debate. DM, 3 (December,
1947), 215-16.   3217

Kegler, Stanley G. Techniques in Teaching Listening for Main
Ideas. EJ, 45 (January, 1956), 30-2.   3218

Kruger, Arthur N. Teaching Analysis to a Debate Squad. G, 39
(November, 1956), 9-11. (On the issues involved in debating a
proposition of policy.)   3219

Ladd, J. W. Educational Debating; "Make it an Active and Dynamic
Force in Our Classrooms." WEJ, 13 (February, 1924), 110-
11.   3220

Lane, Frank H. Faculty Help in Intercollegiate Contests. QJS, 1
(April, 1915), 9-16.   3221

Litsheim, Patricia M. Is Speech a Tinkling Cymbal? F, 44 (May,
1959), 123-25.   3222

Long, Emmett T. Handling Ethical Problems in Coaching Debate.
G, 39 (1957), 45-6, 50.   3223

Lyman, Rollo L. V. Some Suggested Reforms in Intercollegiate Debating. PSR, 3 (January, 1914), 144-54. (Criticizes over-
coached and stereotyped debate procedure.)   3224

MacLatchey, Josephine, ed. Handling Controversial Issues. (A
discussion.) Education on the Air, 1940. Columbus, Ohio State
University Press, 1940.   3225

MacQuilkin, Nona. The Emancipation of the Contest Coach. QJS,
6 (April, 1920), 69-72.   3226

Marcham, Frederick G. Teaching Critical Thinking and the Use of
Evidence. QJS, 31 (October, 1945), 362-8.   3227

Marsh, Charles A. Coaching Debate Teams. G, 13 (January,
1931), 3-6.   3228

_____. Coaching Debate Teams. In A Program of Speech Educa-
tion in a Democracy, ed. by W. A. Cable. Boston, Expression,
1932. Pp. 227-32.   3229

McKean, Dayton D. Woodrow Wilson as a Debate Coach. QJS, 16
(November, 1930), 458-63.   3230

Merry, Glenn N. Should a Debate Team Have a Coach? PSR, 1
(April, 1912), 241-2.   3231

Mills, Glen E.   Argumentation in General Education.   SSJ, 26 (Summer, 1961), 313-17.   3232

Millson, William A. D.   The Shift of Opinion Ballot as a Teaching Tool.   S, 26 (May, 1942), 3-5.   3233

_____.   Using the Shift-of-Opinion Ballot as a Teaching Device.
PN, 7 (January-February, 1941), 5-6.   3234

Murphy, Richard.   Socrates, the Student, and the War.   F, 28 (May, 1943), 117-119, 127.   (On coaching and directing debate.)
                                                                  3235
Nobles, W. Scott.   Criticism in Teaching: Debate.   WS, 28 (Winter, 1964), 35-38.   3236

O'Neill, James M.   Buying Debates.   QJS, 5 (January, 1919), 55-6.   (On the practice, which the author deplores, of hiring teachers to work out briefs for students.)   3237

Palzer, Edward.   Techniques in Adult Speech Instruction.   AEB, 6 (December, 1941), 44-5.   3238

Perry, I. D.   A Unit in Debating.   SEN, 33 (January, 1937), 42-4.
                                                                  3239
Polisky, Jerome B., and Hendrix, J. A.   The "Subject Matter" Coach.   SPG, 3 (January, 1966), 55-56.   3240

Poos, Roberta L.   A Device for Training Contest Speakers.   PN, 3 (April-May, 1937), 15, 30.   3241

Prescott, Herbert.   What I Learned from Ten Years Coaching.   PN, 8 (March-April, 1942), 13-14.   3242

Pross, E. L., and Shirley, John.   Debate Coaches View the Post-War Situation.   SA, 5 (Summer, 1949), 56.   3243

Quimby, Brooks.   Is Directing of Forensics a Profession?   ST, 12 (January, 1963), 41-2.   3244

_____.   Training the Debater.   BDAPC, 21 (December, 1955), 4-8.
                                                                  3245

Rice, George P., Jr.   Aristotle's Rhetoric as an Undergraduate Textbook.   QJS, 33 (April, 1947), 217-19.   3246

Rives, Stanley G.   Rhetoric Project: Implications for Argumentation and Debate.   JAFA, 8 (Spring, 1972), 228-232.   3247

Robinson, Karl F., and Keltner, John.   Suggested Units in Discussion and Debate for Secondary Schools.   QJS, 32 (October, 1946), 385-90.   3248

Rupp, A. E.   The Superior Teacher of Debate.   QJS, 34 (April,

1948), 220-1.   3249

Sandford, William P.   A Laboratory in Persuasion.   QJS, 21
(April, 1935), 188-91.   3250

Sattler, William M.   Some Values of Discussion in the Investigation
and Analysis Phases of Debate.   G, 24-25 (March-May, 1943),
54-5.   3251

Shaw, W. C.   The Crime Against Public Speaking.   QJS, 8 (April,
1922), 138-44.   (The crime referred to is the "toleration and
encouragement that is being given to coaching among academic
teachers of public speaking. ")   3252

Siegel, Seymour N.   Handling Controversial Issues.   In Education
on the Air, ed. by Josephine MacLatchey.   Columbus, Ohio,
Ohio State University Press, 1939.   Pp. 45-80.   3253

Smith, William S.   Coordinating Classroom Instruction in Debate
with the Extracurricular Program.   ST, 6 (September, 1957),
213-16.   3254

Sternberg, William N.   A Project in Argumentation.   HP, 12 (January, 1930), 52-3.   3255

Stone, Arthur P.   Novelties, Real and Fancied, in the Teaching of
Argument.   QJS, 4 (May, 1918), 247-62.   (Replies to articles
by C. H. Woolbert and Mary Yost in QJS, July, 1917, and Janu-
ary, 1918.)   3256

Teaching Argumentation.   Na, 94 (May 9, 1912), 456-7.   3257

Teaching Controversial Issues.   Columbus, Ohio, The Junior Town
Meeting League, 1947.   3258

Townsend, Howard W.   Aristotle and Contemporary Textbooks.   WS,
22 (Summer, 1958), 154-8.   3259

Troxell, E. E.   Argumentation--Its Relation to Debate.   PSR, 2
(March, 1913), 185-7.   (A plan for a "supplementary course" in
argumentation to teach brief-making and argumentative writing.)
                                                                            3260
Trueblood, Thomas C.   A Chapter on the Organization of College
Courses in Public Speaking.   QJS, 12 (February, 1926), 1-11.
                                                                            3261
_____.   Coaching a Debate Team.   PSR, 1 (November, 1911), 84-
5.   3262

_____.   Forensic Training in Colleges.   Ed, 27 (March, 1907),
381-92.   3263

Verderber, R. F.   One-Point Debate: An Addition to the Beginning
Speech Course.   ST, 12 (March, 1963), 125-6.   3264

Walch, J. Weston.   Can You Pick Them?   (An Aptitude Test for
    Debaters.)   PN, 5 (October, 1938), 5-7.   3265

_____.   Debate Them Yourself.   PN, 7 (January-February, 1941),
    10-11.   (Suggests that the debate coach debate his own students
    as a teaching device.)   3266

_____.   Recent Methods in Teaching Debate.   PN, 3 (October,
    1936), 5-6, 18.   3267

Waltz, Waldo E.   Teaching Debate by Attention to Rebuttal.   ArT,
    22 (March, 1934), 199-202.   3268

Warther, George S.   The Rewards of a Debate Coach.   BDAPC, 15
    (December 10, 1948), 2-4.   3269

Watkins, Dwight E.   Coaching Versus Instruction.   PSR, 4 (October,
    1914), 38-43.   (Suggestions to improve quality of teaching.) 3270

Watkins, Lloyd I.   The Social Responsibility of Debate Coaching.
    G, 40 (1957), 3-6.   3271

Wells, Hugh N.   Coaching Debates.   QJS, 4 (March, 1918), 170-
    83.   3272

Wilson, O. J.   Utilization of Textbooks and Handbooks in Teaching
    and Coaching Intercollegiate Debating.   AFAR, 7 (Winter, 1959),
    15-22.   3273

Wisness, Arthur M.   Outline of Activities in a Newly Organized
    Speech Department.   PN, 7 (September, 1940), 18-19.   3274

Woolbert, Charles H.   The Coach Versus the Professor.   QJS, 9
    (June, 1923), 284-5.   3275

_____.   Scholar vs. Advocate.   QJS, 1 (July, 1915), 207-210. 3276

Wright, Donald K.   The Coach's Letter to the Freshman Squad.   F,
    46 (October, 1960), 13.   3277

Zelko, Harold P.   Problems of Debate Coaching--As Our Own
    Coaches Solve Them.   BDAPC, 13 (December 15, 1939), 11-13.
                                                                        3278

XIII. THE DEBATE PROGRAM

A. DIRECTING FORENSICS

1. Books

Faules, Don F., and Rieke, Richard D. Directing Forensics: Debate and Contest Speaking. Scranton, Pa., International Textbook Co., 1968.   3279

Klopf, Donald W., and Lahman, Carroll P. Coaching and Directing
Forensics. Skokie, Ill., National, 1967.   3280

2. Theses and Dissertations

Anderson, Dorothy I. Consideration of Possible Factors Influencing
or Indicating the Success of the State University of Iowa Debaters.
M. A. Iowa. 1931.   3281

Dean, Nancy S. An Analysis of the Inter-Collegiate Forensic Program in the State of Ohio for the Academic Year 1953-54. M. A.
Ohio. 1955.   3282

Dicks, Vivian I. Description of Criteria which Influence Debate
Coaches' Decision when Selecting Tournaments for Teams with
Varying Levels of Experience and Preparation. M. A. Ohio
State. 1968.   3283

Faules, Donald F. A Survey and Analysis of College Audience Debating in Three National Honorary Forensic Societies for 1955-
56. M. A. Southern Illinois. 1957.   3284

Goldman, Robert. A Survey of the Administration and Financing of
Extra-Curricular Debate Programs in the State of Illinois, 1963-
1964. M. A. N. Illinois. 1964.   3285

Grimmer, Betty B. The International Debate Program: 1921-1958.
M. A. Alabama. 1959.   3286

Haston, Bruce. A Survey of Forensics Activities in the Northwest.
M. A. Washington State. 1960.   3287

Lane, Richard A. An Examination of Debate Policies, Procedures,
and Coaching Techniques Employed in Schools Participating in a

237

National Speech Tournament. M. A. Washington. 1962.   3288

Price, Michael J. Grace Mary Walsh: A Case Study of Influences
and Methods of Coaching Forensics. M. A. Marquette. 1968.
                                                                    3289
Stine, Richard L. A Study of Administrators' Attitudes Toward Debate. M. S. Kansas State. 1970.   3290

Wright, Wiley J. The Development, Presentation, and Evaluation
of a Short Training Program in Educational Debate Processes.
M. A. Hawaii. 1968.   3291

3. Articles

Alexander, Boris G. Negroes Can Think as Well as Sing. F, 24
(January, 1939), 42-8.   3292

Allen, Ronald R. The Effects of Interpersonal and Concept Compatibility on the Encoding Behavior and Achievement of Debate
Teams. CSSJ, 14 (February, 1963), 23-26.   3293

Altman, Irwin, and Haythorn, William W. The Effects of Social
Isolation and Group Composition on Performance. HR, 20 (November, 1967), 313-340. (On the effectiveness of compatible and
incompatible persons working singly and in groups. Findings
could help coach in pairing members of a debate team.)   3294

Anapol, Malthon M. A Second Reply to the Need for Standards.
AFAR, 9 (Spring Issue, 1961), 29-30. (An answer to Mader's
"Need for Standards" on the universal use of the AFA ballot.)
                                                                    3295
_____, ed. , and Weaver, Carl H. , assoc. ed. The Forensic
Travel Directory. AFAR, Special issue, 1957. 63 pp.   3296

Anderson, Frederick W. Modern Tendencies in Intercollegiate Debating. JEX, 1 (December, 1927), 167-75.   3297

Armstrong, George R. Intercollegiate Forensic Budget Survey,
1966-1967. JAFA, 4 (Fall, 1967), 87-95.   3298

Auer, J. Jeffery. The College Debater Finds a Public. G, 22
(March, 1940), 50-1.   3299

Baird, A. Craig. The College Debater: 1955. SSJ, 20 (Spring,
1955), 204-11.   3300

_____. How Can We Improve International Debating? QJS, 34
(April, 1949), 228-30.   3301

Baker, George P. Intercollegiate Debating. ER, 21 (March, 1901),
244-57.   3302

Baldwin, Charles S.   Intercollegiate Debate.   ER, 42 (December, 1911), 475-85.   3303

Barber, William S.   Streamlining the Speaker's Bureau.   G, 43 (January, 1961), 18-22, 25-6.   3304

Barefield, Paul A.   "I Coach Debate" or "Whatthehell Is Forensics?"   JAFA, 7 (Spring, 1970), 116-119.   (Humorous description of a year in the life of a debate coach.)   3305

Barry, James J.   Ralph Brownell Dennis.   DM, 3 (March, 1947), 42-3.   3306

Barton, William B.   Some Expedients for Interest in Debate Work. Illinois Association of Teachers of English Bulletin, 17 (March, 1925), 13-18.   3307

Bass, W. W.   Debate as an Extra-Curricular Activity.   KT, 32 (January, 1931), 13.   3308

Bergan, K. W.   Debate: How Shall It Be Organized?   Montana Education, 5 (December, 1928), 28-9.   3309

Berry, Mildred F.   A Survey of Intercollegiate Debate in the Mid-West Debate Conference.   QJS, 14 (February, 1928), 86-94. 3310

Betz, Edward S.   Evaluation of the Intercollegiate Forensic Program.   F, 31 (May, 1946), 95-8.   Also in DM, 3 (September, 1946), 147-8.   3311

_____.   Address to the Convention.   F, 45 (May, 1961), 11-16.
                                                                        3312
Bilski, T.   Directing the Debate Program.   TCJ, 34 (December, 1962), 95-9.   3313

Bos, William H.   The Creed of a Director of Forensics.   F, 50 (March, 1965), 10.   3314

Boyle, Mary J.   Operating a Debate Program in a Large University. BDAPC, 17 (December, 1951), 6-8.   (The program at the University of Pittsburgh.)   3315

Bradley, Bert E., Jr.   Debate--A Practical Training for Gifted Students.   ST, 8 (March, 1959), 134-8.   3316

Bradshaw, Jane A.   The Rochester Plan.   PN, 8 (January-February, 1942), 14.   (For training debaters--students used as teachers.)   3317

Brake, Robert, and Littlefield, Walter.   The Swing Tour: a Re-Discovery.   AFAR, 11 (Spring, 1963), 9-13.   (Recommends early trips for the novice debaters.)   3318

Brembeck, Cole S.   How About the Freshmen?   BDAPC, 10 (December 19, 1940), 20-23.   3319

_____.   Our Brownstone Front.   BDAPC, 12 (January 1, 1943),
6-9.   3320

Breniman, Lester R.   Comments on Speech Activities.   R, 11 (December, 1936), 6-7.   3321

Brooks, William D.   Needed: A Rationale for Debate that is Potent.
F, 47 (March, 1962), 6-7.   3322

Brother Alexander.   Defense of the South.   DM, 1 (October-December, 1945), 111-12.   (On the merits of the debate programs
of Southern California.)   3323

_____.   What Was That Remark about Comparisons?   DM, 1
(April-June, 1945), 92-3.   (On the comparison of debate programs of Northern and Southern California.)   3324

Brown, Ralph A.   Why Doesn't Your School Have Debating?   SchA,
13 (September, 1941), 11-12.   3325

Buehler, E. C.   Drums on the Forensic Front.   G, 28 (November,
1945), 3, 8.   Also in DM, 1 (October-December, 1945), 31-32.
                                                                            3326
_____.   Experimenting in Debate.   G, 14 (May, 1932), 6-7.   3327

_____.   From My Campus to Yours.   G, 41 (January, 1959), 29,
32.   3328

_____.   The Off-Campus Audience as an Adjunct of the Forensic
Program.   G, 30 (January, 1948), 27.   3329

_____.   Ten Commandments for the Debater.   Scholastic Debater,
1 (March, 1945), 1.   Also in G, 27 (May, 1945), 51, 57; and in
DM, 2 (June, 1946), 82-3.   3330

_____.   What Should be the Philosophy and Objective of a Debate
Program?   G, 39 (January, 1957), 31-4.   3331

Cable, W. Arthur.   Financing Intercollegiate Forensics.   G, 11
(January, 1929), 10-13.   3332

Cameron, Donald J.   Backgrounds of Forensic Directors.   JAFA,
1 (May, 1964), 59-61.   3333

Campbell, Gus W.   A Successful Debating Season.   QJS, 20 (April,
1934), 272-75.   3334

Capp, Glenn R.   Comments on Student Evaluation of Intercollegiate
Forensic Program.   DM, 2 (September, 1946), 180, 185.   (Comments on Betz's article.)   3335

_____. Let's Improve Debate. SSJ, 6 (September, 1940), 1-5.
                                                                  3336

Carlile, Clark S. Ask the Men Who Were There. F, 49 (October,
  1963), 9-14. (Transcription of a humorous speech delivered at
  the awards banquet of the Idaho University Debate Tournament.)
                                                                  3337

Carmack, Paul A. Dr. O. J. Wilson: College President - Debate
  Director. AFAR, 7 (Spring, 1959), 4.   3338

_____. Survey of Forensic Finances. SA, 7 (Spring, 1951), 5-7.
                                                                  3339

Carter, Reginald. Debating as an Activity. HER, 21 (November,
  1932), 73-4.   3340

Cathcart, Robert. In Memory of E. R. Nichols. F, 43 (May, 1958),
  103-4. (E. R. Nichols was an author, editor, and teacher, whose
  many works are listed here.)   3341

A Challenge to Debaters. PN, 5 (September, 1938), 30. (From
  F, May, 1938.)   3342

Chambers, Mildred E. Games to Liven Up Your Debate Club Meetings. PN, 4 (September, 1937), 13-14, 20.   3343

Cleary, James W. Debating Technique 1949. G, 32 (January,
  1950), 28, 35.   3344

Cole, John D. Western College Debate Survey. SA, 7 (Summer,
  1951), 45.   3345

College Debating. B, 22 (January, 1906), 528-9.   3346

College Debating, 1931-1932. WLB, 6 (December, 1931), 306. 3347

Committee On International Debating. Arrangements for International Debates. QJS, 35 (October, 1949), 366-68.   3348

_____. QJS, 35 (December, 1949), 519-20.   3349

Cook, Joseph. View of an American Debate Tour of Great Britain.
  S, 45 (November, 1962), 6-9.   3350

Cortelyou, E. H. Preparedness: The Secret of Successful Debating.
  Schol, 31 (October 9, 1937), 23-4.   3351

Cortright, Rupert L. A Balanced Forensic Program. G, 27 (January, 1945), 22-3, 29.   3352

Covelli, Eugene F. James Milton O'Neill: Father of the Modern
  Speech Movement. ST, 13 (September, 1964), 176-183.   3353

_____. Debate: Won or Lost?--James M. O'Neill's Legacy. SPG,
  4 (March, 1967), 60-63. (Recalls O'Neill's defense of debate

during the period, 1912-1918.)   3354

Cripe, Nicholas M.   Intercollegiate Forensic Budget Survey.   JAFA,
1 (May, 1964), 52-58.   3355

_____.   Status of the Profession.   AFAR, 7 (Winter, 1959), 13-
14.   3356

_____.   A Survey of Debate Programs in Two Hundred and Forty-
Six American Colleges and Universities.   ST, 8 (March, 1959),
157-60.   3357

Crocker, Lionel.   The Financial Support of Debating.   QJS, 22
(December, 1936), 603-07.   3358

Curtis, H. S.   Educational Extension Through the Rural Social Center.   Ed, 34 (January, 1914), 290-1.   3359

Dahlberg, W. A.   Forensic Preparation in Action.   WS, 10 (October,
1946), 6-8.   Also in DM, 3 (March, 1947), 6-7.   3360

Davis, Barrett.   Debate: Promotion Problems and Techniques.
BDAPC, 14 (December 14, 1947), 20-21.   3361

Davis, James D.   Why the Debate Institute?   S, 23 (January, 1939),
13-14.   3362

Debater's Code.   SchA, 28 (January, 1957), 146-7.   3363

Debating Practices and Procedures.   BDAPC, 10 (January 15, 1938),
2-5.   3364

Debating's Ten Commandments.   R, 10 (October, 1935), 6.   (Re-
printed from the Minnesota State High School League Bulletin.)
                                                                 3365
Dee, James P.   Bringing the Forensics Program to the Taxpayer.
ST, 4 (September, 1955), 200-3.   3366

Devries, Donna.   George Pierce Baker.   WS, 23 (Winter, 1959),
24-5.   (On the author of one of the first textbooks on debate.)
                                                                 3367
Dobkin, Milton.   The Forensic Director and Citizenship.   WS, 22
(Fall, 1958), 203-6.   3368

Donaldson, Alice.   Experimenting in Debate.   ST, 1 (January, 1952),
42-5.   3369

Douds, J. B.   Debate Managers: Read, Honor, and Obey!   BDAPC,
13 (December 15, 1939), 8-11.   3370

_____.   Taking College Debates to the High Schools.   PN, 8 (Jan-
uary-February, 1942), 7-9.   3371

Douglas, Donald G.   Toward a Philosophy of Forensic Education.
    JAFA, 8 (Summer, 1971), 36-41.   3372

Edney, Clarence W.   Forensic Activities: Strengths and Weak-
    nesses. SSJ, 19 (September, 1953), 2-13.   3373

Ehninger, Douglas.   Six Earmarks of a Sound Forensic Program.
    ST, 1 (November, 1952), 237-41.   3374

Einerson, Mary L.   The Blind Student and Forensics. F, 56
    (March, 1971), 3-5.   3375

Ellery, John B.   Predicting Speaking Success.   G, 32 (November,
    1949), 6, 8.   3376

Ellis, Carroll B.   Financing Forensics. F, 55 (October, 1969),
    14.   (Part of symposium: Advice to Young Coaches.)   3377

Emery, Emogene.   Rehabilitating Women's Debate. SSJ, 17
    (March, 1952), 186-91.   3378

Emperor, John B.   The State as the College Speaker's Forum.
    QJS, 22 (October, 1936), 433-38.   3379

Erickson, Keith.   Calling a Spade a Spade. SPG, 3 (March, 1966),
    62-65.   3380

Esch, Marvin L. , and Ziegelmueller, George W.   Forensics and
    the University Community. G, 41 (January, 1959), 27, 30. 3381

Eubank, Wayne C.   A View of the Forensic Situation. SSJ, 14
    (November, 1948), 108-14.   3382

Eulalia, (Sister) Mary.   Salvaging Time and Talent from the Wreck-
    age of War. BDAPC, 12 (January 1, 1943), 9-11.   3383

Evans, Edward H.   "There's a War On. " F, 29 (April, 1944), 83-
    86.   (On the debate program during wartime.)   3384

Ewbank, Henry L. , Jr.   Debate: A Combined Operation. G, 33
    (2 January, 1951), 34-5.   (Reprinted from the Wisconsin High
    School Forensic Association News Letter, 21 (September, 1949),
    17-19.)   3385

Fest, Thorrel B.   It Doesn't Trickle Down. G, 29 (2 January,
    1947), 21-3.   (On methods of gaining administrative support for
    speech and debate.)   3386

_____ .   A Survey of College Forensics. QJS, 34 (April, 1948),
    168-73.   3387

Foster, William Trufant.   Intercollegiate Debating. Na, 86 (May 7,
    1908), 420-1.   3388

Freeburg, Victor O.   Debating in the College Curriculum.   EJ, 4
(November, 1915), 577-81.   3389

Freeley, Austin J.   The Dusty Pigeonhole.   G, 26 (May, 1944), 53,
64.   3390

_____.   An Examination of the Status Quo.   G, 36 (November,
1953), 8-12.   (On debate budgets.)   3391

_____.   Forensic Budgets and Teaching Load.   G, 39 (November,
1956), 15-16.   3392

_____.   A Further Examination of the Status Quo.   G, 36 (March,
1954), 59-62.   3393

_____.   Public Relations and Forensics.   SA, 7 (Summer, 1951),
43-4.   3394

_____.   A Survey of College Forensics.   G, 33 (March, 1951), 50-
52.   3395

Fulkerson, Richard.   Some Zoological Observations.   F, 49 (October, 1963), 4-6.   (A humorous treatment of the debate program.)
                                                              3396
Garland, J. V.   Squad vs. Seminar.   G, 19 (May, 1937), 61-2. 3397

Gasink, Warren A.   Physical Forensic Facilities Can Be Obtained.
F, 55 (March, 1970), 6-8.   (Outlines appropriate physical facilities for forensics programs.)   3398

Giffin, Kim, and Blubaugh, Jon A.   A Survey of Salary Conditions
in Speech Departments in American Colleges, Universities, and
Junior Colleges.   ST, 13 (March, 1964), 119-127.   (Contains information on forensics directors' salaries.)   3399

Gilbert, Aimie.   The Managing of School Forensics.   NEJ, 7 (October, 1927), 429-30.   3400

Gilman, Wilbur E.   Can We Revive Public Interest in Intercollegiate
Debates?   QJS, 14 (November, 1928), 553-63.   3401

Gislason, H. B.   Ways and Means of Getting a Student Before a Real
Audience.   QJS, 4 (May, 1918), 263-70.   3402

Goetzinger, Charles.   A Simple Case of Adaptation.   G, 38 (November, 1955), 15-17.   (Deplores the fact that college campuses are
so over-organized that the debate program suffers; recommends
various solutions, such as publicizing debate news in the campus
newspaper.)   3403

Goodwin, Fred.   This Business of Bestness.   F, 45 (October, 1959),
3-4.   (Believes there is too much emphasis on winning and producing champions in intercollegiate debate.)   3404

Graham, John. Variations in Speech Activities. AFAR, 10 (Spring, 1962), 21-24.   3405

Gulley, Halbert. Building Audiences for Debate. G, 36 (May, 1954), 98-9.   3406

Haakenson, Robert, ed. Briefly Speaking; A Symposium: How Can Debates Draw Audiences? BDAPC, 17 (December 15, 1951), 38-40. (Contributors include Clayton Schug, Harry F. Bolich, and Samuel B. Shirk.)   3407

Hackett, William A. This Thing Called Debate. EJ, (College Edition), 21 (December, 1932), 810-16. (The responsibility for organizing briefs and gathering material should be the students', not the director's.)   3408

Hamilton, H. W. Popularizing Debate. NEJ, 15 (1935), 43-4. 3409

Hanks, L. D. Comparison, Philosophy, or Situation. DM, 1 (June-September, 1945), 106-8. (Rejoinder to Brother Alexander, supra.)   3410

_____. A Modern Forensics Program. DM, 4 (Summer, 1948), 68-70.   3411

Harkins, William E. Why Keep Debate a Secret? BDAPC, 10 (December 19, 1940), 18-20.   3412

Harkness, P. J. Comment [On Betz's Article.]. DM, 2 (September, 1946), 148-74.   3413

Harrington, Elbert W. A Student Extension Speaking Program. G, 25 (January, 1943), 30-1.   3414

Hayworth, Donald. Debating in 1940. SSJ, 5 (January, 1940), 1-4.   3415

_____. Debating Standards. G, 11 (January, 1929), 15-16. 3416

Hazzard, J. C. Financing Forensics. QJS, 9 (June, 1923), 286-9.   3417

Hellman, Hugo E. Debating--More or Less? DM, 1 (April-May-June, 1945), 1-4.   3418

Hempstead, Walter E., Jr. When a Debater Goes International. G, 14 (January, 1932), 10-11. (On the value of international debate.)   3419

Hensley, Wayne E. A Profile of the NFL High School Forensic Director. JAFA, 9 (Summer, 1972), 282-287.   3420

_____ and Strother, David B. Success in Debate. ST, 17 (September, 1968), 235-237. (Considers the question of whether men are superior to women in debate.)   3421

Hester, J. Gordon.   Motivating Debaters.   PN, 6 (October, 1939),
   23-6.   3422

Hildreth, Richard A.   Bestness Has a Place.   F, 45 (January,
   1960), 3, 6.   (Cf. Fred Goodwin's "This Business of Bestness, "
   supra.)   3423

_____.   A Debate Coaches Institute: An Experiment in Service.
   ST, 13 (September, 1964), 204-207.   3424

Hill, J. Newton.   Post Hoc Propter Hoc.   BDAPC, 10 (December
   19, 1940), 12-14.   (He believes that intercollegiate debating is
   becoming stereotyped.)   3425

Hochmuth, Marie.   Your Gown is Lovely, But---.   BDAPC, 12
   (January 16, 1939), 1-4.   (On women in the debate program.)
                                                      3426

Holm, James N.   Debate in the College of the Future.   DM, 2
   (June, 1946), 79-81.   3427

_____.   Debating, 1958: A Re-examination.   AFAR, 7 (Spring,
   1959), 12-19.   3428

Hopkins, Arthur A.   Conserving the Fundamental Values in Debating.
   SSJ, 10 (November, 1944), 25-28.   3429

Hostettler, Gordon F.   International Debaters Selected.   G, 34 (January, 1952), 26-7.   3430

Howell, William S.   Post War Forensics.   MJE, 27 (September,
   1946), 24-5.   3431

Howes, Raymond F.   Finding Debate Audiences.   QJS, 11 (November, 1925), 364-8.   3432

_____.   Results of a Questionnaire on International Debating in the
   United States.   F, 15 (January, 1930), 381.   3433

_____.   Shall Debating Secede.   EJ, 18, college edition (May,
   1929), 411-15.   (A plea for audience debate.)   3434

_____.   Status of International Debating.   G, 12 (May, 1930), 4-6.
                                                      3435

Hull, B. J.   Building the Junior College Program in Forensics.
   JCJ, 31 (November, 1960), 56-60.   3436

Huseman, Richard C. , Jaksa, James A. , and Steil, Lyman K.
   Budgetary Practices in Intercollegiate Forensic Programs, 1966-
   1967.   JAFA, 5 (Spring, 1969), 53-56.   3437

Intercollegiate Forensic Activities Strand of Western Association at

Denver, November 22 to 24. WS, 1 (November, 1937), 1, 2.
3438

International Debating. HENB, 26 (February, 1951), 28-9.   3439

Irvin, Charles E. Let's Get Together. BDAPC, 10 (December 19, 1940), 14-15.   3440

_____. A Survey of Extension Speaking Programs. BDAPC, 12 (January 16, 1939), 10-13.   3441

Jackson, George S. Reinvigorating Moribund Literary Societies. SSJ, 4 (January, 1939), 8-11.   3442

Jacob, Bruno E. Improving Debate by Discussion. R, 25 (December, 1950), 8-9, 14.   3443

Johnson, Eleanor. Sharing Makes a Squad. F, 46 (March, 1961), 6.   3444

Jones, Howard. Fraternity Speakers' Clubs. S, 25 (May, 1941), 5-6.   3445

Kaltenborn, Helen. Case Studies in the Forensic Program. QJS, 22 (February, 1936), 117-20. (Discusses the use of hypothetical and real cases in debate and discussion.)   3446

Keltner, John. Action Is the Heart of Our Tradition. G, 38 (March, 1956), 55-6, 90.   3447

Kemp, Robert. Publicizing Forensics. ST, 8 (January, 1969), 54-57.   3448

King, Thomas R., and Phifer, Gregg. The College Debater as Seen by Himself and by His Peers. JAFA, 5 (Spring, 1968), 48-52. (Finds no significant difference in image of debaters held by themselves and their non-debating peers.)   3449

Kleinau, Marvin D. New Directions in Forensics. F, 55 (October, 1969), 15-16.   3450

_____. Training the Advocate. F, 57 (March, 1972), 4-6.   3451

Klopf, Donald W. Forensics in the Fiftieth State. G, 41 (May, 1959), 61-2, 4. (Activities and problems in Hawaii.)   3452

_____ and McCroskey, James C. A Study of Certain Characteristics of NFL Chapter Sponsors. R, 38 (February, 1964), 5-7.
3453

_____ and Rives, Stanley. Characteristics of High School and College Forensics Directors. JAFA, 2 (January, 1965), 33-37. 3454

Kruger, Arthur N. Are Debate Coaches Becoming Misologists? JAFA, 10 (Summer, 1973), 47-48.   3455

Kuhr, Manuel I.   Conducting a Two-Week Debate Institute.   ST, 12
(March, 1963), 116-17.   3456

Laase, Leroy T.   A Philosophy for the Director of Forensics.   F,
24 (March, 1939), 69-73.   3457

La Follette, A. C.   The Debate Must Go On.   SSJ, 8 (March, 1943),
109-13.   3458

Lahman, Carroll P.   Compensations for the Debate Coach.   DM, 1
(April-June, 1945), 84-5.   3459

_____.   Criteria for a Wartime Forensic Program.   G, 26 (3
March, 1944), 37-8.   3460

Lambertson, F. W.   What Are We Doing for Freshman Debaters?
G, 17 (March, 1935), 39.   3461

Lewis, Leroy.   One Way to Secure a Debate Audience.   F, 27 (October, 1941), 13-15, 25.   2462

_____.   You Can Have a Debate Audience.   S, 23 (November,
1938), 57.   (On fraternity sponsorship of debate at Duke University.)   3463

Lilienthal, N.   Time for Debate: Uses of the Interval Timer.
SchA, 37 (October, 1965), 19-20.   3464

Lillywhite, Herold.   The "Star System" in Forensics.   WS, 14
(March, 1950), 31-33.   3465

Lloyd, M. Pearl.   More Forensics!   Better Forensics!   G, 2 (November, 1919), 9-11.   3466

Loftus, William K. , and Watkin, Lloyd I.   A Survey of Practices
and Problems Relevant to Novice Debating in Eighty-five D. S. R.
and T. K. A. Affiliated Colleges and Universities.   G, 42 (January,
1960), 29-32.   3467

Lull, Paul E.   Mass Production of Debaters.   QJS, 34 (October,
1948), 374-6.   3468

Lyman, Rollo La Verne.   College Debating.   Ce, 82 (October, 1911),
937-42.   3469

Mader, Thomas.   The Need for Standards.   AFAR, 9 (Winter, 1961),
4-6.   (See Rejoinder by Markgraf, infra, and Mader's reply to
Markgraf, AFAR, 9, Convention Issue, 1961, 16-17.   3470

Mahaffey, Roy D.   Comment from a Western Coach.   DM, 2 (September, 1946), 177, 179.   (On Betz's article.)   3471

Makosky, John D.   Give Debate Back to the Debaters!   BDAPC,

No. 12 (January 16, 1939), 4-6.   3472

Marino, Teresina. Another Survey of Debating. G, 10 (November,
1927), 14.   3473

Markgraf, Bruce. Standards and In-Service Training: A Reply to
the Need for Standards. AFAR, 9 (Spring Issue, 1961), 28-9.
(Reply to Mader, supra.)   3474

Mayer, James. Activity Program in Debating. SchA, 12 (February, 1941), 235-6.   3475

McBath, James H. "Just Call Me Coach. " AFAR, 9 (College
Calendar Edition, 1961), 1.   3476

McConnell, Anne M. A Debate Program for 1943. BDAPC, 12
(January 1, 1943), 14-17.   3477

Merrill, Barbara. Comment by a Student. DM, 2 (December,
1946), 221-2. (On Betz's article.)   3478

Merry, Glenn N. War and Intercollegiate Contests. QJS, 4 (May,
1918), 325-7.   3479

Miller, F. Byers. New Program for Debate. OS, 17 (January,
1939), 16.   3480

_____ . Whither Do We Go? F, 26 (May, 1941), 122-3.   3481

Miller, Edd. The Debater and His Audience. SA, 5 (Winter, 1949),
157-9. (How to overcome the small audience problem.)   3482

_____ . The Status of Debating: 1958. AFAR, 7 (Spring, 1959),
5-11.   3483

Miller, Orville C. Educational Debate and the Extension of the
Classroom. In A Program of Speech Education in a Democracy.
Compiled and edited by W. A. Cable. Boston, Expression Com-
pany, 1932. Pp. 530-32.   3484

Moore, Wilbur E. A Philosophy for Forensics. F, 35 (January,
1950), 37-39.   3485

Moorhouse, Melvin. Get Your Debates before the Public. BDAPC,
15 (December 10, 1948), 27-31.   3486

Moravec, Charles J. Forensics in the Press. S, 23 (January,
1939), 11-12.   3487

Moree, Macy B. , and Lehmann, Richard. Starting a Speech Program. SC, (May, 1969), 34ff.   3488

Moulton, H. G. Debating in the University. University of Chicago

Magazine, 5 (1913), 114-19.   3489

Murphy, James J. "Cirriculum Committees" to Plan Forensics.
WS, 18 (January, 1954), 9-14.   3490

_____ and East, James P. Forensic Activities in the West. WS,
22 (Fall, 1958), 220-4.   3491

Murphy, Ralph M. A Community Speakers' Project. PN, 6 (March-
April, 1940), 4-5.   3492

Murphy, Roy D. Comment on Foregoing Article. DM, 2 (September, 1946), 148-50. (Betz's article on evaluation, supra.) 3493

_____. Do Debaters Make Your Squad or Does Your Squad Make
Debaters? DM, 3 (June, 1947), 76-7.   3494

_____. Don't You Have Time for Debate? F, 31 (October, 1945),
5-6. (Also in DM, 1 (October-December, 1945), 106-8.) 3495

Musgrave, George M. Procedures for Timing Debates. DM, 1
(April-June, 1945), 6-10.   3496

Nelson, Roy C., and Fest, Thorrel B. Administrative Practices in
College Forensic Programs. SA, 512 (Summer, 1949), 90-3.
                                                                    3497
_____ and _____. The Financial Support of Forensics. CSSJ, 2
(November, 1950), 24-32.   3498

_____ and _____. Speech in the West, 1949: Administrative
Practices in College Forensics Programs. WS, 13 (March, 1949),
12-17.   3499

Newell, G. A. Stimulating Interest in Forensics. NEJ, 17 (1937),
43.   3500

Nichols, Egbert R. Debate Organization in the United States. DM,
1 (January-February, 1945), 3-6.   3501

_____. There Were Giants in Those Days. DM, 2 (March, 1946),
17, 54. (On the career of Charles A. Marsh.)   3502

O'Brien, Joseph F. Bring Debate Back to the Campus! BDAPC,
12 (January 16, 1939), 15-16. (Also in G, 21 (January, 1939),
20.)   3503

_____. Let the Audience Participate! S, 25 (January, 1941), 7-9.
                                                                    3504
_____. The Place of Extra-Curricular Speech in the College or
University of Today. QJS, 21 (November, 1935), 579-87. 3505

_____. The Status Quo in Debate. QJS, 20 (June, 1934), 365-77.
                                                                    3506

Oliver, Robert T. Debating for Fun! S, 25 (November, 1940), 4-
   5.   3507

_____. A Student Speakers' Bureau--for What? BDAPC, 13 (De-
   cember 15, 1939), 16-18.   3508

_____. Who Will Listen? BDAPC, 12 (January 16, 1939), 13-15.
                                                            3509

Olson, Donald O. What It Takes to Build a Good Forensic Program. G, 39 (May, 1957), 89-90.   3510

_____, Tompkins, Philip, and Temple, Gloria. A Survey of De-
   bate Practices. G, 39 (May, 1957), 91.   3511

O'Neill, James M. Debating as a College Sport. PSR, 2 (February, 1913), 161-5. (Characterizes debate as a desirable intellectual sport.)   3512

_____. Intercollegiate Debating and the Weekly Journals. G, 7
   (June, 1924), 3-12.   3513

Owen, Gordon R. N. C. D. A. : An Immodest Proposal. F, 58 (October, 1972), 12-15. (Proposes an organization similar to the
   NCAA to regulate competitive debate.)   3514

Palmer, Archie M. Rotary and Student Debating. G, 12 (January,
   1930), 19.   3515

Palzer, Edward. The Gentle Art of Losing. PN, 6 (March-April,
   1940), 6-7, 10. (Discusses students' reactions to losses in debate.)   3516

Pelham, Howard. Should Debate Adopt the Two-Platoon System?
   F, 58 (October, 1972), 7-9.   3517

Pelsma, J. R. Questionnaire on Debating. QJS, 2 (April, 1916),
   130-40.   3518

Perry, I. D. Debating for Every Pupil. QJS, 11 (April, 1925),
   130-5.   3519

Peterson, Owen M. Directing the Extracurricular Forensic Pro-
   gram. In Speech Methods and Resources: A Textbook for the
   Teacher of Speech. Ed. by Waldo W. Braden. New York,
   Harper, 1961. Chapter 10.   3520

Phillips, Gerald M. Experimentation and the Future of Debate.
   G, 45 (November, 1962), 5-7.   3521

_____ and Frandsen, Kenneth D. A Summary of Intercollegiate Debate Practices and Attitudes: 1958-59. AFAR, 8 (College Calendar Issue, 1960), 26-36.   3522

Pinkerton, Herman. Comments on the Betz Article. DM, 2 (September, 1946), 179-80.   3523

Prestwood, Elwood L. Streamlining Extemporaneous Debate. SchA, 11 (March, 1940), 279-81.   3524

Pross, E. L. A Survey of Intercollegiate Forensic Practices and Activities. SA, 5 (1949), 8-11.   3525

Questionnaire on Debate Methods. G, 11 (January, 1929), 23-4.
                                                                   3526
Quimby, Brooks. Yankee Debating. G, 17 (May, 1935), 54-5.3527

Quimby, Clarence P. An Eastern Debate Coach Views the Western Style. PN, 5 (March-April, 1939), 9.   3528

Rahe, Herbert. Toward Better Debating in our Colleges. S, 30 (March, 1948), 4. Also in DM, 3 (Autumn, 1948), 110-11. 3529

Rand, Mark S. A Laboratory Dedicated to Controversy. PN, 6 (December, 1939), 15. (Describes the ideal room for debate.)
                                                                   3530
Rank, Vernon E. Let's Take Debate to the People. ST, 2 (September, 1953), 201-4.   3531

Reid, Ronald F. What It Takes to Build a Good Forensic Program: The Urban University. G, 4 (November, 1958), 7-8.   3532

Reiff, Evan A. Practical Forensics for the Duration. F, 28 (October, 1942), 13-14, 19.   3533

Richards, E. B. The Game of Debate. EJ, 9 (March, 1920), 147-52. (Discusses a plan of interclass debates.)   3534

Ringwalt, Ralph C. How to Improve Intercollegiate Debating. HGM, 9 (March, 1901), 337-9. (Suggests an exchange of briefs before a debate.)   3535

Rives, Stanley, and Klopf, Donald W. Debate Coaches: Why They Quit. CSSJ, 16 (February, 1965), 38-40.   3536

Roberts, Henry G. Intramural Debate, a Sound Investment. G, 17 (March, 1935), 41-2.   3537

Roberts, Mary M. Planning a Forensic Workshop. ST, 12 (March, 1963), 115-16.   3538

Robinson, James L. Are We "Over Legalizing" School Debate? ST, 10 (March, 1960), 111-12.   3539

Robinson, Karl F. Directing Extraclass Speech Activities and Contests. In Teaching Speech in the Secondary School. New York, Longmans, 1951. Pp. 267-351. (Chapter 19: An Orientation to

Activities and Contests; Chapter 20: Individual Activities; Chapter
21: Discussion and Debate.)   3540

Roegiers, Charles L. A Philosophy of Forensics. F, 52 (March,
1967), 13-14.   3541

Ross, Herold T. Long Trips for Debate Teams. EQ, 11 (November, 1930), 19-20.   3542

Roth, Richard W. , and Devlin, L. Patrick. A Survey of Financial
Aid to Debaters. JAFA, 5 (Fall, 1968), 99-105.   3543

Rousseau, Lousene. Great Teachers of Speech: James Milton
O'Neill. ST, 10 (March, 1961), 95-9.   3544

Ruby, Wade. Forensic Preparation in Action. DM, 3 (March,
1947), 8-9. (A rejoinder to Dahlberg's article of the same title.)
                                                                       3545

Russ, William A. , Jr. A Method of Stimulating Attendance.
BDAPC, 7 (May 30, 1936), 3-4.   3546

Samovar, Larry A. A Second Attempt at a Philosophy for an Extra-
curricular Forensic Program--in Dialogue Form. AFAR, 8
(Winter, 1960), 15-20.   3547

Sanborn, Ruth D. Record Attendance at National Convention. PN,
6 (January-February, 1940), 3-7. (A report on debate activities
at the National Association of Teachers of Speech.)   3548

Sandford, W. P. Recent Debate Questionnaire. QJS, 12 (April,
1926), 180-6.   3549

Sattler, William M. Discussion as Preparation for Debate. R, 19
(February, 1945), 6-7. (Also in DM, 1 (April-June, 1945), 14-
17.)   3550

Sayers, Judith. The International Debating Exchange. AFAR, 9
(Spring, 1961), 1-4.   3551

Schmidt, Ralph N. Popularizing Debate in American Schools. DM,
3 (Autumn, 1948), 107-9.   3552

Schonberger, E. D. Debate and the Audience Problem. QJS, 16
(June, 1930), 291-6.   3553

Schopler, John, Gruder, Charles L. , Miller, Mickey, and Rousseau,
Manko. The Endurance of Change Induced by a Reward and a
Coercive Power Figure. HR, 20 (August, 1967), 301-309. (Indicates that debaters with a reward in sight may do better than
those who are forced into debate.)   3554

Schug, Clayton H. Avoiding Abuses in Speech Activities. BDAPC,
19 (December, 1953), 17-20. (Also in BNAP, 38 (January, 1954),

220-3.)   3555

_____. Gaining Administrative Support for Debate. G, 35 (March,
1953), 50-54.   3556

_____. It Need Not Be So! BDAPC, 10 (December 19, 1940), 15-
18. (On problems dealing with scheduling, traveling, and hospi-
tality to visiting teams.)   3557

_____. Our Future in the Field of Forensics. BDAPC, 16 (July
10, 1950), 23-26.   3558

_____. A Study of the Status of Intramural Forensics on the Amer-
ican College Campus. SPG, 5 (March, 1968), 94-98.   3559

Shackson, Rolland. Extra-Curricular Speech Activities in Junior
Colleges. G, 13 (March, 1931), 19-22.   3560

_____. Junior College Debating. JCJ, 2 (December, 1931), 49-
51.   3561

Shannon, J. R. Six Sicknesses of Forensics. SchA, 25 (January,
1954), 147-8.   3562

Sharp, Harry, Jr., and Murphy, James J. Forensic Activities in
the West: 1967-1968. WS, 32 (Fall, 1968), 234-245.   3563

Shelby, H. H. Recruiting Students for Speech. R, 20 (December,
1945), 9.   3564

Sikkink, Donald. The Process of Constitutional Revision. F, 46
(October, 1960), 14, 23.   3565

Sinzinger, Richard A. Selecting a Forensic Institute. JAFA, 9
(Spring, 1973), 464-466.   3566

Smith, Myra A. Debating Problems in High School and College.
Ed, 37 (November, 1916), 160-6.   3567

Smith, Paul W. Intercollegiate Debate and Discussion. QJS, 35
(December, 1949), 520.   3568

Smith, Robert L. Bestness Re-Visited. F, 45 (May, 1960), 3-5.
                                                                      3569

Snowdon, Leroy. Coach Chaperon Chauffeur. PN, 6 (October,
1939), 11-13.   3570

Sommer, Leonard F. Building the Debate Program. CSSJ, 9 (Fall,
1957), 24-26.   3571

Sorensen, Carolyn J. Forensic Recruiting. F, 46 (March, 1961),
7. (By a student.)   3572

Stelzner, Hermann. Debate: Prerequisite to Discussion. WS, 22
(Fall, 1958), 225-9.   3573

Stewart, John R., and Merchant, Jerrold J. Perceived Differences
Between Debaters and Non-Debaters. JAFA, 6 (Spring, 1969),
67-72.   3574

Stonecipher, Nadine. Helps in Financing a Debate Club. PN, 3
(April-May, 1937), 11, 24.   3575

Stonehocker, D. Doyle. Let Us Face the Issue. R, 16 (May,
1942), 10-11.   3576

Streff, Craig R. "Good Men Coaching Well?" JAFA, 6 (Spring,
1969), 106-108.   3577

Sunday, Daniel M. A Debate Clientele. Speech Bulletin. Supplement QJS, 2 (December, 1930), 8-10. (On building an audience
for debate.)   3578

Taylor, Glenn J. Debate Techniques Used by Pennsylvania Colleges.
BDAPC, 10, No. 14 (December, 1940), 26-30.   3579

Thompson, Richard N. Literary and Debating Societies. EJ, 19
(March, 1930), 222-27.   3580

Thompson, Wayne N. Intramural Forensics: One Solution to Our
Wartime Problems. F, 29 (March, 1944), 61-4.   3581

Thornton, Helen G. Improving the Forensics Program: The Students Speak. SSJ, 21 (Winter, 1955), 133-7.   3582

Timmons, Glenn W. The Allegheny Student Speakers' Bureau.
BDAPC, 14 (December 14, 1947), 18-19.   3583

_____. What is Needed in Debate Today? BDAPC, 15 (December
10, 1948), 13-17.   3584

Trout, John M. Debating for Everyone. EJ, 38 (June, 1949), 506-
11.   3585

Trueblood, Elton P. College Credit for Intercollegiate Representatives. PSR, 1 (March, 1912), 208-10. (Results of survey to
determine whether colleges are granting students credit for oratory and debate.)   3586

Trueblood, Thomas C. Forensic Training in Colleges. Ed, 27
(March, 1907), 381-92.   3587

_____. A Panorama of Public Speaking. G, 25 (November, 1942),
11-13, 14.   3588

Utterback, W. E. Extension Audience. QJS, 16 (April, 1930), 194-

200.   3589

Van Buren, Ruth. Bangor Holds a [Debate] Clinic. PN, 8 (January-
February, 1942), 5.   3590

Van Emmerik, Cunera. Discussion on Trial for Its Life. F, 47
(October, 1961), 4-5.   3591

Veatch, W. H. Truthful Publicity for Forensics. F, 14 (March,
1929), 197-8.   3592

Vogel, Alfred T. The Revival of Debating. HP, 20 (September,
1938), 32-5.   3593

Walch, J. Weston. Debating's Ten Commandments. PN, 1 (September, 1934), 2.   3594

_____. How to Fatten Up Your Debate Schedule. PN, 8 (Septem-
ber, 1941), 12-13.   3595

_____. How to Organize and Finance Your Debate Club. Portland,
Maine, Platform, 1936. (Booklet.)   3596

Wall, K. Wayne. Mr. Budget-Cutter. JAFA, 9 (Summer, 1972),
289-291.   3597

Walsh, Grace. Nine Steps to a Good Forensic Program. CSSJ, 9
(Spring, 1958), 35-7.   3598

_____. A Report on Student Reaction to Intercollegiate Discussion.
ST, 7 (November, 1958), 336-39.   3599

Watkins, J. M. Your Best Representative: Debate Squad. JCJ, 38
(April, 1968), 34-37.   3600

Weaver, Andrew T. What Is Over-Emphasis? QJS, 17 (June,
1931), 408-9.   3601

_____. Borchers, Gladys L., and Smith, Donald K. Public Speak-
ing in Co-Curricular Activities, 310-17. Discussion as a Co-
Curricular Activity, 340-4. Debate in the Co-Curriculum, 362-
74. Speech Contests, Chapter 20. In The Teaching of Speech.
New York, Prentice, 1952.   3602

Weaver, James F. AFA Directory for 1972-1973. JAFA, 9 (Fall,
1972), 297-327.   3603

Wenzel, James W. Campus and Community Programs in Forensics:
Needs and Opportunities. JAFA, 7 (Spring, 1971), 253-259. 3604

Westerfield, Hargis. Mass Debating: Incentives and Techniques.
QJS, 26 (October, 1940), 420-26.   3605

White, H. A.   Management of Debate.   G, 11 (January, 1929), 16-
    18.   3606

_____.   The Recent Trend in Debating.   EJ, 18 (College Edition,
    April, 1929), 320-29.   3607

_____.   Some Mile Posts of Progress in Forensics.   G, 13 (No-
    vember, 1930), 5-7.   3608

_____.   Whither the Trend in Debating?   QJS, 17 (February, 1931),
    77-83.   3609

Why Not Public Appearances for all Student Speakers.   PN, 4
    (April-May, 1938), 13, 25.   3610

Wichelns, H. A.   Questionnaires.   QJS, 12 (April, 1926), 197-8.
    (Complains that there are too many questionnaires on debate.)
                                                               3611
Wilkinson, Roy, Jr.   Debating at It Looks from Here.   BDAPC, 14
    (December 14, 1947), 22-26.   3612

Williams, Donald.   The Intramural Program--A Means of Increasing
    Participation in the Speech Activities.   G, 40 (March, 1958), 51-
    53.   3613

Willmington, S. Clay.   A Study of the Relationship of Selected Fac-
    tors to Debate Effectiveness.   CSSJ, 20 (Spring, 1969), 36-39.
    ("Explores the relationship of knowledge to debate theory and ex-
    perience in school debates to debate effectiveness. ")   3614

Wilson, O. J.   Techniques for Stimulating Interest in Debate.   G,
    38 (November, 1955), 11-14, 25.   3615

Winsor, Jerry L.   Recruitment: The Age of the Scholarship.
    JAFA, 7 (Winter, 1971), 247.   3616

Winters, Dennis.   Notes of a North Dakota Neophyte.   F, 51 (Janu-
    ary, 1966), 8-10.   3617

Withington, Robert.   On College Debating.   SchS, 27 (June 30, 1928),
    770-4.   (Why debating has declined; recommends the British sys-
    tem of discussion.)   3618

_____.   College Debating.   WB, 3 (December, 1928), 401-5.   3619

Woolbert, Charles H.   On Certain Proposals for Reforming Debate.
    PSR, 3 (February, 1914), 164-71.   (A rejoinder to R. L. Lyman,
    PSR, January, 1914.)   3620

B.   PROGRAMS AT VARIOUS INSTITUTIONS

1.   Theses and Dissertations

Butcher, Paul A.   Linfield College Tournament of Champions: History and Analysis.   M. A.   Hawaii.   1968.   3621

Davis, Frank B.   The Literary Societies of Selected State Universities of the Lower South.   Ph. D.   L. S. U.   1949.   3622

Dice, Margaret.   A Descriptive Analysis of the Bowling Green Speech Major in Education from 1958-1968.   M. A.   Bowling Green.   1969.   3623

Frederick, Felix.   An Evaluation of the Debate Program at Southwest Louisiana Institute.   M. A.   L. S. U.   1953.   3624

McClure, Leda G.   An Investigation into the Determining Factors Influencing the Evolution of the Speech Program at Bloomsburg State College.   M. S.   Bloomsburg State College.   1969.   3625

Taylor, Nonabeth G.   A Survey of the Speech and Drama Program in the Public Junior Colleges of Texas, 1963-1964.   M. A. Stephen F. Austin State College.   1964.   3626

2.   Articles

Aly, Bower.   The University of Missouri Debate Series.   G, 22 (March, 1940), 54-6.   3627

Ansberry, Merle.   As Others Hear Us.   F, 24 (October, 1938), 1-4.   (The experience of recording debaters at Arizona State Teachers College.)   3628

Auer, J. Jeffrey.   The Oberlin College Forensic Union.   G, 29 (3 March, 1947), 43-5; 31 (March, 1949), 52.   3629

Bates World Debating Tour.   G, 11 (May, 1929), 5-6.   3630

Boyd, R.   Debating in Mississippi Junior Colleges.   JCJ, 4 (December, 1933), 127-29.   3631

Bradley, E. E.   Why Oklahoma's Success in Forensics?   F, 26 (May, 1941), 115-16.   3632

Brose, Dorothy.   We Present: The University of Colorado in Speech and Debate.   DM, 4 (Summer, 1948), 77-83.   3633

Cable, W. Arthur.   A New Pledging System at the University of Arizona.   G, 24 (May, 1942), 71.   3634

Carmack, Paul A., and Randolph, Harland.   College Debating in

India and Pakistan. St, 13 (March, 1964), 103-109.   3635

Chapin, Leland. Stanford's Mellinkoff Medal. G, 38 (March, 1956),
69, 89.   3636

Cowles, Robert. A View of Forensics at Wayne State University.
AFAR, 9 (Winter, 1961), 7-9.   3637

Danberg, Neil. Forensic Activities at Beloit. G, 22 (March, 1940),
57.   3638

Dause, Charles A., and Seltzer, Robert V. Debate and the Black
Student: A Comment on Recruiting. F, 55 (March, 1970), 3-4.
(Compares general and selective recruiting techniques at the Uni-
versity of Detroit.)   3639

Debating at Western Reserve University. SchS, 21 (May 2, 1925),
534.   3640

Debating News. WB, 4 (February-November, 1930), 261-2, 337,
392, 430, 519; 5: 65, 132, 198.   3641

Elizabethtown Initiation (into Delta Sigma Rho-Tau Kappa Alpha).
SPG, 10 (January, 1973), 56.   3642

Emery, Walter B. Forensics at Oklahoma: A Prologue and a Plan.
G, 16 (March, 1934), 43-4.   3643

Evans, Charles F., Jr. Bridgeport Installs Chapter (Delta Sigmo
Rho-Tau Kappa Alpha). SPG, 6 (January, 1969), 60.   3644

Evenson, Judy. Stout Forensics in a Nutshell. F, 53 (March,
1968), 18. (On Stout State University program.)   3645

Ewbank, Henry L. Wisconsin on the Forensic Platform. G, 14
(May, 1932), 4-5.   3646

Friedman, Robert P. Delta Sigma Rho's at the University of Missouri Celebrate Their Golden Anniversary. G, 41 (March, 1959),
35-6, 48.   3647

Fruin, Anthony T. Dutch Student Revives Forensics at Rollins College. F, 31 (October, 1945), 3-4.   3648

Gavin, T. F. State of Catholic College Education. CER, 63 (December, 1965), 609-611.   3649

Gislason, Haldor B. Popular Debating at Minnesota. PSR, 3 (February, 1914), 182-4. (On sending debate teams out into the community.)   3650

Graunke, Dean F. Rollins College Installation (into Delta Sigma
Rho-Tau Kappa Alpha). SPG, 7 (November, 1969), 18.   3651

Guthrie, Warren A.   The Reserve Rostrum.   G, 22 (May, 1940),
    69.   (On the activities of the Western Reserve University Speak-
    er's Bureau.)   3652

Hardy, William G., and Jones, Louis C.   Debate in the Modern
    Curriculum.   EJ, 27 (College Edition, April, 1938), 346-49.
    (Describes the details of a plan for conducting debate at New
    York State College for Teachers in Albany.)   3653

Harvard-Oxford Debate.   HGM, 31 (1922), 216-18.   3654

Hatcher, Caro C.   Results of the Discussion Progression Program
    of the High School Laboratory Group of the University of Denver.
    DM, 1 (July-September, 1945), 63-5.   3655

Hellman, Hugo E.   Marquette Chapter Edits Handbook.   G, 32
    (March, 1950), 54-5, 63.   3656

Hicks, Philip M.   Two Years of Open Forum Debating at Swarth-
    more.   QJS, 10 (November, 1924), 340-45.   3657

Hold 'em Yale; Yale Debaters in South America.   PAM, 43 (Septem-
    ber, 1930), 216-17.   3658

Holstein, George H.   Presenting Rutgers.   DM, 3 (December, 1947),
    210-15.   3659

How Oregon's Debaters Also Made a Globe-Trotting Talking Tour.
    LD, 101 (May 11, 1929), 56-9.   3660

How to Talk Your Way Around the World: Bates College Debating
    Team.   LD, 100 (February 16, 1929), 40-5.   3661

Irvin, Charles E.   Allegheny's Debate Program.   BDAPC, 13 (De-
    cember 15, 1939), 14-16.   3662

Jacob, Bruno E.   Ripon Starts Things.   DM, 10 (December, 1945),
    33-5.   3663

Kain, Richard M.   Open Forum Debating at Swarthmore.   G, 12
    (January, 1930), 17.   3664

Kane, Peter E.   The Origins of Intercollegiate Forensic Competition
    in Southern California.   SPG, 1 (March, 1964), 84-87.   3665

Kiefer, Charles, Jr.   The George Washington Union: The National
    Capitol's Most Recent Political Institution.   G, 20 (March, 1938),
    46-7.   3666

Kleinschmidt, J. Barney.   The University of Chicago Renaissance.
    G, 18 (November, 1935), 12-13.   3667

Kreps, Leslie R.   Forensics at a Land-Grant Institution [Oklahoma

State]. F, 44 (October, 1958), 10-11.   3668

Kruger, Arthur N. Debaters Give College National Publicity. The
   Alumnus of Wilkes College, 1 (Spring, 1955), 8, 15. (On the debating program of Wilkes College.)   3669

Lee, Ralph M. The Citadel. F, 26 (January, 1941), 46-47. 3670

Lefforge, Orlando S. Hawaii's Program. G, 33 (November, 1950),
   7, 18.   3671

Lewis, Leroy. Tau Kappa Alpha Speech Activities Dinner at Duke.
   S, 26 (November, 1941), 14-15.   3672

Linkugel, Wil A. , and Parson, Donn W. The Leavenworth Peniten-
   tiary Debating Society. SPG, 5 (January, 1968), 55-57. 3673

Miller, Edd. The Inter-Society Congress of the University of Texas.
   G, 29 (March, 1947), 67.   3674

Miller, John T. Forensics at Benau. S, 23 (May, 1939), 6. 3675

Murphy, James J. , and East, James R. Forensic Activities in the
   West. WS, 21 (Fall, 1959), 220-24.   3676

Nichols, Egbert R. The Editor in Japan. SA, 9 (Autumn, 1953),
   65, 74.   3677

1959-60 National Debate Topic: Champion Dartmouth. SrS, 76
   (May 11, 1960), 25.   3678

Osterweiss, Rollin G. Yale Develops Intra-University Debate. G,
   32 (March, 1950), 58, 65.   3679

Pace College Installation. SPG, 7 (May, 1970), 142.   3680

Parker, John W. Current Debate Practices in Thirty Negro Colleges. JNE, 9 (January, 1940), 32-8.   3681

_____. The Status of Debate in the Negro College. JNE, 2 (Spring,
   1955), 146-53.   3682

Parrish, W. M. Letter to Editor. QJS, 11 (November, 1925), 388-
   89. (On the debating program at Pittsburgh.)   3683

Phillips, Gerald M. Total Forensics Programming at Washington
   State University. G, 43 (May, 1961), 62-3, 65.   3684

The Pittsburgh Policy in Debating. G, 11 (May, 1929), 8-9. 3685

Public Debates at West Virginia University. SPG, 4 (January,
   1967), 51.   3686

Quimby, Brooks. Bates Revives International Debating. G, 28
(May, 1946), 57.   3687

Reager, Richard. Every Student a Debater at Rutgers. S, 30 (January, 1948), 3-5. Also in DM, 4 (Spring, 1948), 5-6.   3688

Runion, Howard. The Maine Debate Plan. S, 26 (March, 1942),
5-7.   3689

Rutherford, R. Stanley. Geneseo Style of Debating. AFAR, 4 (College Calendar Issue, 1958), 7-10.   3690

Schrier, William. Two Aspects of Intercollegiate Debating at the
University of North Dakota. NDUQJ, 19 (April, 1929), 311-18.
(Discusses non-decision debating and debating before organizations
at the University of North Dakota.)   3691

Shaw, Warren C. Open Forum Debating at Knox. G, 12 (January,
1930), 14-15.   3692

Shields, William S. An Integrated Speech Program at Annapolis.
QJS, 34 (December, 1948), 489-93.   3693

Speer, James P. Machinery and Problems of the George Washington
Union. G, 21 (January, 1939), 26-28.   3694

Stokes, Thomas J. A Note on St. Joseph's Villiger Debating Society.
BDAPC, 12 (January 16, 1939), 22-23.   3695

Stone, Arthur P. Debating at Harvard. HGM, 16 (June, 1908),
620-23.   3696

Stuart, Rex. This Tiny College Has Beaten the World at Debating;
Interview with C. Baird. AMag, 96 (September, 1923), 32-3.
(Bates College.)   3697

Thompson, A. W. Talking Tour: University of Oregon Students Are
Arguing Their Way Around the World. Sun, 60 (January, 1928),
15.   3698

Thompson, G. W. When the Schoolmen Came to Brooklyn. Catholic
World, 142 (1935), 38-44.   3699

Thompson, William J. Speech Instruction at West Point. QJS, 34
(December, 1948), 489-93.   3700

Van Emmerik, Cunera. Iowa Does It That Way. F, 24 (January,
1940), 49-50.   3701

Walsh, Grace. The Case for Eau Claire. F, 57 (January, 1972),
3-4. (On the Wisconsin State College at Eau Claire program.)
                                                                    3702

William Jewel Debaters in Europe. F, 25 (October, 1939), 6-8.

3703

XIV.   DEBATE ORGANIZATIONS:
Fraternities, Leagues, and Associations

Articles

Adams, John Q.   Fixing a Policy [for Delta Sigma Rho].   G, 13
(March, 1931), 12-13.   3704

AFA [American Forensic Association] Constitution.   AFAR, 8 (Spring,
1960), 2-7.   Also in AFAR, 11 (Fall, 1963), 11-18.   3705

AFA Sets New Debate Standards.   Spectra (October, 1971), 8. 3706

The Aims of Delta Sigma Rho.   G, 11 (November, 1928), 4.   3707

Anderson, Jerry.   Comment and Report from the President.   JAFA,
9 (Fall, 1972), 328-334.   (On the American Forensic Association.)   3708

Attractive Plan.   PSR, 3 (May, 1913), 18-19.   (Plan for an inter-
collegiate debating league, adapted from a report by J. A. Winans.)
                                                                          3709
Barker, Burt B.   Debating at Chicago and the Founding of Delta
Sigma Rho.   G, 13 (March, 1931), 10-11.   3710

Basset, Lee E.   Intercollegiate Debates and Debating Societies.
PSR, 2 (January, 1912), 129-35.   3711

Biehle, Martha H.   The National Student Federation and International Debating.   G, 6 (May, 1930), 6-8.   3712

Blyton, Gifford.   The American Forensic Association: A History.
JAFA, 7 (Winter, 1970), 13-16.   3713

_____.   Biographies of Presidents of AFA.   JAFA, 7 (Winter,
1970), 17-19.   3714

Buehler, E. Christian.   The Delta Sigma Rho Golden Jubilee Assembly.   G, 38 (November, 1955), 3-5, 25.   3715

_____.   The Golden Jubilee [of DSR].   G, 38 (May, 1956), 95-97,
114.   3716

_____.   History of Delta Sigma Rho.   S&G, 1 (November, 1963),
12-18.   3717

———. Missouri Valley Debate League. G, 12 (May, 1930), 10-
11.   3718

———. The Missouri Valley Forensic League. G, 28 (May, 1946),
57-58.   3719

———. To Believe or Not to Believe. SPG, 7 (May, 1970), 139-
141. (A reevaluation of the objectives of Delta Sigma Rho-Tau
Kappa Alpha.)   3720

———. Our History, Standards, and Goals. G, 34 (March, 1952),
1-2. (On Delta Sigma Rho.)   3721

———. The State of Delta Sigma Rho and the Fourth Congress.
G, 31 (March, 1949), 43.   3722

———. What Delta Sigma Rho Has Done For Me. G, 45 (May,
1963), 59-60.   3723

Chenoweth, Eugene C. We Salute Delta Sigma Rho. G, 45 (May,
1963), 61-64.   3724

Church, Russell T. The AFA Code: Work Left Undone. JAFA,
9 (Winter, 1973), 378-379.   3725

Constitution and By-laws of the DAPC. BDAPC, 14 (December 14,
1947), 27-30.   3726

Constitution of Delta Sigma Rho. G, 1 (October 15, 1912), 41-51;
1 (May-November, 1915), 237-57; 3 (January, 1920), 9-23; 9
(March, 1927), 10-30; 11 (March, 1929), 9-29; 15 (January,
1933), 13-30.   3727

The Constitution of Delta Sigma Rho-Tau Kappa Alpha. S&G, 1
(November, 1963), 33-40.   3728

Constitution of Pi Kappa Delta (as revised at the 22nd National Convention). F, 47 (January, 1962), 9-18.   3729

Conventions. QJS, 49 (October, 1963), 360-61. (A brief history
of Pi Kappa Delta.)   3730

Cortright, Rupert L. Past Pride and Future Promise; Thoughts
from 1906 to 2020. G, 45 (May, 1963), 70-71. (On Delta Sigma
Rho.)   3731

Cripe, Nicholas M. Sponsored Activities of Tau Kappa Alpha. G,
38 (January, 1956), 35, 49.   3732

Cromwell, Harvey. Resume of National Officers of Pi Kappa Delta:
1913-1965. F, 51 (October, 1965), 4-7.   3733

Debating Societies: Organization and Procedure. University of Wis-

consin Extension Division, Department of Debating and Public
Discussion, 1911.   3734

The Delta Sigma Rho Congress.   DM, 3 (March, 1947), 60.   3735

Discussion Classes.   Chamber's Journal, 9 (February 12, 1948),
    107-9.   (On the value of debate societies.)   3736

Ditty, Mildred A.   An Open Letter to [DSR] Chapter Sponsors.   G,
    36 (May, 1954), 84-88.   3737

Donaho, Melvin W.   A Perspective on Changes Proposed in Pi Kap-
    pa Delta Debating.   F, 53 (October, 1967), 3-5.   3738

Dye, Maxine.   A Survey of Speech Organizations in the U.S.   G,
    13 (November, 1930), 11-12.   3739

Eubanks, Wayne C.   Delta Sigma Rho-Tau Kappa Alpha, Today-To-
    morrow.   SPG, 3 (May, 1966), 81-84.   3740

Ewbank, Henry L.   Bits and Pieces of Delta Sigma Rho History.
    DSR Anniversary Issue.   3741

Faculty Sponsors' Roundtable Considers Future of Delta Sigma Rho.
    G, 38 (May, 1956), 106-8.   3742

Ferson, Merton L.   Beginnings [of DSR].   G, 13 (March, 1931),
    14.   3743

Fest, Thorrel B.   The Future of Controversy on the Campus.   G,
    45 (May, 1963), 65-67.   3744

Files, J. Ray.   Iowa and Delta Sigma Rho.   G, 13 (March, 1931),
    11-12.   3745

Freeley, Austin.   The AFA and the Great Debates.   AFAR, 9
    (Winter, 1961), 1-3.   3746

_____.   Outside the Ivory Tower.   BDAPC, 19 (December, 1953),
    14-16.   (Urges membership in AFA.)   3747

_____.   Procedures, Rules, and Suggestions for the National Con-
    ference of Delta Sigma Rho-Tau Kappa Alpha.   SPG, 5 (Novem-
    ber, 1967), 17-38.   3748

Freshley, Dwight L.   Briefly Speaking; A Symposium: What Can
    We Do to Secure More Members in the DAPC?   BDAPC, 18 (De-
    cember, 1952), 34.   3749

Frizzill, John H.   The Place of the DAPC in the Field of Debate in
    Pennsylvania.   BDAPC, 14 (December 15, 1947), 5-13.   3750

_____.   A Unique Debating Association [DAPC].   BDAPC, 11 (May

25, 1938), 7-10. Also in EQ, 18 (June, 1938), 12-13.   3751

Golden Jubilee Citations [of DSR]. G, 38 (May, 1956), 99-105.3752

Gordon, Harry E. A Bit of History [of DSR]. G, 13 (March, 1931),
9-10.   3753

_____ . Story of the Growth and Development of the National Society [DSR]. G, 1 (circa January, 1912), preliminary no. , 2-4.
(From an article in a bulletin of the Society, February, 1909.)
3754

Hade, William T. Tau Kappa Alpha. SSJ, 5 (January, 1940), 20.
3755

Hagood, Annabel D. Forensic Honor Societies. In Argumentation
and Debate, ed. by J. M. McBath. New York, Holt, rev. ed.,
1963. Pp. 33-47.   3756

_____ . The Merger. S&G, 1 (November, 1963), 3. (On the
merger of Delta Sigma Rho and Tau Kappa Alpha.)   3757

Hanawalt, Dorothy. Speech Training Through Chapter Activity. R,
10 (October, 1935), 10-11.   3758

Hance, Kenneth G. The Perspectives Before Us, Keynote Address,
Sixth National Contress [DSR]. G, 35 (May, 1953), 87-89. 3759

Hansen, Malvin L. The Northern Oratorical League. G, 22 (January, 1940), 34.   3760

Hellman, Hugo E. American Forensic Association: Aims and Objectives. QJS, 37 (February, 1951), 79.   3761

Henning, William C. Delta Sigma Rho: On the Campus. G, 22
(November, 1939), 9.   3762

The History of Pi Kappa Delta. F, 22 (May, 1937), 116-20; 45
(March, 1960), 16-20, 26.   3763

History, Constitution and General Regulations of Delta Sigma Rho.
(Special unnumbered issue, June 1922), 27 pp.   3764

History of Delta Sigma Rho. G, 1 (October 15, 1912), 37-40; 1
(May-November, 1915), 231-35; 3 (January, 1920), 1-7; 9 (March,
1927), 2-9; 11 (March, 1929), 3-8; 15 (January, 1933), 5-12; 38
(March, 1956), 70-78.   3765

Holcomb, Martin. A Word from the National President of PKD [Pi
Kappa Delta]. DM, 3 (March, 1947), 59-60.   3766

Holm, James N. The Function of the Province in Pi Kappa Delta.
F, 29 (January, 1944), 40-41, 44.   3767

Hopkins, H. Dana. The Influence of the Honor Forensic Fraternity.

G, 11 (November, 1928), 5-8.   3768

_____. The Value of the Honor Forensic Fraternity. EQ, 8 (May,
1928), 17-18.   3769

Houck, Stanley B. Delta Sigma Rho Has No Room For Drones. G,
1 (January-March, 1918), 329-31.   3770

_____. Nature and Purpose of Delta Sigma Rho. G, 11 (January,
1929), 5-6.   3771

_____. Traditions of Delta Sigma Rho. G, 13 (March, 1931), 7-
9.   3772

Huber, Robert. Shall the American Forensic Association be Re-
structured? JAFA, 2 (September, 1965), 92-93.   3773

_____. Reaching Maturity. JAFA, 1 (January, 1964), 26-28.
(On the American Forensic Association.)   3774

Jacob, Bruno E. Constitution and Regulations of the National Forensic League. Booklet prepared and distributed by the National Office of the National Forensic League, 1962. (Also contains a
history of the NFL.)   3775

Judson, Lyman S. The Question of the Union of the Forensic Societies. G, 20 (January, 1938), 19-21.   3776

Kane, Peter E. Selecting a Speaker of the Year. SPG, 9 (January,
1972), 48-51. (On the DSR-TKA annual selection.)   3777

Karl, Theodore O. H. Revising Our Constitution [PKD]. F, 48
(January, 1963), 10, 12.   3778

Keltner, John. The Role of Delta Sigma Rho Chapters. G, 37
(November, 1954), 20.   3779

Klingbeil, H. C. Michigan Junior College Debate League. JCJ, 10
(October, 1939), 80-82.   3780

Laase, Leroy T. For the Gavel. G, 45 (May, 1963), 67.   3781

Layton, Charles R. Fifty Years of Tau Kappa Alpha. S&G, 1 (November, 1963), 10-11.   3782

_____. History of Tau Kappa Alpha. In Argumentation and Debate,
ed. by David Potter. New York, Dryden, 1954. Pp. 475-90.
                                                               3783
_____. The Origins and Development of Tau Kappa Alpha: Sister
Society to Delta Sigma Rho. G, 38 (March, 1956), 79-80, 91.
                                                               3784
Loevinger, Gustavus. Some Recollections [of DSR]. G, 13 (May,
1931), 7-8.   3785

Lull, Paul E.   The Five Problems Facing Tau Kappa Alpha.   S,
33 (November, 1950), 11-12.   3786

Lyman, Rollo La Verne.   Debating Societies.   University of Wisconsin General Series 423.   Madison, Wisconsin, University of Wisconsin, 1913.   3787

Makosky, John D.   A Message to the DAPC.   BDAPC, 14 (December 15, 1947), 2-4.   3788

Marsh, Patrick O.   Merger.   G, 45 (May, 1963), 76.   (On the
merger of DSR and TKA.)   3789

Nabors, D. J.   The Provinces--An Overview.   F, 57 (March, 1972),
3.   3790

_____.   The Historians of Pi Kappa Delta.   F, 54 (March, 1969),
8-9.   3791

_____.   The History of Pi Kappa Delta.   CSSJ, 14 (May, 1963),
125-128.   3792

Nagel, Robert H.   Honor Societies: Past, Present, and Future.
SPG, 5 (January, 1968), 58-62.   3793

Nelson, Theodore.   "A Proposal..." Evaluated.   F, 47 (March,
1962), 12-13.   (On national PKD conventions.)   3794

Nichols, Egbert R.   Twenty-four Years of Pi Kappa Delta Records.
DM, 2 (March, 1946), 47-48.   3795

_____.   The History of Pi Kappa Delta.   Division One--From the
Beginning to the First Convention.   F, 34 (March, 1949), 69-77.
Rep. from F, March, 1923.   3796

_____.   The Honorary Speech Fraternity.   In A Program of Speech
Education in A Democracy, ed. by W. A. Cable.   Boston, Expression.   Pp. 553-81.   3797

_____.   Convention Debates.   F, 7 (March-April, 1921), 8.   (Ref-
erence to Pi Kappa Delta Convention.)   3798

Officers of Other Societies Honored by Tau Kappa Alpha.   S, 13
(January, 1928), 7-8.   3799

Olson, Donald.   Sponsors [of DSR] Discuss Forensic Program.   G,
33 (May, 1951), 70-71.   3800

O'Neill, James M.   Debating Societies: Organization and Procedure.
University of Wisconsin Extension Division Bulletin 1115.   Madison, Wisconsin, University of Wisconsin, 1925.   3801

Ottawa University--Mother Chapter of Pi Kappa Delta.   DM, 2 (June,

1946), 104, 109.   3802

Parsloe, Eric. An Englishman at Large at the DSR-TKA Confer-
    ence. SPG, 8 (May, 1971), 122-123.   3803

Phi Rho Pi Resumes Its Place in Forensics. DM, 2 (March, 1946),
    59. (Junior College debate fraternity.)   3804

The Pi Kappa Delta National Convention. DM, 3 (March, 1947),
    56-59.   3805

Proceedings of the Twenty-First National Convention of Pi Kappa
    Delta. F, 44 (May, 1959), 99-105.   3806

Proceedings of the Twenty-Second National Convention of Pi Kappa
    Delta. F, 46 (May, 1961), 3-9.   3807

Professional Standards: The Role of the AFA. JAFA, 3 (Septem-
    ber, 1966), 116-118.   3808

Quimby, Brooks. "The Old Order Changeth... " G, 45 (May,
    1963), 71-72. (On the merging of DSR and TKA.)   3809

_____. A Sponsor Wonders "Why?" G, 38 (March, 1956), 61,
    87.   3810

Rarig, Frank M. , and Greaves, Halbert S. National Speech Organi-
    zations and Speech Education. In History of Speech Education in
    America, ed. by Karl R. Wallace. New York, Appleton, 1954.
                                                                    3811
Rau, Gilbert. Question Asked 182 Chapters [PKD]. F, 44 (October,
    1958), 14-17.   3812

Rives, Stanley, and Klopf, Donald. Characteristics of the Forensic
    Honoraries. F, 50 (March, 1965), 4-5.   3813

_____ and _____. Differences in the Forensic Honor Fraternities.
    SPG, 2 (March, 1965), 83-85.   3814

Rose, Forrest H. Pi Kappa Delta. SSJ, 5 (January, 1940), 17-
    19.   3815

Ross, Herold T. Delta Sigma Rho-Tau Kappa Alpha. SPG, 6 (No-
    vember, 1968), 24-25.   3816

_____. The Faculty Sponsor. G, 43 (May, 1961), 54.   3817

_____. The Merger. SPG, 1 (November, 1963), 4-5. (On the
    merger of Delta Sigma Rho and Tau Kappa Alpha.)   3818

_____. What Do I Get Out of Delta Sigma Rho? G, 41 (January,
    1959), 18, 26.   3819

Rules of the Jubilee Congress of Delta Sigma Rho. G, 38 (March,
  1956), 81-86.   3820

Ryan, Oswald. The Origin of Tau Kappa Alpha. S, 25 (March,
  1941), 3-5.   3821

_____. A Message from TKA's Founders. TKA Golden Anniver-
  sary. National Office of TKA.   3822

A Sample Constitution [for local chapters of PKD]. F, 47 (October,
  1962), 17-18.   3823

Shrout, Clayton H. Delta Sigma Rho Comes to Creighton. G, 17
  (March, 1935), 35, 44.   3824

Sikkink, Donald E. A Proposal for Future National Conventions.
  F, 47 (October, 1961), 9, 14.   3825

Smith, Glenna. Bowling Green University Scene of the Next Pi Kappa Delta Convention. DM, 3 (March, 1947), 34-40.   3826

Smith, Horace G. Northwestern University and Delta Sigma Rho.
  G, 13 (March, 1931), 6.   3827

Smith, H. B. An Idea Whose Time Had Come. G, 38 (May, 1956),
  109-10, 118-19. (On history of Delta Sigma Rho.)   3828

Smith, William S. American Forensic Association. R, 31 (November, 1956), 6-7.   3829

Spiritual·Amalgamation. G, 17 (May, 1935), 1.   3830

Sproule, G. A. Debating Clubs. Agricultural College Bulletin 23.
  Winnipeg, Manitoba, 1917. (15pp.)   3831

The Story of How Redlands Helped Launch Pi Kappa Delta. DM, 1
  (April-June, 1945), 89-91.   3832

Suggested Constitution for Triangular Debating Leagues, rev. ed.
  Madison, Wisconsin, The University, 1911. (10 pp.)   3833

Swartz, James C. Message to Student Members [of DSR-TKA].
  SPG, 8 (March, 1971), 79.   3834

Thomas, Charles E. Honorary and Special Fraternities--With a
  Challenge to Forensic Fraternities. G, 13 (November, 1930),
  13.   3835

Toussaint, Sylvester R. Revision of Membership Requirements. F,
  26 (March, 1941), 73-75. (Pi Kappa Delta.)   3836

Tribute to the Founders of Delta Sigma Rho. G, 15 (November,
  1932), 12-13.   3837

Trueblood, Thomas C.   Delta Sigma Rho: Its Origin and Purposes.
  G, 22 (November, 1939), 8.   3838

_____. The Founding of Delta Sigma Rho. G, 13 (March, 1931),
  5-6.   3839

Up-Dated Constitution and By-Laws [of AFA]. JAFA, 9 (Fall,
  1972), 338-342.   3840

Wagner, Lillian R.   Delta Sigma Rho Merger [with TKA]. G, 45
  (May, 1963), 64.   3841

Wall, K. Wayne. A Research Proposal for Pi Kappa Delta: We
  Need to Prove What We Believe. F, 55 (January, 1970), 3-4.
  (Proposes that PKD establish a research program to determine
  educational benefits of forensics.)   3842

Walsh, Grace. The Twentieth Anniversary [of AFA]. JAFA, 6
  (Fall, 1969), 164.   3743

_____. The Development of Chapters [of Pi Kappa Delta]. F, 55
  (October, 1969), 13-14. (Part of symposium: Advice to Young
  Coaches.)   3844

Wells, Earl W. The Alumni Relations of Delta Sigma Rho. G, 38
  (March, 1956), 63-66.   3845

_____. Forty-Four Years--Auld Lange Syne. G, 45 (May, 1963),
  74-75. (On merger of DSR and TKA.)   3846

What Is Pi Kappa Delta? Pamphlet distributed by the National Council of Pi Kappa Delta. (Other data unavailable.)   3847

Wiley, Francis R. Choosing an Emblem [for DSR]. G, 13 (March,
  1931), 13.   3848

Woodward, Howard S. Delta Sigma Rho. SSJ, 5 (January, 1940),
  15-16.   3849

_____. Values to Stand By. F, 26 (March, 1941), 69-72. (On
  the value of the honor fraternity.)   3850

XV.   CONTESTS AND COMPETITIVE DEBATE

A.   GENERAL PRINCIPLES

1.   Books

Bedichek, Roy, and Winship, F. L.   The Speech Teacher and Competition.   University of Texas Publication No. 4142.   November 8, 1941.   3851

Buys, William E., ed.   Contest Speaking Manual.   Lincolnswood, Ill., National, 1964.   3852

Densmore, Gail E.   Contest Debating.   Ann Arbor, Michigan, Wahr, 1929.   3853

Dressel, Harold.   Introducing Contest Debate.   Flint, Michigan, Mott Foundation, 1959.   3854

Howell, William S., Smith, Donald K., and Thompson, David W. Speech, Debate, Drama in Contests and Festivals.   Minneapolis, Minnesota, 1953.   3855

Klopf, Donald W., and Rives, Stanley G.   Individual Speaking Contests.   Minneapolis, Burgess, 1967.   3856

McGauby, Fern, and McGauby, J. Fred.   Handbook for Students and Coaches of Speech Contests.   Syracuse, New York, The Willis N. Bugbee Co., 1935.   3857

Miller, Orville C.   The Speech Tournament and the Congress of Human Relations.   Nashville, Tennessee, Vanderbilt University, 1938.   3858

Summers, Harrison B., comp. by.   Contest Debating: A Textbook for Beginners.   Reference Shelf, 9. No. 6 (September, 1934), 1-232.   New York, Wilson, 1934.   3859

2.   Theses and Dissertations

Amberg, Walter.   A Comparative Study of Individual Speech Contest Events in Public High Schools of the Thirteen States in the Central States Speech Association.   M. A.   Mankato.   1967.   3860

Gelvin, Elizabeth D.   County Contests and Reflective Thinking.
M. A.   Ohio State.   1929.   3861

Method, Ethel.   An Analytical Comparison and Evaluation of the
Speech Tournament and Speech Festival According to Sound Educational Objectives.   M. A.   Washington.   1944.   3862

Strange, Buford B.   A Study of Certain Personality Traits of Students Participating in Intercollegiate Debating.   M. A.   Mississippi Southern College.   1960.   3863

3.   Articles

Abernathy, Elton.   The Criticism Against Speech Tournaments.
QJS, 28 (October, 1942), 354-56.   3864

Auer, J. Jeffrey, and Shearer, W. W.   Contest Debate.   S, 21
(May, 1937), 6-8.   3865

Baccus, Joseph.   Unique Values of Competitive Debate.   F, 23
(March, 1938), 81-85.   3866

Baker, Virgil L.   "Conscience, Say I..."   S, 24 (March, 1940),
6-7.   (An appraisal of debate practices.)   3867

Barber, Sara M.   Education and Contests.   Speech Bulletin.   Supplement QJS, 3 (December, 1931), 7-9.   3868

Beaird, T. M.   Educational Values in Speech Contests.   R, 12 (December, 1937), 4-5.   3869

Bedichek, Roy.   In Defense of Contests.   SchA, 10 (February,
1938), 25-53.   3870

_____.   Interschool Contest.   CH, (October, 1931), 87-88.   3871

_____.   A Sound Program of Inter-School Contests.   National Uni-
versity Extension Association Proceedings, (1933), 65.   3872

Belfour, C. Stanton.   The Case for Contests.   PN, 5 (November,
1938), 19-20.   Condensed from "Non-Athletic Contests, " CH,
(October, 1937).   3873

Bietry, J. Richard.   Evils of Contest Debating.   Speech Bulletin.
Supplement QJS, 2 (December, 1930), 6-8.   3874

Bolton, F. R.   Expression Demonstration Instead of a Contest.   Sch,
(Elementary Edition), 33 (September, 1944), 54.   3875

Brann, Vincent C. , ed.   Briefly Speaking; A Symposium: What, in
Your Opinion, Is the Least Desirable Characteristic of Intercollegiate Debating, and How Can It Be Changed for the Better?

BDAPC, 20 (December, 1954), 23-27. (Contributors include Miriam E. Dickey, Lloyd H. Fuge, Gordon F. Hostettler, (Sister) Mary Karen, Melvin P. Moorhouse, Samuel V. O. Pritchard, and Irvine N. Smith. The characteristic most frequently cited by the panel as least desirable was tournament debating.)   3876

Burrows, Albert H.   Competition in Forensics.   F, 26 (March, 1941), 76-81.   3877

Committee Blasts Contests.   R, 25 (October, 1950), 2-3.   (Recommendations of the North Central Association of Colleges and Secondary Schools.)   3878

Convention and Contest Rules.   F, 46 (January, 1961), 7-10; 48 (January, 1963), 6-9.   3879

Crocker, Lionel G.   Intellectual Combat; Awards and Rewards in Speech Contests.   VS, 15 (March 15, 1949), 338-41.   3880

Douglas, Franklin C.   Personality Measurement in Forensics.   WS, 6 (January, 1942), 14-17.   3881

Editorial Gleanings.   Speech Bulletin.   Supplement, QJS, 3 (December, 1931), 49-54.   (Comments on contests, benefits, and methods of conducting them.)   3882

Elsen, William J.   Democracy Needs Both.   R, 25 (February, 1951), 4-5.   (On both discussion and debate, in reference to NCA recommendations.)   3883

Ewbank, Henry L.   Speech Contests as Educational Techniques. QJS, 22 (April, 1936), 187-96.   3884

_____.   What's Right with Speech Contests?   EQ, 16 (March, 1936), 13-15.   Also in R, 9 (May, 1935), 5-8; R, 18 (January, 1944), 9-11.   3885

Fostering Dishonesty.   SchR, 34 (May, 1926), 331-2.   (An indictment of championship contests in debating.)   3886

Fuchs, Grover A.   About Speech Contests.   ST, 3 (January, 1954), 53-8.   3887

Hellman, Hugo E.   The Fallacy of the Fisher Report.   R, 25 (December, 1950), 2-4.   (On the NCA recommendations.)   3888

Holm, James N.   The Opposition Is Essential.   F, 28 (March, 1943), 87-9.   3889

Hunt, Everett L.   Debating and College Advertising.   QJS, 1 (October, 1915), 272-5.   (Discusses educational and competitive aspects of debate; recommends a balance between them.)   3890

Jacob, Bruno E.   This Matter of Winning.   R, 9 (February, 1935),
    4-5.   3891

Johnson, Gertrude E.   "As It Was in the Beginning. "   Speech Bul-
    letin.   Supplement, QJS, 3 (December, 1931), 55-7.   (Suggestions
    for improving contests, especially in declamation.)   3892

Kamiat, A. H.   Competitive Debate.   SchS, 19 (May 3, 1924), 525-
    6.   (An indictment of contest debating.)   3893

Karr, Harrison M.   Speech Contests: Good and Not-so-Good.
    CJSE, 15 (February, 1940), 103-7.   3894

Kolberg, O. W.   In Defense of Speech Contests.   SchA, 14 (January,
    1943), 179.   3895

Laase, Leroy T.   A Critical Evaluation of Intercollegiate Forensic
    Contests in Terms of Educational Principles.   F, 24 (January,
    1939), 37-41.   3896

_____.   Some Suggested Revisions in Contest Procedures.   F, 24
    (May, 1939), 101-6.   3897

Lahman, Carroll P.   Recent Trends in Speech Contests.   Education-
    al News Bulletin (Kalamazoo), 3 (January, 1933), 13-16.   3898

Larson, P. Merville.   Speech Cooperation?   S, 22 (January, 1938),
    5-6.   (An evaluation of contest debating.)   3899

Lowell, Abbott L.   Competition in College.   AtM, 103 (June, 1909),
    822-31.   3900

Mangun, Vernon L.   The Mind Bedevilment Caused by Debate.   ER,
    74 (October, 1927), 155-61.   3901

Manning, George A.   A View of Speech Contests.   BNAP, 151 (Jan-
    uary, 1948), 210-11.   3902

Mason, H. C.   How Can Debate Contests be Improved?   WJE, 62
    (December, 1929), 173-4.   3903

Mendenhall, Lawrence C.   Speech Methods--A Conservation of Nat-
    ural Illusions.   Ed, 55 (March, 1935), 440-2.   (Contends that
    contests retard speech education development.)   3904

Mitchell, Harold V.   A Tribute to Oscar.   F, 27 (March, 1942),
    86-7.   (On developing humility in debaters.)   3905

Nichols, Egbert R.   Some Remarks upon Intercollegiate Debate.   F,
    8 (May, 1922), 7.   3906

Objections and Objectives.   Speech Bulletin.   Supplement, QJS, 3
    (December, 1931), 2-4.   (Sixteen alleged evils of speech contests

and how to eliminate them; mentions eight benefits.)   3907

Paget, Edwin H., ed.   A Question-and-Answer Free-for-All.
Speech Bulletin.   Supplement, QJS, 3 (December, 1931), 25-38.
(Speech teachers' replies on values and preparation of speech
contests.)   3908

Parrish, Wayland Maxfield.   A Tirade in the Family Circle.   QJS,
12 (November, 1926), 359-62.   (Notes on contest debating.) 3909

Perkins, Elizabeth.   The Purpose and Function of Criticism.   R,
27 (March, 1953), 4-5.   (On the value of competition.)   3910

Peterson, Court.   Student Reaction to NCA Report.   G, 33 (March,
1951), 53-4.   (See NCA recommendations, QJS, 37 (October,
1951), 347-58.)   3911

A Program of Speech Education: Recommendation of the Contest
Committee of the North Central Association with Respect to
Speech as Submitted by the Speech Association of America.   QJS,
37 (October, 1951), 347-58.   (Criticizes competitive debate.)
                                                                                        3912
Raubicheck, Letitia.   Contest Deficiencies.   Speech Bulletin.   Supplement, QJS, 3 (December, 1931), 4-7.   (On the goals and de-
fects of contests.)   3913

Recommendations of a Committee of the North Central Association,
March, 1950.   SA, 6 (Winter, 1950), 145.   (Critical of debate.)
                                                                                        3914
Recommendations of the Contest Committee of the North Central
Association with Respect to Speech.   R, 26 (October, 1951), 2-3,
13.   3915

Ridgeway, James M.   Educational Principles and Contest Debating.
QJS, 27 (December, 1941), 542-6.   Also in F, 27 (December,
1941), 5-6.   3916

Robinson, Rex E.   North Central Association Committee Charges
Analyzed.   G, 33 (January, 1951), 32.   3917

Rosa, H.M.   The Case Against Debate and Athletics.   Michigan
Educational Association Yearbook: Department of High School
Principals, 1 (1930), 21-31.   3918

Scott, Edna.   Education vs. Contests.   AmT, 15 (May, 1931), 11.
                                                                                        3919
Scott, Preston H.   Contest Values.   Speech Bulletin.   Supplement,
QJS, 3 (December, 1931), 9-11.   (In defense of competition.)
                                                                                        3920
Secord, Arthur E., and Thomas, Ruth H.   Speech Contests Are
Here to Stay.   Schol, 47 (January 7, 1946), sup. 6.   3921

_____.   Types of Speech Contests.   Schol, 48 (February 4, 1946), sup. 3.   3922

Shurter, Edwin Du Bois.   Advantages and Possible Disadvantages of
    Contests in Public Speaking.   QJS, 8 (February, 1922), 49-52.
                                                                     3923
Simonson, Walter E.   Prejudice Is a Two-Way Street.   F, 45
    (March, 1960), 3-4.   (The value of traveling to other areas.)
                                                                     3924
Smith, Carney C.   In Defense of Contests.   S, 22 (January, 1938),
    3-4.   3925

Speech Association of America.   A Program of Speech Education.
    BNAP, 36 (May, 1952), 7-21.   (Includes section on speech con-
    tests.)   3926

Staerkel, W. M.   A Look at the Contest Committee's Speech Recom-
    mendations.   NCAQ, 25 (January, 1951), 254-7.   3927

Stevens, Wilmer E.   Competition a Valid Motive?   S, 24 (January,
    1940), 4-5.   3928

Thayer, Lynne.   Speech Contests.   PSA, 5 (August, 1948), 9-12.
                                                                     3929
Thompson, Richard N.   The Thrill of Achievement in Debate.   PSJ,
    78 (November, 1929), 149.   (Defends competitive debate.)   3930

Toussaint, Sylvester R.   Speech Contests in Trial.   R, 13 (Decem-
    ber, 1938), 4-6.   3931

Votaw, David.   What it Takes to Win.   F, 25 (October, 1939), 9-
    11.   3932

Webster, Marjorie F.   The Value of Speech Contests.   R, 25 (De-
    cember, 1950), 11.   3933

Westerfield, Hargis.   Are There too Many Speech Contests?   KSJ,
    19 (December, 1940), 19-21.   3934

What Some Judges Think.   Speech Bulletin.   Supplement, QJS, 3
    (December, 1931), 39-44.   (Reports on contest debating by well-
    known teachers.)   3935

Whittemore, Irving C.   The Competitive Consciousness.   JASP, 20
    (April, 1925), 17-33.   3936

Williamson, Arleigh B.   Mal-Practice in Speech Contests.   QJS,
    16 (November, 1930), 420-31.   3937

Winans, James A.   Speaking Contest.   PSR, 1 (March, 1912), 212-
    13.   (Discusses the good and bad aspects of contests.)   3938

_____.   What is Good "Contest" Literature?   PSR, 2 (February,
    1913), 165-6.   3939

Wing, Herbert, Jr. The Desirability of Discontinuing Intercollegiate Debating; Negative Position. S, 23 (November, 1938), 10-14.
3940

Witt, Carl. The Mania for Contests. Secondary Education, 5 (January, 1936), 20-4. (The pro's and con's of contests.) 3941

B. DEBATE TOURNAMENTS

1. Books

The Clio Mall Reporter. Rock Hill, South Carolina, Winthrop College, 1938. (A report on the debates in the Dixie Forensic Tournament.) 3942

Hunsinger, Paul, and Wood, Roy V. Managing Forensic Tournaments. Skokie, Ill., National, 1967. 3943

2. Theses and Dissertations

Conklin, Royal F. A History and Analysis of Debate Tournaments in the United States. M.A. Baylor. 1950. 3944

Fausti, Remo P. The Empirical Nature of One-Question Intercollegiate Debating. M.A. State College of Washington. 1947.
3945

Maynard, William T. A Study of the Relation of Tournament Debating Experience to Academic Achievement in Law School. M.A. Kansas. 1960. 3946

Montgomery, Charles L. An Examination of Artistic Ethos in Selected Intercollegiate Debates. M.A. Ball State. 1969. 3947

Murrish, Walter. An Analysis of Interscholastic and Intercollegiate Debate Tournament Procedures. Ph.D. Denver. 1953. 3948

Phelps, Lynn A. An Experimental Study of Debaters' Ethical Argument Selection in Game Theory Tournaments. M.A. Arizona State. 1969. 3949

Swinney, James P. An Experimental Study of the Relative Comprehension of Contemporary Tournament Debate Speeches. Ph.D. S. California. 1967. 3950

Trent, Jimmie D. A Manual for the Beginner in Tournament Debate. M.A. Kansas State Teachers College. 1959. 3951

3. Articles

AFA Debate Program and Debate Tournament Standards for Colleges and Universities. JAFA, 7 (Winter, 1971), 243-245.   3952

Alleman, Benson S. Debate Tournaments and a Small Budget. S,
22 (March, 1938), 11.   3953

Allen, R.R., and Polisky, J.B. The Gorgeous Debating Machine.
QJS, 49 (February, 1963), 75-77. (A satire on tournament debating.)   3954

Alvsow, Frank, and Rau, Gilbert. Random Samplings. F, 50 (May,
1965), 16-19. (Recounts experiences traveling to and from debate
tournaments.)   3955

And Now a National Intercollegiate Tournament. DM, 2 (December,
1946), 263.   3956

Anderson, Kenneth E., and Polisky, Jerome B. The Application of
the Symposium-Forum to Contest Discussion. ST, 9 (March,
1960), 131-34.   3957

Baccus, Joseph H. The November Forensic Tournament--and Beyond. WS, 4 (May, 1940), 22-3.   3958

Baker, Eldon. Nine Simple Ways for Coaches to Win Friends and
Influence People at a Forensic Tournament. F, 45 (March,
1960), 8, 11.   3959

Baker, J. Thompson. Value of Debate Tournaments. F, 16 (January, 1931), 147.   3960

Bane, Laverne. Discussion for Public Service vs. Debate Tournaments. QJS, 27 (December, 1941), 546-49.   3961

Barefield, Paul A. Contemporary Forensics: An Appraisal. SPG,
8 (January, 1971), 35-38.   3962

Barnard, Raymond H. A Deserter Pleads His Own Defense. G,
19 (May, 1937), 59-60, 63.   3963

Bauer, Otto F., and Colburn, C. William. A Challenge Debate
Tournament. JAFA, 5 (Winter, 1968), 1-9.   3964

Beauchamp, George. Problems of a Tournament. S, 23 (May,
1939), 7-8.   3965

Betz, Edward S. Speech Tournaments, 1940-41. F, 27 (October,
1941), 3-11.   3966

Boaz, John K., and Ziegelmueller, George. An Audience Debate
Tournament. ST, 13 (November, 1964), 270-276.   3967

Brand, Richard C. Practice Tournaments Stimulate Interest in Debate. SSJ, 4 (January, 1939), 16-19.   3968

Brockriede, Wayne.   College Debate and the Reality Gap.   SPG, 7
  (March, 1970), 71-76.   3969

_____ and Giffin, Kim.   Discussion Contests vs. Group-Action
  Tournaments.   QJS, 45 (1959), 50-65.   3970

Buehler, E. C., ed.   A Symposium: Debate Tournaments Appraised.
  G, 32 (May, 1950), 75, 82, 83.   (Contributors and articles in-
  clude: Quimby, Brooks--"Deemphasize Tournaments"; Brembeck,
  Winston L. --"Correct the Evils"; Olson, Donald--"Balance the
  Program. ")   3971

Cable, W. Arthur.   A Decalogue of Contest Debating.   QJS, 15
  (April, 1929), 254-6.   (Cf. reply by R. Howes, infra.)   3972

Capp, Glen.   Rules for Convention Contests.   F, 27 (October, 1941),
  16-18.   3973

Chaffin, William W.   Tournaments for Real Novices.   SPG, 5 (January, 1968), 70.   3974

Constans, H. P.   The Role of Intercollegiate Debate Tournaments in
  the Post-War Period.   SSJ, 15 (September, 1949), 38-44.   3975

Cortright, Rupert L.   Tournament Debating; Reply to R. H. Barnard.
  QJS, 15 (February, 1929), 92-94.   3976

Crawford, Richard J.   On Revising the Traditional Debate Format.
  SPG, 4 (January, 1967), 42-44.   3977

Crocker, Lionel.   The Values of Tournament Debating.   SSJ, 3
  (March, 1938), 5-6.   Also in PN, 5 (October, 1938), 21-2. 3978

Dean, Richard.   Tournament Debating: A Case for Guerrilla War-
  fare.   SPG, 8 (November, 1970), 17-19.   3979

Delta Sigma Rho Forensic Tournament.   G, 43 (March, 1961), 42-
  3, 46.   3980

Dickey, Dallas C.   The Southern Speech Association: Part IV. The
  Forensic Tournament.   SSJ, 23 (2 Winter, 1957), 55-60.   3981

Directors of Forensics.   A Statement of the Place of Tournament
  Debating in Speech Education.   QJS, 40 (December, 1954), 435-
  39.   (The directors include those of: Universities of Chicago,
  Illinois, Indiana, Iowa, Michigan, Minnesota, and Wisconsin,
  Michigan State, Northwestern, Ohio State, and Purdue.)   3982

The Featured Tournament--West Point Military Academy Invitational.
  DM, 2 (June, 1946), 120.   3983

First National Delta Sigma Rho Forensic Tournament.   G, 41
  (March, 1959), 37-8, 46-7.   3984

Fisher, Walter. Advisory Rhetoric: Implications for Forensic Debate. WS, 29 (Spring, 1965), 119.   3985

Freeley, Austin J. Boston University Debate Tournament. G, 30
(November, 1947), 16.   3986

_____. The First Biennial Tournament. G, 41 (May, 1959), 55-
7. (Sponsored by Delta Sigma Rho.)   3987

_____. Public Relations in Tournament Debating. G, 31 (Novem-
ber, 1948), 9-10.   3988

Freshley, Dwight L. Tournament Debating During a Fact-Finding
Truce. AFAR, 8 (Convention Issue, 1960), 15-18.   3989

Gabbard, William R. In Defense of the Status Quo. F, 57 (October, 1972), 9-10. (A response to David Walker's criticism of
contemporary intercollegiate debate, infra.)   3990

Gibson, Harold E. An Argument for More Uniform Debate Regulations. R, 9 (June, 1935), 10-11.   3991

Giffin, Kim, and Lashbrook, Brad. An Evaluation of Two Experimental Group-Action Tournaments. SSJ, 26 (Spring, 1961), 241-
44.   3992

_____. An Evaluation of "Group-Action." G, 43 (January, 1961),
30-1.   3993

_____. The University of Kansas Group-Action Tournament. G,
41 (1950), 41-2, 48.   3994

_____ and Linkugel, Wilmer. The Heart of America Debate Tournament. G, 40 (May, 1958), 73-4.   3995

_____ and Megill, Kenneth. A Study of the Use of Key Issues in
Tournament Debates. G, 43 (November, 1960), 3-4, 10-12. 3996

_____ and Rhea, Joseph. An Analysis of Participant Attitudes and
Relationships in the University of Kansas Group-Action Tournament. G, 45 (January, 1963), 34-39.   3997

Gough, Harry B. A New Arrangement for Intercollegiate Debates.
PSR, 3 (March, 1914), 214-15. (Plan devised by Earlham College, Indiana and DePauw Universities.)   3998

Gow, John E. Tournament Debating: A Time for Changes. JAFA,
4 (Fall, 1967), 107-111.   3999

Griffin, Floyd J., Jr. A Proposed Plan for Power-Pairing. SPG,
3 (May, 1966), 112-14.   4000

Guiou, Trula. Thoughts of a Debater. F, 47 (October, 1962), 20,

23. (A humorous selection on why debaters lose tournaments.)
4001

Hansen, John D. The Origin of the Debate Tournament. F, 35 (October, 1949), 21-24. 4002

Hargis, D. E. A Note on Championship Debaters. QJS, 34 (February, 1948), 57-9. 4003

Haston, Bruce M. Have We Forgotten Quality? WS, 24 (Autumn, 1960), 233-5. 4004

Hatch, Hazel. Over-Emphasis in Debate. PN, 7 (December, 1940), 6-7. (Answers the charge that debate detracts from student work, and stresses the value of debate tournaments.) 4005

Henning, J. H. O. K., Johnny, Get Your Gun. F, 29 (October, 1943), 2-4. (On scoring in debate tournaments; does not believe that all decisions should be equally weighted.) 4006

Hopkins, Thomas A. A Case for Writing Critiques at Major Debate Tournaments. G, 39 (January, 1957), 47-8. 4007

Howe, Jack H. Forensics, Tournaments, and the Pursuit of Trophies. F, 44 (October, 1958), 6-9. 4008

Howes, Raymond F. Professor Cable's Decalogue: Reply. QJS, 15 (June, 1929), 413-17. 4009

Hufford, Roger. A Proposal for NDT. JAFA, 6 (Spring, 1969), 103-106. (Suggests that only the last four rounds of NDT be power matched.) 4010

———. Scheduling Debate Tournaments. F, 55 (January, 1970), 9-10. (Outlines a block scheduling system.) 4011

Judson, Lyman S. An Indictment of Large-Scale Tournament Debates. G, 20 (March, 1938), 35. 4012

Karr, Harrison M. vs. Baccus, Joseph H. Should Tournament Debating Be Discontinued? WS, 5 (March, 1941), 6-21. (Karr-- Yes; Baccus--No.) 4013

Kell, Carl L. Power-Matching by Computer. JAFA, 4 (Winter, 1967), 26-27. 4014

Klopf, Donald W. Experiment in Educational Debate. F, 49 (October, 1963), 3-4. (Suggestions for an elimination tournament.)
4015

———. Practices in Intercollegiate Speech Tournaments. JAFA, 1 (May, 1964), 48-52. 4016

Kolberg, O. W. Aiming at Tournament Success. DM, (July-September, 1945), 89-91. 4017

_____ . The Proposed National Debate Tournament. DM, 2 (September, 1946), 170-1.   4018

Kruger, Arthur N. Objectionable Trends in Contemporary Debate. LISA, 5 (January, 1968), 18-21.   4019

_____ . Treating the Ills of Academic Debate. SPG, 11 (November, 1973), 15-19.   4020

Lambertson, F. W. The Mechanics of Tournament Debating. G, 23 (March, 1941), 57-8.   4021

Lashbrook, Brad, and Giffin, K. A Preliminary Evaluation of the University of Kansas Group-Action Tournament. S, 42 (1960), 8-11.   4022

Lawton, J. H. Tournament Debating Controversy. CER, 60 (September, 1962), 392-401.   4023

_____ . National Collegiate Debate Tournament. CER, 62 (November, 1964), 510-516.   4024

Lazzatti, John L., Jr. An Artificial and Inadequate Substitute. AFAR, 5 (Convention, 1957), 11-12. (An answer to R. P. Newman's "The Tournament in a Balanced Debate Program," AFAR, 5 College Calendar Issue, 1957, 3-5.)   4025

Legere, Lawrence J., Jr. The West Point Debate Tournament. QJS, 34 (February, 1948), 54-6.   4026

Letter to Editor. QJS, 28 (February, 1942), 95. (An announcement of various direct-clash debating tournaments.)   4027

Litke, Robert E. Dominance Matrices for Determining Winners of Debate Tournaments. ST, 15 (November, 1966), 295-298.   4028

Lomas, Chas. W. A Speech Tournament within the School. Speech Bulletin. Supplement, QJS, 3 (December, 1931), 63.   4029

Ludlum, Thomas. The Case for Abolishing The National Debate Tournament. SPG, 4 (January, 1967), 45-47.   4030

Mahaffey, Roy D. National--Convention or Tournament? F, 50 (January, 1965), 14-16.   4031

_____ , Karl, Theodore O. H., Long, Emmett T., and Hingston, Albert C. The Western Speech Association Tournament. WS, 22 (Fall, 1958), 198-202.   4032

Mangun, Vernon L. Debating: Sophism Institutionalized. ER, 74 (November, 1927), 195-200. (Criticizes tournament debate and judging.)   4033

Markgraf, Bruce. College Debating. Spectra, 2 (August, 1966),
    3.   4034

Marks, Russell R., and Pearce, Barnett. The Protagoras Memorial
    Debate Tournament. JAFA, 7 (Spring, 1971), 284-287.   4035

Matlon, Ronald J. Debate Program and Tournament Standards.
    JAFA, 9 (Fall, 1972), 347-349.   4036

McCrery, Lester L. Tournament Debating Should Be Abolished.
    G, 37 (March, 1955), 51-55, 67. (See negative stand by New-
    man, infra.)   4037

_____ and Smith, Paul W. WSA's [Western Speech Association]
    Responsibility in the Annual Forensics Tournament. WS, 15
    (March, 1951), 35-8.   4038

Merritt, Frank W. Tournament Debating in Pennsylvania: A Re-
    port. PSA, 11 and 12 (June, 1955), 33-5.   4039

Miller, N. Edd. Competitive Debating Should be Deemphasized.
    G, 36 (May, 1954), 95-7. (See opposing stand by Sommer, in-
    fra.)   4040

_____. Some Modifications of Contest Debating. ST, 2 (March,
    1953), 139-40.   4041

Mills, Glen E. Audiences and Tournaments: Two Forms of Over-
    Emphasis. ST, 9 (March, 1960), 95-8.   4042

_____. Western Conference Women's Discussion-Debate Tourna-
    ment. G, 28 (March, 1946), 44.   4043

Montgomery, Charles L. 1984. JAFA, 8 (Spring, 1972), 225-226.
    (Satirical comment on the delivery of tournament debaters.) 4044

Murphy, Richard. Festival or Tournament? QJS, 27 (October,
    1941), 392-7. (In defense of the speech festival vs. a tourna-
    ment; based on observations of the Colorado State Debating
    League.)   4045

Musgrave, George M. Why Not Hold Your Own Tournament? DM,
    2 (June, 1946), 111, 133.   4046

Nelson, J. Arthur. A Dual Debate Tournament. R, 10 (December,
    1935), 8.   4047

_____. A Plan for a Practice Tournament. R, 9 (February,
    1935), 10-11.   4048

Nelson, John S. That Reality Gap and the Rhetoric of Distortion.
    SPG, 8 (March, 1971), 73-79.   4049

Newman, Robert P.   Tournament Debating Should Not Be Abolished.
    G, 37 (March, 1955), 56-60, 68.   (See affirmative stand by Mc-
    Crery, supra.)   4050

_____ .   The Tournament in a Balanced Debate Program.   AFAR,
    5 (College Calendar, 1957), 3-5.   (See rejoinder by Lazzatti,
    supra.)   4051

Nichols, E. R.   Keeping Debate Educational.   DM, (April-June,
    1945), 78-9.   4052

_____ .   My Mama Done Tole Me.   DM, 2 (December, 1946), 259-
    60.   (A defense of speech tournaments.)   4053

Nobles, W. Scott.   Tournament Debating and Rhetoric.   WS, 22
    (Fall, 1958), 206-10.   4054

Norton, Robert W.   A Tournament in the Woods.   JAFA, 7 (Winter,
    1971), 245-247.   4055

Originator of Debate Tournament Retires From Debate Coaching.
    PN, 6 (November, 1939), 6.   (On Dr. J. Thompson Baker.)4056

Owen, Gordon R.   "Judge Not... ?"   F, 51 (May, 1966), 4-5. 4057

Padrow, Ben.   Let's Stop Calling Them Educational.   ST, 5 (Sep-
    tember, 1956), 205-6.   (A criticism of debate tournaments.)4058

Parkhurst, Charles E.   The Establishment of Low-Cost Practice
    Debate Tournaments.   G, 41 (January, 1959), 25-26.   4059

Phifer, Gregg.   College Leagues and Tournaments.   AFAR, 9 (Con-
    vention Issue, 1961), 6-12.   4060

Phillips, Gerald M.   Imagination--The Answer to Tournament Debate.
    ST, 9 (September, 1960), 207-10.   4061

Prescott, Herbert.   Scoring the Tournament Debates.   PN, 31 (Jan-
    uary, 1937), 9.   4062

Princeton Holds Experimental Tournament.   G, 39 (January, 1957),
    38.   (Impromptu split-team tournament debating.)   4063

Program of Events and Rules of Procedure for the First Annual
    Delta Sigma Rho-Tau Kappa Alpha Forensic Conference.   S&G, 1
    (November, 1963), 29-32.   4064

Radall, Julia D.   A Simultaneous Pentagon of Debates.   EJ, 13
    (June, 1924), 417-19.   (Plans for a debate contest.)   4065

Rau, Gilbert.   Brainstorming on a Bus.   F, 45 (January, 1960), 7-
    8.   (While going to a speech tournament.)   4066

A Report on the Status of the National Debate Tournament.   JAFA,
   3 (September, 1966), 118-119.   4067

Richards, Gale L.   Whither Forensic Tournaments?   WS, 17 (January, 1953), 29-31.   4068

Ritzenhein, Donald N.   A Realistic View of Contemporary Debate:
   A Reply.   SPG, 6 (January, 1969), 55-59.   4069

Roberts, Frank L.   Town Meeting Debate Tournament.   SSJ, 20
   (Summer, 1955), 353-58.   4070

Robinson, Zon.   What Happens to Speech Values in Tournament Debating?   SSJ, 7 (March, 1942), 122-5.   4071

Rose, Forrest H.   Bureaucracy, Common Sense, and the Art of
   Persuasion.   DM, (April-June, 1945), 102-7.   Reprinted from F,
   (March, 1945).   (Urges that the war-time ban on traveling be
   lifted for debate tournaments.)   4072

Row, William H.   Revival.   KT, 37 (May, 1933), 10-12.   (Plans
   for invitational and non-decision debate tournaments.   A brief
   description of five suggested plans of debate: revived Oxford
   plan, courtroom plan, duplicate debate, extemporaneous types,
   and forum debate.)   4073

Semlak, William D.   The Protagoras Memorial Tournament: Some
   Theoretical Considerations.   JAFA, 8 (Winter, 1972), 117-122.
                                                   4074

Shepard, David W.   An Indictment of Debate.   SPG, 2 (November,
   1964), 18-23.   4075

_____.   Report to the Association on the First Annual Fr. Mudge
   National Invitational Debate Tournament.   SPG, 5 (November,
   1967), 8-11.   (Satire on tournament debating.)   4076

Shoberg, Raymond V.   The Tournament Critique.   S, 23 (January,
   1939), 5-6.   4077

Sikkink, Donald, Cohen, Herman, and Richards, Gale.   Recommended
   Modifications for the Competitive Forensic Tournament in the
   Western United States.   WS, 20 (Fall, 1956), 218-21.   4078

Skillman, Billy G.   Hunting the Past with Debaters.   F, 51 (May,
   1966), 8-9.   (On the value of tournament travel.)   4079

Sommer, Leonard.   Competitive Debating Should Not be De-Empha-
   sized.   G, 37 (January, 1955), 36-37, 43.   (See opposing stand
   by Miller, supra.)   4080

Sorber, Edna C.   Tournaments: For Better and Better.   ST, 8
   (July, 1959), 49-52.   4081

Spotts, Carle B.   Must Intercollegiate Debate Change or Perish?
A Case for the Affirmative.   BDAPC, 12 (January 1, 1943), 12-
14.   4082

Statement on the Place of Tournament Debating in Speech Education.
WJS, 40 (December, 1954), 435-9.   4083

Stelzner, Hermann, G.   Tournament Debate: Emasculated Rhetoric.
SSJ, 27 (Fall, 1961), 34-42.   4084

Stromer, Walter F.   One-Man Debate Tournament.   SPG, 2 (March,
1965), 77-78.   4085

The Suitcase Set.   Ne, (May 13, 1963), 96, 99.   (On the 1963 National Tournament at West Point; generally unfavorable to debate
presentation because it emphasizes evidence.)   4086

Swinney, James P.   The Relative Comprehension of Contemporary
Tournament Debate Speeches.   JAFA, 5 (Winter, 1968), 16-20.
(Contends that tournament debating does not provide realistic
training for its participants.)   4087

A Symposium: In the December 1954 issue of the DAPC Bulletin
the majority of those asked to name the greatest weakness in
present day intercollegiate debating responded that it was tournament debating.   If you disagree with this opinion, please explain;
if you agree, what measures would you suggest to correct this
alleged weakness?   BDAPC, 21 (December, 1955), 42-44.   (Contributors included: Maynard J. Brennan; Robert P. Newman;
Clayton H. Schug.)   4088

Symposium: Is tournament debating to be preferred over non-decision debating?   BDAPC, 15 (December 10, 1948), 50-52.   (Harry
F. Bolich; Walter Gerson; Tobias F. Henry.)   4089

Tacey, William S.   Let's Not Exploit Speakers.   ST, 1 (November,
1952), 257-59.   4090

Templer, C. S.   Is It Time to Reappraise the Tournament System?
F, 26 (January, 1941), 37-41, 59.   4091

Thomas, Archie.   The University of Buffalo Debate Tournament.
F, 46 (October, 1960), 8-9, 23.   (A humorous selection on traveling and coaching.)   4092

Thompson, Wayne.   Debate Tournament--Intra-Mural Style.   R, 17
(December, 1942), 2-3.   4093

Tournament Debating--Pro and Con.   PN, 4 (February-March, 1938),
22-24.   (Comments by R. H. Barnard, Karl Mundt, Brooks Quimby, and T. A. Rousse.)   4094

Vote, Bette.   How To Drive Your Colleagues Crazy.   F, 50 (January, 1965), 34-35. (On problems encountered while traveling on tournament debate trips.)   4095

Walker, David. Is Contemporary Debate Educational? F, 56 (January, 1971), 9-10. (A criticism of contemporary intercollegiate debate.)   4096

Walsh, Grace. It May Happen Again. R, 16 (February, 1942), 12. (On an accident which occurred to a team traveling to a tournament.)   4097

_____. Tournaments: For Better or Worse? ST, 6 (January, 1957), 65-7.   4098

Walwik, Theodore S., and Mehrley, R. Samuel. Intercollegiate Debate: An Intrapersonal View. ST, 20 (September, 1971), 192-194.   4099

Weiss, Robert O. Tournament Debating: 1965-1966. SPG, 4 (November, 1966), 18.   4100

The West Point National Invitational Debate Tournament. United States Military Academy, N.D. West Point, New York, West Point Debate Council.   4101

The West Point National Tournament. DM, 3 (March, 1957), 61-3.   4102

Wheater, Stanley B. A Critics' Symposium. WS, 16 (May, 1952), 153-4.   4103

Wheeless, Lawrence R. Two Surveys of Debate Format Preferences of Debaters and Coaches. JAFA, 8 (Winter, 1972), 132-134.   4104

Wigley, Joseph A. The Art of Persuading Whom? G, 43 (May, 1961), 67-68. (A criticism of tournament debating without an audience; see rejoinder by Anita Taylor, G, 44 (November, 1961).)   4105

Windes, Russel R. The Northwestern University-Owen L. Coon National Debate Tournament. G, 40 (March, 1958), 42, 53.   4106

Woolbert, Charles H. Our New Olympics. QJS, 13 (June, 1927), 306-7.   4107

Zimmerman, Gordon I. Intra-Squad Debates at the National Debate Tournament. JAFA, 8 (Summer, 1971), 45-46.   4108

290   Argumentation and Debate

C. OTHER EVENTS

1. Books

Boone, Lester, ed.   New Declamations; Modern Short Speeches on
Current Subjects for Class Study and Speaking Contests.   New
York, Barnes, new ed., 1943.   4109

Buehler, E. C., and Johannesen, Richard L.   Building the Contest
Oration.   New York, Wilson, 1965.   4110

Judson, Lyman S.   Intercollegiate After-Dinner Speaking.   New
York, Noble, 1937.   4111

Pi Kappa Delta Winning Orations.   Published every other year by
Pi Kappa Delta.   4112

Schrier, William, ed.   Winning Hope College Orations, 1941-1966.
Holland, Mich., Hope College, 1966.   4113

Winning Orations of the Interstate Oratorical Association.   Published
annually by the Interstate Oratorical Association.   4114

2. Theses and Dissertations

Cote, Letha.   The State Declamatory Contest in Wisconsin.   M. A.
Wisconsin.   1942.   4115

Ferris, Millicent M.   The Pillsbury Oratorical Contest: A Study
of Seventy-five Years of College Oratory.   M. A.   Minnesota.
1967.   4116

Keesey, Ray.   An Experimental Study of Techniques in College Oratory with Special Emphasis on the Emotional Aspects.   M. A.
Ohio.   1938.   4117

Lieboff, Michael D.   The Relationship between Theory and Practice
in Winning American Legion Orators.   M. A.   Nebraska.   1967.
                                                           4118
McIntosh, Douglas M.   A Study of the Relationship between Classroom Instruction and Contest Practices of Characterization in
Oral Interpretation.   M. A.   Bowling Green.   1966.   4119

Ratliffe, Sharon.   A Critical Survey of Selected Rhetorical Elements
Utilized by the Winning Speakers in the Final Rounds of the An-
nual Interstate Oratorical Association Contests.   M. A.   Wayne
State.   1965.   4120

Rudd, Mary J.   The Status of Individual Events in American Colleges and Universities.   M. A.   Bowling Green.   1967.   4121

3. Articles

Aggertt, O. J.   Case for the Speech Festival.   CE, (October, 1969),
   42-46.   4122

Barefield, Paul A.   Competitive Individual Speaking in Rhetorical
   Criticism.   ST, 16 (March, 1967), 109-114.   4123

Becker, Sam L.   The Ordinal Position Effect.   QJS, 39 (April,
   1953), 217-19.   (On the relation of position on the program and
   rank by judges.)   4124

_____.   The Rating of Speeches: Scale Independence.   SM, 29
   (March, 1962), 38-44.   4125

Beckman, Vernon E.   Is There a Real Place in the Modern Forensic
   Program for Oratory?   AFAR, 11 (Winter, 1963), 7-10.   4126

Benson, James A.   How Should Finalists Be Chosen in Individual
   Events?   SPG, 9 (November, 1971), 14-19.   4127

Betz, Edward.   The Preliminary Rounds in Oratory.   F, 26 (March,
   1941), 82-85.   4128

Blackburn, Mary E.   Preparing Material for Declamation.   R, 12
   (October, 1937), 4-5.   4129

Blommer, Henry H.   Extempore Speaking.   Schol, 48 (March 4,
   1946), supp. 4.   4130

Bouton, Archibald L.   The Oratorical Contest as a College Activity.
   PSR, 1 (October, 1911), 7-13.   4131

Bradley, Earl E., and Mulvany, Annette M.   Logical Reasoning and
   Success in Speech Contest.   F, 50 (October, 1964), 9-15.   4132

Brewer, W. F.   Notes on the History of Extemporaneous Speaking.
   F, 28 (January, 1943), 51-54.   4133

Brigance, William N.   The Twenty-Eight Foremost American Orators.   QJS, 24 (October, 1938), 376-80.   4134

Brother Alexander.   We've Lost Oratory.   R, 20 (December, 1945),
   6-7.   Also in DM, 2 (March, 1946), 42-43.   4135

Buys, William E.   Extemporaneous Speaking in Interscholastic Contests.   In Contest Speaking Manual, ed. W. E. Buys.   Lincolnswood, Ill., National, 1964.   4136

Camp, Leon.   Extemp Speaking.   F, 50 (October, 1964), 17-18.
                                                                       4137
Carr, Robert R.   Current Analysis Approaches for Evaluating Oratory.   AFAR, 10 (Fall, 1962), 1-6.   4138

Casey, William J. Preparing for Individual Speech Events. SchA,
     40 (October, 1968), 17-21. (Gives hints for preparing for ora-
     tory, extemporaneous speaking, interpretative reading, after-
     dinner speaking, and radio speaking.)   4139

Chamberlain, Austen. How Great Speakers Prepare Their Speeches.
     LA, 324 (January 3, 1925), 22-36.   4140

Clark, Robert D. Innovation in the Impromptu Contest. F, 27
     (March, 1942), 79-81.   4141

_____. The Oratory Contest. WS, 4 (November, 1939), 16-18.
                                                                    4142
Clark, Solomon H. A New Contest in Public Speaking. PSR, 2
     (October, 1912), 33-5. Also in SchR, 20 (June, 1912), 379-82.
     (A plan for extemporaneous contests for secondary schools.) 4143

Cobin, Martin. Oral Interpretation and the Intercollegiate Forensics
     Program. AFAR, 11 (Winter, 1963), 11-15.   4144

_____. Serious Dramatic Interpretation in Interscholastic Contests.
     In Contest Speaking Manual, ed. W. E. Buys. Lincolnswood, Ill.,
     National, 1964.   4145

_____. Humorous Dramatic Interpretation in Interscholastic Con-
     tests. In Contest Speaking Manual, ed. W. E. Buys. Lincolns-
     wood, Ill., National, 1964.   4146

Conger, Maybelle. Practicing For Dramatic Declamation. R, 16
     (February, 1942), 10-11.   4147

Cromwell, Harvey. Decisions in Extemporaneous Speaking Contests.
     SSJ, 18 (December, 1952), 116-121.   4148

Curry, Herbert L. A Variant in Intercollegiate Speech. F, 52
     (March, 1967), 7-8.   4149

Davis, William H. The Function of the Speaking Contest. EJ, 4
     (May, 1915), 299-303. (Special reference to declamation con-
     tests.)   4150

Debaters and Orators. Ou, 121 (April 9, 1919), 622-3. (On the
     status of debate and speaking styles of some orators.)   4151

DeBoer, Ray L. Original Oratory /Persuasive Speaking. F, 55
     (May, 1970), 3-6.   4152

Dennis, W. C. Present Day Oratory: What Should It Be? QJS, 27
     (October, 1941), 429-32.   4153

Dickey, Dallas C. Studies in Southern Oratory. SSJ, 8 (September,
     1942), 8.   4154

_____. Were They Ephemeral and Florid? QJS, 32 (February, 1946), 16-20. (On Southern oratory.)   4155

Edwards, G. V. Quintilian on Extemporaneous Speaking. SchR, 10 (May, 1902), 396-8.   4156

Eubank, Wayne C., and Owens, Cullen B. Individual Speaking Events. WS, 22 (Fall, 1958), 215-20.   4157

Extemporaneous Speech Topics. PN, 5 (March-April, 1939), 14.
                                                                     4158

Fernandez, Thomas L. A Tradition in Oratory. F, 46 (March, 1961), 15-17.   4159

Fest, Thorrel B. The Vanishing College Orator? QJS, 29 (February, 1943), 45-8.   4160

Fieg, Eugene, Jr. On After Dinner Speaking. F, 46 (March, 1961), 20. (By a student.)   4161

Fouts, Kenneth B. Once More, With Feeling. F, 51 (October, 1965), 10-11. (On oral interpretation.)   4162

_____. Oral Interpretation, Yes. F, 49 (May, 1964), 10-11. 4163

Freeley, Austin J. Report of a Survey to Determine the Events Desired by the Chapters for the National Conference of Delta Sigma Rho-Tau Kappa Alpha. SPG, 7 (November, 1969), 19-23.   4164

Gilbert, Edna. Declamation Activities; A Survey. North Dakota Teacher, 20 (April, 1941), 13-14.   4165

_____. What is Declamation? North Dakota Teacher, 24 (April, 1945), 15.   4166

Golden, James L. Achieving Excellence in the College Oration. ST, 14 (September, 1965), 184-192.   4167

Goodwin, Fred B. Oratory by the Seat of Your Pants. F, 47 (1906), 12-14.   4168

Gow, John E. Re-Examining Contest Speaking. F, 53 (January, 1968), 3-5. (Criticizes current contest speaking events, particularly oratory; recommends more extemporaneous and manuscript speaking contests.)   4169

Graham, Burdette, and Strubinger, Howard M. Parliamentary Procedure Contests. Agricultural Education Magazine, 13 (December, 1940), 117.   4170

Grant, David M. Orators Judge Each Other. F, 32 (March, 1947), 69-70.   4171

Harris, Therman G.   Coaching for the Extempore Speaking Contest. Schol, 48 (March 4, 1946), supp. 5.   4172

Hellman, Hugo E.   The Greatest American Oratory.   QJS, 24 (February, 1938), 36-9.   4173

Henrikson, E. H.   A Footnote on Impromptu Speaking.   G, 26 (March, 1944), 41.   4174

Hinds, George L.   Developing University Oratory and Extemporaneous Speaking Programs.   G, 36 (November, 1953), 15-16.   4175

Holcomb, J. Rayford.   Why Not Declaim?   TO, 23 (June, 1939), 23-4.   4176

Hope, B. W.   Draw Three.   F, 35 (May, 1950), 79-81.   (On the extemporaneous speaking contest.)   4177

_____.   Draw Three--1950-1965.   F, 50 (March, 1965), 11-13. (On the extemporaneous speaking contest.)   4178

_____   and Hale, Judith C.   The Introduction to the Contest Oration: Is It "Speech" or "Declamation"?   JAFA, 9 (Winter, 1973), 367-370.   4179

Hostettler, Gordon F.   Original Oratory in Pennsylvania.   BDAPC, 14 (December 14, 1947), 14-17.   4180

Huber, Robert B.   Memorandum: To Committee in Charge of DSR-TKA Conference.   SPG, 3 (November, 1965), 20-22.   (On the most popular contest events.)   4181

Hunsinger, Paul.   Oral Interpretation of Prose in Interscholastic Contests.   In Contest Speaking Manual, ed. W. E. Buys.   Lincolnswood, Ill., National, 1964.   4182

_____.   Oral Interpretation of Poetry in Interscholastic Contests. In Contest Speaking Manual, ed. W. E. Buys.   Lincolnswood, Ill., National, 1964.   4183

The Impromptu Speaking Contest.   DM, 1 (January-February, 1945), 71-2.   4184

Irwin, Ramon L.   Taste in Declamation.   SchA, 19 (September, 1947), 5-6.   4185

Jaswal, Alice.   "One Man Speaking"--A Valuable Thing.   F, 58 (January, 1973), 16-17.   (On the advantages of oral interpretation.)   4186

Keiber, A. E.   The Declamation--In or Out?   R, 12 (October, 1937), 5-8.   4187

Klopf, Donald W.   Tournament Competition in the Individual Speaking Events.   JAFA, 3 (January, 1966), 33-36.   4188

Knower, F. H.   A Study of Rank-Order Method of Evaluating Performances in Speech Contests.   JAP, 24 (October, 1940), 633-
44.   4189

Kolberg, Oscar W.   On Writing Orations.   R, 17 (February, 1943),
2, 15.   4190

Kruger, Arthur N.   The Extempore Speaking Contest.   ST, 5 (September, 1956), 214-22.   (Condensed version in R, 31 (February,
1956), 4-6.   Also a supplement to AFAR, vol. 4, No. 3, September 14, 1956.)   4191

Laity, Harry A.   Our Debt of Honor.   (Winning oration).   G, 5
(June, 1922), 3-6.   4192

Lambertson, Floyd W.   The Intramural After-Dinner Speaking Contest.   G, 24 (March, 1942), 52.   4193

Lawver, Kathleen.   The How and Why of Oratory.   R, 16 (September, 1941), 4.   4194

Lee, Irving J.   Four Ways of Looking at a Speech.   QJS, 28 (April,
1942), 148-55.   (Rhetorician, semanticist, logician, and general
semanticist.)   4195

Lomas, Charles W.   The College Oration and the Classic Tradition.
G, 31 (May, 1949), 78-9.   4196

Mahaffey, R. D.   After Dinner Speaking.   WS, 5 (November, 1940),
10-13.   4197

Mann, Ivan C.   So You're Going Out for Extemp.   R, 16 (February,
1942), 8-9.   4198

Mannebach, Wayne C.   Japan's Best English Orator.   F, 57 (May,
1972), 3-5.   (On Miss Keiko Onishi, winner of the National Intercollegiate English Oratorical Contest in Japan and her winning
oration, "This Above All. ")   4199

McCarty, George.   South Dakota Plan of Extempore Speaking.   R,
26 (February, 1952), 4-5.   4200

McCrery, Lester L.   Educational Aims and Dilemmas of the Extempore Speech Contest.   WS, 16 (October, 1952), 233-38.   4201

McLeod, N. B.   Coaching Oratorical Declamation.   R, 16 (February,
1942), 6.   4202

Miles, Hardy L.   Competitive Forensics: A Remedial Program for
the Disadvantaged.   JAFA, 8 (Winter, 1972), 140-141.   4203

Miller, Melvin H. Special Occasion Speeches. In Contest Speaking
    Manual, ed. W. E. Buys. Lincolnswood, Ill., National, 1964.
                                                                4204

Morgan, Robert. Objectives Gained from Participation in the Ex-
    temporaneous Speaking Contest. Supp. QJS, 3 (December, 1931),
    13-14. (A report by a student winner of an Arizona State con-
    test.)   4205

Murphy, Jack W. College Oratory Analyzed. G, 32 (March, 1950),
    52-3, 66.   4206

Nabors, D. J. Historical Perspectives. F, 55 (March, 1970), 12-
    13, 20-22. (On the development of extemporaneous speaking and
    oratory.)   4207

New Extempore Contest Initiated at Kansas State. G, 38 (January,
    1956), 51.   4208

Nichols, Egbert R. I. A Study of College Oratory. DM, 1 (June-
    September, 1945), 44-6.   4209

_____. II. A Study of College Oratory (continued). DM, 1 (Octo-
    ber-December, 1945), 90-5.   4210

_____. III. Elements of Successful Oratory. DM, 2 (March,
    1946), 41-2.   4211

_____. IV. Principles of the College Oration. DM, 2 (June,
    1946), 89-90, 110.   4212

_____. V. Understanding the Kinds of College Orations. DM, 2
    (September, 1946), 183-5.   4213

_____. The Literary Character Type of Oration. DM, 2 (Septem-
    ber, 1946), 183-5.   4214

_____. Those Extra Outside Contests. DM, (January-February,
    1945), 7-8.   4215

O'Brien, Joseph P. A Substitute for Contests in Extemporaneous
    Speaking. SchA, 7 (March, 1936), 29-30.   4216

Paget, Edwin H. Letter to the Editor. QJS, 24 (December, 1938),
    684-6. (Description of three contest forms used by the South
    Atlantic Forensic Association; two others being tested.)   4217

Palzer, Edward. Declamation Takes a Bow. PN, 7 (March-April,
    1941), 13-14.   4218

Pelsma, J. R. Contest Orations. PSR, 2 (February, 1913), 166-
    70.   4219

Pfister, Emil R., and Storey, Alfred W. A Procedure for On-the-

Spot Oral Evaluation of Performances by Students in Speech Contests. ST, 14 (March, 1965), 132-135.   4220

Pirkle, James E. Contest Oratory? Forget It!...If,... JAFA, 8 (Spring, 1972), 226-227.   4221

Proposed "Code for Contests" by the Speech Association of the Eastern States. (Adopted at the 1956 annual convention business meeting of SAES.) PSA, 14 (June, 1957), 52-5. Also in TS, 4 (November, 1956), 30-31. (Criteria for judging the persuasive speech and the extemporaneous speech.)   4222

Purnell, Sandra E., and Wilkes, Raymond S. Ethos in Contest Oratory. ST, 16 (September, 1967), 225-229.   4223

Reeves, J.B. Oratory in the College. G, 14 (March, 1932), 15-16.   4224

Rhodes, Jack. The Selection of Materials for Contests in Oral Interpretation. JAFA, 8 (Winter, 1972), 135-138.   4225

Rock, Kenneth M. A Training Program for the Orator. Speech Bulletin. Supplement. QJS, 3 (December, 1931), 57-8. (Training the contest orator.)   4226

Schilling, Elsa A. The Original Oration. JEX, 4 (September, 1930), 135-40. (Analysis of ten National Oratorical League orations.)   4227

Schindler, C.M. How to Teach Declamation. R, 23 (December, 1948), 3-5, 10.   4228

_____. Practicing for Humorous Declamation. R, 16 (November, 1941), 6-7.   4229

Schrier, William. Coaching Oratory. F, 52 (October, 1966), 11-14.   4230

Scott, Robert L. Oratory in Interscholastic Contests. In Contest Speaking Manual, ed. W.E. Buys. Lincolnswood, Ill., National, 1964.   4231

Settle, Lloyd. The Monroe Doctrine. (Winning oration.) DM, 1 (April-June, 1945), 99-101.   4232

Shaw, Warren C. An Experiment with the Referendum. QJS, 1 (April, 1915), 33-7. (Audience judging of declamation contests.)
                                                               4233
Smith, Margurite. Training for Extemporaneous Speaking. Speech Bulletin. Supplement QJS, 3 (December, 1931), 62-3.   4234

Smith, T.V. In Honor of Oratory. QJS, 34 (April, 1948), 143-49.   4235

_____. Oratory in Modern Dress. NYTM, (August 30, 1942), 12.
Also in G, 26 (November, 1943), 5-6, 12; and DM, 1 (April-
June, 1945), 63-65. ("Our generation has produced some mighty
orators, Roosevelt and Churchill, Hitler and Mussolini--each has
contributed new touches to an ancient art. ")   4236

Sorber, Edna C. On the Other Hand. F, 50 (October, 1964), 16.
(Response to Kenneth Fouts, supra; considers whether debate is
more persuasive than oratory, extemp, and discussion.)   4237

Stoll, Elmer E. Downfall of Oratory; Our Undemocratic Arts.
JHI, 7 (January, 1946), 3-34.   4238

Talley, C. Horton. Manuscripts Win Oratory Contests. AFAR, 11
(Spring, 1963), 14-17.   4239

Thayer, Albert R. Forensics. QJS, 51 (1965), 235-236.   4240

Tompkins, Phillip K., and Baker, Eldon E. Coaching the Contest
Oration. F, 46 (March, 1961), 12-14.   4241

Trueblood, Elton P. A Contest for Extemporaneous Speaking. PSR,
2 (March, 1913), 194-7. (The plan of Earlham College, Richmond, Indiana.)   4242

Van Houton, Edna M. Impromptu Speeches. American Childhood,
31 (February, 1946), 12.   4243

Walch, J. Weston. A Symposium of Ideas on Extemporaneous
Speaking. PN, 3 (November, 1936), 4-5, 20. (Contributors:
T. M. Beaird; C. Stanton Balfour; Walton G. Hinds; Warren Kings-
bury.)   4244

_____. A Symposium of Extemporaneous Speaking Methods, (Part
II). PN, 3 (December, 1936), 11-12, 22, 24. (Contributors:
W. Arthur Cable; J. R. Pelsma; Robert Justice; C. E. Grady.)
                                                              4245
_____. A Symposium of Extemporaneous Speaking Methods, (Part
III). PN, 3 (January, 1937), 12-13, 24, 26-27. (Contributors:
C. C. Diettert; H. A. Dressel, Maudeva McCord; W. A. Mahoney,
J. A. Nelson.)   4246

West, Robert W. Qualities of Contest Orations. QJS, 5 (May,
1919), 258-65. (A study of one hundred undergraduate college
orations.)   4247

_____ and Larsen, Helen. Some Statistical Investigation in the
Field of Speech. QJS, 7 (November, 1921), 375-82. (An experiment with seven hundred and four freshmen at Iowa University;
the relationship of the position on the program to the judges' decisions; problems of grading and evaluation.)   4248

Wilkinson, William J. Requirements for the Extemporaneous Speech.

R, 9 (March, 1935), 5-8.   4249

Williams, D. Terry.   Oral Interpretation--A Forensic Activity?
    F, 49 (March, 1964), 6.   4250

Willis, Edgar E.   College Orations Old and New.   CSSJ, 7 (Spring,
    1956), 18-20.   4251

Winship, Albert E.   Comparing the Oratory of Twenty Years Ago
    with the Public Speaking of Today.   EQ, 3 (June, 1923), 4. 4252

XVI. FORMS OF DEBATE

A. MISCELLANEOUS

1. Books

Lacey, Douglas R. Dissent and Parliamentary Politics in England 1661-1689; A Study in the Perpetuation and Tempering of Parliamentarianism. New Brunswick, N. J., Rutgers, 1969. 4253

Taylor, Eric. The House of Commons at Work. Baltimore, Maryland, Penguin, 4th ed., 1961. 4254

2. Thesis

Stone, Susan J. An Examination of Stylistic Elements in Security Council Debating. M. A. Penn State. 1968. 4255

3. Articles

American Debating. TES, 2242 (May 9, 1958), 743. 4256

Baccus, Joseph H. The Speech Institute. WS, 6 (May, 1942), 7-9. 4257

Brock, Bernard L., and Fieldman, Steven D. The Case Comparison Format: An Experimental Format for Intercollegiate Debate. JAFA, 9 (Spring, 1973), 450-457. 4258

Chenoweth, Eugene C. Courtroom Style Debating. S, 39 (January, 1957), 19-24. 4259

Christian, Orville F. Forensic Experiment Produces Big Results. WJF, 81 (November, 1948), 8. 4260

Clark, Glenn. Popularizing Debate. PSR, 4 (May, 1914), 16-20. (Explains new form: briefs are exchanged and printed on a program. After twelve-minute speeches, rebuttals follow.) 4261

Cowell, Ray. The Problem-Solving Debate. R, 11 (September, 1936), 6-7. 4262

Debate-Panel. In The University Debaters' Annual ed. by E. M. Phelps. New York, Wilson, 1937. Pp. 381-425. (Debate be-

tween Northwestern and Missouri illustrating this type of debate.)
                                                                4263

Dickens, Milton. Newer Types of Debate and Debate-Discussion.
    G, 23 (March, 1941), 52-4.   4264

Dickey, Dallas C. An Experiment in Discussion and Debate. SSJ,
    10 (November, 1944), 36-7.   4265

Direct Clash Debating. G, 24 (March, 1942), 53, 63.   4266

The Direct Clash System of Debate. BDAPC, 1 (June 1, 1933), 4-
    6.   4267

Drushal, J. Garber. Direct Clash Debate as a Teaching Procedure.
    G, 41 (November, 1958), 5-6, 14.   4267a

Eckert, Ralph G. Experiments in Intercollegiate Debate: In Re-
    Valuation of the Place of Speech in the Educational Process.
    Comp. and Ed. by E.R. Nichols. Redlands, California, Univer-
    sity of Redlands Debate Bureau, 1935. Pp. 48-52. (Explains
    the compromise debate plan and parliamentary debate plan.) 4267b

Experiment in Debate. NFL, 5 (October, 1930), 6-7.   4267c

Forensic Progression Planned for Western Speech Conference. PN,
    4 (November-December, 1937), 9-10, 27.   4267d

Guthrie, Warren A. The Reserve Plan for Intercollegiate Discus-
    sion. QJS, 25 (October, 1939), 392-96.   4267e

Hansen, John D. Streamlining Debate. F, 28 (October, 1942), 17-
    19. (On experimenting with two-man Lincoln-Douglas type of de-
    bating.)   4267f

Harding, Harold F. A Debate Symposium. S, 22 (May, 1938), 6.
    (Notes on George Washington University discussion.)   4267g

"Heckling" Type Debate. In The University Debaters' Annual ed. by
    E.M. Phelps. New York, Wilson, 1937. Pp. 471-530. (Debate
    between Pittsburgh and Western Reserve illustrating this type of
    debate.)   4267h

Hendrix, Jerry A., and Schiszik, Keith N. The Mock-Trial Assign-
    ment: A Non-Debate Variation. ST, 21 (November, 1972), 325-
    328.   4267i

Howes, Raymond F. Two Experiments in Debating. G, 11 (May,
    1929), 10-11.   4268

Irvin, Tucker. Direct Clash Debating. (An analysis.) F, 25
    (March, 1940), 88-9.   4269

Johnson, Tom. The Role of Speech in Parliamentary Debate. SPG,

1 (March, 1964), 88-92.   4270

Jordan, H. M.   Tournament Experiment with Debate Types.   F,
    (March, 1946), 75-6.   4271

Julber, Eric, and Christopher, Warren.   "Mail Order" Debating.
    R, 17 (September, 1942), 5.   (Debate by mail to compensate for
    wartime travel restrictions.)   4272

Kellogg, Lincoln L.   The Reality of Debating.   Ou 132 (October 24,
    1922), 354.   (In defense of the American plan of debating.) 4273

Kirn, John F.   The Kirnian-Style Debate.   JAFA, 8 (Spring, 1972),
    224-225.   4274

Lang, Robert A.   The Modern French Parliament.   TS, 5 (April,
    1957), 25-27.   4275

Lawrence, J. H.   Congressional Debate.   F, 13 (March, 1928), 170.
                                                                 4276
Lyon, Leverett S.   Some Types of Public Speech.   EJ, 8 (Decem-
    ber, 1919), 602-9.   4277

Markgraf, Bruce.   Evaluation Debating.   SPG, 3 (November, 1965),
    11-14.   4278

_____.   The Parliamentary Debate in Action.   ST, 12 (September,
    1963), 219-22.   4279

McReynolds, Charles H.   A New System of Debate.   QJS, 26 (Feb-
    ruary, 1940), 6-11.   4280

Miller, Edd.   Special Types of Debate as an Aid in the Analysis of
    a Debate Proposition.   SSJ, 11 (September, 1945), 16-19.   (Also
    in DM, 2 (September, 1946), 145-6, 188.   4281

Moore, Wilbur E.   New Patterns for Debate.   F, 28 (January,
    1943), 43-7.   4282

Mundt, Karl E.   An Experiment Worth Repeating.   R, 12 (6 Febru-
    ary, 1938), 2-3.   (On Murray's forensic progression.)   4283

Murray, Elwood.   The Discussion Progression.   S, 24 (November,
    1939), 18-21.   4284

_____.   The Forensic Experience Progression.   G, 20 (May, 1938),
    56-8.   Also in SchA, 9 (April, 1938), 359-60.   4285

A New Plan for Intercollegiate Debates.   QJS, 3 (April, 1917), 184.
    (Debates to be held in cities other than those in which the colleges
    are located.)   4286

Nichols, E. R.   Boil and Bubble, Toil and Trouble.   DM, 2 (Sep-

tember, 1946), 189-90.   (Attributes new debate forms to criticism of orthodox debate.)   4287

O'Brien, Joseph F.   An Appraisal of Contemporary Forms and
Phases of Forensics in Pennsylvania.   BDAPC, 11 (December 12,
1941), 20-35.   Reprinted with minor revisions in BDAPC, 15
(December 10, 1948), 32-45.   4288

Olds, Stuart, and Sajdak, Kenneth.   The Experiment of Extempore
Debate.   F, 57 (January, 1972), 11-14.   4289

O'Rourke, James.   Contemporary Issues Debate.   SPG, 10 (November, 1972), 2-3.   4290

Orr, Frederick W.   The University of Washington Plan of Problem-
Solving Debate.   PN, 6 (January-February, 1940), 14-16.   4291

_____ and Franzke, A. L.   The University of Washington Plan of
Problem-Solving Debate.   Bulletin of the University of Washington,
Ext. Series, No. 8, January, 1938.   4292

Osborn, Michael M.   A Blueprint for Diversity in Forensic Programs.   ST, 14 (March, 1965), 110-115.   4293

Paget, Edwin H.   The Direct-Clash Debate Plan.   QJS, 27 (February, 1941), 125-8; also QJS, 18 (November, 1932), 648; G, 15
(March, 1933), 12-14.   4294

_____.   Effective Judging and the Direct Clash Debate.   G, 15
(March, 1933), 15-16.   4295

_____.   Rules for the Direct Clash Debate Plan.   QJS, 23 (October,
1937), 431-3.   4296

Pelsma, J. R.   Advantages and Disadvantages of Impromptu Debating.
G, 13 (May, 1931), 6-7.   4297

_____.   Types of Debating.   G, 18 (May, 1936), 56-7.   4298

Pitt, Carl A.   Contemporary Speaking in the House of Commons.
CSSJ, 15 (May, 1964), 117-125.   4299

Problem-Solving Debate.   In The University Debaters' Annual ed. by
E. M. Phelps.   New York, Wilson, 1937.   Pp. 59-95.   (Debate
between University of Washington and Stanford illustrating this
type of debate.)   4300

Reid, Loren D.   Speaking in the Eighteenth Century House of Commons.   SM, 16 (August, 1949), 135-143.   4301

Reynolds, C. H.   A New System of Debate.   QJS, 26 (November,
1940), 6-11.   4302

Roberts, Holland D., and Fox, Helen. Streamlining the Forum and
  Debate. EJ, 26 (April, 1937), 275-82.   4303

Sandford, William P. A Proposed Change in Intercollegiate Speaking. QJS, 19 (June, 1933), 416-18. (Notes on Williamson's
  proposed change, infra.)   4304

Sheffield, Alfred D. Discussion, Lecture-Forum, and Debate.
  QJS, 18 (November, 1932), 517-31.   4305

Some Experiments and Incidents of the Season. BDAPC, 6 (May
  29, 1935), 9-12.   4306

Swanson, Don R. Debate in a Larger Context. F, 54 (October,
  1968), 10-11. (Description of the York University International
  Centennial Debate Tournament, March 31-April 2, 1967, in
  Toronto, Canada.)   4307

Swinney, James P. A Survey of Religious Debate Attitudes. RQ,
  6 (Summer, 1962), 85-91.   4308

_____. A Survey of Religious Debate Practices. RQ, 9 (Summer,
  1966), 91-98.   4309

Two New Styles of Debate Described. S, 17 (November, 1932), 17.
  (Ohio-Oregon plan and the Purdue Congressional Debate Plan.)
                                                                   4310
The University of Washington Plan of Problem-Solving Debate. Bul-
  letin 610. Seattle, University of Washington. June 1, 1940.
                                                                   4311
Weldon, John. Direct Clash Debating: Recent Developments. F,
  26 (January, 1941), 44-5.   4312

Wiley, B. I. Bridging the Gap Between the Decision and the No-
  Decision Type of Debate. QJS, 16 (February, 1930), 114-16.
  Also in JEX, 4 (June, 1930), 75-7. (Recommends split-team de-
  bate.)   4313

_____. Splitting the Teams has Advantages. G, 12 (January,
  1930), 9-10.   4314

Williamson, A. B. A Proposed Change in Intercollegiate Debating.
  QJS, 19 (February, 1933), 192, 200-202.   4315

B. CROSS-EXAMINATION

1. Books

Baer, Jules H., and Balicer, Simon. Cross-Examination and Sum-
  mation. New York, Fallon Law Book Co., 2nd ed., 1948. 4316

Busch, Francis X. Law, Tactics, and Jury Trials. Indianapolis, Bobbs, 1949.   4317

Cornelius, Asher L. The Cross-Examination of Witnesses: Rules, Principles and Illustration. Indianapolis, Indiana, Bobbs, 1929.   4318

Fordham, E. W., Compiler and Annotator. Notable Cross-Examinations. New York, Macmillan, 1952.   4319

Gallagher, William. Technique of Cross-Examination. New York, Practising Law Institute, 1955.   4320

Goldstein, Irving. Trial Techniques. Chicago, Callaghan and Co., 1935.   4321

Lake, Lewis W. How to Cross-Examine Witnesses Successfully. Englewood Cliffs, New Jersey, Prentice, 1957.   4322

Wellman, Francis L. The Art of Cross-Examination. New York, Collier Books, 4th ed., 1962.   4323

2. Thesis and Dissertation

Beard, Raymond S. A Survey of the Theories and Trends in Cross-Examination from Ancient Times to Modern. Ph. D. Northwestern. 1954.   4324

Fredrich, Gustav W. Strategy in Cross-Examination Debating, 1964-1965. M. A. Kansas. 1966.   4325

3. Articles

Beard, Raymond S. A Comparison of Classical Dialectic, Legal Cross-Examination, and Cross-Examination Debate. JAFA, 3 (May, 1966), 53-58.   4326

_____. Legal Cross-Examination and Academic Debate. JAFA, 6 (Spring, 1969), 61-66. (Shows how the writings on legal cross-examination can be applied to academic debate.)   4327

Bond, T. C. Oregon Plan of Debating. R, 9 (March, 1935), 4-5.   4328

Carlson, R. L. Cross-Examination of the Accused. CLQ, 52 (Spring, 1967), 705-722.   4328a

Clark, John H., Jr. Answer Yes or No. NAR, 228 (July, 1929), 84-90.   4329

Confrontation, Cross-examination, and the Right to Prepare Defense. GLR, 56 (May, 1968), 939-975.   4330

Constitutional Right of Cross-Examination--the Unanswerable Question Tactic.   MqLR, 19 (1967), 117-123.   4331

Cross-Examination Debate.   S, 35 (January, 1953), 7.   4332

Ditty, Mildred A., ed.   Briefly Speaking; A Symposium: Should the
Questioner Include Summaries in the Questioning Period of a
Cross-Examination Debate? BDAPC, 16 (July 10, 1950), 31-34.
(Contributors include: Eva M. Cappellanti; Clayton Schug; Dale
L. Van Meter.)   4333

Ehrlich, J.W.   Lost Art of Cross-Examination.   Lincoln Law Review, 5 (June, 1970), 85ff.   4334

Freshley, Dwight L.   A Case for More Cross-Examination Debating.
JAFA, 2 (January, 1965), 21-24.   4335

Fuge, Lloyd H., and Newman, Robert P.   Cross-Examination in
Academic Debating.   BDAPC, 21 (December, 1955), 9-15.   Also
in ST, 5 (January, 1956), 66-70.   4336

Gair, H. A.   Cross-examination.   Tr, 4 (October-November, 1968),
33-36.   (Extended example of cross-examination in the courtroom.)   4337

Grady, C. E.   Debate Must be Realistic! PN, 7 (October, 1940),
15, 18-19.   (A defense of the dynamic style of speech, and an
attack on the cross-examination debate.)   4338

Graham, Gladys M.   Oregon Plan of Debate.   QJS, 13 (June, 1927),
309-10.   4339

Gray, J. Stanley.   The Oregon Plan of Debating.   QJS, 12 (April,
1926), 175-80.   4340

Griffith, Coleman R.   On the Witness Stand.   In his Introduction to
Applied Psychology.   New York, Macmillan, 1935.   Pp. 243-55.
                                                                4341
Grosman, Brian A.   Testing Witness Reliability.   Criminal Law
Quarterly, 5 (1962), 318-27.   (Cross-examination to uncover un-
reliability.)   4342

Hance, Kenneth.   The Dialectical Method in Debate.   QJS, 25 (April,
1939), 243-8.   4343

Horrocks, John E.   Oregon Debate: Its Cross-Examination Feature.
CH, 17 (February, 1943), 342.   4344

Jacob, Bruno E.   Why N. F. L. [National Forensic League] Will Retain Cross-Examination Style.   PN, 7 (December, 1940), 12, 14.
                                                                4345

Johenning, Jean.   Let's Have More Cross-Examination Debate.   F,

52 (March, 1967), 4-6.   4346

Lomas, Charles W.   Audience Interest: A Criterion for the Cross-
Examination. G, 23 (January, 1941), 31-2.   4347

Luvera, P. N., Jr.   How to Cross-examine the Defendant's Doctor
in a "Minor" Whiplash Case. TLQ, 5 (Spring-Fall, 1968), 36ff.
4348
Mann, Ivan C.   Cross-Examination Debate is Modern. R, 15 (February, 1941), 12.   4349

Micken, Ralph A.   The Cross-Examination Method. PN, 5 (March-
April, 1939), 7-8. (Reprint from the Montana News Letter, December 10, 1938.)   4350

Morrill, A. E.   Cross-Examination. ILJ, (May, 1968), 420-496.
4351
_____. Direct Examination. ILJ, (April, 1968), 305-352.   4352

Murphy, H.   How to Cross-Examine Defense Doctors. DIS, 34
(January, 1967), 22-33. (On basic cross-examination technique
for questioning the experienced witness.)   4353

Neely, Gerry.   Cross-Examination Debate. F, 50 (March, 1965),
6-10.   4354

Newman, Robert P.   Oxford and the Cross-Examination Tournament.
G, 37 (November, 1954), 10-12, 17.   4355

Nichols, E. R.   The Oregon Plan of Debate. F, 13 (October, 1927),
88.   4356

O'Brien, Joseph F.   The Oregon Plan of Debating. BDAPC, 2 (January 1, 1932), 2-3.   4357

Palzer, Edward.   Let's Examine "Cross-Examination." G, 24
(January, 1942), 33-5.   4358

Parker, Darrell R.   The Use of Cross-Examination in Debate. QJS,
18 (February, 1932), 97-102.   4359

Reiss, Albert J., Jr. and Black, Donald J.   Interrogation and the
Criminal Process. AAA, 374 (November, 1967), 47-57. (On
the role of interrogation in producing legally admissible evidence;
discusses the newly established criteria for admissibility.) 4360

Robie, Fred S.   Cross-Examination Achieves Debate Objectives Best.
BDAPC, 15 (December 10, 1948), 22-26.   4361

Stewart, Paul.   Cross-Examination--In Debate and in Court. PN,
8 (September, 1941), 18-21.   4362

Swain, Louis H.   Aristotle on Cross-Examination. SSJ, 3 (March,

1938), 24-5.   4363

Symposium: In Cross-Examination Style of Debate How Brief Must
the Answers of the Witness be? BDAPC, 15 (December 10,
1948), 46-8. (Contributors include: Elvin L. Valentine; C. W.
Fink; William W. Hamilton; and Hubert V. Cordier.)   4364

Thomas, Earl T. Cross-Examination of Witnesses. Mississippi
Law Journal, 32 (1961), 243-55.   4365

Veatch, W. H. Cross-Question Debating. G, 15 (March, 1933), 15-
16.   4366

Zelko, Harold P. Can a Pre-Debate Agreement Improve Cross-Examination? G, 24 (March, 1942), 48-51.   4367

_____. Questions, Comment, or Speeches for the Cross-Examiner?
G, 23 (November, 1940), 9-10.   4368

C. BRITISH DEBATE

1. Books

Aitken, Jonathan, and Beloff, Michael. A Short Walk on the Campus.
New York, Atheneum, 1966.   4369

Harris, Kenneth. Travelling Tongues; Debating Across America.
London, Murray, 1950. (The account of an Oxford Union Society
debating team touring the United States. American edition published under title of Innocents From Abroad. Cambridge, Mass.,
Houghton, 1951.)   4370

Hollis, Christopher. The Oxford Union. New York, Hillary House,
1965.   4371

Rules and Regulations of the Oxford Union Society. Oxford, Oxford,
1967.   4372

2. Articles

Acland, Richard. Oxford Debating. G, 12 (May, 1930), 8-10. 4373

American Debating Evaluated. G, 32 (May, 1950), 78, 84. (Short
articles by Robert W. Kingdon, "A Retort to the British;" and
Charles W. Radcliffe, "Debating in Britain.")   4374

Baird, Albert C. British Debating Methods in American Universities. RR, 69 (April, 1924), 439-40.   4375

_____. Shall American Universities Adopt the British System of

Debating? QJS, 9 (June, 1923), 215-22. (Also in WB, 2 (February, 1924), 179-83.)   4376

Barse, Joseph R. British and American Debating--Conflict or
Harmony? G, 35 (January, 1953), 37-9.   4377

Benn, Anthony W., Boyle, Edward, and Harris, Kenneth. American and British Debating. QJS, 34 (December, 1948), 469-72.
                                                               4378
Braden, Waldo W. The British Style of Debating. S, 41 (January,
1959), 10-12.   4379

_____. Notes on Debating in the British Isles. QJS, 44 (October,
1958), 285-93.   4380

Briggs, Nancy E. International Debate Evaluation. JAFA, 5 (Winter, 1968), 25-27.   4381

British Debating is Parliamentary. QJS, 34 (February, 1948), 50-
53.   4382

British Debating Methods in American Universities. RR, 69 (April,
1924), 439-40.   4383

British Debating Team Here. HENB, 24 (October, 1948), 16. 4384

Brittan, L. Oxbridge Style on Tour. Overs, 1 (May, 1962), 9-
12.   4385

Buehler, E. C. British and American Debating. G, 32 (March,
1950), 51, 71.   4386

Carson, Ralph M. The World's Greatest Debating Society. Ou,
132 (October 18, 1922), 281-2. (On experiences in the Oxford
Union.)   4387

Chenoweth, Eugene C., and Good, Voieja Z. The Rise of Women
and the Fall of Tradition in Union Debating at Oxford and Cambridge. SPG, 9 (January, 1972), 31-34.   4388

Crane, Ben. British Debating: a Hardy Perennial. HENB, 29
(February, 1953), 31-35.   4389

Davis, Wayne E. The Oxford Team Visits America. G, 6 (June,
1923), 4-7.   4390

Debates and Beliefs. Editorial. Ou, 132 (September 13, 1922),
54-5. (Editorial comments on the British and American methods
of debating.)   4391

Duniway, Benjamin C. Oxford Union Debates. G, 14 (March,
1932), 14-15.   4392

Dunn, Edward P., and Temple, Norman J. British Students Take
     Debating Seriously. G, 29 (January, 1947), 26-7.   4393

_____ and _____. International Debating Resumes. DM, 2 (De-
     cember, 1946), 223-5.   4394

Ehninger, Douglas. Outline of Procedure for the English-Style of
     Debate. G, 30 (March, 1948), 51, 53.   4395

Eton Wins the Mace; Sixth Form Debating Team. N. Y. Times
     Educ. Sup., 2557 (May 22, 1964), 1435.   4396

Freeth, D. K.; Cradock, P.; Lull, P. E.; Buehler, E. C.; Perritt,
     H. H.; Eubank, Wayne C.; and Larson, P. Merville. American
     Versus British Debating. QJS, 35 (December, 1949), 427-34.
                                                                  4397
Guptill, Charles H. Organization and Tone of British Debating.
     G, 11 (May, 1929), 7-8.   4398

Harris, Kenneth. University Debating. National and English Re-
     view, 150 (1958), 196-7. (An evaluation of debating done at
     some English universities.)   4399

Herklots, Hugh G. G. Debating in England. PN, 3 (September,
     1936), 4-5, 212.   4400

Howes, Raymond F. American and English Debating. QJS, 11
     (February, 1925), 45-8.   4401

_____. The English Debates. QJS, 14 (February, 1928), 112-6.
                                                                  4402
Hunt, E. L. English Debating Reconsidered. QJS, 21 (February,
     1935), 98-102.   4403

International Debating Resumes. DM, 2 (December, 1946), 223-5,
     261.   4404

Is the English Debate System Superior to that of the United States?
     F, 14 (October, 1928), 122.   4405

King-Hamilton, M. A. B. The Union Societies of Oxford and Cam-
     bridge. G, 11 (November, 1928), 11-12.   4406

Lloyd, I. S., and Richmond, W. A. L. The 1947 Cambridge Union
     Tour. QJS, 34 (February, 1948), 46-9.   4407

McBath, James H. Oxford Views American Debating. QJS, 50
     (February, 1964), 93-95.   4408

Moore, G. L. Where Men Debate Beliefs, Not Statistics. Ou, 132
     (September 13, 1922), 55-6. (On the British methods of debate.)
                                                                  4409
Norton, Aloysius. Why We Lost (and Why We Will Probably Go on

Losing).   AFAR, 9 (Spring, 1961), 26-7.   (American style versus the Canadian (British) style of debate; favors latter.)   4410

Oxford Students to Debate Here.   SchS, 16 (September 9, 1922), 295-6.   4411

Oxford: Two Views in Vivid Contrast.   NYTM, (April 30, 1950), 26.   (Criticism of Oxford by Rhodes scholar E. Burdick and rebuttal by Balliol Don M. Dick.)   4412

Oxford Union of Debaters at Eastern Colleges.   SchS, 18 (October 6, 1923), 408-9.   4413

Parsloe, Eric.   Take a British View.   F, 57 (October, 1972), 6-7. (Author was former president of the Oxford Union and a member of the Oxford debate team which toured America in 1970.)   4414

Prichard, Samuel V. O. , and McCroskey, James C.   An Empirical Look at an International Debate.   JAFA, 4 (Winter, 1967), 21-25.   4415

Quimby, Brooks.   Can We Learn from Debating with the British? QJS, 33 (April, 1947), 159-61.   4416

Radcliffe, Charles W.   Let's Adopt British-Style Debating.   G, 34 (January, 1952), 30-1.   4417

Rebuttal Notes on British and American Debating.   QJS, 36 (February, 1950), 10-15.   (Comments by: George D. Stoddard; Virgil M. Hancher; Carter Davidson; Erwin D. Canham; William T. Foster; and Norman Temple.)   4418

Replies from American Debaters.   QJS, 36 (February, 1950), 15-22.   (On British and American Debating; respondents include: Alfred Makulec; Elizabeth B. Flory; Roger Cozens; William F. Buckley, Jr.; Howard E. Goldfarb; Charles E. Lilien; Harry B. Stutts; Irwin Kuhr; Charles Radcliffe; Frederick M. Peyser, Jr., and C. David Cornell.)   4419

Skorkowsky, George R. , Jr.   British University Debating.   QJS, 57 (October, 1971), 335-343.   4420

Stockdale, Allen A.   How They Debate in English Universities.   EQ, 3 (April, 1923), 3-4.   4421

Temple, Norman, and Dunn, Edward.   British Debating Is Parliamentary.   QJS, 34 (February, 1948), 50-3.   4422

Vickery, J.   Debating: British Style.   IIENB, 33 (September, 1957), 23-5.   4423

D. BROADCASTING DEBATE: RADIO AND TELEVISION

1. Thesis and Dissertation

Howell, William S.   The Relative Effectiveness of the Radio Round
    Table and the Radio Forum.   M. A.   Wisconsin.   1938.   4424

Mortensen, Calvin D.   A Comparative Analysis of Political Persua-
    sion on Four Telecast Program Formats in the 1960 and 1961
    Presidential Campaigns.   Ph. D.   Minnesota.   1967.   4425

2. Articles

Aarnes, Hale.   Training for Radio.   SSJ, 13 (September, 1947),
    14-20.   (Also DM, 4 (Spring, 1948), 52-5.)   4426

Bartlett, Kenneth G.   Radio Debating as the Program Director Sees
    It.   G, 17 (January, 1935), 26-7.   4427

Bowrey, Paul B.   What about Television?   DM, 2 (March, 1946),
    49-52.   (Also in DM, 2 (June, 1946), 95-6.)   4428

Brockriede, Wayne E., and Strother, David B.   Televised Foren-
    sics.   ST, 6 (January, 1957), 30-35.   4429

Cherne, Leo M.   Biggest Question on Television Debates.   NYTM,
    (March 2, 1952), 14, 35-6.   4430

Clark, Kenneth R., and East, James R.   Television Debate.   WS,
    22 (Fall, 1958), 211-15.   4431

Commager, Henry S.   Washington Would Have Lost a Television
    Debate.   NYTM, (October 30, 1950), 13, 79-80.   4432

Dickens, Milton.   Adapting Debate to the Air.   QJS, 27 (April,
    1941), 225-61.   4433

_____.   Better Radio Debate.   EQ, 19 (February, 1939), 9-10.
                                                             4434
Emery, Walter B.   FCC Practices and Problems in Regulating Ra-
    dio and Television Programs.   F, 46 (May, 1961), 35-7.   4435

Goldstein, Walter.   Network Television and Political Change: Two
    Issues in Democratic Theory.   WPQ, 20 (December, 1967), 875-
    887.   (On the effect of network TV coverage on the Viet Nam de-
    bate; concludes that the networks must make news, and therefore
    distort it.)   4436

Guthrie, Warren.   New Patterns in Radio and Television Debate.
    G, 32 (March, 1950), 57, 64.   4437

Haakenson, Robert.   Adapting Debate to Television.   WS, 17 (May,

1953), 165-73.   4438

———. Your First Telecast? BDAPC, 20 (December, 1954), 19-
22.   4439

Halley, Donald L., and Jamison, Frank R. A Television Forensic
Event. F, 51 (October, 1965), 12-14.   4440

Hansen, Howard C. Discussion Takes the Air. DM, 3 (December,
1947), 221-2.   4441

———. Interpreting for Radio. Players Magazine, 24 (December,
1947), 63. (Also in DM, 4 (Summer, 1948), 91-2.)   4442

Holland, Dewitte T. Debate Tournament Televised. F, 47 (October,
1961), 10, 14.   4443

Lomas, Charles W. Television in British Political Debate. CSSJ,
17 (May, 1966), 97-105.   4444

McBath, James H. Debating on Television. QJS, 50 (April, 1964),
146-152.   4445

Miller, N. Edd. Possible Formats for Presenting Debate to Television Audiences. G, 40 (January, 1958), 25-26.   4446

———. Presidential Campaign 1960: A Symposium (Part II). Contest for the Presidency: Overview. QJS, 46 (December, 1960),
355-6.   4447

Mills, Glen E. Debate as Educational Television. G, 39 (May,
1957), 87, 90.   4448

Millson, William A. D. Radio Debating; a New Form. S, 24 (November, 1939), 9-10.   4449

Musgrave, G. M. Account of the MIT Radio Season. DM, 2 (September, 1946), 58-61.   4450

Newcomer, Lloyd R. Radio's Influence on Debate Practice. WS,
12 (April, 1948), 13-14. (Also in DM, 4 (Summer, 1948), 92-
3.)   4451

Quimby, Brooks. Adaptation of Debate to Radio. G, 27 (January,
1945), 24, 32. (Also in DM, 1 (April-June, 1945), 13-14.) 4452

Rexroth, Kenneth. Debating the Great Debates. Na, 191 (November 5, 1960), 344.   4453

Roberts, John B. Adapting Forensic Activities for Radio. BDAPC,
13 (March 1, 1947), 14-18.   4454

Shayon, R. L. Puppy Dogs and Dialectics; International Championship Debate on the NBC. SaR, 45 (June 28, 1952), 32.   4455

Sibley, Carroll. Radio Debating. G, 16 (2 January, 1934), 22-3.
                                                                  4456

Stanton, Frank. The Case for Political Debates on TV, NYTM,
    (January 19, 1964), 16, 68-70.   4457

Stasheff, Edward. The Campaign on the Air. QJS, 30 (December,
    1952), 412.   4458

_____ and Miller, Edd. Televising a Debate in a Courtroom Set-
    ting. ST, 3 (September, 1954), 215-19.   4459

Stevenson, Adlai. Plan for a Great Debate. This Week, (March
    6, 1960), 14-15.   4460

Summers, H. B. Radio Debating. G, 13 (January, 1931), 6-8. 4461

Television has "Little Debates" Too. Business Week, (October 29,
    1960), 34.   4462

Those Atrocious Great Debates. Reporter, 23 (November 10, 1960),
    2.   4463

TV Debates. SPG, 1 (March, 1964), 99.   4464

Van Buren, Ruth. Give 'Em the Air. PN, 9 (January-February,
    1942), 10-11. (On broadcasting debate.)   4465

Vickrey, James F., Jr. Debating on a Statewide Educational Tele-
    vision Network. SSJ, 33 (Winter, 1967), 108-112.   4466

Waltz, Waldo E. Broadcasting the Spoken Argument at Illinois. G,
    16 (January, 1934), 24-5.   4467

WCBS Gets Acceptances for Political Debates. Broadcasting, 60
    (June 5, 1951), 62.   4468

Welden, Terry A. Educational Television and the University of
    Pittsburgh's Debate Program. PSA, 13 (May, 1956), 41-3. 4469

Wenger, D. A. Great Debate: The Producer's View. ES, 45 (Feb-
    ruary, 1966), 25. (An interview with K. Gammerman.)   4470

Willis, Edgar E. Little Television Debates in Michigan. QJS, 48
    (February, 1962), 15-23.   4471

E.   FORUMS, CONFERENCES, CONGRESSES, AND CONVENTIONS

1.   Books

Judson, Lyman S., ed.   The Student Congress Movement.   New
York, Wilson, 1940.   4472

Overstreet, H. A., and Overstreet, Bonaro.   Town Meeting Comes
to Town.   New York, Harper, 1938.   4473

2.   Thesis

Dlugach, Martha N.   A History and Analysis of Legislative Debating
in the United States.   M. A.   Baylor.   1967.   4474

3.   Articles

Adams, Edwin W.   Youth Points the Way.   JNEAJ, 33 (November,
1944), 190-1.   (Description of a Junior Town Meeting.)   4475

Agard, Walter R.   Freshman Forum at Wisconsin.   SchS, 58 (December 18, 1943), 477-8.   4476

Alexander, Fred G.   Let's Have a Student United Nations.   DM, 3
(September, 1947), 139-43.   4477

Alexander, John W., and Berger, M.   Is the Town Meeting
Finished?   AMe, 69 (August, 1949), 144-51.   4478

Allen, Harold B.   Film Forums; an Experiment in Community Discussion.   QJS, 31 (October, 1945), 300-3.   4479

Allen, Ronald R.   The Model Security Council Conference.   G, 45
(1 November, 1952), 7-9.   4480

Aly, Bower.   Report of the D. S. R. Student Congress.   G, 21 (May,
1939), 78-9.   4481

American and English Students Discuss Post-War Education over the
Air; First Trans-Atlantic Broadcast of a Junior Town Meeting.
SchS, 61 (May 19, 1945), 325.   4482

Andersen, Kenneth E.   The Student Congress: An Evaluation and a
Proposal.   SPG, 6 (March, 1969), 77-81.   4483

_____.   Student Congress: Retrospect and Prospect.   SPG, 5 (Jan-
uary, 1968), 51-54.   4484

Anderson, Jerry M., and Andersen, Kenneth E.   Student Congress
on Trial.   SPG, 3 (November, 1965), 27-32.   4485

Bachman, John W.   Bringing the Public into Public Discussion.
DM, 3 (Autumn, 1948), 146-7.   4486

_____.   The Significance of the Junior Town Meeting Movement to
the Evolving Secondary School Curriculum.   Ed, 57 (May, 1947),
571-7.   4487

Baird, John E.   Try Conference Debate.   F, 55 (January, 1970),
5-7.   (Advocates a conference setting for scholastic debate.)4488

Balduf, E. W.   Public Affairs Education Through Forums.   AEB, 4
(January, 1940), 127-30.   Condensed version in the NEA Proceedings, 1940, 195-8.   4489

Bekker, John A.   Wanted: Forums for Adults.   SchS, 52 (August
17, 1940), 110-11.   4490

Beyer, Bertha S.   Student Forums Find Favor.   SchA, 12 (January,
1941), 197.   4491

Binney, James.   Debating for Truth, Not Decisions.   SchA, 10
(May, 1939), 389-91.   4492

Brandes, P. D.   The Mississippi Youth Congress.   SSJ, 16 (September, 1950), 40-9.   4493

Brewster, Harold L.   Town Meeting Goes to Town.   CJSE, 18
(March, 1943), 183-4.   4494

Bright, Hazel.   Moorhead State Experimental Coffee Forum.   S,
25 (May, 1941), 4.   4495

Bristow, William H.   Forum in Family Life Education.   AEB, 3
(April, 1939), 11-12.   4496

Brown, Frances.   English Class Tackles World Problems.   CH, 14
(September, 1939), 19-24.   (The forum method in English class.)
                                                               4497
Brundin, A. S.   New Social Invention.   I, 90 (1917), 248.   4498

Buehler, E. C.   The Third National Congress of D. S. R.   G, 29
(March, 1947), 38-42.   4499

_____.   To Scuttle or Not to Scuttle the Student Congress.   SPG,
3 (November, 1965), 15-19.   4500

Bunch, David A.   Possibilities of High School Forum Clubs.   SchA,
13 (February, 1942), 213-15.   4501

Caffyn, Walter W.   Open Air Forum, St. Petersburg, Florida.   Re,
40 (August, 1948), 257-8.   4502

Camden, Blanche.   Little Town Hall in Session.   SoS, 30 (April,

1939), 171-2.   4503

Campbell, William G.   Making Forums Function.   ASBJ, 105 (October, 1942), 29-30.   4504

Champlin, Carrol D.   Forums and Subversive Propaganda.   ERF, 3 (January, 1939), 181-4.   4505

Chastian, Charlotte.   United Nations Assembly... Collegiate Level. G, 41 (May, 1959), 52-4.   (The author was an undergraduate when she wrote this article.)   4506

Chenoweth, Eugene C.   The Discussion Conference; Value and Preparation.   S, 30 (March, 1948), 3.   4507

Clemens, Richard, and Caffrey, Francis.   Forum Enters into the Curriculum.   HP, 27 (February, 1945), 57-61.   4508

Coleman, G. W.   Get Together in the Open Forum.   Pu 22 (1919), 871-3.   4509

Collins, Sherod J.   The Student Assembly.   F, 27 (May, 1942), 126-127, 162.   (Of Pi Kappa Delta.)   4510

Conger, (Mrs.) Edwin, and others.   High School Forum: Training for Tomorrow's Citizens.   EJ, 36 (April, 1947), 196-7.   4511

Corbett, H. G.   Forum Meeting Presents Points of View of Many City Interests.   La Crosse, Wisconsin.   AC, 55 (February, 1940), 91.   4512

County Youth Forum Organized by Students in High Schools of Dallas County, Iowa.   EV, 1 (July 1, 1942), 14.   4513

Davis, H. N.   Social Values of the Open Forum.   SSR, 13 (1929), 256-64.   4514

Denny, George V., Jr.   Forums and Morale.   SaR, 25 (July 4, 1942), 7-8.   4515

De Zafra, Carlos, Jr.   Batavia's Public Forum.   NYSEJ, 28 (February, 1941), 353-4.   4516

Dickens, Milton.   Intercollegiate Convention Debates in New York. G, 19 (May, 1937), 51-4.   4517

_____.   Intercollegiate Convention Debating.   QJS, 20 (February, 1934), 30-37.   4518

_____.   The National Student Congress of D. S. R.   G, 21 (January, 1939), 22-3.   4519

_____.   Origin and Development of the National Student Congresses of Delta Sigma Rho.   D. S. R.   Golden Anniversary Issue.   4520

Diem, W. Roy.   Student Conference on Public Affairs.   G, 18
(March, 1936), 42-3.   4521

Dolbear, Frank T.   Arranging Pupil Forums.   NSch, 24 (November,
1939), 66.   4522

Drury, J. W.   Impressions of the National D. S. R. Student Congress.
G, 21 (May, 1939), 82.   4523

Ehninger, Douglas, and Graham, Mary.   The Student Congress
Movement Comes of Age.   G, 20 (November, 1947), 6-7, 11.
4524
Ely, Mary L.   Talking it Over: The Old Town Meeting Reincar-
nated.   SuG, 74 (January, 1938), 57-9.   4525

Eversule, Frank L.   Public Forum and the College.   JHE, 11 (May,
1940), 242-6.   4526

Ferris, Frances.   The Student Congress.   R, 27 (December, 1952),
6, 8.   4527

Forum in Small Country Town.   Sur, 41 (1919), 538.   4528

Forums Organized in the Schools.   EV, 1 (June 15, 1942), 15-16.
4529
Freeley, Austin J.   The Eighth Delta Sigma Rho Congress.   G, 40
(May, 1958), 61, 66.   4530

Frizzell, John H.   The Parliamentary Discussion.   G, 18 (November, 1935), 7.   4531

_____.   The Pennsylvania State Debaters' Convention.   BDAPC, 7
(May 30, 1936), 9-10.   4532

Gaffney, Matthew, W.   Student Forums in Democratic Education.
SoE, 4 (March, 1940), 168-9.   4533

Gage, L. J.   Open Forum.   Sur, 43 (1920), 485-86.   4534

Garvey, Neil F.   Forum--an Instrument of Democracy.   IE, 29
(September, 1940), 11-12.   4535

Goetzinger, Charles.   Death Comes to an Old Friend?   SPG, 2
(May, 1965), 103-105.   (On the student congress.)   4536

Goodman, Louis S.   Film Forum: a Technique in Adult Education.
ES, 20 (October, 1941), 330-2.   4537

Gordon, Dorothy.   Wanted: Youth Forums.   PaM, 23 (February,
1948), 28-9.   4538

Gorst, H. E.   Girls' Parliaments, an Experiment in Education.   FR,
121 (May, 1924), 708-20.   4539

Grant, Percy S.   Objects and Methods of the International Forum.
CO, 64 (1918), 287.   4540

_____.   Open Forum in America as a Safeguard Against Revolution.
CO, 64 (1918), 142-3.   4541

_____.   Open Forum Movement.   NAR, 203 (1916), 81-92.   4542

Gutmans, Theodore M.   Language Difficulties on the International
Forum.   QJS, 35 (December, 1949), 435-40.   (On U. N. interpretations.)   4543

Haiman, Franklyn S.   Northwestern's Mock United Nations Conference.   G, 29 (January, 1927), 24-5.   4544

Harvey, C. C.   Questions for Student Forums and Discussion Groups.
SchA, 15 (March, 1944), 230-1.   4545

Have You a Forum in Your Town?   Schol, 35 (October 16, 1939),
5.   4546

Hayden, F. S.   Civic Training by Means of Student Forums.   CJSE,
15 (March, 1940), 141-2.   4547

High, Stanley.   America Talks it Over.   RD, 32 (April, 1938), 73-
5.   4548

Hopkins, H. Dana.   The Public Forum.   DM, 2 (December, 1946),
209-12.   4549

Hornady, C.   Live and Useful Forum.   Talledega, Alabama, AC,
55 (September, 1940), 64.   4550

Hughes, R. O.   Junior Town Meeting.   SchA, 17 (October, 1945),
43-4.   4551

The Intercollegiate Forum.   BDAPC, 4 (February, 1934), 4-7. 4552

Jeffrey, Robert C.   The Ninth Delta Sigma Rho Congress.   G, 42
(May, 1950), 49, 62.   4553

_____.   The Tenth Delta Sigma Rho Congress.   G, 44 (May, 1962),
50-3.   4554

Johnson, C. L.   The West Point Conference on United States Affairs.
QJS, 36 (April, 1950), 226-31.   (Cf. Eighty-six page report
printed by U. S. M. A., 1950.)   4555

Johnson, Janet B.   Open Forum Club Experiments.   SchA, 12 (November, 1940), 103-4.   4556

_____. Open Forum Club Stresses Good Citizenship. BBE, 17
(September, 1939), 23-4.   4557

Johnson, Katharine. "Should be Continued." G, 21 (May, 1939),
    65. (On the National Student Congress.)   4558

Junior Forums; Public Debate Adapted to Classroom and Assembly
    Practices. Schol, 49 (October 14, 1946), 2.   4559

Kaye, Stephen R. Ivy League Tries New Meeting. G, 34 (Novem-
    ber, 1951), 10-11. (The debate conference.)   4560

Keltner, John. Backward or Forward? SPG, 2 (May, 1965), 109-
    110. (On student congress.)   4561

Kennon, Sudie. Student Forums and the Library. EM, 19 (Decem-
    ber, 1939), 188-90.   4562

Klopf, Donald. Experience in Parliamentary Conduct. G, 41
    (March, 1959), 39-40, 47.   4563

Kolberg, Oscar W. How to Operate a Successful Student Congress.
    DM, 1 (October-December, 1945), 101-3.   4564

_____. Stimulating Discussion Through a Student Congress. DM,
2 (December, 1946), 254-5.   4565

Laase, Leroy T. The Nebraska Debate and Discussion Conference.
    G, 28 (May, 1946), 53-54.   4566

Lahman, Carroll P. A One-Day Student Legislative Assembly. G,
    25 (January, 1943), 33-4.   4567

Lake, Richard. Organization of a Forum. AEB, 4 (January, 1940),
    60-3.   4568

Lamb, H. D. Broadcasting Forums. EV, 1 (May 15, 1943), 7-8.
                                                                   4569
Lomas, Charles W. Parliamentary Debate at the University of
    Michigan. G, 28 (May, 1946), 55.   4570

Lyman, R. L. The Forum as an Educative Agency. QJS, 1 (April,
    1915), 1-8.   4571

Maple, Glen W. Student Forums and Discussion Clubs. SoS, 30
    (March, 1939), 109-11.   4572

Mason, John B. Public Forums vs. Propaganda. SchS, 46 (1937),
    311-13.   4573

_____. For Forum Leaders. JAD, 11 (October, 1939), 429-31.
                                                                   4574
Matthews, C. P. Rural Teacher and the Farm Radio Forums. Sch

(Elementary and Secondary Editions), 32 (April, 1944), 676-7.
4575

Maze, Lavelle T.   Open Forum for Business Students.   JBE, 17 (March, 1942), 17-18.   4576

McKenzie, Ruth I.   Community Action Through Farm Forum.   CF, 28 (June, 1948), 49-60.   4577

Means, Ruth D.   Alumni Forums in Colorado.   JAD, 11 (June, 1939), 274-5.   4578

Melick, W.   National Heckle Hour: America's Town Meeting of the Air.   RD, 28 (June, 1936), 42-6.   4579

Menser, C. L.   On the Open Forum.   QJS, 10 (November, 1924), 346-49.   4580

Miller, Edd.   Michigan Tries Participation Experiment.   G, 34 (November, 1951), 5.   4581

Minelli, Philip.   Forum Discussion Brings Safety Results.   MJE, 26 (May, 1946), 387-8.   4582

_____.   Forum Method.   SE, 26 (February, 1947), 14-15.   4583

Montgomery, Keith S.   The National Student Conference and Student Council.   TKA Golden Anniversary issue.   National office of TKA.   4584

Morris, D. W.   The Intercollegiate Forum.   QJS, 24 (April, 1938), 212-20.   4585

Muehl, E. William.   An Adaptation of the Congress Plan.   G, 26 (January, 1944), 24-26.   4586

The National Student Congress of D. S. R.   G, 28 (3 March, 1946), 38-41.   4587

Nelson, Thomas L.   Growing Importance of Public Forums.   CJSE, 14 (May, 1939), 273-5.   4588

New Solvent for Antagonisms.   Sur, 36 (1916), 234.   4589

New York State Forums.   JAD, 11 (October, 1939), 463-4.   4590

Nichols, Walter S.   Planning Public Forums.   ASBJ, 103 (September, 1941), 19-21.   4591

Nuesse, C. J.   Will Student Forums Grow?   SchA, 13 (March, 1942), 271-2.   4592

O'Brien, Joseph F.   The American Students Constitutional Convention: A Unique Parliamentary Assembly.   ST, 7 (January, 1958),

35-39.   4593

_____. Pennsylvania State Debaters' Convention. BDAPC, 11
(May 25, 1938), 11-13.   4594

_____ and Carlson, Fred S., Jr. The Fourth Annual Pennsylvania
State Debaters' Convention. BDAPC, 12 (January 16, 1939), 23-
26. Also in G, 21 (May, 1939), 80-82.   4595

_____ and Young, Fred L., Jr. The Third Annual Pennsylvania
State Debaters' Convention. BDAPC, 10 (January 15, 1938), 11-
13.   4596

Open Forum and its Influence. Ou, 110 (1915), 357-8.   4597

Oppy, Gene B. Public Speaking Forum for High Schools. OS, 17
(December, 1939), 481.   4598

Paddock, Howland. Kenosha Organizes Town Hall. AmT, 25 (December, 1940), 23.   4599

Peterson, M. O. Des Moines Holds Public Forums. LJ, 58 (1933),
453-54.   4600

Peterson, Owen. Forum Debating. ST, 14 (November, 1965), 286-
290.   4601

Pettegrew, C. W. The Junior Town Meeting Movement. PSA, 3
(May, 1946), 21-4.   4602

Princeton Debate Groups Unite in Model Congress. PN, 4 (January,
1938), 18.   4603

Proffitt, Maris M. Adult Civic Education Through Public Forums.
USOEB, (1937), 58-72.   4604

Putnam, Miriam. Film Forums - an Adventure in Adult Education.
ES, 22 (November, 1943), 334-6.   4605

Quinlan, Geraldine E. A Realistic Approach. G, 21 (May, 1939),
84-5. (On the DSR student congress.)   4606

Ray, Robert F. The Iowa University Student Senate. QJS, 32 (December, 1946), 454-57.   4607

Reid, Ronald F. Impressions of Impressions: a View of Student
Reaction to the Eighth Congress. G, 40 (May, 1958), 67-70.
(Delta Sigma Rho congress.)   4608

Report of the Committee on Evaluation of the Congress. G, 40
(May, 1958), 71-2, 85. (On the 8th DSR congress.)   4609

Resolutions of the Eighth Congress. G, 40 (May, 1958), 63-4, 85.

(On the ith DSR congress.)   4610

Rhode Island Schools Conduct Annual Model Congress. PN, 4 (January-February, 1941), 18-19.   4611

Rice, Philip B.   How to Get a Better Congress; Ohio Democratic
   Forum.   Na, 158 (April 8, 1944), 413-15.   4612

Robbin, Joseph J.   School Forum--a Social Service Force.   OS, 19
   (November, 1941), 378-9.   4613

Roper, Ralph C.   Let People Talk.   Multiple Group Forum Plan.
   Na, 157 (October 23, 1943), 469-70.   4614

Rose, Forrest H.   So You're Going to Invite the Convention.   F,
   27 (March, 1942), 76-8.   4615

Rowland, A. Westley.   TKA National Discussion Conference and
   Congress.   S, 30 (November, 1947), 3-4.   4616

Rules of the Ninth National Delta Sigma Rho Congress.   G, 42 (3
   March, 1960), 34-9.   4617

Rules of the Tenth National Delta Sigma Rho Congress.   G, 44 (3
   March, 1962), 35-47.   4618

Rummel, Lynda.   Critical Look at a Concept.   SPG, 2 (May, 1965),
   106-108.   4619

Sampson, Harold P.   Midwest Conference Debate.   F, 52 (March,
   1967), 9-10.   4620

Schlesser, George E.   Organizing Community Forums.   SchS, 68
   (August 21, 1948), 113-18.   4621

Seger, Ralph, and Oaks, Diane.   The Speaker and Clerk Look at
   the Congress.   G, 40 (May, 1958), 65-6.   (By the students who
   acted as speaker and clerk at the 8th DSR congress.)   4622

Sharp, Margaret M.   Experiment with Community Forums.   AEB,
   12 (December, 1947), 43-4.   4623

Shepard, Grace F.   Symposium Rather than Debate.   Ed, 52 (December, 1931), 211-13.   (The merits of symposium contrasted
   with those of competitive debate.)   4624

Shepard, Warren.   Three Types of Conference.   EJ, 19 (June,
   1930), 487-89.   4625

Slappey, George H.   Youth Forums as a Means of Teaching Civics.
   SocS, 30 (January, 1939), 33-4.   4626

Steinbarger, Helen T.   A Capital Forum Experiment.   JAD, 11

(January, 1939), 61-3.   4627

Stringer, William.   Forums Make Democracy Think.   CSMM, (July 19, 1941), 7.   4628

Studebaker, J. W.   Des Moines Forum Experiment.   SL, 18 (May, 1933), 175.   4629

_____.   Freedom to Find Out; an Improved Citizenship is Needed. VS, 5 (June 15, 1939), 523-5.   4630

_____.   Ideas Have a Chance in Des Moines.   NEAJ, 22 (May, 1933), 152.   4631

_____.   A Nation-wide System of Public Forums.   WS, 1 (June, 1937), 1, 4.   4632

_____.   What I Mean by Public Forums.   SL, 21 (October, 1935), 33-34.   4633

_____.   Why I Believe in Public Forums.   PN, 3 (October, 1936), 9-10, 19.   4634

_____ and Williams, Chester.   Forum Planning Handbook.   USOEB, 17 (1939), 1-71.   4635

Symposium.   In University Debaters' Annual, ed. by E. M. Phelps. New York, Wilson, 1937.   Pp. 156-98.   (Students from Kansas State, West Virginia, and Texas Universities present a symposium on the question "Should Athletes be Paid?")   4636

Terkel, Meyer.   Town Hall Meeting of the Air Auditorium Program in an Elementary School.   Ed, 61 (September, 1940), 38-9. 4637

Terman, Earle L.   Building for Democracy Through School Forums. SchS, 31 (March, 1940), 10-11.   4638

The Third National Student Congress of DSR.   G, 29 (3 March, 1947), 38-42.   4639

Thomas, Harrison C.   Place of Student Forum in Training for Democratic Citizenship.   HP, 21 (December, 1939), 47-57.   4640

Tompkins, Miriam D.   Film Forums and Adult Education in the Library.   ALAB, 35 (May, 1941), 320-2.   4641

Town Hall of Washington.   SL, 20 (December, 1934), 74-5.   4642

Vandenberg, Arthur H.   A Device to Put Men's Minds in Gear. NYTM, (September 16, 1945), 9.   (On the use of conference method at the United Nations Charter Meeting in San Francisco.)
                                                                   4643
Wagner, Russell H.   Making Democracy Work.   BDAPC, 11 (De-

cember 12, 1941), 8-11.   (On the intercollegiate conference.)
                                                                          4644

Walker, Harvey.   Communication in the Legislative Assembly.
   AAA, 250 (March, 1947), 59-69.   4645

Walsh, John J.   New York State Debate Assembly.   G, 20 (January,
   1938), 22-3.   4646

Wass, Philmore B.   School-Community Cooperation in a Community
   Forum.   SoE, 11 (December, 1947), 346-7.   4647

Williams, Byron B.   Junior Forum, a Rising Tide.   TO, 28 (August, 1944), 23-4.   4648

Williams, Dorothy.   Film Forums at Atlanta University.   LJ, 68
   (June 1, 1943), 469-70.   4649

Williams, Nicholas W.   Youth Defines the Issue.   KSJ, 18 (December, 1939), 25-7.   4650

Wolgamuth, Dale E.   A Local Forensics Conference--Some Advantages.   G, 41 (November, 1958), 9-10.   4651

Wood, Herbert J.   A Canadian-American Student Conference.   F,
   28 (January, 1943), 48-50.   4652

Woodward, Emily B.   Forums, Why and How.   Athens, Georgia,
   University of Georgia, 1943.   (A pamphlet).   4653

Wright, Charles F.   The National Speech Tournament and Student
   Congress.   WS, 3 (January, 1939), 20-1; (May, 1939), 15. 4654

Wyer, Malcom G.   Union Seeks Library's Aid; Public Forum, Denver Public Library.   LJ, 70 (June 1, 1945), 524.   4655

Yeager, W. Hayes.   Conference Speaking.   In A Program of Speech
   Education in a Democracy, ed. by W. A. Cable.   Boston, Expression, 1932.   Pp. 257-68.   4656

Zander, Eugene.   The Student Congress Movement.   R, 15 (October,
   1940), 3-6.   4657

F.   PARLIAMENTARY PROCEDURE

1.   Books

Auer, J. Jeffery.   Essentials of Parliamentary Procedure.   New
   York, Appleton, 3rd ed.   1959.   4658

Bosmajian, Haig A.   Readings in Parliamentary Procedure.   New
   York, Harper, 1968.   4659

Chaffe, Edith T.   Parliamentary Law.   New York, Crowell, 1930.
4660

Chambers, George F.   Handbook for Public Meetings.   London,
Stevens, 1907.   (Includes rules for debate.)   4661

Cruzan, Rose M.   Practical Parliamentary Procedure.   Bloomington, Illinois, McKnight, 1947.   4662

Cushing, Luther S.   Cushing's Manual of Parliamentary Practice,
rev. by Albert S. Bolles.   Philadelphia, Winston, 1947.   4663

Davidson, Henry A.   Handbook of Parliamentary Procedure.   New
York, Ronald, 1955.   4664

Demeter, George G.   Manual: How to Master the Rules of Parliamentary Law and Procedure.   Boston, Mosher, 1947.   4665

Freeman, William M., and Abbott, J. Carson.   ABC of Parliamentary Procedure; a Handbook for Use in Public Debate.   London,
Butterworth, 1906.   4666

Gray, John W., and Rea, Richard G.   Parliamentary Procedure:
A Programed Introduction.   Chicago, Scott, 1963.   4667

Gregg, Fred M.   Handbook of Parliamentary Law.   Boston, Ginn,
rev. ed.   1940.   4668

Hall, Alta B., and Sturgis, Alice F.   Textbook on Parliamentary
Law.   New York, Macmillan, 1923.   4669

Hamilton, William G.   Parliamentary Logic.   Introduction and Notes
by Courtney S. Kenny.   Reprint Series No. 1.   Cambridge, Heffer, 1927.   (How to become a good parliamentary debater.) 4670

Hawley, Edward W.   How to Learn Parliamentary Law Easily--and
Remember It.   Minneapolis, Minn., Northwestern, 1932.   4671

Henry, William H. F., and Seeley, Levi.   How to Organize and How
to Conduct a Meeting.   Rev. ed.   New York, Noble, 1938. 4672

Hoogestraat, Wayne E., and Sikkink, Donald E.   Modern Parliamentary Practices.   Minneapolis, Minn., Burgess, 1963.   4673

Howe, Frank W.   Howe's Handbook of Parliamentary Usage.   New
York, Noble, 6th ed.   1932.   4674

Johnston, James.   Westminster Voices: Studies in Parliamentary
Speech.   London, Hodder, 1928.   4675

Jones, Ossie G.   Parliamentary Procedure at a Glance.   New York,
D. Appleton, 1933.   4676

Lacock, John K.   Outline of Parliamentary Law.   Boston, Expression, 1936.   4677

Lehman, Warren. Parliamentary Procedure. New York, Double-
    day, 1962.   4678

Leigh, Robert D. Modern Rules of Parliamentary Procedure. New
    York, Norton, 1937.   4679

MacKelvey, Elizabeth G. Ritual Parliamentary Law for Ordinary
    Assemblies. New York, Macmillan, 1934.   4680

Mason, Paul. Mason's Manual of Legislative Procedure. New
    York, McGraw, 1953.   4681

Menderson, Melanie F. Parliamentary Procedure Simplified. Cin-
    cinnati, Dale Press, 3rd ed. 1957.   4682

Moore, Zoe S., and Moore, John B. Essentials of Parliamentary
    Procedure. New York, Harper, 1944.   4683

Morin, Victor. Chairman's and Debater's Guide in Deliberative As-
    semblies. Toronto, Ontario, Canada. Carswell, 1947.   4684

Nolan, William J. Guide to Parliamentary Practice. Minneapolis,
    Minn., Northwestern, 1938.   4685

O'Brien, Joseph F. Parliamentary Law for the Layman. New
    York, Harper, 1952.   4686

Ponsonby, Arthur. Hints for Platform and Parliamentary Speaking.
    London, Allen, 1938.   4687

Ransom, D.M. The Chairman and Debater's Handbook. London,
    Routledge, 1931.   4688

Reeves, J. Walter. Parliamentary Procedure. Boston, Heath,
    1931.   4689

Riddick, Floyd M. Congressional Procedure. Boston, Chapman,
    1941.   4690

Robert, Henry M. Parliamentary Law, Method of Transacting Busi-
    ness in Deliverative Assemblies, Uses of the Various Motions,
    Method of Conducting Elections, etc. New York, Century, 1923.
    ("Detailed, comprehensive treatment of the broad field of parlia-
    mentary law. The master volume from which the simplified
    rules are derived. ")   4691

_____. Parliamentary Practice: An Introduction to Parliamentary
    Law. New York, Century, 1925. (Companion volume to Rules
    of Order and Parliamentary Law.)   4692

_____. Rules of Order Revised, 75th Anniversary Edition. Chicago, Scott, 1951.   4693

Stevenson, Fred G.   Pocket Primer of Parliamentary Procedure.
    Boston, Houghton, 1952.   4694

Sturgis, Alice F.   Learning Parliamentary Procedure.   New York,
    McGraw, 1953.   4695

_____.   Sturgis' Standard Code of Parliamentary Procedure.   New
    York, McGraw, 1950.   4696

Thomas, Peter D. G.   The House of Commons in the Eighteenth
    Century.   Oxford, Clarendon, 1971.   4697

Whitney, Bryl A.   Please Come to Order.   Anandale, Virginia,
    Turnpike Press, 1966.   4698

_____.   Whitney's Parliamentary Procedure.   Washington, D. C.,
    Luce, 1962.   4699

Wiksell, Wesley.   How to Conduct Meetings.   New York, Harper,
    1966.   4700

2. Thesis and Dissertation

Davis, Robert E.   The Characteristic Parliamentary Practices of
    the Fourth Party.   Ph. D.   Illinois.   1959.   4701

White, William P.   The History and Philosophy of the Quorum as a
    Device of Parliamentary Procedure.   M. A.   Montana.   1967.
                                                                        4702

3. Articles

Adult Education Association of the United States.   Streamlining Par-
    liamentary Procedure.   (Chicago, 1957), A Symposium by Knowles,
    English, O'Brien, Lacey, Auer, Mason, and Sturgis, Reprinted
    from AL, (December, 1956), 177-193.   4703

Alexander, Henry M.   School for State Legislators.   StG, 14 (Feb-
    ruary, 1941), 39-40.   4704

Amato, Philip P.   Programmed Instruction in Teaching Parliamen-
    tary Procedure.   ST, 17 (March, 1968), 145-149.   4705

Balgooyen, Theodore J.   Unusual Procedures for Extending Debate
    in the U. N. General Assembly.   SSJ, 32 (Summer, 1967), 296-
    303.   4706

Borchers, Gladys L.   Radio Dramatizations in Parliamentary Law.
    CH, 7 (October, 1932), 77-81.   4707

Callaghan, J. Calvin. Precedence in Parliamentary Motions. QJS, 51 (October, 1965), 301-303.   4708

Carmack, Paul A. Evolution in Parliamentary Procedure. ST, 11 (January, 1962), 26-39.   4709

Civics Class Becomes the U. S. House of Representatives. CD, 11 (October, 1932), 252-3; 11 (November, 1932), 286-7.   4710

Cleary, James W. A Rationale for a College Course in Parliamentary Procedure. JAFA, 1 (January, 1964), 12-20.   4711

Crocker, Lionel. The Strategy of Parliamentary Procedure. TS, 4 (November, 1956), 17-18.   4712

Davis, William H. Parliamentary Procedure and Formal Debating. QJS, 12 (February, 1926), 11-22.   4713

Everhart, Rodney W. Scrap Parliamentary Procedure? TS, 11 (November, 1963), 20-21.   4714

Glossary of Parliamentary Terms. CD, 5 (November, 1926), 301.
4715

Gray, Giles W. Implementing the Philosophy of Parliamentary Practice. ST, 10 (January, 1961), 13-21.   4716

_____. A Philosophy of Parliamentary Law. QJS, 27 (October, 1951), 437-41.   4717

_____. Points of Emphasis in Teaching Parliamentary Procedure. ST, 13 (January, 1964), 10-15.   4718

Gregg, Fred M. Inter-Relations of Parliamentary Motions and Questions. SchA, 14 (November, 1942), 109.   4719

Hall, Alta B. Curricular Training in Parliamentary Law. In W. A. Cables' A Program of Speech Education in a Democracy. Boston, Expression, 1932. Pp. 322-41.   4720

_____ and Sturgis, Alice F. Parliamentary Law in the Speech Curriculum. QJS, 21 (February, 1935), 85-8.   4721

Harrison, Frederic. Parliamentary Procedure. NCA, 55 (April, 1906), 553-64.   4722

Ilbert, C. P. History of English Parliamentary Procedure. Con, 89 (January, 1906), 14-20.   4723

Jackson, George S. An Experiment in the Teaching of Parliamentary Law. QJS, 24 (February, 1938), 45-8.   4724

Jenkins, Jon E. "I Move That..." SchA, 14 (November, 1942), 92.   4725

Judson, Lyman S.   Combining Debate and Parliamentary Practice.
    JEX, 4 (June, 1930), 71-4.   4726

Knowles, Malcolm S.   Move Over, Mr. Robert!   AL, 1 (June,
    1952), 2.   4727

Laine, Joseph B.   Requirements and Procedures for the "Richards
    Primary Law" Debates.   CSSJ, L (Winter, 1962), 96-99.   4728

Mason, Paul.   The Legal Side of Parliamentary Procedure.   TS, 4
    (November, 1956), 9-14.   4729

Meyer, Frank.   Parliamentary Current Events.   SoE, 5 (March,
    1941), 194-5.   4730

O'Brien, Joseph.   The Chairman and His Job.   TS, 4 (November,
    1956), 19-20.   4731

_____.   Don't Shove, Mr. Knowles, Parliamentary Law is Basical-
    ly Sound.   TS, 2 (January, 1954), 2-4.   4732

_____.   Henry M. Robert as a Presiding Officer.   QJS, 42 (April,
    1956), 157-62.   4733

_____.   The Place of Parliamentary Procedure in the Department
    of Speech.   QJS, 26 (February, 1940), 26-30.   4734

_____.   The Use and Abuse of Parliamentary Procedure.   AL, 5
    (December, 1956), 178-82.   4735

Pannell, Charles.   Disorder in the House.   NSta, 55 (1958), 192-4.
    (Discusses abuse of parliamentary procedure in the House of
    Commons.)   4736

Parsons, E. Dudley.   Experiment in Teaching Parliamentary Prac-
    tice.   EJ, 32 (May, 1943), 273-4.   4737

Peters, J. , and Mayhew, P. B. B.   This House Believes...   IIENB,
    29 (May, 1954), 27-29.   4738

Rea, Richard G. , and Gray, John W.   Teaching Parliamentary Pro-
    cedure through Programed Instruction.   ST, 13 (January, 1964),
    21-24.   4739

Reeves, J. Walter.   Knowing Parliamentary Procedure.   EQ, 10
    (May, 1930), 12.   4740

_____.   Value of Parliamentary Law.   QJS, 17 (April, 1931), 261-
    4.   4741

Smith, Bromley.   Parliamentary Law and Public Speaking.   QJS, 3
    (October, 1917), 327-31.   4742

Sturgis, Alice F.   American Voluntary Associations: Our Informal
    Government.   TS, 4 (November, 1956), 7-9.   4743

Van Zandt, James E.   What a Congressman Needs to Know about
    Parliamentary Procedure.   TS, 4 (November, 1956), 5-7.   4744

Walker-Smith, Derek.   New Procedure in Parliament.   FR, 167
    (1947), 425-32.   4745

Watkins, R.   Parliamentary Organization in the Classroom.   EJ,
    24 (September, 1935), 584-6.   4746

Watson, J. Steven.   Parliamentary Procedure as a Key to the Under-
    standing of Eighteenth Century Politics.   Burke Newsletter, 3
    (1962), 108-28.   4747

Wills, Gayle V., and Rea, Richard G.   Status of Parliamentary
    Procedure in Southern Colleges and Universities.   SSJ, 36 (Fall,
    1970), 43-46.   4748

XVII. JUDGING DEBATE

1. Book

Holm, James N. How to Judge Speech Contests. Portland, Maine, Platform, 1938.   4749

2. Theses and Dissertations

Anapol, Malthon M. An Experimental Study of the Reliability and Validity of Certain Non-Professional Debate Judges. M. A. Temple. 1953.   4750

Barker, Larry L. A Comparative Analysis of Debater-Judge Ratings. M. A. Ohio. 1963.   4751

Callaway, Byron C. The Relationship between the Theoretical and the Actual Criteria for Determining Decision Debate. M. A. North Texas State. 1964.   4752

Delozier, Sister Mary Linus. An experimental Study of the Competency of Debate Judges. M. A. Hawaii. 1964.   4753

Esch, Marvin L. A Comparative Study of the Shift-of-Opinion Ballot, Audience Evaluation, and Critic-Judge Systems of Debate Decisions. M. A. Michigan. 1951.   4754

Evans, Diane R. An Experimental Study of Student and Trained Judges of Oratory. M. A. Hawaii. 1963.   4755

Farley, Fern. The Decisionless Debate. M. A. Northwestern. 1926.   4756

Gibson, James W. The Construction and Testing of a Forced Choice Scale for Debate Judging. M. A. Ohio State. 1960. 4757

Holcomb, Martin. A Study of the Critic-Judge System. M. A. Northwestern. 1931.   4758

Holm, James N. An Outline of Standards and Techniques in Judging Speech Contests. Ph. D. Wisconsin. 1937.   4759

Infante, Dominic A. The Perceived Educational Value of the AFA Form C and Flow-Sheet Debate Ballots. M. A. Kent State.

1969. (Abstracted by Kenneth Anderson in JAFA, 7 (Spring, 1971), 308-310.)   4760

Jacob, Bruno. Factors Responsible for Unsatisfactory Debate Decisions. M. A. Denver. 1936.   4761

Miller, Wayne L. A Study of Judging Standards in Contest Debating. M. S. Purdue. 1950.   4762

O'Connor, John R. , Jr. The Objectivity of Intercollegiate Debate Judges. M. A. Indiana. 1966.   4763

Pearce, W. Barnett. An Analysis of the Communicative Efficacy of Debate Ballots. M. A. Ohio. 1968.   4764

Pic'l, Melvin E. A Critical Study of Judges and Judgments in Intercollegiate Debate Tournaments. M. A. Pepperdine College. 1962.   4765

Rausch, Anthony L. A Systematic Method of Evaluating the Strengths and Weaknesses of Debaters Through the Debate Ballots. M. A. Bowling Green. 1968.   4766

Roever, James E. A Study to Determine to What Extent Academically Defensible Criteria Are Employed in the Judging of Debate Tournaments. M. A. Kansas. 1958.   4767

Schunk, John F. Probability and Desirability Determinants of Relationships Among Beliefs in Rhetorical Propositions. Ph. D. Illinois. 1967.   4768

Scott, Robert. A Study of the Objectivity of Debate Judges. M. A. Nebraska. 1951.   4769

Steinfatt, Thomas M. A Factor Analytic Study of the Evaluation of College Debates. M. A. Michigan State. 1966.   4770

Travis, John C. An Investigation of the Audience-Judge Agreement Factor in College Debate. M. A. Montana State. 1958.   4771

Wilmington, Sidney C. A Study of the Relationship of Selected Factors to Debate Effectiveness and to Debate Rating Reliability. M. A. Northwestern. 1967.   4772

3. Articles

Anapol, Malthon M. , and Towne, Ralph L. The Use of the Demurrer in Debating: A Proposal. JAFA, 7 (Fall, 1970), 125-129.
                                                                                4773
Baccus, Joseph. Debaters Judge Each Other. QJS, 23 (February, 1937), 74-80.   4774

Baird, John E.   Attorney Judges: A Communication Problem for
    Debaters.   F, 56 (January, 1971), 3-7.   4775

Baker, J. Thompson.   The New Ballot in Debate.   PN, 6 (January-
    February, 1940), 9-10.   4776

Baker, Roy T.   "...Shall Provide Qualified Judges." F, 44
    (March, 1959), 67-68.   4777

Barker, Larry L.   An Investigation of Judging Practices in Debate.
    SPG, 2 (November, 1964), 22-23.   4778

_____.   A Comparative Analysis of Debater-Judge Ratings.   JAFA,
    2 (January, 1965), 17-20.   4779

Barnard, P.E.   Concerning Judges.   G, 8 (January, 1925), 21-23.
                                                               4780
Bartlett, Kenneth G.   'To a Decision." G, 12 (January, 1930), 22-
    23.   4781

Bauer, Otto F., and Colburn, C. William.   The Maverick Judge.
    JAFA, 3 (January, 1966), 22-25.   4782

Bawcom, David.   What Are the Characteristics of an Ideal Debate
    Judge? SPG, 7 (May, 1970), 145.   4783

Becher, Edmond T.   Shall the Audience Decide? EJ, 16 (March,
    1927), 203-12.   4784

Berthold, Carol A.   A Descriptive Study of Selected Characteristics
    of Debate Judges' Ballots.   JAFA, 7 (Winter, 1970), 30-35.   (On
    how debate judges use their ballot for rendering a decision.)4785

Betz, Edward S.   Analysis of Tournament Ballots.   WS, 4 (January,
    1940), 16-17.   4786

_____.   A Study of Debate Standards.   F, 25 (May, 1940), 108-
    112, 181.   (With regard to judging.)   4787

Bostrom, Robert N.   Dogmatism, Rigidity, and Rating Behavior.
    ST, 13 (November, 1964), 283-287.   4788

Bowen, Roger.   Where Bad Decisions Come From.   G, 37 (January,
    1955), 41-42.   4789

Brann, Vincent C.   The Art of Judgemanship, or, How to Survive
    a Debate Tournament.   BDAPC, 20 (December, 1940), 9-14.4790

Brick, Adolph H.   Suggestions for Improving Debate Judging.   F, 6
    (January, 1921), 1.   4791

Brooks, William D.   Judging Bias in Intercollegiate Debate.   JAFA,
    7 (Winter, 1971), 197-200.   4792

Carter, Reginald. The Non-Decision Debate. HER, 23 (March, 1935), 204-205.   4793

———. The Use of the Critic-Judge in Debating. HER, 20 (October, 1931), 34.   4794

Chenoweth, Eugene C. Debate Judging Ballot. F, 32 (October, 1946), 1-4. Also in DM, 3 (March, 1947), 47-49. (Rejoinder to Betz, supra.)   4795

Christopherson, Merrill G. If Judges Can't Agree, Make Them Debate. F, 39 (May, 1954), 99-100.   4796

Clark, William K. Debate Judging: Implications of the James Study. AFAR, 9 (Convention Issue, 1961), 1-5. (See James article, infra.)   4797

Clevenger, Theodore, Jr. Retest Reliability of Judgments of General Effectiveness in Public Speaking. WS, 26 (Autumn, 1962), 216-22.   4798

———— and King, Thomas R. A Comparison of Debate Results Obtained by Participant and Critic-Judging. SSJ, 25 (Spring, 1960), 223-32.   4799

Cohen, A. R. Cognitive Tuning as a Factor Affecting Impression Formation. JPer, 29 (1961), 235-245.   4800

Corder, Kenneth W. Students Prefer Judged Debates. G, 12 (January, 1930), 5-6. Also in NFL, 4 (March, 1930), 6-7.   4801

Crocker, Lionel. Debate Judging. S, 30 (January, 1948), 6.   4802

Cunningham, C. C. A Ballot Comparison. G, 18 (November, 1935), 10.   4803

Daily, R. C. From Lower Mississippi Way. F, 30 (May, 1945), 86-7. (On judging in tournaments.)   4804

Davis, William H. A Ray of Hope as to Judges. QJS, 9 (April, 1923), 195-96.   4805

Decisionless Debate with the Open Forum. QJS, 7 (June, 1921), 279-91. (Reports of six directors of debate in Western universities.)   4806

Diem, W. Roy. The Task of the Critic Judge. G, 15 (March, 1933), 10-12.   4807

Drake, Ormond J. Instructions for Debate Judges. QJS, 25 (February, 1939), 130.   4808

Drum, Dale D. The Debate Judge as a Machine. TS, 4 (April,

1956), 28-31. (Believes that judges should not have to take notes at a debate tournament; advocates less "dry logic" by debaters. See rejoinders by R. P. Friedman, infra, and A. N. Kruger, "The Debate Judge as a Critical Thinker," infra.)   4809

Dunne, Dennis P., Mack, Herschel L., and Pruett, Robert. Empirical Evidence on the "Logical"-"Proficiency" Dichotomy in Debate Judging. JAFA, 7 (Winter, 1971), 201-207.   4810

Dwyer, Charles A. Judging Debates. G, 14 (March, 1932), 19-20.   4811

Ellis, Dean S., and Minter, Robert. How Good Are Debate Judges? JAFA, 4 (Spring, 1967), 53-57.   4812

Erskine, William C. Informal Debating. G, 12 (January, 1930), 15-16.   4813

Ewbank, Henry L. Departments and Activities. QJS, 11 (February, 1925), 101-102. (On judging debate.)   4814

Fotheringham, Wallace C. Measuring Speech Effectiveness. SM, 23 (March, 1956), 31-37.   4815

Freshley, Dwight L. Report of the PSA [Pennsylvania Speech Association] College Forensic Section on "A Standard Debate Ballot for Pennsylvania." BDAPC, 18 (December, 1952), 2-3.   4816

Friedman, Robert P. Reflections of an Incompetent Judge. JAFA, 8 (Winter, 1972), 123-126.   4817

_____. Why Not Debate Persuasively? TS, 5 (January, 1957), 32-34. (Comment on Drum's article, supra.)   4818

A Further Comparison of the "Individual Ballot" with the Audience "Team Ballot," and the Judges' Decision. G, 16 (January, 1934), 23.   4819

Giffin, Kim. A Study of the Criteria Employed by Tournament Debate Judges. SM, 26 (March, 1959), 69-71.   4820

_____ and Warner, Donald. A Study of the Influence of Note-Taking by Tournament Judges on Debaters' Attitudes. G, 45 (March, 1963), 42-43, 56. (Concludes that debaters expect judges to take notes.)   4821

Gilkinson, Howard A. Departments and Activities. QJS, 11 (February, 1925), 100-101. (On judging debate.)   4822

Graham, Donald L. Private Debate Vs. Public Speaking. F, 45 (October, 1959), 8-12.   4823

Gregory, Joyce R. A Method of Speech Improvement (Northwest

Speech Judges' Association).   R, 13 (April, 1939), 12.   4824

Grether, Ewald T.   No-Decision Debates.   G, 11 (January, 1929),
14.   4825

Haakenson, Robert, ed.   Briefly Speaking; a Symposium: What Are
the Most Important Criteria for Judging a Debate and Why?
BDAPC, 17 (December 15, 1951), 35-37.   (Contributors include
Mary H. Purcell, Mahlon H. Hellerich, and Bruce Carlton.) 4826

Hadaller, J. A.   The One-Judge System in Debate.   F, 10 (May,
1924), 380-81.   4827

Halstead, William P.   Who Wins Debates; A Statistical Study of
1320 Debates.   QJS, 26 (April, 1940), 213-20.   4828

Harvey, P. Casper.   How Shall Debates Be Judged?   NEAJ, 13
(March, 1924), 106.   (See rejoinder by W. W. Parker, infra.)
                                                              4829
Haston, Bruce M.   Have We Forgotten Quality?   G, 43 (November,
1960), 5-6.   (On poor debate judging.)   4830

Hayes, Michael T., and McAdoo, Joe.   Debate Performance: Differences Between Male and Female Rankings.   JAFA, 8 (Winter,
1972), 127-131.   4831

Henrikson, E. H.   The Split Decision Ballot.   G, 23 (March, 1941),
59-60; G, 24 (November, 1941), 12-13.   4832

Hill, Sidney R., Jr.   A Study of Participant Evaluations in Debate.
JAFA, 9 (Winter, 1973), 371-377.   4833

Holcomb, Martin.   The Critic-Judge System.   QJS, 19 (February,
1933), 28-38.   4834

_____.   The Critic-Judge System of Deciding Debates.   G, 14
(March, 1932), 17-19.   Also in F, 17 (March, 1932), 224-25.
                                                              4835
_____.   Standards Used by Critic-Judges.   G, 15 (March, 1933),
18.   4836

Hollister, R. O. T.   Faculty Judging.   QJS, 3 (July, 1917), 235-41.
                                                              4837
Holm, James N.   Judging the Cross-Examination Debate.   PN, 7
(November, 1940), 6-9.   4838

_____.   The Contest Judge as Educator.   PN, 4 (April-May, 1938),
3, 29.   4839

_____.   A Philosophy of Judging Debate.   SSJ, 5 (January, 1940),
5-11.   4840

Hoogestraat, Wayne E.   Should Debate Judges Take Notes?   F, 52

(March, 1967), 11.   4841

How to Judge a Debate.   Extension Bulletin 282.   Madison, Wisconsin, The University, 1911.   4842

Howes, Raymond T.   What Price Judging?   G, 12 (January, 1930),
7-8.   4843

Hufford, Roger.   Toward Improved Tournament Judging.   JAFA, 2
(September, 1965), 120-125.   4844

_____.   Tie Breaking: The Quality-Point System.   JAFA, 5 (Win-
ter, 1968), 21-24.   (Proposes the use of quality-points instead
of speaker points for breaking tie records in tournaments.) 4845

Hunter, E.R.   The Judge's Scoresheet.   F, 14 (March, 1929), 199.
                                                                     4846
Infante, Dominic A.   The Perceived Educational Value of the AFA
Form C and Fiow-Sheet Debate Ballots.   JAFA, 7 (Spring, 1971),
308-310.   4847

Jackson, George S.   Why Not Have a Decision?   S, 24 (November,
1939), 6.   4848

James, Herbert L.   Standards for Judging Refutation.   AFAR, 9
(Spring, 1961), 21-25.   Also in S, 44 (November, 1961), 15-19.
                                                                     4849
Johnson, T. Earle.   How Should Debate Be Judged?   QJS, 21
(June, 1935), 396-99.   .   4850

Judson, Lyman S.   A Judgment Based on Individual Excellency in
Debating and Speaking.   G, 15 (March, 1933), 8.   4851

Kelley, W.D.   Objectivity in the Grading and Evaluation of Speech.
ST, 14 (January, 1965), 54-58.   4852

Klopf, Donald, Evans, Diane, and DeLozier, Sister Mary Linus.
The Controversy Over Judges' Qualifications.   F, 51 (March,
1966), 7-10.   4853

_____, _____ and _____.   Comparative Studies of Students, Lay-
men, and Faculty Members as Judges of Speech Contests.   ST,
14 (November, 1965), 314-318.   4854

Krueger, Richard F.   The Reliability of Debate Judges.   G, 32
(November, 1949), 7-9.   4855

Kruger, Arthur N.   The Debate Judge as Critical Thinker.   TS, 5
(January, 1957), 29-31.   (Rejoinder to Drum's article, supra.
Believes that since debate is complex, a competent judge should
take notes during the course of a debate.)   4856

_____.   An Evaluation of Tournament Debate Judging.   PSA, 14

(June, 1957), 39-51.   (Introduces a scale for comparing and rating debate judges.)   4857

_____. It Was Only a Dream! BDAPC, 21 (December, 1955), 16-
20.   (A satire on debate judging, or how not to judge a debate.)
                                                                       4858
_____. Judging the Judging at Meadville. BDAPC, 21 (December,
1955), 30-35.   (Use of scale to evaluate judges at annual DAPC
tournament.)   4859

_____. Judging the Tournament Debate Judge. G, 37 (January,
1955), 31-35, 43.   (Explanation of a rating scale to compare
and evaluate debate judges.)   4860

_____. Judging Results of the 1956 DAPC Tourney. BDAPC, 22
(December, 1956), 16-19.   (Judges evaluated by new scale.) 4861

Kuperstein, Hyman. Who Is Judging What? S, 29 (May, 1947), 5-
6.   4862

Laase, Leroy T. An Evaluation of the Quality Rating System in
Measuring Debate Achievement. QJS, 28 (December, 1942), 422-
30.   4863

_____. A Standard for Judging Debates. F, 16 (March, 1931),
192.   4864

_____, Siekman, Harold L., and McGee, Gale. Instructions to
Judges. R, 14 (October, 1939), 12-13.   4865

Lamers, William M. This Business of Debate Judging. G, 20
(May, 1938), 59-62.   4866

_____. The Personal Equation in Debate Judging. G, 15 (March,
1933), 7.   4867

Layton, Charles R. How Can We Secure More Uniformity in Debate
Judging in 1948-1949? S, 31 (November, 1948), 4-7.   4868

Lichtenfels, Paul J. The Judging of Public Speaking Contests.
Ohio Teacher, 48 (February, 1928), 267-70.   4869

Long, Emmett. The Debate Judge and the Rhetorical Critic. WS,
16 (January, 1952), 21-23.   4870

Lyman, Rollo La Verne. How to Judge a Debate. University Bulletin No. 423. Madison, Wisconsin, The University, 1913. 4871

Marino, Teresina. Consensus in Debate. QJS, 15 (June, 1929),
421-22.   (Criticism of open-forum, decisionless debating.) 4872

Markgraf, Bruce. Debate Judging and Debater Adaptation: A Reply.
JAFA, 3 (January, 1966), 37-39.   (A rejoinder to Henry von

Moltke's article "Decision Debating: A Judge's Point of View, "
infra.)   4873

Mazzola, John P.   Judging a Debate.   BDAPC, 6 (May 29, 1935),
  3.   4874

McBride, Lida.   Why We Favor Non-Decision Open-Forum Debates.
  G, 12 (November, 1929), 5-6.   4875

McCarty, Leon.   The Expert Judge of Debating.   QJS, 15 (June,
  1929), 417-20.   4876

McCroskey, James C. , and Camp, Leon R.   Judging Criteria and
  Judges' Bias in Debate.   JAFA, 3 (May, 1966), 59-62.   4877

_____ and _____.   A Study of Stock Issues, Judging Criteria, and
  Decisions in Debate.   SSJ, 30 (Winter, 1964), 158-168.   (Concludes that judges and debaters consider the need issue to be the
  most important one in most debates.)   4878

Melzer, Dorothy G.   Suggestions for Improving Debate Judging.
  SSJ, 18 (September, 1952), 43-51.   4879

Miller, Arthur B.   Instruction of Debate Judges: A Case History.
  JAFA, 6 (Winter, 1969), 24-26.   4880

Miller, Edd.   I Believe in Decisions.   G, 12 (January, 1930), 16.
  Also in NFL, 5 (November, 1930), 4-5.   4881

Miller, Gerald R.   Some Factors Influencing Judgments of the Logical Validity of Arguments: A Research View.   QJS, 55 (October,
  1969), 276-286.   4882

Monroe, Alan.   The Statistical Reliability and Validity of the Shift-
  of-Opinion Ballot.   QJS, 23 (December, 1937), 577-85.   4883

Moore, Wilbur E.   Worst Faults of Debaters and Judges.   DM, 3
  (Autumn, 1948), 111-12.   4884

Mundt, Karl E.   An Answer to Critics.   R, 11 (December, 1936),
  2.   (Critics referred to are those of decision-debating.)   4885

_____ .   The Fallacy of No-Decision Debates.   NFL, 3 (February,
  1929), 1-3.   Also in F, 15 (May, 1929), 273.   4886

_____ .   Why Decision Debating?   NFL, 9 (December, 1934), 3.
                                                                                     4887

Murphy, Jack W. , and Hensley, Wayne E.   Do Debaters Know Why
  They Win or Lose?   ST, 15 (March, 1966), 145-147.   4888

Musgrave, George M.   An Attempt to Answer Some Questions on
  Judging.   DM, 2 (December, 1946), 246-7, 265.   4889

_____. Debate Judging. DM, 2 (June, 1947), 78-80.   4890

_____. The Double-Summary Method of Judging Debates. DM, 1 (January-February, 1945), 11-15.   4891

_____. Elements of Double-Summary Judging. DM, 4 (Summer, 1948), 95-97.   4892

_____. The Pepperdine-U. S. C. Debate: A Critique. DM, 1 (July-September, 1945), 39-43.   4893

_____. Quiz for Judges. DM, 4 (Summer, 1948), 97-99.   4894

_____. The Wells-O'Neill Controversy. DM, 2 (December, 1946), 218-20, 251-54. (A complete review of a well-known controversy on debate judging.)   4895

Myers, W. Grading a Debate. SchA, 15 (March, 1944), 232.   4896

Newell, Clarence A. Uniform Rules for Debating. QJS, 24 (October, 1938), 483-85. Also in BDAPC, 12 (January 16, 1939), 6-8. (Suggested instructions to debate judges.)   4897

Newman, Robert P. Construction and Use of Debate Ballots. BDAPC, 18 (December, 1952), 4-12.   4898

Newton, W. T. Elements of Good Debating; A Guide for Judges. WB, 3 (January, 1927), 43-46.   4899

Nichols, Egbert R. The Composite Judge System. F, 9 (March, 1924), 318.   4900

_____. A Three to Two Decision. F, 30 (March, 1945), 54-55.
                                                             4901
Nicholson, Harold. Marginal Comment: Judging a Competition in Public Speaking. Sp, 174 (February 2, 1945), 102.   4902

Ojala, Dorothy, and Shinnick, Fred. The Debaters' Bill of Rights. ST, 4 (March, 1955), 98-100. (A humorous skit on debate judging.)   4903

Olson, Donald O. Suggestions for Judging Debates. G, 41 (November, 1958), 13.   4904

O'Neill, James M. Able Non-Debaters. QJS, 1 (July, 1915), 201-205.   4905

_____. Comment on Judge Wells' Last Manuscript. QJS, 4 (October, 1918), 410-21.   4906

_____. Judging Debates. QJS, 3 (October, 1917), 336-55; 4 (January, 1918), 76-92.   4907

_____. Judges Again. QJS, 1 (October, 1915), 305-307.   4908

_____. Judges for Intercollegiate Debates. PSR, 2 (January, 1913), 135-38.   4909

_____. The Juryman's Vote in Debate. QJS, 3 (October, 1917), 346-55.   4910

_____. A Sensible System. QJS, 2 (April, 1916), 198. (On the use of a single critic-judge.)   4911

Paget, Edwin H.   The Audience Vote.   EJ, (College Edition) 17 (April, 1928), 320-25.   4912

_____. Non-Decision Debates. QJS, 13 (February, 1927), 53-54.
                                                              4913
Parker, W. W.   Why Should Debates Be Judged?   Reply to P. C. Harvey.   NEAJ, 13 (November, 1924), 301.   (See Harvey's article, supra.)   4914

Parlette, John W.   Overcoming Dislike for No-Decision Debates. G, 12 (January, 1930), 8.   4915

Pearce, W. Barnett.   Communicating the Reasons for Decision by the Ballot.   JAFA, 6 (Spring, 1969), 73-77.   4916

Pease, Raymond B.   Audience as the Jury.   QJS, 3 (July, 1917), 218-23.   4917

_____. Can We Have a More Scientific Basis for Judging Debates? G, 1 (January-March, 1918), 331-33. ("Why not make the audience the jury?")   4918

Perry, F. M.   The National Catalogue of Debate Judges.   QJS, 11 (April, 1925), 173-74.   4919

Petelle, John L.   A Comparison of Team Quality Ratings Against Strong Versus Weak Opposition.   JAFA, 4 (Fall, 1967), 104-106.
                                                              4920
_____ and Olson, Donald O.   The Effect of Time Variation on Team Quality Ratings.   JAFA, 6 (Winter, 1969), 21-23. (Studies the effect of time of day on debate ratings.)   4921

Plantz, Earl.   Judges--Blind or Instructed?   R, 10 (September, 1935), 6-7.   4922

Radcliffe, Barbara M.   A Plea for Uniform Judging.   R, 31 (January, 1957), 4.   4923

Raum, Richard D.   What Are the Characteristics of an Ideal Debate Judge?   SPG, 7 (May, 1970), 144.   4924

Reeves, Mary, and Osborn, Lynn R.   Judges of High School Debate

Tournaments: Sources, Criteria, and Orientation. ST, 14 (January, 1965), 59-62.   4925

Roberts, Mary. Make It Legible. F, 47 (January, 1962), 21. (Complains about illegible comments on debate ballot.)   4926

Robinson, Frederick B. Coach and Judges. PSR, 3 (April, 1914), 236-37.   4927

Roever, James, and Giffin, Kim. A Study of the Use of Judging Criteria in Tournament Debate. AFAR, 8 (Winter, 1960), 12-14.   4928

Sarett, Lew R. The Expert Judge of Debate. QJS, 3 (April, 1917), 135-39.   4929

_____. A Juryman-Critic's Vote. QJS, 4 (October, 1918), 428-33.   4930

Schunk, John F. A Quantitative Study of Decision-Making in Academic Debate. JAFA, 7 (Spring, 1971), 271-277.   4931

Scott, Robert L. The Problem of the Prima Facie Case: A Reply to Mr. Markgraf. SPG, 2 (March, 1964), 81-83.   4932

_____. The Objectivity of Debate Judges. G, 37 (November, 1954), 14-15.   4933

Sebald, H. Limitations of Communication: Mechanisms of Image Maintenance in Form of Selective Perception, Selective Memory, and Selective Distortion. JC, 12 (1962), 142-149.   4934

Seeley, Kenneth B. Who Is Best Qualified to Judge Debates? G, 12 (January, 1930), 20.   4935

Shaw, Warren C. A Basis for Judging Debates. PSR, 3 (April, 1914), 232-36.   4936

Shirley, Kathy. What Are the Characteristics of an Ideal Debate Judge? SPG, 7 (May, 1970), 143-144.   4937

Shrier, William. Are Not No-Decisions Real Tests After All? G, 12 (January, 1930), 10-11. Also in NFL, 5 (November, 1930), 5-6.   4938

_____. Shifting the Emphasis: An Argument for No-Decision Debating. QJS, 15 (June, 1929), 364-74.   4939

Sillars, Malcolm O. A Note on Tournament Judging. AFAR, 8 (Spring, 1960), 21-22.   4940

Simonson, Walter E., and Strange, Bennett. A Reconsideration of Debate Judging. F, 46 (October, 1960), 10-12.   4941

Smelser, J. N.   Why Have a Decision?   S, 25 (November, 1940), 5.
4942

Steiner, Ivan D.   Reactions to Adverse and Favorable Evaluations
of One's Self.   JPer, 36 (1968), 553-563.   4943

Student Forum: What Are the Characteristics of the Ideal Debate
Judge?   SPG, 7 (May, 1970), 143-145.   (Contributors: Tim
Wright, Kathy Shirley, Richard D. Raum, Tom Walsh, and
David Bawcom.)   4944

Taylor, Carl.   Decisionless Debating.   G, 12 (January, 1930), 13-
14.   Also in NFL, 5 (December, 1930), 7.   (Comments of a
graduate student.)   4945

Thomas, D. A.   Instructions for Debate Judges on Preparing for Debate Tournaments.   SchA, 39 (November, 1967), 4-5.   4946

Thompson, Wayne.   Is There a Yardstick for Measuring Speaking
Skill?   QJS, 29 (February, 1943), 87-91.   4947

Toch, H., and MacLean, M. S., Jr.   Perception, Communication,
and Educational Research: A Transactional View.   AVCR, 10
(1962), 55-77.   4948

Trueblood, Thomas C.   I Prefer Decisions.   G, 12 (January, 1930),
6.   4949

_____.   More About Judges.   PSR, 3 (May, 1913), 24-25.   (Dis-
cusses a method for choosing judges.)   4950

Unruh, A.   Evaluation Blank.   SchA, 21 (October, 1949), 43-44.
4951

Utterback, William E.   Decisionless Debates Are Becoming Popular.
G, 12 (January, 1930), 21.   4952

_____.   News of the Departments.   QJS, 10 (June, 1924), 315-16.
(On judging debate.)   4953

Valentine, Elvin L.   Judging Debate.   BDAPC, 13 (March 1, 1947),
8-14.   4954

Verderber, Rudolph.   Judges' Criteria and Debater Adaptation:
Empirical Evidence.   JAFA, 5 (Winter, 1968), 28-30.   (On tournament designed to permit greater audience adaptation by debaters.)   4955

von Moltke, Henry.   Decision Debating: A Judge's Point of View.
JAFA, 1 (September, 1964), 97-101.   4955a

Walch, J. Weston.   Debates Are Judged by Human Beings.   SchA,
22 (September, 1950), 24-25.   4956

Walker, J. E., and Olson, W. H.   Debate Judges Should Remain

Awake.   CH, 28 (February, 1954), 367-69.   4957

Wanted: Judges.   PN, 3 (March, 1937), 15-16, 30.   (An exchange
of views on the problem of securing efficient judges for speech
contests; answers to a questionnaire.)   4958

Weinschenk, Franz.   Bless Those "Lay" Judges.   AFAR, 10 (Spring,
1962), 25-27.   4959

Weiss, Robert O.   Judgment and Decision-Making.   JAFA, 1 (May,
1964), 43-47.   4960

Wells, Hugh N.   Comment on Professor O'Neill's Latest Manuscript.
QJS, 4 (October, 1918), 422-27.   4961

_____.   Judging Debates.   QJS, 3 (October, 1917), 336-45.   4962

_____ and O'Neill, James M.   Judging Debates.   QJS, 4 (January,
1918), 76-92.   4963

_____, _____ and Sarett, Lew R.   Juryman or Critic; Three Re-
buttal Arguments and a Decision.   QJS, 4 (October, 1918), 398-
433.   4964

West, Robert W.   Methods Used in Computing Contest Scores.   QJS,
5 (October, 1919), 319-33.   4965

Westerfield, Hargis.   Decision Debating: A Philosophy.   QJS, 28
(February, 1942), 24-27.   4966

Westfall, Alfred.   The Critic-Judge Arrives at His Decision.   G,
15 (March, 1933), 5-7.   4967

_____.   The Judges, the Honorable Judges, If You Please.   F, 5
(March-April, 1919), 3-6.   4968

Whan, Forrest L.   Charging or Choosing the Judges.   G, 13 (January, 1931), 14-15.   4969

Wheater, Stanley B.   A Critics' Symposium.   WS, 16 (May, 1952),
153-158.   (Recommends that judges should give opinions of their
judging criteria before a tournament begins; six sample statements.)   4970

White, H. Adelbert.   Some Objections Against Judged Debates.   G,
10 (November, 1927), 10.   4971

Wiley, Earl W.   Debate as Competition.   G, 12 (January, 1930),
11.   4972

Williams, Frederick, Clark, Ruth A. , and Wood, Barbara S.
Studies in the Dimensionality of Debate Evaluation.   JAFA, 3
(September, 1966), 95-103.   4973

_____ and Webb, Sally A.   Factors in Debate Evaluation: A Pilot Study.   CSSJ, 15 (May, 1964), 126-128.   4974

Wilmington, S. Clay.   A Study of the Relationship of Selected Factors to Debate Effectiveness.   CSSJ, 20 (Spring, 1969), 36-39.
                                                                          4975
Winans, James A.   Judging Debates.   PSR, 2 (March, 1913), 187-91.   4976

Wing, Herbert J.   Criteria for Judging Oregon-Style Debates.   BDAPC, 10 (December 19, 1940), 7-11.   4977

Wise, Charles N.   Relationship Among Certain Rating Judgments on the Form C Ballot.   JAFA, 7 (Spring, 1971), 305-308.   4978

Wisner, Harold E.   Judging the Negative Counterplan.   CSSJ, 2 (March, 1951), 11-14.   4979

Woodward, Howard S.   Debating Without Judges.   QJS, 1 (October, 1915), 229-33.   4980

Woolbert, Charles H.   Contest Judging and Professional Solidarity.   QJS, 8 (April, 1922), 167-68.   4981

_____.   The Decisionless Debate With the Open Forum.   QJS, 7 (June, 1921), 279-91.   4982

_____.   On Critic Debate Decisions.   QJS, 11 (June, 1925), 286-88.   4983

The Worst Faults of Debate Judges.   F, 33 (March, 1948), 49-51.
                                                                          4984
Wright, Tim.   What Are the Characteristics of an Ideal Debate Judge?   SPG, 7 (May, 1970), 143.   4985

XVIII. HIGH SCHOOL FORENSICS

1. Books

Frederick, W. J. , and Wilcox, Ruth. Teaching Speech in High
Schools. New York, Macmillan, 1953.   4986

Gibson, Harold E. , and Sheppard, Victor H. Practical High School
Debating. Minneapolis, Minn. , Northwestern, 1934.   4987

Hannum, Elizabeth C. Speak! Read! Write! Boston, Little,
1935. (A high school debate text.)   4988

High School Debater. Extension Bulletin. New Brunswick, New
Jersey, Rutgers University Press, 1929.   4989

Immel, Ray K. , and Whipple, Ruth H. Debating for High Schools.
Boston & New York, Ginn, 1929.   4990

Jacobson, Paul. The American Secondary School. New York,
Prentice, 1952.   4991

Laycock, Craven. Manual of Argumentation for High Schools and
Academies. New York, Macmillan, 1906.   4992

_____ and Spofford, A. Keith. Manual of Argumentation. New
York, Macmillan, 1908. (A high school text.)   4993

Lyon, Leverett S. Elements of Debating. Chicago, Ill. , Chicago,
1932. (A manual for high school.)   4994

McKinney, Frank C. , and Mary E. A Case Book in Discussion;
Explanatory and Argumentative. Composition. New York, Ronald, 1930. (A case book on argumentation for high school.)4995

Melzer, Arnold. High School Forensics, an Integrated Program.
New York, Wilson, 1940.   4996

Ontario Department of Education. Debates and Public Speaking in
Schools. Toronto, Ontario, Canada, Department of Education,
1936.   4997

Prenner, Manuel, Rogoff, Bernard M. , and Sternberg, William N. ,
eds. Concurrence and Dissent; Some Recent Supreme Court
Cases. New York and Chicago, Merrill, 1933. (For use in the

study of argumentation in senior high schools.)   4998

Reed, A. G., and Adams, J. Q. Suggestions for High School De-
    baters. L. S. U. Bulletin, 51, No. 2, part 2. Baton Rouge,
    L. S. U., 1914.   4999

Robbins, Edwin C. The High School Debate Book. Chicago, Ill.,
    A. C. McClurg Co., 1939.   5000

Robinson, Karl F. Teaching Speech in the Secondary School. New
    York, Longmans, 1954.   5001

Walch, J. Weston. High School Debating: Its Aims and Adminis-
    tration. Portland, Me., Platform News, 1940.   5002

2. Theses and Dissertations

Amberg, Walter. A Comparative Study of Individual Speech Contest
    Events in Public High Schools of the Thirteen States in the Cen-
    tral States Speech Association. M. A. Mankato. 1967.   5003

Anderson, H. H. An Evaluation of High School Debating in Oklahoma
    in the Light of Modern Objectives. M. A. S. California. 1930.
                                                                   5004
Armstrong, George. A Forensic Class Course Outline for High
    Schools of Southern California. M. A. Redlands. 1959. 5005

Bagenstos, Pearl E. An Evaluation of Contests in Speaking in the
    Secondary Schools. M. A. Iowa. 1930.   5006

Barber, George B. An Analysis and Evaluation of Forensic Contests
    as Conducted in the Secondary Schools within the Area of the
    North Central Association. Ph. D. Ohio State. 1953.   5007

Baugh, Ronald L. Summer High School Debate Institutes 1969: A
    Survey and Analysis. M. A. Eastern Michigan University.
    1969.   5008

Bedichek, Ray. Interscholastic Non-athletic Contests. M. A.
    Texas. 1927.   5009

Bonner, John T. A Survey of Contest Extemporaneous Speaking in
    the High School Speech Leagues of the United States. M. A.
    Ohio State. 1946.   5010

Brannan, Roger D. A Survey of the Educational Background of
    Coaches of Debate in Kansas Secondary Schools. M. A. Kansas
    State. 1969.   5011

Brockhaus, Herman H. The History of the Wisconsin High School
    Forensic Association. Ph. D. Wisconsin. 1949.   5012

Brown, Jackie L.   History of the West Virginia State High School
    Forensic Tournament.   M. A.   West Virginia.   1968.   5013

Bursack, Lois.   The Effects of High School Debating on Knowledge
    of the Subject, Attitude Toward Issues and Critical Thinking.
    M. A.   Washington State.   1961.   5014

Cain, Catherine L.   An Application of Hammond's Error-Choice
    Technique to a Study of Attitudes of High School Debaters and
    Non-Debaters toward Debate.   M. A.   Ohio.   1966.   5015

Capel, Robert B.   The Effects of High-School Debating on the Atti-
    tudes of Debaters and Listeners.   M. A.   Wisconsin.   1939. 5016

_____.   The Effectiveness of High School Debate in Providing In-
    formation and Influencing Attitudes.   Ph. D.   Wisconsin.   1941.
                                                                 5017
Champ, Beulah G.   A Comparative Study of the Content of Magazine
    Articles and Winning Northern Oratorical League Contest Orations.
    M. A.   Northwestern.   1928.   5018

Claggett, Harlow M.   A Study in the Ethical Use of Evidence in
    High School Debating.   M. A.   Michigan State.   1966.   5019

Clark, Carolyn.   A Descriptive Study of Declamation in the High
    Schools in Ohio.   M. A.   Bowling Green.   1966.   5020

Coffield, Martha E.   The Integration of Discussion and Debate in a
    High School Forensic Program.   M. A.   Baylor.   1954.   5021

Curry, E. Thayer.   A Study of Differential Background Factors Pos-
    sibly Accounting for Varying Levels of Achievement of Inter-
    scholastic Debaters in the Finals of the Iowa High School Foren-
    sic League of 1935-36.   M. A.   Iowa.   1936.   5022

Curry, Mary B.   A Study of the Value of Speech Contests in the
    High School Curricula.   M. A.   S. California.   1934.   5023

Dollar, David L.   Kansas High School Debate Judging, 1967, 1968:
    An Examination of the Importance Assigned Criteria of Debate
    Evaluation by Groups of Judges According to Educational Level
    and Subject Area Studied.   M. S.   Kansas State.   1968.   5024

Dorsey, David M.   A Study of Factors Involved in the Direction of
    Speech Activities in Selected High Schools in Minnesota.   M. A.
    St. Cloud.   1962.   5025

Duggan, Bessie.   Organization and Establishment of High School De-
    bate Program.   M. A.   Kansas State Teachers College.   1957.
                                                                 5026
Elliott, Phyllis J.   A Study of the Growth and Development of the
    National Forensic League.   M. A.   Nebraska.   1967.   5027

Evans, Robert W.   A Critical Analysis of Programs of Extemporaneous Speaking in Selected Member Schools of the Iowa High School Forensic League.   M. S.   Iowa.   1958.   5028

Garnett, Donald T.   A Critical Look at High School Debate.   M. A. Texas Technological College.   1964.   5029

Gibbs, Gwendolyn E.   A Critical Study of the Constitutional Regulations Governing Declamatory Contests in the High Schools of the United States.   M. A.   Wisconsin.   1939.   5030

Gravholt, Loy E.   A History of Speech Training at Yankton High School, Yankton, South Dakota.   M. A.   S. Dakota.   1965.   5031

Gruner, Charles R.   A Study of Objectivity of High School Debaters as Demonstrated in Self-Evaluation Projects.   M. S.   S. Illinois. 1956.   5032

Hale, Mabel M.   A Study of Interscholastic Debate: Its Potentialities and Deficiencies in the Present-day High School Curriculum. M. A.   Colorado.   1952.   5033

Hamilton, Mary E.   A History of the Colorado State Speech League from 1914 to 1967.   M. A.   Colorado.   1969.   5034

Hartman, Maryann.   A Survey of Current Opinions and Practices in Declamation Contests of High School Speech Leagues.   M. A. Kent State.   1965.   5035

Helgesen, Charles R.   An Investigation of the Relationship Between the Debate Effectiveness of Michigan High School Debaters and a Number of Other Variables.   Ph. D.   Denver.   1962.   5036

Hess, Myron D.   An Analysis of Debate Programs in Selected Minnesota High Schools.   M. A.   St. Cloud.   1962.   5037

Hope, Ben W.   The Interscholastic Extempore Speaking Contest: A Survey and Analysis of Procedures.   M. A.   Iowa.   1947.   5038

Howell, William S.   The Effects of High School Debating on Critical Thinking Ability.   Ph. D.   Wisconsin.   1942.   5039

Hullinger, James L.   A Case Study of the Second Summer Debate Institute Sponsored by the University of Nebraska at Omaha. M. A.   Nebraska at Omaha.   1970.   5040

Johnson, John A.   A Study of Related Aspects of Debate Programs of the Public Schools of Minnesota.   M. S.   Mankato.   1965. 5041

Keeling, Russell M.   An Analysis of Refutation and Rebuttal in Interscholastic Debate.   M. A.   Baylor.   1959.   5042

Kvasmicka, Gerald A.   An Evaluation of Inter-Scholastic Forensics.

M. A.   Nebraska.   1935.   5043

Kyker, Rex Paton.   A History and Evaluation of the Forensic Divi-
    sion of the University Interscholastic League of Texas.   M. A.
    Iowa.   1946.   5044

Lambert, A. Edward.   A Survey of the State High School Speech
    Leagues Cooperating with the N. U. E. A. Committee on Debate
    Materials and Interstate Cooperation.   M. A.   Colorado.   1948.
                                                                    5045
Lane, Ralph L.   A History and Analysis of Illinois High School
    State Contests in Speech.   Ph. D.   Northwestern.   1967.   [Ab-
    stract: SM, 35 (August, 1968), 33.]   5046

Lee, Dale.   The Academic and Experiential Qualifications of Coaches
    of Extra-Curricular Speech Activities in Schools Belonging to the
    Wisconsin High School Forensic Association.   M. S.   Wisconsin.
    1969.   5047

Lockwood, Bonnie J.   A Survey of Debating in the Senior High
    Schools of the Los Angeles District.   M. A.   S. California.   1931.
                                                                    5048
Londergran, Margaret J.   The Organization and Direction of High
    School Forensic Tournaments.   M. A.   Bradley.   1956.   5049

Long, David K.   Speech Education in the Public Secondary Schools
    of Northeastern Ohio 1968-69.   M. A.   Akron.   1969.   5050

Madsen, Sandra.   A Study of the Use of Specified Criteria by Twen-
    ty-Four Judges in Evaluating Tournament Debates at the Begin-
    ning and the End of the 1968-69 Wisconsin High School Debate
    Season.   M. A.   Wisconsin State.   1969.   5051

Martin, George W.   An Administrative Appraisal of High School De-
    bating in Three Mid-Western States.   M. A.   Iowa.   1946.   5052

McDonald, Priscilla M.   An Analysis of Debate Programs in Se-
    lected Missouri High Schools.   M. A.   Univ. of Missouri at Kan-
    sas City.   1966.   5053

McPhee, Rodreck F.   A Survey of Championship Debate Programs
    in American High Schools.   M. A.   Wisconsin.   1953.   5054

Moeller, George A.   An Analysis and Evaluation of Selected Original
    Orations as Presented in the Iowa High School Forensic League of
    1938-1939.   M. A.   Iowa.   1942.   5055

Mole, Olema.   A Critical Study of Eight High School Textbooks in
    Argumentation and Debate.   M. A.   Iowa.   1925.   5056

Moore, Mary E.   A Sociological Study of Debating in Northeast
    Junior High School, Reading, Pa.   M. S.   Teachers College, Co-
    lumbia.   1928.   5057

Mortimer, James R.   A Comparison of the Difference in Personality Change between High School Novice Debaters and Their Peers.
M. A.   Missouri, Kansas City.   1970.   5058

Mraz, Thomas.   An Analysis of Written Comments Given to Selected Students of Burnsville High School in Oral Interpretation
Contests.   M. A.   Mankato.   1967.   5059

Murphy, John W.   A Content Analysis of Northern Oratorical
League Orations.   M. S.   Wisconsin.   1948.   5060

O'Brien, Thomas F.   An Analysis of the Development of the Montana State High School Speech Tournament, 1904-1964.   M. A.
Montana.   1968.   5061

O'Malley, Charles J.   The Organization of and Procedure in Selected High School Forensic Programs.   M. S.   Emerson College.
1968.   5062

Parkerson, James W.   The Place of Logical Reasoning in Representative Works of Argumentation, Debate, and Discussion, of the
High School Level.   M. A.   Iowa.   1949.   5063

Parks, Mack.   A Comprehensive Analysis of the Multi-Organization-
al Structure of the California High School Forensic Program as
It Affects the Novice Director of Forensics.   M. A.   Whittier
College.   1969.   5064

Paulson, Jon R.   A Study of Support Material in Selected High
School Orations.   M. S.   Mankato.   1966.   5065

Pierson, William.   Policies and Practices of Secondary School Debating in the United States.   M. A.   Nebraska.   1962.   5066

Polk, Lillian G.   A Debating Program for Louisiana High Schools,
Based on Current Debating League Practices.   M. A.   L. S. U.
1939.   5067

Reeves, Mary M.   A Descriptive Study of the Relationship between
Training and Experience Factors of Selected Kansas High School
Debate Judges and the Criteria Employed in Determining Their
Debate Decisions.   M. A.   Kansas.   1965.   5068

Schnoor, Larry G.   An Investigation of the Nature and Importance
of Ethical Standards in Minnesota High School Debating.   M. A.
Mankato.   1964.   5069

Shellen, Wesley N.   A Study of Verbatim Memorization of Original
High School Orations in the Southwestern Forensic Championship
Tournament.   M. A.   Arizona State Univ.   1968.   5070

Smith, Don K.   An Experiment in Teaching Critical Thinking in a
High School Speech Class.   M. S.   Wisconsin.   1942.   5071

Smith, Walter R.   A Survey of Successful High School Forensic Programs in Wisconsin.   M. S.   Wisconsin.   1950.   5072

Soli, Audrey.   A History of Statewide Speech Contests in Illinois.
   M. A.   N. Illinois.   1959.   5073

Sorum, Lynn D.   An Analysis of the Curricular Background in
   Speech of the Judges of the Iowa Interscholastic Speech Association.   M. A.   S. Dakota.   1969.   5074

Sparks, Donna J.   A Descriptive Study of the Sacramento Valley
   Forensic League.   M. A.   Sacramento.   1968.   5075

Stephans, Thomas W.   A Survey of Judging Standards in High School
   Speech Contests of Northern and Central California.   M. A.   College of the Pacific.   1950.   5076

Stockdale, Robert.   A Study of the Value to the Participants of
   Inter-School Speech Activities at Ravenna High School, 1928-1949.
   M. A.   Kent State.   1950.   5077

Thompson, Mary E.   The Wisconsin Idea in the Wisconsin High
   School Forensic Association.   Ph. D.   Northwestern.   1960. 5078

True, Bert G.   Inter-school Debate.   M. A.   Florida.   1929. 5079

Webb, Sally A.   Factors on Judgment in the Evaluation of High
   School Debate.   M. S.   Wisconsin.   1964.   5080

Welsch, J. Dale.   Evaluation of the Activities of High School Debating Leagues.   M. A.   Iowa.   1929.   5081

Wolvin, Darlyn.   A Study of the Events in Interscholastic Speech
   Contests in the United States.   M. A.   Nebraska.   1965.   5082

Wrenn, Charles.   Which of a Selected Series of Factors Character-
   istically Differentiated "Winning" and "Losing" Ohio High School
   Debate Programs, 1967-1968?   M. A.   Kent State.   1968.   5083

3. Articles

Active Michigan Team Broadcasts.   PN, 5 (December, 1938), 21.
   (Eastern High School, Lansing, Mich.)   5084

Adams, Walter H.   The Selection of the Proposition for Debate in
   the High School.   SchR, 35 (September, 1927), 538-47.   (A questionnaire study.)   5085

Alderfer, R. D.   Value of High School Debate.   NEAJ, 56 (March,
   1967), 39.   5086

Alicia, (Sister) M. R. S. M.   Debating in Junior High Schools.   CaSJ,

48 (June, 1948), 211-12.   5087

Bach, Mayme. Debate Project of Six Weeks for an English III
    Class. SER, 16 (February, 1931), 141-54.   5088

Baker, George P. Teaching Argumentative Discourse in High School.
    Proceedings of the National Education Association, 1903. Pp.
    460-70. (See article with same title by Charles S. Hartwell,
    infra.)   5089

Barber, G. Bradford. Analysis and Evaluation of Forensic Contests
    as Conducted in the Secondary Schools Within the Area of the
    North Central Association. NCAQ, 28 (January, 1954), 313-17.
    Also printed simultaneously in ST, 3 (January, 1954), 20-22.
                                                                    5090
Barksdale, E. C. Notes on High School Debating. SchA, 7 (April,
    1936), 5-7.   5091

_____. What the High School Debater Needs. G, 12 (November,
    1929), T-2.   5092

Barnard, Raymond H. A Plea for the Short High School Debate.
    QJS, 14 (February, 1928), 117-19.   5093

_____. The Evils of High School Debating. CH, 12 (December,
    1937), 211-14. (Contends that debates are devoid of humor.)
                                                                    5094
_____. The Tournament Idea in High School Debating. QJS, 14
    (April, 1928), 269-71.   5095

Barr, W. M., and Lintz, O. L. Our Personal Experience With Mil-
    burn's Open Forum. CH, 12 (December, 1937), 214-17. (Refer-
    ence to Milburn, New Jersey, High School.)   5096

Bass, W. W. Debate as an Extra-Curricular Acticity. KT, 32
    (1931), 13.   5097

Beaird, T. M. A Word for High School Debaters. QJS, 18 (Novem-
    ber, 1932), 658.   5098

_____. National High School Debating Project. G, 13 (November,
    1930), 8-9. Also in NFL, 5 (December, 1930), 3-4.   5099

A Beginner's Tournament. PN, 8 (October, 1941), 9-10. (Ponca
    City High School novice tournament.)   5100

Behrens Debating Society [Canisius High School, Buffalo, New York]
    Presents Debates Via Radio. PN, 4 (April-May, 1938), 6-7,
    27.   5101

Blount, Ralph E. The Chicago High School Literary Union. QJS,
    7 (June, 1921), 258-60. (Reports changes in debate, extempora-
    neous speaking, declamation, and reading contests.)   5102

Bode, C. J.   High School Debate as Seen by a Bystander.   WJE, 69
(December, 1936), 206-7.   5103

Bolenius, Emma M.   Oral Composition.   Ed, 31 (March, 1911),
449-55.   (Recommendations for speech projects, including debating, in high school English courses.)   5104

Bond, T. C.   How Ohio Does It.   R, 29 (December, 1944), 8-10.
5105
Bowdoin College Again Sponsors High School Forum.   (Forum of the
Bowdoin Inter-Scholastic Debating League) PN, 7 (December,
1940), 19-20.   5106

Bradford, A. L.   Can the Debate Idea be Saved?   CH, 9 (December,
1934), 219-22.   (See rejoinder by W. A. Dahlberg, infra.)   5107

Brendel, Ida May.   Directing a High School Forensic Program.
AFAR, Special High School Issue (1957), 1-4.   5108

Breniman, L. R. N. F. L.   Initiation Ceremony.   R, 10 (October,
1935), 8-9, 15.   5109

Brockhaus, Herman H.   Administration of High School Forensics in
Wisconsin.   CSSJ, 6 (Fall, 1954), 7-8.   5110

Broud, Richard C.   A High School Practice Debate Tournament.
West Virginia School Journal, 65 (February, 1937), 12-13.   5111

Brown, Frank E.   Some Difficulties in Teaching Argumentation and
Debating in the High School.   PSR, 2 (November, 1912), 65-8.
5112
Brown, G. Victor.   Debating at the Alexander Hamilton High School.
HP, 9 (June, 1927), 8-17.   (On how debate serves the school
and community.)   5113

Bruntz, G. G.   Inter-Scholastic Debate in the High Schools.   SEN,
26 (April, 1930), 61.   5114

Bryant, Donald C.   High-School Prize Speaking Contest.   QJS, 15
(April, 1929), 166-70.   Also in NFL, 4 (October, 1929), 4-6.
(A study of the New York State contests and suggestions for im-
provements.)   5115

Buehler, E. C.   Whither High School Contest?   G, 33 (November,
1950), 1-2.   5116

Canisius [Buffalo] High School Debaters Want Opposition.   PN, 3
(February, 1937), 18-19.   5117

Canisius High School Debate Season Gets Underway.   PN, 3 (April-
May, 1937), 12-13.   5118

Carmack, Paul A.   The Development of State High School Speech

Leagues. ST, 3 (November, 1954), 264-8.   5119

Carroll, Herbert A.   The Psychological Story of an Interscholastic
   Debate. EJ, 20 (November, 1931), 756-60. (What goes on in a
   debater's mind while preparing a debate.)   5120

Cass, Frank H.   Debate Work in the Small High School. Washington Educational Journal, 10 (February, 1931), 180-1.   5121

Cate, Roscoe.   Speech is Still Free. PN, 7 (March-April, 1941),
   10-11.   (Condensed from The Daily Oklahoman, Oklahoma City;
   a history of speech and debate in Oklahoma with reference to the
   N. F. L. Tournament.)   5122

Change in Points for Debate.   N. F. L., 4 (February, 1930), 2-3.
   (On rating high school debaters.)   5123

Churchill, George B.   Public Speaking Work in the Secondary School.
   SchR, 11 (April, 1903), 269-87.   5124

Clark, G. A., Jr.   Let Them Have Their Say in Debate. Instruction, 74 (November, 1964), 14.   5125

Clark, Lydia.   N. F. L. Goes to Northwestern. R, 15 (November,
   1940), 10, 12.   5126

Coffman, George R.   A New Plan for High School Debating in Montana.   EJ, 6 (February, 1917), 108-10.   5127

Confusion in High School Debating.   OS, 11 (1933), 9.   5128

Constitution and Rules for County, District and State Contests in Debate, Declamation, Speaking, Essay Writing, Music Memory, and
   Athletics.   Austin, The University of Texas Bulletin, (1928).5129

Cooper, Lean M., and Konigsberg, Ephraim. N. F. L. Goes to Denver. R, 15 (December, 1940), 10-11.   5130

Cordell, Christobel M.   So You're Going to the Tournament
   [N. F. L.]. PN, 4 (January, 1938), 3, 30.   5131

Cortright, Rupert L.   The Debate Class in High School. JEX, 2
   (September, 1928), 163-70.   5132

Cote, Letha J.   Forensics in the Smaller High School. WJE, 74
   (November, 1941), 148.   5133

Creedon, J. J.   Junior High Debating; No Longer Debatable. SchA,
   31 (April, 1960), 239-41.   5134

Dahlberg, W. A.   The Debate Idea Can be Saved. CH, 9 (April,
   1935), 497-9.   (Rejoinder to A. L. Bradford, supra.)   5135

Damon, Verne L.   High School Debating.   WEJ, 7 (September,
1927), 20-1.   5136

Davies, John.   National Tournament Trip Financed by Student
Pledges.   PN, 3 (April-May, 1937), 18-19.   (Kenosha, Wisconsin, High School.)   5137

Debating Picks Up in New England.   PN, 2 (March, 1936), 13, 23.
(On the N. F. L. Tournaments.)   5138

Densmore, Gail E.   The Educational Advantages of the Michigan
High School Debate League.   Michigan Educational Association
Yearbook, Department of High School Principals.   1 (1930), 17-
21.   5139

_____.   Interscholastic Debating Has Greater Goal.   Michigan Edu-
cational Journal, 6 (February, 1929), 348-9.   5140

Douds, J. B.   High School Debating Within our [DAPC] Association
Bounds.   BDAPC, 10 (December 19, 1940), 24-26.   5141

Draxton, Nina.   The Speech Teacher Needs a Conscience.   PN, 8
(January-February, 1942), 13-14.   (Believes that since the in-
tricacies of debate are beyond most high school students, the
speech teacher must teach them other aspects of speech.)   5142

Drum, Jean, and Drum, Dale D.   A Survey of Parent Attitudes Toward High School Forensics.   WS, 19 (March, 1955), 63-8. 5143

Dudley, L. P.   Get Them Interested in Junior High School.   PN, 7
(December, 1940), 10-11.   5144

Engleman, Buryl F.   Problems of the High School Debate Coach.
HST, 4 (February, 1928), 82.   5145

Evans, Robert W.   Extemporaneous Speaking in Iowa High Schools.
AFAR, 9 (College Calendar Edition, 1961), 10-13.   5146

Favel, William.   Four-Round Debate to a Decision.   SrS, 56 (April
26, 1950), 18.   5147

Fox, Albert.   What About High School Debate?   WEJ, 10 (October,
1930), 54; 10 (March, 1931), 204.   5148

Gardner, Bertha L.   Debating in the High School.   SchR, 19 (October, 1911), 534-45; 20 (February, 1912), 120-4.   (Typical criticism of high school debating; see rejoinder by E. C. Hartwell,
infra.)   5149

Gibson, James.   AFA and the High Schools.   AFAR, 9 (Convention
Issue, 1961), 13.   5150

Gosling, Thomas W.   The Reorganization of Methods of Debate in

High School. EJ, 9 (April, 1920), 147-52.   5151

Grady, C. E. [An interview with]. How Debate Champions Are
    Made! PN, 6 (November, 1939), 10-11, 29. (Grady was a suc-
    cessful high school debate coach.)   5152

Graham, W. B. A Ten-Year Experiment: Debating at Lewis and
    Clark High School. WS, 14 (May, 1950), 31.   5153

Graves, R. D. Justification of Debate in High School. SchA, 32
    (September, 1960), 17-18.   5154

Gray, Giles W. Aims and Values of High School Speaking Contests.
    High School Quarterly (Georgia), 17 (July, 1929), 173-83. 5155

_____ and Bagenstos, Pearl. The Declamatory Contest. Univer-
    sity of Iowa Extension Bulletin 259. Iowa City, The University,
    1931. (64 pp.)   5156

Greene, Guy S. Speech Contests in the Technical School. JEX, 6
    (February, 1932), 52-6.   5157

Hagie, C. E. The Tragedy of Inter-School Debating. CoSJ, 43
    (April, 1928), 29-31.   5158

Hanley, Chuck. How Now Speech Program. SC, 15 (October, 1968),
    42-43. (On the status of interscholastic forensic programs in
    Missouri high schools.)   5159

Happe, R. J. Proposed Revision of N. F. L. Program. R, 26 (Octo-
    ber, 1951), 11.   5160

Harrington, Elbert W. A Sense of Direction in High School Debating.
    QJS, 24 (December, 1938), 627-33.   5161

Harrington, Frederic C. An Effective Debate Program for High
    School. QJS, 27 (February, 1941), 52-60.   5162

Harris, Therman G. Forensics Program at Eastern High School.
    BNAP, 38 (January, 1954), 193-6.   5163

_____. The Michigan State College Debate League [Michigan High
    School Forensic Association]. PN, 8 (November, 1941), 19-22.
                                                              5164
Hart, Hubert N. Debating at the Boys' High School. HP, 14 (Octo-
    ber, 1932), 58-9.   5165

Hartwell, Charles S. Teaching Argumentative Discourse in High
    School. Proceedings of the NEA, 1903. Pp. 446-459. (See arti-
    cle with the same title by Baker, George P., supra.)   5166

Hartwell, E. C. Debating in the High School. SchR, 19 (December,
    1911), 689-93. (Rejoinder to B. L. Gardner, supra.)   5167

Henderson, John C.   The Shortridge High School Senate.   PSR, 3
    (October, 1913), 33-6.   (Twenty-six years in existence, it is
    modeled after the United States Senate, at Shortridge High
    School.)   5168

Hensley, Wayne E.   Budgetary Trends in Kansas High School Foren-
    sics Programs.   KaSJ, 32 (Spring, 1971), 2-6.   5169

_____ .   Ohio High School Forensic Budgetary Practices, 1969-1970.
    OSJ, 9 (1971), 12-15.   5170

Higgins, Roger W.   A Century of Debating at Phillips Academy, An-
    dover.   S, 23 (March, 1939), 8.   5171

Highfill, F. J.   High School Debating, Why?   SEN, 28 (May, 1932),
    46.   5172

Highshaw, James L.   Interscholastic Debates in Relation to Political
    Opinion.   QJS, 2 (October, 1916), 365-82.   5173

Hopkins, Richard.   Speech Teacher's Assignments in Secondary
    Schools.   WS, 34 (1970), 144-48.   (On Colorado speech teachers'
    assignments, including their work in forensics.)   5174

How Debating Grew in One Eastern High School [Donora, Pa.].   PN,
    5 (October, 1938), 25.   5175

How I Reached the National Speech Tournament.   (Denton Harvey,
    Visalia High School, 11-12.   Max Cope, Portland High School,
    11; 23.)   PN, 3 (September, 1936), 11-12, 23, 28.   5176

How Michigan Does It.   [Michigan High School Forensic Associa-
    tion].   PN, 7 (December, 1940), 14-15.   5177

Howell, William S.   The Effects of High School Debating on Critical
    Thinking.   SM, 10 (1943), 96-103.   Condensed versions in R, 19
    (October, 1944), 10-11; and in DM, 1 (April-June, 1945), 10-12.
                                                                     5178
_____ .   Teaching Critical Thinking in the High School Speech Pro-
    gram.   BNAP, 38 (January, 1954), 43-8.   5179

Howes, Raymond F.   What the Inexperienced High School Debater
    Should Know.   R, 10 (December, 1935), 4-7.   5180

Howett, L. C. , and O'Connor, J. R.   Junior High School Pupils En-
    gage in Inter-School Debate.   HP, 44 (May, 1962), 58-64.   5181

Huston, Ruth E.   Debate Coaching in High School, Benefits and
    Methods.   QJS, 10 (April, 1924), 127-43.   5182

_____ .   Modern High School Debating Society.   QJS, 11 (April,
    1925), 135-9.   5183

Instructions to Judges, Southern California Debate League. DM, 1
(April-June, 1945), 98-9.   5184

Isbell, Ruth.   Speech Courses at Lincoln High School Offer Unusual
Variety of Devices.   PN, 4 (November-December, 1937), 5-6,
20.   5185

Jackson, L. E.   Coaching a High School Debate Team.   QJS, 22
(October, 1936), 429-33.   5186

Jacob, Bruno E.   First National High School Speech Tournament.
G, 14 (November, 1931), 15.   5187

_____.   History of the National Forensic League, Constitution and
Regulations.   (Booklet prepared and distributed by the National
Office of the National Forensic League, 1962.)   5188

_____.   More About Credit Points.   R, 22 (January, 1948), 8-9.
                                                                            5189
_____.   The National Forensic League.   SSJ, 5 (January, 1940),
12-14.   5190

_____.   Should We Change Our Credit Points System?   NFL, 3
(January, 1929), 1-4.   5191

Karner, E. F.   Debate Team Should be Seen and Heard.   SchA, 26
(December, 1954), 123.   5192

Keiber, A. E.   High School Debates.   PSR, 1 (January, 1912), 138-
9.   (On the Davenport, Iowa High School Debate Society.)   5193

Kemp, Robert.   Publicizing Forensics.   ST, 18 (January, 1969),
54-57.   (On promoting high school forensics in Iowa.)   5194

Kennedy, Allan J.   Directory of Universities and Colleges Conduct-
ing Summer High School Speech Communication Institutes--1969.
JAFA, 6 (Spring, 1969), 91-100.   Ibid. --1970.   JAFA, 7 (Winter,
1970), 21-29.   Ibid. --1971.   JAFA, 7 (Winter, 1971), 224-233.
                                                                            5195
Kingsbury, Warren T.   The Educational Objectives of the High
School Speech Contest.   QJS, 23 (October, 1937), 474-7.   5196

Kittredge, H. W.   The Function of the Debating Society or High
School Lyceum.   SchR, 10 (April, 1902), 292-7.   5197

Klein, Maurice.   Ravenna's Chapter Records.   R, 24 (February,
1950), 6.   5198

Klopf, Donald W.   Ban Summer Institutes?   SPG, 2 (January, 1965),
63-65.   5199

_____ and Ogitani, Betty.   Curricular Practices and Procedures in
Summer Institutes.   ST, 14 (January, 1965), 67-71.   5200

Konigsberg, Evelyn.   What Should be Our Objective in High School
    Debating? QJS, 21 (June, 1935), 392-6.   5201

Kourilsky, M. , and Phelps, W.   Employing Debate in the High
    School Social Science Curriculum.   JSE, 43 (March, 1968), 134-
    142.   5202

Lambertson, Floyd W.   Debate-Discussion Program for Iowa High
    Schools.   Midland Schools, 57 (November, 1942), 82.   5203

_____.   Non-Decision Debates in the High School.   QJS, 18 (Novem-
    ber, 1932), 653.   5204

Lamers, William M.   Non-Decision Debates in the High School.
    QJS, 18 (November, 1932), 653-7.   5205

Larson, P. Merville.   Some Suggestions for High School Forensics.
    ST, 1 (January, 1952), 52-4.   5206

Laudick, David, and Beers, Larry.   A Discriminative Study of the
    Debate Program of the State of Kansas.   KaSJ, 27 (April, 1966),
    34-38.   5207

Lewis, Grace T.   Extemporaneous Speaking in the High School.   EJ,
    13 (December, 1921), 720-3.   (Details of an extemporaneous
    speaking contest.)   5208

Lewis, Leroy.   The College Coach Looks at the High School Debater.
    SSJ, 7 (January, 1942), 69-73.   5209

_____.   The Effect of High School Debating on College Speech Train-
    ing.   QJS, 28 (February, 1942), 27-30.   5210

Little, R. C.   Debating in the High School.   The High School Quar-
    terly, (1918), 93.   5211

Livingston, Kathryn H.   Counteracting Foreign Ideology Through the
    High School Speaker's Bureau.   Ed, 59 (June, 1939), 608-9. 5212

Loeb, Helen, and Weisman, Anna.   High School Debating.   QJS, 20
    (June, 1934), 419-21.   5213

Lowry, Sara.   A Speech Institute for High School Students.   QJS,
    26 (April, 1940), 189-92.   5214

Lowther, James B.   Some Suggestions on High School Debate.   G,
    24 (March-May, 1943), 56; 68.   5215

Lull, Paul E.   High School Debaters' Conference at Purdue Univer-
    sity.   S, 29 (March, 1947), 3-9.   5216

Lyon, Clarence E.   Contacts with High School Debating.   G, 14
    (January, 1932), 16-17.   5217

Lyon, Leverett S.   Inter and Intra High School Contests.   Ed, 33
(September, 1912), 38-49.   5218

Maaske, Roben J.   The Symposium Method in High-School Teaching.
SchR, 57 (1949), 217-22.   5219

MacMurray, W. B.   Class Debates.   Sch (Elementary and Secondary
Education), 24 (September, 1935), 59-60.   5220

Mantell, M.   Teen-Agers Develop Skills While Debating the Issues
in a Junior High Forensic League.   NYSEJ, 15 (February, 1964),
14-16.   5221

Marshall, Iva R.   The Value of Debate in High School.   HSJ, 6
(October, 1923), 159-60.   5222

Mauller, C. T.   A Solution for Public Speaking in the High School.
Ed, 34 (November, 1913), 162-8.   (Notes and rules for extem-
poraneous speaking contests, which the author prefers to debate.)
                                                            5223
McCall, Lottye K.   Reflections of a High School Debate Coach.
SSJ, 2 (October, 1936), 26-28.   5224

McDermott, E. E.   Minnesota High School Debating League, Fifth
Annual Report, 1906.   (Specimen Speeches and Constitution;
League founded in 1901.)   5225

McLaughlin, G. L.   High School Oratory in Outer Space.   CER, 55
(April, 1957), 250-7   5226

McLeod, Norman B.   Debate in Our High Schools.   LASJ, 20 (November 30, 1936), 7-8.   5227

McMonagle, James A.   Shall We Coach to Win?   As answered by
Flint Northern High School.   Sp. Bul. Supp. QJS, 2 (December,
1930), 2-3.   5228

Mendiola, John A., and Gibson, James W.   Participation and
Achievement in Ohio High School Individual Events.   AFAR, 9
(College Calendar Issue, 1961), 6-9.   5229

Michigan Debate League.   G, 11 (May, 1929), 6.   (Contains questionnaire.)   5230

Miller, Carl G.   High School Debate: 1930 Model.   JEX, 3 (September, 1929), 143-6.   5231

_____.   Tradition.   Speech Bulletin.   Supp. QJS, 2 (December,
1930), 14-15.   (Tradition in debate in high school.)   5232

Miller, Robert E.   Some Aspects of High School Debating.   Montana Education, 3 (December, 1926), 17-18.   5233

Mills, Glenn E.   Abolish High School Speech Contests.   SN (Fall,
  1950), 9-12.   Also in R, 25 (October, 1950), 4-6.   (On NCA
  recommendations.)   5234

_____.   Extemporaneous Speaking and Oratorical Declamation as
  Speech Activities in the Secondary Schools.   BNAP, 36 (May,
  1952), 127-31.   5235

_____.   Should Interscholastic Contests be Abolished?   WJE, 83
  (February, 1951), 6-8.   5236

Mixon, H. D.   Promoting High School Debate.   SchA, 38 (October,
  1966), 4-6.   5237

_____ and Brewer, R. S.   Coaching High School Debate.   SchA, 39
  (October, 1967), 5-9.   5238

Monaghan, John P.   Directing a Debate Program in the Secondary
  Schools.   LISA, 4 (May, 1967), 14-18.   5239

Montana High School Debating League; Announcements for the Year
  1906-1907.   Helena, Montana, 1906.   (Bulletin of the University
  of Montana.)   5240

Mundt, Karl E.   Where Do We Go From Here?   R, 12 (November,
  1937), 2-3.   (On the NFL.)   5241

National Speech Tournament.   NFL, 5 (September, 1930), 1-2. 5242

NFL Plans First National Students Congress.   PN, 4 (April-May,
  1938), 11.   5243

Nelson, J. Arthur.   Debate at Benson High School [Omaha, Nebras-
  ka].   PN, 6 (October, 1939), 9-10.   5244

Nelson, Theodore F.   Debating in Illinois High Schools.   QJS, 21
  (April, 1935), 246-251.   5245

_____.   Methods of Conducting Debate Activities in Illinois High
  Schools.   G, 17 (March, 1935), 42-3.   (Reprinted from the
  Illinois Speech News.)   5246

New High School Honor Society Makes Rapid Climb.   PN, 7 (November, 1940), 20, 22.   ("Mask and Gavel" reports ninety chapters
  in thirty-two states.)   5247

Nichols, Egbert R.   Consider the High School Debater.   DM, 1
  (January-February, 1945), 7.   5248

_____.   The High School Debater Chooses His College.   DM, 3
  (June, 1947), 80-1.   5249

Nichols, Ralph G.   Should Interscholastic Speech Competition Be

Abolished? PN, 8 (December, 1941), 8-10.   5250

Nolin, L. L.   Debating in a California Junior High School.   SEN,
26 (February, 1930), 29.   5251

The North Judson Plan For Financing Forensic Activities.   NFL, 9
(December, 1934), 8.   5252

N. U. E. A. to Support National Speech Tournament.   NFL, 5 (December, 1930), 1-2.   5253

O'Brien, Joseph.   Group Discussion as a Substitute for the Conventional High School Contest in Extemporaneous Speaking.   G, 18
(January, 1936), 19-20.   5254

O'Neill, James M.   Coaches for High School Contests.   PSR, 2
(March, 1913), 193-4.   (Plan of the New Hampshire Debating
League [under the direction of the Public Speaking Department at
Dartmouth], undergraduate debaters sent out at request of high
schools.)   5255

Open Forum Policy and Practice in Milburn High School.   SchR,
44 (June, 1936), 408-9.   5256

Otis, A. T.   Appreciation and Management of High School Debates.
EJ, 3 (February, 1914), 94-8.   5257

Palzer, Edward.   Debating Is on the Upgrade at Moorehead [Minne-
sota].   PN, 8 (October, 1941), 18-19.   (An interview with the
debate coach.)   5258

Pane, O. E.   Debate as a High School Elective.   HSJ, 19 (February,
1936), 39-40.   5259

Patton, Bobby R.   A Descriptive Analysis of Successful High School
Debaters in Kansas.   AFAR, 10 (Fall, 1962), 10-13.   5260

Pence, James W. , Jr.   Directory of Universities and Colleges Conducting Summer High School Speech Communication Institutes --
1973.   JAFA, 9 (Winter, 1973), 405-411.   Ibid. --1972.   JAFA,
8 (Winter, 1972), 168-174.   5261

Pomona High School Organizes Indaba Club.   PN, 5 (September,
1938), 26.   (Indaba is the African name for "conference. ") 5262

Pore, O. E.   Debate as a High School Elective.   HSJ, 19 (February,
1936), 39-40.   5263

Powers, Raymond A.   Method of Pupil Effort in High School Forensics.   HST, 9 (September, 1933), 262-3.   5264

Present Speech Contests.   Speech Bulletin.   Supp. QJS, 3 (December, 1931), 14-25.   (A listing by states of known inter-school

contests.)   5265

Pruett, Robert.   Problems in Achieving Institutes.   CDE Forum, 2
(January, 1971), 5-7.   5266

_____ .   The Student's Perception of the Effects of a Summer High
School Debate Institute.   JAFA, 9 (Summer, 1972), 279-281.5267

Radabaugh, J. S.   Speech Activities in Today's Schools.   SoS, 51
(January, 1960), 12-15.   5268

Reavis, William C.   Interscholastic Non-Athletic Activities in Selected Secondary Schools.   SchR, 41 (June, 1933), 417-38.   5269

Reed, Marion E.   Does Debate Have a Place in our Schools?   CJSE,
12 (May, 1937), 300-02.   5270

Reed, Thomas D.   Sportsmanship at the National Forensic League
Tournaments.   NFL, 9 (December, 1934), 4-5.   5271

Resolved: that ----.   Schol, 28 (March 21, 1936), 3.   5272

Reutter, D. C.   Let the Small School Win.   R, 13 (October, 1938),
6-7.   (The South Dakota Plan for giving all schools a fair chance.)
                                                                     5273
_____ .   Providing High School Students with Debate and Discussion
Topics.   ST, 12 (September, 1963), 233-7.   5274

Robinson, Karl F.   Facts Regarding Practices in Secondary School
Contests.   SchA, 19 (March, 1948), 211-12.   5275

Rooney, Ethel M.   Debating in the Long Island Schools.   NYSEJ, 18
(December, 1930), 390.   5276

Round Table.   Speech Bulletin.   Supp. QJS, 2 (December, 1930),
35-46.   ("... in which practical problems and questions raised by
secondary school debate directors are treated in the light of the
actual experience and practice of other directors of debating. ")
                                                                     5277
Rowe, J. Wyant.   An Experiment in Interscholastic Debating.   SchA,
10 (September, 1938), 11-12.   5278

Rules for National Speech Tournament.   NFL, 5 (January, 1931),
1-7.   5279

Rupp, A. E.   How I Teach High School Debate.   Ohio Teacher, 52
(April, 1932), 221.   5280

Schrier, William.   High School Debate as I See It.   SER, 20 (January, 1935), 116-25.   5281

Schwartz, P. L.   Through Games to Debating; Putting Bait into Debating for the Under-Sixteen-Year-Old Group.   Re, 33 (December,

1939), 515-16.   5282

Scott, Almere L.   Debating as an Intellectual Activity in Our High
    Schools; Debating Societies in Wisconsin.   SL, 16 (November,
    1930), 43-44.   5283

_____.   Speech Institutes for High School Students.   QJS, 23 (Feb-
    ruary, 1923), 80-81.   5284

Shelby, H. H.   Recruiting Rostrum Students for Speech.   DM, 2
    (March, 1946), 59-60.   5285

Shurter, Edwin Dubois.   State Interscholastic Organizations and Con-
    tests in Debate and Declamation.   PSR, 3 (November, 1913), 21-
    22.   (Debate and Declamation League of Texas.)   5286

_____.   State Organization for Contests in Public Speaking.   QJS,
    1 (April, 1915), 59-64.   5287

Sibley, R. P.   Intellectual Contests for High Schools.   PSR, 1
    (March, 1912), 213-15.   (The Lake Forest College plan for read-
    ing and oral discussion contests.)   5288

Sikkink, Donald E.   Attitude Change on the 1960-61 High School De-
    bate Topic.   AFAR, 10 (3 Fall, 1962), 7-9.   5289

Simley, Anne.   Should the Present Rules in Speech Activities of the
    Minnesota State High School League Be Continued?   Yes.   MJE,
    20 (May, 1940), 368.   5290

Simonson, Walter E., and Strange, Bennett.   An Analysis of High
    School Debate Programs in the Southeast United States.   SSJ, 26
    (Spring, 1961), 235-40.   5291

_____.   Better Prepared Coaches for State's High School Debaters
    Recommended.   NYSEJ, 48 (November, 1960), 16-17.   5292

_____.   High School Debate Activity.   Ed, 50 (December, 1961),
    156-7.   5293

_____.   High School Debate in Missouri.   SC, 46 (January, 1960),
    30-1.   5294

Smith, Carney C.   Practical Procedures in Coaching High School
    Debate.   QJS, 29 (April, 1943), 222-34.   5295

Smith, Robert L.   NFL: A Perversion of Values.   CSSJ, 11 (Au-
    tumn, 1959), 7-10.   5296

Stang, Richard E.   Student's Viewpoint on the Point System.   R, 23
    (November, 1948), 2.   5297

Stansfield, E. J.   High School Debate.   Virginia Journal of Education,

62 (November, 1968), 19-21.   5298

Stenius, A.   Eenie, Meenie, Minie, Mo and Debating.   HSJ, 19
(1936), 41-5.   5299

Stephens, Lucille.   The Poughkeepsie Plan.   R, 23 (December,
1948), 2, 10.   5300

Stowe, A. Monroe.   The Motivation of Debate in Our Secondary
Schools.   SchR, 19 (October, 1911), 546-9.   5301

Stratton, Clifford.   The Story of Topeka High's Impressive Speech
Record.   PN, 3 (November, 1936), 12, 16.   5302

A Symposium: Have Western Debaters Anything that Easterners
Haven't?   PN, 6 (November, 1939), 7-9, 29.   (Contributors and
articles include: R. Paul Hobbs, "Eastern vs. Western Debating
in the High School," 7-8; W. Francis English, "Western Viewpoint," 8-9, 29.)   5303

A Symposium: More About Successful Western Debate Practices.
PN, 6 (December, 1939), 7-9.   (Russell L. Caldwell, "Presenta-
tion," 7-8; R. S. Cartwright, "Adaptation," 8-9; H. B. Mitchell,
"Experience," 9.)   5304

Tacey, W. S.   How to Win a High School Debate Contest.   SchA, 27
(October, 1955), 55-7.   5305

Tatlock, Abraham.   Debate in Indiana High Schools.   Indiana Teacher, 70 (May, 1929), 10-11.   5306

These Western Schools Stress Wide Student Participation in Debate.
PN, 7 (January-February, 1941), 8-9.   5307

Thomas, Gorden L.   A Survey of Debate Practices in Michigan High
Schools.   CSSJ, 16 (May, 1965), 129-135.   5308

Thomas, Katharine.   A Workable High School Speech Contest.
Sierra Educational News, 30 (May, 1934), 37-8.   5309

Thompson, Leslie.   Topeka's Forensic Record.   R, 11 (6 February,
1937), 8-10.   5310

Thompson, Richard N.   The Intelligence of High School Debaters.
QJS, 17 (June, 1931), 403-5.   5311

_____.   Stage Management of Decision Debates.   Ed, 51 (June,
1931), 602-4.   (Description of the "Carbondale Plan" where teams
are not identified to the audience or judges and the audience is
not permitted to applaud at the end of each speech.)   5312

_____.   Strangling Debating.   Ed, 50 (May, 1930), 555-8.   (How
educators often contribute to debate problems.)   5313

_____. A Study of the Intelligence of High School Debaters. NFL, 5 (February, 1931), 4-7.   5314

Tooze, Russell. Intramural vs. Interscholastic Contests. SchA, 14 (April, 1943), 292-4.   5315

_____. Who Wins Interscholastic Debates? NSch, 30 (September, 1942), 45.   5316

Tower, Donald M. The Binghamton Course in Debate. EQ, 10 (March, 1930), 20. (Binghamton, New York, high school syllabus.)   5317

Tucker, Elaine. The Secret of Oklahoma. R, 15 (November, 1940), 11-12.   5318

Tufts, J. A. Debate at Exeter. G, 14 (2 January, 1932), 15-16.   5319

Turner, Robert G. Whither High School Forensics? QJS, 27 (December, 1941), 550-54.   5320

Upchurch, R. L. Debating in Junior High Science. Science Teacher, 32 (April, 1965), 46.   5321

Wagner, R. J. Confusion in High School Debating. OS, 11 (January, 1933), 9. (Suggests reforms.)   5322

Walch, J. Weston. How Charleroi Does It. PN, 7 (September, 1940), 27-8. (An interview with L. D. Schreiner by J. Weston Walch.)   5323

_____. The National Tournament. PN, 7 (October, 1940), 22-3.   5324

Walsh, Grace. Vitalizing Debate Procedures in the High School. QJS, 25 (December, 1949), 539-45.   5325

War Suspends National Tournament. R, 16 (January, 1942), 3. 5326

Watkins, Dwight E. Group Systems in Interscholastic Debating. Ed, 34 (March, 1914), 416-20. (The development and benefit of debate programs.)   5327

_____. High School Debating League. PSR, 1 (December, 1911), 112-13. (The league organized by the author in Illinois.)   5328

Weaver, Andrew T. Argumentation and Debate in High Schools. QJS, 4 (March, 1918), 160-9.   5329

_____. The Interschool Forensic Contest. QJS, 2 (April, 1916), 141-8. (On the values and aims of high school contests.)   5330

_____. The Quality of High School Debating. QJS, 18 (June, 1932), 456-57.   5331

Weber, Natalie.   What the NFL Tournament Means to Us.   R, 31
   (December, 1956), 5.   5332

Welch, F. A.   Our Debating and Declamatory Leagues.   PSR, 2
   (January, 1913), 138-43.   5333

Welch, J. D.   Debating in the Secondary Schools.   HST, 5 (January,
   1929), 5-8.   5334

Wells, Earl W.   The Pacific Forensic League.   G, 11 (January,
   1929), 7-10.   5335

White, H. Adelbert.   Debating in Our High Schools.   SchS, 28 (November 24, 1928), 660-2.   5336

_____.   Judging High School Debates.   G, 15 (March, 1933), 19-
   23.   5337

Wilds, Elmer H.   A Practical High School Speaking Contest.   QJS,
   3 (April, 1917), 178-83.   (Extemporaneous contest at Dakota
   Wesleyan University.)   5338

_____.   Interschool Contests in American High Schools.   SchR, 40
   (June, 1932), 429-41.   5339

Wilmington, S. Clay, and Swanson, Linda A.   A Televised High
   School Debate Tournament.   ST, 15 (November, 1966), 299-302.
                                                                           5340
Williams, Frederick, Webb, Sallyann, and Clark, Ruth A.   Dimensions of Evaluation in High School Debate.   CSSJ, 17 (February,
   1966), 15-21.   (Reports that argument is the dominant factor in
   judging.)   5341

With the Debate Leagues.   Speech Bulletin.   Supp. QJS, 2 (December, 1930), 46-60.   (Reports from nineteen state debating
   leagues.)   5342

Witt, W. H.   Nationwide High School Debating.   NEAJ, 22 (January,
   1933), 13-14.   5343

Wood, Kenneth S.   Is the Decision Element a Detriment to High
   School Debating Objectives?   QJS, 25 (April, 1939), 254-61. 5344

Wright, Chas. F.   The National Speech Tournament and Student Congress.   WS, 3 (May, 1939), 15.   5345

Young, Cladys E.   From Maine to Idaho.   PN, 3 (February, 1937),
   9, 26.   (The experience of a high school debate coach who
   changed schools for a year and found the change stimulating.)
                                                                           5346

XIX. CRITICAL ANALYSES OF DEBATES AND DEBATERS

1. Books

Avins, Alfred. The Reconstruction Amendments' Debates: The Legislative History and Contemporary Debates in Congress of the 13th, 14th, and 15th Amendments. Richmond: Virginia Commission on Constitutional Government, 1967. 5347

Clark, Glenn, ed. The World's Greatest Debate. St. Paul, Macalester Park Pub. Co., 1940. 5348

Crocker, Lionel. An Analysis of Lincoln and Douglas as Public Speakers and Debaters. Springfield, Ill., Thomas, 1968. 5349

Friedman, Leon, ed. Argument: The Oral Argument before the Supreme Court in Brown v. Board of Education of Topeka, 1952-1955. New York, Chelsea House, 1969. 5350

Grover, David H. Debaters and Dynamiters: The Story of the Haywood Trial. Corvallis, Oregon, Oregon State, 1964. 5351

Heckman, Richard A. Lincoln vs. Douglas: The Great Debates Campaign. Washington, D. C., Public, 1967. 5352

Johanessen, Robert, ed. The Lincoln-Douglas Debates of 1858. New York, Oxford, 1965. 5353

Kraus, Sidney, ed. The Great Debates. Bloomington, Indiana, Indiana, 1962. (Kennedy-Nixon debates.) 5354

Newman, Robert P. Recognition of Communist China? A Study in Argumentation. New York, Macmillan, 1961. 5355

Rhine, Robley D. The Debate on the Foote Resolution, U. S. Senate, 1829-1830. Madison, Wisconsin, Wisconsin, 1967. 5356

Thomas, Peter E. G. Sources for Debates of the House of Commons, 1768-1774. London, 1959. 5357

Ziegler, Donald J., ed. Great Debates of the Reformation. New York, Random, 1969. 5358

2. Theses and Dissertations

Abernathy, M. Elton.   An Evaluation of Alexander Campbell's Debating Techniques.   M. A.   Iowa.   1937.   5359

Alder, George.   Alexander Campbell's Invention in the Debate with
   Robert Owen.   M. A.   San Jose State College.   1959.   5360

Alexander, Fred.   Debate in the 1953 Michigan Legislature.   Ph. D.
   Wisconsin.   1955.   5361

Ashley, Fred C.   A Historical Analysis of the Johnson-Long, Cough-
   lin Debate of 1935.   M. A.   Michigan.   1958.   5362

Bakke, John P.   The Debates on the Fox and Pitt East India Bills,
   1783-1784: A Case Study in the Rhetoric of the House of Commons.   Ph. D.   Iowa.   1966.   5363

Bane, Laverne C.   A Critical Study of Selected Senate Debates of
   W. E. Borah.   M. A.   Iowa.   1930.   5364

Barnes, Arthur M.   A Rhetorical Analysis of the Speeches of
   Stephen A. Douglas in the Lincoln-Douglas Debates.   M. A.   Iowa.
   1937.   5365

Bauer, Otto F.   A Study of the Political Debate between Dwight D.
   Eisenhower and Adlai E. Stevenson in the Presidential Campaign
   of 1956.   Ph. D.   Northwestern.   1959.   5366

Beem, C. H.   Study of the Persuasive and Logical Elements in the
   Beveridge-Hoar Debates on the Philippine Question.   M. A.   Iowa.
   1931.   5367

Belton, Lois H.   A Rhetorical Analysis and Criticism of the Available Arguments in the Ranney-Dennison Joint Gubernatorial Debates
   in Ohio in 1859.   M. A.   Ohio State.   1946.   5368

Benson, Thomas W.   Congressional Debates on the Dies Committee,
   1937-1944.   Ph. D.   Cornell.   1966.   5369

Blatt, Stephen J.   The Rhetoric of Dissent: An Identification of the
   Arguments Used in Selected Anti-War Speeches Delivered During
   the Mexican War, 1846-1848.   M. A.   Ohio.   1967.   5370

Bowser, Anita O.   One Man, One Vote: An Analysis of an Argument.   M. A.   Purdue.   1967.   5371

Brandenburg, Earnest S.   An Analysis and Criticism of the Argumentative Techniques of Jonathan P. Dolliver in the Senate Tariff Debates of 1909.   M. A.   Iowa.   1941.   5372

Brandes, Paul D.   Evidence and Its Use by Selected United States
   Senators.   Ph. D.   Wisconsin.   1953.   5373

Brown, Wayne E.   An Analysis of Congressional Debate Leading to
    the Passage of Public Law 87-447.   M. A.   Central Missouri.
    1964.   5374

Bryant, Russell.   An Analysis of Alexander Campbell's Ethos in the
    Debate with Robert Owen, April 13, 1829.   M. A.   California,
    Long Beach, 1968.   5375

Buell, James R.   An Analysis of the Argumentation of Percy Fore-
    man in the Candy Mossler, Melvin Powers Murder Case.   M. A.
    Bowling Green.   1970.   5376

Cable, W. A.   Webster-Hayne Debate, a Critical Study in Argumen-
    tation.   M. A.   Iowa.   1925.   5377

Cain, Earl R.   An Analysis of the Debates on Neutrality Legislation
    in the United States Senate, 1935-1941.   Ph. D.   Northwestern.
    1950.   5378

Callaghan, J. Calvin.   The Lend-Lease Debate.   Ph. D.   Wisconsin.
    1949.   5379

Camp, Leon R.   The Senate Debates on the Treaty of Paris of
    1898.   Ph. D.   Penn State.   1969.   5380

Case, Theodore.   The Debate Strategy of William Edgar Borah.
    Ph. D.   Wisconsin.   1933.   5381

Casey, William J.   A Case Study of the Debate Over the Re-Opening
    of the African Slave Trade; Southern Commercial Convention,
    Montgomery, Alabama, 1858.   M. A.   Alabama.   1954.   5382

Chester, Giraud.   The Senate Debate on the Selective Service Bill
    of 1940.   M. A.   Wisconsin.   1943.   5383

Choy, Timothy Y. C.   A Critical Analysis of Palmerston's Defense
    in the Don Pacifico Debates.   M. A.   Penn State.   1966.   5384

Cronen, Vernon E. • Consistency and Change in the Political Theory
    of John C. Calhoun: A Study of Arguments.   M. A.   Illinois.
    1968.   5385

Cross, Lois.   Persuasion in the Debates in Congress on the League
    of Nations.   M. A.   Ohio Wesleyan.   1934.   5386

Curry, Herbert La Vere.   An Evaluation of the Debating of John C.
    Calhoun in Representative Pro-Slavery Speeches, 1847-50.   M. A.
    Iowa.   1936.   5387

Dean, Richard L.   An Analysis of Senatorial Debate on the Labor-
    Management Relations Act of 1947.   M. A.   L. S. U.   1949.   5388

Dedmon, Donald Newton.   An Analysis of the Arguments in the De-

bate in Congress on the Admission of Hawaii to the Union. Ph. D.
Iowa. 1961. 5389

De Haven, Jean. An Investigation of William E. Borah's Use of
Argumentation in Congressional Debate. M. A. S. Dakota.
1939. 5390

De Mougeot, William R. Argumentation in the National Health Insurance Movement, 1932-40. Ph. D. Cornell. 1959. 5391

Dreyfus, Lee S. Persuasion Techniques in Modern Congressional
Debate. Ph. D. Wisconsin. 1957. 5392

Duncan, Charles F. Alexander Campbell as a Controversialist as
Revealed in Debate with Robert Owen. M. A. Illinois. 1952.
5393

Ellis, Carroll. The Alexander Campbell and John B. Purcell Religious Debate. M. A. L. S. U. 1945. 5394

Engdahl, Lynn H. A Study of Debate in the United States Senate:
The 1957 Debate over Civil Rights. Ph. D. Iowa. 1969. 5395

Ertzman, Carol. An Original Historical Drama on the Lincoln-
Douglas Debate at Charleston. M. A. Penn State. 1958. 5396

Fisher, Walter R. An Analysis of the Arguments in the Senate Debate on the Crittenden Compromise Resolutions, 1860-1861.
Ph. D. Iowa State. 1960. 5397

George, Geneva P. A Critical Analysis of Sir James Mackintosh
as a Forensic Speaker in the Trial of Jean Peltier. M. A. Iowa.
1936. 5398

Gilchrist, Mary D. The Philippine Annexation Debate: As Contained in Four Selected Speeches. M. A. Michigan State. 1958.
5399

Goetzinger, Chas. S. An Analysis of the "Validity" of Reasoning
and Evidence in Four Major Foreign Policy Speeches. M. S.
Purdue. 1952. 5400

Gonchar, Ruth M. William S. Buckley, on the 1965 New York City
Mayoralty Campaign Debates. M. A. Temple. 1967. 5401

Greenagel, Heather A. An Analysis of the Arguments Used by Cor-
win, Cass, and Calhoun to Support Their Positions in the Senate
Debate on the Three Million Bill during the Mexican War. M. A.
Minnesota. 1969. 5402

Greene, Harry W. The Debates and Religious Forums of Clarence
Darrow. M. S. N. Illinois. 1970. 5403

Gronbeck, Bruce E. The British Parliamentary Debate on the
Regency, 1788-1789: A Rhetorical Analysis. Ph. D. Iowa.

1970.   5404

Gross, Bertram W.   An Analysis of Suez Debates in the U. N. Se-
    curity Council.   M. A.   Temple.   1966.   5405

Grover, David H.   Debaters and Dynamiters: The Rhetoric of the
    Haywood Trial.   Ph. D.   Oregon.   1962.   (1907 Trial of William
    D. Haywood, labor leader.)   5406

Hansen, Merrill Christian.   The Role of Rhetoric in the Mormon
    Suffrage Debate in Idaho, 1880-1906.   Ph. D.   Stanford.   1958.
                                                                           5407
Hatch, Robert D.   The Pratt-Newman Debate.   M. S.   Brigham
    Young.   1961.   5408

Hayes, Merwyn A.   The Andrew Johnson Impeachment Trial: A
    Case Study In Argumentation.   Ph. D.   Illinois.   1966.   5409

Hedeman, Richard A.   The Douglas-Lincoln Campaign of 1858.
    Ph. D.   Indiana.   1960.   5410

Hopkins, Arthur A.   The Fox-Pitt Debate Concerning the Rejection
    of Napoleon's Overtures.   M. A.   Iowa.   1928.   5411

Huesemann, Theodore, Jr.   A Study of the Rhetoric in the Dennison-
    Ranney Debate at Tiffin, Ohio, 1859, together with a Study of
    Audience Adaptation of Major Issues in the Remaining Debates,
    and Including the Text of the Tiffin Debate.   M. A.   Ohio State.
    1949.   5412

Ilardo, Joseph A.   An Analysis of the Congressional Debates on the
    Removal Bill, 1830.   M. A.   Queens.   1966.   5413

_____.   The Bradlaugh Case: A Study of the Parliamentary Debates
    Concerning the Affirmation-Oath Controversy, 1880-1891.   Ph. D.
    Illinois.   1969.   5414

Ingalls, Mary.   The Aspect of the Argument in the Nixon-Kennedy
    Debate.   M. A.   Arkansas.   1964.   5415

Irwin, Ramon B.   Congressional Debates of the James K. Polk Ad-
    ministration--A Study in Factionalism.   Ph. D.   Minnesota.
    1946.   5416

Jones, James L.   An Analysis of Alfred E. Smith's Speaking, Using
    Aristotle's and Toulmin's Systems of Argument.   M. A.   Cornell.
    1965.   5417

Jones, Warren C.   G. C. Brewer: Lecturer, Debater, and Preach-
    er.   Ph. D.   Wayne.   1959.   5418

Jordan, Harriet P.   The Lincoln-Douglas Debates of 1858:   A Pres-
    entation of the Rhetorical Scene and Setting with a Pilot Film

Script of the Ottawa Debate. Ph. D. Illinois. 1958.   5419

Kane, Peter E. The Senate Debate on the 1964 Civil Rights Act.
Ph. D. Purdue. 1967.   5420

Katter, Nafe E. An Analysis of the Stassen-Dewey Debate in 1948,
"Should the Communist Party in the U. S. Be Outlawed?" M. A.
Michigan. 1951.   5421

King, Lois M. A Criticism of the Stassen-Dewey Debate on Communism on May 17, 1948 at Portland, Oregon. M. A. Ohio
State. 1952.   5422

Kirk, Glenn G. The Kennedy-Nixon Joint Radio-Television Programs: A Form of Oral Discourse. M. A. Florida. 1965.
                                                               5423
Kleinau, Marvin D. Senator Erwin's Speaking on Supreme Court
Segregation Decisions: A Study in Evidence. M. A. Illinois.
1960.   5424

Laine, Joseph B. Public Joint Debates Under the Richards Primary
Law. M. A. S. Dakota. 1952.   5425

Lashley, Warren L. The Debate Over Imperialism in the United
States, 1898-1900. M. A. Northwestern. 1966.   5426

Lewis, Thomas R. The Debating Technique of Thomas Hart Benton
with Special Reference to Invention. M. A. Iowa. 1938. 5427

Lucas, William D. A Study of the Speaking and Debating of Joseph
G. Cannon. Ph. D. Northwestern. 1948.   5428

Mader, Diane C. The Argumentation in the Trade Union Movement
between 1902 and 1935. Ph. D. Northwestern. 1966.   5429

Maloney, Martin. Clarence Darrow's Forensic Speaking. Ph. D.
Northwestern. 1941.   5430

Manzer, Margaret. A Descriptive and Rhetorical Analysis of the
Brownlow-Pryne Debates. M. A. Virginia. 1957.   5431

Martin-Trigona, Helen Vasiliou. Logical Proof and Imaginative
Reason in Selected Speeches of Francis Bacon. Ph. D. Illinois.
1968.   5432

Marzolf, Arnold H. William Lemke's Use of Evidence: An Analysis of Some of His Speeches. M. A. N. Dakota State. 1964.
                                                               5433
Maw, Herbert B. Methods of Refutation Adopted by Great Lawyers
in Arguments before Juries. M. A. Northwestern. 1926. 5434

Mazza, Joseph M. A Toulmin Analysis of Robert Kennedy's Use of
Argument in the Presidential Primaries of 1968. M. A. Mis-

souri.   1969.   5435

McCoy, Ford H.   Methods of Refutation Used by Daniel Webster in
his Replies to Hayne.   M. A.   Northwestern.   1931.   5436

McCoy, Pressley C.   An Analysis of the Debates on Recognition of
the Union of Soviet Socialist Republics in the U. S. Senate, 1917-
1934.   Ph. D.   Northwestern.   1954.   5437

McDiarmid, James L.   An Analysis of Selected Speeches by Herbert
Hoover in the 1932 Presidential Campaign According to Stephen
Toulmin's System of Logical Analysis.   M. A.   Nebraska.   1968.
                                                             5438
McGuire, Gale A.   An Examination of the Issues in the Debates of
the House of Commons during the Reign of James II.   M. A.   San
Jose.   1966.   5439

McPhail, Thomas L.   Parliamentary Debates on Confederation of the
British North American Provinces: 1865.   M. A.   SUNY at Buffalo.   1966.   5440

Medley, William L., Jr.   A Structural Analysis of the Senate Debate
on Roosevelt's Plan to Enlarge the Supreme Court.   M. A.   Iowa.
1965.   5441

Meyers, Alice.   Persuasion in the Cooper-Morrison Debates.   M. A.
Nebraska.   1961.   5442

Micken, Ralph A.   A Rhetorical Study of the Senate Debates on the
League of Nations.   Ph. D.   Northwestern.   1948.   5443

Millas, Joseph.   An Analysis of Daily Adjournment Debating in the
House of Commons, 1962-1963 Session.   M. A.   L. S. U.   1966.
                                                             5444
Miller, Joseph B.   An Analysis of the Debate on the Seating of the
Georgia Delegation before the Republican National Convention,
July 10, 1952.   M. A.   Ohio.   1961.   5445

Mills, Norbert H.   A Study of Selected Speeches in the Debate on
U. S. Policy in Viet Nam.   M. A.   Bowling Green.   1967.   5446

Monroe, Craig.   The Structure of Presidential Debates.   M. S.
Kansas State.   1966.   5447

Montgomery, Charles L.   An Examination of Artistic Ethos in Selected Inter-Collegiate Debates.   M. A.   Ball State.   1969.   5448

Moore, W. I.   Analysis and Criticism of Madison as a Debater in
the Virginia Federal Constitution Convention.   M. A.   Iowa.
1932.   5449

Newburn, Robert M.   Argumentative Proof in Selected Speeches of
Douglas MacArthur Given After His Speech to Congress, 1951.

M. A. Florida. 1964.   5450

O'Brien, James D. A Rhetorical Examination of the Use of Refutation in the Series of Nationally Broadcast Debates Between Vice-
President Richard M. Nixon and Senator John F. Kennedy During
the 1960 Presidential Campaign. M. A. Oregon. 1962.   5451

Olmstead, Marvin L. An Analysis of the Argumentation of the
Alaskan Boundary Tribunal. Ph. D. Washington. 1969.   5452

Olson, Donald O. The Debate in Congress on the Kansas-Nebraska
Bill: A Study in Persuasion. Ph. D. Wisconsin. 1959.   5453

Palmer, Ann L. A Toulmin Analysis of the Argumentation of the
American Anarchist, Emma Goldman. M. A. Kansas. 1967.
                                                                          5454

Parsons, Donald W. The First Kennedy-Nixon Debate: A Study in
Textual Accuracy. M. S. Wisconsin. 1961.   5455

Perritt, H. Hardy. An Analysis of the Senatorial Debate on Neutrality Legislation in the 1939 Special Session of Congress. M. A.
L. S. U. 1942.   5456

Peterson, Gary. A Critical Edition of the Lincoln-Douglas Debates
of 1858. Ph. D. Ohio. 1965.   5457

Pierce, M. Scheffel. An Analysis of the Argumentation of the U. S.
Senate Debate on the North Atlantic Pact. M. S. Wisconsin.
1952.   5458

Polisky, Jerome B. The Kennedy-Nixon Debates: A Study in Political Persuasion. Ph. D. Wisconsin. 1965.   5459

Polk, Lee R. An Analysis of Argumentation in the Virginia Slavery
Debate of 1832. Ph. D. Purdue. 1967.   5460

Porter, Priscilla A. A Comparative Analysis of Structural and Content Variables in the West Point Championship Debates. M. A.
Bowling Green. 1966.   5461

Ranta, Richard R. The Argumentation of John Quincy Adams on the
Abolitionists' Rights of Petition and Free Speech, 1835-1844.
M. A. Cornell. 1967.   5462

Ray, Jack L. An Investigation of the Course and Pattern of the Debate in the Senate Over the Truman Doctrine. M. A. Iowa.
1959.   5463

Reeves, Clyde E. The Debates on the War of 1812: Parliament
and Congress Compared. Ph. D. Illinois. 1958.   5464

Rehn, Judith K. The Refutative, Stylistic, and Presumptive Aspects
of Six United Nations Arab-Israeli Debates. M. A. Ohio State.

1970.   5465

Reynolds, Beatrice K.   Ideas and Arguments of Selected Speeches of Pierre Vergniaud in the Years 1791-1793.   Ph. D.   Penn State. 1967.   5466

Reynolds, William M.   Deliberative Speaking in Ante-Bellum South Carolina: The Idiom of a Culture.   Ph. D.   Florida.   1960. 5467

Rhine, Robley D.   The Debate on the Foote Resolution, U. S. Senate, 1829-30.   Ph. D.   Wisconsin.   1967.   5468

Rives, Stanley G.   Dialectic and Rhetoric in Congress: A Study of Congressional Consideration of the Labor-Management Relations Act of 1947.   Ph. D.   Northwestern.   1963.   5469

Rock, Kenneth M.   Relative Use of Formal and Material Logic in the Lincoln-Douglas Debates.   M. A.   S. California.   1934. 5470

Rogge, Edward A.   Two Pre-Civil War Senate Debates on Slavery and States' Rights.   M. S.   Wisconsin.   1950.   5471

Rose, George H.   The Use of Persuasion in the Lincoln-Douglas Debates.   M. A.   S. California.   1929.   5472

Samovar, Larry A.   Ambiguity and Unequivocation in the Kennedy-Nixon Television Debates.   M. A.   Purdue.   1962.   5473

Sanbonmatsu, Akira.   Adaptation and Debate Strategies in the Speaking of Clarence Darrow and Alexander Rorke in New York vs. Gitlow.   Ph. D.   Penn State.   1968.   5474

Sanders, Gerald H.   The Wishart-Bryan Controversy on Fundamentalism: A Study in Argumentation.   M. A.   Texas Technological Univ.   1969.   5475

Sanders, Keith R.   An Empirical Study of the Integrity of Evidence Used in John A. Stormer's None Dare Call It Treason.   Ph. D.   Pittsburgh.   1968.   5476

Scharf, George P.   Topics of the Senate Debate on the Taft-Hartley Labor Bill, April-June, 1947.   M. A.   Illinois.   1950.   5477

Schmidt, John W.   The Gulf of Tonkin Debates, 1964 and 1967: A Study in Argument.   Ph. D.   Minnesota.   1969.   5478

Schwartz, Howard.   Kennedy-Nixon Joint Television Appearances.   M. A.   Emerson.   1961.   5479

Schwartz, Ruth E.   A Descriptive Analysis of Oral Argument before the U. S. Supreme Court in the School Segregation Cases, 1952-1953.   M. A.   S. California.   1966.   5480

Settle, Joyce H. Analysis of the Clashes in the Nixon-Kennedy Television Debates in the 1960 Presidential Campaign. M. A. Hawaii. 1962. 5481

Shelby, Annette N. A Study of Evidence: The Quemoy-Matsu Issue in the Great Debates of 1960. M. A. Alabama. 1962. 5482

Shepard, Carol M. Abolition of the Slave Trade, April 2, 1772: A Comparison of Arguments. M. A. S. Dakota. 1965. 5483

Sherman, Roger N. An Objective Analysis of Language Choice in the First Nixon-Kennedy Debate. Ph. D. Michigan. 1965. 5484

Silliman, Elizabeth R. Ronald Reagan's 1966 Gubernatorial Campaign: An Analysis of Ideas and their Logical Support as a Means of Persuasion in Selected Speeches. M. A. Sacramento. 1968. 5485

Skelly, Loretta. A Comparison of Rhetorical Devices Used in Twelve Intercollegiate Debates with Accepted Textbook Principles. M. A. L. S. U. 1937. 5486

Slover, John C. A Rhetorical Study of Disraeli's Debating Technique in Selected Reform Bill Speeches of 1867. M. A. Iowa. 1939. 5487

Slutzky, Julius. A Rhetorical Analysis of the Lincoln-Douglas Debates. M. A. Brooklyn. 1939. 5488

Smith, Robert G. The Arguments over Abolition Petitions in the House of Representatives in December, 1835: A Toulmin Analysis. Ph. D. Minnesota. 1962. 5489

Strother, David B. Evidence, Argument, and Decision in Brown vs. Board of Education. Ph. D. Illinois. 1958. 5490

Stupp, Vicki. The Debating Techniques of Richard Nixon, 1947-1960. M. A. Penn State. 1961. 5491

_____. The Parliamentary Speaking of Sir Robert Peel from 1835-1841. Ph. D. Penn State. 1968. 5492

Venanzio, Ayne C. A Comparative Analysis of Argument in Selected Speeches by Robert Welch and Carl McIntire. M. A. Penn State. 1966. 5493

Warren, James A. A Study of the Congressional Debate Concerning the Oregon Question. Ph. D. Washington. 1962. 5494

Watkins, Lloyd. The Argumentation of Thomas Erskine in the Trial of Thomas Hardy. M. A. Wisconsin. 1951. 5495

Weathersby, Manaway C. An Analysis of the Argument in the 1962

West Point Final Debate Between Baylor and Ohio State.   M. A.
Pittsburgh.   1964.   5496

Weckesser, Ernest P., Jr.   Forensic Analysis of the Kennedy-Nixon Debates.   M. A.   Bowling Green.   1961.   5497

Weise, Selene H. C.   British Parliamentary Debates on the Suez
Canal (1876).   M. A.   Syracuse.   1968.   5498

Welch, Mary J.   A Description and Evaluation of the Evidence Used
in the 1964 Senate Debate on the Gulf of Tonkin Resolution.   M. A.
Bowling Green.   1970.   5499

Weldon, Lloyd W.   Rhetorical Aspects of the Silver Debate in Missouri: 1896.   M. A.   Missouri.   1948.   5500

Whyte, James P.   The Senate Debate on the Fair Employment Practices Act, January 17-February 9, 1948.   M. A.   Syracuse.
1948.   5501

Williams, Jamye C.   A Rhetorical Analysis of Thurgood Marshall's
Arguments before the Supreme Court in the Public School Segregation Controversy.   Ph. D.   Ohio State.   1959.   5502

Wrage, Naomi H.   A Study of Representative Anti-War Arguments
Presented in Congressional Debates During Specified Periods Between 1809 and 1941.   M. A.   Northwestern.   1946.   5503

Yarborough, Carolyn H.   A Study of the Debate Techniques Utilized
by Selected Senators in Selected Speeches from the 85th Congress,
Second Session.   M. A.   Houston.   1960.   5504

Yoder, Jess.   A Critical Study of the Debate Between the Reformed
and the Anabaptists, Held at Frankenthal, Germany, in 1571.
Ph. D.   Northwestern.   1962.   5505

3.   Articles

Adams, C. F.   Undeveloped Function (Political Debate).   American
Historical Association Report.   1 (1901), 47-93.   5506

Anderson, Floyd D., and Hayes, Merwyn A.   Presumption and Burden of Proof in Whately's Speech on the Jewish Civil Disabilities
Repeal Bill.   SM, 34 (June, 1967), 133-136.   5507

Andrewes, A.   The Mytilene Debate: Thucydides 3. 36-49.   Ph, 16
(Summer, 1962), 64-85.   5508

Andrews, James R.   Sacrifice and Identity: The Australian Conscription Debate, 1916.   CSSJ, 22 (Summer, 1971), 110-117.
                                                                  5509
Arnold, Carroll C.   Invention in the Parliamentary Speaking of Ben-

jamin Disraeli, 1842-1852.   SM, 14 (1947), 66-80.   5510

Barnard, Raymond H.   Wendell Phillips as a Debater.   G, 21 (May,
     1939), 70.   5511

Bartholomew, Paul C.   The Supreme Court of the United States,
     1966-1967.   WPQ, 20 (December, 1967), 841-855.   (Reviews
     each major decision of the Supreme Court for the past year and
     includes majority and dissenting arguments.)   5512

Bauer, Marvin G.   Persuasive Methods in the Lincoln-Douglas De-
     bates.   QJS, 13 (February, 1927), 29-39.   5513

Beeman, Richard R.   Unlimited Debate in the Senate: The First
     Phase.   POQ, 83 (1968), 419-34.   (Examines the history of un-
     limited debate, culminating in the defeat of the 1856 amendment
     requiring a senator "to confine himself to the question under de-
     bate.")   5514

Berquist, Goodwin F., Jr.   The Kennedy-Humphrey Debate.   TS, 8
     (September, 1960), 2-3.   5515

Blankenship, Jane.   State Legislator as Debater: Lincoln, 1834-
     1842.   JAFA, 2 (January, 1965), 28-32.   5516

Bowers, John W.   Deliberative Speech in a Forensic Context: An-
     drew Hamilton at the Peter Zenger Trial.   CSSJ, 16 (August,
     1965), 164-172.   5517

Braden, Waldo W.   Speaking in the House of Commons.   SSJ, 24
     (Winter, 1958), 67-74.   5518

_____.   Contemporary Debating in the House of Commons.   SSJ,
     27 (Summer, 1962), 261-72.   5519

_____.   The Senate Debate on the League of Nations, 1918-1920:
     An Overture.   SSJ, 25 (Summer, 1960), 273-81.   5520

Bradley, Bert E.   Refutative Techniques of John C. Calhoun.   SSCJ,
     37 (Summer, 1972), 413-423.   5521

_____ and Tarver, Jerry L.   John C. Calhoun's Argumentation in
     Defense of Slavery.   SSJ, 35 (Winter, 1969), 163-175.   (Con-
     cludes "that Calhoun was guilty of using enthymematic reasoning
     based on unsupported and unacceptable premises and inductive
     reasoning based on simple assertions, biased samples, or faulty
     analysis.")   5522

Brommel, Bernard J.   The Debates for the Governorship of Iowa in
     1859.   ST, 13 (September, 1964), 232-239.   5523

Cain, Earl R.   A Method of Rhetorical Analysis of Congressional
     Debate.   WS, 18 (March, 1954), 91-95.   5524

_____. Is Senate Debate Significant?   TS, 3 (April, 1955), 10-
12.   5525

_____. Why Analyze Congressional Debate?   S, 37 (May, 1955),
11-14, 24.   5526

Carmack, Paul A.   The Lane Seminary Debates.   CSSJ, 1 (March,
1950), 33-9.   5527

Chester, Giraud.   Contemporary Senate Debate.   QJS, 31 (December, 1945), 407-11.   5528

The Civic Debate.   Ed, 34 (1914), 290-91.   5529

Commager, Henry S.   Today's Events in the Light of History: Congressional Debates and the Course of Events.   Schol, 30 (March
17, 1941), 10.   5530

Corder, Jim W.   Ethical Argument and Rambler No. 154.   QJS,
54 (December, 1968), 352-356.   5531

Covey, Frank M., Jr.   The Role of Oral Argument in the American
Appellate Courts.   G, 45 (November, 1962), 9-11.   5532

Daley, Mason G.   The Lincoln-Douglas Clash in Perspective.   G,
29 (May, 1947), 65-6.   5533

Dause, Charles A.   Analysis of a Debate: Two Perspectives.
CSSJ, 23 (Summer, 1972), 86-91.   (Analysis of a 1937 public debate over Franklin D. Roosevelt's "court packing" proposal.)
                                                                   5534
Debate in the British House of Commons on Public Order Bill.   November 16, 1936.   IC, 326 (January, 1937), 5-110.   5535

Dedmon, D. N.   Functions of Discourse in the Hawaiian Statehood
Debates.   SM, 33 (March, 1966), 30-39.   5536

Dickens, Milton, and Schwartz, Ruth E.   Oral Argument before the
Supreme Court: Marshall v. Davis in the School Segregation
Cases.   QJS, 57 (February, 1971), 32-41.   5537

Ellis, Carroll.   Background of the Campbell-Purcell Religious Debate of 1837.   SSJ, 11 (November, 1945), 32-41.   5538

Fitzpatrick, John R.   Congressional Debating.   QJS, 27 (April,
1941), 251-5.   5539

Florer, J. H.   Major Issues in the Congressional Debate of the Morrill Act of 1862.   History of Education Quarterly, 8 (Winter,
1968), 459-478.   5540

Freeley, Austin J.   Presidential Debates and the Speech Profession.
QJS, 47 (February, 1961), 60-4.   5541

_____. Who Won the Great Debates of 1960? AFAR, 9 (College Calendar Issue, 1961), 29-30.   5542

Freshley, Dwight L. , ed. Briefly Speaking: A Symposium: Was There Real Debating of Issues in the 1952 Political Campaign? BDAPC, 18 (December, 1952), 35-37. (Contributors include Leighton Peters and Elliot Barnett.)   5543

Gain, Earl. Debate in Modern Politics: The United States Senate. AFAR, 11 (Winter, 1963), 1-6.   5544

Gipson, Lawrence H. The Great Debate in the Committee of the Whole House of Commons on the Stamp Act, 1766, as Reported by Nathaniel Ryder. Pennsylvania Magazine of History and Biography, 86 (1962), 10-41.   5545

Gough, H. B. Indiana-DePauw Educational Debates. QJS, 16 (November, 1930), 414-20.   5546

Goulding, Daniel J. The Role of Debate in Parliament: A Nineteenth Century View. WS, 33 (Summer, 1969), 192-198.   5547

Graham, Gladys Murphy. The House of Lords Debates the Naval Treaty. QJS, 16 (November, 1930), 414-20.   5548

Gwin, Stanford P. Argument for the League of Nations: John Sharp Williams in the Senate, 1918-1920. SSJ, 31 (Spring, 1966), 226-243.   5549

Hagan, Michael R. A Debate on the "Death of God. " SPG, 5 (January, 1968), 63-66. (Critique of a debate held at the University of Chicago between Thomas J.J. Altizer and John Warwick Montgomery.)   5550

Hargis, Donald E. The Issues in the Broderick-Gevin Debates of 1859. CHSQ, 32 (1953), 313-25.   5551

Hemmer, James J. , Jr. The Charleston Platform Debate in Rhetorical-Historical Perspective. QJS, 56 (December, 1970), 406-416.   5552

Highlander, John P. , and Watkins, Lloyd I. A Closer Look at the Great Debates. WS, 26 (Winter, 1962), 39-48.   5553

Huber, Robert B. A College Debater Carries On. S, 25 (November, 1940), 3. (On Wendell Wilkie.)   5554

Hudson, Roy F. Debate in the Bible. G, 38 (January, 1956), 47-49.   5555

Insalata, S. John. The Young Titans: Early Forensic Careers of Supreme Court Justices. F, 45 (May, 1960), 11-12.   5556

Jeffrey, Robert C. Republican Credentials Committee Debates,
    1952. SM, 28 (November, 1961), 265-73.   5557

Jones, James L. Alfred E. Smith, Political Debater. QJS, 54
    (December, 1968), 363-372.   5558

Juleus, Nels. Aram's Defense. G, 43 (March, 1961), 37.   5559

Kane, Peter E. Evaluating the "Great Debates." WS, 30 (Spring,
    1966), 89-95. (On the Kennedy-Nixon debates.)   5560

_____. Extended Debate and Rules of the U.S. Senate. QJS, 57
    (February, 1971), 43-49.   5561

_____. Senate Vietnam Debate March 7, 1968. SPG, 5 (May,
    1968), 148-152.   5562

Kelley, Stanley, Jr. Campaign Debates: Some Facts and Issues.
    POQ, 26 (1962), 351-66.   5563

Kerr, Harry P. The Great Debates in a New Perspective. TS, 9
    (November, 1961), 9-11, 28. (On the Kennedy-Nixon debates.)
                                                               5564
Knepprath, E., and Clevenger, Theodore, Jr. Reasoned Discourse
    and Motive Appeals in Selected Political Speeches. QJS, 51
    (April, 1965), 152-56.   5565

Kraus, S. Presidential Debates in 1964. QJS, 50 (February, 1964),
    19-23.   5566

Lockhart, A.M. Seventy Years of Debates of the Month. Ro, 82
    (January, 1953), 26-7.   5567

Lofgren, Charles A. Mr. Truman's War: A Debate and Its After-
    math. RP, 31 (1969), 223-241. (Issues over the Korean War
    are traced from Truman to Eisenhower; political debate includes
    Truman, Taft, Morse, Lucas, Byrd, Acheson, and Douglas.)
                                                               5568
Maloney, Martin. The Forensic Speaking of Clarence Darrow. SM,
    14 (1947), 111-26.   5569

A Matter of Debate. ScM, 47 (March, 1910), 378-9. (On American
    Congressional Debate.)   5570

McPherson, Elizabeth G. Reporting the Debates of Congress. QJS,
    28 (April, 1942), 141-48.   5571

_____. Reports of the Debates of the House of Representatives
    During the First Congress, 1789-1791. QJS, 30 (February, 1944),
    64-71.   5572

Meredith, E.E. Debates of 1901. H, 56 (June, 1951), 17.   5573

Micken, Ralph A.   Forensics at the Grass Roots.   G, 31 (March, 1949), 50-51.   5574

_____.   The Triumph of Strategy in the Senate Debate on the League of Nations.   QJS, 37 (February, 1951), 49-54.   5575

_____.   Western Senators in the League of Nations Debate of 1919-1920.   WS, 16 (October, 1952), 239-44.   5576

Middleton, Russell.   National TV Debates and Presidential Voting Decisions.   POQ, 26 (1962), 426-9.   5577

Miller, William L.   The Debating Career of Richard M. Nixon. Rep, 14 (April 19, 1956), 11-17.   5578

Mitgang, Herbert.   Echoes of Mr. Lincoln and Mr. Douglas. NYTM, (February 9, 1958), 17, 32, 34, 36, 39.   (A brief account of the issues of the Lincoln-Douglas debates.)   5579

Montgomery, Kirt E.   Thomas Brackett Reed: Exemplification of Effective Debating.   G, 30 (March, 1948), 45-6.   5580

_____.   Thomas B. Reed's Theory and Practice of Congressional Debating.   SM, 17 (March, 1950), 65-74.   5581

Moore, Wilbur E.   The Development of the Debater, James Madison. F, 34 (January, 1949), 38-42.   5582

Mundt, Karl E.   A Speech Teacher Looks at Congress.   G, 25 (March-May, 1943), 52-3, 60.   (By the former President of the NFL and U. S. Senator from South Dakota.)   5583

Murphy, James J.   Saint Augustine and the Debate about a Christian Rhetoric.   QJS, 46 (December, 1960), 400-410.   5584

Oxford vs. Norfolk.   T, 58 (December 31, 1951), 40.   5585

Paget, Edwin H.   Napoleon and Forensic Strategy.   Speech Bulletin. Supp. QJS, 2 (December, 1930), 15-18.   (On debate strategy with reference to R. A. Hall's Studies in Napoleonic Strategy.)   5586

Pease, Jane H. , and Pease, William H.   Black Power--the Debate in 1840.   Phylon, 29 (1968), 19-26.   5587

Perego, Ina.   Analysis of a Debate on Evolution.   QJS, 12 (February, 1926), 23, 30.   5588

Pitt, Carl A.   Wendell Wilkie, Debater.   SA, 5 (1949), 99-101.   5589

Ray, Robert F.   Thomas E. Dewey: The Great Oregon Debate of 1948.   In American Public Address, Studies in Honor of Albert Craig Baird, ed. by Loren Reid.   Columbia, Missouri, Missouri, 1961, 245-267.   5590

Reid, Loren. Gladstone's Theory of Parliamentary Debating.
BDAPC, 20 (December, 1954), 4-7.   5591

Richards, Gale L. Invention in John Marshall's Legal Speaking,
1782-1800. SSJ, 19 (December, 1953), 108-115.   5592

Rives, Stanley G. Congressional Hearings: A Modern Adaptation
of Dialectic. JAFA, 4 (Spring, 1967), 41-46.   5593

Salant, Richard S. The Television Debates: A Revolution that De-
serves a Future. POQ, 26 (1962), 335-50.   5594

Samovar, Larry H. Ambiguity and Unequivocation in the Kennedy-
Nixon Television Debates: A Rhetorical Analysis. WS, 29 (Fall,
1965), 211-218.   5595

_____. Ambiguity and Unequivocation in the Kennedy-Nixon Tele-
vision Debates. QJS, 48 (October, 1962), 272-279.   5596

Seldes, Gilbert. The Future of National Debates. TQ, 1 (August,
1962), 62-68.   5597

Smith, Charles D. Debate in the House of Commons. TS, 5
(April, 1957), 21-23.   5598

_____. Lord North, a Reluctant Debater: The Making of a Cabinet
Minister, 1754-1767. QJS, 53 (February, 1967), 17-26.   5599

Sparks to Fly When Salem Meets Salem in Debate. LD, 88 (February 13, 1926), 81-4.   5600

Stern, Philip M. The Debates in Retrospect. NR, 137 (November
21, 1960), 18-19.   (On the 1960 presidential debates.)   5601

Tooth and Tongue; Oxford Union vs. North Texas State University.
Ne, 60 (June 16, 1962), 51.   5602

Tucker, Raymond K. The Nixon-Kennedy Debates and the Freeley
Committee. G, 43 (March, 1961), 47-48, 52.   5603

Voorhis, Jerry. Effective Speaking in Congress. QJS, 34 (December, 1948), 462-64.   5604

Waites, Margaret C. Some Features of the Allegorical Debate in
Greek Literature. HSCP, 23 (1912), 1-46.   5605

Wiley, Earl W. A Footnote on the Lincoln-Douglas Debates. QJS,
18 (April, 1932), 216-24.   5606

XX.   COLLECTIONS OF DEBATES

1. Books

Canopy, Williard B.   Burlesque Debates for High Schools, Clubs, Colleges, or What Have You?   Chicago, Denison, 1932.   5607

Craig, Asa H., and Edgerton, Alice C.   Both Sides of Thirty Public Questions Completely Debated.   New York, Noble, 1926. 5608

Danner, Vernice E.   Danner's Book of Debates, Series I.   Oklahoma City, Oklahoma, V. E. Danner, 1916.   5609

Eldridge, Mabel E.   Nonsense Debates.   Franklin, Ohio, and Denver, Colorado, Eldridge Entertainment House, Inc., 1936.   5610

Finley, G. W., ed.   Pi Kappa Delta Official Biennial Winning Debates, Orations and Speeches.   New York, Noble, 1933-1939. 7 vols.   5611

Kruger, Arthur N., and Windes, Russell R.   Championship Debating.   Portland, Maine, Walch, 1961.   (Final rounds of West Point National Invitational Debate Tournament, with critiques by well-known debate teachers.)   5612

_____ and _____.   Championship Debating, Vol. 2.   Portland, Maine, Walch, 1967.   5613

Lampson, Godfrey L., ed.   Oratory, British and Irish, the Great Age (from the Accession of George III to the Reform Bill, 1832). Piccadilly, A. L. Humphreys, 1918.   (Fifteen orators show skill as debaters and thinkers.)   5614

Long Beach High School Debates.   Published by the Board of Debate Control.   Long Beach, California, Poly High School Print Shop, 1925.   5615

McBath, James H., ed.   T. V. Championship Debates.   Portland, Maine, Walch, 1964.   5616

Miller, Marion M., ed.   Great Debates in American History. Metuchen, New Jersey, Mini-Print Corp., 1970.   3 vols.   5617

_____, ed.   American Debate.   2 vols.   New York, Current, 1916.   5618

Nichols, Egbert Ray, ed. Intercollegiate Debates. Vols. 2-19.
   Redlands, California, Nichols Publishing House, 1920-1938. (Formerly: New York, Noble.)   5619

_____. Intercollegiate Debates of the War Interim, 1941-1947.
   Redlands, California, Nichols Publishing House, 1947.   5620

Pearson, Paul M., ed. Intercollegiate Debates. New York, Noble,
   1909. (First volume of series; later edited by E. R. Nichols,
   supra.)   5621

Percival, Milton, and Jelliffe, R. A., comp. Specimens of Exposition and Argument. New York, Macmillan, 1908.   5622

Phelps, Edith M., ed. University Debaters' Annual. New York,
   Wilson, 1924-1946. (Co-editor with Ruth Ullman, Ibid., 1947-
   1951.)

(1924-25: 1-416	1934-35: 1-453	1943-44: 1-342
1925-26: 1-407	1935-36: 1-442	1944-45: 1-324
1926-27: 1-417	1936-37: 1-533	1945-46: 1-332
1927-28: 1-437	1937-38: 1-503	1946-47: 1-316
1928-29: 1-464	1938-39: 1-498	1947-48: 1-325
1929-30: 1-471	1939-40: 1-435	1948-49: 1-343
1930-31: 1-473	1940-41: 1-517	1949-50: 1-355
1931-32: 1-393	1941-42: 1-459	1950-51: 1-256)
1932-33: 1-467	1942-43: 1-368	5623

Pi Kappa Delta. Winning Intercollegiate Debates and Orations. Fort
   Collins, Colorado, The Express-Courier Publishing Co., 1926.
                                                               5624
Taft, Robert A., and Smith, T. V. Foundations of Democracy.
   Chicago, Chicago, 1939. (Thirteen broadcast debates on political
   topics.)   5625

Ziegler, Donald J. Great Debates of the Reformation. New York,
   Random, 1969.   5626

2. Thesis

Horn, Robert M. A Compilation and Analysis of Various Types of
   Intercollegiate Debates and Discussions. M. A. Northwestern.
   1938.   5627

XXI.   GENERAL INTEREST

A.   DECISION-MAKING

1.   Books

Anscombe, G. E. M.   Intention.   Oxford, Blackwell, 1957.   5628

Boulding, Kenneth E.   Conflict and Defense: A General Theory.
    New York, Harper, 1962.   5629

Braybrook, David, and Lindblom, Charles E.   A Strategy of Deci-
    sion.   New York, Free, 1963.   5630

Brim, Orville, et al.   Personality and Decision Processes: Studies
    in the Social Psychology of Thinking.   Stanford, California, Stan-
    ford, 1962.   5631

Churchman, C. W.   Theory of Experimental Interence.   New York,
    Macmillan, 1948.   5632

Diesing, Paul.   Reason in Society: Five Types of Decisions and
    Their Social Conditions.   Urbana, Illinois, Illinois, 1962.   5633

Edelman, Murray.   The Symbolic Uses of Politics.   Urbana, Illinois,
    Illinois, 1964.   5634

Frank, Jerome.   Law and the Modern Mind.   New York, Brentano's,
    1930.   5635

Gamson, William.   Power and Discontent.   Homewood, Illinois,
    Dorsey Press, 1968.   5636

Hampshire, S.   Thought and Action.   London, Chatto and Windus,
    1959.   5637

Johnson, Donald M.   The Psychology of Thought and Judgment.   New
    York, Harper, 1955.   5638

Kaplan, Abraham.   The Conduct of Inquiry.   San Francisco, Chand-
    ler Pub. Co., 1964.   5639

Kaufmann, Arnold.   The Science of Decision-Making.   New York,
    Academic, 1968.   5640

Melden, A.   Free Action.   London, Routledge, 1961.   5641

Parsons, Talcott.   Structure and Process in Modern Societies.
Glencoe, Illinois, Free, 1957.   5642

Rapoport, Anatol.   Fights, Games, and Debates.   Ann Arbor, Michigan, Michigan, 1960.   5643

Rescher, Nicholas, ed.   The Logic of Decision and Action.   Pittsburgh, Pittsburgh, 1967.   5644

Schelling, Thomas C.   The Strategy of Conflict.   Oxford, Oxford,
1969.   5645

Schubert, Glendon, ed.   Judicial Decision-Making, Vol. 4, International Yearbook of Political Behavior Research.   New York,
Free, 1963.   5646

Simon, Herbert A.   The New Science of Management Decision.
New York, Harper, 1960.   5647

Snyder, Richard C., et al., eds.   Foreign Policy Decision-Making.
New York, Free, 1962.   5648

Sorensen, Theodore C.   Decision-Making in the White House: The
Olive Branch or the Arrows.   New York, Columbia, 1963.   5649

2.   Theses and Dissertations

Fisher, Aubrey B.   Decision Emergence: A Process Model of
Verbal Task Behavior for Decision-Making Groups.   Ph. D.   Minnesota.   1968.   5650

Forston, Robert F.   The Decision Making Process in the American
Civil Jury: A Comparative Methodological Investigation.   Ph. D.
Minnesota.   1969.   5651

Gouran, Dennis S.   Variables Related to Consensus in Group Discussions of Questions of Policy.   Ph. D.   Iowa.   1968.   5652

Heun, Richard E.   Inference in the Process of Cognitive Decision
Making.   Ph. D.   Southern Illinois Univ.   1969.   5653

Kaufman, Rebecca L.   The Effect of Self-Esteem in Decision-Making
in Debate.   M. A.   Ohio State.   1967.   5654

Luck, James I.   Trial Jury Decision-Making Research: A Synthesis
and Critique.   M. A.   Georgia.   1970.   5655

Schreiner, Philip J.   An Exploratory Study of the Nature of Advocacy and Inquiry in Problem-Solving.   Ph. D.   UCLA.   1966.
                                                            5656

3. Articles

Anderson, Norman H. , and Shanteau, James C.   Information Integration in Risky Decision Making. JExP, 84 (1970), 441-451. (On
the usefulness of a decision theory for making judgments about
uncertain events.)   5657

Berman, Marilyn, Fraser, Malcolm R. , and Theios, John.   Learning a General Maximum Likelihood Decision Strategy. JExP, 86
(1970), 393-397. (On "the effects of various types of information
feedback upon the ability of subjects to approximate optimal decision behavior. ")   5658

Bernbach, Harley A. Decision Processes in Memory. PsyR, 76
(November, 1967), 462-480.   5659

Brilhart, John K. An Experimental Comparison of Three Techniques
for Communicating a Problem-Solving Pattern to Members of a
Discussion Group. SM, 33 (June, 1966), 168-177.   5660

Brownoski, J. The Logic of the Mind. American Scientist, 54
(Spring, 1966), 4ff.   5661

Dahl, Robert A. Decision-Making in a Democracy: the Supreme
Court as a National Policy Maker. JPL, 6 (1957).   5662

Ducharme, Wesley M. Response Bias Explanation of Conservative
Human Inference. JExP, 85 (1970), 66-74. (Explains human
"conservatism" in terms of decision theory rather than as a function of misinformation or poor reasoning.)   5663

Dyke, C. Collective Decision-Making in Rousseau, Kant, Hegel,
and Mill. Eth, 80 (October, 1969), 21-37.   5664

Epstein, Fanny. Beyond Determinism and Irrationalism. PhT, 2
(Spring, 1967), 38-46. (On the role of motives in decision-making.)   5665

Fisher, B. Aubrey. Decision Emergence: Phases in Group Decision-Making. SM, 37 (March, 1970), 53-66.   5666

_____. The Process of Decision Modification in Small Discussion
Groups. JC, 20 (1970), 51-64. (On the patterns by which small
groups make decisions.)   5667

Gagnon, V. N. Legal Reasoning in Judicial Decision-Making. PoLR,
2 (Fall, 1966), 123ff.   5668

Gerard, Harold. Choice Difficulty, Dissonance, and the Decision
Sequence. JPer, 35 (1967), 91-108.   5669

Gorden, William J. Academic Games. TS, 19 (Summer, 1971),
27-34.   5670

Hanson, Roger A.   A Formal Analysis of a Constitutional Decision-
Making Argument.   MJPS, 14 (1970), 596-625.   (On how logic
can be applied to Hobbes' conditions for constitution making.)
5671

Hart, H. L. A. , and Hampshire, S.   Decision, Intention, and Certainty.   Mi, 68 (1958), 1-12.   5672

Heslin, Richard, and Streufert, Siegfried.   Task Familiarity and
Reliance on the Environment in Decision-Making.   PsyRd, 18
(1968), 629-637.   5673

Houlgate, Laurence D.   Knowledge and Responsibility.   APQ, 5
(April, 1968), 109-119.   (On the conditions under which ignorance
may or may not excuse one from responsibility for his acts.)
5674

Howard, J. Woodford, Jr.   Adjudication Considered as a Process of
Conflict Resolution: A Variation on Separation of Powers.   JPL,
18 (1969), 339-370.   (Adjudication in U. S. courts compared with
the legislative process.)   5675

Hughes, G.   Rules, Policy, and Decision-Making.   YLJ, 77 (January, 1968), 411-439.   (On the role of the legal system in reaching good decisions.)   5676

Kiesler, Charles, Kiesler, Sara B. , and Pallak, Michael.   The Effect of Commitment to Future Interaction on Reactions to Norm
Violations.   JPer, 35 (1967), 585-599.   5677

Kline, John.   Indices of Opinionated and Orienting Statements in
Problem-Solving Discussions.   SM, 37 (November, 1970), 282-
286.   5678

Lamm, Helmut.   Will an Observer Advise Higher Risk-Taking after
Hearing a Discussion of the Decision Problem?   JPSP, 6 (1967),
467-471.   5679

Lin, Nan.   Information Flow, Influence Flow and the Decision-Making
Process.   JQ, 48 (Spring, 1971), 33-40.   5680

Lundsteen, Sara.   Listening, Reading and Qualitative Levels of
Thinking in Problem-Solving.   CJER (November, 1968), 219-230.
(On the relative importance of listening and reading in problem-
solving.)   5681

Maier, Norman R. F.   Assets and Liabilities in Group Problem-
Solving: the Need for an Integrative Function.   PsyR, 74 (July,
1967), 239-249.   5682

McNassor, Donald.   Decision-Making Process in a Revolution.
CJSE, 44 (October, 1969), 265-270.   5683

Michalos, Alex C.   Rational Decision-Making in Committees.   APQ,
7 (April, 1970), 91-106.   5684

Neimark, Edith D., and Lewis, Nan. The development of Logical Problem-Solving Strategies. ChD, 38 (March, 1967), 100-117.
5685

Ornstein, Allan C. On High School Violence: the Teacher-Student Role. CJSE, 45 (March, 1970), 99-105. (On authoritarian teachers who by-pass rational decision-making and thereby provoke dissatisfied students into violent and irrational behavior.) 5686

Penfold, D. M., and Aborn-Hatab, F. A. H. The Factorial Dimensions of Verbal Critical Thinking. JEE, 36 (Winter, 1967), 1-12. (On the research done and educational value of instruction in critical thinking.) 5687

Raack, R. C. When Plans Fail: Small Group Behavior and Decision-making in the Conspiracy of 1808 in Germany. JCR, 14 (1970), 3-19. 5688

Rapoport, Anatol, and Orwant, C. Experimental Games: A Review. BS, 7 (January, 1962), 1-37. 5689

Rickborn, Ida, and Lundsteen, Sara. The Construction of and Acquisition of Reliability Data for a Test of Qualitative Levels of Creative Problem-Solving. CJER (March, 1968), 53-59. 5690

Shubik, Martin. Studies and Theories of Decision-Making. ASQ, 3 (December, 1958), 289-306. 5691

Smith, Robert D. Heuristic Simulation of Psychological Decision Processes. JAP, 52 (August, 1968), 325-333. (Demonstrates that computers can be programmed to use a decision process like that used in human argumentation.) 5692

Stone, Vernon A. A Primacy Effect in Decision-Making by Jurors. JC, 19 (September, 1969), 239-247. ("An experiment varied the order of presentation of ostensible trial testimony.") 5693

Thalberg, I. Foreknowledge and Decision in Advance. An, 24 (1963-1964), 49-53. 5694

Wetherick, N. A Further Study of the Inferential Basis of Concept Attainment. British Journal of Educational Psychology (November, 1968), 431-436. (On problem-solving capacity with respect to age and familiarity with subjects.) 5695

Wilder, Larry, and Harvey, Donald J. Overt and Covert Verbalization in Problem-Solving. SM, 38 (August, 1971), 171-176. 5696

Wroblewski, Jerzy. Comments on Gideon Gottlieb and the Logic of Choice. LoA, 51 (1970), 379-384. 5697

B.   BELIEFS AND VALUES

1.   Books

Allport, Gordon W.   The Nature of Prejudice.   New York, Anchor
    Doubleday, 1958.   5698

Berry, Thomas E., ed.   Values in American Culture: Statements
    from Colonial Times to the Present.   New York, Odyssey, 1966.
                                                                 5699
Griffiths, A. Phillips, ed.   Knowledge and Belief.   London, Oxford,
    1967.   5700

Heider, Fritz.   The Psychology of Interpersonal Relations.   New
    York, Wiley, 1958.   5701

Insko, Chester.   Theories of Attitude Change.   New York, Appleton,
    1967.   5702

Kluckhohn, Clyde.   Anthropology and the Classics.   Providence,
    R. E., Brown, 1961.   5703

_____.   Culture and Behavior (ed. by Richard Kluckhohn).   New
    York, Free, 1962.   5704

Quine, W. V., and Ullian, J. S.   The Web of Belief.   New York,
    Random, 1970.   5705

Rokeach, Milton.   Beliefs, Attitudes, and Values.   San Francisco,
    Jassez-Bass, 1968.   5706

Schiller, F. C. S.   Problems of Belief.   New York, Doran, 1924.
                                                                 5707

2.   Theses and Dissertations

Barnes, Vernon.   An Experimental Study of Certain Relationships
    between Debaters' Attitudes and Win-Loss Records.   M. A.   Kan-
    sas State.   1954.   5708

Brooks, Robert D.   An Investigation of the Relationship between
    Personal Values and the Selection of Rhetorical Arguments.
    Ph. D.   Cornell.   1965.   5709

Rose, Robert E.   A Comparison of the Power of Four Measuring
    Instruments to Detect Shifts in Attitude.   M. A.   Iowa.   1967.
                                                                 5710

3.   Articles

Albert, Ethel M.   The Classification of Values: A Method and an
    Illustration.   AA, 58 (1956), 221-248.   5711

Armstrong, J. H. S. Knowledge and Belief. An, 13 (1952-1953),
111-117. 5712

Braithwaite, R. B. Belief and Action. PAS, supp. vol. 20 (1946),
1-19. 5713

_____. The Nature of Believing. PAS, 33 (1932-1933), 129-146.
5714

Brooks, Robert D. The Generality of Early Reversals of Attitudes
Toward Communication Sources. SM, 37 (June, 1970), 152-155.
5715

Brown, Steven R. Consistency and the Persistence of Ideology:
Some Experimental Results. POQ, 34 (Spring, 1970), 60-68.
(A study of the relative persistence of political belief systems.)
5716

Clark, Ruth A., and Hynes, Geraldine. The Relationship of Judgments of Desirability and Likelihood. SM, 37 (August, 1970),
199-206. 5717

Dobkin, Milton. Social Values and Public Address: Some Implications for Pedagogy. WS, 26 (1962), 140-146. 5718

Dodd, Stuart C. On Classifying Human Values: A Step in the Prediction of Human Valuing. ASR, 16 (1951), 645-653. 5719

Firth, R. Chisholm on the Ethics of Belief. PR, 68 (1959), 493-
506. 5720

Fishbein, M., and Raven, B. H. The AB Scales: An Operational
Definition of Belief and Attitude. HR, 15 (February, 1962), 35-
44. 5721

Griffiths, A. Phillips. On Belief. PAS, 63 (1962-1963), 167-186.
5722

Hearn, Thomas K., Jr. Norman Kemp Smith on "Natural Belief."
SJP, 7 (Spring, 1969), 3-7. (An attempt to clarify Smith's treatment of natural belief and to divorce it from Hume's position.)
5723

Heider, Fritz. Attitudes and Cognitive Organization. JPsy, 21
(1946), 107-112. 5724

Jones, Stanley E. Attitude Changes of Public Speakers during In-
vestigative and Expressive Stages of Advocacy. SM, 33 (June,
1966), 137-146. 5725

Landesman, C. A Note on Belief. An, 24 (1963-1964), 180-182.
5726

Mace, C. A. Belief. PAS, 29 (1928-1929), 227-250. 5727

Malcolm, Norman. Knowledge and Belief. Mi, 51 (1952), 178-189.
5728

_____. On Knowledge and Belief. An, 14 (1953-1954), 94-98.
5729

Margenau, Henry, and Oscanyan, Frederick. A Scientific Approach
   to the Theories of Values. JVI, 3 (Fall, 1969), 163-172. (Argues that value systems can systematically be derived and measured.)   5730

Martin, R. M.   On Knowing, Believing, Thinking.   JPhil, 59 (1962),
   586-600.   5731

Mayo, Bernard.   Belief and Constraint.   PAS, 64 (1963-1964), 139-
   156.   5732

Mehrley, R. Samuel, and McCroskey, James C.   Opinionated Statements and Attitude Intensity as Predictors of Attitude Change and
   Source Credibility.   SM, 37 (March, 1970), 47-52.   5733

Murphree, Iris.   Experimental Nature of Belief.   JPhil, 60 (1963),
   309-317.   5734

Newcomb, Theodore.   An Approach to the Study of Communicative
   Acts.   PsyR, 60 (1953), 393-404.   5735

Paulson, Stanley F.   Social Values and Experimental Research in
   Speech.   WS, 26 (1962), 133-140.   5736

Price, H. H.   Some Considerations about Belief.   PAS, 35 (1934-
   1935), 229-252.   5737

_____.   Belief and Will.   PAS, supp. vol. 28 (1954), 1-26.   5738

Rescher, Nicholas.   The Study of Value Change.   JVI, 1 (Spring,
   1967), 12-23.   5739

Ryle, Gilbert.   Knowing How and Knowing That.   PAS, 46 (1945-
   1946), 1-16.   5740

Scott, W. A.   Attitude Change through Reward of Verbal Behavior.
   JASP, 55 (1957), 72-75.   (Study of effect on attitude of winning
   or losing a debate.)   5741

_____.   Attitude Change by Response Reinforcement: Replication
   and Extension.   So, 22 (1959), 328-335.   (Replication of previous
   study, supra.)   5742

Sesonske, A.   On Believing.   JPhil, 66 (1959), 486-492.   5743

Stein, Waltraut J.   How Values Adhere to Facts: An Outline of a
   Theory.   SJP, 7 (Spring, 1969), 65-74.   (Argues that values
   arise out of man's encounter with facts; they do not originate and
   reside in the "heaven beyond the heavens. ")   5744

Taylor, R.   A Note on Knowing and Belief.   An, 13 (1952-1953),
   143-144.   5745

White, Alan R.   On Claiming to Know.   PR, 66 (1957), 180-192.
$\hspace{11cm}$ 5746

Woozley, A. D.   Knowing and Not Knowing.   PAS, 53 (1952-1953),
151-172.   5747

C.   MISCELLANEOUS

1.   Books

Auer, J. Jeffrey.   Introduction to Research in Speech.   New York,
Harper, 1959.   5748

Brewer, David J. , ed.   The World's Best Orations.   Metuchen,
New Jersey, Scarecrow, 1970.   5749

Capaldi, Nicholas, ed.   Clear and Present Danger: The Free
Speech Controversy.   New York, Pegasus, 1969.   5750

Fabrizio, Ray, Karas, Edith, and Menmuir, Ruth, eds.   The Rhetoric of No.   New York, Holt, 1970.   5751

Freedman, Leonard, ed.   Issues of the Sixties.   Belmont, California, Wadsworth, 2nd ed. , 1965.   5752

Haiman, Franklyn S.   Freedom of Speech: Issues and Cases.   New
York, Random, 1965.   5753

Hughes, Richard E. , and Duhamel, Albert P. , eds.   Persuasive
Prose: A Reader.   Englewood Cliffs, New Jersey, Prentice,
1964.   5754

O'Neill, Robert M.   Free Speech: Responsible Communication under
Law.   Indianapolis, Bobbs, 1966.   5755

Osborn, Albert S.   The Problem of Proof.   Newark, Essex Press,
1926.   5756

Peterson, William, and Matza, David, eds.   Social Controversy.
Belmont, Cal. , Wadsworth, 1963.   5757

Rice, George P. , Jr.   Law for the Public Speaker.   Boston,
Christopher Publishing House, 1958.   5758

Schubert, Glendon A.   Quantitative Analysis of Judicial Behavior.
New York, Free, 1959.   5759

Skornia, Harvey, and Kitson, Jack, eds.   Problems and Controversies in Television and Radio.   Palo Alto, Cal. , Pacific Books,
1968.   5760

2. Theses and Dissertations

Lotz, John. A Study of the Use of Argumentation as a Dramatic
Convention in One Ancient and One Modern Drama. M. A.
Akron. 1966.   5761

Overking, Michael. An Investigation of Effects of Instruction in
Two Argument Models upon Critical Thinking Ability. M. A.
Ohio. 1968.   5762

Smith, Virgil J. Speech Education in Australian Colleges and Universities. Ph. D. Texas. 1970.   5763

Terris, Walter F. The Right to Speak: Massachusetts, 1628-1685.
Ph. D. Northwestern. 1962.   5764

Wills, Beatrice B. A Survey of Graduate Research in Debate.
M. A. S. California. 1952.   5765

Winick, Charles. The Psychology of Juries. In Legal and Criminal
Psychology, ed. by Hans Toch. New York, Holt, 1961.   5766

Zwerling, Stanley A. The Relationship of Dogmatism to Experience
and Winning in Debate. Ph. D. Bowling Green. 1965.   5767

3. Articles

Ahrendts, Harold L. American Debating Societies Below the Secondary School Level. F, 45 (May, 1960), 6-10.   5768

Anderson, Ray L. The Letter to the Editor: An Exercise in "Argumentative Composition. " SPG, 7 (November, 1969), 14-17.
                                                                5769
Annerose, (Sister) M. (O. S. B.) Wastelands in the Field of Debate.
AFAR, 9 (College Calendar, 1961), 1-5. (On the need for research in debate.)   5770

Ash, Michael. The Growth of Justice Black's Philosophy on Freedom of Speech: 1962-1966. WiLR (Fall, 1967), 840-862.
(Legal aspects of freedom of speech.)   5771

Australian Debaters. IIENB, 27 (January, 1952), 34.   5772

Bahm, Archie J. Some Neglected Aspects of Dialectic. NSchol,
43 (Spring, 1969), 276-281.   5773

Bailey, J. R. Defense Counsel Incompetence in Criminal Trials:
Past--Present--Future. STLJ, 10 (1968), 14ff.   5774

Bankers Are Debating Too! (American Institute of Banking Sponsors
Extensive Debate Program.) PN, 3 (December, 1936), 8, 19.
                                                                5775

Bergsten, Fred. Forensics in Europe: A Lost Art. F, 46 (October, 1960), No. 1, 3-5.   5776

Bevan, William, et al. Jury Behavior as a Function of the Prestige of the Foreman and the Nature of His Leadership. JPL, 7 (1958), 419-449.   5777

Bloomfield, M. Law vs. Politics: The Self-image of the American Bar. AJLH, 12 (October, 1968), 306-323. (History of the interrelations between lawyer and politician between 1830-1860.) 5778

Boren, D., and Webster, M. Debate as a Form of Creative Expression in the Elementary Grades. TO, 16 (February, 1932), 26-7.   5779

Bosmajian, Haig A. The Nazi Attitude Toward Parliamentary Procedures. G, 44 (January, 1962), 25-28.   5780

Boulding, Kenneth E. Towards a Theory of Protest. Etc, 24 (March, 1967), 49-58. (Discusses situations where protest is likely to arise and under what conditions it is likely to be successful and unsuccessful.)   5781

Bouska, James W. The Prosecutor's Closing Argument in Kansas. KLR, 17 (1968-69), 419-436.   5782

Brett, P. Free Speech, Supreme Court Style: A View from Overseas. TxLR, 46 (April, 1968), 668-705. (Comparison of free speech in the U.S., Australia, and England.)   5783

Bristow, C.A. Debate Brings Book Characters to Life. SchA, 19 (November, 1947), 85-6. (Also in DM, 3 (December, 1947), 205-6.)   5784

Broeder, Dale. The University of Chicago Jury Project. NLR, 38 (1959), 744-760. (A comparison of judges' and jury decisions.)
                                                                   5785
Brown, Kenneth S., and Kelly, Douglas S. Playing the Percentages and the Law of Evidence. The University of Illinois Law Forum (1970), 23ff.   5786

Brown, L. Jury Instructions: Issues, Burden of Proof; Rules of the Road; Willing and Wanton Conduct; Imputed Negligence and Defenses. ArLR, 21 (Spring, 1967), 104-121.   5787

Brown, Ralph S., Jr. Legal Research: the Resource Base and Traditional Approaches. ABS, 7 (December, 1963), 3-6.   5788

Burger, W.E. Remarks on Trial Advocacy: A Proposition. WaLR, 7 (Fall, 1967), 15-24.   5789

Cady, T.C. Moot Court Program at West Virginia. WVLR, 70 (December, 1967), 40-49.   5790

Carmack, Paul A., and Randolph, H. L.   College Debating in India
and Pakistan.   ST, 13 (March, 1964), 103-109.   5791

Chaffee, Steven H.   Salience and Homeostasis in Communication
Process.   JQ, 13 (Autumn, 1967), 439-444.   5792

Cook, John W.   Hume's Scepticism with Regard to the Senses.
APQ, 5 (January, 1968), 1-17.   (Argues that Hume's scepticism
about the continued existence of physical objects derives from a
tautology since there is no empirical evidence for the sceptic's
doubt.)   5793

Cordell, Christobel M.   On Bringing Up a Magazine.   PN, 2
(March, 1936), 1-2; 29.   (On editing a magazine devoted to debate.)   5794

Cromwell, Harvey.   Responsible Choice.   F, 56 (March, 1971), 7-
9.   (Transcription of a speech on the importance of freedom of
speech in a democracy.)   5795

Crow, Stan.   The Perfect Affirmative.   F, 50 (January, 1965), 21.
(Married debate partners.)   5796

Dee, James P.   Communication Needs of the Active Union Member.
JC, 18 (March, 1968), 65-72.   (On the communication needs of
the union member, including bargaining.)   5797

DeRoche, Edward F.   Effectiveness of Creative Exercises on Creative Thinking.   CER (January, 1968), 41-51.   (On the relationship between intelligence and creativity; believes that certain exercises can improve creative thinking.)   5798

Douglas, Donald G.   A Need for Review: Forensic Studies in Contemporary Speech Education.   JAFA, 8 (Spring, 1972), 178-181.
                                                              5799

Dovre, Paul J., and Wenburg, John R.   Experimental Research in
Forensics: New Resources.   JAFA, 8 (Summer, 1971), 47-51.
                                                              5800

Drum, Dale.   The Power of Defensive Thinking.   TS, 6 (January,
1958), 7-9.   (Analyzes why people argue back.)   5801

Drushal, J. Garber.   A Sonnet to the Time Keeper.   TS, 11 (April,
1963), 15.   5802

Eagly, Alice H.   Leadership Style and Role Differentiation as Determinants of Group Effectiveness.   JPer, 38 (1970), 509-524.
                                                              5803

Ellis, Dean S.   Debate in Japan.   JAFA, 5 (Fall, 1968), 95-98.
                                                              5804

_____ and Frank, Erick.   The Australian Program.   JAFA, 7
(Spring, 1970), 111-114.   5805

Elms, Alan C.   Role Playing, Incentive, and Dissonance.   PB, 68

(August, 1967), 132-148.   5806

Epstein, Seymour, and Taylor, Stuart P.   Instigation to Aggression
     as a Function of Degree of Defeat and Perceived Aggressive In-
     tent of the Opponent.   JPer, 35 (1967), 265-289.   5807

Fletcher, G. P.   The Role of the Defense Counsel in the Soviet
     Criminal Procedings.   WiLR (1968), 806-900.   (Detailed explana-
     tion of Soviet legal system.)   5808

Foley, George, Jr.   An Experiment in Seventh and Eighth Grade De-
     bating.   PN, 7 (1 September, 1940), 20-1.   5809

Francke, Donald C.   The Assessment and Improvement of Organiza-
     tional Understanding.   JEE, 36 (Winter, 1967), 59-63.   5810

Freeley, Austin J.   Plans for Future National Conferences.   SPG,
     4 (March, 1967), 64-65.   5811

Gabbard, Anne S.   The Use of Persuasive Argumentation in the
     Oresteian Trilogy.   M. A.   Texas Woman's Univ.   1966.   5812

Gallagher, Michael R.   Delicate Aspects of the Lawyer-Trial Judge
     Relationship.   Insurance Council Journal, 36 (1969), 586-609.
     (Analyzes attitudes, language and arguments as they interrelate
     between lawyer and trial judge in formal courtroom situations.)
                                                           5813
Goedecke, Robert.   What Are the Principles of American Constitu-
     tional Law?   Eth, 78 (October, 1967), 17-31.   (Discusses Amer-
     ican Constitutional Law as evolving from deliberation and debate
     between jurists.)   5814

Goldman, Sheldon.   Backgrounds, Attitudes, and the Voting Behavior
     of Judges.   JPol, 31 (1969), 214-222.   ("An evaluation and com-
     mentary on Grossman's theories about social backgrounds and
     judicial decisions.")   5815

Goodure, W. S.   A Motivating Method Used in Practice Teaching;
     Tenth-Grade History Class Study of Napoleon.   Ed, 57 (January,
     1937), 294-8.   5816

Goolsby, T. M., Jr.   Study of the Criteria for Legal Education and
     Admission to the Bar.   JLE, 20 (1968), 175-177.   5817

Gordon, Robert I.   A Study in Forensic Psychology: Petit Jury
     Verdicts as a Function of the Number of Jury Members.   Ph. D.
     Oklahoma.   1968.   5318

Gordon, R. I., and Temerlin, M. K.   Forensic Psychology: the
     Judge and the Jury.   J, 52 (1969), 328.   5819

Goulding, Daniel J.   Dialogue and Discussion: The Challenge of the
     Sixties.   SPG, 3 (November, 1965), 2-5.   5820

Gray, Giles W.   Research on the History of Speech Education.
QJS, 35 (April, 1949), 156-63.   5821

Griffith, J. A. G.   Judges in Politics: England.   GO, 3 (Autumn,
1968), 485-498.   (Observations about factors affecting presumptions in the minds of British judges.)   5822

Gronow, Jukka, and Hilppo, Jorma.   Violence, Ethics and Politics.
JPR, 7 (1970), 311-320.   (An attempt to define violence and to
show its importance to human behavior.)   5823

Grosman, B. A.   The Role of the Prosecutor.   CBJ, 11 (November,
1968), 580-590.   (On the role of the prosecutor in English and
Canadian courts.)   5824

Grossman, Joel B.   Dissenting Roles on the Warren Court: a
Study in Judicial Role Behavior.   JPol, 30 (1968), 1068-1090.
(On forensic decision-making from the perspective of role theory.)
                                                                  5825
Hale, Robert.   Daily Themes and College Debating.   Na, 101 (De-
cember 23, 1915), 10-11.   5826

Hayes, Merwyn A., and Huseman, Richard C.   Georgia Symposium
Series.   ST, 16 (November, 1967), 306-308.   5827

Henderson, Ward G.   Debate Manners.   PN, 5 (January-February,
1939), 6-7.   5828

Hill, Mary A.   Good Manners in Debate.   F, 23 (January, 1938),
45-46.   (With emphasis on avoiding sarcasm.)   5829

Holmes, F.   Lincoln D. Pump Priming.   G, 21 (May, 1939), 60.
(Humorous poem.)   5830

Hurley, Neil P.   Satellite Communications: a Case Study of Tech-
nology's Impact on Politics.   JPol, 30 (April, 1968), 170-190.
(On the potential of world-wide communication and its effect on
politics.)   5831

Hurst, J. W.   Lawyers in American Society.   MqLR, 50 (June,
1967), 594-606.   5832

James, Rita M.   Status and Competence of Jurors.   AJS, 64 (1959),
563-570.   5833

Jones, Stanley E.   Directivity vs. Nondirectivity: Implications of
the Examination of Witnesses in Law for the Fact-Finding Interview.   JC, 19 (March, 1919), 64-75.   ("The results of an examination of the literature on directive and nondirective inter-
viewing are compared to the content of the literature on the examination of witnesses in legal proceedings.")   5834

Karcher, J. T.   Advice to Young Lawyers: Become a Trial Lawyer.

ABAJ, 54 (January, 1968), 41-44. (Traces the various stages
of a trial and the demands on an attorney at each stage.)   5835

Kelley, A. H.   Constitutional Liberty and the Law of Libel: A Historian's View.   AHR, 74 (December, 1968), 429-452.   (Summarizes the development of the law of libel since 1798.)   5836

Knapp, Mark L., and McCroskey, James C.   Communications Research and the American Labor Union.   JC, 18 (June, 1968),
160-172.   (A survey of labor attitudes toward needs and offerings
in oral communication training.)   5837

Lawson, R. G.   Personality Tests for Prospective Jurors.   KLJ,
56 (Summer, 1967-68), 832-854.   (Discusses the pros and cons
of giving personality tests to prospective jurors.)   5838

Linehan, K.   Debates Can Be More Than Talk.   Grade Teacher,
86 (February, 1969), 62.   5839

London, Harvey, Meldman, Philip J., and Lanckton, A. Van C.
The Jury Method: How the Persuader Persuades.   POQ, 34
(Summer, 1970), 171-83.   (Suggests that persuasion is not a
function of intelligence, prediscussion conviction, ability or volu-
bility, but of the expression of confidence during the discussion
itself.)   5840

Lowin, Aaron.   Approach and Avoidance: Alternate Modes of Selective Exposure to Information.   JPSP, 6 (1967), 1-9.   5841

Luschen, Gunther.   Cooperation, Association and Contest.   JCR, 14
(1970), 21-34.   (Analyzes the contest as a special social situation.)   5842

Maechling, Charles, Jr.   The Right to Dissent in a Free Society.
ABAT, 55 (1969), 848-852.   (Attempts to define the legal and
ethical boundaries of dissent.)   5843

Martin, G. Arthur.   Closing Argument to the Jury for the Defense
in Criminal Cases.   CrLQ, 10 (November, 1967), 34ff.   5844

McClatchey, J. F.   Trial, Evidence and Proof of Damages.   CiLR,
38 (1969), 306ff.   5845

Miller, A. S.   Myth of Objectivity in Legal Research and Writing.
CULR, 18 (1969), 290ff.   5846

Mills, C. Wright.   The Powerless People: The Social Role of the
Intellectual.   AAUPB, 31 (Summer, 1945), 231-243.   5847

Monaghan, J.   When Were the Debates First Published?   Journal
of the Illinois State Historical Society, 42 (1949), 344-347.   (On
Lincoln's use of published debates.)   5848

Morrill, A. E.   Voir Dire Examination.   ILJ (March, 1968), 190-
    256.   (On persuasion in the courtroom.)   5849

Nagel, Stuart.   Ethnic Affiliations and Judicial Propensities.   JPol,
    24 (1962), 92-110.   5850

Neimark, Edith, and Lewis, Nan.   Development of Logical Problem-
    Solving: A One-Year Retest.   ChD, 39 (June, 1968), 527-536.
                                                                   5851
Nichols, Ralph G.   Debate Coach Looks at Drama.   SchA, 15 (May,
    1944), 311-312.   5852

Norton, Lawrence E.   Research Directions in Debate.   AFAR, 8
    (Spring, 1960), 8-11.   5853

Pease, Raymond B.   The Audience as the Jury.   JPS, 3 (1917),
    218-233.   5854

Polk, Lee R.   Historical Research in Forensics: Its Status and
    Guidelines for the Future.   JAFA, 7 (Winter, 1970), 36-41. (On
    how historical research can help forensics; proposes a history
    program for forensics.)   5855

Radcliffe, Barbara M.   The Debate Journey.   R, 31 (December,
    1956), 4.   (Poem.)   5856

Rau, Gilbert.   Three Journals Go to Press.   F, 56 (January, 1971),
    12-14.   (An account of the editors, cost, and circulation of the
    three forensic journals sponsored by the leading honorary debat-
    ing fraternities: The Forensic, Speaker and Gavel, and Per-
    suader of Phi Rho Pi, the national organization of Junior Col-
    leges.)   5857

Redmont, Robert S.   Psychological Views in Jurisprudential Theories.
    PLR, 107 (1959), 472-513.   5858

_____.   Pantascopic View of Law and Psychology.   JLE, 10 (1958),
    436-451.   5859

Reynolds, E.   Worthy Opponent.   Instruction, 78 (March, 1969), 51.
                                                                   5860
Rheingold, P. D. , and Gans, A. F.   Analysis of a Case (Do I Have
    a Case?).   AbLR, 29 (January, 1968), 104ff.   5861

Rhine, Jennie.   The Jury: A Reflection of the Prejudices of the
    Community.   HLJ, 20 (1968-69), 1417-1445.   (On jury selection
    process, with suggestions for reform.)   5862

Rinsky, L.   Let's Debate.   Instruction, 76 (November, 1966), 34-
    35.   5863

Rothman, Richard M.   The Best American Debater of My Acquaint-
    ance.   F, 51 (January, 1966), 4-5.   5864

_____. Thoughts While Riding on a Bus. F, 47 (January, 1962),
19. (While enroute to a debate tournament.)   5865

Salter, Leonard M. The Well-Tempered Advocate. ABAJ, 54 (February, 1968), 177-179.   5866

Sanborn, Ruth D. Browsing Around in Last Spring's Speech Magazines. PN, 8 (September, 1941), 3-5. (A review of articles on debate.)   5867

Saunders, John T. The Temptations of "Powerlessness." APG, 5 (April, 1968), 100-108.   5868

Sessions, C. C. Trial Lawyer of the Future. TnLR, 35 (Spring, 1968), 442-451.   5869

Seymour, M. A. Debating Clubs for Grammar Schools. JEd, 84 (December 7, 1916), 578.   5870

Shillan, David. Public Speaking in the Upper Fourth. JEd (London), 65 (December, 1933), 762-3.   5871

Sibley, R. P. A Neglected Form of Argument. EJ, 10 (January, 1921), 35-8. (A plea for more use of the written argumentative dialogue.)   5872

Smith, J. C. Law, Language and Philosophy. BCLR, 3 (May, 1968), 59ff.   5873

Tauro, G. P. Law School Curricula Must Change to Give Bar More Trial Lawyers. Tr, 4 (October-November, 1968), 48-49.   5874

Taylor, James S. A Study of Group Discussion in Selected American Colleges and Universities. SSJ, 33 (Winter, 1967), 113-118.
                                                                   5875

Thayer, Lynn W. Radio in the Pennsylvania Forensic and Music League. DM, 3 (September, 1947), 159-60.   5876

Tillman, Frank A. On Being Fair to Facts. PhS, 19 (January-February, 1968), 1ff.   5877

Ulmer, S. S. Analysis of Behavior Patterns in the U. S. Supreme Court. JPol, 22 (November, 1960), 629-653.   5878

Walsh, Grace. The Irish National Debate Championship. JAFA, 7 (Spring, 1970), 114-116.   5879

Walwik, Theodore J. Research in Forensics: An Overview. JAFA, 6 (Spring, 1969), 43-48.   5880

Welden, Terry A. A Congruity Prediction of Attitude Change from Debate Win-Loss Record. JAFA, 3 (May, 1966), 48-52.   5881

Whittaker, James O.   Perception and Judgment in the Political Ex-
   tremist.   JC, 17 (June, 1967), 136-141.   5882

Winans, J. A.   The Need for Research.   QJS, 1 (April, 1915), 17-
   23.   5883

Wolfson, Lester M.   On Selecting Subjects for Graduate Research.
   SSJ, 20 (Fall, 1954), 37-41.   5884

Wright, E. A.   Courtroom Decorum in the Trial Process.   J, 51
   (May, 1968), 378ff.   5885

Zdep, Stanley, and Wilson, Warner.   Recency Effects in Opinion
   Formation.   PsyRt, 23 (1968), 195-200.   5886

XXII. BIBLIOGRAPHIES

1. Books

A Bibliography of Parliamentary Debates of Great Britain. London,
Her Majesty's Stationery Office, 1956.   5887

Brockett, Oscar G., Becker, Samuel L., and Bryant, Donald C.
A Bibliographical Guide to Research in Speech and Dramatic Art.
Chicago, Scott, 1963.   5888

Cain, Earl R., et al., ed. Speech Abstracts, Vol. I. Long Beach,
Dept. of Speech Communication, California State College, Long
Beach, 1970.   5889

Childs, Harwood L. A Reference Guide to the Study of Public Opinion. Princeton, N.J., Princeton, 1934.   5890

Cleary, James W., and Haberman, Frederick W., eds., with the
assistance of Shearer, Ned A. Rhetoric and Public Address: A
Bibliography 1947-1961. Madison and Milwaukee, Wisconsin,
1964.   5891

Dow, Clyde W., ed. An Introduction to Graduate Study in Speech
and Theatre. East Lansing, Michigan, Michigan, 1961.   5892

Dunham, Robert E., and Harms, L.S. Index and Table of Contents
of the Southern Speech Journal, 1935-1960; Western Speech Journal, 1937-1960; Central States Speech Journal, 1949-1960; and
Today's Speech, 1953-1960. Central States Speech Association,
Speech Association of the Eastern States, Southern Speech Association, 1962.   5893

Gray, Giles W. Index to the Quarterly Journal of Speech, Volumes
1 to 40, 1915-1954. Dubuque, Iowa, Brown, 1956.   5894

Johnsen, Julia E., comp. Debate Index; Supplement. (New rev.
ed.) Reference Shelf, 14 (1941), 1-90. (Reference Shelf series
published by H.W. Wilson Co.)   5895

Knower, Franklin H. Table of Contents of the Quarterly Journal of
Speech, 1915-1960; Speech Monographs, 1934-1960; and the Speech
Teacher, 1952-1960. Speech Association of America, 1961. 5896

Lasswell, Harold D., Casey, Ralph D., and Smith, Bruce L.

Propaganda and Promotional Activities; An Annotated Bibliography. Minneapolis, Minn., Minnesota, 1935. (Continued in B. L. Smith, H. D. Lasswell, and R. D. Casey's Propaganda, etc., infra.)5897

McCoy, Ralph E. Freedom of the Press: An Annotated Bibliography. Carbondale, Ill., Southern Illinois, 1968.   5898

Milic, Louis T., ed. An Annotated Bibliography of Style and Stylistics. New York, Macmillan, 1967.   5899

Mudge, Isadore G. Guide to Reference Books. Chicago, American Library Association, 6th ed., 1936.   5900

Mulgrave, Dorothy I., Marlor, Clark S., and Baker, Elmer E. Bibliography of Speech and Allied Areas. Philadelphia and New York, Chilton Company Book Division, 1962.   5901

Phelps, Edith M., ed. Debate Index, also Bibliographies... on Current Subjects. Reference Shelf, 8 (October, 1932), 1-110. 5902

_____. Debate Index, Revised. Reference Shelf, 12, No. 9 (1939), 1-130.   5903

_____. Debate Index Supplement; and Supplementary Bibliographies on Current Debate Topics. Reference Shelf, IQ (May, 1935), 7-49. (Reference Shelf Series published by H. W. Wilson Co.)5904

_____. Debaters' Manual. New York, Wilson, 6th ed. rev., 1929.
                                                                   5905
Shearer, Ned A., ed. Bibliographic Annual in Speech Communication. 1970 Annual. New York, Speech Communication Association, 1971. Ibid., 1971. 1972. (Supersedes bibliographies contained annually in Speech Monographs up to the year 1970. Contains sections on doctoral dissertations, graduate theses and dissertation titles, bibliography of rhetoric and public address, and miscellaneous bibliographies.)   5906

Smith, Bruce L., Lasswell, Harold D., and Casey, Ralph D. Propaganda, Communication and Public Opinion; A Comprehensive Reference Guide. Princeton, N. J., Princeton, 1946.   5907

Thompson, Wayne N. Quantitative Research in Public Address and Communication. New York, Random, 1967.   5908

Thonssen, Lester, Fatherson, Elizabeth, and Thonssen, Dorothea. Bibliography of Speech Education. New York, Wilson, 1939.5909

_____, Robb, Mary M., and Thonssen, Dorothea. Bibliography of Speech Education; Supplement, 1939-1948. New York, Wilson, 1950.   5910

Wasserman, Paul, and Silander, Fred S. Decision-Making: An Annotated Bibliography. Ithaca, New York, Cornell, 1958. 5911

Winchell, Constance. Guide to Reference Books. Chicago, American Library Assn., 8th ed., 1967. 5912

2. Theses and Dissertations

Foster, Teddy J. A Bibliography of Experimental Studies Related to Persuasion Published in English Language Journals: 1914-1964. Ph.D. Ohio. 1967. 5913

Kaufman, Ileen. An Annotated Bibliography on the Work of Arthur N. Kruger. M.A. C.W. Post. 1974. 5913a

Thornton, Gayle E. An Analysis of Discussion and Debate Articles in the Quarterly Journal of Speech, 1915-1945. M.A. Iowa. 1955. 5914

Wills, Beatrice B. A Survey of Graduate Research in Debate. M.A. S. California. 1952. 5915

3. Articles

Anderson, Kenneth E. Quantitative Research in Debate. JAFA, 3 (September, 1966), 112-115. 5916

Aubert, Vilhelm. Researches in the Sociology of Law. ABS, 7 (December, 1963), 16-20. 5917

Auer, J. Jeffrey. Doctoral Dissertations in Speech: Work in Progress, 1951. SM, 18 (June, 1952), 162-72.
Ibid., 1952. SM, 19 (June, 1952), 103-111.
Ibid., 1953. SM, 20 (June, 1953), 108-119.
Ibid., 1954. SM, 21 (June, 1954), 136-141.
Ibid., 1955. SM, 22 (June, 1955), 136-141.
Ibid., 1956. SM, 23 (June, 1956), 79-83.
Ibid., 1957. SM, 24 (June, 1957), 77-83.
Ibid., 1958. SM, 25 (June, 1958), 77-83.
Ibid., 1959. SM, 26 (June, 1959), 79-86.
Ibid., 1962. SM, 29 (August, 1962), 182-188.
Ibid., 1963. SM, 30 (August, 1963), 265-301.
Ibid., 1964. SM, 31 (August, 1964), 340-349.
Ibid., 1965. SM, 32 (August, 1965), 385-392.
Ibid., 1966. SM, 33 (August, 1966), 356-363. 5918

_____ and Pic'l, M. E. Doctoral Dissertations in Speech: Work in Progress, 1967. SM, 34 (August, 1967), 377-383. 5919

_____ and Waldhart, Enid S. Doctoral Dissertations in Speech: Work in Progress, 1968. SM, 35 (August, 1968), 338-347.
Ibid., 1969. SM, 36 (August, 1969), 315-323. 5920

Baird, A Craig, comp. A Selected Bibliography of American Oratory. QJS, 12 (November, 1926), 352-56.   5921

Braden, Waldo. The Concept of Southern Oratory: A Selected
Bibliography. SSJ, 29 (Winter, 1963), 141-145.   5922

Clark, Alvan W. The Debater's Guide to Magazines in the Normal
Library, and the Public Library of San Jose, California. San
Jose, Cal., A. W. and U. S. Clark, 1911.   5923

Cleary, James W. A Bibliography of Rhetoric and Public Address
for the Year 1956. SM, 24 (August, 1957), 181-211.
Ibid., 1957. SM, 25 (August, 1958), 177-207.
Ibid., 1958. SM, 26 (August, 1959), 183-216.
Ibid., 1959. SM, 27 (August, 1960), 201-238.
Ibid., 1960. SM, 28 (August, 1961), 157-189.
Ibid., 1961. SM, 29 (August, 1962), 147-181.
Ibid., 1962. SM, 30 (August, 1963), 137-174.
(Continuation of series begun by F. W. Haberman, infra.)   5924

_____ and Shearer, Ned A., eds., with the assistance of Theodore
O. H. Karl, and Laurence E. Norton. A Bibliography of Parliamentary Procedure. Thomas Jefferson Parliamentarian, 5 Special Issue (May, 1962), 1-44.   5925

Conklin, Forrest, ed. A Bibliography of Argumentation and Debate
for 1967. JAFA, 5 (Fall, 1968), 85-94.
Ibid., 1968. JAFA, 6 (Fall, 1969), 119-135.
Ibid., 1969. JAFA, 7 (Fall, 1970), 159-187.
Ibid., 1970. JAFA, 8 (Fall, 1971), 81-104.
Ibid., 1971. JAFA, 9 (Spring, 1973), 426-459.   5926

Debate Index. Pittsburgh, Pa., Carnegie Library, 1912. Revised
editions, 1915, 1917, and 1919.   5927

Debate Index Supplement. Carnegie Library of Pittsburgh Monthly
Bulletin, 8 (1913), 445-62.   5928

Debating: A List of Books for Libraries, High Schools, and Debating Societies. Raleigh, N. C., North Carolina Library Commission, 1915. (7 pps.)   5929

Debating: A List of Books on Debating. Raleigh, N. C., North
Carolina State Library, 1915.   5930

Dow, Clyde W. Abstracts of Theses in Speech and Drama. SM,
13, No. 1 (1946), 99-121.
Ibid., II. SM, 14 (1947), 187-218.
Ibid., III. SM, 15, No. 2 (1948), 188-249.
Ibid., IV. SM, 16 (September, 1949), 290-363.
Ibid., V. SM, 17 (August, 1950), 227-329.
Ibid., VI. SM, 18 (June, 1951), 121-134; (August, 1951), 173-
250.
Ibid., VII. SM, 19 (June, 1952), 112-156; (August, 1952), 157-

203.

Ibid., VIII.   SM, 20 (June, 1953), 120-156; (August, 1953), 157-205.

Ibid., IX.   SM, 21 (June, 1954), 142-156; (August, 1954), 143-226.

Ibid., X.   SM, 22 (June, 1955), 142-156; (August, 1955), 157-216.

Ibid., XI.   SM, 23 (June, 1956), 84-156.

Ibid., XII.   SM, 24 (June, 1957), 84-151.

Ibid., XIII.   SM, 25 (June, 1958), 84-150.

Ibid., XIV.   SM, 26 (June, 1959), 87-148.

Ibid., XV.   SM, 27 (June, 1960), 77-152; (August, 1960), 239-59.

Ibid., XVI.   SM, 28 (June, 1961), 71-130.

Ibid., XVII.   SM, 29 (June, 1962), 85-145.

Ibid., XVIII.   SM, 30 (August, 1963), 175-257.

Ibid., XIX.   SM, 31 (August, 1964),

Ibid., XX.   SM, 32 (August, 1965), 253-335.   5931

Ehninger, Douglas.   A Classified Title and Author Index to the Southern Speech Journal, Volumes I-XXII (1935-1957).   SSJ, 23 (Spring, 1958), 142-64.   5932

Erlanger, Howard S.   Jury Research in America.   LSR, 4 (1970), 345-370.   (Bibliographical essay on research relating to juries.)
                                                                                                             5933

Eubanks, Ralph T., and Baker, V. L.   A Bibliography of Speech and Theatre in the South for the Year 1954.   SSJ, 20 (Summer, 1955), 323-31.

Ibid., 1955.   SSJ, 21 (Summer, 1956), 262-71.

Ibid., 1956.   SSJ, 22 (Summer, 1957), 248-56.   5934

————, ————, and Golden, James.

Ibid., 1957.   SSJ, 23 (Summer, 1958), 211-19.

Ibid., 1958.   SSJ, 24 (Summer, 1959), 236-46.

Ibid., 1962.   SSJ, 28 (Summer, 1963), 288-301.

Ibid., 1963.   SSJ, 29 (Summer, 1964), 326-341.   5935

————, ————, and Towns, Stuart.   A Bibliography of Speech and Theatre in the South for the Year 1964.   SSJ, 30 (Summer, 1965), 335-349.

Ibid., 1965.   SSJ, 31 (Summer, 1966), 302-314.   5936

Ewbank, Henry L.   A Bibliography of Periodical Literature on Debating and Discussion.   QJS, 24 (December, 1938), 634-41.   5937

Getchell, Charles M.   Southern Graduate Study in Speech and Theatre from 1941 to 1950.   SSJ, 15 (May, 1950), 297-306.

Ibid., 1951.   SSJ, 18 (December, 1952), 125-31.   5938

Gibson, James W., and Kibler, Robert J.   Creative Thinking in the Speech Classroom: A Bibliography of Related Research.   ST, 14 (January, 1965), 30-34.   5939

Gilkinson, Howard.   Experimental and Statistical Research in General Speech: II. Speakers, Speeches, and Audiences.   QJS, 30
(April, 1944), 180-186.   5940

Gillis, Herbert R.   A Classified Bibliography of References and
Aids for Teaching Speech and Language Arts in the Elementary
and Secondary Schools.   LISA, 5 (January, 1968), 29-47.   5941

Gray, Giles W.   An Index to Speech Monographs, Volumes I-XXVI.
SM, 27 (Special Issue, 1960), 154-200.   5942

Haberman, Frederick W.   A Bibliography of Rhetoric and Public
Address for the Year: 1947.   QJS, 34 (October, 1948), 277-99.
Ibid., 1948.   QJS, 35 (April, 1949), 127-48.
Ibid., 1949.   QJS, 36 (April, 1950), 141-63.
Ibid., 1950.   SM, 18 (June, 1951), 95-121.
Ibid., 1951.   SM, 19 (June, 1952), 79-102.
Ibid., 1952.   SM, 20 (June, 1953), 79-107.
Ibid., 1953.   SM, 21 (June, 1954), 79-107.
Ibid., 1954.   SM, 22 (June, 1955), 79-110.
Ibid., 1955.   SM, 23 (August, 1956), 157-188.
(Continued under the editorship of J. W. Cleary, supra.)   5943

An Index to Articles in the Register [American Forensic Associa-
tion].   AFAR, 11 (Fall, 1963), 24-26.   5944

Knower, Franklin H.   Earned Degrees in Speech and Dramatic Arts
Conferred by Higher Educational Institutions.   CSSJ, 1 (Novem-
ber, 1949), 12-17.
Ibid., 1947-1948 and 1948-1949.   WS, 14 (October, 1950), 15-20.
An Index of Graduate Work in the Field of Speech from 1902 to
1934.   SM, 2 (1935), 1-49.
Ibid., II.   SM, 3 (1936), 1-20.
Ibid., III.   SM, 4 (1937), 1-16.
Ibid., IV.   SM, 5 (1938), 1-15.
Ibid., V.   SM, 6 (1939), 1-19.
Ibid., VI.   SM, 7 (1940), 1-21.
Ibid., VII.   SM, 8 (1941), 1-22.
Ibid., VIII.   SM, 9 (1942), 1-27.
Ibid., IX.   SM, 10 (1943), 1-12.
Ibid., X.   SM, 11 (1944), 1-8.
Ibid., XI.   SM, 12 (1945), 1-8.
Graduate Theses--A Combined Index of Reports of Graduate Work
in the Field of Speech and Dramatic Art, XII, 1902-1944.   SM,
12 (1945), 9-29.
Graduate Theses--An Index of Graduate Work in Speech and Dra-
ma, XIII.   SM, 13, No. 1 (1946), 122-29.
Ibid., XIV.   SM, 14 (1947), 219-22.
Ibid., XV.   SM, 15 No. 2 (1948), 250-62.
Ibid., XVI.   SM, 16 (September, 1949), 364-80.
Ibid., XVII.   SM, 17 (June, 1950), 180-207.
Ibid., XVIII.   SM, 18 (June, 1951), 135-161.
Ibid., XIX.   SM, 19 (August, 1952), 204-34.

Ibid., XX.   SM, 20 (August, 1953), 206-34.
Ibid., XXI.   SM, 21 (June, 1954), 108-135.
Ibid., XXII. SM, 22 (June, 1955), 111-35.
Ibid., XXIII. SM, 23 (August, 1956), 189-215.
Ibid., XXIV. SM, 24 (August, 1957), 155-80.
Ibid., XXV.   SM, 25 (August, 1958), 151-76.
Ibid., XXVI. SM, 26 (August, 1959), 155-82.
Ibid., XXVII. SM, 27 (August, 1960), 259-78; (November, 1960), 328-39.
Ibid., XXVIII. SM, 28 (August, 1961), 190-221.
Ibid., XXIX. SM, 29 (August, 1962), 189-222.
Ibid., XXX.   SM, 30 (August, 1963), 265-301.
Ibid., XXXI. SM, 31 (August, 1964),
Ibid., XXXII. SM, 32 (August, 1965), 336-384.
Ibid., XXXIII. SM, 33 (August, 1966), 307-355.
Ibid., XXXIV. SM, 34 (August, 1967), 321-376.
Ibid., XXXV. SM, 35 (August, 1968), 348-399.
Ibid., XXXVI. SM, 36 (August, 1969), 324-386.   5945

_____. Bibliography of Communications Dissertations in American Schools of Theology. SM, 30 (June, 1963), 108-136.   5946

_____. A Selected Bibliography of Bibliographies for Students of Speech. SSJ, 17 (December, 1951), 141-53.   5947

Lahman, Carroll P. Topical Index of the Gavel (1940-1947). G, 30 (January, 1948), 28-30, 40.   5948

Long, H. S. A Bibliographical Survey of Recent Work on Aristotle (1945-). Classical World, 51 (1957), 47-51, 57-60, 69-76. 5949

McCroskey, James C. Fifty Articles in Fifty Years. JAFA, 1 (May, 1964), 67-69. (On judging debate.)   5950

McGlone, Edward L. Toward Improved Quantitative Research in Forensics. JAFA, 6 (Spring, 1969), 49-54.   5951

McGrew, J. Fred. A Bibliography of the Works on Speech Composition in England During the 16th and 17th Centuries. QJS, 15 (June, 1929), 381-412.   5952

McKean, Dayton D. A Bibliography of Debating. QJS, 19 (April, 1933), 206-210.   5953

Minnick, Wayne C. Graduate Study and Research in Propaganda. SSJ, 18 (September, 1952), 39-42.   5954

Murphy, James J. The Medieval Arts of Discourse: An Introductory Bibliography. SM, 29 (1962), 71-78.   5955

Nelson, Max. Abstracts of Dissertations in the Field of Speech, 1965. SM, 33 (August, 1966), 233-306.
Ibid., 1966. SM, 34 (August, 1967), 221-320.

Ibid., 1967.   SM, 35 (August, 1968), 255-338.
Ibid., 1968.   SM, 36 (August, 1969), 215-315.   5956

O'Neill, James M.   A Bibliographical Introduction to Graduate Work
in Speech.   QJS, 13 (February, 1927), 39-48.   5957

Petrie, Charles R., Jr.   Informative Speaking: A Summary and
Bibliography of Related Research.   SM, 30 (June, 1963), 79-91.
                                                                    5958
Phelps, Edith M.   Forty Years of Debate Publishing.   QJS, 34
(April, 1948), 162-67.   (An account of the materials provided
for debaters by the H. W. Wilson Company.)   5959

_____.   Reference Tools for the Teacher of Speech.   WS, 6 (No-
vember, 1941), 5-8.   5960

Savage, Lillian, comp.   A Brief Bibliography for the Contests Director.   Speech Bulletin.   Supp.   QJS, 3 (December, 1931), 44-
49.   5961

Schubert, Glendon.   Behavioral Research in Public Law, A Bibliographical Essay.   APSR, 57 (June, 1963), 433-445.   5962

Shearer, Ned A., and Haberman, F. W.   A Bibliography of Rhetoric
and Public Address for the Year 1965.   SM, 33 (August, 1966),
187-222.
Ibid., 1966.   SM, 34 (August, 1967), 187-220.
Ibid., 1967.   SM, 35 (August, 1968), 203-254.
Ibid., 1968.   SM, 36 (August, 1969), 171-214.   5963

Swem, Earl G.   A List of Some Books on Debating in the Virginia
State Library.   Richmond, Va., D. Bottom, 1915.   (30 pps.)
Also, Bulletin of the Virginia State Library, 8 (January, 1915).
                                                                    5964
Tauber, Abraham.   A Guide to the Literature of Speech Education.
QJS, 20 (November, 1934), 507-24.   5965

Thompson, Wayne N.   An Assessment of Quantitative Research in
Speech.   QJS, 55 (February, 1969), 61-68.   5966

_____.   An Evaluative Summary of Quantitative Research Published
in Speech Monographs from July 1, 1964, to July 1, 1965.   SM,
32 (June, 1965), 91-94.   5967

Thonssen, Lester.   A Selected List of Reference Works for Students
of Public Speaking.   QJS, 27 (April, 1941), 215-22.   5968

Towns, Stuart, and DeMarco, Norman.   A Bibliography of Speech
and Theatre in the South for the Year 1967.   SSJ, 34 (Fall, 1968),
61-70.
Ibid., 1968.   SSJ, 35 (Fall, 1969), 71-80.
Ibid., 1969.   SSJ, 36 (Fall, 1970), 71-78.   5969

_____. Eubanks, Ralph T. , and DeMarco, Norman. A Bibliogra-
phy of Speech and Theatre in the South for the Year 1966.   SSJ,
33 (Fall, 1967), 50-60.   5970

_____ and Wright, Thomas K.   A Bibliography of Speech and Theatre in the South for the Year 1970.   SSCJ, 37 (Fall, 1971), 84-
91.
Ibid. , 1971.   SSCJ, 38 (Fall, 1972), 91-103.   5971

White, H. A.   Alphabetical List (by Authors) of Articles in the
Gavel, March, 1927-May, 1933.   G, 16 (May, 1934), 67-68.5972

2005, 3183, 3281
Anderson, Dwight 2404
Anderson, Floyd D. 2006
Anderson, Floyd D.; and Anderson 2007
Anderson, Floyd D.; and Hayes 5507
Anderson, Frederick W. 3297
Anderson, H. H. 5004
Anderson, Hurst A. 456
Anderson, Jerry 5, 3708
Anderson, Jerry M.; and Andersen 4483
Anderson, Jerry M.; and Thomas 1223
Anderson, John R. 2405
Anderson, Loren A. 1320
Anderson, Norman H.; and Lampel 1374
Anderson, Norman H.; and Shanteau 5657
Anderson, Paul R. 457
Anderson, Ray L. 458, 5769
Anderson, Ray L.; and Anderson 2007
Anderson, Ray L.; and Mortensen 1623, 1781
Anderson, William S. 2008
Andrewes, A. 5508
Andrews, James R. 5509
Angell, Clarence S. 2446, 3086
Angell, Ernest 2407
Angell, Richard B. 1428
Annerose, (Sister) M. (O. S. B.) 5770
Ansberry, Merle 3628
Anscombe, G. E. M. 5628
Anshen, Ruth M. 2904
Anton, John P. 1429
App, Austin J. 1246, 1624, 3087
Aristotle 279, 1247, 1430, 1865-66
Armstrong, D. J.; and Feather 2485
Armstrong, George R. 3298, 5005
Armstrong, J. H. S. 5712
Armstrong, Robert L. 1624
Arnauld, A. 264
Arnold, Carroll C. 2408-2409, 5510
Arnold, John H. 6

Arnold, William B.; and McCroskey 1322
Arnold, William E. 459
Aronson, Elliot; and Golden, 2410
Asch, S. E.; Block; and Hertzman 2411
Ash, Michael 5771
Ashley, Fred C. 5362
Askew, John B. 995
Atgeld, John P. 2183
Aubert, Vilhelm 5917
Auer, J. Jeffery 460-61, 2184, 2993, 3299, 3629, 4658, 5748, 5918
Auer, J. Jeffrey; and Banninga 2009
Auer, J. Jeffrey; Eisenson; and Irwin 2213
Auer, J. Jeffrey; and Ewbank 59, 593
Auer, J. Jeffrey; and Pic'l 5919
Auer, J. Jeffrey; and Shearer 3865
Auer, J. Jeffrey; and Waldhart 5920
Aurbach, Joseph; and McBath 958
Auser, Cortland P.; and Bayless 3184
Austin, George A.; Bruner; and Goodnow 1442
Austin, J. L. 2905
Avery, A. E. 1431
Avins, Alfred 5347
Ayer, A. J. 2906

Babcock, C. Merton 2994
Babcock, Maud M. 3185
Babcock, Robert W.; and Powell 7
Baca, Albert R. 2010
Baccus, Joseph H. 3866, 3958, 4257, 4774
Baccus, Joseph H.; and Nichols 125
Bach, Mayme 5088
Bachman, John W. 4486-87
Backes, James G. 1924, 2011
Backus, Robert 1925
Bacon, Cecil F. 238

418

Bacon, Francis 265
Baer, Jules H.; and Balicer 4316
Bagehot, Walter 239
Bagenstos, Pearl E. 5006
Bagenstos, Pearl E.; and Gray 5156
Baggaridge, James B.; and Masel 8
Bahm, Archie J. 5773
Baier, Kurt 914
Bailey, Dudley 2185
Bailey, J. R. 5774
Bain, Alexander 28, 266
Baird, A. Craig 9-11, 462-466, 2186, 2858, 3300-01, 4375-76, 5921
Baird, A. Craig; and Thonssen 2305
Baird, John E. 467, 4488, 4775
Baker, Eldon E. 3959
Baker, Eldon E.; and Redding 2412
Baker, Eldon E.; and Tompkins 4241
Baker, Elmer E.; Mulgrave; and Marlor 5901
Baker, George P. 200-202, 240, 3302, 5089
Baker, George P.; and Hart 213
Baker, George P.; and Huntington 12
Baker, J. Thompson 468, 3960, 4776
Baker, Roy T. 4777
Baker, Virgil L. 3867
Baker, Virgil L.; and Eubanks 2483, 5934
Baker, Virgil L.; Golden; and Eubanks 5935
Baker, Virgil L.; Towns; and Eubanks 5936
Bakke, John P. 5363
Balduf, E. W. 4489
Baldwin, Charles S. 2413, 3303
Balfour, Arthur J. 469
Balgooyen, Theodore 2710, 4706
Balicer, Simon; and Baer 4316
Ball, V. C. 1626
Ballantine, Arthur A. 470
Ballantine, W. G. 1432
Bane, Laverne 3961, 5364
Banks, Marion S. 2319a

Banninga, Jerald L.; and Auer 2009
Barber, George B. 5007, 5090
Barber, Sara M. 3868
Barber, Sharla J. 1092, 1110
Barber, William S. 3304
Barefield, Paul A. 3305, 3962, 4123
Barker, Burt B. 471, 3710
Barker, Larry L. 4751, 4778-79
Barker, Stephen F. 1433
Barksdale, Ethelbert C. 13, 5091-92
Barnard, P. E. 4780
Barnard, Raymond H. 472, 1323, 2995, 3088, 3963, 5093-95, 5511
Barnard, Raymond H.; and Taylor 986
Barnes, Arthur M. 5365
Barnes, Vernon 5708
Barnett, Suzanne E. 2320
Barr, W. M.; and Lintz 5096
Barra, E. R. 473
Barrett, Edward F. 2790
Barron, H. M. 14-15
Barrows, L. D. 203
Barry, Brian 1434
Barry, James J. 3306
Barse, Joseph R. 4377
Bartlett, Kenneth G. 4427, 4781
Bartolomew, Paul C. 5512
Barton, William B. 3307
Barwind, Jack 1585
Barwind, J. Alan; and Blubaugh 1627
Basehart, John; and Miller 2606
Baskerville, Barnet 2414
Bass, W. W. 3308, 5097
Basset, Lee E. 3711
Bassett, T. Robert 2859
Bastian, Wright 474
Bauer, E. Jackson 2415
Bauer, Marvin G. 5513
Bauer, Otto F. 16, 319, 349, 5366
Bauer, Otto F.; and Colburn 3964, 4782
Bauer, Raymond A. 2416-17
Baugh, Ronald L. 5008

Baulding, Kenneth E.   5629
Bawcom, David   4783
Baxter, P. G.   1324
Bayliss, C. A.; and Bennett 1436
Beach, Lee Ray; and Peterson 1399
Beaird, T. M.   1325, 3869, 5098-99
Beam, Jacob N.   298
Bean, Charles H.   1111
Beard, Raymond S.   4324, 4326-27
Beardsley, Monroe C.   1435
Beauchamp, George   3965
Becher, Edmond T.   4784
Beck, Clive   924
Becker, Samuel L.   2418, 4124-25
Becker, Samuel L.; Bryant; and Brockett   5888
Beckman, Vernon E.   422, 475, 4126
Bedichek, Roy   3870-72, 5009
Bedichek, Roy; and Winship 3851
Beem, C. H.   5367
Beeman, Richard R.   5514
Beers, Larry; and Laudick 5207
Behl, William A.   18, 1112
Beisecker, Thomas   2996
Bekker, John A.   4490
Belfour, C. Stanton   925, 3873
Bell, Edwin   19
Belloc, Hillaire   476-79
Beloff, Michael; and Aitken 4369
Belton, Lois H.   5368
Benedict, Ted W.   2321
Benjamin, Robert L.   1044, 1306, 2907, 2997
Benn, Anthony W.; Boyle; and Harris   4378
Bennett, A. A.; and Bayliss 1436
Bennett, Charles E.   2012
Bennett, Guy V.   996
Bennett, K. R.; and Pearson 1291
Bennett, Rodney   167
Bennett, William   20, 2421
Benson, Frank T.   1926

Benson, James A.   1307, 1326, 4127
Benson, Thomas W.   5369
Benson, Thomas W.; and Prosser   2187
Beighley, Kenneth C.   2419-20
Bergan, K. W.   3309
Berger, Margaret A.; and Weinstein   1422
Bergsten, Fred   5776
Berkhof, Louis   997
Berlo, David K.; and Gulley 2422
Berman, Eleanor D.; and McClintock   2013
Berman, Marilyn; Fraser; and Theios   5658
Berman, Sanford I.,   1586
Bernays, Edward L.   2188-89, 2433
Bernbach, Harley A.   5659
Berne, Eric   1437
Berquist, Goodwin F., Jr. 2014, 2853, 3089, 5515
Berry, George   1628
Berry, Mildred F.   3310
Berry, Thomas E.   5699
Berthold, Carol A.   4785
Bertoletti, John   1629
Best, William M.   1273
Bettinghaus, Erwin P.   2190, 2424-25, 2322, 3090
Bettinghaus, Erwin P.; Miller; and Steinfatt   1630
Betz, Edward S.   2791, 3311-12, 3966, 4128, 4786-87
Beutel, Frederick   2998
Bevan, Edwyn R.   2015
Bevan, William; et al.   5777
Bevilacqua, Vincent M.   186, 2016-19
Beyer, Bertha S.   4491
Bickford, Ethel S.   3186
Biddick, William   411, 480
Biddle, Phillips R.   481, 1093, 2323
Biehle, Martha H.   3712
Bietry, J. Richard   3874
Bilski, T.   3313
Bilsky, Manuel   1438
Binney, James   4492
Bird, Otto   1632-35
Bishop, Brad   1327

Bitzer, Lloyd F. 1328, 1636, 1927
Black, Donald J.; and Reiss 4360
Black, Edwin 2020
Black, John W. 2426
Black, Max 1046, 1439, 2908-09
Blackburn, Mary E. 4129
Blackman, Charles B. 1329
Blackwell, Barbara 482
Blair, Hugh 281, 1885
Blandshard, Brand 1440
Blankenship, Jane 5516
Blatt, Stephen J. 2324, 5370
Block, Helen; Asch; and Hertzman 241
Block, Ralph 2427
Blommer, Henry H. 4130
Bloom, Margaret 2428
Bloomfield, M. 5778
Blount, Ralph E. 5102
Blubaugh, Jon A.; and Barwind 1627
Blubaugh, Jon A.; and Giffin 3399
Bluhm, Jeanette 483
Blumenstock, Dorothy; and Lasswell 2245
Blyth, John W. 1441
Blyton, Gifford 484, 3713-14
Boas, George 1443
Boase, Paul H. 350
Boast, William M. 1928
Boaz, John K.; and Ziegelmueller 3967
Bode, B. H. 1444
Bode, C. J. 5103
Bodenheimer, Edgar A. 1637
Bogoslavski, Boris 21
Bohman, George V. 351
Bois, J. Samuel 2999
Bolenius, Emma M. 5104
Bolich, Harry F. 3407
Boller, Paul F. 1274
Bolton, F. R. 3875
Bolton, Janet 2021, 2158
Bond, David J. 1047
Bond, T. C. 4228, 5105
Bonner, John T. 5010
Bonner, Stanley F. 299, 2429
Boole, George 267, 1445
Boone, Lester 4109

Borchers, Gladys L. 2984, 3091, 4707
Borchers, Gladys L.; Smith; and Weaver, 3175, 3602
Borden, Richard C.; and Busse 22
Boren, D.; and Webster 5779
Boren, Robert A. 1242
Bormann, Ernest G. 1637, 2022
Bos, William H. 3314
Bosanquet, Bernard 268, 1446, 1447
Bosmajian, Haig A. 23 2191, 4659, 5780
Bostrom, Robert N. 2430, 4788
Bostrom, Robert N.; and Tucker 1330
Boucher, Daniel K. 1094
Boulding, Kenneth E. 5779
Bouska, James W. 5782
Bouton, Archibald L. 4131
Bowen, Roger 4789
Bowers, John W. 2325, 2431-2432, 3000, 5517
Bowers, John W.; and Osborn 3001
Bowers, John W.; and Phillips 2433
Bowman, Georgia 485, 3187
Bowman, John S.; and Graves 2218
Bowra, D. 2860
Bowser, Anita O. 5371
Bowser, Hallowell 486
Bowrey, Paul B. 4428
Boyd, R. 3631
Boyle, Edward Harris; and Benn 4378
Boyle, Mary J. 3315
Brack, Harold A. 487-488, 3092
Braden, Waldo W. 352, 489-490, 4379-4380, 5518-5520, 5922
Braden, Waldo W.; and Brandenburg 24
Braden, Waldo W.; and Tewell 404
Bradford, A. L. 5107
Bradley, Bert E., Jr. 1929, 3316, 5521

Bradley, Bert E.; and Tarver 5522
Bradley, E. E. 3632
Bradley, Earl E.; and Mulvany 4132
Bradley, F. H. 1448
Bradley, Mark E.; and Daniel 25
Bradshaw, Jane A. 3317
Braithwaite, R. B. 5713-5714
Brake, Robert J. 2023-2025, 2434
Brake, Robert; and Littlefield 3318
Brand, Richard C. 3968
Brandenburg, Ernest 2435, 2792, 5372
Brandenburg, Ernest; and Braden 24
Brandes, Paul 489, 1331, 2026, 3188, 4493, 5373
Brandt, William J. 26
Brann, Vincent C. 491, 3876, 4790
Brannan, Roger D. 5011
Braybrook, David; and Lindblom 5630
Breal, M. J. A. 2910
Brehm, J. W.; and Jones 2553
Breitenbach, Harold P. 1867
Brembeck, Cole S. 3319-3320
Brembeck, Winston L. 423, 492, 2192, 2436, 3189-3190
Brendel, Ida M. 5108
Breniman, Lester R. 3151, 3321, 5109
Brentlinger, Brock W. 1930
Brett, P. 5783
Brewer, David J. 5749
Brewer, R. S.; and Mixon 5238
Brewer, Robert; and Willett 3191
Brewer, W. F. 4133
Brewster, Harold L. 4494
Brick, Adolph H. 1048, 4791
Bridgman, Donald S. 493
Bridgman, P. W. 1449, 2911
Brigance, William N. 494-496, 2437-2438, 3093-3094, 3192, 4134
Briggs, Nancy E. 4381
Bright, Hazel 4495
Brilhart, John K. 5660

Brim, Orville, et al. 5631
Brink, T. L.; and Ritter 1075
Bristow, C. A. 5784
Bristow, William H. 4496
Brittain, Dennis F. 1095
Brittan, L. 4385
Brittin, Marie E. 1308
Broad, C. D. 1638
Broadie, Alexander 1639
Broadrick, King 1640
Brock, Bernard L. 926, 1113-1114
Brock, Bernard L.; Chesebro; Cragan; and Klumpp 1084
Brock, Bernard L.; and Fieldman 4258
Brock, T. C.; and Osterhouse 2631
Brockhaus, Herman H. 5012, 5110
Brockriede, Wayne E. 1641, 2027, 2439-2440, 3869
Brockriede, Wayne E.; and Ehninger 56, 1642
Brockriede, Wayne E.; and Giffin 3970
Brockriede, Wayne E.; and Strother 4429
Brodt, Philip E. 241
Broeder, Dale 5785
Brokette, Oscar G.; Becker; and Bryant 5888
Brommel, Bernard J. 5523
Brookings, Walter D.; and Ringwalt 999
Brooks, George E. 1115, 2193
Brooks, Robert D. 5709, 5715
Brooks, William D. 3322, 4792
Brose, Dorothy 3633
Brother Alexander 3095, 3323-3324, 4135
Broud, Richard C. 5111
Brown, Charles T. 497-498, 1116, 1587, 2441
Brown, C. W. 27
Brown, Frances 4497
Brown, Frank E. 5112
Brown, G. Victor 5113
Brown, Hazel L. 1868
Brown, J. A. C. 2194
Brown, Jackie L. 5013
Brown, Kenneth S.; and Kelly 5786

Brown, L. 5787
Brown, M. Ralph 2195
Brown, Ralph A. 3325
Brown, Ralph S., Jr. 5788
Brown, Robert 1643
Brown, Roger 2913
Brown, Steven R. 5716
Brown, W. 1450
Brown, Wayne E. 5374
Brownoski, J. 5661
Brownstein, Oscar L. 2028
Bruce, Lee 2781
Brumbaugh, Jesse F. 28, 1451
Brundin, A. S. 4398
Brundridge, Jerry A. 1096
Bruner, Jerome S.; Goodnow;
  and Austin 1442
Brunton, M. E. 1931
Bruntz, G. G. 5114
Brutian, George 1644
Bryant, Donald C. 1869, 2029-
  2030, 2196-2197, 2442, 2443,
  5115
Bryant, Donald C.; Brokett; and
  Becker 5888
Bryant, Russell 5375
Bryngelson, Bryng 3002
Buchanan, Bruce G.; and Church-
  man 1657
Buchanan, Paul S. 1645
Buck, Gertrude 204
Buck, Gertrude; and Mann 29
Buckham, John W. 242
Buckley, James M. 243-246
Buckley, William F., Jr. 4419
Buehler, Ezra Christian 499-
  502, 1000, 1332, 3096-3097,
  3193, 3326-3331, 3715-3723,
  3971, 4386, 4397, 4499-4500,
  5116
Buehler, Ezra Christian; and
  Johannesen 4110
Buell, James R. 5376
Bump, Malcolm A. 30
Bunch, David A. 4501
Burger, W. E. 5789
Burgess, Parke G. 491, 2326
Burke, Kenneth 2031, 2198
Burke, Kenneth W.; Diehl; and
  White 3101
Burke, Richard J. 1646
Burkowsky, Mitchell R. 1932
Burks, Don M. 2327, 2793

Burns, James M. 2861
Burns, Janette M. 503, 3749
Burrowes, Hillier M. 504-
  505, 867
Burrows, Albert H. 506, 3877
Bursack, Lois 5014
Bursch, James F. 507
Burtt, E. A. 1452
Burtt, Harold E. 2199
Burtt, Harold E.; and Falken-
  berg 2444
Busch, Francis X. 4317
Busse, Alvin C.; and Borden
  22
Butcher, Paul A. 3621
Butler, Harold E. 1870
Butler, J. D. 1647
Butler, J. F. 1049
Butler, Jack H. 2445
Button, Karl 2912
Buys, William E. 31, 3852,
  4136
Byers, Burton H. 508, 2794
Byker, Donald 1933

Cabat, Richard C. 3098
Cable, W. Arthur 3194, 3332,
  3634, 3972, 5377
Cady, T. C. 5790
Caffrey, Francis; and Clemens
  4508
Caffyn, Walter W. 4502
Cahalan, John C. 1648-1649
Cain, Catherine L. 5015
Cain, Earl R. 5378, 5524-
  5526
Cain, Earl R.; et al. 5889
Caldwell, Evelyn 320
Caldwell, Russell L. 5304
Callaghan, J. Calvin 1333,
  2446, 4708, 5379
Callahan, Charles W.; Walker;
  and Olsen 894
Callaway, Byron C. 4752
Callender, W. P., Jr. 509
Callison, Norman 321
Camden, Blanche 4503
Cameron, Donald J. 3333
Camp, Leon R. 4137, 5380
Camp, Leon R.; and McCroskey
  4877-4878
Campbell, Ernest Q. 2448

423

Campbell, George 282, 1885
Campbell, Gus W. 3334
Campbell, Karlyn K. 2200
Campbell, W. A. 1334
Campbell, William G. 4504
Canham, Erwin D. 854, 4418
Cannon, Martin A. 1117
Canopy, Williard B. 5607
Cantril, Hadley; and Allport 3085
Capaldi, Nicholas 5750
Capel, Robert B. 2795, 5016-5017
Capel, Robert B.; and Hayworth 79
Capp, Glenn R. 32, 322, 510, 521, 1136, 3003, 3195, 3335, 3336, 3973
Capp, Glenn R.; and Allen 451
Capp, Glenn R.; and Capp 33, 34
Capp, Glenn R.; and Courtney 42
Capp, Thelma R.; and Capp 33, 34
Care, N. S. 1650
Carey, Thomas J. 205
Carleton, William G. 511-513
Carlile, Clark S. 3337
Carlsmith, James M.; and Festinger 2869
Carlson, Fred S., Jr.; and O'Brien 4595
Carlson, H. S. 1453
Carlson, R. L. 4328a
Carmack, Paul A. 353, 1248, 3338, 3339, 4709, 5119, 5527
Carmack, Paul A.; and Crocker 2206
Carmack, Paul A.; and Randolph 3635, 5791
Carmack, William R., Jr. 424
Carmack, William R., Jr.; and Phifer 2449
Carmen, M. J. 514
Carnap, Rudolph 1454, 2914-2915
Carney, James D.; and Scheer 1455
Carpenter, Oliver C. 1001
Carpenter, Ronald H. 3004-3005
Carr, Clarence F.; and Stevens 35

Carr, Robert R. 4138
Carrell, Martha 515
Carrino, Elnora 1934
Carroll, Herbert A. 5120
Carson, David 491
Carson, Ralph M. 4387
Carter, Elton S. 1588
Carter, Jack 3177
Carter, Reginald 3240, 4793-4794
Cartier, Francis A. 2450
Cartwright, R. S. 5304
Case, Keith 36
Case, Theodore 5381
Casey, Ralph D.; Smith; and Lasswell 5897, 5907
Casey, William J. 4139, 5382
Cashman, P. H.; and Shepard 154
Cass, Frank H. 5121
Cassirer, Ernst 2916
Castell, Alburey 1456
Castell, John L. 1651
Caswell, George 516
Cate, Roscoe 5122
Cathcart, Robert S. 1335, 2328, 3006, 3341
Cathcart, Robert S.; and Church 1656
Centore, F. F. 1652
Cerino, Dorothy V. 1935
Cervin, V. B.; and Henderson 2451
Cessna, R. W. 517
Chafee, Zechariah, Jr. 518
Chaffe, Edith T. 4660
Chaffee, Steven H. 5792
Chaffin, William W. 3974
Chamberlain, Austen 302, 4140
Chambers, George F. 4661
Chambers, Mildred E. 3343
Champ, Beulah G. 5018
Champlin, Carrol D. 4505
Chapel, Ralph E. 2329
Chapin, Leland 3636
Chapman, F. M.; and Henle 1457
Chapman, Hugh H., Jr. 2452
Charlton, Kenneth 1871
Chase, Stuart 1458, 2917-2918
Chastian, Charlotte 4506
Chattopadhyaya, Debiprasad 1653

Chen, William K. C. 2453
Cheng, Chung-Ying 1654
Chenoweth, Eugene C. 37-38,
1118-1119, 3724, 4259, 4507,
4795
Chenoweth, Eugene C.; and Good
4388
Cherne, Kenneth R.; and East
4430
Chesebro, James W. 1120-
1121, 2796
Chesebro, James W.; Brock;
Cragan; and Klumpp 1084
Chester, Giraud 5383, 5528
Chesterton, Cecil 520
Childs, Harwood L. 5890
Childs, Ralph D.; and Koch
1655
Chisholm, R. 1459
Choy, Timothy Y. C. 5384
Christensen, N. E. 2919
Christian, Orville F. 4260
Christian, William K. 1936
Christie, G. C. 1122
Christopher, Warren; and Julber
4272
Christopherson, Merrill G. 522,
3007-3008, 4796
Christopherson, Myrvin F. 2772
Church, Carrie E. 523
Church, David A.; and Cathcart
1656
Church, Russell T. 3725
Churchill, George B. 5124
Churchman, C. West 5632
Churchman, C. West; and
Buchanan 1657
Cicero, Marcus T. 283-285
Claggett, Harlow M. 5019
Clark, Alvan W. 5923
Clark, Anthony J. 2330
Clark, Carolyn 5020
Clark, Donald L. 354-355,
1872
Clark, Fred G. 2201
Clark, G. A., Jr. 5125
Clark, Glenn 4161, 5348
Clark, Lydia 5026
Clark, Patricia A. 3178
Clark, Robert D. 524-525,
4141-4142
Clark, Ruth A.; and Hynes 5717
Clark, Ruth A.; Williams; and

Webb 5341
Clark, Ruth A.; Wood; and Wil-
lians 4973
Clark, Solomon H. 4143
Clark, William K. 4797
Clarke, Edwin L. 1460
Clarke, Martin L. 356, 1873
Clarke, Peter; and James 2454
Clarke, Presley W. 3196
Clausen, Bernard C. 866
Cleary, James W. 425, 1123,
3344, 4711, 5924
Cleary, James W.; and Haber-
man 5891
Cleary, James W.; and Shearer
5925
Cleave, J. P. 1658
Clemens, Richard; and Caffrey
4508
Clevenger, Theodore, Jr. 526,
2202, 3099, 4798
Clevenger, Theodore, Jr.; and
Anderson 2406
Clevenger, Theodore, Jr.; and
King 4799
Clevenger, Theodore, Jr.; and
Knepprath 5565
Cloer, Roberta K. 1937
Cobin, Martin 4144-4146
Cockerham, Louis W. 1589,
1938
Coffa, J. Alberto 1659
Coffee, Thomas G. 527
Coffield, Martha E. 5021
Coffman, George R. 5128
Cohen, Arthur R. 2203, 4800
Cohen, Herman 1939, 2032,
2157
Cohen, Herman; and Nobles 780
Cohen, Herman; Sikkink; and
Richards 4078
Cohen, Morris R. 1461
Cohen, Morris R.; and Nagel
1462
Cohn, G. Bernard 2797
Colbourn, Frank E. 39
Colburn, C. William 39a
Colburn, C. William; and Bauer
3964, 4782
Cole, John D. 3345
Cole, Nancy 528
Cole, Terry 1590
Coleman, E. B. 3009

425

Coleman, G. W. 4509
Colister, E. G., Jr. 1336
Collie, M. J. 2455
Collier, Christopher 1337
Collins, George R. 2456, 3197
Collins, George R.; and Morris 40
Collins, Sherod J. 4510
Colston, John R. 206
Colum, Padraic 2033
Columbia Associates in Philosophy 1462
Combs, Walter H.; and McCroskey 1765
Commager, Henry S. 4432, 5530
Comstock, Alzada 531
Conant, James B. 532
Condon, John C. 2920
Conger, (Mrs.) Edwin 4511
Conger, Maybelle 4147
Conklin, Forrest, 5926
Conklin, Royal F. 3944
Connelly, Robert E. 491, 2888
Constans, H. P. 3975
Cook, John W. 5793
Cook, Joseph 3350
Cook, Thomas D. 2457
Cook, Walter W. 1660-1661
Cooke, Peter J. 207
Cooley, Roger W. 1085
Cooper, Lane 2034
Cooper, Lean M.; and Konigsberg 5130
Coors, D. Stanley 533, 866
Cope, E. M. 286
Copi, Irving M. 1464
Corbett, Edward P. J. 2204
Corbett, Edward P. J.; and Golden 1885
Corbett, H. G. 4512
Cordell, Christobel M. 534, 927, 2798, 5131, 5794
Corder, Jim W. 2205, 5531
Corder, Kenneth W. 4801
Cordier, Hubert V. 4364
Corey, Kathy 1050
Cornblath, N. 861
Cornelius, Asher L. 4318
Cornell, David C. 4419
Cortelyou, E. H. 3351
Cortright, Rupert L. 535, 3352, 3731, 3976, 5132

Cortright, Rupert L.; and O'Neill 129
Cosper, Russell 41
Costello, Charles S. 2331
Costigan, J. 1124
Costley, Dan L. 2332
Cote, Letha J. 4115, 5133
Coulter, E. Merton 300
Courter, Gene W. 426
Courtney, Luther W.; and Capp 42
Cousins, R. B. 536
Covelli, Eugene F. 3353-3354
Covey, Frank M., Jr. 5532
Covington, Harry F. 43-45, 2458
Cowan, Phillip A.; Weber; Hodinott; and Klein 2459
Cowden, D. J.; and Croxton 1275
Cowell, Ray 4262
Cowles, Robert 3637
Cowperthwaite, Lowery L. 323
Cozens, Roger 4419
Cradock, P. 4397
Cragan, John F.; Brock; Chesebro; and Klumpp 1084
Cragan, John F.; and Shields 1125
Craig, Asa H. 208
Craig, Asa H.; and Edgerton 1126, 5608
Crampton, Angela C. 2862
Crane, Ben 4389
Crane, Edgar 2460
Crane, Loren D. 2461
Crane, Wilder W., Jr. 537
Crawford, C. C.; and Michael 3140
Crawford, John W. 1940
Crawford, Richard J. 928, 3977
Creedon, J. J. 5134
Creighton, J. E. 1465
Creighton, J. E.; and Smart 1466
Cripe, Nicholas 2863, 3355-3357, 3732
Cripe, Nicholas; and McBath 3138
Cripe, Nicholas; and Walwik 929
Crocker, Lionel 46, 47, 538-

547, 1340, 1874, 2206, 2462-
2463, 2799-2801, 3358, 3880,
3978, 4712, 4802, 5349
Cromwell, Harvey 548-551,
1014, 1250, 2464-2467, 3733,
4148, 5795
Cronen, Vernon E. 552-553,
1128, 5385
Cronin, Michael W. 1591
Cronkhite, Gary L. 930, 1662,
2207, 2468-2469
Cross, Edward W. 866
Cross, Ira B. 866
Cross, Lois 5386
Crow, Stan 5796
Croxton, F. E.; and Cowden
1275
Crump, James I.; and Dreher
2037
Cruzan, Rose M. 4662
Cryan, Mary E. 2333
Cullison, A. D. 1129
Culp, Ormond S. 554
Culp, Richard 555
Cunningham, C. C. 4803
Cunningham, J. V. 2802
Curry, E. Thayer 5022
Curry, Herbert L. 556, 4149,
5387
Curry, Mary B 5023
Curtis, H. S. 3359
Cushing, Luther S. 4663
Cypher, Patricia M. 1592

Dabbs, James M.; and Albert
2401
Dagget, Naphthali 301
Dahl, Norman O. 1051
Dahl, Robert A. 5662
Dahlberg, W. A. 557, 3360, 5135
Dahlstrom, Carl 2803
Daily, R. C. 4804
Daley, Lowrie J. 1875
Daley, Mason G. 5533
Damon, Verne L. 5136
Danberg, Neil 3638
Dance, Frank E. X. 3021
d'Angelo, Gary 1663
Daniel, David W.; and Bradley 25
Danner, Vernice E. 5609
Darnell, Donald K. 3010
Dause, Charles A. 5534

Dause, Charles A.; and Seltzer
3639
Davidson, Carter 4418
Davidson, Donald 1664
Davidson, Donald; and Vendler
1665
Davidson, Henry A. 4664
Davidson, Hugh M. 1876
Davies, John 5137
Davis, Barrett 558, 631, 3361
Davis, Frank B. 357, 3622
Davis, H. N. 4514
Davis, Henry C.; and Smith 48
Davis, James D. 3362
Davis, Margaret; and Ross 980
Davis, Robert E. 4701
Davis, Wayne E. 4390
Davis, William H. 49, 559-561,
4150, 4713, 4805
Day, Dennis G. 2334, 2470,
2804
Dean, Nancy S. 3282
Dean, Richard L. 3979, 5388
Dearin, Ray D. 2471
De Armond, Frederick F. 2208
De Boer, Halle G. 187
De Boer, Ray L. 4152
Dedmon, Donald N. 5389, 5536
Dee, James P. 3366, 5797
Deering, Ivah E. 52
de Haan, Henry; Thistelthwaite;
and Kamenetzky 2712
De Haven, Jean 5390
Delia, Jesse G. 1666
Dell, George W. 2865
Delozier, (Sister) Mary L. 4753
Delozier, (Sister) Mary L.;
Klopf; and Evans 4853-4854
De Marco, Norman; and Towns
5969
De Marco, Norman; Eubanks;
and Towns 5970
Demarest, Theodore 1467
Demeter, George C. 4665
Demetrius 1877-1879
De Morgan, A. 1468
Demos, Raphael 2472
De Mougeot, William R. 1052,
2335, 5391
Denney, Joseph; Duncan; and
McKinney 53
Dennis, W. C. 4153
Denny, George V., Jr. 4515

Durkee, J. Stanley 572
Durkin, Helen E. 1135
Dutton, Joseph 361
Dwight, Charles A. S. 1673
Dwight, Theodore, Jr. 209
Dwyer, Charles A. 4811
Dye, Maxine 3739
Dyke, C. 5664

Eagly, Alice H. 5803
Eakins, Barbara 2039
Earney, Michael D. 188
East, James R. 1942
East, James R.; and Cherne 4430
East, James R.; and Murphy 3491
Eaton, R. M. 1476
Eckert, Ralph G. 4260
Ecrayd, Donald H. 189
Eddy, P. 1853
Edelman, Murray 5634
Edgerton, Alice C.; and Craig 1126, 5608
Edney, Clarence W. 1674, 1943, 3373
Edwares, A. L. 2477
Edwards, Allen; and Kilpatrick 2478
Edwards, G. V. 4156
Edwards, Paul 2922
Edwards, William A. 1882
Eggeling, Rae 3179
Ehninger, Douglas 489, 573-576, 1675, 1944, 2212, 2040-2046, 2479-2480, 2866, 3274, 4395, 5932
Ehninger, Douglas; and Brock-riede, 56, 1644
Ehninger, Douglas; and Graham 4524
Ehninger, Douglas; and Smith 399
Ehrensberger, Ray 2337, 2481
Ehrlich, J. W. 4334
Ehrlich, Larry G. 577
Ehrsam, Theodore G. 578
Eichmeier, Herman C. 1097
Einerson, Mary L. 3375
Eisenberg, Abne M.; and Ilards 57
Eisenberg, J. A. 1676

Eisenberg, Meyer 2867
Eisenson, Jon 3074
Eisenson, Jon; Aver; and Irwin 2213
Eisenstadt, Arthur 580-581
Eldridge, Mabel E. 5610
Elms, Alan C. 5806
Ellery, John B. 3376
Elliott, Phyllis J. 5027
Ellis, A. Carroll 2807
Ellis, B. D. 1677
Ellis, Carroll B. 3377, 5394, 5538
Ellis, Dean S. 5804
Ellis, Dean S.; and Frank 5805
Ellis, Dean S.; and Minter 4812
Elsen, William J. 3883
Ely, Mary L. 4525
Emerson, James G. 362-363, 1137
Emery, Emogene 3378
Emery, V. J. 250
Emery, Walter B. 3643, 4435
Emperor, John B. 582, 3379
Empson, William 2923
Emswiler, Thomas, Jr. 3015
Endsley, Lorraine 583
Engdahl, Lynn H. 5395
England, Frank 584
Engleman, Buryl F. 5145
English, C. D. 251
English, W. Francis 3103, 5303
Enholm, Donald K. 1243
Eppinga, Peter L. 3104
Epstein, Fanny 5665
Epstein, Seymour; and Taylor 5807
Erasmus 2076
Erhart, Joseph F. X. 3105
Erickson, Keith 3380
Erickson, Richard O. 1595
Ericson, Jon M.; and Murphy 119
Erlanger, Howard S. 5933
Ernest, Carole H. 2482
Erskine, William C. 4813
Ertle, Charles 2338
Ertzman, Carol 5396
Esch, Marvin L. 4754
Esch, Marvin L.; and Ziegel-mueller 3381
Eskridge, James B. 1883

Ettlich, Ernest 2047-2048, 2157
Eubank, Wayne C. 1136, 3382, 3740, 4397
Eubank, Wayne C.; and Owens 4157
Eubanks, Ralph T.; and Baker 2483, 5934
Eubanks, Ralph T.; Baker; and Golden 5935
Eubanks, Ralph T.; De Marco; and Towns 5970
Eulalia, (Sister) Mary 3106, 3383
Evans, Charles F., Jr. 585, 3644
Evans, Diane R. 4755
Evans, Diane R.; Klopf; and De Lozier 4853-4854
Evans, D. L.; and Gamerts-felder 1477
Evans, Edward H. 3384
Evans, Robert O.; and Patrick 2958
Evans, Robert W. 5028, 5146
Evenson, Judy 3645
Everett, G. A.; and Phipps 58
Everhart, Rodney W. 4714
Eversule, Frank L. 4526
Ewbank, Henry L. 364, 586-592, 1138, 3646, 3741, 3884-3885, 4814, 5937
Ewbank, Henry L.; and Aver 59, 593
Ewbank, Henry L., Jr. 2808, 3385
Ewing, T. N. 2484

Fabrizio, Ray; Karas; and Men-muir 5751
Fadely, L. Dean 1139
Fairbanks, Grant; Guttman; and Miron 3108-3110
Fairbanks, Grant; and Kodman 3107
Falkenberg, D. B.; and Burtt 2444
Faries, Clyde J. 3111
Fariley, John A. 303
Fariley, William B.; and Finklestein 1347
Faris, Ellsworth 2214

Farley, Fern 4756
Farnham, Joseph R. 1098
Farnsworth, P. R.; and Saadi 2671
Fatherson, Elizabeth; Thonssen; and Thonssen 5909
Faules, Donald F. 1252, 3284
Faules, Donald F.; and Rieke 3279
Fausti, Remo P. 594, 3945
Fausti, Remo P.; and Miller 115
Favel, William 5147
Fawcett, Harold P. 1679
Faxon, Glen S. 595
Fay, Paul J.; and Middleton 3112-3114
Fearnside, W. Ward; and Holther 1478
Feather, N. T.; and Armstrong 2485
Feather, N. T.; and Jeffries 2486
Feigel, Jerry D. 1680
Fenner, Frances 596
Ferguson, C. L. 304
Feris, F. F. 597
Fernandez, Thomas L. 4159
Ferris, Frances 4527
Ferris, Millicent M. 4116
Ferson, Merton L. 3743
Feshbach, S.; and Janis 2544
Fest, Thorrel B. 598-601, 936, 2487, 2868, 3386-3387, 3744, 4160
Fest, Thorrel B.; and Nelson 3497-3499
Fest, Thorrel B.; and Schind-ler 602
Festinger, Leon 2215
Festinger, Leon; and Carlsmith 2869
Festinger, Leon; and Walster 2741
Fieg, Eugene, Jr. 4161
Field, Peter B.; and Janis 2545
Fieldman, Steven O.; and Brock 4258
Fields, Marsh 427
Files, J. Ray 3745
Finfgeld, Thomas E. 3016
Fink, Cornelius W. 603, 1131,

4364
Finklestein, Michael O.; and Fairley 1347
Finley, G. W. 937-938, 5611
Firth, R. 5720
Fischer, David H. 1479
Fisher, B. Aubrey 2049, 5650, 5666-5667
Fisher, Walter 1681, 2488-2489, 3017, 3985, 5397
Fishbein, M.; and Raven 5721
Fiske, George C.; and Grant 1884
Fitzpatrick, John R. 5539
Flemming, Edwin G. 2050
Flesch, Rudolph 1480, 2924
Fletcher, G. P. 1140-1141, 5808
Flew, A. G. N. 2925
Florer, J. H. 5540
Florey, Elizabeth B. 4419
Flynn, Lawrence J. 2051, 2809
Flynt, Wayne 2810
Fogelin, Robert J. 1276, 1682
Foley, George, Jr. 5809
Fordham, E. W. 4319
Forston, Robert F. 5651
Fort, Lyman M. 60-61
Foster, George M. 1099
Foster, Teddy J. 1596, 5913
Foster, William H. 62
Foster, William T. 63-64, 3388, 4418
Fotheringham, Wallace C. 1348-1349, 2216, 4815
Foulke, E.; and Sticht 3115
Foulkes, William R. 605
Fouts, Kenneth B. 4162-4163
Fowler, Russell 3018
Fox, Albert 5148
Fox, Andrew N. 65
Fox, Helen; and Roberts 4303
Fox, Wayne 606
Fractenberg, David; and Kendall 950
Francke, Donald C. 5810
Frandsen, Kenneth D.; and Phillips 3522
Frank, Erick; and Ellis 5805
Frank, Glenn 607
Frank, Jerome D. 2489, 5635
Franklin, Benjamin 608
Franzke, A. L.; and Orr 4292

Franzwa, Helen H. 2985, 3019
Frase, Lawrence T. 1683
Fraser, Malcolm P.; Theios; and Berman 5658
Frederick, Felix 3624
Frederick, W. J.; and Wilcox 4986
Fredrich, Gustav W. 4325
Freeburg, Victor O. 3389
Freedman, Leonard 5752
Freedman, Philip I 2491
Freeley, Austin J. 66, 609-610, 854, 939-941, 3390-3395, 3746-3748, 3986-3988, 4164, 4530, 5541-5542, 5811
Freeman, William M.; and Abbott 4666
Freeth, D. K. 4397
French, Warren G. 2870
Freshley, Dwight L. 1053, 1142-1143, 3749, 3989, 4335, 4816, 5543
Fretwell, E. K. 611
Frick, F.; and Janis 1719
Fried, Edrita 2492
Fried, Esther 1597
Friedman, Leon 5350
Friedman, N. 1684
Friedman, Robert P. 3020, 3647, 4817-4818
Frieze, Henry S. 287
Fritz, Charles A. 67-68
Frizzell, John H. 3750-3751, 4531-4532
Fromm, Eric 2773
Fruin, Anthony T. 3648
Frye, A. M.; and Levi 1481
Fuchs, Grover A. 3887
Fuge, Lloyd H.; and Newman 4336
Fulkerson, Richard 3396
Fulton, R. Barry 2493
Funk, Alfred A. 2811
Furbay, Albert L. 2494
Furtado, Manuel 612

Gabbard, Anne S. 5812
Gabbard, William R. 3990
Gabriel, Charles 2339
Gaffney, Matthew W. 4533
Gage, L. J. 4534
Gagnon, V. N. 5668

Gain, Earl 5544
Gair, H. A. 4337
Gallagher, F. X. 1100
Gallagher, Michael R. 5813
Gallagher, William 4320
Gamertsfelder, W. S.; and Evans 1477
Gamson, William 5636
Gans, A. F.; and Rheingold 5861
Gantt, Vernon 2340, 2782
Gard, Willis L. 2495
Gardiner, John H. 69
Gardner, Bertha L. 5149
Garland, J. V. 1350, 3397
Garn, Harvey A. 1144
Garnett, Donald T. 5029
Garrett, H. E. 1277
Garrett, J. 861
Garrison, Stewart L.; and Stone 169
Gartland, Henry J. 1351
Garvey, Neil F. 4535
Gasink, Warren A. 1685, 3398
Gates, Thomas S. 614
Gavin, Tif 3649
Geary, (Sister) Theophane 3203
Gellner, Ernest 2926
Gelvin, Elizabeth D. 3861
Genung, John F. 288-290, 2217
George, Geneva P. 5398
Gerard, Harold 5669
Gerard, W. A. 2052
Getchell, Charles M. 5938
Giannon, Carlo 1686
Gibbons, Frederick
Gibbs, Gwendolyn E. 5030
Gibson, Boyce 1687
Gibson, George M. 615
Gibson, Harold E. 1145, 1241, 1253-1256, 1688, 3991
Gibson, Harold E.; and Sheppard 4987
Gibson, James 616, 2341, 3021, 4757, 5150
Gibson, James W.; Gruner; and Kibler 3026
Gibson, James W.; and Kibler 5939
Gibson, Laurence M. 70
Gietzen, Albin J. 1945
Giffin, Kim 617, 2496, 4820
Giffin, Kim; and Blubaugh 3399
Giffin, Kim; and Brockriede 3970
Giffin, Kim; and Lashbrook 3992-3994, 4022
Giffin, Kim; and Linkugel 618, 3995
Giffin, Kim; and McKee 1352
Giffin, Kim; and Megill 1146-1147, 3996
Giffin, Kim; and Rhea 3997
Giffin, Kim; and Roever 4928
Giffin, Kim; and Warner 2497, 4821
Gilbart, James W. 269
Gilbert, Aimie 3400
Gilbert, Edna 4165-4166
Gilbert, Russell W. 3116
Gilchrist, Mary D. 5399
Giles, Leona H. 365
Gilkinson, Howard S. 2497, 4322, 5940
Gilkinson, Howard S.; Paulson; and Sikkink 2499, 3022
Gillen, (Mrs.) Richard D. 2853
Gillis, Herbert R. 324, 5941
Gilman, Wilbur E. 1689, 3401
Gipson, Lawrence H. 5545
Gislason, Haldor B. 71, 2500, 3402, 3650
Glasgow, George M. 3117
Glenn, Norval D. 1353
Glenn, Robert 1946
Glossop, Ronald J. 1054
Glover, Samuel 1006
Goedecke, Robert 5814
Goetz, Emily 2342
Goetzinger, Charles 3403, 4636, 5400
Goguen, J. A. 1690
Goldberg, Murray A. 620
Golden, Burton W.; and Aronson 2408
Golden, James L. 1947, 2053-2054, 4167
Golden, James L.; and Corbett 1885
Golden, James L.; Eubanks; and Baker 5935
Goldfarb, Howard E. 4419
Goldman, Robert 3285
Goldman, Sheldon 5815
Goldstein, Irving 4321
Goldstein, J. H.; and Rosnow 2664

Goldstein, Stephen; and Kaufmann 1727
Goldstein, Walter 4436
Gonchar, Ruth M. 2501, 5401
Gonzalez, Frank S. H. 3080
Good, I. J. 1691
Good, Voieja Z. ; and Chenoweth 4388
Goodfellow, Donald M. 2055
Goodman, C. ; and Schanck 2678
Goodman, Louis S. 4537
Goodman-Malamuth, Leo 3081
Goodnow, Jacqueline J. ; Bruner; and Austin 1442
Goodure, W. S. 5816
Goodwin, Fred B. 3404, 4168
Goolsby, T. M. , Jr. 5817
Gorden, William I. 3118, 5670
Gordon, Albert I. 72
Gordon, Dorothy 4538
Gordon, Elizabeth M. 2986
Gordon, Harry E. 3753-3754
Gordon, Robert I. 5818
Gordon, Robert I. ; and Temerlin 5819
Gordy, J. P. 252
Gore, James H. 211
Gorman, Margaret 3023
Gorst, J. E. 4539
Gosling, Thomas W. 5151
Goss, Blaine 2343
Gough, Harry B. 1148, 2871, 3998, 5546
Goulding, Daniel J. 1692, 5547, 5820
Gouran, Denis S. 2502, 5652
Gow, John E. 3899, 4169
Grady, C. E. 4238, 5152
Graham, Burdette; and Strubinger 4170
Graham, Donald L. 4823
Graham, Gladys M. 621, 1693-1698, 2503, 4239, 5548
Graham, John 622-23, 3204, 3405
Graham, Mary W. 325, 942
Graham, Mary W.; and Ehninger 4524
Graham, W. B. 1149, 5153
Grandy, Adah G. 3205
Granneberg, Audrey G.; and Menefee 2605
Grannell, Lee E. 624
Grant, Alexander 291

Grant, C. K. 3024
Grant, David M. 4171
Grant, Mary A.; and Fiske 1884
Grant, Percy S. 4540-4542
Grant, W. B. 2872
Grant, W. Leonard 2812
Graunke, Dean F. 3651
Graves, Harold F. 73, 2504
Graves, Harold F.; and Bowman 2218
Graves, Harold F.; and O'Brien 1699
Graves, Harold F.; and Oldsey 74
Graves, Harold F.; and Spotts 75
Graves, R. D. 5154
Graves, Wallace 2056, 2158, 2219
Gravholt, Loy E. 5031
Gray, C. T.; and Votaw 1278
Gray, Clifton D. 625
Gray, Giles W. 2505-2506, 3119, 4716-4718, 5155, 5821, 5894, 5942
Gray, Giles W.; and Bagenstos 5156
Gray, J. Stanley 4340
Gray, John W.; and Rea 4667, 4739
Greaves, Halbert S.; and Rarig 3811
Green, Charles P. 2344
Green, Clarence 626
Green, E. W. 305
Green, Mark 1007
Green, Thomas F. , Jr. 1354
Greenagel, Heather A. 5402
Greenberg, Bradley S.; and Mc-Ewan 2597
Greenberg, Bradley S.; and Miller 2057
Greene, Guys 5157
Greene, Harry W. 5403
Greenough, J. B.; and Kittredge 2927
Greenwald, Anthony G. 2508, 2873
Greenwood, James G. 2057
Greg, John B. 1597a
Gregg, Fred M. 4668, 4719
Gregg, Richard B. 1309, 1355,

1700, 2058
Gregory, Joshua 2509
Gregory, Joyce R. 4824
Gregory, Kathleen M. 3025
Grether, Ewald T. 627, 4825
Griffin, Floyd J., Jr. 4000
Griffin, Robert S. 2345
Griffin, Whitmore 628
Griffin, Wycliffe 1053
Griffith, Coleman R. 4341
Griffith, J. A. G. 5822
Griffiths, A. Phillips 5700, 5722
Grimmer, Betty B. 3286
Grisdorf, Georges 2774
Grisez, Germain G. 2813
Grissinger, James A. 2346, 2510
Grissom, Mary A. 1101
Gronbeck, Bruce E. 1055, 1102, 2059, 3206, 5404
Gronow, Jukka; and Hilppo 5823
Grosman, Brian A. 4342, 5824
Gross, Bertram W. 5405
Grossman, Joel B. 5825
Grover, David H. 5351, 5406
Gruder, Charles L.; Miller; Rousseau; and Schopler 3554
Gruner, Charles R. 2511-2513, 5032
Gruner, Charles R.; Huseman; and Luck 629
Gruner, Charles R.; Huseman; and Ware 672
Gruner, Charles R.; Kibler; and Gibson 3026
Gruner, Charles R.; and Willett 1272
Gruner, Rolf 1701-1702
Guilford, J. P. 1279-1280
Guiliani, Allesandro 2514
Guiou, Trula 4001
Gulley, Halbert 76, 630, 2347, 3406
Gulley, Halbert; and Berlo 2422
Gunderson, Robert G. 366, 3207
Guptill, Charles H. 4298
Guterman, Norbert; and Lowenthal 2254
Guthrie, Warren A. 1948, 2060, 3652, 4263, 4437
Gutmans, Theodore M. 4543

Guttman, Newman; Fairbanks; and Miron 3108-3110
Gwin, Stanford P. 5549
Gwynn, Aubrey O. 1886

Haakenson, Robert 631, 1150, 3307, 4438-4439, 4826
Haarhoff, Theodore 1887
Haberman, Frederick W. 2061, 5943
Haberman, Frederick W.; and Cleary 5891
Haberman, Frederick W.; and Shearer 5963
Hack, Roy K. 2062
Hackett, William A. 3408
Hadaller, J. A. 4827
Hade, William T. 3755
Hagan, Michael R. 2515, 5550
Hagie, C. E. 5158
Hagood, Annabel D. 489, 3756-3757
Haiman, Franklyn S. 632, 2348, 2814-2815, 3120, 4544, 5753
Haitema, John S. 2816
Hale, Edward E., Jr. 2063
Hale, Judith C.; and Hope 4179
Hale, Mabel M. 5033
Hale, Robert 633, 5826
Hall, Alta B. 4720
Hall, Alta B.; and Sturgis 4669, 4721
Hall, Charles C. 212
Halladay, John 634
Halle, Louis J. 2516
Halley, Donald L.; and Jamison 4440
Halley, Richard D. 2349
Hallie, P. P. 3027
Halstead, William P. 4828
Hamblin, Charles L. 1482
Hamburg, John H. 3028
Hamilton, H. W. 3409
Hamilton, Mary E. 1131, 5034
Hamilton, Peter K. 2987
Hamilton, William W. 270, 4364, 4670
Hammond, Lewis M. 2517
Hampshire, S. 5637
Hampshire, S.; and Hart 5672

434

Hanawalt, Dorothy 3758
Hance, Kenneth G. 635-637, 1949, 2064, 3121, 3208, 3759, 4343
Hancher, Virgil M. 638, 4418
Haney, Thomas K. 77
Haney, William V. 2350
Hanks, L. D. 639, 3410-3411
Hanley, Chuck 5159
Hannum, Elizabeth C. 4988
Hansen, Edna 2351
Hansen, Howard C. 4441-4442
Hansen, John D. 944, 3902, 4264
Hansen, Malvin L. 3760
Hansen, Merrill C. 5407
Hansen, Norman J. 2352
Hanson, Roger A. 5671
Happe, R. J. 5160
Harding, Harold F. 640, 1950, 2060, 3122, 4265
Harding, Harold F.; and Utterback 1845, 2518
Harding, Harold F., Jr. 641
Hardy, William G.; and Jones 3653
Hare, R. M. 915
Hargis, Donald E. 1356, 4003, 5551
Harkins, William E. 3412
Harkness, P. J. 1257, 3313
Harlan, Roy E. 78
Harmon, Carol 3209
Harms, L. S. 2519, 3123
Harms, L. S.; and Dunham 5893
Harries, O. 1151
Harrington, Elbert W. 642, 2220, 2520-2521, 3414, 5161
Harrington, Frederic C. 5162
Harris, Albert M. 1357
Harris, James F. 1703
Harris, Kenneth 4370, 4399
Harris, Kenneth; Benn; and Boyle 4378
Harris, Robert T.; and Jarrett 2928
Harris, Seymour E. 854
Harris, Therman G. 4172, 5163-5164
Harris, Thomas E.; and Smith 643
Harrison, Carolyn P. 326
Harrison, Frederic 4722

Harshbarger, H. C. 644
Hart, Albert B. 999
Hart, Albert B.; and Baker 213
Hart, H. L. A.; and Hampshire 5672
Hart, Hubert N. 5165
Hart, Peter 1358
Harte, Thomas B. 1310, 1359
Harter, D. Lincoln; and Sullivan 2221
Hartman, Maryann 5035
Hartmann, George W. 2522, 2523
Hartwell, Charles S. 5166
Hartwell, E. C. 5167
Harvey, C. C. 4545
Harvey, Donald J.; and Wilder 5696
Harvey, Jan 2222
Harvey, P. Casper 4829
Harwood, Kenneth A. 3124-3125
Hasbettler, Gordon A. 3129
Hastings, Arthur 1056, 1598, 3029, 3210
Hastings, Arthur; and Windes 183
Haston, Bruce M. 3287, 4004, 4830
Hatch, R. W. 3211
Hatch, Robert D. 5408
Hatcher, Caro C. 1026, 3655
Hatlen, Theodore 3126
Hausman, Alan 1704
Hawkins, Gary J.; and Sereno 2691
Hawley, Edward W. 4671
Hay, D. 2524
Hay, Denys 306
Hayakawa, S. I. 2929-2932
Hayden, F. S. 4547
Hayes, Harold B. 2353
Hayes, Merwyn A. 5409
Hayes, Merwyn A.; and Anderson 5507
Hayes, Merwyn A.; and Huseman 5827
Hayes, Michael T.; and McAdoo 4831
Hayhurst, J. S. 645
Haythorn, William W.; and Altman 3294

435

Hayworth, Donald 3315-3316
Hayworth, Donald; and Capel 79
Hazlett, Henry 1483
Hazzard, J. C. 3417
Healy, Alice 1053
Hearn, Thomas K., Jr. 5723
Heckman, Richard A. 5352
Hedeman, Richard A. 5410
Hefferline, Ralph F. 2817
Heidbreder, E. F. 1705
Heidelberger, Herbert 1706-1707
Heider, Fritz 5701, 5724
Heidt, Raymond 1599
Heinberg, Paul 2525, 3127
Heisey, D. Ray 2526, 3212
Helgesen, Charles R. 5036
Heller, John L. 2066
Hellerich, Mahlon H. 646, 3213
Hellman, Hugo E. 647-648, 945, 1057-1061, 1152, 1360, 3656, 3761, 3888, 4173
Hellman, J. C. 3418
Helm, George M.; and Shurter 159
Hemmer, James J., Jr. 5552
Hempstead, Walter E., Jr. 3419
Henderson, G. P.; and Cervin 2451
Henderson, John C. 5168
Henderson, Richard D. 649
Henderson, Ward G. 5828
Hendrix, Jerry A.; and Polisky 3240
Hendrix, Jerry A.; and Schiszik 4267
Henle, Mary 1708
Henle, P.; and Chapman 1457
Henning, J. H. 1103, 4006
Henning, William C. 3762
Henrikson, E. H. 4174, 4832
Henry, David D. 854
Henry, William H. F. 214
Henry, William H. F.; and Seeley 4672
Hensley, Wayne E. 3420, 5169-5170
Hensley, Wayne E.; and Murphy 4888
Hensley, Wayne E.; and Strother 3421
Hepp, Maylon H. 1484
Herklots, Hugh G. G. 4400

Herrick, Marvin T. 2067
Hertzman, Max; Asch; and Block 2411
Herzog, E. G. 1153
Hesler, J. Gordon 1154
Heslin, Richard; and Streufert 5673
Hess, Maurice 3214
Hess, Myron D. 5037
Hester, J. Gordon 3422
Hetlinger, Duane F.; and Hildreth 650
Hettinger, E. 2354
Heun, Richard E. 5653
Hewgill, Murray A.; and Miller 2607
Hewlett, Marilyn N. 1951
Hibbon, J. G. 1485
Hicks, Philip M. 652, 3657
Hicks, Wreatha 327
Higgins, Albert J., Jr. 190
Higgins, Howard H. 2223, 2527-2529
Higgins, Roger W. 5171
High, Stanley 4548
Highfill, F. J. 5072
Highlander, John P.; and Watkins 5553
Highshaw, James L. 5173
Hildebrandt, Herbert W. 2068
Hildebrandt, Herbert W.; and Stevens 3128
Hildreth, Richard A. 1952, 2355, 3423-3424
Hildreth, Richard A.; and Hetlinger 650
Hill, Adam S. 292-293
Hill, Charles L. 1953
Hill, David J. 2224
Hill, Forbes I. 2933
Hill, J. Newton 3425
Hill, Mary A. 5829
Hill, Didney R., Jr. 4833
Hillbruner, Anthony 2069
Hilliard, Otis L. 3215
Hilppo, Jorma; and Gronow 5823
Hinds, George L. 653, 4175
Hingston, Albert C.; Karl; Mahaffey; and Long 4032
Hinks, D. A. G. 2070
Hoag, C. G. 1709
Hobbes, Thomas 279

Hobbs, R. Paul 5303
Hochnuith, Marie 2530, 3426
Hodinott, B. A.; Cowan, Weber;
and Klein 2459
Hoffer 2225
Hogstrom, Harold R. 654
Holcomb, J. Rayfore 4176
Holcomb, Martin 521, 3766,
4758, 4834-4836
Holladay, Howard 655
Holland, Delbitte T. 4443
Holland, L. Virginia 1888,
1954
Hollander, Katherine R. 656,
3030
Hollingworth, H. L. 1062, 1486,
2226
Hollis, Christopher 4371
Hollister, R. O. T. 4836
Holm, James N. 80-83, 657-
658, 1710, 3427-3428, 3767,
3889, 4749, 4759, 4838-4840
Holm, James N.; and Kent 84-5
Holmes, F. Lincoln D. 5830
Holmes, Roger W. 1487
Holstein, George H. 3659
Holt, H. Q. 659
Holther, William B.; and Fearn-
side 1478
Holton, Robert F. 2783
Holtzman, Paul D. 2531
Holtzoff, A. 2818
Holyoke, George J. 215-216
Hoogestraat, Wayne E. 660,
4841
Hoogestraat, Wayne E.; and Mc-
Cleary 3031
Hoogestraat, Wayne E.; and
Sikkink 4673
Hook, J. N. 1711
Hook, Sidney 417, 2819
Hoover, Kenneth H. 661-662
Hope, Ben W. 1155, 4177-
4178, 5038
Hope, Ben W.; and Hale 4179
Hope, Walter E. 663
Hopkins, Arthur A. 3429, 5411
Hopkins, H. Dana 3768-3769,
4549
Hopkins, Jon 1132
Hopkins, Richard 5174
Hopkins, Thomas A. 1053,
2888, 4007

Horn, Gunnar 1361
Horn, Robert M. 5627
Hornady, C. 4550
Horrocks, John E. 664, 4244
Hoshor, John P. 1955-1956,
2532
Hospers, John 2934-2935
Hostettler, Gordon F. 1132,
1221, 3129-3330, 4080
Houck, Stanley B. 3670-3672
Houlgate, Laurence D. 5574
Hovland, Carl I. 2227
Hovland, C. I.; and Janis 2228
Hovland, C. I.; Janis; and Kelley
2229
Hovland, C. I.; and Kelman 2558
Hovland, C. I.; Lumsdaine; and
Sheffield 2230
Hovland, C. I.; and Mandell 2533
Hovland, C. I.; and Weiss 2534
Howard, D. D.; and Scott 2295
Howard, Hal 947
Howard, J. Woodford, Jr. 5575
Howe, Frank W. 4574
Howe, Jack 665, 948, 1362,
3908
Howell, Wilbur S. 1712, 1889-90,
2071-74, 2231, 2536, 2874
Howell, William S. 666-68,
1713, 3431, 4424, 5039,
5178-79
Howell, William S.; and Brem-
beck 2192
Howell, William S.; and Smith
850
Howell, William S.; Smith; and
Thompson 3755
Howes, Raymond F. 86, 1891,
2537-8, 3332-35, 3909, 4168,
4301-2, 4742, 4843, 5080
Howett, L. C.; and O'Connor
5081
Hubbeling, H. G. 1063
Huber, Paul 1957
Huber, Robert 87, 1136, 1156,
3673-3674, 4081, 5454
Huber, Walter G. 2875
Huby, Pamela M. 2075
Hudson, Hoyt H. 2076-2078,
2539-2540
Hudson, Hoyt H.; and Reeves
147
Hudson, Hoyt H.; and Winans

181
Hudson, Roy F. 1714, 2079, 5455
Hudson-Williams, H. L. I. 2080
Huebner, Lee W. 669
Huesemann, Theodore, Jr. 5312
Huff, Darrell, 1363
Hufford, Roger 1364-1365, 1715, 4010-4011, 4844-4845
Hughes, G. 5676
Hughes, Paul 670
Hughes, R. O. 4551
Hughes, Richard E.; and Duhamel 5754
Hughes, Thomas 328
Hull, B. J. 3436
Hullinger, James L. 5040
Hultzer, L. S. 1157
Hummel, Paul; and Huntress 2232
Humphrey, Chris 1064
Humphrey, Hubert H. 671, 854
Hungerford, Herbert 88
Hunsaker, David M.; and Smith 163
Hunsinger, Paul 4182-4183
Hunsinger, Paul; and Wood 3943
Hunt, Everett L. 1716, 2081- 2084, 2541, 3890, 4403
Hunter, E. R. 4846
Huntington, Henry B. 1158
Huntington, Henry B.; and Baker 12
Huntress, Keith; and Hummel 2232
Hurley, Neil P. 5831
Hurst, J. W. 5832
Husband, Richard W. 2233
Huse, H. R. 2936
Huseman, Richard C. 1958, 2085-2087
Huseman, Richard C.; Gruner; and Luck 629
Huseman, Richard C.; and Hayes 5827
Huseman, Richard C.; Jaksa; and Steil 3337
Huseman, Richard C.; Ware; and Gruner 672
Huston, Ruth F. 5182-5183
Hutton, Ralph 673, 3217
Hyman, Herbert H.; and Sheats- ley 2542

Hynes, Geraldine; and Clark 5717
Hyslop, James H. 272-273

Ihde, Ira C. 674
Ilbert, C. P. 4723
Illardo, Joseph A. 5413-5414
Illardo, Joseph A.; and Eisen- berg 57
Immel, Ray L. 3151
Immel, Ray K.; and Whipple 4990
Infante, Dominic A. 949, 1717, 4760, 4847
Ingalls, Mary 5415
Innes, James 675
Insalata, S. John 1366, 5556
Insko, Chester 5702
Irvin, Charles E. 1258, 2543, 3440-3441, 3662
Irvin, Tucker 4269
Irvine, James R. 2088-2089
Irwin, James R. 328
Irwin, John V.; Eisenson; and Auer 2213
Irwin, Ramon L. 2356, 4185, 5416
Isaacs, Mildred H. 1104
Isaeus 1894
Isbell, Ruth 5185
Isocrates 1895

Jackson, George S. 3442, 4724, 4848
Jackson, James H. 3082
Jackson, L. E. 5186
Jackson, Teddy R. 428
Jacob, Bruno E. 1027, 2820, 3443, 3663, 3775, 3891, 4345, 4761, 5187-5191
Jacobson, Clarence 677
Jacobson, Paul 4991
Jaeger, Werner 2090-2091
Jafee, C. L.; and Lucas 3135
Jager, Ronald 1718
Jaksa, James A.; Steil; and Huseman 3437
James, Herbert L. 1959, 4849
James, Jim; and Clarke 2454
James, Rita M. 5833
James, William 1896

438

Jamison, Frank R.; and Halley 4440
Janis, Irving L.; and Feshbach 2544
Janis, Irving L.; and Field 2545
Janis, Irving L.; and Frick 1719
Janis, Irving L.; and Hovland 2230
Janis, Irving L.; Hovland; and Kelley 2228
Janis, Irving L.; and King 2876-2877
Janis, Irving L.; and Lumsdaine 2586
Janis, Irving L.; and Milholland 2546
Jarrett, James L.; and Harris 2928
Jarrett, R. F.; and Sheriffs 2547
Jastrow, Joseph 1488-1489, 2234-2235
Jaswal, Alice 4186
Jay, J. A. 678
Jeffrey, Richard 1490
Jeffrey, Robert C. 4553-4554, 5557
Jeffries, D. G.; and Feather 2486
Jelliffe, R. A.; and Percival 5622
Jenkins, Jon E. 4725
Jennes, Larry 679
Jenness, Arthur 2548
Jensen, J. Vernon 2821
Jensen, Leonard 429
Jensen, Otto C. 1491
Jepson, R. W. 1492
Jerome, H. 1281
Jersild, A. T. 3032
Jespersen, Otto 2937
Jevons, W. S. 1493-1495
Johannesen, Richard L. 2236, 2549, 2775
Johannesen, Richard L.; and Buehler 4110
Johannesen, Richard L.; and Zacharias 410
Johannesen, Robert 5353
Johenning, Jean 4346
John of Salisbury 307
Johnsen, Julia E. 1367, 5895
Johnson, Alexander B. 2938
Johnson, Allen 1282

Johnson, Alma 1720, 2550
Johnson, C. L. 4555
Johnson, Donald E. 5638
Johnson, Donald M. 1721
Johnson, Eleanor 3444
Johnson, Francis R. 2092
Johnson, George E. 680
Johnson, Gertrude E. 3892
Johnson, Janet B. 4556-4557
Johnson, John A. 5041
Johnson, Katharine 4558
Johnson, Oliver A. 1722
Johnson, Prescott 1065
Johnson, Robert 2784
Johnson, T. Earle 4650
Johnson, Tom 4270
Johnson, Wendell 2237, 2939
Johnson, W. E. 1496
Johnson-Laird, P. N. 1723
Johnston, James 4675
Johnston, M. M. 681
Johnstone, Henry W., Jr. 1497-1498, 1724, 2551
Johnstone, Henry W., Jr.; and Natanson 121
Joiner, Charles W. 1086
Jones, Alfred K. 430
Jones, Cecil H. 682
Jones, Elbert W. 1960
Jones, Ernest 2552
Jones, Howard 3445
Jones, James L. 5417, 5558
Jones, John G. 218
Jones, Leo 89
Jones, Louis C.; and Hardy 3653
Jones, Marshall R. 2238
Jones, Merritt B. 2357
Jones, Ossie G. 4676
Jones, R. A.; and Brehm 2553
Jones, Richard F. 2554
Jones, Robert W. 683
Jones, Stanley E. 5725, 5834
Jones, Warren C. 5418
Jones, William M. 1600
Jordan, Harriet P. 5419
Jordan, Howard M. 4271
Jordan, Howard M.; and Wheeler 2752
Jorgenson, J. 1499
Joseph, H. W. B. 1500
Judd, Larry 2358
Judson, Lyman S. 684, 2555,

3776, 4012, 4111, 4472,
4726, 4851
Julber, Eric; and Christopher
4272
Juleus, Nels 685, 5559

Kadish, Mortimer R. 1369
Kahane, Howard 1501, 1501a
Kahn, Theresa G.; and Murphy
90
Kain, Richard M. 3664
Kaltenborn, H. V. 686, 2902
Kaltenborn, Helen 3446
Kamenetzky, Joseph; de Haan;
and Thistlewaite 2712
Kamenetzky, Joseph; and Thistle-
waite 1267
Kamenetzky, Joseph; Thistle-
waite; and Schmidt 1268
Kamiat, A. H. 3893
Kane, Peter E. 3665, 3777,
5402, 5560-5562
Kanouse, David E.; and Abelson
3033
Kantner, Claude E. 2853
Kanungo, R. N. 3130
Kaplan, Abbott 1725
Kaplan, Abraham 5639
Karas, Edith; Fabrizio; and
Menmuir 5751
Karcher, J. T. 5835
Karl, Theodore O. H. 3778
Karl, Theodore O. H.; Mahaffey;
Long; and Hingston 4032
Kariins, M.; and Abelson 2239
Karner, E. F. 5192
Karns, C. Franklin 1726
Karr, Harrison M. 3894
Katter, Nafe E. 5421
Katz, Daniel E. 2240, 2556
Kaufman, Ileen 5913a
Kaufmann, Arnold 5640
Kaufmann, Harry; and Goldstein
1727
Kaufmann, Rebecca L. 5654a
Kay, Lilian 2557
Kaye, Stephen R. 4560
Keane, Helen 1961
Keatinge, Maurice W. 2241
Kecskemeti, Paul 2940
Keele, Reba L. 431
Keeling, Russell M. 5042

Keesey, Ray E. 1961, 4117
Keeton, Morris T. 1066
Kegler, Stanley G. 3218
Keiber, A. E. 1028, 4187,
5193
Keil, Charles R. 1601
Kehm, Harold D. 687
Kell, Carl L. 4014
Keller, I. C. 3131
Kelley, A. H. 5736
Kelley, Harold H.; Hovland;
and Janis 2228
Kelley, Hubert 688
Kelley, Stanley, Jr. 2242,
5563
Kelley, Truman L. 1283
Kelley, W. D. 4852
Kellogg, Lincoln L. 689, 4273
Kelly, Douglas S.; and Brown
5786
Kelman, H. C.; and Hovland
2558
Kelso, Robert W. 690
Keltner, John 3447, 3779,
4561
Keltner, John; and Robinson
3248
Kemp, Robert 3448, 5194
Kendall, Richard H.; and Frac-
tenberg 950
Kennedy, Allan J. 5195
Kennedy, George 367, 1897,
2095
Kennedy, J. E. 1728
Kennon, Sudie 4562
Kent, Robert; and Holm 84-85
Kerr, Harry P. 1502, 1729,
2559, 5564
Ketcham, Victor A. 91-92
Key, Percy C. 93
Keynes, John Maynard 1503,
1504, 2243
Kibler, Robert J.; and Gibson
5939
Kibler, Robert J.; Gruner; and
Gibson 3026
Kiefer, Charles, Jr. 3666
Kiepe, Paul E. 2359
Kiesler, Charles; Kiesler; and
Pallak 5677
Kiesler, Sara B.; Kiesler; and
Pallak 5677
Kilpatrick, F. P.; and Edwards

440

2478
Kimball, Emily A. 2360
King, Bert T.; and Janis 2876-2877
King, Lois M. 5422
King, Thomas R.; and Clevenger 4799
King, Thomas R.; and Phifer 691, 3449
King, Thomas S. 2560
Kingdon, Robert W. 4374
King-Hamilton, M. A. B. 4406
Kingsbury, Warren T. 5196
Kinnamon, A. J. 219
Kinney, Richard 692
Kinsey, O. P. 220
Kipp, Eugene W. 2361
Kirk, Glenn G. 5423
Kirkendall, Lester 2561
Kirn, John F. 4274
Kirwan, Christopher 1730
Kitson, Jack; and Skornia 5760
Kittredge, George L. L and Greenough 2927
Kittredge, H. W. 5197
Klapper, Joseph T. 2562
Klapper, Paul 2563
Klein, J.; Cowan; Weber; and Hodinatt 2459
Klein, Maurice 5198
Klein, Willette C. 1963
Kleinan, Marvin D. 3450-3451, 5424
Kleinschmidt, J. Barney 3667
Kleiser, Grenville 94-95
Klemke, E. D. 1731
Kline, Donald F. 3132
Kline, John 1311, 1370-72, 5678
Kline, R. E. 96
Klingbeil, Henry C. 693, 3780
Klopf, Donald W. 694, 3452, 4015, 4016, 4188, 4463, 5099
Klopf, Donald W.; Evans; and de Lozier 4853-4854
Klopf, Donald W.; and Lahman 3280
Klopf, Donald W.; and McCroskey 97, 1384, 2822, 2878, 3453
Klopf, Donald W.; and Ogitani 5200
Klopf, Donald W.: and Rives 3813-3814. 3454, 3536, 3856

Klubertanz, George P. 1505
Kluckholm, Clyde 5703-5704
Klumpp, James F.; Brock; Chesebro; and Cragan 1084
Knapp, H. G. 1732
Knapp, Mark L.; and McCroskey 5837
Kneale, W. C. 1506
Knee, (Mrs.) Robert C. 695
Knepprath, E.; and Clevenger 5565
Knoll, P. X. 696, 1160
Knower, Franklin H. 1161-1162, 2564-2566, 4189, 5896, 5945-5947
Knowles, James S. 221
Knowles, Malcolm S. 4727
Knox, John J. 1733
Koch, Gustav A.; and Childs 1655
Kodman, Frank, Jr.; and Fairbanks 3107
Koehler, Jerry W.; Mlady; and Tucker 881, 2731
Kolb, J. H.; and Wileden 98
Kolberg, O. W. 1163, 3895, 4017-4018, 4190, 4564-4565
Konigsberg, Ephraim; and Cooper 5130
Konigsberg, Evelyn 5201
Konrad, Richard 1067
Korzybski, Alfred 2941
Kosman, L. A. 1734
Kostlin, Bertram; and Moos 2616
Kourilsky, Marilyn 922
Kourilsky, Marilyn; and Phelps 5202
Kowitz, Albert C. 1312
Kozy, John, Jr. 1735
Kramer, D. N. 1373
Kraus, Sidney 5354, 5566
Kreps, Leslie R. 3668
Kretsinger, Elwood A. 2567
Kriesberg, Martin 2568
Krueger, Richard F. 4855
Kruger, Arthur N. 99-101, 631, 951-952, 1068-1069, 1166-1173, 2569, 2823, 2879-2880, 3034, 3219, 3455, 3669, 4019-4020, 4191, 4856-4861
Kruger, Arthur N.; and Manicas 1518-1519

Kruger, Arthur N.; and Windes 5612-5613
Krugman, Herbert E.   2570
Kuebler, Roy R.   368
Kuenzel, B.   861
Kuhr, Irwin   4419
Kuhr, Manuel I.   3456
Kully, Robert D.   697
Kulp, D. H.   2571
Kuperstein, Hyman   4862
Kurth, William C.; and Dieter 2035
Kvasmicka, Gerald A.   5043
Kyburg, Henry E., Jr.   1507, 1736
Kyburg, Henry E., Jr.; and Nagel   1508
Kyburg, Henry E., Jr.; and Smokler   1509
Kyker, Rex P.   5044
Kyle, Judy M.   330

Laase, Leroy T.   3457, 3781, 3896-3897, 4566, 4863-4864
Laase, Leroy T.; Siekman; and McGee   4865
Lacey, Douglas R.   4253
Lacock, John K.   4677
Ladd, J. W.   3220
La Follette, A. C.   3458
Lahman, Carroll P.   191, 698-699, 3173, 3459-3460, 3898, 4567, 5948
Lahman, Carroll P.; and Klopf 3280
Laine, Joseph B.   1964, 4728, 5425
Laity, Harry A.   4192
Lake, Lewis W.   4322
Lake, Richard   4568
Lakoff, George   1737
Lamb, H. D.   4569
Lamb, John H.   1965
Lambert, A. Edward   5045
Lambertson, Floyd W.   1070, 1174-1175, 2572-2573, 3133, 3461, 4021, 4193, 5203-5204
Lamers, William M.   4866-4867, 5205
Lamers, William M.; and Dewey 700
Lamm, Helmut   5679

Lampel, Anita K.; and Anderson 1374
Lampson, Godfrey L.   5614
Lanckton, A. Van C.; London; and Meldman   5840
Landers, Audrey D.; Lundy; and Simonson   2588
Landesman, C.   5726
Lane, Frank H.   3221
Lane, Ralph L.   5046
Lane, Richard A.   3288
Lane, Robert A.   4275
Langer, Susanne K.   1510, 2942
Lantz, William C.   3083
Larmer, Larry E.   1105
Larmon, Sigurd S.   701
Larrabee, H. A.   1511
Larson, Carl E.   702, 2785
Larson, P. Merville   703-704, 3899, 4397, 5206
Larson, R. G.   1738-1739
La Russo, Dominic   2096, 2157, 2574
Lashbrook, Brad; and Giffin 3992-3994, 4022
Lashley, Warren L.   5426
Lasswell, Harold D.   1740, 2244
Lasswell, Harold D.; and Blumenstock   2245
Lasswell, Harold D.; Casey; and Smith   5897, 5907
Laudick, David; and Beers 5207
Laughlin, Mary F.   1898
Lawrence, J. H.   4276
Lawson, Robert G.   1176, 2575, 5838
Lawton, J. H.   705, 4023-4024
Lawver, Kathleen   4194
Laycock, Craven   4992
Laycock, Craven; O'Neill; and Scales   130
Laycock, Craven; and Scales 102
Laycock, Craven; and Spafford 4993
Layton, Charles R.   3782-3784, 4868
Lazzatti, John L., Jr.   4025
Leathers, Dale G.   2097
Leavenworth, Russell E.; and

Pitt 1528a
Le Blanc, H. 1741
Lechner, Joan M. 1899
Lee, Albert S. 222
Lee, Alfred M.; and Lee 2246
Lee, Dale 5047
Lee, Elizabeth B.; and Lee 2246
Lee, Irving J. 706, 1966, 2576, 2943-2945, 3035-3036, 4195
Lee, Josh 707
Lee, Ralph M. 3670
Lefford, A. 1742
Lefforge, Orlando S. 3671
Legere, Lawrence J., Jr. 4026
Lehman, Warren 4678
Lehmann, Richard; and Moree 3488
Lehrer, Keith 1743-1745
Leigh, Robert D. 4679
Lembke, Russell W. 1177
Lemmon, Martha L. 2577
Lepley, Ray 917-918
Leppman, Walter 711-712, 854, 2249-2250
Lerbinger, Otto 2247
Letke, Robert E. 4028
Level, Dale, Jr. 432, 708
Leventhal, Howard; and Perloe 2578
Levi, A. W.; and Frye 1481
Levi, Edward 1512
Levi, Isaac 1746
Levine, I. N. 709
Levitas, Louise 1178
Levy, B. H. 1513
Lewin, Kurt 2248
Lewis, Albert 1747
Lewis, C. I. 1514
Lewis, George C. 223
Lewis, Grace T. 5208
Lewis, H. D. 2946
Lewis, J. U. 1748
Lewis, Leroy 3462-3463, 3672, 5209-5210
Lewis, Nan; and Neimark 5685, 5847, 5851
Lewis, Thomas R. 5427
Leys, Wayne A. R. 2776
Lichtenfels, Paul J. 4869
Lieboff, Michael D. 4118
Lighthall, Barbara 1021
Lilien, Charles E. 4419
Lilienthal N. 710, 3464

Lillich, Richard B. 369
Lillywhite, Herold 2824-25, 3465
Lin, Nan 5680
Lindblom, Charles E.; and Braybrook 5630
Lindquist, E. F. 1284
Lindsley, Charles F. 2579, 3134
Lineham, K. 5839
Ling, David A.; and Seltzer 1179
Link, Alma T. 192
Linkugel, William A.; and Giffin 618, 3995
Linkugel, William A.; and Parson 2779, 3673
Linsky, Leonard 2947
Lintz, O. L.; and Barr 5096
Litsheim, Patricia M. 3222
Little, A. G.; and Pelster 308
Little, R. C. 5211
Littlefield, Walter; and Brake 3318
Livingston, Kathryn H. 5212
Lloyd, G. E. R. 1900
Lloyd, I. S.; and Richmond 4407
Lloyd, M. Pearl 3466
Locke, Charlton 2362
Lockhart, A. M. 5567
Lockridge, Ross F. 103
Lockwood, Bonnie J. 5048
Lockwood, D. P. 2098
Loeb, Helen; and Weisman 5213
Loevinger, Gustavus 3785
Loevinger, Lee 1749
Lofrgen, Charles A. 5568
Loftus, William K.; and Watkins 3467
Logue, Cal M. 2580
Lomas, Charles W. 713-717, 2363, 4029, 4196, 4347, 4444, 4570
Londergran, Margaret J. 5049
London, Harvey; Meldman; and Lanckton 5840
Long, Chester C. 2581
Long, David K. 5050
Long, Emmett 3223, 4870
Long, Emmett; Karl; Mahaffey; and Hingston 4032
Long, H. S. 5949

444

1518-1519
Mann, Ivan C. 4198, 4349
Mann, Kristine; and Buck 29
Mannebach, Wayne C. 4199
Manning, George A. 3902
Manning, Peter K. 1377
Manning, Robert N. 724
Mantell, M. 5221
Manzer, Margaret 5431
Maple, Glen W. 4572
Marcham, Frederick G. 3227
Marderosian, Haig Der 331
Margenau, Henry; and Oscanyan 5730
Margolis, Joseph 954, 1072, 1758
Marino, Herman J. 1759
Marino, Teresina 3473, 4872
Markert, M. G. 1181
Markgraf, Bruce 725, 955, 1182, 3474, 4034, 4278-4279, 4873
Marks, Russell R.; and Pearce 4035
Marlor, Clark S.; Baker; and Mulgrave 5901
Marple, C. H. 2590
Marriott, James W. 107
Marsh, Charles A. 3228-3229
Marsh, Patrick O. 1183-1187, 2260, 2368, 3789
Marsh, Robert 2102
Marsh, Thomas H. 2103
Marshall, Iva R. 5222
Marshall, K. D.; and Mitchell 117
Martin, Boyd N. 332
Martin, G. Arthur 5844
Martin, George W. 5052
Martin, Howard H. 1132, 2104, 2827
Martin, R. M. 1378, 2949, 5731
Martin-Trigona, Helen V. 1602, 5432
Marts, Arnaud C. 726
Marzolf, Arnold H. 5433
Masel, Philip; and Baggaridge 8
Maslow, A. H. 2591
Mason, H. C. 3903
Mason, John B. 4573-4574
Mason, Paul 4681, 4729
Matlon, Ronald J. 4036
Matson, Henry 1008
Matthews, C. P. 4575

Matthews, Jack 2592-2593
Matza, David; and Peterson 5757
Mauller, C. J. 5223
Mauser, Anthony 956
Maw, Herbert B. 5434
Maxcy, Carroll L. 1087
Maxwell, Paul A. 1760
Maxwell, Pearl 728
Mayer, James 3475
Mayer, J. Edmund 729-730
Mayhew, P. B. B.; and Peters 4738
Maynard, William L. 3946
Mayo, Bernard 5732
Mays, Morley J. 3136
Maze, Lavelle T. 4576
Mazza, Joseph M. 5435
Mazza, Joseph M.; and Polisky 1260
Mazzola, John 957, 4874
McAdoo, Joe; and Hayes 4831
McAdoo, William G. 731
McBath, James H. 108-109, 732, 3137, 3476, 4408, 4445, 5615
McBath, James H.; and Aurbach 958
McBath, James H.; and Cripe 3138
McBride, Lida 4875
McBride, Sara A. 331
McBurney, James H. 733, 1603, 1761-1762, 2105
McBurney, James H.; and Mills 110
McBurney, James H.; O'Neill; and Mills 111
McBurney, James H.; and O'Neill 131
McCain, John W., Jr. 2106
McCall, Lottye K. 5224
McCall, Marsh H., Jr. 1902
McCall, Sorrs 1763
McCarty, Dwight G. 2261
McCarty, George 4200
McCarty, Leon 4876
McClatchey, J. F. 5845
McClaugherty, John 734
McCleary, William R.; and Hoogestraat 3031
McClelland, Samuel D. 735
McClintock, E. C., Jr.; and

Berman 2013
McClung, Thomas; and Sharp 2692
McClure, Leda G. 3625
McCole, Mary M. 867
McConnell, Anne M. 3477
McConnell, Harry 1968
McCord, Clarence W. 2107
McCormick, M. 1380
McCoy, Ford H. 5436
McCoy, Pressley C. 5437
McCoy, Ralph E. 5898
McCoy, Thomas R. 1764
McCracken, Anna; and Templin 1563
McCrery, Lester L. 4037, 4201
McCrery, Lester L.; and Smith 4038
McCroskey, James C. 736, 1286, 1381-1383, 1765, 2369, 2594, 2882, 5950
McCroskey, James C.; and Arnold 1322
McCroskey, James C.; and Camp 4877-4878
McCroskey, James C.; and Combs 1766
McCroskey, James C.; and Dunham 2595
McCroskey, James C.; and Klopf 97, 1384, 2822, 2878, 3453
McCroskey, James C.; and Knapp 5837
McCroskey, James C.; and Mehrley 2596, 5733
McCroskey, James C.; and Prichard 4415
McCulloch, Catherine W. 737
McCurdy, Frances L. 1903
McDermott, Douglas 2108
McDermott, E. E. 5225
McDiarmid, James I. 5438
McDonald, Daniel 112, 2950
McDonald, Priscilla M. 5053
McEdwards, Mary G. 1767
McElligott, James N. 225, 253
McEwan, W. J.; and Greenberg 2597
McGauby, Fern; and McGauby 3857
McGauby, J. Fred; and McGauby 3857
McGee, Gale; Laase; and Siek-

man 4865
McGlone, Edward L. 5951
McGrew, J. Fred 1969, 5952
McGuckin, Henry E. 738-739, 2988, 3038
McGuire, Gale A. 5439
McGuire, William J. 2598-2599
McGuire, William J.; and Papageorgis 2109, 2636
McIntosh, Douglas M. 4119
McKay, Frederick B. 740
McKean, Dayton D. 741-742, 2600, 3230, 5953
McKee, Paul R. 1313
McKee, Paul R.; and Giffin 1352
McKenzie, Ruth I. 4577
McKeon, Richard 1768, 2110-2112, 2601
McKinney, Frank C.; Denney; and Carson 53
McKinney, Frank C.; and McKinney 4995
McKinney, Fred 3139
McKinney, Mary E.; and McKinney 4995
McKown, Harry C. 3174
McLaughlin, G. L. 5226
McLaughlin, Ted J. 1970
McLeod, Norman B. 4202, 5227
McMahon, Fred R. 1971, 2113, 2158
McMonagle, James A. 5228
McNally, James R. 371
McNassor, Donald 5683
McPhail, Thomas L. 5440
McPhee, Rodreck F. 5054
McPherson, Elizabeth G. 5571-5572
McReynolds, Charles H. 4280
Mead, G. H. 2951
Meader, Clarence L.; and Pillsbury 2277
Meader, Prentice A. 372, 1769-1770, 2114-2115
Means, Ruth D. 4578
Measell, James S. 1604-1605
Mechling, Richard 2888
Medley, William, Jr. 5441
Megill, Kenneth; and Giffin 1146-1147, 3996

Mehling, Reuben 2602
Mehrley, R. Samuel; and Mc-
Croskey 2596, 5733
Meiklejohn, Alexander 854
Melden, A. 5641
Meldman, Philip J.; London; and
Lanckton 5840
Melick, W. 4579
Mellinkoff, David 2952
Melzer, Arnold 4996
Melzer, Dorothy G. 4879
Mendenhall, Lawrence C. 3904
Menderson, Melanie F. 4682
Mendiola, John A. 5229
Menefee, Selden C. 2603-2604
Menefee, Selden C.; and Granne-
berg 2605
Menmuir, Ruth; Fabrizio; and
Karas 5751
Menniger, Karl A. 2262
Menser, C. L. 4580
Merchant, Jerrold J.; and
Stewart 857, 3577
Meredith, E. E. 5573
Meriwether, Colyer 309
Merrill, Barbara 3478
Merrill, Beverley J. 1606
Merritt, Frank W. 743, 1221,
4039
Merry, Glenn N. 3231, 3479
Merton, Robert K. 2263
Messner, Carolann G. 2370
Method, Ethel 3862
Meyer, Frank 4730
Meyer, Samuel L. 744
Meyerhoff, Arthur E. 2264
Meyers, Alice 5442
Michael, William; and Crawford
3140
Michaelis, Clayton 745
Michalos, Alex C. 1520a, 1771,
5684
Micken, Ralph A. 4350, 5443,
5574-5576
Middleton, Russell 5577
Middleton, Warren C.; and Fay
3112-3114
Miles, Hardy L. 4203
Milholland, H. C., Jr; and Janis
2546
Milic, Louis J. 5899
Mill, John Stuart 274, 413
Millas, Joseph 5444

Miller, A. S. 5846
Miller, Arthur B. 4880
Miller, Arthur B.; and Fausti
113
Miller, Carl G. 114, 5231-
5232
Miller, Clyde R. 470, 2265
Miller, D. F. 294
Miller, E. W. 194
Miller, Edd 569, 3039, 3482-
3483, 3674, 4281, 4446-4447,
4581, 4881
Miller, Edd; Drushal; Ralph;
and Schug 569
Miller, Edd; and Stasheff 4459
Miller, Emerson W. 746
Miller, Enid 334
Miller, F. Byers 1772, 3480-
3481
Miller, Fred R. 2371
Miller, Gerald R. 959, 1773,
2116, 4882
Miller, Gerald R.; and Basehart
2606
Miller, Gerald R.; Bettinghaus;
and Steinfatt 1630
Miller, Gerald R.; and Green-
berg 2507
Miller, Gerald R.; and Hewgill
2607
Miller, Gerald R.; and Nilsen
115
Miller, Gerald R.; Siegel; and
Woting 2696
Miller, H. B. 1385
Miller, John T. 960, 3675
Miller, Joseph B. 5445
Miller, Joseph M.; and Vorr
3169
Miller, Justin 747
Miller, Marion M. 254, 5617-
5618
Miller, Melvin H. 4204
Miller, Mickey; Rousseau;
Schopler; and Gruder 3554
Miller, N. 4040-4041
Miller, Orville C. 3484, 3858
Miller, Robert E. 5233
Miller, Wayne L. 4762
Miller, William L. 5578
Milliken, Joyce; and Sharp 841
Mills, C. Wright 5847
Mills, Frederick C. 1287

Moulton, H. G. 3489
Mowder, Barbara J. 335
Mraz, Thomas 5059
Mudd, Charles S. 1782
Mudge, Isadore G. 5900
Muehl, E. William 2267, 4586
Mulgrave, Dorothy I.; Marloi;
  and Baker 5901
Mulvaney, Annette M. 435
Mulvaney, Annette M.; and Brad-
  ley 4132
Mundt, Karl E. 374, 631, 756-
  762, 1783, 2884, 3142-3144,
  4283, 4885-4887, 5241, 5583
Munn, Norman L. 2618
Munro, Harry C. 763
Munsterberg, H. 1522
Mure, Geoffrey R. 1905
Murphree, Iris 5734
Murphy, Arthur E. 1523
Murphy, Gardner 3076
Murphy, H. 4353
Murphy, Jack 764
Murphy, Jack W. 4206
Murphy, Jack W.; and Hensley
  4888
Murphy, James J. 375, 1906,
  2122-2128, 3490, 3676, 5584,
  5955
Murphy, James J.; and East
  3491
Murphy, James J.; and Ericson
  119
Murphy, James J.; and Sharp
  3563
Murphy, Jeffrie G., 1784, 1785
Murphy, John W. 436, 5060
Murphy, Ralph M. 3492
Murphy, Richard 765, 961,
  2830-2831, 2885-2887, 3235,
  4045
Murphy, Richard; and Kahn 90
Murphy, Roy D. 766, 962,
  3493-3495
Murray, Edward J. 2268
Murray, Elwood 2832, 3077,
  4284-4285
Murray, Frank S. 1389
Murray, Jerry B.; Shaugnessy;
  and Vince 767
Murrish, Walter H. 2619, 3948
Musafer, Sherif 2269
Muscio, Bernard 1390

Musgrave, George M. 120, 768,
  1189-1198, 1391, 1786, 3041,
  3496, 4046, 4450, 4889-4895
Muskie, Edmund S. 769
Musselewhite, D. C. 1787
Musser, William M., Jr. 770
Myers, W. 4896
Myers, Wilfred 1199

Nabers, D. J. 336, 771, 3790-
  3792, 4207
Nadeau, Ray 376, 1200, 1973,
  2129-2130, 2620
Nagel, Ernest 1462, 1788,
  1789
Nagel, Ernest; and Kyburg
  1508
Nagel, Robert H. 3793
Nagel, Stuart 5850
Natanson, Maurice 2621-2622
Natanson, Maurice; and John-
  stone 121
Naylor, G. K.; and Naylor 122
Naylor, T. E.; and Naylor 122
Neale, John V. 1974
Nebergall, Roger E. 1201,
  2372, 3042
Nebergall, Roger E.; Sherif;
  and Sherif 2297
Neely, Gerry 4354
Neely, Thomas B. 226
Neimark, Edith D.; and Lewis
  5685, 5847, 5851
Nelson, Everett J. 1790
Nelson, J. Arthur 4047-4048,
  5244
Nelson, John S. 4049
Nelson, Max 5956
Nelson, Norman E. 2131
Nelson, Roy C. 1073
Nelson, Roy C.; and Fest
  3497-3499
Nelson, Theodore F. 3794,
  5245-5246
Nelson, Thomas L. 4588
Nelson, William F. 1607, 1791
Nesbitt, F. F. 2955
Ness, Ordean G. 2446
Neurath, Otto 1392
Newburn, Robert M. 5450
Newcomb, Theodore 5735
Newcomer, Lloyd R. 4451

Newell, Clarence A. 4897
Newell, G. A. 3500
Newman, Dale R.; and Newman 1289
Newman, John D. 2623
Newman, Robert P. 123, 491, 772, 964, 1202-1203, 2833-2834, 2888, 4050-4051, 4355, 4898, 5355
Newman, Robert P.; and Fuge 4336
Newman, Robert P.; and Newman 1289
Newman, Robert P.; and Sanders 1393
Newton, Kenneth 1106
Newton, W. T. 4899
Nichols, Alan 124, 773, 1074
Nichols, Egbert R. 377, 521, 774-776, 965-967, 1204-1205, 1394, 3043, 3501-3502, 3678, 3795-3798, 3906, 4052-4053, 4209-4125, 4287, 4356, 4900-4901, 5248-5249, 5619-5620
Nichols, Egbert R.; and Baccus 125
Nichols, Henry W. 777
Nichols, Marie H. 2270
Nichols, Ralph G. 2624, 5250, 5852
Nichols, Walter S. 4591
Nicholson, Harold 4902
Nilsen, Thomas R. 195, 778-779, 2777
Nilsen, Thomas R.; and Miller 114
Nishiyama, Kazuo 2625
Nobles, W. Scott 2132, 3236, 4054
Nobles, W. Scott; and Cohen 780
Nolan, William J. 4685
Nolin, L. L. 5251
Norman, Nelson F. 781
Norrall, Chrysouia; and Schulman 2684
Norris, George W. 854
Northrop, F. S. C. 1524
Northwall, John H. 2787
Norton, Aloysius 4410
Norton, Lawrence E. 1031, 5853
Norton, Robert W. 2373, 4055
Nuesse, C. J. 4592

Oaks, Diane; and Seger 4622
Oates, Whitney J. 2778
O'Brien, James D. 5451
O'Brien, Joseph F. 1131, 1221, 3503-3506, 4288, 4357, 4593-4594, 4686, 4731-4735, 5254
O'Brien, Joseph F.; and Carlson 4595
O'Brien, Joseph F.; and Graves 1699
O'Brien, Joseph F.; and Young 4596
O'Brien, Joseph P. 4216
O'Brien, Thomas F. 5061
O'Connell, Sandra E. 1608
O'Connor, John R., Jr. 4763
O'Connor, John R., Jr.; and Howett 5181
O'Connor, Lillian 312
Odegard, Peter H. 2271
Ogden, C. K.; and Richards 2956
Ogden, R. M. 2626
Ogitani, Betty; and Klopf 5200
Ojala, Dorothy; and Shinnick 4903
Olbrechts-Tyteca, L.; and Perelman 139
Oldenquist, Andrew 1792
Olds, Stuart; and Sajdak 4289
Oldsey, Bernard S.; and Graves 74
Olgivie, John S. 126
Olian, J. Robert 2133
Oliver, J. Willard 1793
Oliver, Robert T. 313, 782, 970, 2272-2731, 2627-2629, 2835, 3044, 3507-3509
Olmstead, Marvin L. 5452
Olson, Donald O. 337, 783, 1205, 1262, 3510, 3800, 4904, 5453
Olson, Donald O.; and Petelle 2630, 4921
Olson, Donald O.; Tompkins; and Temple 1395, 3511
Olson, Elder J. 2134
Olson, Ronald H. 2889
Olson, William H.; and Walker 4957
Olson, William H.; Walker; and Callahan 894

450

O'Malley, Charles J. 5062
O'Meara, Julia A. 784
O'Neil, Marion R. 1975
O'Neill, James M. 127-128,
  785, 3237, 3512-3513, 3801,
  4905-4911, 5255, 5957
O'Neill, James M.; and Cort-
  right 129
O'Neill, James M.; Laycock;
  and Scales 130
O'Neill, James M.; and Mc-
  Burney 131
O'Neill, James M.; McBurney;
  and Mills 111
O'Neill, James M.; Sarett; and
  Wells 4964
O'Neill, James M.; and Wells
  4963
O'Neill, Robert M. 5755
O'Neill, Robert N.; and Windes
  184
Oppy, Gene B. 4598
Ornstein, Allan C. 5686
O'Rourke, James 4290
Orr, Frederick W. 4291
Orr, Frederick W.; and Franzke
  4292
Orvis, M. B. 1396
Orwant, C.; and Rapaport 5689
Osborn, Albert S. 5756
Osborn, Lynn R.; and Reeves
  4925
Osborn, Michael M. 4293
Osborn, Michael M.; and Bowers
  3001
Osborne, Margherita O., 132
Osborne, Wilbur J.; and Ross
  981
Oscanyan, Frederick; and
  Margenau 5730
Ostergaard, H. 971
Ostergren, Carl F. 786
Osterhouse, Robert; and Brock
  2631
Ostermeier, Terry H. 2374,
  2632
Osterweiss, Rollin G. 3679
Ostler, Margaret E. 1976
Ostlund, Leonard A. 787
Otis, A. T. 5257
Overking, Michail 5762
Overstreet, Harry A. 789,
  1794-1795, 2274

Overstreet, Harry A.; and
  Overstreet 4473
Owen, Chester D. 790
Owen, Gordon R. 3514, 4057
Owens, Cullen B.; and Eubank
  4157
Owens, Joseph 1796

Pacilio, John, Jr.; and Stites
  133
Pack, Roger 2135
Paddock, Howland 4599
Padrow, Ben 4058
Page, William T. 1797
Paget, Edwin H. 791, 1798,
  2633, 3908, 4217, 4294-
  4296, 4912-4913, 5586
Palgrave, Reginald F. D. 227
Pallak, Michael; Kiesler; and
  Kiesler 5677
Palmer, Ann L. 5454
Palmer, Archie M. 3515
Palmieri, Ron 792
Palzer, Edward 793, 1263-
  1264, 1799-1800, 2634, 3045-
  3048, 3145-3151, 3238, 3516,
  4218, 4358, 5258
Pane, O. E. 5259
Pannell, Charles 4736
Pap, Arthur 2957
Papageorgis, Demetrius 2635
Papageorgis, Demetrius; and
  McGuire 2110, 2636
Parker, Darrell R. 4359
Parker, John P. 2637
Parker, John W. 3681-3682
Parker, M. J. 1107
Parker, W. B. 2638
Parker, W. W. 4914
Parkerson, James W. 5063
Parkhurst, Charles E. 1265,
  4059
Parks, E. Patrick 2135
Parks, Edelbert 1907
Parks, Mack 5064
Parks, Sara R.; and Prentiss
  806
Parlette, John W. 4915
Parrella, Gilda 3049
Parrish, Wayland Maxfield
  1032, 2136, 2639, 3152,
  3583, 3809

2449
Phifer, Gregg; and King 691, 3449
Philbrick, F. A. 2960-2961
Phillips, David C. 2647
Phillips, Gerald M. 799, 1980, 3521, 3684, 4061
Phillips, Gerald M.; and Frandsen 3522
Phillips, Robert L. 2648
Phillips, William A.; and Bowers 2433
Phipps, G. R.; and Everett 58
Pic'l, Melvin E. 4765
Pic'l, Melvin E.; and Aver 5919
Pierce, John R.; and Shurter 160
Pierce, M. Scheffel 5458
Pierson, William 5066
Pigors, Paul 2276
Pillsbury, Walter B.; and Meader 2277
Pinkerton, Herman 3523
Pirkle, James E. 4221
Pitchell, Robert J. 800
Pitkanen, Allan M. 801
Pitkin, William M. 2989
Pitt, Carl A. 802, 803, 1400, 4299, 5589
Pitt, Jack; and Leavenworth 1528a
Pittenger, William 1009
Plantz, Earl 4922
Plato 1908
Platz, Mabel 1909
Plummer, Robert N. 804
Poffenberger, A. J. 1401, 2649
Poincare, H. 1529
Pokorny, Gary F. 2375
Polisky, Jerome B. 5459
Polisky, Jerome B.; and Allan 3954
Polisky, Jerome B.; and Anderson 3957
Polisky, Jerome B.; and Hendrix 3240
Polisky, Jerome B.; and Mazza 1260
Polk, Lee R. 382, 5460, 5855
Polk, Lillian G. 5067
Pollock, Art 805
Pollock, Wallace S. 1981
Pomeroy, Ralph S. 1808

Ponsonby, Arthur 4687
Poos, Roberta L. 3241
Popper, Karl R. 1809
Pore, O. E. 5263
Porter, Ebenezer 3155
Porter, Priscilla A. 5461
Porter, William C. 974
Post, Robert M. 383
Postman, Leo 2650
Potter, David 141, 314, 384-392
Powell, Frederick 2651
Powell, John H., Jr.; and Babcock 7
Powers, Francis F. 2652
Powers, Raymond E. 5264
Prado, C. G. 1810
Pratt, Jerie M. 1811
Prenner, Manuel; Rogoff; and Sternberg 4998
Prentiss, Henrietta; and Parks 806
Prescott, Daniel A. 2278
Prescott, Herbert 3242, 4062
Preston, Ivan L. 1812
Prestwood, Elwood L. 3524
Pribil, Rosemarie 3180
Price, H. H. 5737-5738
Price, Michael J. 3289
Price, Paula 338
Prichard, H. H. 1530
Prichard, Samuel V. O. and McCroskey 4415
Prior, A. N. 1813
Probert, Walter 2653, 3051
Proffit, Maris M. 4604
Pross, Edward L. 2376, 2838, 3525
Pross, Edward L.; and Shirley 3243
Prosser, Michael H.; and Benson 2187
Pruett, Robert E. 1209-1210, 5266-5267
Pruett, Robert E.; Dunne; and Mack 4810
Przelecki, Marion; and Wojcicki 1814
Pullinger, Anne B. 867
Purnell, Sandra E. 1314
Purnell, Sandra E.; and Wilkes 4223
Putnam, Miriam 4605

Quimby, Brooks 143-145, 807-810, 2891, 3244-3245, 3527, 3687, 3809-3810, 4416, 4452
Quimby, Clarence P. 854, 3528
Quimby, Frank B. 339
Quine, Willard V.O. 1531-1532, 2962
Quine, Willard V.O.; and Ullian 5705
Quinlan, Geraldine E. 4606
Quintilian 1870, 1910-1911, 2156
Quist, Allen J. 1107a

Raack, R.C. 5688
Rabbitt, Patrick M. 1402
Radabaugh, J.S. 5268
Radall, Julia D. 4065
Radcliffe, Barbara M. 4923, 5856
Radcliffe, Charles W. 4417, 4419, 4374
Radin, Max 1292, 1533
Rafferty, Ruth S. 812
Ragsdale, J. Donald 1815, 3156-3157
Rahe, Herbert 2654, 3529
Rahskopf, Horace G. 975, 2137
Raines, Lester C. 2282
Rainolde, Richard 1912
Ralph, David C.; Drushal; Schug; and Miller 569
Ralph David C.; and Thomas 2713
Ramsey, Benjamin 2655, 3052
Rand, Mark S. 3530
Randolph, H.L.; and Carmack 3635, 5791
Rank, Vernon E. 2656, 3531
Ransom, D.M. 4688
Ranta, Richard R. 5462
Rapaport, Anatol 414, 2963, 5643
Rapaport, Anatol; and Orwant 5689
Rarig, Frank M.; and Greaves 3811
Rashdall, Hastings 1913
Ratliffe, Sharon 4120
Rau, Gilbert 3812, 4066, 5857
Rau, Gilbert; and Alvsow 3955
Raubicheck, Letitia 3913

Raum, Richard D. 4924
Rausch, Anthony L. 4766
Raven, B.H.; and Fishbein 5721
Ray, Jack L. 2657, 5463
Ray, Robert F. 4607, 5590
Ray, William T.D. 438, 813
Rayment, Charles S. 393
Rea, Richard G.; and Gray 4667, 4739
Rea, Richard G.; and Wills 4748
Reader, Mark 2658
Reager, Richard 3688
Reavis, William C. 5269
Rebstock, Eugene; and Tucker 1618
Redding, W. Charles 2659
Redding, W. Charles; and Baker 2412
Redding, W. Charles; and Steele 2707, 2710
Redfern, Donna D. 1609
Redmont, Robert S. 5858-5859
Reed, A.G.; and Adams 4999
Reed, Marion E. 5270
Reed, Marshall R. 814
Reed, Thomas D. 5271
Reeves, Clyde E. 5464
Reeves, J.B. 4224
Reeves, J. Walter 146, 815, 4689, 4740-4741
Reeves, J. Walter; and Hudson 147
Reeves, Mary M. 5068
Reeves, Mary M.; and Osborn 4925
Rehn, Judith K. 5465
Reichenbach, Hans 1816
Reid, Loren 4301, 5591
Reid, Ronald F. 3532, 4608
Reiff, Evan A. 3533
Reinhardt, L.R. 976
Reinsch, N. Laram, Jr. 3053
Reiser, Oliver L. 1534, 2660
Reiss, Albert J., Jr.; and Black 4360
Reiss, Samuel 2964
Remmers, H.H. 2283
Rescher, Nicholas 5644, 5739
Reuther, Jean 1405
Reutter, D.C. 5273-5274
Rexroad, Chloe E. 198

Rexroth, Kenneth 4453
Reynolds, Beatrice K. 5466
Reynolds, C. H. 4302
Reynolds, E. 5860
Reynolds, William M. 5467
Rhea, Joseph; and Giffin 3997
Rheingold, P. D.; and Gans 5861
Rhine, Jennie 5862
Rhine, Robley D. 5356, 5468
Rhoads, John K. 1817
Rhodes, Jack 4225
Rice, George P. 817-818,
2138, 3246, 5758
Rice, P. Jeannine 340
Rice, Philip B. 4612
Richards, Darrel S. 819
Richards, E. B. 3534
Richards, Gale L. 4068, 5592
Richards, Gale L.; Cohen; and
Sikkink 4078
Richards, Ivor A. 2284
Richards, Ivor A.; and Ogden
2956
Richardson, Don R. 2377
Richman, Robert J. 1818
Richmond, W. H. L. 820
Richmond, W. H. L.; and Lloyd
4407
Rickard, Paul B. 2378
Rickborn, Ida; and Lundsteen
5690
Rickey, John T. 821
Riddell, George A. R. 148
Riddick, Floyd M. 4690
Ridgeway, James M. 3916
Ried, Paul E. 1982, 2139
Rieke, Richard D.; and Faules
3279
Rieke, Richard D.; and Smith
2840
Rigg, John 149
Riggs, Francis B. 822
Riggs, Joseph H. 491
Rignani, Eugenio 1535
Riley, Floyd K. 2140
Ringwalt, Ralph C. 256, 823,
1011, 1088, 1819, 3535
Ringwalt, Ralph C.; and Brook-
ings 999
Rinsky, L. 5863
Ritchie, A. D. 1536
Ritchie, David G. 257
Ritter, John; and Brink 1075

Ritzenhein, Donald N. 4069
Rivers, William H. 2285
Rives, Stanley G. 1076, 2841,
3247, 5469, 5593
Rives, Stanley G.; and Klopf
3454, 3536, 3813, 3814,
3856
Roach, Helen P. 315, 394
Robb, Mary M.; Thonssen; and
Thonssen 5910
Robbin, Joseph J. 4613
Robbins, Edwin C. 824, 5000
Robbins, James 3054
Robert, Henry M. 4691-4693
Roberts, Frank L. 4070
Roberts, Henry G. 3537
Roberts, Holland D.; and Fox
4303
Roberts, John B. 4454
Roberts, Mary 3538, 4926
Roberts, W. Rhys 2141-2142
Robertson, Roger 825
Robie, Fred S. 1211, 4361
Robinson, Daniel S. 1537-1538
Robinson, Edward J.; and Ros-
now 2287
Robinson, Frederick B. 1212,
1403, 4927
Robinson, James A. 862, 1404
Robinson, James H. 1539
Robinson, James L. 3539
Robinson, Karl F. 3151, 3540,
5001, 5275
Robinson, Karl F.; and Keltner
3248
Robinson, Kenneth W. 1983
Robinson, R. 1043
Robinson, Rex E. 439, 3917
Robinson, William 228
Robinson, Zon 4071
Rock, Kenneth M. 4226, 5470
Rockey, Edward 1984
Roegiers, Charles L. 3541
Roegiers, Charles L.; and
Tubbs 827
Roerig, Ronnie A. 2379
Roethlisberger, F. J. 3055
Roever, James E. 4767
Roever, James E.; and Giffin
4928
Roff, M.; and Weld 1423
Rogers, A. K. 2842
Rogers, Clement F. 3056

Rogge, Edward A. 2843-2844, 5471
Rogoff, Bernard M.; Prenner; and Sternberg 4998
Rohrer, Daniel 341
Rokeach, Milton 5707
Roma, Emilio, III 1077
Romano, Joseph J. 1820
Rooney, Ethel M. 5276
Rooney, M. T. 1821
Roosevelt, Theodore 2893, 2902
Roper, Ralph C. 4614
Rosa, H. M. 3918
Rose, Forrest H. 977-979, 1038, 3815, 4072, 4615
Rose, George H. 5472
Rose, Robert E. 5710
Rosenbaum, Milton 828
Rosenthal, Paul I. 2661-2662
Rosenthal, Solomon P. 2286
Rosenzweig, Sandford; Shearn; and Sprague 3160
Rosnow, Ralph L. 2663
Rosnow, Ralph L.; and Goldstein 2664
Rosnow, Ralph L.; and Robinson 2287
Ross, C. C. 1293
Ross, Edward A. 2288
Ross, Herold T. 829, 2665, 3542, 3816-3819
Ross, Raymond S. 342
Ross, Raymond S.; and Davis 980
Ross, Raymond S.; and Osborne 981
Rossman, George 2289
Roth, Richard W.; and Devlin 3543
Rothman, Richard M. 2666, 2894, 3158, 5864-5865
Rousse, Thomas A.; Summers; and Whan 170
Rousseau, Lousene G. 2143, 3544
Rousseau, Manko; Schopler; Gruder; and Miller 3554
Row, William H. 4073
Rowe, J. Wyant 5278
Rowell, Edward Q. 1213, 1822, 2667
Rowland, A. Wesley 1610, 4616
Rowton, Frederick 229-230

Rowton, Frederick; and Payne 231
Rubinstein, Ronald 1294
Ruby, Lionel 1540-1541
Ruby, Wade 3545
Rudd, Mary J. 4121
Rudin, John J. 2845
Ruechelle, Randall C. 2668
Rugg, Harold O. 1295
Rummel, Lynda 4619
Runion, Howard 3689
Runkel, Howard W. 2859
Rupp, A. E. 3249, 5280
Russ, Wm. A. 3546
Russell, Bertrand 1542-1543, 2669-2670, 2965
Russell, Bertrand; and Whitehead 1576
Russell, Jensen E. 1315
Rutherford, Lewis R. 1611
Rutherford, R. Stanley 3690
Ruys, Constance R. 1985
Ryan, Oswald 3821-3822
Rycenza, John A.; and Schwartz 2292
Ryle, Gilbert 5740
Rynin, David 3057

Saadi, M.; and Farnsworth 2671
Sacksteder, William 1823
Sajdak, Olds; and Stuart 4289
Salant, Richard S. 5594
Salmon, Wesley C. 1544, 1824
Salomon, Louis B. 2966
Salper, Donald 2672
Salsbury, Martha 831
Salter, Leonard M. 5866
Samovar, Larry A. 3547, 5473, 5595-5596
Samovar, Larry A.; and Tompkins 2724
Samples, Eual M. 2380
Sampson, Harold P. 4620
Sanbonmatsu, Akira 5474
Sanborn, George A. 2673
Sanborn, Ruth D. 3548, 5867
Sanders, Gerald H. 5475
Sanders, J. W. 1406
Sanders, Keith R. 1407, 5476
Sanders, Keith R.; and Newman 1393

457

3923, 5286-5287
Shurter, Edwin D.; and Taylor 1012
Shurter, Robert L.; and Helm 159
Shurter, Robert L.; and Pierce 160
Sibley, Carroll 4456
Sibley, Edward C. 3062
Sibley, R. P. 5288, 5772
Sidgwick, Alfred 232, 1551-1552, 2968
Sidis, Boris 2298
Siegel, Elliot R.; Miller; and Wating 2696
Siegel, Seymour N. 3253
Siekman, Harold L.; Laase; and McGee 4865
Siever, George O. 2146
Sikkink, Donald E. 845, 2697-2698, 2896, 3565, 3825, 5289
Sikkink, Donald E.; Cohen; and Richards 4078
Sikkink, Donald E.; Gilkinson; and Paulson 2499, 3022
Sikkink, Donald E.; and Hoogestraat 4673
Silander, Fred S.; and Wasserman 5911
Sillars, Malcolm O. 343, 1218, 2699, 4940
Silliman, Elizabeth R. 5485
Silverman, Franklin 846
Silverman, Irwin; and Shulman 2700
Simley, Anne 5290
Simmons, Henry T. 1090
Simmons, James R. 1828
Simon, Herbert A. 5647
Simon, Rita J. 1829
Simons, Herbert W. 2701
Simonson, Norman R.; Lundy; and Landers 2588
Simonson, Solomon 1614, 1830, 2383
Simonson, Walter E. 3924, 5291-5294
Simonson, Walter E.; and Strange 4941
Simrell, V. E. 2849
Sims, John G., Jr. 161, 416
Singer, R. G. 3063
Sinzinger, Richard A. 3566

Skelly, Loretta 3064, 5486
Skillman, Billy G. 4079
Skorkowsky, George R., Jr. 4420
Skornia, Harvey; and Kitson 5760
Slappey, George H. 4626
Sloan, J. R., Jr. 162
Sloan, Thomas O. 440, 2147
Sloan, Thomas O.; and Talley 847
Sloman, Aaron 1081
Slover, John C. 5487
Slutzky, Julius 5488
Smallwood, Osborne T. 1266
Smart, H. R. 1553
Smart, H. R.; and Creighton 1466
Smelser, J. N. 4942
Smith, Bromley 396, 397, 398, 2148, 2149, 2150, 4642
Smith, Bromley; and Ehninger 399
Smith, Bruce L.; Lasswell; and Casey 5897, 5907
Smith, Carney C. 848, 849, 2850, 3925, 5295
Smith, Charles D. 2446, 5598, 5599
Smith, Craig R.; and Hunsaker 163
Smith, David H.; and Rieke 2840
Smith, Donald K. 400, 2897, 5071
Smith, Donald K.; and Howell 850
Smith, Donald K.; Howell; and Thompson 3855
Smith, Donald K.; and Scott 2702
Smith, Donald K.; Weaver; and Borchers 3175, 3602
Smith, Elmer W. 164
Smith, Glenna 3826
Smith, G. J. 258
Smith, G. M. 1296
Smith, H. B. 1554, 3828
Smith, Harold E. 1411
Smith, Henry P. 851
Smith, Horace G. 852, 3827
Smith, J. C. 5873
Smith, Margurite 4234

Smith, Mary J. 1615
Smith, Myra A. 3567
Smith, Paul W. 3568
Smith, Paul W.; and McCrery 4038
Smith, Raymond G. 2703
Smith, Reed; and Davis 48
Smith, Robert D. 5692
Smith, Robert G. 1219, 5489
Smith, Robert L. 3569, 5296
Smith, Robert M.; and Harris 643
Smith, Robert W. 853, 1220, 1412, 2704, 2851
Smith, Roy M. 166
Smith, T. V. 2705, 4235, 4236
Smith, T. V.; and Taft 5625
Smith, Virgil J. 5763
Smith, Walter R. 5072
Smith, William S. 489, 1555, 1831, 1832, 3254, 3829
Smokler, Howard E.; and Kyburg 1509
Smullyan, A. 1833
Snoddy, Rowena 1991
Snowdon, Leroy 3570
Snyder, Henry N. 401
Snyder, Richard C.; et al. 5648
Sochatoff, A. Fred 2151
Soli, Audrey 5073
Solmsen, Friedrich 1834, 2152
Sommer, Leonard F. 3571, 4080
Sondel, Bess 2969
Sonnino, Lee A. 1917
Soper, Paul 1413
Sorber, Edna C. 4081, 4237
Sorenson, Carolyn J. 3572
Sorenson, Theodore C. 5649
Sorum, Lynn D. 5074
Spalding, William; and Waldstein 296
Sparks, Donna J. 5075
Speer, Diane P. 2153
Speer, James P. 3694
Speer, Richard 2154
Spencer, Floyd A. 1997
Spicer, Holt V. 1616
Spicher, Lynn 199
Spoffard, A. Keith; and Laycock 4993
Sponberg, Howard E. 2384, 2706

Spotts, Carle B. 168, 4082
Spotts, Carle B.; and Graves 75
Sprague, Robert; Shearn; and Rosenzweig 3160
Sproule, G. A. 3831
Stachowiak, Ray J. 2385
Stack, George J. 1082
Staerkel, W. M. 3927
Staley, Dilbert M. 2299
Stang, Richard E. 5297
Stansfield, E. J. 5298
Stanton, Frank 4457
Starbuck, E. D. 1835
Starika, Beverly 1021
Stasheff, Edward 4458
Stasheff, Edward; and Miller 4459
Stebbing, L. Susan 1556, 1557
Steele, Edward D. 2155, 2710
Steele, Edward D.; and Redding 2707
Steer, Max D.; and Tiffin 3065
Steil, Lyman K.; Houseman; and Jaksa 3437
Stein, Waltrout J. 5744
Steinbarger, Helen T. 4627
Steiner, Ivan D. 4943
Steinfatt, Thomas M. 4770
Steinfatt, Thomas M.; Betting-haus; and Miller 1630
Stelzner, Hermann G. 3575, 4084
Stenius, A. 5299
Stephans, Thomas W. 5076
Stephens, Frank F. 316
Stephens, Lucille 5300
Stern, Philip M. 5601
Stern, William 1414
Sternberg, William N. 3255
Sternberg, William N.; Rogoff; and Prenner 4998
Stevens, Edwin L.; and Swallow 862
Stevens, Frederick E.; and Carr 35
Stevens, Walter W.; and Hilde-brandt 3128
Stevens, Wilmer E. 855, 2708, 3928
Stevenson, Adlai 4460
Stevenson, Charles 919, 920
Stevenson, Fred G. 4694

Stevenson, Robert Louis 259
Stewart, Daniel K. 1836
Stewart, Irwin 856
Stewart, John R. 2990
Stewart, John R.; and Merchant 857, 3574
Stewart, Paul 4362
Sticht, T. G.; and Foulke 3115
Stiles, Karl A. 858
Stinchfield, Sara M. 2300
Stine, Richard L. 3290
Stirling, Brents; and Pellegrini 135
Stites, Ruth E. 402
Stites, William H.; and Pacilio 133
Stockdale, Allen A. 4421
Stockdale, Robert 5077
Stoddard, George D. 4418
Stokes, Thomas J. 3695
Stoll, Elmer E. 4238
Stone, Arthur P. 3256, 3696
Stone, Arthur P.; and Garrison 169
Stone, Julius 1558
Stone, Susan J. 4255
Stone, Vernon A. 5693
Stonecipher, Nadine 3575
Stonehocker, D. Doyle 3576
Storey, Alfred W.; and Pfister 4220
Stovall, Richard L. 3181
Stovall, Thera 2156
Stowe, A. Monroe 5301
Strange, Bennett; and Simonson 4941
Strange, Buford B. 3863
Stratton, Clifford 5302
Strawson, P. F. 1559
Streeter, Don 859
Streff, Craig R. 3577
Stretch, Evelyn A. M. 1993
Streufert, Siegfried; and Heslin 5673
Stringer, William 4628
Stromer, Walter F. 985, 4085
Strother, David B. 5490
Strother, David B.; and Hensley 3421
Strubinger, Howard M.; and Graham 4170
Stryker, Lloyd P. 2301
Stuart, Rex 3697

Stuart, Sajdak; and Olds 4289
Studebaker, John W. 2970, 4629, 4630, 4631, 4632, 4633, 4634
Studebaker, John W.; and Williams 4635
Stupp, Vicki 5491, 5492
Sturgis, Alice F. 4695, 4696, 4743
Sturgis, Alice F.; and Hall 4669, 4721
Stutts, Harry B. 4419
Sullivan, Daniel J. 1560
Sullivan, John; and Harter 2221
Summers, Dorothy 1994
Summers, Harrison B. 2709, 3859, 4461
Summers, Dorothy B.; Whan; and Rousse 170
Sunday, Daniel M. 3578
Swain, Louis H. 4363
Swallan, Alan; and Stevens 862
Swanson, Don R. 4307
Swanson, Linda A.; and Wilmington 5340
Swartz, James C. 3834
Swem, Earl G. 5964
Swift, Edgar J. 2302
Swift, Walter B. 863, 3161
Swigeit, J. Mack 864
Swinney, James P. 3162, 3950, 4087, 4308, 4309
Sykes-Marshall, J. G. 865
Symonds, Percival M. 1561

Tacey, William S. 4090, 5305
Taft, Robert A.; and Smith 5625
Tallet, Jorge 1837
Talley, C. Horton 2386, 4239
Talley, C. Horton; and Sloan 847
Talley, Paul M. 2159
Tallmadge, John A. 867
Tame, Ellwood R. 441
Tammelo, I. 1838
Tanner, J. R. 302
Tarski, Alfred 1562
Tarver, Jerry L. 1415
Tarver, Jerry L.; and Bradley 5522
Tatlock, Abraham 5306

Tauber, Abraham 868, 5965
Tauro, G. P. 5874
Taylor, Anita 1839
Taylor, Carl 4945
Taylor, Carl; and Barnard 986
Taylor, Carl; and Shurter 1012
Taylor, Eric 4254
Taylor, Glenn J. 3579
Taylor, Harold C. 3164
Taylor, James S. 5875
Taylor, John A. 403
Taylor, Nonabeth G. 3526
Taylor, R. 5745
Taylor, Stuart P.; and Epstein 5807
Taylor, Vernon L. 171, 2387
Taylor, W. S. 2711
Temerlin, M. K.; and Gordon 5819
Temple, Gloria; Olson; and Tompkins 1395, 3511
Temple, Norman 4418
Temple, Norman; and Dunn 4393, 4394, 4422
Templer, C. S. 4091
Templin, Olin; and McCracken 1563
Terkel, Meyer 4637
Terman, Earle L. 4638
Terris, Walter F. 987, 988, 5764
Terry, Donald R. 172
Tewell, Fred 344
Tewell, Fred; and Braden 404
Thalberg, I. 5694
Thaler, Margaret 3182
Thayer, Albert R. 173, 4240
Thayer, James B. 234
Thayer, Lee 2971
Thayer, Lynn W. 3929, 5876
Theios, John; Berman; and Fraser 5658
Thistlethwaite, Donald L. 1840
Thistlethwaite, Donald L.; de Haan; and Kamenetzky 2712
Thistlethwaite, Donald L.; and Kamenetzky 1267
Thistlethwaite, Donald L.; Kamenetzky; and Schmidt 1268
Thomas, Archie M. 2853, 4092
Thomas, Charles E. 3735
Thomas, David A. 1222, 4946

Thomas, David A.; and Anderson 1223
Thomas, Earl T. 4365
Thomas, Gordon L. 5308
Thomas, Gordon L.; and Ralph 2713
Thomas, Harrison C. 4640
Thomas, J. D. 2899
Thomas, Katharine 5309
Thomas, Ota 345
Thomas, Peter D. C. 4697, 5357
Thomas, R. H.; and Secord 839
Thomas, Ralph W. 174
Thomas, Sid B., Jr. 1224
Thomas, Stafford H. 3165
Thompson, A. W. 3698
Thompson, Claud A.
Thompson, David W.; Howell; and Smith 3855
Thompson, Ernest 1225, 2714, 2715
Thompson, G. W. 3699
Thompson, Janna L. 1841
Thompson, Leslie 5310
Thompson, Mary E. 5078
Thompson, Morris L. 442
Thompson, Richard N. 869, 870, 2716, 3580, 3930, 5311, 5312, 5313, 5314
Thompson, Wayne N. 175, 871, 872, 989, 1226, 1227, 2161, 2717, 3581, 4093, 4947, 5908, 5966, 5967
Thompson, William J. 3700
Thomson, Mehran K. 2303
Thonssen, Dorothea; Thonssen; and Fatherson 5909
Thonssen, Dorothea; Thonssen; and Robb 5910
Thonssen, Lester W. 873, 874, 2162, 2304, 2718, 5968
Thonssen, Lester W.; and Baird 2305
Thonssen, Lester W.; Fatherson; and Thonssen 5909
Thonssen, Lester W.; Robb; and Thonssen 5910
Thorndike, Edward L. 2306, 2719
Thorne, E. J. 2720, 2721
Thornton, Gayle E. 5914
Thornton, Helen G. 3582

Thouless, Robert H. 1564, 1565, 2307
Thurber, E. 1416
Thurston, L. L. 2722
Thurstone, Louis L. 1297
Tiffany, Albert C. 2388
Tiffin, Joseph; and Steer 3065
Tillman, Frank A. 5877
Timmons, Glenn W. 3583, 3584
Timmons, William M. 875, 1417
Tinkcom, H. M. 876
Toch, H.; and MacLean 4948
Todd, W. 1842
Tompkins, Miriam D. 4641
Tompkins, Philip K. 2723
Tompkins, Philip K.; and Baker 4241
Tompkins, Philip K.; Olson; and Temple 1395, 3511
Tompkins, Philip K.; and Samovar 2724
Tooze, Russell 877, 878, 5315, 5316
Topliss, Patricia 1918
Torrence, Donald L. 990, 1195, 1228, 2725
Toulmin, Stephen E. 176, 1566, 1567
Toussaint, Sylvester R. 1269, 3836, 3931
Tower, Donald M. 5317
Towne, Ralph L.; and Anapol 4773
Towns, Stuart; and DeMarco 5969
Towns, Stuart; Eubanks; and Baker 5936
Towns, Stuart; Eubanks; and DeMarco 5970
Towns, Stuart; and Wright 5971
Townsend, D. E. 879
Townsend, Howard W. 3259
Tozier, R. B. 405
Tracey, John E. 1298
Trautman, P. A. 1418
Travis, John C. 4771
Treat, Jimmie D. 1617, 1843, 3951
Treolar, A. E. 1299
Tressider, Angus 2726
Trew, Marsha A. 443

Trout, John M. 3585
Troxell, E. E. 3260
True, Bert G. 5079
Trueblood, C. K. 2727
Trueblood, Elton P. 3586, 4242
Trueblood, Thomas C. 406, 1419, 3261, 3262, 3263, 3587, 3588, 3838, 3839, 4949, 4950
Tubbs, Stewart L. 2728
Tubbs, Stewart L.; and Roegiers 827
Tucker, Charles O. 880
Tucker, Elaine 5318
Tucker, Raymond K. 2389, 2730, 3066, 5603
Tucker, Raymond K.; and Bostrom 1330, 2430
Tucker, Raymond K.; Koehler; and Mlady 881, 2731
Tucker, Raymond K.; and Rebstock 1618
Tucker, Raymond K.; and Ware 2729
Tufts, J. A. 5319
Turner, Frederick H., Jr. 3166
Turner, Robert G. 5320
Tussman, Joseph 882

Uberweg, F. 275
Ullian, J. S.; and Quine 5705
Ullman, Stephen 2972, 2973, 2974
Ulmer, S. S. 5878
Underwood, Willard A. 883, 1316
Unruh, A. 4951
Upchurch, R. L. 5321
Urban, W. M. 2975
Utterback, William E. 884, 1844, 2163, 2732, 2733, 2734, 2735, 2736, 2737, 3067, 3589, 4952, 4953
Utterback, William E.; and Harding 1845, 2518
Utterback, William E.; and Winans 182
Utterback, William E.; and Yeager 912
Utzinger, V. A. 2390

Ware, Paul D.; and Tucker 2729
Warford, Aaron A. 235
Warner, Donald; and Giffin 2497, 4821
Warnock, Henry Y. 489
Warren, Irving D. 2745
Warren, James A. 5494
Warther, George S. 3269
Wasby, Stefn L. 2746
Wass, Philmore B. 4647
Wasserman, Paul; and Silander 5911
Waterman, Thomas H. 318
Watkins, Dwight E. 3270, 5327, 5328
Watkins, J. M. 3600
Watkins, Lloyd I. 1271, 2853, 3271, 5495
Watkins, Lloyd I.; and Highlander 5553
Watkins, Lloyd I.; and Loftus 3467
Watkins, R. 4746
Watling, Thomas O. 2394
Watson, J. Steven 4747
Watts, Lowell 895
Weathersby, Manaway C. 5496
Weaver, Andrew T. 896, 3601, 5329, 5330, 5331
Weaver, Andrew T.; Borchers; and Smith 3176, 3602
Weaver, Andrew T.; and Shaw 153
Weaver, Carl H.; and Anapol 3296
Weaver, James F. 3603
Weaver, Richard L. 347
Weaver, Richard M. 1302
Webb, Sally A. 5080
Webb, Sally A.; Clark; and Williams 5341
Webb, Sally A.; and Williams 4974
Weber, Earl 1851
Weber, J.; Cowan; Hodinott; and Klein 2459
Weber, Natalie 5332
Webster, M.; and Boren 5779
Webster, Marjorie F. 3933
Weckesser, Ernest P., Jr. 5497
Wecter, Dixon 897
Wedeking, Gary A. 1852

Weedon, Jerry L. 2174
Weekley, E. 2977
Wegener, Ruth A. 2991
Weil, R. 1573
Weiler, G. 3070
Weinberg, Harry L. 2747, 2854, 2978
Weinscheuk, Franz 4959
Weinstein, Jack B.; and Berger 1422
Weinstein, Jack B.; Morgan; and Maguire 1288
Weise, Selene H. C. 5498
Weisman, Anna; and Loeb 5213
Weiss, Franklin R. 2748
Weiss, R. F. 2749
Weiss, Robert O. 2750, 4100, 4960
Weiss, Walter 2751
Weiss, W.; and Hovland 2538
Welch, Charles E. 2395
Welch, Dale D. 2000
Welch, F. A. 5333
Welch, J. D. 5334
Welch, Mary J. 5499
Weld, H. P.; and Roff 1423
Welday, John D. 178
Welden, Geraldine S. 2857
Welden, Terry A. 2396, 4469, 5881
Weldon, John 4312
Weldon, Lloyd W. 5500
Wellman, Carl 921
Wellman, Francis L. 4323
Wellman, R. R. 1853
Wells, Earl W. 1108, 1231, 3845, 3846, 5335
Wells, Hugh N. 3272, 4961, 4962
Wells, Hugh N.; and O'Neill 4963
Wells, Hugh N.; O'Neill; and Sarett 4964
Welsch, J. Dale 5081
Wenburg, John R.; and Dovre 5800
Wenger, D. A. 4470
Wenzel, James W. 3604
Werkmeister, W. H. 1574
Wertheimer, Max 1575
West, Robert W. 898, 4247, 4248, 4965
Westerfield, Hargis 3605,

3934, 4966
Westfall, Alfred 899, 900, 901, 4967, 4968
Weston, John R. 2397
Wetherby, Joseph C. 902
Wetherick, N. 5695
Wetzel, William A. 903
Whan, Forrest L. 4969
Whan, Forrest L.; Summers; and Rousse 170
Whately, Richard 186, 236, 277, 1885
Wheater, Stanley B. 4103, 4970
Wheatly, Jon 1854
Wheeler, David; and Jordon 2752
Wheeless, Lawrence R. 2752, 4104
Wheelwright, Philip 2979
Whipple, Ruth H.; and Immel 4990
White, Alan R. 5746
White, H. Adelbert 1232, 1233, 2754, 3606, 3607, 3608, 3609, 4971, 5336, 5337, 5972
White, (Mrs.) H. M. S. 2001
White, Jacqueline A. 348
White, Richard C.; Diehl; and Burk 3101
White, Richard C.; Diehl; and Satz 3100
White, Trumbell 904
White, Wendell 2310
White, William P. 4702
Whitehead, Alfred N.; and Russell 1576
Whitehead, Jack L., Jr. 1424, 2755
Whitney, Bryl A. 4698, 4699
Whittaker, James O. 2756, 5882
Whittemore, Irving C. 3936
Whittier, Duane H. 2757
Whorf, Benjamin L. 2980
Whyte, James P. 5501
Wichelns, H. A. 1425, 1855, 2758, 3611
Wick, Robert 1234
Wick, Warner A. 1856
Wickert, Frederic 2759
Wieman, Henry N.; and Walter 2855
Wiener, F. B. 1857
Wiener, Norbert 2311
Wiese, M. J. 420

Wiggam, A. E. 1235
Wigley, Joseph A. 4105
Wigmore, John H. 1303, 1304, 1577, 1578
Wiksell, Wesley 4700
Wilbur, William A. 1579
Wilcox, Ruth; and Frederick 4986
Wilcox, Stanley 2175, 2176, 2177
Wilcox, W. C. 1858
Wilder, Larry; and Harvey 5696
Wilds, Elmer H. 5338, 5339
Wileden, A. F.; and Kolb 98
Wiley, B. I. 4313, 4314
Wiley, Earl W. 1859, 4972, 5606
Wiley, Francis R. 3848
Wilkes, Raymond S.; and Purnell 4223
Wilkie, Walter 2760
Wilkinson, Ray, Jr. 3612
Wilkinson, William J. 4249
Willett, Thomas H. 1244
Willett, Thomas H.; and Brewer 3191
Willett, Thomas H.; and Gruner 1272
Willhoft, Waldo O. 179
Williams, A. M. 262
Williams, Byron B. 4648
Williams, Chester; and Studebaker 4635
Williams, D. C. 1580
Williams, Donald E. 405, 407, 906, 3613
Williams, D. Terry 4250
Williams, Dorothy 4649
Williams, Frederick 1581
Williams, Frederick; Clark; and Wood 4973
Williams, Frederick; and Webb 4974
Williams, Frederick; Webb; and Clark 5341
Williams, H. M. 905
Williams, Hazel B. 2900
Williams, Jayme C. 5502
Williams, Terry W. 446
Williamson, Arleigh B. 3837, 4315
Williamson, Colwyn 1860

Willis, Edgar E. 2761, 4251, 4471
Wills, Beatrice B. 5765, 5915
Wills, Gayle V.; and Rea 4748
Wills, John W. 2398
Wilmington, S. Clay 3614, 4772, 4975
Wilmington, S. Clay; and Swanson 5340
Wilson, Harold S. 2178, 2179
Wilson, J. C. 1582
Wilson, Louis R. 180
Wilson, O. J. 3273, 3615
Wilson, Thomas 1921
Wilson, W. A. 992
Wilson, Warner; and Zdep 5886
Winans, James A. 2762, 3938, 3939, 4976, 5883
Winans, James A.; and Hudson 181
Winans, James A.; and Utterback 182
Winchell, Constance 5912
Windes, Russel R., Jr. 2901, 4106
Windes, Russel R., Jr.; and Hastings 183
Windes, Russel R., Jr.; and Kruger 5612, 5613
Windes, Russel R., Jr.; and O'Neill 184
Wing, Herbert J. 3940, 4977
Wingate, J. D. 907
Winick, Charles 5766
Winks, Robin W. 1305
Winship, Albert E. 4252
Winship, F. L.; and Bedichek 3851
Winslow, C. N.; and Scheffler 2679
Winsor, Jerry L. 1083, 3516
Winterowd, W. Ross 2763
Winters, Dennis 3617
Wise, Charles N. 1620, 4978
Wishart, Charles F. 908
Wisner, Harold E. 4979
Wisness, Arthur M. 3274
Withington, Robert 909, 3618, 3619
Witt, Carl 3941
Witt, W. H. 5343
Wittig, John W. 2002
Wittig, Robert G. 2003

Wojcicki, Ryszard; and Przelecki 1814
Wolf, A. 1583, 1584
Wolfson, Lester M. 5884
Wolgamuth, Dale E. 4651
Wolvin, Darlyn 5082
Wood, Barbara S.; Williams; and Clark 4973
Wood, E. O. 521
Wood, Herbert J. 4652
Wood, Kenneth S. 5344
Wood, Roy V. 185
Wood, Roy V.; and Hunsinger 3943
Woodward, Emily B. 4653
Woodward, Howard S. 2764, 3849, 3850, 4980
Woodward, Michael L. 1045
Woolbert, Charles H. 910, 1861, 2765, 2766, 2767, 2768, 2769, 3172, 3275, 3276, 3620, 4107, 4981, 4982, 4983
Woozley, A. D. 5747
Workun, Arthur E. 447
Worsham, James A. 2312
Woting, Edward; Miller; and Siegel 2696
Wrage, Ernest J. 911
Wrage, Naomi H. 5503
Wrenn, Charles 5083
Wright, Charles F. 4654, 5345
Wright, Donald K. 3277
Wright, E. A. 5885
Wright, Philip Q. 2313
Wright, Thomas K.; and Towns 5971
Wright, Tim 4985
Wright, Warren E. 2770
Wright, Wiley J. 3291
Wroblewski, Jerzy
Wyer, Malcolm G. 4655

Yarborough, Carolyn H. 5504
Yeager, W. Hayes 4656
Yeager, W. Hayes; and Sandford 150
Yeager, W. Hayes; and Utterback 912
Yeager, Raymond 1236, 1862
Yoakam, Doris G. 408

467

Yoder, Jess   409, 5505
Yost, Mary   1863
Young, Fred L., Jr.; and
    O'Brien   4596
Young, Gladys E.   5346
Young, Kimball   2314, 2315,
    2316
Young, Paul   2317

Zacharias, Donald W.; and
    Johannesen   410
Zander, Eugene   4657
Zarefsky, David   1091, 1237
Zdep, Stanley; and Wilson   5886
Zelko, Harold P.   913, 993,
    2771, 2856, 3071, 3278,
    4367, 4368
Ziegelmueller, George W.; and
    Boaz   3967
Ziegelmueller, George W.; and
    Esch   3381
Ziegler, Donald J.   5358, 5626
Ziff, Paul   2981
Zimmerman, Gordon I.   4108
Zimmerman, Leland L.   448
Zwerling, Stanley A.   5767

school debating 5052
Administrative support for debate, gaining 3286
Administrators' attitudes toward debate 3290
Adversary system, and ethics 2790
Advertising, and belief 2649
and rhetoric 2676
Advisory rhetoric 2488
Advocacy 2289
art of 2301
in the courtroom 2443
ethics of 2819, 2848
in problem solving 5656
(See also Persuasion)
Affirmative approaches 1096
and burden of proof (see Burden of proof)
to case, proving 1156
to plan 1132, 1232
placement of 1106
and speakers, duties of 1136
African slave trade debate (1858) 5382
After-dinner speaking 4111, 4161, 4197
contest in 4193
Agricola, Rudolph, dialectical system of 371
Aims of debate 462 (See also Objectives)
Alaska Boundary Tribunal, argumentation by 5452
Alcidamas, and contemporary sophistic 1904
Alexander Hamilton High School debate program 5113
Allegheny College, debate program 3662
speaker's bureau 3583
Allegorical debate in Greek literature 5605
Alumni forums 4578
Ambiguity, in Kennedy-Nixon debates 5473, 5595-5596
in persuasion, role of 2658
in reasoning 1723
America, rhetorical theory in (1635-1850) 1948, 2060
American colonial rhetoric 2105
American debaters' tour of Britain 3350
American debating 4256, 4374
American Forensic Association 3829
aims and objectives of 3761
code of 3725
constitution and by-laws of 3705, 3840

directory of (1972-73) 3603
and the great debates 3746
growth of 3774
and the high schools 5150
history of 3713
new standards of 3706
presidential report on 3708
presidents of 3714
program of, and tournament standards 3952
restructuring of 3773
standards of 3808
twentieth anniversary of 3842
value of 3747
American history, controversial speaking in 353
American Institute of Banking 4
American Legion oratorical contest 4118
American Lyceum, beginnings of (1826-1840) 352
history of 320
in Michigan (1818-1860) 347
in Ohio 325
American oratory 4134, 4173
bibliography of 5922
Amplification, in Massilon 1945
Analogy 1810
in debate, use of 1624
definition and implications of 1848
effects of, on attitude change 1765
on source credibility 1765
in Greek mathematics and rhetoric 1604
and persuasion 1693
in philosophy and rhetoric 1605
and polarity 1901
a psychological consideration 2577
a rationale for 1741
reasoning by 1735
St. Thomas Aquinas on 1505
teaching of 1775
Analysis, of argument 1231
of debate, discussion for 3251
of issues 1216
of policy questions, teaching 3219
studies in 1157
Analytic statements 951, 956
Analyticity, problem of 1814
Ancient Greece, rhetoricians of 1869
Ancient rhetoric, Aristotelian tradition in 2152
arrangement, theories of, in 1951
audience, views of, in 1975
disposition, concepts of, in 1934
ethos in, concepts of 2144
in modern speech course 2066
Ancient Rome, rhetoricians of 1869

Argumentation (cont'd)
a bibliography of 5926
course in 3194
a rhetorical project for 3247
textbooks, treatment of enthymeme in 1597a, treatment of
logic in 5063
as a dramatic convention 5761
in early Greece 1901
formal logic, role of, in 1629
in general education 748, 3232
honors course in 3212
as humanistic subject 463
in legal education 906
and logic 1696, 1806, 1844
nature of 1828
objectives of 462
and persuasion 1839, 2627, 2667
positive and negative, and attitude
change 2341
a project in 3255
prolegomena to 1822
psychological view of 2735
student opinion, effects on, of 443
teaching of 258, 3257
use of,
in John Quincy Adams' speeches
5412
by Alaska Boundary Tribunal
5422
in John C. Calhoun's defense of
slavery 5522
by Percy Foreman in Mossler-
Powers case 5376
in Andrew Johnson's impeachment trial 5409
in the Kennedy-Nixon debates
5415
in National Health Insurance
Movement (1932-1940) 5391
in the Orestian Trilogy 5812
in the Trade Union Movement
(1902-1935) 5429
in the Wishart-Bryant debate on
fundamentalism 5475
(See also Argument and Persuasion)
Argumentative analysis 1213, 1231
Aristides, as influenced by Isocrates
1892
Aristotle 291, 1905
on arrangement 1922
bibliography of recent work on
5949
Kenneth Burke's rhetorical theory
as influenced by 1954
and contemporary textbooks 3259
contrariety, theory of 1429
on cross-examination 4363

dialectic of 1997
on disputation, art of 307
on emotional and ethical persuasion
2001
enthymeme of 1606, 1636, 1692
recent interpretations of 1762
on ethical proof 1970
in modern speech literature
1965
on ethics of speaking 2809
on ethos 2838
on evidence 1331
on inconvertible modal propositions
1734
on invention 1931
on language 2111
on limits of argument 1646
on logic, and belief 1998
and good 1730
on logos in oral communication
1612
on mean, doctrine of 2006
and rhetorical style 2085
and the modern rhapsode 2103
modes, theory of, and forms of
proof 1611
on moral good, criteria of 1230
on poetics 2071
on public speaking 2104, 2141
on psychology 2099
of argument 2163
rhetoric of, concept of choice in
2155
composition and preservation of
2126
early history of 2067
functional interpretation of, a
2162
intended uses of 2133
introduction to 286
and introductory public address
2138
in the middle ages 2127
normative terms in 1988
as a textbook 3246
theory of 1888, 1959, 1974,
2000, 2034, 2051, 2071, 2142,
2439, 2601, 2083
on rhetoricians 2083
on scientific method 1768
on stasis, theory of 2011
on style 2050
on syllogism 1526, 1671
topics of 1635
date of 2075
modern approaches to 2086,
2087
as sources of proof 1236, 1862

472

tradition of, in ancient rhetoric 2152
on truth, in rhetorical discourse 1930
for the undergraduate 3188
and value, problem of 2778
Arizona State Teacher College debate program 3628
Arrangement 1966
in rhetorical theory 1969
a theory of 246
theories of, of ancient rhetoricians 1951
   of Aristotle, Cicero, Quintilian, and Winans 1922
   of John Quincy Adams 1991
Artifact, and attitude change 2700
"Artificial reason," Coke's Theory of 1748
Assertion and truth 1718
Athletics and debate 536
Atlanta University film forums 4649
Attack and defense (see Refutation and Rebuttal)
Attention 3168
Attic oratory, legal aspects of 2057
Attitude(s) 2283, 2402
and beliefs 2235
and cognitive organization 5724
credibility, effect of, on 2740
of debaters 5708
   and non-debaters, toward debate 5015
debating, effect of, on 5016, 5017
directive and non-directive procedures, effects of, on 2712
information-seeking as affected by 2454
instability of, and persuasibility 2342
and judgments 2411
measurement of, and debate 2524
and motivation 2306
of parents toward forensics 5143
and prestige and suggestion 2582
radio delivery, effect of, on 2473, 2761
reasoning as affected by 1840
scales, construction of 2478
of students, as affected, by organization 2703
   by propaganda 2453
theory, and Toulmin's model of argument 1663
and values 5706
Attitude change 2239, 2297
during advocacy 5725
analogy, effects of, on 1765

arguments, effects of, on 2457
conflict-arousing 2368
evaluation of 2385
opposing, acknowledgment of 2640
oral 2564
printed 2565
and artifact, concept of 2700
and audience comprehension 2502
debate, effect of, on 2547
determination of 2474
disorganization, effects of, on 2596
ethos, effects of, on 2340, 2457
evidence, effects of, on 1330, 2430, 2738
an experimental design for 2464
experimental studies of 2566
toward high school debate topic (1960-1961) 5289
and language intensity 2325, 2432
and majority attitude 2381
measurement of 5710
non-fluency, effects of, on 2596, 2691
oral communication, effects of, on 2422
and personality 2430
and positive and negative argumentation 2341
predictors of 5733
prestige, effects of, on 2640
propaganda, effect of, on 2547
reference, effect of, on 2374, 2632
refutation, effect of, on 1267, 1268, 2598, 2599
response reinforcement, effect of, on 2688, 2689, 5742
scale and intensity analysis in studying 2448
and social influence 2203
toward sources 5715
theories of 5702
by verbal behavior 5741
and win-loss record 5881
(See also Opinion change)
Attitudinal inherency 1179
Attorney debate judges 4775
Audience, the 2765
ability of, to distinguish between, sincerity and insincerity 2355
   inferential and descriptive statements 2350
to evaluate argument 1630
to apply tests of evidence 1359
to recognize emotional and logical appeals 2668
for academic debate 2709, 3299, 3302, 3306, 3307, 3329, 3432,

Audience, the (cont'd)
3486, 3503, 3504, 3509, 3515,
3531, 3553, 3578
desires of 2716
adaptation to, by debaters 2555,
2647, 3116
affinities of 2634
analysis of 2202, 2659, 2758
ancient rhetoricians on 1975
anticlimax order, effect of, on
2697
argumentative speeches, effect of,
on 2465-2467
authoritative assertion, effect of,
on 1424, 2697
bodily movement, effect of, on
2567
and the communicator 2416
comprehension of, and attitude
change 2502
loaded language, effect of, on
2592
concept of, in rhetoric of Perelman,
Johnstone, and Natanson 2405
credibility techniques, effects of,
on attitude of 2584
debate and discussion, relative effects of, on 2347
debating, effect of, on 2529
debating for 3102
explicit and implicit conclusions,
effects of, on 2728
humor, effect of, on 2513
interpretation of, by 2367
interest, factors of, to, in debate
2352
negative and positive argument,
effect of, on 2351
non-fluency, effects of, on 2691
obstinate 2417
opinion, measurement and analysis
of 2764
orientation of, and opinion change
2394
party preference, influence of, on
2498
provocative language, effects of,
on 2363
proximity, effect of, on persuasion
2713
psychology of 2226
reaction of, to cross-examination
debate 2610
experimental work in 2608
measurement of, to argumentation 2737
problems in measuring 2609
to symposium and debate 2611

scattered vs. compact seating, effect of, on 2494
speech rate, effect of, on 2357,
2497
status cues, judgments of, by
2519
syllogisms, judgments of, by 1719
visual aids, effects of, on 1410
Auer, J. Jeffrey, on discussion and
debate 575
Augustine, Aurelieus, rhetoric of
2035
Augustine, influence on, by Cicero
1883
Australia, speech education 5763,
5805
Australian Conscription Debate (1916)
5509
Australian debaters 5772, 5805
Authoritative evidence 1306
in academic debate 1332
audience, effect on, of 1424, 2697
persuasion, effect on, of 2319,
2499
tests for 1408
Authority, group position and attitudes
toward 2679
Axiology of rhetoric, an 2483

-B-

Babylonian Talmudic academies, rhetorical theory in (70-500) 1980
Bacon, Francis, on communication
and rhetoric 1920
on fallacies 1830
logical proof in speeches of 1602,
5432
public address, theory of 1999
rhetoric, concept of 2169
contribution to 2170
on understanding, reason and rhetoric 2173
Bain, Alexander, rhetoric, philosophy
of 1938
theory of 1989
Baird, A. Craig, course in debating
of 3199
Baker, George P., argumentation theory of 196, 1609, 1729
contribution to debate of 3367
Baker, Thomas, criticism of rhetoric
by 2116
Ballot, shift of opinion 3233, 3234
(See also Debate ballot)
Barron, William, language in 1967
Bary, René, on rhetoric 1932

Bates College 10
  former debaters of 809, 810
  international debate tour of 3630,
    3661, 3687, 3697
Baylor University 17
Beattie, James, rhetorical theory of
  2018
Beecher, Henry Ward, rhetorical
  theory of 1874
Begging the question 1722 (See also
  Fallacies)
Behavioral change, effect of persuasion on 2508
Behavioral research in law, bibliography of 5962
Belief 5705, 5714, 5722, 5726, 5727,
  5737, 5743
  and action 5713
  and attitudes 2235
    definition of 5720
    and values 5706
  basis of 1432
  condition of, in advertising 2649
  and constraint 5732
  ethics of 5721
  experimental nature of 5734
  and knowledge 5700, 5712, 5728,
    5729, 5731, 5745
  and personality 2727
  problems of 5707
  psychology of 2257, 2587, 2638
  test of 257
  and values 5698, 5747
  and will 5738
Beloit, forensic activities at 3638
Benau, forensics at 3675
Bennett, William H., on debate and
  speech 2569
Benson High School debate program
  5244
Bentham, Jeremy, criticism of rhetoric by 2027
Benton, Thomas Hart, debating technique of 5427
Best evidence, appraisal of 1339
Beveridge-Hoar debates on Philippine
  question 5367
"Beyond reasonable doubt" 1829
Biased authoritative assertions 1320
Bible, the, debate in 5555
Bibliographies 5887-5963
  bibliography of 5947
Binghamton course in debate, the
  5317
Black, Hugo, on freedom of speech
  5771
Black power debate (1840) 5587
Blair, Hugh 1915, 2041, 2042

on language 1967
practice of rhetoric 1946
rhetoric, theory of 1939, 1946
  philosophical assumptions under-
    lying 2017
Bloomsburg State College speech program 3625
Bodily movement, effect of, on audience interest 2567
Borah, William E., argumentation of,
  in Congressional debate 5390
  debate strategy of 5381
  Senate debates of 5364
Boston University debate tournament
  3986
Boswell, James, on rhetoric 2055
Bowdoin College's sponsorship of high
  school forum 5106
Bowling Green State University, as
  site for PKD Convention 3826
  speech program of 3622
Boylston Chair of Rhetoric and Oratory 1982, 2053, 2139
Boys' High debate program 5165
Brevity, and persuasiveness 3156
Brewer, G. C., as a debater 5418
Bridgeport Univ. debate fraternity
  3644
Brief(s) 1087-1089
  affirmative and negative 1161
  for debate 997-999, 1001, 1003,
    1011, 1012
  distribution of 1357
  in law 1086
  making of 1451
    and use of lawbooks 1085
    new techniques of 1212
  as related to argument 1158
British debate 4369-4423 (See also
  Oxford Union and Parliamentary de-
  bate)
  collection of 5614
British Parliamentary debate on the
  Regency (1788) 5404
Broadcasting, debate 4424-4471
  discussion 2648
  forums 4569
Broadhus, John A., on rhetoric 1957
Brockriede, Wayne, on Stephen Toulmin 1595
Broderick-Gevin debates (1859) 5551
Brooks, Phillips, on rhetoric 1949,
  2064
Brown vs. Board of Education 5350
  evidence and argument in 5490
Brownlow-Pryne debates 5431
Bryant, William J., argument of, in
  fundamentalism debate 5475

Buckley, William S., debate techniques of, in N.Y. mayoralty campaign 5401
Budget survey for forensics (1966-1967) 3298 (See also Financing forensics)
Budgeting high school forensics 5169, 5170
Burden of proof 1117, 1118, 1220, 1234, 1643, 5787
 and counterplan 1226
 in criminal law 1141
 and the negative 1218
 and presumption 1093
 as related to statutes 1214
Burke, Kenneth, on perspective 2100
 on rhetoric 1888, 2100, 2530
 influence of Aristotle on 1954
Burlesque debates, collection of 5608

-C-

Calhoun, John C., arguments of, in defense of slavery 5522
 in political theory of 5385
 debating of, in pro-slavery speeches 5387
 refutation used by 5521
 in Senate debate on Three Million bill 5402
California high school(s), forensic program in 5064
 judging speech contests in 5076
California junior high school debating 5251
Cambridge disputations 398
Cambridge Union 302, 4388, 4406, 4407
Campaign debates (1960) 5563
Campbell, Alexander, debate techniques of 5359
 in Robert Owen debate 5375, 5393
 in John B. Purcell religious debate 5394
  background of 5538
 rhetorical theory and practice of 1990
Campbell, George 2041, 2042, 2048
 and the classical tradition 2109
 on emotional and ethical persuasion 2001
 on evidence 1328
 Hume's influence on 1927
 on language 1967
 William Leechman's influence on 2032
 on logical truth 1674

psychological background of 2118
 on public address 1943
 and revolution in inventional theory 2045
 rhetorical theory of 1926, 1940, 2016, 2096, 2157
 and rhetorical tradition 2046
 on taste 2036
Canadian-American student conference 4652
Canisius High School debate program 5101, 5118
Cannon, Joseph G., debate techniques of 5428
Capitol forum 4627
Caplan, Harry, studies in honor of 1919
Carbondale debate plan 5312
Cardozo, Benjamin, on legal thinking 1513
Carnap, Rudolph, the philosophy of 1824
Carpenter, Nathaniel, on dialectic and rhetoric 2074
Case, analysis of 1115, 1116
 comparison debate 4258
 construction of, in tournament debates 1147
Cass, in Senate debate on Three Million bill 5402
Cassiodorus, on rhetoric 1972
Catholic colleges, education at 3649
Causal analysis, history of, before Mill 1726
 and rhetoric 1726
Causal explanation, and action 1756
Causal proposition 1794
 proving 1648, 1649
Causal reasoning, in academic debate 1591
 in medical testimony 1787
 treatment of, in argumentation 1586
  in debate textbooks 1596
Causal relations 1664, 1685, 1750, 1752
Causes 1850
 actions and reasons 1664
 plurality of 1701
 and reasons 1768, 1818
Central States Speech Assn. speech contests 3860
Chambers of rhetoric, the Netherlands 1985
Championship debates, collection of 5612, 5613
 characteristics of 4003
 programs of, in American high

476

high school debate 5210
Colonial debating 309, 314
Colonial disputation 309
Colonial New England town meetings 392
Colorado high schools, coaching debate in 5174
Colorado State, Debating League 4045
  Speech League, history of 5034
Columbia College, debating societies at 241, 394
  speech education, history of, at 315
Command arguments 1852
Common ground 2501 (See also Identification)
Communications, dissertations in theology 5946
  limitations of 2690
  and logic 1835
  psychological barriers to 2556
  psychology of 2213
  rationalization in 2656
  reference guide to 5907
  and rhetoric 2410
  study of 5735
Community forums 4621, 4623, 4647
Comparative advantage case, the 1091, 1113, 1114, 1121
  attitudes of judges and debaters towards 1094, 1101, 1107a
  classification of 1128
  in debate textbooks 1097
  Arthur N. Kruger on 1104, 1091, 1114, 1186
  negative approaches to 1125, 1133, 1222, 1223
  and public policy decision-making 1084
  and the traditional case 1237
  validity of 1139
  weakness of 1166, 1167
Competitive debate 3851-4252
  criticism of 3893, 3901, 3918
  de-emphasis of, debate on 4040, 4080
  value of 3866, 3916, 3930, 3940, 4080
  (See also Academic debate)
Competitive forensics, for the disadvantaged 4203
Composition, practice of, by Thucydides and Isocrates 2080
Comprehension, credibility, effects of, on 2724
  listening rate, effects of, on 3108
  loss of, effects on persuasion 2753

message structure, effect of, on 2715
pitch change, effects of, on 3100, 3101, 3107, 3109, 3110, 3115
sentence length, effects of, on 3009
sentence order, effects of, on 3010
speech rate, effects of, on 3124, 3169
speech summaries, effects of, on 3166
speech variables, effects of, on 2419, 2420
Compromise, context and limits of 2705
Conciliation, psychology of, the 2573
Conclusion-drawing 2537 (See also Inference)
Conclusions and introductions 3039
Conference, types of 4625
Conference debate 4488, 4560
Conference method at U.N. 4643
Conference speaking 4656
Confirmation, Hempel's logic of 1659
  theorem of, and probability 1842
Conflict 5643, 5645
  and defense 5629
  resolution of 5675
Conflict-arousing arguments, and attitude change 2368
Conformity and persuasibility 2588
Congressional debate(s) (debating) 5539, 5570, 5583, 5593, 5604
  on the admission of Hawaii to Union 5389
  analysis of, method for 5524, 5526
  anti-war arguments in (1809-1941) 5503
  of William E. Borah 5390
  on the Dies Committee (1937-1944) 5369
  effect of 5530
  on the Kansas-Nebraska Bill 5453
  on Labor-Relations Act of 1947 5649
  on the League of Nations 5386
  on the Morrill Act (1862) 5540
  on the Oregon question 5494
  persuasive techniques in 5392
  on the James K. Polk administration 5416
  on Public Law 87-447, 5374
  of Thomas Brackett Reed 5580, 5581
  on the Removal Bill (1830) 5413
  reporting of 5571, 5572
  on the War of 1812 5464

478

on evolution 5588
on FDR's court enlargement
proposal (1937) 5534
on the Foote Resolution 5356
Fox-Pitt, on East India Bills
(1783-1784) 5363
on Napoleon 5411
for the Governorship of Iowa
(1859) 5523
on Gulf of Tonkin 5478
on Hawaiian Statehood 5536
in the Haywood trial 5351, 5406
on impeachment of Andrew
Johnson 5409
on imperialism (1898-1900) 5426
Indiana-DePauw educational 5546
intercollegiate 5448, 5461, 5496
Johnson-Long-Coughlin (1935)
5362
Kennedy-Humphrey 5515
Kennedy-Nixon (1960) 5354, 5415,
5423, 5451, 5455, 5459, 5473,
5479, 5481, 5484, 5497, 5541,
5542, 5553, 5560, 5564, 5594-
5596, 5601
on Quemoy-Matsu 5482
on Korean War 5568
Lane Seminary 5527
Lend-Lease 5379
of Abraham Lincoln, as state
legislator 5516
Lincoln-Douglas (1858) 5349,
5352, 5353, 5365, 5410, 5419,
5457, 5472, 5488, 5513, 5533,
5579, 5606
at Charleston 5396
of James Madison, at Virginia
Convention 5449
in Michigan Legislature (1953)
5361
on Mormon Suffrage, in Idaho
(1880-1906) 5407
Mytilene, the 5508
on national health insurance
(1932-1940) 5391
during N.Y. mayoralty campaign
(1965) 5401
(1901) 5573
Parliamentary, on the affirmation oath controversy 5414
on confederation of British
North American Provinces
(1865) 5440
on daily adjournment (1962-
1963) 5444
during James II reign 5439
on the Naval treaty 5548
on Public Order Bill (1936)

5535
on the Regency (1788-1789)
5404
(1768-1774) 5357
on the Stamp Act (1766) 5545
on the Suez Canal (1876) 5498
on the War of (1812) 5464
in the trial of Jean Peltier 5398
Pratt-Newman 5408
presidential debates 5447
public joint debates under Richards Primary Law 5425
Ranney-Dennison gubernatorial
debates (1859) 5368, 5412
on recognition of Red China
5355
on Reconstruction amendments
5347
of the Reformation 5358
between Reformed and Ana-
baptists (1571) 5505
of Republican Credentials Committee (1952) 5557
Senate, of William E. Borah
5364
on Civil Rights (1957) 5395
(1964) 5420
on Crittenden Compromise
(1860-1861) 5397
of 85th Congress 5504
on Foote Resolution (1829-30)
5468
on FEPC (1948) 5501
Gulf of Tonkin resolution
5499
on Labor-Management Rela-
tions (1947) 5388
on League of Nations 5443,
5520, 5549, 5575-5576
on neutrality legislation (1935-
1941) 5378
(1939) 5456
on North Atlantic Pact 5458
on Philippine annexation 5399
on recognition of U.S.S.R.
(1917-1934) 5437
on Roosevelt's plan to enlarge
Supreme Court 5441
on Selective Service Bill (1940)
5383
on slavery and states' rights
5471
on Taft-Hartley Bill (1947)
5477
on tariff (1909) 5372
on Three Million Bill 5402
on treaty of Paris (1898) 5380
on Truman Doctrine 5463

Debate(s)(ing)
  judging (cont'd)
    criteria for 4820, 4826, 4829,
      4864, 4877, 4878, 4928, 4970
    debate on 4895
    debater-judge ratings compared
      in 4751, 4779
    double-summary 4891, 4892
    evaluation of 4812, 4857, 4859-
      4861
    forced choice scale for 4757
    ideal characteristics of 4924,
      4937, 4944, 4985
    improving, suggestions for 4791
    instructions for 5184
    in Kansas high schools 5024
    objectivity of 4763, 4769, 4933
    practices in 4778
    study of 4765
  in junior high school 5321
  language of 3034, 3043, 3048
  leagues 4060, 5081, 5333
    of Colorado State 4045
    of Michigan 5230
      high schools 5139
      of junior colleges 3780
    of Michigan State College 5164
    of Minnesota high schools 5225
    of Montana high schools 5240
    plan for 3709
    of Texas 5286
  and lecture-forum 4305
  and legal profession 459, 471, 483,
    680, 692, 749, 770, 853, 867, 882
  and liberal education 636, 637, 738
  and literary societies 3580
    of the south 357
  and logic 3105
  magazine, editing of 5794
  management of 3606
  manners 5829
  men and women in, relative effec-
    tiveness of 3421
  mental attitudes in 863
  as method 576
  methods of 567
  and ministry 857
  in modern education, place of 618
  modes of, in Roman rhetorical
    theory 1984
  as molder of public opinion 756
  of the month 5567
  motivation for 3422, 3554
  Negroes in 3292
  new aims for 868
  new ideals in 806
  new patterns of 1710
  new program for 3480

  in (1940) 3415
  in (1958) 3428
  non-academic, coaching of 3217
  and non-academic life 559
  objectives of 462, 584, 708, 721,
    788, 792, 796, 860
  in the old South 300
  organization of 3309
  organization of ideas in 672
  overemphasis in 3569, 3601
  parliamentary (see Debates, analy-
    sis of)
  and parliamentary procedure 4726
  and personal success 795
  and personality development 729
  role of persuasion in 2533
  philosophic risk in 579
  philosophy of 499, 679, 871
    for Americans 2620
  and politics 612, 693, 800
  popularizing of 3409
  practices 3364
    survey of 3511
  preparation for life 619
  in prison 610, 790
  procedures of schools in national
    speech tournaments 3288
  program(s) in 3519
    of Alexander Hamilton High
      School 5113
    of Allegheny College 3662
    of American colleges and uni-
      versities 3357
    of American Institute of Banking
      5775
    of Annapolis 3693
    of Arizona, University of 3634
    of Arizona State Teachers Col-
      lege 3628
    of Australia 5805
    of Bates College 3630, 3661,
      3687, 3697
    of Beloit College 3638
    of Benan 3675
    of Benson High School 5244
    of Bowling Green University
      3826
    of Boys' High School 5165
    of Bridgeport University 3644
    building of 3571
    of California junior high schools
      5251
    of California, northern and
      southern 3323, 3324
    of Cambridge University 302
    of Canisius High School 5101,
      5118
    of Charleroi High School 5323

484

485

Debate(s)(ing)
  program(s) in (cont'd)
    of Rockford 402
    of Rollins College 3648, 3651
    of Rutgers University 3659, 3688
    of St. Albans 305
    of St. Joseph's College 3695
    of Southwestern College in Kansas 321
    of Southwest Louisiana Institute 3624
    standards for 4036
    of Stanford University 3636
    of Stephen F. Austin College, history of 346
    of Stout State University 3645
    of S.U.N.Y., at Albany 3653
    of Swarthmore College 3657, 3664
    of Texas, University of 3674
    of Topeka High School 5302, 5310
    of Trinity College, Dublin (18th century) 383
    of Virginia, University of 380
    during wartime 3284
    of Washington State University 3684
    of Wayne State University 328, 3637
    of western colleges, survey of 3345
    of West Point 3700
    of Western Reserve University 3641
    of West Virginia University 3686
    of Wilkes College 3669
    of William Jewell College 3703
    of Wisconsin State College at EauClaire 3702
    of Wisconsin, University of 3646
    of Yale University 301, 3658, 3679
  promoting 585, 794, 3361
  and propaganda recognition 793, 833
  propaganda techniques in 3014
  proposition(s) 996, 997, 1024, 1029, 1032, 1035, 1039, 1040
    analysis of 1057
    attitude change toward 982, 5289
    characteristics of 952
    classifying 947, 986-988
    definition of 1048, 1058-1060, 1069
    fifty years of 1025
    for (1922-1923) 932
    for (1927-1928) 1036
    for (1931-1932) 1034

  phrasing of 934, 974
  relevancy of 942
  requisites of 965
  selection of 934, 962, 980, 981
    in high school 5085
    by Pi Kappa Delta 937, 973
  shortcomings of 970
  types of 933
  variety of 966
  and professional soldier 687
  and psychiatric nursing 834
  publicizing of 3412
  and public interest 759
  published materials for 5959
  purpose of 536, 644 (See also Debate, aims of; and Debate, objective of)
  and radio 895
  a rationale for 3222
  recruitment for 3564, 3572, 3616
  reference 1351
  and reflective thinking 672
  of the Reformation 5358
  reforms for 3620
  regulations for 3991
  in the Renaissance 306
    medieval antecedents of 379
  research in 5770, 5852, 5855
  research for 1417
    upgrading 1400
  revised art of, the 486
  revival of, the 3593
  rules of 3216
  and salesmanship 2682
  satire, use of, in 2655
  scheduling of 3595
  and scientific attitude 1651
  scope of 536
  and selling life insurance 745
  general semantics for 3003
  skill in 469
    gained from English and political science 3178
  and social action 912
  and social adjustment 558, 802, 803
  and social rehabilitation 610
  society(ies) 50, 259, 410, 3711, 3787, 3801, 5768
    Cambridge Union 302
    of Davenport High School 5193
    Edinburgh 303
    function of 5197
    Ladies' Edinburgh 310
    Magpie and Stump 304
    organization and procedure of 3734
    at Princeton University 389
    at St. Albans 305

value of 3736
Village 259, 260
(See also Debate organizations)
in southern California, origins
of 3665
in the space age 465
and speech communication 697,
844, 2422, 2569
and speech objectives 430
speech rate, and judgments in
2357
standards of 3416
between Stanford and California 362
statistics, use of, in 1349, 1411
status of (1958) 3483
strategy in 1217
students' view of 634
style in 3087
and emphasis 3005, 3006
suggestion, use of, in 2458
and superior student, the 859
a systems analysis of 643
teaching of 3179, 3307
criteria for 3249
criticism in 3236
problems in 3197
recent methods of 3267
in Pennsylvania colleges 646
rebuttal in 3268
by students 3317
by telephone 3191
"teaching cycle," adapting of, to
3208
as a teaching method 662
teams, trips for 3542
techniques of 1124, 3344
of James Madison 5582
of Napoleon 5586
of Richard M. Nixon 5578
(1947-1960) 5491
of Lord North 5599
in Pennsylvania colleges 3579
of Wendell Phillips 5511
of selected Senators 5504
of Alfred E. Smith 5558
of Wendell Wilkie 5554, 5589
textbooks, new aspects of 3210
argument, study of, in 1615
causal reasoning, study of, in
1591, 1596
comparative advantage case,
study of, in 1098
criteria for selecting 3181
definition of major terms in 1045
ethymeme, study of in 1597a
ethics, treatment of, in 2781,
2786
induction, study of, in 1619

medieval 375
presumption and burden of proof
in 1093
timing of 3496
tournament 3942-4108
audience for 2750
beginner, instructions for, in
3951
at Boston Univ. 3986
at Buffalo Univ. 4092
criticism of 3950, 3954, 4033,
4036, 4046, 4075-4077, 4082,
4084, 4086, 4087, 4096, 4105
debate coaches, behavior of, at
3959
and debate leagues 4060
evaluation of 3962, 3971, 3976,
4081, 4083, 4088, 4091, 4094,
4097, 4099, 4100, 4103
financing of 3953
function of 3975
history of, in the U.S. 3944
management of 3943
and non-decision debating 4089
at Northwestern Univ. 4106
origin of 4002
over-emphasis in 4042
power-matching by computer in
4014
problems of 3965
procedures of 3948
and public discussion 3961
recommended changes for 4078
revising traditional format of
3977
scheduling of 4011
scoring in 4006
standards for 3952
television of 5340
travel to 3955, 4066, 4079,
4095, 4098, 5865
type(s) of 4065
audience, 3967
challenge 3964
courtroom 4073
direct-clash 4027
dual 4047
duplicate 4073
elimination 4015
extemporaneous 4073
forum 4073
group-action 3992-3994, 3997
versus discussion contests
3970
evaluation of 3994
participant attitudes in
3997
impromptu split-team 4063

Debate(s)(ing)
  tournament
    type(s) (cont'd)
      novice 3974
      one-man 4085
      Oxford 4073
      practice 3968, 4048, 4059
        a plan for 4048
      values of 3960, 4005
      at West Point 3983, 4026
      of the Western Speech Assn.
        4032
      winners of, determing 4028
      written critiques at 4007
    training in, of Supreme Court
      judges 5556
    recent trends in 3607, 3609
    and the truth 580
    unit in, a 3239
    in the U.N. General Assembly 4706
    use and abuse of 4735
    value of 61, 536, 540, 545, 572,
      592, 628, 651, 658, 663, 673,
      686, 710, 776, 812, 866, 885,
      886, 896, 897, 3418, 3429
      academic 440, 493, 568, 676,
        681
      for advocacy 641
      after-college 777
      for "allness" behavior 437
      in armed forces 504
      for articulate leadership 836
      in business 454, 493, 767
      for character development 730,
        865
      for citizenship 495, 566
      for the clergy 814
      for college presidents 519
      to Congressmen 723, 747, 769
      in current affairs 543
      debaters, as seen by 451
      in a democracy 489, 500, 505,
        511, 514, 538
      in domestic life 596
      educational 742
      for engineers 887
      and finance 483
      for freedom of speech 544
      for freshman entrance examina-
        tions 447
      for general education 546
      for gifted students 3316
      for group thinking 507
      to an historical novelist 670
      and the honors program 551
      in human relations 588, 694, 787
      in industrial relations 843
      for leadership 542, 547

      and the legal profession 515,
        556
      for legislators 891
      in life activities 510, 848, 913
      in mind, training of 879
      in national crisis 631
      in national defense 494
      need for research on 845
      and open-mindedness 444
      permanent 716
      for personality 498
      for the physician 554
      in post-war service to democ-
        racy 464
      for practical education 753
      for preaching 539, 682
      as pre-ministerial training 488
      in public administration 595
      for public service 769
      in public speaking course 623
      for radio career 485
      as reported, by former debaters
        426, 427, 433
        by sponsors of Pi Kappa Delta
          432
      and scholarship 506
      in schools 509
      for the scientist 744
      for social inquiry 461
      for social integration 434
      as social methodology 508
      for social and political leader-
        ship 523
      statements on, anthology of 609,
        854, 899
      for student leadership 480
      to teacher in training 503
      for U.S. Senate 803
      for vocational success 439
      in wartime 862, 894
    voice as factor in 3097
    in wartime 782, 804, 3479
    winning of, dogmatism in 5767
    women in 3278, 3421, 3426
    of yesteryear 361
Debater(s), achievement of 453, 3293
  advice to, by statesmen 634
  attitudes of, toward debating 888
  from Australia 5772, 5805
  characteristics of, at Iowa Univ.
    3281
  code for 3363, 3365
  duties of 1163
  and evidence, law of 1348
  faults of 521
  financial aid for 3543
  freshmen, training of 3319
  guidelines for 3330

5175
Don Pacifico debates, the 5384
Double-summary technique 1189
Douglas, Stephen A., as public
speaker and debater 5349
speeches of 5365 (See also Lin-
coln-Douglas debates)
Dramatic declamation 4147
Dramatic interpretation, contests in
4145, 4146
Duke Univ., debate fraternity at
3672

-E-

Early English rhetoricians, on rhe-
torical prose 2171
Early humanist rhetoric, and George
of Trebizond 2179
Early rhetorical instruction 2177
Eastern High School forensics pro-
gram 5163
Eastern style debate 5303
Edinburgh debating society 303
for ladies 310
Education, at Catholic colleges 3649
and debate 578
in Renaissance England 1871
Educational debate 3220, 3291 (See
also Academic debate)
Ehninger, Douglas, on Stephen
Toulmin 1595
Eisenhower-Stevenson debates (1956)
5366
Elder Seneca, the, on rhetoric 2151
Electronic "opinion meter" 2346
Elecutio, in 17th cent. England 2101
Elizabethtown College debate fraternity 3642
Emerson College, history of debating
at 331
Emerson, Ralph Waldo, on philosophy of rhetoric 1937
Emphasis, analysis of 3065
modes of, in public speaking
2337, 2481, 3032
and style, in debate 3005, 3006
Empirical knowledge 1836
Emotion, in persuasion 2468
and reasoning 1742, 2628
in the rhetorical tradition 2030
Emotional appeals, in advertising
2233
and logical appeals, audience
recognition of 2668
relative effects of 2641
on Negro 2674

research on 2418
in rhetorical theory 1966, 2576
Emotional conflict, effect of, on persuasion 2648
Emotional persuasion 2001
"Emotional" and "rational" political
leaflets compared 2523
Emotionally-loaded argument, effect
of, on recall 2644
Emotions, facial expressions as key
to 2618
England, invention in, rhetorics of
(1550-1600) 1987
(1600-1800) 1815
(1759-1828) 1944
rhetorical theory in (1700-1750)
1950
(1950-1900) 2044
style, concepts of, in (1600-1700)
1971
English morals and uses of rhetoric
2056
English Renaissance mind, the 2172
English Renaissance rhetoric 2158
English rhetorics 2754 (See also
England)
Entailment 1813
Enthymeme 1597a, 1622
Aristotle's treatment of 1636, 1692
recent interpretations of 1762
compared with Toulmin's mode
of argument 1606
and cognitive theory 1666
definitions of 1592
and logical validity 1783
and persuasion 1859
as rehtorical argument 1662
in rhetorical theory 1603, 1761
uses of 1681
Epicheireme, the 1680, 1769
in Greek and Roman rhetoric 1656
Minucian on 1770
Erskine, Thomas, use of argument in
Thomas Hardy trial 5495
Ervin, Sam, speeches on segregation
decisions 5424
Ethical analysis 919
Ethical argument(s) 1753
in game theory tournaments 3949
Ethical judgments (see Propositions
of value)
Ethical language 2993
Ethical persuasion 2001
Ethical proof, Aristotle's view of
1965, 1970
in debate 2845
Quintilian's view of 1952
principles of 1955

Ethical proof (cont'd)
(See also Ethos)
Ethical standards, in Minnesota High
School debate 5069
Ethics, of academic debate 2785,
2788, 2816, 2820
  of advocacy 2790, 2819, 2848
  of argument 2834, 2841
  of belief 5721
  of coaching debate 3223
  of communication, basis for 2852
    evaluating 2796
    standards of 2824, 2825
  of controversy 2818
  of debate 2797, 2804, 2822, 2829,
    2837, 2846, 2853
  debate code of 2795
  of debating both sides 2863
  and evidence 2840
  of expression 242
  of language 914, 915, 918, 919,
    921
  of persuasion 654, 2814, 2815,
    2823, 2827, 2830, 2832, 2833,
    2835, 2843, 2844, 2847
    and adversary system 2790
    analysis of 2855
    and appropriateness 2813
    and Birmingham crisis 2810
    classical and modern concepts
      of 1925
    contemporary concepts of 2783
    and existentialism 2787
    suggestion for 2789, 2805, 2806
    teaching of, in speech courses
      2784
  for policy questions 2776
  of politics 2842
  psychology of 2772
  of public speaking 2836
    Aristotle's basis for 2809
    semantic approach to 2854
    teaching 2821
  of rhetoric 1302
  of speech contest 2828
  of teaching speech content 2808
Ethos, analysis of 2376
  in ancient rhetoric 2144
  and argument 2388
  Aristotle's concept of 2838
  artistic and non-artistic, interac-
    tion of 2318
  attitude change, effect on 2340,
    2457
  of Alexander Campbell, in Owen
    debate 5375
  comparative effects of 2370
  as a confounding element 2531,

2595, 2723
  in contest oratory 4223
  and credibility proneness 2696
  in debate 3121
  and ethical proof 2630
  experimental research in 2406
  factors of 2755
  an experimental study of 2323,
    2348, 2349
    of Jack L. Whitehead 2687
  humor, effect of, on 2512
  in intercollegiate debates 5448
  in international propaganda 2353
  and language usage 2982
  measurement of 2393, 2594
    scales for 2433
  of John Milton, in a polemic 2153
  non-fluency, effects of, on 2607,
    2691
  opinionated statements, effect of,
    on 2606
  organization, effects on, of 2339,
    2343, 2692
  in persuasion, concept of 2661,
    3121
  presentation, effect of, on 2686
  public speaking, effects in, of
    3120
  effect of, on recall of information
    2560
  effect of reference on 2374, 2632
  relevant and irrelevant aspects of,
    effects of 2408
  in rhetoric, concept of 1986
  and the sleeper effect 2684
  social status as a factor of 234
  and subjective probability 2395
  treatment of, in speech textbooks
    2319a, 2334
  and vocal variations 3084
European education in middle ages
  1913
Evaluation in parliamentary procedure 4709
Evaluative dynamic language 3019
Evidence, in advocacy, speeches of
  2328, 2336
  in Aristotle's rhetoric 1331
  and attitude change 1330, 2430
  from authority 1306
  in Brown vs. Board of Education
    5490
  George Campbell's doctrine of 1328
  in civil law 1406
  in common law 1285
  cooperative file for 1395
  in debating 1307, 1313-1316, 1326,
    1343, 1352, 1403, 1419, 5019

492

1819

Grant, W. B. , on debating both sides 2895, 2900

Graphs (see Visual aids)

Great debaters, style of 3008

Greco-Roman education, rhetoric in 1872

Greece, speech education in 367

Greek rhetoric, epicheireme in 1656

Grierson, H. J. C. , on rhetoric 2526

Group-action debate tournament, at Kansas Univ. 3994, 3997, 4022

Group decision-making 5666, 5667, 5688

Group forum 4614

Group opinion, compared with expert opinion 2590
    effect of, on individual opinion 2752

Group persuasion, experiments in 2407

Group position, and attitudes toward authority 2679

Group problem-solving 5681

Group systems in high school debate 5327

Gulf of Tonkin debates, argument in 5478

-H-

Hamilton, Andrew, speaking of, at Peter Zenger trial 5517

Handbooks 1409

Hardy, Thomas, trial of, argument in 5495

Harvard, debating at 240, 3696
    history of disputation at (1700-1800) 345

Harvard-Oxford debate 3654

Harvard-Yale debate, history of 349

Harvey, Gabriel, on rhetoric 2178

Hawaii, Univ. of, debating at 3671

Hawaiian statehood debates, language of 5536

Haywood trial, the 5351, 5406

Hearsay evidence 1412

Heart of America debate tournament 3995

Hemple's logic of confirmation 1659

Heraclitus, on logic in oral communication 1612

Hermogenes on stock issues 376

Heywood, John, on logic and rhetoric 2107

High school debate(s) 4987, 4989, 4992, 5021, 5050, 5054, 5079, 5091,
5092, 5097-5099, 5103, 5107, 5114, 5125, 5136, 5148, 5149, 5167, 5180, 5192, 5193, 5211, 5213, 5215, 5217, 5227, 5231, 5233, 5248, 5257, 5270, 5281, 5283, 5293, 5298, 5299, 5307, 5313, 5316, 5329, 5334, 5336, 5343
    administration of 5002
    and the American Forensic Assn. 5150
    coaching of 5238, 5239, 5295
    collection of 5615
    confusion in 5128, 5322
    critical thinking, effects on, of 5178, 5179
    direction of 5161
    effect of, on attitudes 5016, 5017
        on critical thinking 5039
        on college speech training 5210
    an effective program for 5162
    ethical standards in 5069
    evaluation of 5029, 5033, 5043, 5080, 5094, 5331
        by administrators 5052
        in Oklahoma 5004
    evidence, use of, in 5019
    experiment in 5278
    goals of, 5002, 5140, 5172
        as affected by decisions 5344
    group systems in 5327
    institute for, at Nebraska, Univ. of 5040
    justification of 5154
    league(s) of 5119, 5328
    manual for 4992-4995, 4998-5000
    motivation for 5301
    new plan for, in Montana 5127
    in Pennsylvania 5141
    policies and practices of 5066
    and political opinion 5173
    preparation for 5120
    program, organization of 5026
        in southeastern U. S. 5291 (See also Debate program)
    promoting 5237
    refutation and rebuttal in 5042
    reorganizing methods of 5151
    society 5183
    teaching 5280
    textbooks, evaluation of 5056
    tournament, television of 5340
    tradition in 5232
    tragedy of 5158
    value of 5086, 5222
    vitalizing 5325

High school debaters, conference of, at Purdue Univ. 5216
    intelligence of 5311, 5314
    objectivity of 5032 (See also De-

497

ity 2756
Induction 1569
Rudolph Carnap on 1824
and consistency 1743, 1744
current issues of 1508
in debate textbooks 1619
design of 1657
grounds of, the 1580
justification of 1653
metaphysical presuppositions of 1790
and non-rational factors 1779
Charles Peirce on 1654
and probability 1506, 1570
proof by 1432
Inductive logic and inductive reasoning (see Induction)
Inexact concepts, logic of 1690
Inference, in decision-making 5653
and information 1746
validity of 1846
Inferential and descriptive statements 2350
Information, and inference 1746
versus persuasion 2455
recall of, and organization 2371
Information-seeking, effects of 2454
Informative speaking, a bibliography of 5958
Inherency 1165, 1168, 1171, 1179, 1203, 1209
Inquiry, John Dewey on 1853
nature of 5639
in problem-solving 5656
value of 909
Instructions for debate judges 5184
Intellect and emotion, a behavioristic account of 2766
Intelligence, effects of, on false beliefs 2652
of high school debaters 5311, 5314
and voice 3140
Intelligibility, and monotonous delivery 3165
Intemperate language (see Unethical language)
Intensity, analysis of, and attitude change 2448
of language 2983, 3000
of message, effects of 2597
Intention 5628
DeQuincey on 2159
theory of 2539
Interaction between speaker and audience 2485, 2486
Intercollegiate conference 4644
Intercollegiate contests, faculty help in 3221

Intercollegiate debate(s)(ing) 823
artistic ethos in 5448
collections of 5612, 5613, 5616, 5619-5621, 5623, 5627
contribution of 491
criticism of 450
evolution of 403
history of 336
at Iowa, Univ. of 439
in Ohio 358
as persuasion, training in 529
practical values of 827
rational philosophy of, a 522
rhetorical devices used in 5846
value of 452
(See also Debate and Academic debate)
Intercollegiate discussion, reserve plan for 4267e
Intercollegiate forum 4585
Interest, factors of, in debate 2352
Internal summaries 3041
International debate(s)(ing) 339, 819, 3419, 4394, 4404, 4411, 4415
arrangements for 3249, 3348
committee on 3249, 3348
exchange for 3551
improvement of 3301
and National Student Federation 3712
program, of Bates College 3630, 3697
(1921-1958) 3286
of Oregon, Univ. of 3660, 3698
proposition for 1038
status of 3435
tournament, at York Univ. 4307
in the U.S. 3433
International debaters, selection of 3430
International forum 4540, 4543
International propaganda, effect of ethos in 2353
Interpersonal persuasion 2625
Interpersonal relations, psychology of 5701
Interscholastic debate, criticism of 531
Interscholastic debater, achievement of 5022
Interscholastic League of Texas, forensic program of 5044
Interscholastic speech contests, in dramatic interpretation 4145, 4146
in extemporaneous speaking 4136
in oral interpretation 4182, 4183
in oratory 4230
Interstate Oratorical Assn., winning orations of 4114, 4120

Interview data, interpreting 1378
Intramural debate 3537, 3613, 5315
Intramural forensics 3559
   in wartime 3481
Introductions and conclusions 3039
Inventio(n) 1966
   John Q. Adams on 1994
   Aristotle on 1931
   in Thomas Hart Benton's debates 5427
   in A. Campbell's debate with R. Owen 5360
   Cicero on 1931
   classical doctrine of 2043
   and disposition, modern views of 2335
   in B. Disraeli's speeches 5510
   in English rhetorics (1550-1600) 1987
      (1600-1800) 1815
      (1759-1828) 1944
   in John Marshall's speaking 5592
   a modern approach to 2521
   Quintilian on 1931
   in rhetorical theory 1960
   study of 2220
Iowa high schools, debating in 5203
   extemporaneous speaking in 5146
   forensic league of 5022
   orations of 5055
Iowa Interscholastic Speech Assn., judges in 5074
Iowa, Univ. of, debate program 3701
   debaters of, characteristics of 3281
Irish national debate championship 5879
Irrelevancy 1787
Irrelevant information 1402
"Is" and "should" relationship 1046, 1077, 1079
Isocrates, fellow rhetoricians of 2176
   influence of, in antiquity 1997
      on Cicero, Dionysius, and Aristides 1892
   on method of composition 2080
   precepts of 2014
   on rhetoric 1928, 2091, 2166
Isodorus of Seville, on rhetoric and dialectic 1935
Issue(s), analysis of 1208, 1216
      teaching 1211
   of constitutionality 1142
   of debate 1131
   of the (1960's) 5752
   ways of confusing 1151

Izelgrinus, Jacobus, on rhetoric 1898

-J-

Japan, forensic activities in 3678
Jargon, in debate 2959, 3020, 3034, 3043, 3048, 3064
Jefferson, Thomas, and rhetoric 2013
Jewel, John, on rhetoric 2078
John of Salisbury, on rhetoric 2154
Johnson, Andrew, debate on impeachment of 5409
Johnson-Long-Coughlin debate 5362
Johnson, Samuel, on rhetoric 2120
Johnson, Wendell, on semantics 3012
Johnstone, Henry W., Jr., on the audience 2405
   on philosophical argumentation 1724
Judges, background of, in Iowa Speech Assn. 5074
   and juries, decisions of, compared 5785
   the language of 2653
Judging, applied logic in debate 1641
   debate 4749-4985
      a bibliography on 5950
      criteria for 4752, 4761, 4762, 4767, 5080, 5337, 5341
         in Kansas high schools 5068
         in Wisconsin high schools 5051
   speech contests 4749
      in California high schools 5076
Judgment, and attitudes 2411
   and thought 5638
Judicial behavior, analysis of 5759
Judicial decision-making 5646
   primacy effect in 5693
   reasoning in 5668
Judicial proof 1467, 1577
Judicial rhetoric 2770
Judicial thinking 1740
Junior college, debating in 3560, 3561
   objective of 703
   forensic program in 3436
   speech program in, in Texas 3626
Junior forum 4648
Junior high school, debate in 5087, 5134, 5180, 5282, 5321
   forensics in 5144
   forensic league 681, 5221
Jury, psychology of 5766
   research in, bibliography of 5933
Juvenal, and Quintilian 2008

Mader, Thomas, on the AFA ballot 3295

Madison, James, as a debater 5449, 5582

Maine, Univ. of, debate program 3689

Major change of status quo 1172

Majority attitude, and attitude change 2381

estimate of, and persuasion 2675

Majority and expert opinion compared 2615

Majority opinion, and religious attitudes 2444

Management decision 5647

Manuscript delivery 3128

Many-valued logic 1837

Marquette Univ. debate program 342, 3656

Marsh, Charles A., forensic career of 3502

Marshall, John, invention in speeches of 5592

Marshall, Thurgood, arguments of, in segregation issue 5502, 5537

Mass debating 3605

Massilon, amplification in 1945

Mass media, and attitudes 2562

Mass persuasion, theories of 1936

Master index, the 1327

Material, and comprehension 2482

Maurus, Rabanus, and medieval rhetoric 2125

Maverick debate judge 4782

McElligott's American Debater 410

McIntire, Carl, argument in speeches of 5493

Mean, the, Aristotle's doctrine of 2006, 2085

Medical causation 1789

Medieval arts of discourse, bibliography of 5955

Medieval debate 379

Medieval logic 1632

Medieval rhetoric 2124, 2125

Medieval university, the (1200-1400) 1875

Melanchton, Philip, on rhetoric 1953

Mellinkoff Medal for debate, the 3636

Message structure, and comprehension 2715 (See also Organization)

Metaphor 2909, 2979, 3001, 3029

and simile, in persuasion 3053

Miami Univ., speech program of 340

Michigan Debate League 5230

Michigan Junior College Debate League 3780

Michigan high schools, debate in 5308

debaters in, effectiveness of 5036

debate league of 5139

forensic assn. of 5164, 5177

Michigan State College, debating at 328

debate league sponsored by 5164

Michigan, Univ. of, parliamentary debate at 4570

Microphone technique 3149

Middle Ages, European education in 1913

Midwest Conference debate 4620

Milburn High School, open forum at 5256

Milburn, William H., on rhetoric 2022

Mill, John Stuart, rhetorical theory and practices of 1924

on utility of debate 685

Mills, G. E., and Petrie, H. G., on logic in debate 1827

Milton, John, ethos in polemic of 2153

on rhetoric 2102

Minnesota high schools, ethics of debate in 5069

debate league of 5225, 5290

Minuchian on the epicheireme 1770

Mississippi junior colleges, debating in 3631

Missouri high schools, debating in 5053, 5294

forensics in 5159

Missouri, history of 316

Univ. of, debate fraternity at 3647

Missouri Valley Debate League 3718, 3719

Modern congress in Rhode Island schools 4611

Modern rhapsode, and Aristotle 2103

Modern speech course, ancient rhetoric in 2066

Monotonous delivery, and intelligibility 3165

Montaigne, on rhetoric 2023, 2024

Montana, debating in 5127

Montana high school debate league 5240

Montana State high school speech tournament 5061

Moore, Wilbur E., on debate 1710

Moorehead High School debate program 5258

Moot court debate at West Virginia 5790

Moral judgments, support of 1792 (See also Propositions of value)

Moral studies, and rhetoric 2019

Non-decision debating 4793, 4806,
4825, 4875, 4886, 4887, 4913,
4915, 4938, 4939, 4945, 4952,
4980, 4982
  vs. decision debating 4089
  in high school 5204, 5205
Non-fluency, effects of 2596, 2607,
2691
Non-logical proofs 188
Non-professional debate judges 4750
Nonsense debates, collection of 5610
Non-verbal communication 3163
Norfolk Prison debaters 610
Normative terms, in Aristotle's
rhetoric 1988
Norms 1063
  analysis of 1129, 1776
North Carolina Univ. debate program
373
North Dakota Univ. debate program
3691
North Judson plan for financing
forensics 5252
Northeastern Ohio high schools,
speech education in 5050
Northern Oratorical League 3760
  orations of 5060
Northwestern Univ., debate program
of 319, 334
  and Delta Sigma Rho 3827
  U.N. mock conference of 4544
Notes, use of 3129
N.U.E.A. 1325, 5045
  and the NFL 5253

-O-

Oberlin College, forensic union of
3629
  young ladies literary society of
341
Objectives of debate, and argumentation 462
  according to sponsors of Pi Kappa
Delta 432
Objectivity, of debate judges 4763,
4769, 4833
  of high school debaters 5032
Obstinate audience, the 2417
Ockham's logic, topics in 1634, 1635
Ohio, forensic programs in 3282
  intercollegiate debate in 358
Ohio high schools, debate in 5083
  forensic programs of 5170
  individual events in 5229
Ohio State Univ., speech activities at
330

Ohio Univ., debate at 348
Ohio Wesleyan, debate at 359
Oklahoma, debate in 365, 5122
  high schools of, debate in 5004
Oklahoma State Univ., forensics at
3668
Oklahoma, Univ. of, forensics at
3643
Old debate topics 991
One- and two-sided presentation compared 2338, 2553
O'Neill, James M., on contribution
to speech 3354
  on defense of debating 3353
  as teacher of debating 3544
Open- and closed-mindedness 2651
Open forum 5096
  at Knox College 3692
  at Milburn High School 5256
Opinion, change of, and argumentation
443
  and audience orientation 2394
  conference, effect of, on 2736
  and ethos 2408
  and evidence 1502
  in Iowa 138
  factors affecting 2484
  formation of, from legal evidence
1423
    effects of recency in 5886
  and group opinion 2752
  measurement of 2722
  in public controversy 2415
  research in, and public policy 2568
  "sleeper" effect in 2751
  and social influences 2548
  (See also Attitude change)
Opinionated statements, and ethos
2606
"O" proposition 1652
Opposing arguments, and attitude
change 2640
Oral argument, and attitude change
2564
  improvement of 1857
Oral communication, and attitude
change 2422
Oral interpretation 4162, 4163
  benefits of 4186
  contests in 4182, 4183, 5059
    characterization in 4119
    selecting material for 4225
  role of, in forensics 4144, 4250
Oral presentation, types of, and comprehension 2378
Oral style 2948, 2986, 3091
Oral vocabularies, compared with
written 3026

Oral and written discourse 3172
Orations, collections of 5749
  evaluating 4195
  evidence in 5065
  of Hope College 4113
  of the Interstate Oratorical
    Assn. 4114, 4120
  of the Iowa High School Forensic
    League 5055
  of the National Oratorical League
    4227
  of the Northern Oratorical League
    5060
  of Pi Kappa Delta 4112
    collections of 5611, 5624
  of the Southwest Forensic Cham-
    pionship Tournament 5070
  writing of 4190
Oratorical contest, of the American
  Legion 4118
  in college 4131
  the Pillsbury 4116
Oratorical declamation, coaching of
  4202
  in high school 5235
Oratory 4235, 4236
  analysis of 4153
  coaching of 4230
  in college 4117, 4160, 4167, 4168,
    4175, 4224
    contest in 4142, 4231
    manuscripts for 4239
    preliminary rounds in 4128
  downfall of 4238
  evaluation of 4138
  and forensics 4126
  John Heywood on 2106
  in high school 5226
  judgment of, by orators 4171
  on the Missouri Frontier 1903
  and persuasive speaking 4152
  preparation for 4140
  political, in pre-Revolutionary
    America 351
  Quintilian on training for 1961
  student and trained judges of 4755
  technique of 4194
  a tradition in 4159
  types of 4252
Order of presentation 1739, 2227,
  2228, 2229, 2499, 2583
  climax and anti-climax 2697, 2706
  and familiarity and saliency 2664
Ordinal position, the 4124
Oregon, Univ. of, international debate program 3698
Organization, effects of 1225
  on attitudes and retention 2396,

2397
  on college students 2703
  on comprehension 2637
  on ethos 2339, 2343, 2692
  on memory 2650
  in oral communication 2714
  on recall of information 2371
Original oratory, in Pennsylvania
  4180
Ottawa Univ., and founding of Pi
  Kappa Delta 3802
"Ought" (see "Should")
Outlines (see Briefs)
"Overhead" persuasive communications 2740
Overstatement and understatement
  2614
Overstreet, Harry A., on criticism
  of debaters 893
Owen L. Coon National Debate Tournament 4106
Oxford-Harvard debate 3654
Oxford, terra filial disputations at
  399
  theological disputation at 308
Oxford Union, the 311, 4370-4372,
  4387, 4388, 4392, 4406, 4413

                    -P-

Pace College debate fraternity 3680
Pacific forensic league 5335
Pakistan, academic debating in 3635,
  5791
Palmerston, defense of, in Don
  Pacifico debates 5384
Paraphrasing quotations 3028
Parliamentary assembly 4593
Parliamentary conduct 4563
Parliamentary and Congressional debates, on War of (1812) 5464
Parliamentary debate(s) 4253, 4254,
  5598
  on the affirmation oath controversy
    5414
  a bibliography of 5887
  on confederation of British North
    American Provinces 5440
  on daily adjournment 5444
  Gladstone's theory of 5591
  during James II reign 5439
  at Michigan, Univ. of 4570
  on the Naval Treaty 5548
  Nazi attitude toward 5780
  in the 19th cent. 5547
  on Public Order Bill 5535
  on the Stamp Act (1776) 5545

2730
and majority attitude 2675
materials of 2516
motivation in 2493
motive appeals in 2360
and oratory 4152
and order of presentation 1739,
  2499
other available means of 2446
philosophy of 2613
physical distance in 2401
place of 2487
Plato on 1933, 1963
power of 2683
principles and methods of 2768
and problem-solving 2580
psychology of 2579
race in 2491
recent theories of 2361
resistance to, forewarning as 2109
satire in 2511, 2512
a schematic interpretation of 2646
self-contradiction in 2685
Richard Sibbe on 2079
social facilitation in 2447
for social movements 2701
statistical theory of 2451
tallness, effects of, in 2412
teaching of 3190
    at U.S. Air Force Academy
    3184
    motivation in 2702
techniques of 2492
unity of 2673
value system as premise for 2707
verbal fluency in 2390
warning, effect of, on 2635, 2636
Peter Zenger trial, Andrew Hamilton
speaking at 5517
Phi Rho Pi, activities of 3804
Philippine Annexation debate 5399
Phillips Andover Academy debate program 5171
Phillips, Wendell, as a debater 5511
Philodemus on rhetoric 1893, 2089
Philosophical argumentation 1724,
1736
Philosophy and rhetoric 2551
Photius on Attic orators 2164
Physical distance, in persuasion 2401
Pi Kappa Delta 3812, 3815
changes proposed in 3738
constitution of 3729
conventions of 435, 3794
    at Bowling Green Univ. 3826
    debates at 3798
    21st national 3806
    22nd national 3807

development of chapters of 3844
founding of, at Ottawa Univ. 3802
historians of 3791
history of 3730, 3763, 3792, 3796
membership requirements of 3836
national convention of 3805
national officers of 3733
national president of 3766
nature of 3847
origin of, at Redlands Univ. 3832
provinces of 3790
    function of 3767
research proposal for 3842
revising constitution of 3778
sample constitution for local chap-
    ters of 3823
sponsors of, on debate objectives
    432
twenty-four-year record of 3795
winning debates of, collection of
    5611, 5624
winning orations of 4112, 5611
Piccolomini, Aneas Silvius, on rhetoric 2010
Pillsbury Oratorical contest, the 4116
Pioneer women's oratory 312
Pitch change, and comprehension 3100
Pittsburgh, Univ. of, debate program
3315
Plan and counter-plan, in policy questions 1174
Plato 2160
dialectic of 1997, 2028, 2052
on dispositio 2007
influence of, on Cicero 2145
paradoxical attitude of, toward
    rhetoric 2132
on persuasion 1963
on philosophy of natural law 1933
on public speaking 2103
on rhetoric 1959, 2020, 2090
    and rhetoricians 2082, 2083
    source of ideas 2161
    truth in 2069
Platonism, logic with 1628
Pleading, and rhetoric 2514
Poetics, Aristotle and Horace on 2071
    De Quincey on 2073
    Peter Ramus on 2131
Polarity, and analogy 1900
Policy propositions 951, 975
analysis of 1148, 1164-1174
case possibilities for 1192
in economics 922
ethics for 2776
foreign, debating of 950
obligations of negative in 1207
teaching analysis of 3219

Policy propositions (cont'd)
  underlying assumptions of 1122,
  1169-1173, 1188
Political argument 1434
Political debate 5506
  collection of 5625
  on the Korean War 5568
Political ethics 2842
Political motives, goals as 2522
Political opinion, and high school
  debate 5173
Polylogic 1644
Ponca City High School debate tour-
  nament 5100
Poor decisions, cause of 4761, 4789
Popular opinion campaign slogans
  2617
Port Royal rhetoric 2040
Positions, Cicero on 1590
Positive and negative argumentation
  2341
Poughkeepsie plan of debate 5300
Practical problem-solving 1760
Practical reasoning 1805
Practical syllogism 1639
Practice debate tournament 5111
Pratt-Newman debate 5408
Precedence in parliamentary motions
  4708
Pre-Han persuasion 2037
Prejudice 5698
  and persuasion 2320
Pre-Revolutionary American oratory
  351
Presentation, and ethos 2686
Presidential debates (1964) 5566
  and the speech profession 5541
  structure of 5447
Prestige, and attitude change 2640
  measurement of 2571, 2589
  and suggestibility 2589
  suggestion from 2557, 2582
  and political leadership 2616
Presumption 1160, 5822
  and burden of proof 1093, 1643
  in law 1176
  in problem-solving 1103
  Richard Whately on 1102
  in Richard Whately's speech
    5507
  in criminal law 1122, 1127
  of innocence, in Soviet Union 1140
  law of 1738
Primacy, influence of 2719
  law of 2663
  in the courtroom 2575
  test of 2364
Prima facie case 1182, 1183

in academic debate 1098
in judging 4932
meaning of, in debate 1215
Primary research 1405
Primary sources, as debate evidence
  1384
Princeton Univ., American Whig Society of 298
  old debating societies at 389
Printed argument and attitude change
  2565
Prison debate 610, 790
Probability 1301, 1503
  and certainty 1706
  and confirmation 1842
  Corax on 2148
  and induction 1506
  and non-demonstrative inference
    1789
  and rational belief 1507
  theory of 1788
    and proof 1626
Problem, discussion of a 1119
Problem-solving 1149, 1561, 5690
  advocacy and inquiry in 5656
  and debate 435
  an experimental study of 1135
  listening in 5681
  logical strategies for 5685
  modern account of 1721
  opinionated statements in 5678
  pattern of, communicating 5660
  persuasion in 2580
  reasons used in 1707
  and reflective thinking 841
  verbalization in 5696
Progressive rhetoric 2717
Proof, Aristotle on modes and forms
  of 1611
  burden of 1093, 1643
  by Liebniz 1732
  nature of 1679
  principles of, in college debate 194
  problem of 5756
  sources of, and Aristotle's topics
    1962
  standards of, and probability theory
    1626
  in public discussion 1597
Propaganda 411, 2189, 2221, 2279,
  2404
  analysis of 2232
    and public speaking 2550
  annotated bibliography on 5897
  art of 2246
  and attitude change 2547
  detection of 2535
  devices of 2760

Quintilian (cont'd)
  and ethical proof 1952
  on extemporaneous speaking 4156
  and forensics 2121
  and the good orator 2792
  Institutions of 287
  on invention 1931
  and Juvenal 2008
  on oratorical training 1961
  on rhetoric 1959, 2012
  Vir Bonus of 2114
  witnesses of 2065
Quotations 3119
  paraphrasing of 3028
  use and abuse of 1274

-R-

Rabelais and Cicero 2146
Race, and persuasion 2491
Radio broadcast of debates 4426,
  4427, 4433-4435, 4437, 4449, 4450-
  4452, 4454, 4456, 4461, 4465, 4467,
  5101
Radio delivery, and attitudes 2473,
  2761
Radio dramatizations in parliamentary
  procedure 4707
Rainolde, on rhetoric 2092
Ramus, Peter, on logic and rhetoric
  2131
Ranney-Dennison gubernatorial debates 5368, 5412
Rate of speaking 3093
  and comprehension 2482, 3101,
    3107, 3109-3110, 3115
  effect of, in debate 2497
Rating of speeches 4125
Rational belief, and probability 1481,
  1507
Rationalization 2552
  in communication 2656
  social significance of 2711
Ravenna High School debate program
  5077, 5198
Reading ease, and persuasibility 2987
Reagan, Ronald, logic in speeches of
  5485
Reason(s)(ing), with ambiguous sentences 1723
  by analogy 1735, 1741
  appeal to 1803
  attitude, effect of, on 1840
  Francis Bacon on 2173
  and causes 1664, 1758, 1818
  Rene Descartes on 1849
  and emotion 2628

in judicial decision-making 5668
in law 1451
modes of 1620
non-logical factors of 2602
in practice 1687
psychology of 2495
test for 1673
use of, in foreign policy speeches
  5400
  in political speeches 5565
Rebuttal, some problems of 1270
  role of, in teaching debate 3268
Recognition of Red China debate 5355
Recognition, effect on, of political
  contexts 2477
Reconstruction Amendment debates
  5347
Redlands Univ., and origin of Pi
  Kappa Delta 3832
Reed, Thomas B., debate techniques
  of 5580, 5581
Reference books, guide to 5900, 5912
Reference, ethos, and attitude change
  2374, 2632
Reflective thinking, analysis of 1720
  and county speech contests 3861
  and discussion 841
Reformation debates, collection of
  5626
Reformed and Anabaptists debate 5505
Refutation, of affirmative case 1253
  and attitude change 1267, 1268,
    2598, 2599
  in criminal law 1249
  and evidence 1251
  judging of, standards for 4849
  methods of, in championship de-
    bates 1247
  of negative case 1254
  of psychological egoism in rhetori-
    cal theory 2327
  and rebuttal, in academic debate
    5042
    use of topoi for 1243
  skill in, measuring 1252
  strategy in 1264
  in team debating 1269
  technique of 1248
  use of, by John C. Calhoun 5521
    in jury trials 5434
    in Kennedy-Nixon debates 5451
    in U.N. Arab-Israel debates
      5465
    by Daniel Webster 5436
Register, index to 5944
Relations, Hume's theory of 1704
Relevancy, rules for 1422
Religious attitudes, influences on 2444

510

Religious debate, attitudes toward
4308
  between Campbell and Purcell
  5394
  practices of 4309
Religious disputation 409
Reluctant testimony 1320, 1322
Renaissance, commonplaces of 1899
  debate 306, 379
  England, education in 1871
  rhetoric textbooks of 2092
Repetition in public address 2462
Republican Credentials Committee debates (1952) 5557
Research, in debate, historical-
critical 360
  for debate 1417
  in forensics 5880, 5883, 5884
  methods of, upgrading 1400
  in sociology of law 5917
  in speech 5748
    a bibliography of 5888
    and social values 5736
Response reinforcement, and attitude
change 2688, 2689
Rhetoric 2472, 2479
  as act 2699
  John Quincy Adams on 2009, 2137,
  2143
  and advertising 2676
  in America, development of (1635-
  1850) 1948, 2060
  in American colleges (1915-1954)
  1964
  in the American colonies 2104
  in the ancient world 2015
  for anti-rhetoricians 2428
  Aphthonius on 2092
  of argumentation 26
  of Aristotle 1865, 1867, 1888,
  1959, 1974, 2000, 2034, 2051,
  2071, 2083, 2142, 2439, 2601
    choice, concept of, in 2155
    composition of 2026
    early history of 2067
    functional interpretation of 2162
    intended uses of 2133
    in the Middle Ages 2127
    and public address 2138
    as a textbook 3246
  arrangement in 1966
  art of 1921, 2538
  Augustine, St. on 2140
  Aurelius Augustine on 2035
  axiology of 2482
  in Babylonian Talmudic academies
  (70-500) 1980
  Francis Bacon on 1919, 2169, 2173

Alexander Bain on 1938, 1989
René Bary on 1932
James Beattie on 2018
Henry Ward Beecher on 1874
Hugh Blair on 1939, 1947, 2017
James Boswell on 2054
Boylston Chair of 1982
John A. Broadus on 1957
Phillips Brooks on 1949, 2064
Kenneth Burke on 1888, 1954,
  2100, 2530
Alexander Campbell on 1990
George Campbell on 1926, 1940,
  2016, 2096, 2157
  Hume's influence on 1927
Cassiodorus on 1972
Edward T. Channing, on definition
  of 2005
  on teaching of 1923, 3183
Christianization of, and St. Augustine 2123
Cicero on 1959, 1979, 2143
classical traditions of, and speech
  training 2072
college teaching of 2413
of commitment 2704
and communication 2410
conservative or progressive 2741
contemporary theories of 2236
in the courtroom 2748
and criticism 2270
  by Thomas Baker 2111
  by Jeremy Bentham 2027
  by John Jewel 2078
and cybernetics 2645
in defense of 2537
definition of 2489, 2654
  and John F. Genung 2048
delivery, concepts of, in 2344
Thomas De Quincey on 2038, 2061,
  2073, 2077
and dialectic 2517
dimensions of 2440
first discussion of, in English 2122
of dissent, and Isaac Watts 2003
earliest teaching of, at Oxford 2128
education in, in Italy 2574
the Elder Seneca on 2151
Ralph W. Emerson on 1937
emotional appeal in 1966, 2030,
  2576
enemies of 2403
in England (1500-1700) 1889
  (1700-1750) 1950
in English 2754
and English morals 2056
in the English Renaissance 2158
the enthymeme in 1761

Rhetoric (cont'd)
ethos in 1986
of evidence 1355
evolution of 2039
an experimental study of 2372
Thomas Farnaby on 1973
field of 2540
the flowers of 2695
and formal argument 2693
form and content in 2333
Harry E. Fosdick on 2463
function of 2476
and general education 2541, 2563
John F. Genung on 2004, 2048
Chauncey A. Goodrich on 1956,
2532
Gorgias on 2059
in Greco-Roman education 1872,
1873
H. J. G. Grierson on 2526
Gabriel Harvey on 2178
John Heywood on 2106
historical study of 1891
Horace on 2071
John Huarte on 2088
illustration in 2387
the imaginative component of 2672
invention in 1966
invention of, by Corax and Tisias
2070
Isocrates on 1928, 2091, 2166
Isodorus of Seville on 1935
Jacobus Izelgrinus on 1898
and Thomas Jefferson 2013
John of Salisbury on 2154
Samuel Johnson on 2120
Notker Labeo on 1941
Bernard Lami on 2040
Brunetto Latini on 1942
and law of evidence 2514
John Lawson on 1961
for lawyers 2770
legal 294
as a liberal art 2472
the limits of 2621
literary association in 2030
and logic 1684, 1711, 1715, 1774
lost canon of, and Hippias 2149
Philip Melanchton on 1953
mentalist concept of 2088
in the Middle Ages 2112
William H. Milburn on 2022
John Milton on 2101
Montaigne on 2023, 2024
and moral studies 2019
Morley on 2119
motive appeals in 1960
old and new 2031

orations on, of Gabriel Harvey
2178
and oratory, John Q. Adams on
2009
Blaise Pascal on 1918
Chaim Perelman on 2408, 2471
Philodemus on 1893, 2089
and philosophical argumentation
2622
philosophy of 2284
and philosophy 2551
Aeneas Silvius Piccolomini on 2010
Plato on 1959, 2020, 2082, 2083,
2090, 2132
Plato's sources on 2161
and poetics, Aristotle and Horace
on 2071
Gorgias on 2059
and political protest 2559
and political science 2746
progressive 2717
project of, and debate 3247
prospect of 2280
psychological approach to 2734
and public address, Francis Bacon's
contribution to 2170
a bibliography of 5891, 5924,
5943, 5963
and public opinion 2767
purpose of 2383
Quintilian on 1959, 2012
Rainolde on 2092
Peter Ramus on 2131
and rational man, John Locke on
2174
recent literature on 2718
a redefinition of 2747
refutation of psychological egoism
in 2327
Renaissance textbooks of 2092
renaissance of, in 12th cent. 2111
and rhetoricians, Aristotle on 2083
Plato on 2082, 2083
in Rome, as legal training 2135
Bertrand Russell on 1995, 2775
in Russia 2445
and F. S. C. Schiller's logic 2058
and scientific method 2220
Scottish school of 262
and semantics 2623
William G. T. Shedd on 1981
Sherry on 2068
in 16th cent. 1917, 2063
Adam Smith on 2053
social responsibility in 2326
stasis in 1099
style in 1966, 2030
the substance of 2581, 2657, 2666,

2739
survey of (1950-1970) 2379
and sympathy, from Hume to
Whately 1946
teaching of, by John Q. Adams
1996
truth in, Plato and Korzybski on
2069
uses of 2205
and value theory 2710
John Ward on 1929
Richard Weaver on 2549
Daniel Webster on 2117
Richard Whately on 1993, 2097,
2136
Thomas Wilson on 2167, 2168
James Winans on 2437
Rhetorical argument, enthymeme as
1662
Rhetorical devices in intercollegiate
debate 5486
Rhetorical practices of John Stuart
Mill 1924
Rhetorical propositions 923, 949
Rhetorical prose, structure of 2171
Rhetorical scholarship 2442
Rhetorical schools in Rome 356
Rhetorical style 2382 (See also Style)
Rhetorical theory (see Rhetoric)
Rhetorical tradition, intellectual as-
pects of 2029
Rhetoricians, of ancient Greece and
Rome 1869
and Cicero 2033
Plato on 2082, 2083
Richards, I. A., on context of lan-
guage 2049
Ridicule in controversy 3056
Ripon College debate program 3663
Robert, Henry M., as presiding of-
ficer 4733
Rockford, debating at 402
Rogge, Edward, on ethics of per-
suasion 2851
Rollins College, forensics at 3648,
3651
Roman declamation 299, 393
value of 355
Roman education, from Cicero to
Quintilian 1886
Roman rhetoric, epicheireme in 1656
as legal training 2098, 2135
modes of delivery in 1984
Roman speech education 372
Roosevelt, Franklin D., debate on
proposal of, to enlarge Court 5534
Roosevelt, Theodore, on debating
both sides 2871

Rorke, Alexander, debate strategy of
5474
Rose, Forrest, memorial service for
3187
Rules, for debate 3216, 5129
for national speech tournament 5279
Russell, Bertrand, on rhetoric 1995,
2725
Russian rhetoric 2445
Rutgers Univ. debate program 3659,
3688

-S-

Sacramento Valley forensic league
5075
St. Augustine, and Christianization of
rhetoric 2123
and debate on Christian rhetoric
5584
and genesis of medieval rhetoric
2125
as rhetorician and public speaker
2140
St. Joseph's College debating society
3695
Salaries of forensics directors 3299
Salesmanship, and debate 2682
and teaching 2720, 2721
Satire 3052
in argumentation 2375
in debate 2655
in persuasion 2511, 2512
"Satisfactory" and "unsatisfactory" evidence compared 1342, 2336
Scare words, effect of 2604
Scattered vs. compact seating compared 2494
Schiller, F. S. C., on logic and rhetoric 2058
School debates 822 (See also Academic
debate)
School forums 4638
School segregation debates, argument
in 5480
Science, Thomas De Quincey on 2073
Scientific attitude, and debate 1651
Scientific evidence, and the law 1318,
1373
Scientific method, Aristotle's concept
of 1768
and rhetoric 2220
Scientific proof, methods of 1678
Scottish school of rhetoric 262
Scripture, effect of, in persuasion
2380
Seating of Georgia delegation debate

513

5271
"Spread," attitudes on the 1205
Stanford Mellinkoff medal for debate
3636
Stasis 1180
    Aristotelian and Stoic influences
    on 1200
    Aristotle's theory of 2011
    development of, in deliberative
    speaking 1099
    theory of, in treating issues 1107
Stassen-Dewey debate 5421, 5422
State colleges of Louisiana, debating
  at 344
State debating leagues 5342
State forensic organizations 5287
State high school speech leagues,
  and NUEA 5045
SUNY at Albany, debate program of
  3653
Statements, controversial, nature of
  951
    dogmatic, effects of 2671
    inferential and descriptive 2350
    opinionated, and ethos 2606
    (See also Propositions)
Statistics 1275, 1277-1281, 1283,
  1284, 1287, 1291, 1293, 1295-
  1297, 1299, 1301, 1399
    abuse of 1363
    in debate 1349, 1365, 1411
    judicial use and abuse of 1368
    presentation of 3046
    reasoning with 1581
Status cues, audience judgments of
  2519
Status quo, indictment of 1170
  major change of 1172
Stephen F. Austin State College de-
  bate program 346
Stereotyped words, and political
  judgments 2603
Stock issues 1148
    analysis of 1202
    and analysis of debate proposition
    1105
    Hermogenes on 376
    in tournament debates 1146
Stockton, Dale, memorial service for
  3187
Stormer, John A., use of evidence by
  5476
Stout State Univ., forensics at 3645
Strategy, in debate 1100, 1164, 1217
    elements of 1138
    of parliamentary procedure 4712
Student conference 4521
Student congress 4524, 4527, 4536,

4558, 4564, 4565, 4586, 5612, 4654,
4657
    of Delta Sigma Rho 4472, 4481,
    4483-4485, 4493, 4499, 4500,
    4519, 4520, 4523, 4530, 4553,
    4554, 4561, 4587, 4606, 4608-
    4610
    of NFL 5243
    and National Speech Tournament
    5345
    at Princeton 4603
Student constitutional convention 4593
Student forum 4491, 4501, 4508,
  4510, 4511, 4513, 4522, 4529, 4533,
  4538, 4547, 4552, 4556, 4557, 4559,
  4562, 4571, 4572, 4576, 4592, 4598,
  4640
    questions for 4545
Student judges of oratory 4755
Student legislative assembly 4567
Student senate, at Iowa Univ. 4607
Style 1966, 2382, 2763
    Cicero and Aristotle on 2050
    classical discussion of 1983
    concepts of, in England 1971
    contemporary notions of 3157
    in debating 3087
    definition of 3011
    De Quincey on 2159
    and emphasis in debate 3005, 3006
    logic of 3025
    in persuasion 3017
    in rhetorical theory 1960, 2030
    stylistics, bibliography of 5899
Stylistic errors 3031, 3050
Subjective probability 1509
    and ethos 2395
Sublime, Longinus on the 2134
Substantive evidence, false statements
  as 1346
Successful debaters, in Kansas high
  schools 5260
Successful debating, art of 1126
Suez debates, in the U.N. 5405
Sufficiency of evidence 1418
Suggestion 2633
    in argumentation and debate 2458
    and prestige 2557, 2582, 2616
    psychology of 2298
Summer high school debate institutes
  5008, 5195, 5199, 5200, 5214, 5261,
  5266, 5267, 5284
Support forms of 1356 (See also Evi-
  dence)
Supreme Court, arguments in deci-
  sions of the 5512
    debate before the, on segregation
    5502, 5537

Truman Doctrine, debate on 5463
Truth, Aristotle's concept of 1930
　and assertion 1718
　and debate 578
　and evidence 1745
　through personality 2801
　in rhetorical theory 2069
　theory of 1705
Truth-telling, and voice 3113
TV debates, collection of 5616
Type, the, as a logical form 1817

-U-

Understanding, Francis Bacon on
　2173
Understatement and overstatement
　2614
Unethical language 3018, 3068, 3071
Unethical practices in academic de-
　bate 2782
Unfair debate decisions 4858
Unfamiliar strategy 1196
U. N. Arab-Israeli debates, refutation
　in 5465
U. N. mock conference at North-
　western 4544
U. N. Security Council debates on
　Suez 5405
U. S. policy in Viet Nam, debate on
　5446

-V-

Vagueness, and the excluded middle
　1847
Validity, and differential certainty
　1733
　in logical systems 1658
　as moral obligation 2480
Valuation, and knowledge 1514
Value(s), in America 5699
　and attitudes 5706
　change of 5739
　classification of 5711, 5719
　of debate 452
　　for academic adjustment 440
　　for "allness" behavior 437
　　in armed forces 504
　　in business 493
　　for citizenship 495
　　to college presidents 456, 457,
　　519
　　and critical thinking 422, 423,
　　441
　　according to debaters 451

in a democracy 464, 489, 500,
　505, 511
in finance 483
according to former debaters
　426, 433, 436
and freshman entrance examina-
　tions 447
for leadership in business 454
in legal profession 515
in life activities 510
in national defense 494
and open-mindedness 444
for personality 498
for pre-ministerial training 488
and problem-solving 435
for radio career 485
ratings of 446
and scholarship 506
in schools 509
for scientific group thinking 507
as social inquiry 461
for social integration 434
as social methodology 508
for social and political leader-
　ship 523
for student leadership 480
for teacher in training 503
and vocational success 439
and facts 919, 1047, 1065, 1071,
　1082, 5744
　Humes's view of 1067
Value judgment, vs. logic, in law
　1764 (See also Propositions of value)
Verbal fluency, in persuasion 2390
Verbal repetition, effects of 3130
Vergniaud, Pierre, speeches of,
　argument in 5466
Virginia Slavery debate, argument in
　5460
Visual aids 1374, 1394
　in argument 1392
　effects of 1410
Vocabulary, of academic debaters
　3021
Vocal pitch, and meaning 3117
Vocal variations, and ethos 3084
Voice, in debate 3097
　and intelligence 3140
　and personality 3085, 3114, 3141
　and sociability 3112
　and truth-telling 3113

-W-

Wallace, Karl R., on substance of
　rhetoric 2434, 2581, 2657, 2666
Walsh, Grace M., and coaching

520